From Ivory Towers to Ebony Towers: Transforming Humanities Curricula in South Africa, Africa and African-American Studies

From Ivory Towers to Ebony Towers: Transforming Humanities Curricula in South Africa, Africa and African-American Studies

Edited by Oluwaseun Tella and Shireen Motala

First published by Fanele, an imprint of Jacana Media (Pty) Ltd, in 2020

10 Orange Street
Sunnyside
Auckland Park 2092
South Africa
+27 11 628 3200

www.jacana.co.za

© for this edition – Institute for Pan-African Thought and Conversation, 2020
© for individual chapters – individual contributors, 2020

All rights reserved.

ISBN 978-1-4314-2955-4

Editing by Glenda Younge
Cover design by publicide
Layout by Aimèe Armstrong
Proofreading by Russell Martin
Index by Tessa Botha
Set in Bembo 10.9/14pt
Job no. 003667

Printed by **novus print**, a division of Novus Holdings

See a complete list of Jacana titles at www.jacana.co.za

Contents

Contributors	vii
Acronyms and abbreviations	xv
Ackowledgements	xix

Section I Introduction

Chapter 1 Transforming humanities curricula in South Africa, Africa and African-American studies – *Oluwaseun Tella* — 1

Chapter 2 Vanquishing the ghost of Cecil Rhodes: Historical struggles to transform South Africa's humanities curriculum – *Adekeye Adebajo* — 13

Section II The Challenges of Transforming South Africa's Higher Education Sector

Chapter 3 The significance of the decolonial turn in South African higher education – *Crain Soudien* — 33

Chapter 4 Turn inwards to connect outwards: South Africa's universities in historical perspective – *Ahmed Bawa* — 48

Chapter 5 Equity in higher education and education for all: Critical considerations – *Shireen Motala* — 66

Chapter 6 The challenges of transforming South Africa's historically black universities – *Bheki R Mngomezulu* — 81

Section III Lessons from South Africa's Student Movement

Chapter 7 South Africa's student movement: A Wits perspective – *Musawenkosi Hemelton Malabela* — 101

Chapter 8 South Africa's student movement: A Rhodes perspective – *Corrine Knowles* — 118

Chapter 9 South Africa's student movement: A UCT perspective – *Sandile Ndelu* — 136

Section IV Transforming South Africa's Humanities Curriculum

Chapter 10 The aporias of 'decolonisation' in the South African academy – *Joel Modiri* — 157

Chapter 11 Going to Sokoto to look for something in the pocket of your ṣòkòtò: The curious case of African sociology and decolonisation – *Jimi Adesina*   174

Chapter 12 Transforming South Africa's curricula through African philosophy – *Philip Higgs*   192

Section V African Schools of Thought

Chapter 13 The Ibadan School of History – *Toyin Falola*   211

Chapter 14 The Dar es Salaam School of Political Economy – *Severine M Rugumamu*   228

Chapter 15 The Dakar School of Culture – *Samba Buri Mboup*   255

Section VI African Transformation Initiatives

Chapter 16 Decolonisation, the Heinemann African Writers Series and the making of a trans-national, Pan-African literary audience – *Harry Garuba*   269

Chapter 17 Ghanaian transformation efforts – *David Owusu-Ansah*   283

Chapter 18 Ugandan transformation efforts – *Pamela Khanakwa*   301

Chapter 19 The development of contemporary literature in East Africa – *Chris Wanjala*   314

Section VII Lessons from African-American Studies

Chapter 20 De-colonising the 'pre-history' of African and African-American studies: Confronting racism in the American episteme – *Zine Magubane*   329

Chapter 21 The Atlanta School of Sociology – *Aldon Morris*   342

Chapter 22 The Howard School of International Affairs – *Krista Jihnson*   357

Chapter 23 Righteous struggle: Historically black colleges and universities in the United States – *Walter R Allen, Chantal Jones and Gadise Regassa*   377

Section VIII Conclusion

Chapter 24 Key lessons for South Africa's curriculum transformation in the humanities from Africa and African-American studies – *Shireen Motala*   399

Index   409

Contributors

Adekeye Adebajo
Adekeye Adebajo is the Director of the Institute for Pan-African Thought and Conversation (IPATC) at the University of Johannesburg (UJ) in South Africa. Professor Adebajo served on United Nations missions in South Africa, Western Sahara, and Iraq, and is the author of six books including *The Curse of Berlin: Africa after the Cold War*; *Thabo Mbeki: Africa's Philosopher-King*; and *The Eagle and the Springbok: Essays on Nigeria and South Africa*. He is co-editor or editor of nine books. He obtained his doctorate from Oxford University in England where he studied as a Rhodes Scholar.

Jimi Adesina
Jimi Adesina is the Holder of the Department of Science and Technology (DST) and the National Research Foundation (NRF), South African Research Chairs Initiative (SARChI) Research Chair in Social Policy at the College of Graduate Studies at the University of South Africa (UNISA). He served on the Executive Committee of the Dakar-based Council for the Development of Social Science Research in Africa (CODESRIA), and was Chair of its Programme Sub-Committee. Professor Adesina was educated at the University of Ibadan in Nigeria, and Warwick University in Britain. His research interests include Endogeneity and Modern Sociology; Social Policy; and the Political Economy of Africa's Development.

Walter Allen
Walter Allen is Allan Murray Carter Professor of Higher Education and Distinguished Professor of Education, Sociology, and African-American Studies at the University of California, Los Angeles (UCLA), in the US. He co-directs the Center for Capacity Building which conducts empirical research to improve equity, diversity, inclusion, and excellence in higher education in California, the US, and internationally. A prolific author, editor, and writer, Allen's more than 200 publications include *As the World Turns: Implications of Global Shifts in Higher Education for Theory, Research and Practice*; and *Everyday Discrimination in a National Sample of Incoming Law Students*.

Ahmed Bawa
Ahmed Bawa is the Chief Executive Officer of Universities South Africa. He was previously the Vice-Chancellor and Principal of Durban University of Technology (DUT). Professor Bawa was a faculty member of the Department

of Physics and Astronomy at Hunter College in New York. He served as the Programme Officer for Higher Education in Africa with the Ford Foundation in Johannesburg, and during this time, led and coordinated the Foundation's African Higher Education Initiative. Professor Bawa holds a doctorate in Theoretical Physics from the University of Durham in Britain. He is a Fellow of the Royal Society of South Africa, as well as the Academy of Science of South Africa.

Toyin Falola
Toyin Falola is a University Distinguished Teaching Professor and the Jacob and Frances Mossiker Chair in the Humanities at the University of Texas at Austin in the US. Professor Falola is currently working on 20 handbooks on various issues related to Africa, with three already published: *The Handbook of African Politics*; *The Handbook of African Philosophy*; and *The Handbook of Colonial and Post-Colonial History*. He is also working on a book, *The Character and Composition of Evil*. Professor Falola is a recipient of 10 honorary doctorates and over 20 life-time career awards, including the Distinguished Africanist Award awarded by the African Studies Association (ASA) of the US.

Harry Garuba
Harry Garuba teaches in the School of African and Gender Studies, Anthropology, and Linguistics at the University of Cape Town (UCT) in South Africa. He has served as Director and Head of Department of the Centre for African Studies; Director of the School of African and Gender Studies, Anthropology, and Linguistics; and acting Dean of the Faculty of Humanities, all at UCT. Professor Garuba served as a member of the International Editorial Board of the Heinemann African Writers series. He has published widely in the fields of African and Post-Colonial Literature with four co-edited books, one edited anthology of poetry, two poetry monographs, as well as over 50 journal articles and book chapters.

Philip Higgs
Philip Higgs is an Emeritus Professor and Research Fellow in the College of Education at the University of South Africa. He holds two doctorates in the areas of Philosophy of Religion from the University of Natal, and Philosophy of Education from the University of South Africa. Professor Higgs was the Series Editor of the International Heinemann Philosophy of Education Series. His book publications include *African Voices in Education*; *Re-thinking Our World*; *Re-thinking Truth*; *Philosophy of Education Today: An Introduction*; and *A Reader in Philosophy of Education*. Professor Higgs has also published in many academic journals.

Krista Johnson

Krista Johnson is an Associate Professor and Director of Graduate Studies in the Department of African Studies at Howard University in Washington D.C. in the US. She received her doctorate in Political Science from Northwestern University, Evanston, in the US and has published on a wide range of topics including Health Policy; Gender and HIV Prevention; and Global Health Governance in Africa. She has lived and travelled extensively throughout Southern Africa, completed a Fulbright Fellowship in 2012 at the Centre for the Study of HIV and AIDS at the University of Botswana; and has been a Visiting Scholar at the University of Cape Town and the University of the Western Cape.

Chantal Jones

Chantal Jones is a doctoral candidate in the Higher Education and Organisational Change (HEOC) programme in the Graduate School of Education and Information Studies at the University of California, Los Angeles (UCLA), in the US. Ms Jones received her Master of Arts degree from UCLA; her Master's of Education in Post-secondary Administration and Student Affairs from the University of Southern California; and her Bachelor of Fine Arts in painting from Arizona State University, all in the US. Her research interests include Higher Education; Critical Race Theory; and Law.

Pamela Khanakwa

Pamela Khanakwa is a Lecturer in the Department of History, Archaeology, and Heritage Studies at Makerere University in Kampala, Uganda. She holds Master's and Doctoral degrees in African History from Northwestern University, Evanston, in the US. Dr Khanakwa is a recipient of several grants including the African Peacebuilding Network Individual Grant. She has published on Ritual Male Circumcision and Constructions of Masculinities, and Ethnicity and Political Identity among the Bagisu. Her current research project focuses on the Dilemmas of the Survivors of Landslides and Mudslides in Bududa district in Eastern Uganda.

Corinne Knowles

Corinne Knowles is a Lecturer in the Humanities Extended Studies Programme at Rhodes University in Grahamstown, South Africa. She previously served as chair of the Women's Academic Solidarity Association at Rhodes. Ms Knowles is a gender and social justice activist, and has been an active member of various progressive staff collectives. She teaches courses on African feminism, academic support for Politics and Sociology, and Butler's Performance Theory. She has published a book of poetry, *Said and Done*; and written an award-winning play, *Bus Stop*. She is completing her doctorate at Rhodes University.

Zine Magubane

Zine Magubane is a Professor of Sociology at Boston College in the US. She taught at the University of Cape Town between 1996 and 1997, and served as a Research Associate with the Human Sciences Research Council (HSRC) in Tshwane (Pretoria) between 1998 and 2000. Her areas of specialisation include Social Theory; Sociology of Post-Coloniality; Race and Ethnicity; Globalisation; Race and Popular Culture; Gender and Sexuality; and the Sociology of African Societies. Professor Magubane is the author of *Bringing the Empire Home: Race, Gender and Class in Britain and Colonial South Africa*. She completed her Master's and Doctorate in Sociology at Harvard University in the US.

Musawenkosi Malabela

Musawenkosi Malabela is a Researcher at the Chris Hani Institute (CHI) in Johannesburg. He previously worked as a Researcher at the National Labour and Economic Institute (NALEDI), and as an Assistant Lecturer at the University of Johannesburg. Mr Malabela holds a Master's degree in Political Sociology, and Bachelor of Arts and Honours degrees in Industrial Sociology, all from the University of the Witwatersrand in Johannesburg, South Africa. He is pursuing a Doctorate in Industrial Sociology at the University of the Witwatersrand. His research interests include Organisations' Internal Democracy; Trade Unions; Local Government Politics; and Student Politics.

Samba Mboup

Samba Mboup is an Associate Professor at the Centre for Diplomatic and Strategic Studies, and Head of the Department of Languages and Culture, at the Pan-African Cultural and Research Institute (PACRI), both in Senegal. He was previously an Associate Professor at the University of South Africa (UNISA) and a founding member of the Thabo Mbeki African Leadership Institute (TMALI) at UNISA. He served as Ambassador of Senegal to Southern Africa between 2001 and 2006. Professor Mboup holds a Doctorate in General and Comparative Literature, and a University Diploma in Swahili/Bantu Language and Civilisation, from the Sorbonne University in Paris, France.

Bheki Mngomezulu

Bheki Mngomezulu is a Professor of Political Science and Deputy Dean of Research at the University of the Western Cape (UWC) in South Africa. He has published five books including *The President for Life Pandemic in Africa*, ten book chapters, and several journal articles. He previously served as the Chief Executive Officer (CEO) of the Mzala Nxumalo Centre, and as Senior Lecturer and Academic Leader of the International and Public Affairs Cluster at the University of KwaZulu-Natal (UKZN), both in South Africa. His research interests include International Relations; Comparative African Politics; Higher Education; and Traditional Leadership.

Joel Modiri
Joel Modiri is a Senior Lecturer in the Department of Jurisprudence at the University of Pretoria (UP) in South Africa. He holds a doctorate in Legal Theory from the University of Pretoria. His research interests include Critical Race Theory; Critical Pedagogy; Critical Theories of Rights; Constitutionalism; African Jurisprudence; Black Political Thought; and Feminist Theory. He is working on a book titled *The Thought of Steve Biko in the Context of Post-1994 Law and Society*.

Aldon Morris
Aldon Morris is the Leon Forrest Professor of Sociology and African-American Studies at Northwestern University in the US. Professor Morris is the author of the award-winning book, *The Origins of the Civil Rights Movement*, which won the Distinguished Contribution to Scholarship Award from the American Sociological Association in 1986; and *The Scholar Denied: W.E.B. Du Bois and the Birth of American Sociology*, which in February 2015 won the R.R. Hawkins Award from the Association of American Publishers. Professor Morris is the current President of the American Sociological Association. His interests include Race; Social Inequality; Religion; Politics; W.E.B. Du Bois; and Social Movements.

Shireen Motala
Shireen Motala is Senior Director of the Postgraduate School: Research and Innovation Division, and Professor in the Faculty of Education at the University of Johannesburg. She has worked extensively in research and research management, and provided leadership for regional and international partnerships. Professor Motala served on the South African Council of Higher Education (CHE), the Ministerial Task Team to review the national Senior Certificate examination, and South Africa's United Nations Educational, Scientific, and Cultural Organisation (UNESCO) Commission. Her research interests and expertise are in Education Financing; Internationalisation; Postgraduate Pedagogies; Decolonisation; and Globalisation.

Sandile Ndelu

Sandile Ndelu is a South African black trans feminist writer, speaker, and public interest lawyer. She is currently working as a Candidate Attorney and Bertha Justice Fellow at the University of the Witwatersrand's Centre for Applied Legal Studies (CALS). Ms Ndelu holds a Bachelor of Arts degree in Media and Writing Studies and a postgraduate degree in Law, both from the University of Cape Town (UCT). Sandile is a co-founder of Trans* Collective at UCT, and founder of the Trans University Forum (TUF!).

David Owusu-Ansah

David Owusu-Ansah is an Associate Provost for Diversity and Executive Director for Faculty Access and Inclusion at James Madison University in Virginia in the US. He is a Professor of African History and a founding member of the institution's African, African-American, and Diaspora Studies Minor. He earned his Master's degree in Islamic Studies at McGill University in Montreal, Canada, and obtained a Doctoral degree from Northwestern University in Evanston, US. Professor Owusu-Ansah is the author of *Islamic Talismanic Traditions in Nineteenth Century Asante*; *Islamic Learning, the State, and the Challenges of Education in Ghana*; and three editions of the *Historical Dictionary of Ghana* in 1995, 2005, and 2014.

Gadise Regassa

Gadise Regassa is a Doctoral student in the Graduate School of Education and Information Studies at the University of California, Los Angeles (UCLA), in the US. Her research interests include the lived experiences of black college students, and anti-blackness in organisational change. At UCLA, she co-founded a collective of black graduate and professional women/femme students called Sisters in Scholarship (SIS). Ms Regassa holds a Master's degree in Higher Education and Student Affairs from Ohio State University in the US.

Severine Rugumamu

Severine Rugumamu is Deputy Vice-Chancellor at Kampala International University in Tanzania. He previously served as the Executive Secretary of the African Association of Political Science (AAPS). Professor Rugumamu is the author of three recent books: *Globalization Demystified: Africa's Possible Development Futures*; *Lethal Aid: The Illusion of Socialism and Self Reliance in Tanzania*; and *Finnish-Value Added: Boon or Bane to Aid Effectiveness?* He has also taught at the universities of Maryland in College Park; North Carolina at Chapel Hill; and Bennett College, all in the US. He obtained his Doctorate in Political Science from the University of Maryland.

Crain Soudien

Crain Soudien is the Chief Executive Officer (CEO) of the Human Sciences Research Council (HSRC), and a former Deputy Vice-Chancellor at the University of Cape Town (UCT), where he remains an Emeritus Professor in Education and African Studies. He holds a doctorate from the State University of New York (SUNY) in the US. His publications in the areas of social difference, culture, education policy, comparative education, educational change, public history, and popular culture include four books, four edited collections, and over 200 articles, reviews, reports, and book chapters, including a 2017 publication entitled *Nelson Mandela: Comparative Perspectives of his Significance for Education*.

Oluwaseun Tella

Oluwaseun Tella is a Senior Researcher at the Institute for Pan-African Thought and Conversation at the University of Johannesburg in South Africa. He holds a Doctorate in Political Science from the University of KwaZulu-Natal in South Africa. Dr Tella has edited a book entitled *Nigeria–South Africa Relations and Regional Hegemonic Competence*; and published two book chapters, and over 20 mostly single-authored journal articles in *Politikon*, *Journal of Asian and African Studies*, *Journal of Black Studies* and elsewhere. His research interests include Foreign Policy; International Relations; Soft Power; Peace and Conflict Studies; African Politics; and South African Higher Education.

Chris Wanjala

Chris Wanjala was a Professor of Literature at the University of Nairobi, and the founder of the Department of Literature at Egerton University, both in Kenya. He died in October 2018. He previously served as the Director of the Institute of African Studies at the University of Nairobi. Professor Wanjala was the author of several journal articles, poems, and books. His publications include *Ingwe: The Oral Literature of Western Kenya*; *The Season of Harvest*; *For Home and Freedom*; *Drums of Death*; and *Memories We Lost*. He received the Elder of the Order of the Burning Spear (EBS) from the President of Kenya for his cultural contributions in 2012. He earned a doctorate in East African Literature from the University of Nairobi.

Acronyms and abbreviations

AADS	African and African Diaspora Studies
AALS	Academy of African Languages and Science (at UNISA)
ACLALS	Association for Commonwealth Literature and Language Studies
ANC	African National Congress
ANCYL	ANC Youth League
ASA	American Sociological Association
AWS	African Writers Series (Heinemann)
BAC	Black Academic Caucus (UCT)
BSI	black-serving institution (United States)
BSM	Black Student Movement (Rhodes University)
CCWG	Curriculum Change Working Group (UCT)
CHE	Council on Higher Education
CHET	Centre for Higher Education Transformation
CODESRIA	Council for the Development of Social Science Research in Africa
CPU	Campus Protection Unit (Rhodes University)
CPUT	Cape Peninsula University of Technology
CRT	critical race theory
CSVR	Centre for the Study of Violence and Reconciliation
DACST	Department of Arts, Culture, Science and Technology
DHET	Department of Higher Education and Training
DUT	Durban University of Technology
EAC	East African Community
EALB	East African Literature Bureau
EFF	Economic Freedom Fighters
EFFSC	Economic Freedom Fighters Student Command
FRELIMO	Mozambique Liberation Front
GNU	Government of National Unity (South Africa)
HBCU	historically black colleges and university (United States)
HBLGU	historically black land-grant university (United States)
HBU	historically black university
HESA	Higher Education South Africa
HSRC	Human Sciences Research Council
HWLGU	historically white land-grant universities (United States)
HWU	historically white university
IAS	Institute of African Studies (University of Ghana)
ICL	income contingent loans
IEU	Islamic Education Unit (Ghana)

IMF	International Monetary Fund
IPATC	Institute for Pan-African Thought and Conversation (University of Johannesburg)
IPEDS	Integrated Postsecondary Education Data System (United States)
ISC	International Science Council
KOLA	Kenya Oral Literature Association
Medunsa	Medical University of South Africa (now Sefako Makgatho Health Sciences University)
MPLA	People's Movement for the Liberation of Angola
MUT	Mangosuthu University of Technology
NBC	New Black Consciousness
NCHE	National Commission on Higher Education
NH	New Humanism
NIC	newly industrialised country
NMMU	Nelson Mandela Metropolitan University
NP	National Party
NRF	National Research Foundation
NSFAS	National Student Financial Aid Scheme
NUSAS	National Union of South African Students
OBE	Outcomes-Based Education
OCED	Organisation for Economic Co-operation and Development
PAC	Pan Africanist Congress
PYA	Progressive Youth Alliance
RDP	Reconstruction and Development Programme
SAP	Structural Adjustment Programme
SAPSE	South African Post-School Education
SARChI	South African Research Chairs Initiative
SASCO	South African Student Congress
SASO	South African Students Organisation
SPU	Sol Plaatje University
SRC	Student Representative Council
STEM	science, technology, engineering, and mathematics
SUN	Stellenbosch University
SWAPO	South West Africa People's Organisation
TEFSA	Tertiary Education Fund for South Africa
TUT	Tshwane University of Technology
TVET	technical and vocational education and training
UCKAR	University Currently Known As Rhodes
UCT	University of Cape Town
UEA	University of East Africa

UJ	University of Johannesburg
UKZN	University of KwaZulu-Natal
UL	University of Limpopo
UM	University of Mpumalanga
Unisa	University of South Africa
UNITRA	University of Transkei
UNIVEN	University of Venda
UNIZUL	University of Zululand
USAf	Universities South Africa
USARF	University Students' African Revolutionary Front (Dar es Salaam)
USKAR	University Still Known As Rhodes
UWC	University of the Western Cape
VUT	Vaal University of Technology
WAISER	West African Institute for Social and Economic Research
WASU	West African Students Union
WSU	Walter Sisulu University
ZANU	Zimbabwe African National Union
ZAPU	Zimbabwe African People's Union

Ackowledgements

Writing is by its very nature a solitary activity. Responding to curriculum transformation in the humanities in South Africa, Africa and African-American studies was by its nature a social undertaking, particularly for an Institute for Pan-African Thought and Conversation (IPATC), based at the University of Johannesburg (UJ) in South Africa, and committed to social transformation in Africa as well as building bridges with the Diaspora. Thus, even in the deepest solitude, the editors of this volume depended on the support and input of many others. First, we would like to thank all the contributors to this volume for their patience and perseverance.

In recent times, curriculum transformation has attracted increasing attention in South Africa, Africa, the United States (US) and globally, as exemplified by the #RhodesMustFall and #BlackLivesMatter movements in South Africa and the US, respectively. This book provides a comprehensive examination of these issues for post-apartheid South Africa's curriculum transformation efforts, drawing lessons from post-colonial African countries including Nigeria, Ghana, Senegal, Uganda, Kenya and Tanzania as well as African-American studies in the post-civil rights era. Thus, this volume provides the platform for diverse voices including established scholars, mid-career academics and student activists from South Africa, Africa and the United States. We owe a profound debt of gratitude to these 25 contributors for their responsiveness and dedication to the project. Our persistent demand for revision of chapters was graciously accepted, thus ensuring the academic rigour of this peer-reviewed volume.

We would like to acknowledge that this project was funded by Carnegie Corporation of New York and we particularly thank Claudia Frittelli and Alloya Elwadie for supporting this project so enthusiastically. It is also important to note that this is the first project that Carnegie has funded at the University of Johannesburg. We would like to extend our sincere gratitude to Professor Adekeye Adebajo, Director, IPATC, whose consistent critique, input and support contributed significantly to the substance of this book. We are also grateful to Jacana Media, particularly its formidable publishing director, Bridget Impey, and colleagues Kelsey Matus and Megan Mance for their unwavering support throughout the editing, layout and proofreading stages. We also express our deep gratitude to our meticulous copy-editor, Glenda Younge, whose fingerprints appear on almost all the pages of this book.

We would further like to use this medium to express our condolences to the families of Professors Chris Wanjala and Harry Garuba. The prolific Kenyan and Nigerian scholars died during the editing process. Their chapters here on 'The development of contemporary literature in East Africa' and 'Decolonisation, the Heinemann African Writers Series and the making of a trans-national, Pan-African literary audience' are clear testament to their life-long commitment and dedication to the transformation project across Africa and its Diaspora.

We hope that this contribution will help to foster a better understanding of the challenges of curriculum transformation in South African universities and transformation efforts in other African countries and African-American studies in the US. We also hope that this book will shape the decisions of policymakers around curriculum transformation in higher education in South Africa, Africa and across the globe. *Aluta Continua, Victoria Acerta!*

Oluwaseun Tella and Shireen Motala
Johannesburg, November 2019

Section I: Introduction

Chapter 1

Transforming humanities curricula in South Africa, Africa and African-American studies

Oluwaseun Tella

Background and context: South Africa's curriculum transformation efforts

South Africa celebrated 25 years of black majority rule in 2019. While there has been visible transformation in the composition of the country's governing elite, other spheres, including economic and social frameworks, remain mostly untransformed. This is particularly evident in the country's higher education system, as South African universities continue to embrace international practices to be well positioned in global university rankings (Dlamini, 2016). Despite two-and-a-half decades of black majority rule, South African higher education continues to embrace European models and paradigms. Paradoxically, concepts such as Africanisation, indigenisation and decolonisation of the curriculum have become buzzwords, especially after 2015 (Mahabeer, 2018). Nonetheless, in general, the country's universities continue to reflect Eurocentric, colonial and apartheid designs, and concerns have been expressed about over-representation of white academics and Western scholarship in the upper echelons of academia.

The #MustFall campaigns, student-led protests which began at the University of Cape Town (UCT) in 2015 and reverberated across the country's universities, ignited recent calls for curriculum transformation, the abolition of Eurocentric epistemologies, and for indigenous knowledge systems to be embraced (see Malabela, Chapter 7, Knowles, Chapter 8, and Ndelu, Chapter 9, in this volume). The protests also raised issues around access, fees and the slow pace of transformation across South African higher education institutions (see Motala, Chapter 5, in this volume). The country's universities are thus seen as sites of oppression, where Western literature and Eurocentric world-views are prioritised at the expense of African positionality. Universities are, therefore, failing in their primary responsibility to enhance social change as higher education spaces continue to perpetuate marginalisation and exclusion (Kotze, 2018).

The legacies of the apartheid regime's 'separate development' are visible in South African higher education in the democratic era. In 1949, the apartheid government set up the Eiselen Commission on Native Education, which was saddled with the primary responsibility of modifying the content and form of the curriculum taught to black South Africans. Its recommendations led to the passing of the Bantu Education Act in 1953, which created a segregated schooling system, and the subsequent 1959 University Extension Act, which extended the Bantu Education system to higher education institutions, giving rise to historically black universities (HBUs) such as Limpopo and Zululand. Relative to the historically white universities (HWU) – such as the universities of Cape Town, Pretoria and the Witwatersrand – these institutions are underfunded and ill-equipped, with negative impacts on the quality of research and teaching (see Adebajo, Chapter 2, Motala, Chapter 5, and Mngomezulu, Chapter 6, in this volume).

Successive governments since 1994 have adopted various policies and initiatives to transform the South African higher education sector, including the 1995 National Commission on Higher Education (NCHE) and the 1997 Education White Paper 3: *A Programme for Higher Education Transformation* (see Mngomezulu, Chapter 6, in this volume). Several institutions to fast-track the transformation of the higher education system have also been established. These include Higher Education South Africa (HESA), created in 2005 – now Universities South Africa – and the Centre for Higher Education Transformation (CHET), established in 1996. The CHET in particular aims to tackle the bottlenecks inhibiting transformation in this sector. However, South African universities remain significantly untransformed as Eurocentric world-views remain dominant. This has led to calls for curricula that speak to the socio-economic and political realities of the post-apartheid era. While curriculum transformation does not necessarily imply delinking from Western epistemologies, it advocates putting Africa at the centre of curriculum design and delivery. This manifests not only in the composition of academic staff, but also in the content of the curricula. As Nigerian academic Harry Garuba rightly notes, the racial composition of an institution does not always determine success in terms of curriculum transformation (Garuba, 2015). Transformation should go beyond fees reduction or free education, or the removal of the statues of colonial administrators and renaming institutions. Genuine transformation calls for serious engagement with knowledge production and delivery, and a disruptive shift that has been labelled 'a decolonial turn in the academic space' (Zondi, 2018). One way in which South African universities have perpetuated Eurocentrism is the reward system, which offers academics financial rewards for publishing in accredited journals. While this is commendable, it suffers from two shortcomings. First, Western journals are more valued and rewarded (Melber, 2018). Preference for international journals reinforces Western epistemic hegemony. Second, there has been an alarming increase in the number of South African academics publishing in predatory journals that appear on accredited lists. While the bodies responsible for compiling lists of accredited publications are culpable, academics that publish in these journals are also to blame.

Earlier decolonial and transformation efforts include attempts by academics like the late South African anthropologist Archie Mafeje, who vigorously argued for curriculum reforms as early as 1968 (Mngomezulu and Hadebe, 2018), and the 1976 student protests against the use of Afrikaans as the language of instruction in schools and oppressive Bantu Education. The development of isiZulu and isiXhosa as languages of instruction at the University of KwaZulu-Natal and Rhodes University, respectively, is a recent concrete attempt towards decolonisation (Rossouw, 2018). It is believed that the use of indigenous languages would facilitate better understanding of academic concepts and theories, and also enable students to relate well to content because many of them think in their indigenous languages. However, it remains to be seen if these efforts will yield the desired results, given the slow pace of the implementation of this initiative at the University of KwaZulu-Natal.

South Africa's 1997 Higher Education Act notes the need to redress past discrimination and ensure representativeness and equal access (South African Government, 1997). However, the overarching theme of curriculum transformation debates is the re-awakening of indigenous knowledge, practices and languages that have been relegated to the background. It is important that Africa-centred scholarship is embraced in order to thwart the hegemony of Western episteme. While Western scholarship is critical for the development of the West, it does not sufficiently capture the African experience (Matthews, 2018). The salience of transformation stems from the hegemonic notion that Western epistemologies are universal and that indigenous knowledge systems are of less value. Decolonisation and transformation thus connote the struggle against epistemicides with the ultimate objective of understanding other knowledge systems. South African scholar Lesley le Grange (2016) highlighted five key factors that could transform South African curricula: (1) assessing the relevance of Western disciplines for domestic African contexts; (2) creating transdisciplinary knowledge that incorporates indigenous communities; (3) developing a curriculum that reflects local and regional realities; (4) teaching students about the Cradle of Humankind; and (5) drawing lessons from the Inter-cultural University of the Indigenous Nations and Peoples, Amawtay Wasi, in Ecuador. The last approach – learning from the experiences of other countries – forms the crux of this book. Beyond the use of internally constructed strategies to foster curriculum transformation in South Africa, it would add value to draw lessons from the curriculum transformation efforts of other African countries and African-American studies in the United States.

Lessons from the experiences of other African countries: Nigeria, Ghana, Senegal, Uganda, Kenya and Tanzania

The end of colonialism in Africa from the 1950s and 1960s witnessed the rise of struggles to transform the continent's universities. This marked the most important era in curriculum transformation efforts in African higher education, evident in the rise of leading scholars such as Nigeria's Kenneth Dike, Guyana's Walter Rodney and Senegal's Cheikh Anta Diop, who championed decolonial schools: the Ibadan School of History, the Dar es Salaam School of Political Economy and the Dakar School of Culture, respectively. These centres used rigorous research techniques, such as nationalist historiography and oral sources, to challenge Eurocentric epistemologies (see Falola, Chapter 13, Rugumamu, Chapter 14, and Mboup, Chapter 15, in this volume). However, these schools were criticised on many levels. The Ibadan School was chastised for presenting a narrow historical perspective, while detractors pointed to the Dar es Salaam school's emphasis on economic determinism (see Falola, Chapter 13, and Rugumamu, Chapter 14, in this volume).

Beyond the efforts of these scholars and their schools, many first-generation African scholars vigorously fought Western epistemological dominance. These included political scientists such as Kenya's Ali A Mazrui and Nigeria's Claude Ake; anthropologists such as South Africa's Archie Mafeje and Ghana's Maxwell Owusu; geographers like Kenya's Simeon Ominde; historians like Ghana's Adu Boahen and Nigeria's Jacob FA Ajayi; and literary scholars such as Nigeria's Chinua A Achebe, Senegal's Ousmane Sembène, Kenya's Ngũgĩ wa Thiong'o and Uganda's Okot p'Bitek (Arowosegbe, 2014a). South Africa could draw lessons from these African countries and create similar schools, as well as adopt research techniques such as nationalist historiography and oral sources to capture the socio-economic and political realities of contemporary South Africa.

However, the efforts of these schools of thought and first-generation scholars have been eroded as many African universities, such as the University of Ibadan, the University of Dar es Salaam and the University of Dakar (Cheikh Anta Diop University), continue to perpetuate the hegemony of Western thought and wallow in epistemic crises, as seen in their continuous academic dependence on Europe and the United States. This is compounded by the fact that Africa's research funding and its volume of internationally recognised publications are infinitesimal (Arowosegbe, 2014b). This challenge was especially daunting in the 1980s when the International Monetary Fund (IMF) and the World Bank imposed structural adjustment programmes. The emergence of military regimes and the attendant human rights abuses, as well as Cold War politics across Africa, further dampened academic freedom (Mazrui, 2003).

The West remains the generator and exporter of concepts and theories that are tested in Africa. It continues to attract many students from Africa, and African scholars continue to pride themselves on the validation of their scholarship in the West through publication in so-called 'high impact journals' (Ndlovu-Gatsheni, 2018). Kenyan academic Ali Mazrui (2003: 147) poignantly noted that 'African universities have been the highest transmitters of Western culture in African societies. The high priests of Western civilization in the continent are virtually all products of those cultural seminaries called "universities".' It is against this backdrop that a Nigerian scholar, Claude Ake (1979), argues that Western social science perpetuates imperialism, although it embraces a subtle academic rather than forceful economic imperialism.

Ugandan academic Mahmood Mamdani (2018) argues that the African university emerged as an integral part of the Western colonial agenda to build institutions and individuals that would champion 'excellence', irrespective of domestic context. However, after decolonisation, intellectuals emerged who prioritised relevance over excellence. These scholars were primarily concerned with the specificities of their domestic context (Mamdani, 2018). But, as noted earlier, the efforts of this generation of African academics have largely vanished. This is another important lesson for South Africa. It is not only important to call for curriculum transformation, but the process must also be internalised and institutionalised to guarantee generational mobility.

Lessons from African-American studies
The African-American scholar Molefi Kete Asante has often argued that the education offered to African Americans alienates them from their culture and traditions, and glorifies Western culture. An emancipatory education would take cognisance of the need to engage Africa's and America's history, using Afrocentricity as a framework. Thus, teaching and research must be framed from an African standpoint. This implies that African Americans should be the subjects rather than the objects of education to counteract inferiority and marginalisation (Asante, 1991).

Historically black colleges and universities (HBCUs) were founded primarily to offer education to African Americans. In a country that confronts racial discrimination, HBCUs seek to, among other things, maintain black traditions, serve as a source of leadership for the black community and produce competent black graduates (Brown and Davis, 2001). Similar to the realities in apartheid South Africa, before the American Civil War (1861–65) higher education was racially segregated and African-American students were denied access to education through institutional and legal frameworks such as Jim

Crow laws and Black Codes (see Morris, Chapter 21, and Allen, Jones and Regassa, Chapter 23, in this volume). It is not therefore surprising that by 1865, literate African Americans accounted for only 5 per cent of a total black population of around 4.5 million (Brown and Davis, 2001). This period saw the burgeoning of HBCUs. However, in contrast to the realities in South Africa's post-apartheid era, there was significant financial support for HBCUs in the post-Civil War period, and these institutions emerged as veritable sources of socio-economic and political mobility among black Americans (see Allen, Jones and Regassa, Chapter 23, in this volume). Thus, HBCUs are critical to African Americans' influence and roles in a society that is exclusionary and discriminatory. Nevertheless, these institutions remain underfunded in comparison to 'historically white universities and colleges' (HWCUs).

The development of African studies in America was directly linked to the independence of African countries and the civil rights movement in the United States in the 1960s (Ferreira, 2010). While independence resulted in more African students attending American universities, the civil rights movement ignited the entry of African Americans into predominantly white universities and colleges. However, these students and academics were shocked by the racism they experienced in these institutions. This led to the embrace of Pan-Africanism and calls for curriculum transformation, relevance and social justice (Zeleza, 2011). Interest in African studies and area studies was also propelled by Cold War politics. The US government was actively involved in the development of African studies with the aim of promoting national security and global hegemony. For example, the 1958 National Defense Education Act VI provided for the teaching of African languages (Ferreira, 2010). Thus, African studies during this period were shaped by US foreign policy as Washington attempted to universalise Euro-American knowledge across the globe, including Africa.

African-American studies emerged in the United States as a Pan-African project and focused on decolonisation in Africa and civil rights struggles in America in the post-Second World War era (Zeleza, 2011). Two important schools emerged, namely, the Atlanta School of Sociology championed by individuals such as W.E.B. Du Bois and Richard Wright, and the Howard School of International Affairs with prominent scholars such as Ralph Bunche and Merze Tate (see Morris, Chapter 21, and Johnson, Chapter 22, in this volume). Both schools relied on rigorous research techniques – surveys, field interviews and ethnography – to debunk the notion of black inferiority. The onus lies with South African academics to take a cue from this approach to confront the ubiquitous legacies of apartheid in higher education.

Approach and content

This book of 24 chapters is structured in seven sections. The first two introductory chapters present an overview of the major themes of the book. This chapter lays the foundation of, and provides a background to, the study. In Chapter 2, Nigerian scholar Adekeye Adebajo notes that South Africa has continued to adopt Western models in the democratic era. This is evident in the challenges the country confronts in its quest to decolonise the humanities curriculum and free the country's higher education from Eurocentrism. The author argues that, while there have been reform efforts on the part of post-apartheid governments such as the 1995 National Commission on Higher Education and the 2000 National Student Financial Aid Scheme, South Africa's higher education remains largely untransformed. Adebajo offers potential lessons for South Africa's higher education sector from other African countries and African-American studies in the United States.

Section II comprises four chapters, which engage the challenges that confront transformation efforts in South Africa's higher education sector. South African scholar Crain Soudien's chapter locates the student protests between 2015 and 2017 within broader epistemological and ontological issues. He opines that, while epistemological considerations are well-engaged in South Africa, ontological issues have been largely neglected. Despite the fact that ontological considerations have identified racism to be a major challenge in contemporary South Africa, they have been unable to engage its psychological effects, particularly the 'phenomenon of black pain'. In Chapter 4, South African educationist Ahmed Bawa observes that to understand the rationale for the heavy reliance of South Africa's higher education system on Western epistemologies, there is an urgent need to investigate the conditions that led to the emergence of South African universities. He uses transformation efforts at the former University of Natal as a case study to illustrate these points.

In Chapter 5, South African scholar Shireen Motala reveals that successive South African governments in the post-1994 democratic era have supported equity in higher education, despite declining government revenues. However, high levels of inequality persist, begging the question of the efficacy of government policies on equity. To address this issue, the author engages four key themes: (1) fee-free education and free higher education; (2) education as a public and private good; (3) expansion, equity and quality of education; and (4) equitable funding models and approaches. Section II concludes with a chapter by another South African academic, Bheki Mngomezulu, who argues that the apartheid education system was characterised by a glaring dichotomy between the advantaged historically white institutions and the disadvantaged historically black institutions. Despite the efforts of successive post-apartheid governments to improve the academic administration and capacity at the HBUs such as the universities of Limpopo, Walter Sisulu and Zululand, the author notes that these institutions remain confronted by greater challenges than the HWUs in terms of funding, infrastructure, research and teaching. These challenges have stymied transformation efforts at the HBUs.

The three chapters in Section III present the lessons that can be drawn from South Africa's student movements. Relying on primary data supplemented with media reports, former South African student activist Musawenkosi Malabela assesses student protests at the University of the Witwatersrand (Wits) between 2015 and 2016. Two key issues that emerge in this chapter include the call for transformation and a decolonised curriculum, and the response of university management. The student protests at Rhodes University are the subject of Chapter 8 by Zambian–South African scholar Corrine Knowles. She argues that, without carefully constructed and implemented policies around teaching, working and living spaces at Rhodes, the university will continue to embrace neoliberal ideas, thus circumscribing transformation efforts. Knowles then deploys three concepts – embodiment, collectivism and recentring – to engage the nexus between the student protests and transformation discourses.

Another South African scholar-activist, Sandile Ndelu, engages the 'Fallist' student protests at the University of Cape Town (UCT) in Chapter 9. She notes that the call for a decolonised curriculum at UCT must be seen in the light of marginalisation and epistemic violence experienced by black students who refuse to 'whiten up' at the University. She then outlines the demands of the movement, most especially the removal of Cecil Rhodes's statute in 2015 and the call for a decolonised curriculum. The events that followed led the movement and university management to engage with 'what the university teaches, who teaches it, and how it teaches' (see Ndelu, Chapter 9, in this volume).

Section IV highlights the issues around the transformation of South Africa's humanities curriculum. South African academic Joel Modiri considers the conditions that can enhance the success of the decolonisation of the education project in South Africa in Chapter 10. The author argues that efforts to decolonise the curricula in the country will only be meaningful if they take cognisance of the struggle for a decolonised world. Modiri submits that the deployment of decolonisation by academics and policy-makers must take cognisance of South Africa's peculiar settler–colonial past. In Chapter 11, Nigerian scholar Jimi Adesina argues that while the teaching and learning of sociology must be embedded within an African context, there is still an over-reliance on Western theories and models, which are often taught out of context. The author debunks the widespread idea that there is a lack of African scholarship on sociology.

He submits that this reflects ignorance and neglect of African social science scholarship. South African scholar Philip Higgs argues in Chapter 12 for the revival of indigenous African knowledges – which have been relegated to the back-burner – in the quest for curriculum transformation in the discipline of philosophy. This is critical for the socio-economic circumstances of South Africans to find expression in the country's educational spaces. In contrast to scholars who have argued for Africa to de-link from Western thought, Higgs advocates what he refers to as a 'fusion of epistemologies', that is, a synthesis of indigenous African knowledges and Western epistemologies.

Section V of this volume offers potential lessons for South Africa that can be drawn from African schools of thought, including the Ibadan, Dar es Salaam and Dakar schools. Nigerian historian Toyin Falola discusses the Ibadan School of History in Chapter 13. The author notes that the appointment of Kenneth Dike at the University College, Ibadan, resulted in an intellectual struggle against a Eurocentric view of African history that had dominated the university's School of History. Deploying oral sources and nationalist historiographies, Dike challenged the negative depiction of Africa by Western historians, and sought to ensure that the continent's history was more objectively portrayed by its own scholars. Other important academics of this school included Adiele Afigbo, Obaro Ikime, Tekena Tamuno and Bolanle Awe. They analysed topics ranging from indirect rule to African leadership and institutions. In Chapter 14, Tanzanian scholar Severine Rugumamu presents the Dar es Salaam School of Political Economy, which emerged in 1964. Some of the prominent members of this school included Guyana's Walter Rodney and Congo's Jacques Depelchin and Ernest Wamba-dia-Wamba. These scholars ascribed Tanzania's and, by extension, Africa's underdevelopment to colonialism and capitalism. Rugumamu illustrates that the internal contradictions of the capitalist system in the 1970s, the East Asian miracle by the 1980s and the disintegration of the Soviet Union by 1991, resulted in the decline of the Dar es Salaam School of Political Economy. Chapter 15 by Samba Mboup, a Senegalese researcher, examines the Dakar School of Culture. The rise of the school was directly linked to the scholarship of Cheikh Anta Diop from Senegal and Samir Amin from Egypt. The school also benefited from the works of scholars such as Congo's Théophile Obenga, Senegal's Abdoulaye Ly and Ghana's Ayi Kwei Armah. Their progressive scholarship helped to shape societal transformation. However, this chapter focuses on how Cheikh Anta Diop adopted Afrikology to transform curriculum and research methods in the humanities and social sciences.

Section VI provides lessons from other parts of Africa, including Ghana, Kenya and Uganda. It also discusses the influence of the Heinemann African Writers Series. Nigerian scholar Harry Garuba argues that despite the criticisms levelled against the Heinemann African Writers Series in terms of its monopoly on the publication of African literature – especially between the 1960s and the 1990s – South Africa could draw lessons from this project in terms of decolonisation and higher education. Garuba notes that lessons can be drawn in areas such as accessibility, the publication of low-cost paperbacks and the republication of the classics. In Chapter 17, Ghanaian scholar David Owusu-Ansah opines that there is a need for a strong relationship between higher education institutions and society. For him, knowledge production across African universities ought to be informed by societal challenges. It is within this context that Owusu-Ansah focuses on the nexus between Ghana's post-colonial societal challenges and knowledge production. The author submits that the regime of Kwame Nkrumah, the founding Ghanaian leader (1957–66), focused on building an educational system from scratch to serve the cause of national development.

Ugandan academic Pamela Khanakwa traces the process of Africanisation at Makerere University in the 1960s and 1970s in Chapter 18. She engages transformation efforts in terms of the Africanisation of both academic and administrative staff at the institution, as well as in the context of curriculum transformation. She uses archival documents gathered from the Makerere University Library, supplemented by other relevant literature. In Chapter 19, Kenyan academic Chris Wanjala highlights the transformation efforts of scholars such as Kenya's Ngũgĩ wa Thiong'o, Uganda's Okot p'Bitek and Uganda's Taban Lo Liyong at the University of Nairobi in Kenya, and in the East African sub-region more broadly, from the 1970s. The author explores how these literary figures used oral and popular literature that revolved around African people, society and history to challenge Eurocentric ideas across East Africa.

African-American studies are the focus of Section VII. South African-American scholar Zine Magubane examines the 'pre-history' of the disciplines in African studies in the United States. She explores the development of concepts for the study of Africans and the African diaspora, and notes the spread of the disciplines of African studies and, by extension, Western epistemologies across the globe. Magubane highlights the 'intellectual confrontations' and 'social particularities' that determined how the history of people of African descent was researched before the emergence of African and African-American studies in the United States. African-American academic Aldon Morris shows how the Atlanta School of Sociology, which emerged in a black university, prided itself on the principle of 'accurate scholarship that would disprove black inferiority and lay the foundation for black activism that produced liberation movements, thus enabling blacks to reach their full potential'. Prominent members of this school included W.E.B. Du Bois, Richard Wright and Monroe Nathan. The school adopted rigorous research techniques to study black people and the oppression they encountered in America.

In Chapter 22, another African-American scholar, Krista Johnson, also acknowledges the need for curriculum transformation in higher education. She examines the epoch of widespread racial segregation in the United States between the 1930s and 1950s. She focuses particularly on the Howard School of International Affairs and the work of eminent black academics, including Ralph Bunche, Alain Locke, Merze Tate and Eric Williams. These academics sensitised the broader public to issues of racism while acting as public intellectuals. In Chapter 23, American scholars Walter Allen, Chantal Jones and Gadise Regassa engage the emergence of HBCUs in the United States. They argue that the emergence of institutions such as Howard and Fisk was sparked by the racism and oppression experienced by black people in America. The authors note that HBCUs became – and remain – critical to the social mobility of more than 40 million black people in the United States.

In the concluding chapter, South African academic Shireen Motala offers a synthesis and summarises the book's major findings and conclusions focusing on the five main themes of transformation, developing agency, decolonising the curriculum, making knowledge accessible in African scholarship and implementing change in African-American studies.

References

Ake, C (1979) *Social Science as Imperialism: The theory of political development*. Ibadan: Ibadan University Press.
Arowosegbe, J (2014a) African studies and the bias of Eurocentricism, *Social Dynamics*, **40**(2): 308–21.
Arowosegbe, J (2014b) Introduction: African studies and the universities in postcolonial Africa, *Social Dynamics*, **40**(2): 243–54.
Asante, M (1991) The Afrocentric idea in education, *The Journal of Negro Education*, **60**(2): 170–80.
Brown, M and Davis, J (2001) The historically black college as social contract, social capital and social equalizer, *Peabody Journal of Education*, **76**(1): 31–49.
Dlamini, R (2016) The global ranking tournament: A dialectic analysis of higher education in South Africa, *South African Journal of Higher Education*, 30(2): 53–72.
Department of Education (1997) Education White Paper 3: A Programme for the Transformation of Higher Education. Tshwane: South African Department of Education. Available at: http://www.che.ac.za/sites/default/files/publications/White_Paper3.pdf (accessed 25 October 2019).
Ferreira, R (2010) The institutionalization of African studies in the United States: Origin, consolidation and transformation, *Revista Brasileira de História*, **30**(59): 71–88.
Garuba, H (2015) What is an African curriculum? *Mail & Guardian*, 17 April. Available at http://mg.co.za/article/2015-04-17-what-is-an-african-curriculum/ (accessed 18 August 2019).
Kotze, J (2018) On decolonisation and revolution: A Kristevan reading on the Hashtags student

movements and Fallism, *Politikon*, **45**(1): 112–27.

Le Grange, L (2016) Decolonising the university curriculum, *South African Journal of Higher Education*, **30**(2): 1–12.

Mahabeer, P (2018) Curriculum decision-makers on decolonising the teacher education curriculum, *South African Journal of Education*, **38**(4): 1–13.

Mamdani, M (2018) The African university, *London Review of Books*, **40**(14): 29–32.

Matthews, S (2018) Confronting the colonial library: Teaching political studies amidst calls for a decolonised curriculum, *Politikon*, **45**(1): 48–65.

Mazrui, A (2003) Towards re-Africanising African universities: Who killed intellectualism in the post-colonial era? *Alternatives: Turkish Journal of International Relations*, **2**(3 & 4): 135–63.

Melber, H (2018) Knowledge production and decolonisation: Not only African challenges, *Strategic Review for Southern Africa*, **40**(1): 4–15.

Mngomezulu, B and Hadebe, S (2018) What would the decolonisation of a Political Science curriculum entail? Lessons to be learnt from the East African experience at the Federal University of East Africa, *Politikon*, **45**(1): 66–80.

Ndlovu-Gatsheni, S (2018) The dynamics of epistemological decolonisation in the 21st Century: Towards epistemic freedom, *Strategic Review for Southern Africa*, **40**(1): 16–45.

Rossouw, J (2018) South Africa's enduring colonial nature and universities, *Strategic Review for Southern Africa*, **40**(1): 65–81.

South African Government (1997) Higher Education Act 101. Pretoria: South African Government.

Zeleza, P (2011) Building intellectual bridges: From African studies and African-American studies to Africana studies in the United States, *Afrika Focus*, **24**(2): 9–31.

Zondi, S (2018) Decolonising international relations and its theory: A critical conceptual meditation, *Politikon*, **45**(1): 16–31.

Chapter 2
Vanquishing the ghost of Cecil Rhodes: Historical struggles to transform South Africa's humanities curriculum

Adekeye Adebajo

Although I studied as a Rhodes Scholar from Nigeria at Oxford University in England, I have always justified my acceptance of the scholarship as a pragmatic decision – to take a slice of the wealth plundered from Africa by the imperial robber-baron to pursue anti-colonial causes in order to bite the hand that fed me. Cecil John Rhodes, the greatest individual historical symbol of imperialism until his death in 1902, dreamed of building a railway from the Cape to Cairo. He described Africa north of the Limpopo as South Africa's 'natural hinterland', extending railways and telegraph poles northwards. This ruthless diamond and gold magnate sought to spread what he saw as 'enlightened' British culture, values and institutions to as much of Africa as possible. As prime minister of the Cape Colony between 1890 and 1895, Rhodes also introduced social segregation (later called apartheid from 1948) for 'non-whites' in schools, hospitals, theatres, prisons, sports and public transport. This forced blacks to carry passes (a precursor of apartheid's 'dumb pass') and removed thousands of members of these groups from the colony's electoral rolls. Two South African universities are heavily influenced by the legacy of Rhodes: the University of Cape Town (UCT), built on part of his Groote Schuur estate by 1918; and Rhodes University, built from endowments from the Rhodes Trust in 1904, and named after its benefactor.[1]

From Rhodes to Mbeki
South Africa's post-1945 leaders were thus, in a genuine sense, the heirs of Cecil Rhodes. South African premier between 1948 and 1954, DF Malan, spoke of 'preserving Africa for white Christian civilization' (Nolutshungu, 1975: 298), and believed that Euro-Christians needed to establish a trusteeship

---
1 See Magubane, B (1996) *The Making of a Racist State.* Trenton, NJ: Africa World Press; Maylam, P (2005) *The Cult of Rhodes: Remembering an imperialist in Africa.* Cape Town: David Philip; Rotberg, R (2002) *The Founder: Cecil Rhodes and the pursuit of power.* Johannesburg: Jonathan Ball; Samkange, S (1967) *On Trial for My Country.* London: Heinemann; and Thomas, A (1996) *Rhodes: The race for Africa.* Johannesburg: Jonathan Ball.

over Africans (Nolutshungu, 1975). Apartheid governments saw themselves as very much part of the West, members of the 'white dominions' (with Australia, Canada and New Zealand) sharing Western culture, economic systems and security concerns (Barber and Barrett, 1990: 6). Hendrik Verwoerd, the Grand Wizard of apartheid and the architect of the 1953 Bantu Education Act – which provided inferior and only basic education for blacks – claimed that whites had brought civilisation, education, economic development and order to Africa, and that South Africa would determine the continent's destiny (Barber and Barrett, 1990: 2). Even before President Thabo Mbeki (1999–2008) and his concept of the 'African Renaissance' (Adebajo, 2016), these were colonial 'Renaissance men' seeking to spread enlightenment to a 'Dark Continent'. Such patronising thinking was very much a feature of South African political thought from Cecil Rhodes to FW de Klerk.

Despite Thabo Mbeki's efforts to integrate South Africa into the rest of Africa, these efforts have not been deeply entrenched within South African society, as demonstrated by the xenophobic attacks against mostly black African citizens, which killed an estimated 350 people between 2008 and 2015 (*The Economist*, 2015). Many black South Africans still talk about the rest of Africa as if they were not part of it. The fact that so many symbols of apartheid still litter South Africa's political landscape, two-and-a-half decades after the end of apartheid, astonishes many African visitors. Streets still bear the names of racist colonial and apartheid stalwarts like Jan Smuts and Hendrik Verwoerd. Statues of imperial rogues, such as Cecil Rhodes, are ubiquitous in Cape Town. Military monuments in Tshwane (Pretoria) celebrate white supremacy in the wars of dispossession of the black majority. Most astonishingly, outside South Africa's Parliament – the deliberative body of Africa's greatest hope – stands a statue of Louis Botha, a white military conqueror, on horseback. Nothing could better symbolise South Africa's cultural limbo, caught in a shameful past of arrogant European racism and struggling to arrive at a future as the midwife of Africa's Renaissance (Adebajo, 2010).

Paradoxically, South Africa is both the most Pan-African and the least Pan-African country in Africa. Its national anthem starts with the words 'God bless Africa'; its ruling party is called the African National Congress (ANC); its other main black liberation movement is called the Pan Africanist Congress (PAC); and many of the leaders of its liberation movement grew up in exile in Lusaka, Gaborone, Mbabane, Harare and Dar es Salaam. But many of South Africa's white leaders viewed the country as a European outpost, a kind of Australia in Africa, and many South Africans still hold the image of Africa as a 'Dark Continent' of conflicts and diseases from which they are apart (Adebajo, 2010).

Thabo Mbeki's own vision of an African Renaissance was inspired by his shock at what he regarded as the 'slave mentality' of black South Africans after his return home from exile in 1990. As he put it:

> The beginning of our rebirth as a Continent must be our own rediscovery of our soul... It was very clear that something had happened in South African society, something that didn't happen in any other African society. The repeated observation is that 'These South Africans are not quite African, they're European' (Gevisser, 2009: 221).

Mbeki also criticised the black intelligentsia, many of whose members he felt were timid and too deferential to their white colleagues. He further sought to use the Renaissance vision to convince fellow South Africans – who had for decades been indoctrinated by racist white rulers – to embrace not just a new South African identity, but also a new African identity (Mbeki, 2001: 4–5). As Mbeki told his fellow South Africans in 1999:

> No longer capable of being falsely defined as a European outpost in Africa, we are an African nation in the complex process simultaneously of formation and renewal... We will work to rediscover and claim the African heritage, for the benefit especially of our young generation (Mbeki, 2001: 4–5).

As Kenyan scholar Ali Mazrui noted, no African leader other than a black South African president could have made Mbeki's famous 1996 'I am an African' speech without being marched off to an asylum.[2]

After two-and-a-half decades of a black-led government in South Africa, the country's education system is still stalked by the ghost of Cecil Rhodes and his heirs. Colonial epistemologies and the dominance of Western thought are still ubiquitous throughout South Africa's education system while African epistemologies are marginalised. This book thus explicitly seeks to draw on transformation lessons from post-colonial Africa and post-civil rights African-American studies in an effort to contribute to the literature on, and policies for, transforming South Africa's curriculum in the field of humanities. Such lessons obviously need to be carefully applied to post-apartheid South Africa's own specific and idiosyncratic context.

The 2015 student-led #RhodesMustFall and similar movements at South African universities were at the forefront of more contemporary efforts to transform these institutions, their curricula and institutional cultures, to

---

2   This statement was made at a presentation by Ali Mazrui, which I attended in 2004.

rename colonial and apartheid-era buildings and generally fight the cause of disadvantaged black students.[3] It is thus critical to have an inter-generational debate between established and emerging scholars to ensure that new voices are part of important discourses and debates, which are often dominated by the same voices. It is important, however, to note that an estimated R1 billion of damages was recorded during the unrest on various campuses,[4] and this movement has not always demonstrated discipline and restraint in its activism. Nevertheless, this book seeks to contribute positively to shaping South Africa's education policies in the area of curriculum transformation.

The heirs of Cecil Rhodes: The South African context
Post-apartheid transformation policies

Despite the rhetoric of 'transformation', post-apartheid South Africa tends to look to the West for its models. For example, the country's post-1994 outcomes-based education (OBE) system was borrowed from Australia, Canada and New Zealand, while its first cabinet office in the presidency was borrowed from Britain. Due to the failure of economic policies and political autocracy in countries like Zambia and Tanzania, where many South African leaders were exiled during the apartheid era, there was a tendency not to look to Africa, but rather to the West for models for South Africa's post-apartheid governance. This context helps to explain the stubborn persistence of Eurocentric curricula in South African universities in the post-apartheid era.

South Africa's higher education sector reflects an inheritance of over three-and-a-half centuries of both colonial and apartheid domination of a European-descended white minority over a 90 per cent black majority. Apartheid produced socio-economic inequalities, and not just discriminatory laws. It also deeply entrenched patronising political and cultural attitudes, which permeated South Africa's historically white universities such as the universities of Cape Town, Stellenbosch, the Witwatersrand (Wits), Pretoria, Rhodes, and the Rand Afrikaans University (RAU), from which the black majority was largely excluded during the apartheid era.

Thirty-six universities and technikons were inherited from the apartheid government in 1994, which were later reduced to 26 through mergers and incorporations. As South African academic Philip Higgs recognised in 2016,

---

3   See, for example, Tabensky, P and Matthews, S (eds) (2015) *Being at Home: Race, institutional culture and transformation at South African higher education institutions*. Pietermaritzburg: University of KwaZulu-Natal; and the student-driven and -written book, *Rioting and Writing: Diaries of Wits Fallists* (Society, Work and Politics Institute (SWOP), Wits University, Friedrich Ebert Stiftung and Ford Foundation, June 2017).

4   I thank Ahmed Bawa for providing me with this statistic.

South Africa's education sector still mirrors colonial education paradigms and the hegemony of Western thought, with African knowledge systems and the voices of African indigenous populations marginalised: a phenomenon which critics have described as 'epistemicide' (Higgs, 2016; Lange, 2017; see also Higgs, Chapter 12, in this volume). As Cameroonian scholar Achille Mbembe noted, the demand after the end of apartheid in 1994 was, therefore, to transform the universalisation of Western thought and instead achieve 'pluriversalism'.[5]

Given this difficult inheritance, South Africa's black-led governments after 1994 had an obligation to support the development of a university curriculum that radically moved away from white domination and Eurocentric epistemologies, and instead reflected the aspirations, cultures and experiences of the long-subjugated black majority. Transformation debates revolved around two perspectives: demographic change in terms of race, gender and language, as well as changing the traditional culture of privilege and power, which marginalised black students. A second view argued that an ideological process was needed to overturn a structural process of domination. Scholars like South Africa's Crain Soudien (who chaired a committee on transformation and the elimination of discrimination in South African higher education institutions in November 2008) rightly argued that both changes were needed (Soudien, 2010; see also Chapter 3 in this volume).

A National Commission on Higher Education (NCHE) was established by the Nelson Mandela government in 1995, which submitted its report, 'An Overview of a New Policy Framework for Higher Education', a year later (NCHE, 1996). This document proposed that South Africa seek to establish a single, coordinated national education system, harnessed to increasing access to education for the previously disadvantaged black majority. A Green Paper on Higher Education Transformation was subsequently published in 1996, and the Education White Paper 3 a year later.[6] The focus was on massification to increase the number of students in the sector. However, by 1999, there were 140 000 fewer students in higher education than expected by the NCHE report, despite increasing enrolment in historically white universities. The number of students in historically black universities such as Fort Hare, Limpopo, Walter Sisulu, Venda and Zululand declined, and they continued to suffer from a lack of administrative capacity (see Mngomezulu, Chapter 6, in this volume). While

---

5   See Mbembe, A (2016) Decolonizing the University: New directions, *Arts and Humanities in Higher Education*, **15**(1): 29–45.

6   Green Paper on Higher Education Transformation, December 1996; and General Notice 1196 of the 1997 Education White Paper 3, *A Programme for the Transformation of Higher Education*, South African Ministry of Education, Tshwane, 24 July 1997. Available at: http://www.che.ac.za/sites/default/files/publications/White_Paper3.pdf (accessed June 2018).

UCT's recurrent expenditure was R2.9 billion in 2016, the University of Limpopo's was R1.5 billion in the same year.[7]

Although the 1997 government White Paper highlighted the need to advance 'all forms of knowledge and scholarship and … address the diverse problems and demands of the local, national and Southern African contexts',[8] curricula remained stubbornly untransformed, as faculties in historically white universities continued to be mostly white (typically about 70 per cent), and there continued to be resistance to transforming established curricula.

The National Student Financial Aid Scheme (NSFAS), implemented by 2000, provided bursaries and loans. The 2001 National Plan for Higher Education pushed for equity and increased access: staff and students were to reflect South Africa's demographics; black student graduation rates (at less than 50 per cent) were to be increased; black representation in academic and administrative positions was to be improved; and more students were to be admitted from southern Africa[9] (the number of students from the sub-region increased from 7 497 in 1995 to 35 725 a decade later) (Badat, 2010: 8). A National Research Foundation (NRF) was also established in April 1999 to fund research, including on indigenous knowledge systems. Despite these initiatives, by 2019 an alarming 80 per cent of 18- to 24-year-olds, mostly black South Africans, remained outside the university system.[10] Other critical issues involved the protection of African language studies; the urgency of reversing the underfunding of humanities, social sciences and the arts; the challenge of correcting the funding imbalance between historically white universities and historically black universities; and the need for South Africa's Department of Higher Education and Training (DHET) and its Department of Science and Technology to coordinate their efforts more closely to develop a joint strategy for transforming the country's higher education sector (these ministries were merged by President Cyril Ramaphosa in June 2019) (Badat, 2010).

A new generation of academics also needs to be trained to promote genuine curriculum transformation by equipping them with the knowledge to teach courses related directly to the African context. The sizeable number of African academics in South African universities can provide rich resources to achieve these goals, until enough black South Africans can be trained. As

---

7   These figures are from the published annual reports of the universities of Cape Town and Limpopo.

8   Education White Paper 3.

9   South African Ministry of Education, National Plan for Higher Education in South Africa. Pretoria, February 2001. Available at: http://www.dhet.gov.za/HED%20Policies/National%20Plan%20on%20Higher%20Education.pdf (accessed September 2019).

10   I thank Ahmed Bawa for providing me with this information.

South African academic Saleem Badat has further consistently noted, funding of higher education (including for curriculum innovation and post-graduate studies) remains a major problem, evidenced by the student-led #FeesMustFall movement, which emerged in 2015, calling for free education (Badat, 2010: 18). In December 2017, South Africa's outgoing president, Jacob Zuma, announced that the government would extend fully subsidised free higher education to poor and working-class students from 2018. Following this significant development, the government announced an allocation of an additional R57 billion for fee-free higher education for the poorest learners on a means-tested basis (Motala, 2017; see also Chapter 5 in this volume.)

Despite many government initiatives over the last two-and-a-half decades, government-funded universities – the traditional sites for the production of knowledge and waging intellectual debates – such as UCT and Wits, Stellenbosch and Pretoria, have remained stubbornly untransformed. White-dominated institutions typically continue to lack a sense of a Pan-African intellectual awareness or identification with their African geographical roots. Many have wondered why it took so long for a debate to emerge at UCT on Cecil Rhodes' blighted legacy (Magubane, 1996; Maylam, 2005). Rhodes University – named after the colonial plunderer – removed a statue of Rhodes from its main entrance as South Africa entered a democratic era, although an effort by British-South African academic Roger Southall to change the name of the university in August 1994 was soundly defeated in the institution's senate (Maylam, 2005).

The fall of Rhodes

So, why did it take so long for a debate to emerge at UCT on the legacy of Cecil Rhodes? It was only in March 2015 that Rhodes' colossal statue fell from the main entrance of the university, marking the beginning of South Africa's own student awakening. This lit the fuse that has ignited other student movements like it in the Western Cape, Johannesburg, Durban, Grahamstown and other university towns and cities across the country (see chapters 7 to 9 in this volume). The #RhodesMustFall movement also spread globally to universities in England (Oxford, Cambridge, the School of Oriental and African Studies [SOAS], Queen Mary, University College London [UCL]) and the United States (Harvard and Princeton) where the transformation of Eurocentric curricula was also placed on the agenda (Chantiluke, Kwoba and Nkopo, 2019).

If one listened to the students at UCT, the removal of Rhodes' statue in 2015 appeared to be a metaphorical call for the transformation of the university's curriculum, culture and faculties, which many blacks felt were alienating and still reflected a Eurocentric heritage. UCT's Student Representative Council (SRC) noted in March 2015:

> For too long, the narrative at this university has silenced the voices of black (coloured, Indian and African) students and black history. This university continues to celebrate, in its institutional symbolism, figures in South African history, who are undisputably white supremacists. Rhodes has been praised for donating this land to the university, building the South African economy and bringing 'civilisation' to this country. But for the majority of South Africans this is a false narrative, how can a colonizer donate land that was never his in the first place? (Office of the President, University of Cape Town Students' Representative Council Statement, 11 March 2015).

Mamphela Ramphele, the first black and first female Vice-Chancellor of UCT between 1996 and 2000, put her thoughts in writing in her 2013 memoir, *A Passion for Freedom*. As deputy vice-chancellor, she had attended marathon meetings with students. Ramphele noted, somewhat disdainfully, about these sessions, that students should only comment on academic issues and not on university decision-making. Many black male students particularly opposed her candidacy to become vice-chancellor because – according to her – she had been tough on sexual harassment, set boundaries on transformation and insisted on 'excellence'. She dismissed these criticisms as representing the 'psychology of the oppressed', arguing that these views were based on the fear of students that they would not be academically good enough. Ramphele's constant talk of 'excellence' and 'raising standards' employs terms that are often used to equate competence with whiteness. While she cited as her greatest achievement the changing of UCT's institutional culture (Ramphele, 2013), many would challenge this claim, with students continuing to complain about a Eurocentric culture and curriculum, and only about five black full professors out of more than 200 by 2015. Based on these figures, critics have argued that Ramphele and her successor, Njabulo Ndebele, were effectively in office rather than in power.

I had an exchange with one of Mamphela's successors as UCT, Vice-Chancellor Max Price, published in *The Sunday Independent* in March and April 2015. Although Price conceded that Rhodes' 'values and his ruthlessness, and his willingness to take the view that imperial ends were justified by any means, were appalling', he went on to make the extraordinary statement:

I do believe there's a risk of simplifying Rhodes ... it's important to examine why he came to be viewed as a great man. He achieved an enormous amount by the time he died ... a businessman, diplomat and Prime Minister of the Cape, a military strategist, and a philanthropist very committed to education, and in all these things he was successful.

Price later sought to distance himself from his own statement by unconvincingly arguing that he had been quoted out of context.[11] The views of these two vice-chancellors of UCT are, however, for this author, some of the reasons why the university's institutional culture has remained so stubbornly untransformed.

Ugandan scholar Mahmood Mamdani noted after an unhappy stint at UCT between 1996 and 1999 that the most powerful weapon of apartheid's leaders was to create enforced identities, which still linger into the present. These identities are reproduced in academia, the media and the popular imagination. As Mamdani put it:

It was the white intelligentsia that took the lead in creating apartheid-enforced identities in the knowledge they produced. Believing that this was an act of intellectual creativity unrelated to the culture of privilege in which they were steeped, they ended up defending an ingrained prejudice with a studied conviction (Mamdani, 1999).

Mamdani further noted that English-speaking institutions in South Africa had intellectual freedom, but lacked social accountability.

The 'hidden curriculum' in these historically white universities has also allowed many of their academics to remain gatekeepers in preserving the status quo. Excellence is often equated with race, and autonomy is used to defend white privilege (Mamdani, 1999). South African scholar Joel Modiri more recently noted, on the issue of curriculum transformation, that 'one of the more noteworthy revelations of the Fallist student movement has been its exposure of the mediocrity and ignorance – not of the students but of South African academics' (Modiri, 2016; see also Chapter 10 in this volume.) He went on to bemoan the depiction of knowledge in South African universities as predominantly Western, thus ignoring the contributions of African, Chinese and Indian scholars in fields such as medicine, physics, astronomy

---

11   See Michael Morris's interview with Max Price (2015) The student statue protest is significant, but the greater debate is what really matters, *The Sunday Independent*, 22 March 2015; Adebajo, A (2015) Why Price is wrong over Rhodes, *The Sunday Independent*, 29 March; Max Price, A false picture of UCT head's views on Rhodes, *The Sunday Independent*, 25 April; Adekeye Adebajo, Price has resorted to intellectual cowardice, *The Sunday Independent*, 12 April.

and mathematics (Modiri, 2016). There is thus an urgent need for a systematic formulation of what a decolonised curriculum would look like (Falola and Jennings, 2002).

The Eurocentric curriculum in South Africa has been so internalised that some scholars talk decolonisation while doing the exact opposite. For example, when South African academic Candice Moore reviewed my 2018 co-edited book on South African foreign policy, she did not understand that 'critical' non-South African perspectives meant 'important' Pan-African and other perspectives; she understood this to mean that South African scholars were incapable of being critical. More significantly, even as Moore calls for 'new African theories and perspectives', she advocates a focus on Western schools of thought – realism, constructivism and/or liberalism – before singling out British scholar Ian Taylor's 2001 book on South African foreign policy as the only one that has convincingly used a single theoretical framework, chastising my introduction for not citing Taylor's apparently seminal volume (Moore, 2019).

However, these Eurocentric schools of thought should not be our intellectual gods on the scholarship on the foreign policy of an African state. Chapter 8 in this volume by African-American scholar Krista Johnson presents an excellent example of the sort of decolonisation that is more convincing than Moore's unconscious Eurocentrism. Focusing on the work of black scholars such as Merze Tate, Ralph Bunche and Eric Williams at the Howard School of International Affairs from the 1930s to the 1950s, Johnson shows their 'epistemic and methodological commitment to the colonised and subaltern, and their treatment of slavery and colonialism as constitutive of the contemporary world system'. She further explains how this work 'centres race and its interlocking modalities of capitalism and imperialism in its interrogation of international relations and the international system'. Bunche thus deconstructs the theory of racism in global politics; Tate engages issues of race-ordering, hierarchy and exclusion in understanding race and empire; while Williams shows how the transatlantic slave trade directly contributed to Britain's expansion of trade, industrialisation and prosperity. This is the sort of scholarship that could credibly contribute to decolonising curricula and scholarship on Africa's international relations, rather than an unconscious reversion to Eurocentrism.

The heirs of Kenneth Dike: Lessons from the rest of Africa

African countries, other than South Africa, had universities created by their European colonial powers only from about 1948. These countries embarked on the decolonisation and Africanisation of these institutions from the 1950s, replacing both foreign staff and Eurocentric curricula. There were efforts to build African nationalist historiographies to support nation-building and to challenge Eurocentric history in Nigeria (Ibadan), Senegal (Dakar), Tanzania (Dar es Salaam), Kenya (Nairobi), Uganda (Makerere) and Ghana (Legon). In the process, these universities created some centres of excellence of African knowledge production, such as the Ibadan School of History, the Dakar School of Culture and the Dar es Salaam School of Political Economy (Adesina, 2005).

The Ibadan School of History emerged in the 1950s, and was one of the earliest efforts to create a 'nationalist historiography' that sought to counter European misrepresentations of African history as 'primitive', backward and lacking in agency. Members of this school included scholars such as Kenneth Dike, AE Afigbo, JFA Ajayi and Obaro Ikime. They innovatively used oral sources and sought to write the history of the pre-colonial and colonial periods from an African perspective, and in the process of writing about the achievements of the country's pre-colonial history, they helped to forge a Nigerian identity. These authors produced many of the textbooks on Nigerian history at all levels of education (see Falola, Chapter 13, in this volume.) However, the Ibadan School did have its critics, like Nigerian scholar Peter Ekeh, who argued that it was too empiricist, not theoretical enough, and tended to promote an elitist 'history from above' (Falola, 2001).

Tanzania's Dar es Salaam School of Political Economy emerged in 1964 from efforts to build a nationalist historiography (see Rugumamu, Chapter 14, in this volume.) The school was led by Marxist scholars like Guyana's Walter Rodney, who, in his famous 1972 book, *How Europe Underdeveloped Africa*, traced the roots of Africa's underdevelopment to European colonialism. He thus advocated African self-reliance and self-sustainability, condemning the African 'comprador class' that collaborated in their continent's exploitation, while placing ultimate responsibility in reversing this situation on Africans themselves (Rodney, 1982). Members of the Dar es Salaam School, such as the East Africans IN Kimambo and AJ Temu, also wrote on indigenous economic production, class, social formation and the impact of capitalism on Tanzania and Kenya (Falola, 2001). Critics of the school, such as Kenya's Ali Mazrui, however, complained about the lack of intellectual diversity of this largely Marxist school (Mazrui, 1967),[12] while others noted that its work on the colonial period focused too much on African citizens, and not enough on the colonial structure (Falola, 2001).

The Dakar School of Culture at the University of Dakar was led by Senegal's Cheikh Anta Diop, who was a forerunner of the Afrocentric approach which became part of African-American and Africology studies in the United States

---

12 Mazrui, A (1967) Tanzaphilia: A diagnosis, *Transition*, **31**(June–July): 20–26.

by the 1980s, led by scholars such as Molefi Asante and Leonard Jeffries. Diop challenged the cultural bias in Western scientific research, and what he felt was the racist view of Eurocentric scholarship in the 19th century and the first half of the 20th century.[13] Other scholars of the Dakar School included Théophile Obenga and Boubacar Barry. Diop's critics, however, accused him of an Afrocentric essentialism, while his linguistic research on the links between Wolof and ancient Egyptian languages was challenged as flawed (Falola, 2001; also see Mboup, Chapter 15, in this volume).

In Kenya in 1968, a group of three young academics in the English department at the University of Nairobi – Ngũgĩ wa Thiong'o, Henry Owuor-Anyumba and Taban Lo Liyong – led efforts to Africanise the curriculum. They argued that just adding literature in English from other parts of the world was insufficient to transform the curriculum, and that, since Africa was not an extension of the West, a concentric circle of Kenya, East Africa and Africa needed to be placed at the centre of reconceptualising a new curriculum. This led to a major transformation of curricula throughout East Africa (Garuba, 2015; see Wanjala, Chapter 19, in this volume). Similar to the arguments by Nigeria's Chinua Achebe and Palestinian-American Edward Said, this was not a call to delink from the rest of the world, but rather an effort to view the world from a Global South perspective.[14]

In 1958, Chinua Achebe published *Things Fall Apart* in reaction to what he regarded as the misrepresentation of Africa by Western authors such as Joyce Cary and Joseph Conrad in their novels, such as *Mister Johnson* (1939)[15] and *Heart of Darkness* (1902).[16] This eventually resulted in the birth of modern African literature under the Heinemann African Writers Series, which began in 1962. Heinemann produced 273 books, which essentially became Africa's literary canon, with writers such as Wole Soyinka, Nadine Gordimer, Tayeb Salih, Bessie Head and Ousmane Sembène (Currey, 2008). This was the first generation of modern African writers who transformed literature curricula across the continent (see Garuba, Chapter 16, in this volume). Penguin South Africa acquired the local rights to the African Writers Series, while Exclusive Books – the country's biggest bookstore with about 40 stores in 2018 – created

---

13 See Diop, CA (1963) *The Cultural Unity of Negro Africa*. Paris: Présence Africaine, English translation (1989) *The Cultural Unity of Black Africa: The domains of patriarchy and of matriarchy in classical antiquity*. London: Karnak House; and Diop, CA (1974) *African Origins of Civilization: Myth or reality*. Chicago, IL: Lawrence Hill Books.
14 See Achebe, C (1988) An image of Africa: Racism in Conrad's Heart of Darkness, in C Achebe (1990) [1988] *Hopes and Impediments: Selected essays*. New York: Anchor Books; and Said, EW (1994) [1993] *Culture and Imperialism*. New York: Vintage Books.
15 Cary, J (1962) [1939] *Mister Johnson*. New York: Time Life.
16 Conrad, J (2012) [1902] *The Heart of Darkness*. London: Penguin.

a Pan-African writers' series section with many of these and other writings in all of its stores, thus highlighting the potential of these books to help transform South Africa's literature curriculum and reading culture.

The heirs of W.E.B. Du Bois: Lessons from African-American studies

There are many parallels between the struggles of black South Africans for the transformation of their humanities curriculum and that of African Americans. The key difference, of course, is that while African Americans constitute only about 13 per cent of the US population, black South Africans comprise 90 per cent of the population in their country and also mostly run the government. It is thus important to interrogate the lessons that South African universities can learn from the efforts to create Departments of African-American Studies in the United States. *The African American Studies Reader* – edited by Nathaniel Norment, Jr and published in 2007 – is an 850-page anthology with 73 essays by leading African-American scholars who have traced the evolution of this discipline over four decades (Norment, 2007). Producing similar comparative research, based on African and African-American experiences, could provide valuable lessons for South Africa in transforming its humanities curriculum. This book on South Africa, Africa and African-American studies is also seeking to capture the key debates in the evolution of Africanised curricula on the continent and African-American studies over the last six decades to assist curriculum transformation efforts in South Africa.

As was the case in South Africa after apartheid ended in 1994, it was after the civil rights struggles from the 1950s that black American students entered predominantly white institutions in large numbers. This led to demands for 'Black Studies' courses by the first generation of African-American students alienated by white institutions with Eurocentric curricula, which often did not recognise black history and culture (see Magubane, Chapter 20, in this volume). From the 1970s, there was much criticism directed at 'Black Studies' programmes – including from prominent African-American scholars and activists such as Martin Kilson, Bayard Rustin and A Philip Randolph, who argued against what they regarded as the 'ghettoisation' of African-American studies and raised concerns about the rigour of these courses. Critics thus advocated that these programmes should be aligned to major disciplines such as history, politics and sociology. One of the most distinct aspects of this activist scholarship – with potential lessons for South Africa – was that they consistently argued that the curriculum and education in 'Black Studies' must be practical and linked to alleviating social problems in African-American communities (Norment, 2007).

Black feminist scholars like Angela Davis, Alice Walker and bell hooks also forced the establishment of Black Women's Studies by the late 1970s, successfully arguing that their narratives had been marginalised in Black Studies curricula. Another point of potential relevance to South Africa was that part of the goals of Black Studies curricula in the United States was to help white students overcome inherited racism and prejudice in order to build a more harmonious society (Norment, 2007). Two African-American schools of thought are thus of potential relevance to South Africa: the Atlanta School of Sociology (led by scholars such as Richard Wright Sr, W.E.B. Du Bois, Monroe Work and George Edmund Haynes)[17] and the Howard School of International Affairs (led by scholars such as Alain Locke, Ralph Bunche, Merze Tate and Eric Williams).[18]

The Atlanta School of Sociology was pioneered in the 1890s by Richard Wright and W.E.B. Du Bois with the explicit goal of using rigorous research methods of social science – including fieldwork in poor black communities – to disprove racist claims by white social scientists of black inferiority. The direct aim of this activist scholarship was thus to contribute to the dismantling of Jim Crow segregationist laws and racial discrimination in the United States (Morris, 2015). Du Bois' 1899 *The Philadelphia Negro*, in a genuine sense, was a pioneering work that heralded the birth of modern sociology (Du Bois, 1973; see Morris, Chapter 21, in this volume). The Howard School of International Affairs in the 1920s and 1930s saw African-American and Afro-Caribbean scholars challenging conventional Western ideas about empire and race in international relations (see Johnson, Chapter 22, in this volume.) In both the Howard and Atlanta schools, this scholarship was marginalised by mainstream Western sociology and international relations.

Lessons from transforming curricula at America's historically black colleges and universities, such as Atlanta, Howard, Fisk, Morehouse and Lincoln (see Chapter 23 in this volume), can also be potentially beneficial to transforming humanities curricula in South Africa's universities.

Conclusion

The schools of thought in both Africa and African-American studies had largely disappeared by the late 1970s, as new intellectual fads and ideas took hold and as new challenges arose to which academics in both locations were forced to respond. Many of the authors of these schools have since died, and a new generation of scholars has focused on new and emerging issues (governance,

---

17   See, for example, Morris, AD (2015) *The Scholar Denied: W.E.B. Du Bois and the birth of modern sociology.* Oakland, CA: University of California Press.
18   See, for example, Vitalis, R (2015) *White World Order, Black Power Politics: The birth of American International Relations.* Ithaca, NY: Cornell University Press.

conflict management, regional integration, poverty and single-mother households, institutionalised racism, etc.) based on their own contemporary challenges. Many African-American studies departments have also suffered from financial cuts and lost the intellectual dynamism of earlier years. In the African context, the enforced cuts in higher education linked to the Structural Adjustment Programmes (SAPs) of the 1980s, combined with widespread university closures, strikes and a weakening of the autonomy of universities across Africa, led to a mass exodus of many of the best academics from the continent, mostly to American universities, and inflicted great damage on research output in African universities, from which the continent is yet to recover.[19]

These lessons are particularly relevant to South Africa: recognising the need to continue to invest in higher education (and particularly in the field of humanities); maintaining the autonomy of universities from heavy-handed government intervention; and ensuring that institutions of higher education allow innovative ideas to flourish, that recognise and borrow from South Africa's geographical location in Africa.

Finally, the transformation of South Africa's humanities curriculum is not a theoretical issue and one must never assume that everyone is in support of it, but somehow it is simply not happening due to some invisible systemic failures. If transformation is to succeed, it is clear that it will have to be fought for. Senior black South African academics have often failed to take the lead in waging transformation battles, with many appearing to be comfortable with the perks and privileges of office. However, victory will not be handed to reformers on a silver platter. In my 16 years in South Africa, I have met many students of development studies who have never heard of Nigeria's Adebayo Adedeji or Malawian-Swede Thandika Mkandawire; literature students who think Nigeria's Buchi Emecheta and Ghana's Ama Ata Aidoo are traditional cures; politics students who think Kenya's Ali Mazrui and Nigeria's Bolanle Awe are exotic fetishes; sociologists who have not heard of South Africa's Ben Magubane and Archie Mafeje; undergraduate students who have not been taught by any black professors. This is clearly not a sustainable situation, and even the syllabi of some of the most supposedly progressive black professors have often failed to reflect the intellectual diversity and geographical location of South Africa in Africa. There is so much to do, and so little time to do it, if the ghost of Cecil Rhodes, which continues to stalk South Africa's intellectual life, is finally to be vanquished.

---

19 See, for example, Mamdani, M (2007) *Scholars in the Marketplace: The dilemmas of neo-liberal reform at Makerere University, 1989–2005*. Dakar: Council for the Development of Social Science Research in Africa [CODESRIA]; and Tshwane: Human Sciences Research Council [HSRC], 2008).

References

Achebe, C (1990) [1988] *Hopes and Impediments: Selected essays*. New York: Anchor Books

Adebajo, A (2010) Mandela and Rhodes: A monstrous marriage, in A Adebajo, *The Curse of Berlin: Africa after the Cold War*. New York: Columbia University Press; London: Hurst; Pietermaritzburg: University of KwaZulu-Natal Press, pp. 215–32.

Adebajo, A (2015a) Why Price is wrong over Rhodes, *Sunday Independent*, 29 March.

Adebajo, A (2015b) Price has resorted to intellectual cowardice, *Sunday Independent*, 12 April.

Adebajo, A (2016) *Thabo Mbeki: Africa's Philosopher-King*. Johannesburg: Jacana; Ohio: Ohio University Press, 2016.

Adesina, JO (2005) Realising the vision: The discursive and institutional challenges of becoming an African university, *African Sociological Review*, **9**(1): 23–39.

Badat, S (2010) The Challenges of Transformation in Higher Education and Training Institutions in South Africa. A report commissioned by the Development Bank of Southern Africa.

Barber, J and Barrett, J (1990) *South Africa's Foreign Policy*. Cambridge: Cambridge University Press.

Cary, J (1962) [1939] *Mister Johnson*. New York: Time Life.

Chantiluke, R, Kwoba, B and Nkopo, A (eds.) (2019) *Rhodes Must Fall: The struggle to decolonise the racist heart of empire*. London: Zed Books.

Conrad, J (2012) [1902] *The Heart of Darkness*. London: Penguin.

Currey, J (2008) *Africa Writes Back*. Oxford: James Currey.

Diop, AC (1963) *The Cultural Unity of Negro Africa*. Paris: Présence Africaine. English translation: *The Cultural Unity of Black Africa: The domains of patriarchy and of matriarchy in classical antiquity*. London: Karnak House, 1989.

Diop, AC (1974) *African Origins of Civilization: Myth or reality*. Chicago: Lawrence Hill Books.

Du Bois, WEB (1973) [1899] *The Philadelphia Negro*. New York: Kraus-Thompson.

Economist, The (2015) Blood at the end of the rainbow, 25 April (www.economist.com).

Falola, T (2001) *Nationalism and African Intellectuals*. Rochester, NY: University of Rochester Press.

Falola, T and Jennings, C (eds) (2002) *Africanizing Knowledge: African studies across the disciplines*. New Brunswick and London: Transaction.

Garuba, H (2015) What is an African curriculum? *Mail & Guardian*, 17 April (https://mg.co.za).

Gevisser, M (2009) *Thabo Mbeki: The dream deferred*. New York: Palgrave Macmillan.

Higgs, P (2016) The African Renaissance and the transformation of the higher education curriculum in South Africa, *Africa Education Review*, **13**(1): 87–101.

Jansen, J and Motala, S (eds) (2017) *Curriculum Stasis, Funding and the 'Decolonial Turn' in Universities: Inclusion and exclusion in higher education in South Africa*, Special Issue, *Journal of Education*, **68**: 15–30.

Lange, L (2017) 20 years of higher education curriculum policy in South Africa, Special Issue, *Journal of Education*, **68**: 31–57.

Magubane, BM (1996), *The Making of a Racist State*. Trenton, NJ: Africa World Press.

Mamdani, M (1999) There can be no African Renaissance without an Africa-focused intelligentsia, in MW Makgoba (ed.) *African Renaissance: The new struggle*. Johannesburg: Tafelberg, pp. 131–32.

Mamdani, M (2007) *Scholars in the Marketplace: The dilemmas of neo-liberal reform at Makerere University, 1989–2005*. Dakar: Council for the Development of Social Science Research in Africa (CODESRIA); and Tshwane: Human Sciences Research Council (HSRC) 2008.

Maylam, P (2005) *The Cult of Rhodes: Remembering an imperialist in Africa*. Cape Town: David Philip.

Mazrui, A (1967) Tanzaphilia: A diagnosis, *Transition*, **31** (June–July): 20–26.

Mbeki, T (2001) *Mahube: The Dawning of the Dawn. Speeches, lectures and tributes*. Johannesburg: Skotaville Media.

Mbembe, A (2016) Decolonizing the university: New directions, *Arts and Humanities in Higher Education*, **15**(1): 29–45.

Modiri, J (2016) In the fall: Decolonisation and the rejuvenation of the academic project in South Africa, *Daily Maverick*, 16 October (www.dailymaverick.co.za).

Moore, C (2019) Book Review: *Foreign Policy in Post-Apartheid South Africa: Security, Diplomacy and Trade*, *South African Journal of International Affairs*, **26**(2): 317–18.

Morris, AD (2015) *The Scholar Denied: W.E.B. Du Bois and the birth of modern sociology*. Oakland, CA: University of California Press.

Morris, M, interview with Max Price, The student statue protest is significant, but the greater debate is what really matters, *The Sunday Independent*, 22 March 2015.

Motala, S (2017) Achieving 'free education' for the poor: A realisable goal in 2018? In A Jansen and S Motala (eds) *Curriculum Stasis, Funding and the 'Decolonial Turn' in Universities: Inclusion and exclusion in higher education in South Africa*, Special Issue, *Journal of Education*, **68**: 15–30.

National Commission on Higher Education (NCHE) (1996) An Overview of a New Policy Framework for Higher Education, 22 August.

Nolutshungu, S (1975) *South Africa in Africa: A study in ideology and foreign policy*. Manchester: Manchester University Press.

Norment, N (ed.) (2007) *The African American Studies Reader*, 2nd edition. Chapel Hill, NC: Carolina Academic Press.

Office of the President, University of Cape Town Students' Representative Council Statement, 11 March 2015.

Ramphele, M (2013) *A Passion for Freedom*. London: IB Tauris.

Rodney, W (1982) *How Europe Underdeveloped Africa*. Washington DC: Howard University Press; originally published in London: Bogle-L'Ouverture Publications and Dar es Salaam: Tanzanian Publishing House, 1972.

Rotberg, R (2002) *The Founder: Cecil Rhodes and the pursuit of power*. Johannesburg: Jonathan Ball.

Said, EW (1994) [1993] *Culture and Imperialism*. New York: Vintage Books.

Samkange, S (1967) *On Trial for My Country*. London: Heinemann.

Soudien, C (2010) Transformation in Higher Education: A Briefing Paper. A report commissioned by the Development Bank of Southern Africa (DBSA).

SWOP (2017) *Rioting and Writing: Diaries of Wits Fallists*. Society, Work and Development Institute, University of the Witwatersrand; Friedrich Ebert Stiftung and Ford Foundation, June 2017.

Tabensky, P & Matthews, S (eds) (2015) *Being at Home: Race, institutional culture and transformation at South African higher education institutions*. Pietermaritzburg: University of KwaZulu-Natal Press.

Thomas, A (1996) *Rhodes: The race for Africa*. Johannesburg: Jonathan Ball.

Vitalis, R (2015) *White World Order, Black Power Politics: The birth of American International Relations*. Ithaca, NY: Cornell University Press.

Section II: The Challenges of Transforming South Africa's Higher Education Sector

Chapter 3

The significance of the decolonial turn in South African higher education

Crain Soudien

Introduction

The significance of the decolonial turn in South African higher education is interpreted principally in relation to the post-apartheid project. This project is largely described in much of the critical commentary as a continuation of the colonial discourse of South Africa's long experience of white dominance. Using a set of questions that emerged out of recent debates around the student uprising of the 2015–16 period, I attempt to situate the significance of the uprising in a larger set of related problematics. These problematics are both epistemological and ontological. They are about our understanding of life – how we explain the nature of the world in which we live, our languages, discourses, interpretative frameworks and the 'social' itself. This 'social' is what we understand by the nature of everyday human life, what we understand of ourselves and others when we are in engagement with each other, what we see in ourselves and what we see in others.

This chapter is stimulated by the conversation that took place after a presentation I delivered at the University of Pretoria. It provides a description of the context in which the questions in that discussion arose and attempts to locate in those questions the significance of the 'decolonial turn' in its larger context. It argues that two distinct positions have emerged out of the discussion. The first of these is New Black Consciousness and the second is New Humanism. I show, firstly, what these positions stand for and how they differ from each other and, secondly, what they help us understand and what their blind-spots may be.

The structure of this chapter pivots on the issues that arose in the discussion at the University of Pretoria. I have used these to frame the commonalities and differences between the positions that I outline in the decolonial movement.

Provocation one: A debate between Africanists

In 2017, I gave a talk at a South African university on the debates and the positions that were emerging in the decolonial discussion in South Africa. The purpose of the talk was to develop an exploratory mapping of the discussion and to suggest the major positions that were beginning to take shape. Two analytic questions framed the mapping. The first was sociological. I was, and remain, deeply interested in the sociological frameworks that were being developed. I asked: what analytic propositions with respect to the social were being assumed? How did they understand and explain the nature of South African society? And what could be extracted from them as their distinguishing features? The second was to ask about the significance of these positions for curriculum development in South African higher education.

With respect to the sociological question, I suggested that there was general agreement – a kind of consensus – on the points of departure of the decolonial movement. In that agreement was a range of ideological positions. Contributors included traditional academics, social commentators and activists. Among the most prominent were Ndlovu-Gatsheni (2015), Garuba (2015), Naidoo (2015; 2016), #RhodesMustFall (#RMF)1 (2015), Gamedze and Gamedze (2015), Essop (2016), Hendricks and Leibowitz (2016), Kamanzi (2017), Rudin (2016), Mbembe (2016), Nyathi (2016), Pityana (2016), Sopazi (2016), Ntombini (2017), Prah (2017), Tabisher (2017) and Jansen (2017). They all agreed about the need for re-centring enquiry and the making of knowledge in higher education around the full historical and cosmological experience of Africa in response to Eurocentrism. Common to them all was the insight that Eurocentrism had produced and was being expressed through the epistemological displacement, subjugation, delegitimation and, ultimately, erasure of all other forms of knowing the world (see also Modiri, Chapter 10, Adesina, Chapter 11, and Higgs, Chapter 12, in this volume). There was the realisation of the imperative to put the African experience on the front burner. More specifically, the agreement raised the following:

- a rejection of the marginalisation of the African voice;
- a rejection of the positioning of Africa as a 'place to learn about and not from' (Hendricks and Leibowitz, 2016: para 7); and
- a rejection of the objectification of Africa as a site for Western scrutiny (Garuba, 2015: para 12; see also Kamanzi, 2016: para 8).

Achille Mbembe (2016: 3) argues that racism is the discursive frame holding Eurocentrism together. 'Racism gave whiteness its cosmological hubris and its resultant blindness.' He explained: 'we are ... calling for the demythologisation of whiteness because democracy in South Africa will either be built on the ruins of those versions of whiteness that produced Rhodes or it will fail.'

---

1   #RhodesMustFall or #RMF refers, of course, to the social movement. This contribution is written by the #RMF Collective.

And so, he explained, 'For these reasons, the emerging consensus is that our institutions must undergo a process of decolonisation both of knowledge and of the university as an institution' (Mbembe, 2016: 10).

Important as this agreement was, I argued that distinct positions were evident in the discussion. The first was New Black Consciousness (NBC) and the second, New Humanism (NH). I argued that blackness was privileged in the first. In the second, it was the interest in an exploration of the limits of being human that activates the discussion. Both positions were complex and had within them a variety of accents and emphases.

In contrast to older forms of black consciousness, NBC is characterised by strong echoes of the global decolonial movement such as the focus on the 'black body' picked up from the Black Lives Matter movement in the United States and developed into conceptual conversation with the contributions of key decolonialists such as Ramon Grosfoguel (2011; 2013), Santos (2007) and Mignolo (2001). I sought to argue that NBC brought these contributions together into an anti-Cartesian and an anti-white normativity view of the world. White bodies carried the affordances of whiteness, black bodies carried only baggage – the baggage of inferiority. It rejects hegemonic explanations of the world which secure the privileging of the white body and the denigration of the abject black body and the reification of whiteness as the normative standard (see Grosfoguel, 2011: paras 6–8).

The NHs were concerned about a re-nativisation of ideas of 'race' and tribe. Prah (2017), for example, argued against the racial ways in which the idea of Africa was being used in popular discussion. He argued that simply installing black people into positions of authority reproduced the conflation of 'race' with culture:

> the Africanisation or localisation (as it is sometimes called) of positions which were previously held by colonial personnel does not in itself necessarily translate as outstanding progress. It must be remembered that Africanisation wherever it has been pursued on this continent is a policy which mainly affects the fortunes of the elite (Prah, 2017: 1).

His central argument was that development was a question of culture and not colour: 'the centering of African culture at the heart of the development endeavour is crucial' (Prah, 2017: 2).

Similarly, Mbembe (2016: 1) urged caution with respect to dealing with the complexity of whiteness: they 'want to finally bring white supremacy to its knees. But the same seems to go missing when it comes to publicly condemning the extra-judicial executions of fellow Africans on the streets of our cities and in our townships.' He suggested that historically a conflation of decolonisation and Africanisation underpinned sociological thinking, which had the political effect of 'the transfer into native hands of those unfair advantages which were a legacy of the colonial past' (Mbembe, 2016: 11). They amounted to a 'racketeering' or predatory project, a moment when 'the nation is passed over for the race, and the tribe is preferred to the state' (Mbembe, 2016: 11). What was needed, instead, he argued, was a process of 'taking back of our humanity … They are struggles to repossess, to take back, if necessary by force, that which is ours unconditionally and, as such, belongs to us' (Mbembe, 2016: 12). Mbembe argues for the democratisation of the world beyond anthropocentric understandings of life. His framing of the issues and the problems sought to include life in all of its variety and complexity.

Having made these arguments, I had hoped that the discussion would focus on the curriculum and the implications of decolonised thinking for what the academics and the students in the room needed to teach and be taught. It turned, instead, on the positions in the debate about the social. This development in the discussion, largely led by students, I want to suggest, was absolutely correct. It is the *prior* clearing of the ground which needs to be had in South African and, indeed, global discussions about the major political debates that take place about the past, present and future. A key issue, to illustrate the point, and to which I shall return in this contribution, was what a student described as Mbembe's ecological focus. He took issue with the politics of this focus and placed it within an essentially liberal perspective that was typical of European philosophy. The critique, by implication, was of Mbembe's understanding of the nature of the social – relationships between people. It remained, so the criticism went, in a Eurocentric logic. What was suggested was the need to break with Eurocentrism and the development of a way of explaining the world that was framed by our African reality.

Almost predictably, the discussion continued outside of the formal space of the lecture theatre. Persistently the question arose of how we made meaning of the social space in which we found ourselves. I would like to reference this discussion as the basis for developing a response to the question I pose for this contribution. Opening up the discussion, a participant (whom I shall not name for reasons of privacy) sent me the following e-mail:

> Decolonising was framed as a project opposed to or critical of positivism. As a result, it, in many ways, seemed like an epistemological project at least somewhat related to post-structuralists (or other post-positivists). The push for a plurality of 'knowledges' and the importance of recognising the relevance of experience are just two of the aspects you raised in this

regard. This also includes the reference you made to Latour, who in my understanding, tries to unmask the constructed nature of the subject/object dichotomy of positivism (and its opponents), arguing the whole distinction between objective and subjective is an unnecessary battle line of disciplines. Both black intersectionalism and post-humanism appear to be concerned primarily with a critique of a colonial enlightenment hegemony that can be associated with a particular set of epistemologies that prefer grand narratives to heterogeneous and complex realities.

I discerned two elements in my interlocutor's question that I thought called for a continued conversation. These I pursue here as rubrics for placing the question of decoloniality in a larger set of problematics. The first was relatively explicit. It related to the politics of knowledge discussion in decoloniality. At the heart of my interlocutor's question was whether decoloniality was 'fundamentally an epistemological shift, or whether there is also some merit in a subversive project of epistemological appropriation' (e-mail reference). What lay behind the question was unclear, but it raised for me the question of the value of what is referred to as European philosophy and particularly the capacity for this philosophy to explain the African condition. Was this whole corpus of thinking about the social – about human beings and their relationships with and to one another – so tainted by its historical provenance and its spatial location that a complete break from it was required? Did it have within its expansive reach nothing of use for thinking about the black condition?

The second issue I engage here was raised less explicitly but was one that had provided much of the engagement around decoloniality in South Africa through its tone and register. That tone and register, seen at the talk I gave and on many other occasions, was essentially a racial one. I approach it here as a question about the ontological assumptions inherent in what we think of as the European tradition.

I focus in this discussion on the first question and offer only exploratory comments on the second. In conclusion, I suggest that the conversations around the first, and herein lies the contemporary contribution of the decolonial discussion, have been productive in South Africa. They have been able to cut to the quick of the knowledge debate in South Africa and globally. With respect to the second question, the ontological one, I suggest that the discussion has struggled. While it has been able to locate and identify the phenomenon of racism in modern institutions, it has struggled to open up the bigger question of racism and its psychosocial effects, particularly the phenomenon called 'black pain'. I argue that the issue of 'black pain' remains inadequately theorised.

Knowledge claims

The first element of my interlocutor's question is crucial in so far as it references particular strains of European philosophy, which argue that a major contribution of the European Enlightenment was essentially a methodological one. The Enlightenment gave the world 'the scientific method'. This methodological approach has come to be described as 'positivism'. In contrast to earlier and other forms of knowledge formation, this method places its central claims on scientific reasoning – the process through which 'truth' is arrived at. It is described as the objective observation and measurement of phenomena:

> For example, in order to explain the reaction of a particular chemical to heat, it is necessary to provide exact measurements of temperature, weight and so on. With the aid of such measurements it will be possible to accurately observe the behaviour of matter and produce a statement of cause and effect... Once it has been shown that the matter in question always reacts in the same way under fixed conditions, a theory can be devised to explain its behaviour (Haralambos, 1985: 18–19).

My colleague's e-mail draws attention to European positivism's claims to have arrived at the ultimate routes and pathways to 'truth'. For many people, in this claim is the major and most objectionable feature of particular forms of European thought. It presumes a break from sense-making procedures in what are described as 'primitive societies', where the spheres of the cultural and the social are undifferentiated: 'The sacred is immanent in the profane ... nature and the spiritual remain undifferentiated in animism and totemism' (Lash, 1990: 6). The scientific method establishes the domains of the natural, the social and the spiritual as distinct and, as Lash (1990: 9) argues, with their own rules of legitimation and of proof and warrant. Drawing on Weber, Lash describes these rules as self-legislation. The process of self-legislation finds its legitimacy in its conscious and articulated rules of reasoning; and so the aesthetic is distinct from the cultural and, likewise, distinct from the scientific. It is in the method of the scientific that claims for what is true and real move beyond the arbitrary and are rooted in scientific measurement and verification.

The argument I am seeking to make is that 'self-legislation' is inherent in every example of 'truth-making'. There is a great deal to be said here, but the central issue is how one group of people's self-legislation procedures have become the template for the rest of the world and how these have become universalisms at the expense of all other forms of meaning-making. The philosopher AJ Ayer (1976: 179) is useful in helping us get to the heart of the issues quickly. Using an example of deductive reasoning – the very methodology marking Europe's distinctiveness – he shows how easily the universalisation of a hypothesis, using Aristotelian methods of reasoning, can be disproved:

> The moral of such examples, however they are formulated, is that whatever the evidence, we always have some latitude in the choice of the hypotheses which we are going to project… If anyone maintains that the choice of different hypotheses … will serve us better in the future, we cannot prove that he is wrong; we can only wait upon the event (Ayer, 1976: 178–79).

In managing this discussion, the point to be made about self-legislation procedures is not whether they are right or wrong but, simply, their ability to locate themselves historically. Critical, then, is our self-consciousness in making hypotheses. The discussion, at this point, becomes extremely contentious. It is here that decoloniality has an important contribution to make. Whether it warrants a break from the corpus of thinking that has come out of Europe over the last 500 years or not is an important question to stay with. An elaboration of the question in my colleague's e-mail is pertinent at this point. He continued to ask:

> I guess the aspect of my question that this is trying to formulate is whether decolonising of more positivist disciplines (and maybe the institutional structure more generally) necessitates an epistemological departure, or whether there is not also a need for a decolonised empiricism? Whatever this might mean. Can we draw on the very positivist methodologies that were part of the colonial oppression to subvert that very bulwark and dismantle it not only from the 'outside', but also the 'inside'?

A response to the question is that both are required. There is a need for both a larger understanding of what constitutes knowledge and of how that knowledge can be acquired. But a prior issue around the history of science needs clarification. That issue is simply, as the Librarian Emeritus of the Alexandria Library, Ismail Serageldin, recently explained, the falsehood of the narrative of a pristine European discovery of the scientific method and of science. Serageldin's speech at the founding meeting of the International Science Council (ISC) in 2018 questioned the 'origins' narrative of the history of knowledge, that it was Muslim, Greek or Roman: 'that narrative is Eurocentric. That the Greeks invented everything is not correct' (notes taken at the ISC meeting, Paris, 5 July 2018; see also Mboup, Chapter 15, in this volume). He noted that the process of knowledge-making involved 'the passing of the torch'. The European

Renaissance, he explained, depended on centuries-long history of knowledge production in North Africa. It did not arise and develop by itself.

'The passing of the torch' metaphor is a reaction to the European idea of its precedence and superiority. I would like to use my interlocutor's use of the term 'appropriation' to explain what Eurocentrism has done. It has taken the whole store of human knowledge – what we have learnt everywhere as a human community – and appropriated it under the label of European and 'Western'. This insight about the appropriation of the complex roots of our knowledge stores is important. It is important because what is happening is that at the very moment that this European project claims for itself the right to speak for the whole of humankind and to appropriate to itself the status of 'first-of-all-people', it loses its capacity to see. Self-consciousness, awareness of itself, is decidedly wanting. And so, what it constitutes as knowledge and the procedures for collecting that knowledge present themselves as partial and incomplete. The issues, it must be said, are crucial for the development of life on the planet. Serageldin understands this. He insists on working with a heightened sense of the multiplicity and plurality of our knowledge affordances. He argues for the defence of values in thinking about knowledge. Six values, he suggests, are crucial (notes from the ISC meeting, 5 July 2018):

1. commitment to truth even as we acknowledge that there are multiple ways of coming to what we understand to be the truth;
2. embracing the values of honour in what we say and what we claim, that we acknowledge that others have explanations of complex realities;
3. a valuing of creativity and imagination and a realisation that imagination is more important than knowledge;
4. the cultivation of constructive subversiveness;
5. tolerance of engagement and breaking with the practice of listening to what people say as opposed to reading them through the colour of their skins or their gender; and, finally,
6. holding fast to the principles of the arbitration of disputes through evidence and logic, not insult and denigration.

An important decolonial response to this appropriation, against which Serageldin warns us, is provided by Catherine Odora Hoppers, the former Chair of Development Education at the University of South Africa (UNISA). She offered the idea of 'enlargement'. She questions the objectification of knowledge that has taken place in dominant European explanations of truth and reality and asks us to confront the reality that what is counted as knowledge in this appropriation has been exclusionary and hierarchising. Her argument is that what is needed

> is not so much to rewrite the Western script that African universities are using but to enlarge it so that Africa, too, has a voice… The Western package … is inadequate to the task of bringing up children who have other frames of reference. The system as we have it is too limited for the drama that confronts a growing African child… No one has complete answers… [The problem with Eurocentric knowledge was that] it bites a little piece of what is possible; it spits out and ignores the rest (South African Research Chairs Initiative [SARChI] Chair, 2009b).

Western logic was, in this argument, exclusionary and managed on a basis of contempt for others not European. *Enlargement* is both about the content of our knowledge and its methodologies: 'No one has complete answers. It is about how your one-tenth of the solution can link with that one-tenth and that two-fifths and so on' (SARChI Chair, 2009b). This requires, Odora Hoppers argues, a hospitality to all knowledge forms, critically the knowledges of so-called high Western modernity, quantum physics, and those of

> the rural child, barefoot and in tattered clothes, who has a botanical garden coming right to her doorstep. She is naturally evolving inside a system that is integrated with nature, with a grounding in plant, weather and soil systems. Western science needs to build on the knowledge the African child already has by linking up with the child's lived world (SARChI Chair, 2009b).

The methodology for this is transdisciplinarity. Transdisciplinarity in this context is, however, more than the disciplines of the Western archive. It includes the full repertoire of critical thought available to human beings: 'The deeper you specialise in a specific discipline, the deeper you dig yourself into the silo… Unless you dig sideways, you lose the capability to converse with other disciplines' (SARChI Chair, 2009b). The commitment to working with multiple knowledges and knowledge approaches – transdisciplinarity – is the ambit of her *transformation by enlargement* [all the emphases in the following quotation are in the original]. This implies that all key concepts and ideas driving or anchoring policy and the academy are revisited with a view to expanding their understanding to include ways of seeing that had been previously excluded:

The result is that *new theoretical and conceptual advances are introduced which in turn help to provide more nuanced conceptions and interpretations of hitherto poorly understood dimensions of livelihood in the African context.* These include expanding the understanding of innovation from only scientific laboratories and the related economic parameters, to notions such as 'social innovations', 'cultural capital', 'innovative practices in relation to livelihoods', 'innovations from below', the 'social good' and the 'commons'. It calls for revolutions not only in technology, *but also in the way we THINK about issues.* It furthermore enables the introduction of dynamic conceptual reversals that give dignity to rural people (SARChI Chair, 2009b).

In this expanded understanding of knowledge and its real and existing potential, Odora Hoppers sought to introduce into the university the provocation of moving beyond its narrow cultural horizons and to venture into a transterritorial mode of thinking about itself and how it works. The transgressive requirement for the world was to cross the bounded lines of time and space, with all their exclusionary inclinations, into a new, enlarged human commons. What was critical moreover about this transgressive commitment was, as Odora Hoppers argued, an openness 'to understand the weaknesses [of the knowledge affordances available to humankind] and to [see] where enlargement can happen' (SARChI Chair, 2009a). She argued in this same document:

> I zoom in on where I think humanity is losing out and I do not do duels... Once people have torn up a new idea, everyone is happy. No, I only want serious thinkers who can go beyond thinking in terms of critique and make a collective contribution in creating a safe space for code determination. I am not interested in polemic at this stage; I don't have time to waste (SARChI Chair, 2009a).

What is important in understanding what this 'transformation by enlargement' approach does is to give effect to Serageldin's six values, which present a view of the world that constitutes a distinct rupture from hegemonic thinking. The question of whether decoloniality should break with hegemonic thinking is answered in practical terms. It already is a break. But it is also simultaneously a deep subversion. To the idea of origins and differentiation of the world into its binary classifications of 'primitive' and 'advanced', and 'superior' and 'inferior', it offers radical connectedness. I would argue that it is a view that simultaneously breaks with elements of the hegemonic narrative but builds on others.

What does Odora Hopper's 'integrated' and 'enlarged' view of knowledge offer then in response to my interlocutor's dichotomy between a 'break' and a 'subversion'? I shall return to this in conclusion, but a quick comment on the ontological assumptions present in the Eurocentrism evident in the European discussion might help to deepen the argument on the value of the decolonial moment.

Provocation two: The existential urgency
Related to the earlier discussion about knowledge is the persistent question about the contending knowledge regimes' understanding of what it means to be human – the question of 'race' in particular. The criticism made against Mbembe's liberalism above was implicitly about his capacity to understand the issue of 'race'. He did not understand 'black pain'. However, the hard edge of the decolonial critique of the 'whiteness' of the academy is noteworthy. Mbembe, in this critique, was captured by this whiteness.

I have argued elsewhere that typifications of the academy as homogeneously and irredeemably white are both ahistorical and problematic (see Soudien, 2017). The academy has, from its very inception – even in the discursively freighted space of racialised South Africa – been a contested space. In that contestation not only have there been alternatives to dominant ways and modes of thinking, but people have also taken and developed subversive social identities. The academy has always been, as a result, a fecund space of debate. We would, however, be naïve to underplay or fail to recognise racism and the role of the academy in promoting it (see Modiri, Chapter 10, in this volume). The idea of 'race' is a powerful construction of fields such as anthropology and biology in South Africa. This idea, we have to confront, has been dominant in the ways, habits and cultures of the South African university. Odora Hoppers is useful again in explaining what it is and how it works. Her idea deserves a lengthy quotation:

> Yes as modern [institutions], … like all the academies throughout the continent, they've had problems with their constitutive rules that govern knowledge production, that govern the work of the academy. The way all disciplines are structured still retain core pin codes of the European thinking, the cultural drives are European. Core pin codes drive the thinking for example in higher education, research, teaching, learning, content and curriculum, and so on and so forth. And in the South African situation it is even more pungent because of the history of apartheid of course. But I take it that the challenge is the thinking behind the race and the unwritten, the unspoken part about the superiority of the west [*sic*] which is the problem. It is not really race, it is something

deeper than that because an African can get trained inside a university and behave exactly the same. So I'm not tackling the problem which I call mine. I'm not functioning at the level of first-level indigenisation. First-level indigenisation is a replacement of colour and that is not my mandate. Many people can deal with that, there are legislations, there are all manners of equity things. For me the problem is in the default drive itself, the cultural drive of the systems, the intolerance of other ways of seeing, the closure within that, the hierarchicisation of IKS, the absolutely exclusivist way in which the production is framed, that is what I am taking on (SARChI Chair, c. 2009c).

Significant in Odora Hoppers' explanation is how to make sense of the racial experience in the university. The problem, she explains, is 'not really race'; rather 'race' is the symptom of something deeper. That deeper issue is what she calls the 'default drive'. While her understanding of 'race' is not clear, she clarifies how racialisation works. The 'default drive' is the explicit racial capture of the university and the knowledge project. This makes the decolonial turn in South Africa significant. It is calling for a decoupling of the university from the racial ways in which dominant approaches to knowledge formation have evolved within it.

It is at this point, I suggest, that the decolonial project needs further development. The problem raised by Biko is exactly what the students at my talk were alluding to. It is the state of mind – the consciousness – produced inside these regimes of knowledge formation, the conditions of *certainty* possessed and displayed by some, and their opposites – the sense of self-*doubt* and personal insecurity of and among others. Certainty is the sense individuals and groups have of their wishes, desires and dreams being fulfilled. It can take many forms. In racialised societies, it takes the form of whiteness with all of its conceits and presumptions. It is a state of mind in which belief in self is accompanied by constant anxiety. Biko (2004: 30) himself put it like this:

> One should not waste time here dealing with manifestations of material want of the black people. A vast literature has been written on this problem. Possibly a little should be said about spiritual poverty. What makes the black man fail to tick? Is he convinced of his own accord of his inabilities? Does he lack in his genetic make-up that rare quality that makes a man willing to die for the realisation of his aspirations? Or is he simply a defeated person? ... To a large extent the evil-doers have succeeded in producing at the output end of their machine a kind of black man who is man only in form.

The students were making the point that Mbembe did not address this issue. It was the central feature of the current black experience. The problem, however, was that they themselves were not assisting in elucidating the question of 'black pain'. Their approach – and, indeed, that of the larger community of scholars and activists engaged in the decolonial discussion – is what can be described as an ostensive one. An *ostensive* explanation is essentially one that invokes what are thought to be examples of a phenomenon to define and explain the phenomenon itself: 'a definiens is communicated by either literally pointing to or otherwise indexing a case in which the definiendum is thought to be in evidence... Thus, one may give an ostensive definition of "pain" by pointing to a person in the throes of a toothache and saying... "This is what pain is like"' (Royzman, McCauley and Rozin, 2005: 27). A stipulative definition constructs the content of the phenomenon and then goes to look for it (Royzman et al, 2005: 22). It is essentially self-validating. 'Black pain' in most explanations rests on whatever a subject says it is. This is where, I suggest, decoloniality in South Africa struggles.

Conclusion

What then is the significance of the decolonial turn here in South Africa? The major point to make is that decoloniality has brought to the fore the urgency to attend to the politics of our contemporary knowledge affordances. While, critically, its analysis of the ethnocentric nature of our approaches to knowledge is not new, it is responsible for pushing the issues into the centre of the decision-making and policy-making sites of power in the academy. This development is by itself crucial. It is significant, moreover, in the way it has joined existing critiques of dominant narratives of science, such as poststructuralism, postcolonialism and phenomenology; hallmarked in the contributions of contemporary philosophers such as Foucault, Derrida and Deleuze; and put all of contemporary philosophy on notice for its inattention to the complexity of modern racism. It has, through the examples of scholars such as Fanon, worked with critical theory in the Western oeuvre – Marx and Freud in the main – to critique sometimes obscured and hidden elements of ethnocentrism in those theories. Decoloniality has brought, poignantly, to the fore the question of the black body, particularly the black female body. In doing this, it has signalled the need, as I suggest earlier, for both a break with dominant epistemology's universalisation of its ontic imagination and, simultaneously, a critical subversion of its epistemological founding assumptions. The framework has – through the scholarship of a range of decolonial scholars – significantly opened up the discussion about knowledge.

I suggest, however, that it has struggled, as much as contemporary sociology and psychology have, with the challenge of modern racism and its effects. It has remained inside an ostensive tradition of theorising. The large questions of the persistence of racism and the classificatory and hierachising stratagems it recognises. It has also not developed a significant discursive frame and set of analytic procedures for unpacking the complexity of racism. It has pointed to the trauma of racism but not how – and this is what is needed – human beings manage their agency in their consciousness. That racism, like indeed other stimuli such as love and hate, may stimulate complex responses in human beings – and not simply submission – is the hard task of social analysis to explain and account for. This work still needs to be done.

References

Ayer, A J (1973) *The Central Questions of Philosophy*. London: Penguin.

Biko, S (2004) *I Write What I Like*. Johannesburg: Picador.

Essop, A (2016) Decolonisation debate is a chance to rethink the role of universities, in *The Conversation*, 16 August 2016. Available at: http//theconversation.com/decolonisation-debate-is-a-chance-to-rethink-the-role-of-universities-63840 (accessed March 2017).

Gamedze, T and Gamedze, A (2015) Salon for what? *The Johannesburg Salon*, 9: 1–2.

Garuba, H (2015) What is an African curriculum? Available at: https://mg.co.za/article/2015-04-17-what-is-an-african-curriculum/ (accessed March 2017).

Grosfoguel, R (2011) Decolonizing post-colonial studies and paradigms of political economy: Transmodernity, decolonial thinking and global coloniality, *Transmodernity: Journal of Peripheral Cultural Production of the Luso-Hispanic World*, **1**(1): no page nos.

Grosfoguel, R (2013) The structure of knowledge in Westernised universities: Epistemic racism/sexism and the four genocides/epistemicides of the long 16th century, *Human Architecture: Journal of the Sociology of Self-Knowledge*, **11**(1): 72–90.

Haralambos, M (1985) *Sociology: Themes and perspectives*. London: Unwin Hyman.

Hendricks, C and Leibowitz, B (2016) Decolonising universities isn't an easy process – but it has to happen, in *The Conversation*, 23 May 2016. Available at: http://theconversation.com/decolonisng-the-universities-isnt-an-easy-process-but-it-has-to-happen-59604 (accessed March 2017).

Jansen, J (2017) *'As by Fire': The end of the South African university*. Cape Town: Tafelberg Publishers.

Kamanzi, B (2016) Decolonising the curriculum: The silent war for tomorrow, in *The Daily Maverick*, 28 April 2016. Available at: https://dailymaverick.co.za/opnionista/2016-04-28-decolonising-the-curriculum-the-silent-war-for-tomorrow/ (accessed March 2017).

Lash, S (1990) *The Sociology of Postmodernism*. London: Routledge.

Mbembe, A (2016) Decolonising knowledge and the question of the archive. Available at: https://wiser.wits.ac.za/system/files/Achille%20Mbembe%20-%20Decolonizing%20Knowledge%20and%20the%20Question%20of%20the%20Archive.pdf (accessed March 2017).

Mignolo, W (2001) Coloniality and subalternity, in I Rodriguez (ed.) *The Latin American Subaltern Studies Reader*. Durham, NC: Duke University Press, pp. 224–44. Naidoo, L-A (2015) Needing to learn: #RhodesMustFall and the decolonisation of the university. Available at: http://www.dhet.gov.za/SiteAssets/Latest%20News/Independent%20Thinking%20Second%20Edition/dhetpage7.pdf (accessed March 2017).

Naidoo, L-A (2016) Needing to learn: #RhodesMustFall and the decolonisation of the university, in *DHET News eBulletin*, 29 March. Available at: http://www.dhetnews.co.za/

needing-to-learn-rhodes-must-fall-and-the-decolonisation-of-the-university/ (accessed March 2017).

Ndlovu-Gatsheni, S (2013) *Coloniality of Power in Postcolonial Africa: Myths of decolonisation.* Dakar: CODESRIA Press.

Ntombini, K (2017) Reflections on the lecture by Ngũgĩ wa Thiong'o in Baxter Theatre, *Black Opinion,* Tuesday, 14 March. Available at: http://blackopinion.o.za/2017/03/06/reflections-lecture-ngugi-wa-thiongo-baxter-theatre/ (accessed March 2017).

Nyathi, N (2016) Decolonising the Curriculum: The only way through the process is together, *Moneyweb,* 27 December. Available at: http://www.moneyweb.co.za/news/south-africa-decolonising-the curriculum-the only-way-through-the-process-is-together/ (accessed March 2017).

Odora Hoppers, C and Richards. H (2012) *Rethinking Thinking: Modernity's 'other' and the transformation of the university.* Pretoria: UNISA Press.

Pityana, B (2016) The 2015 student revolts in South Africa: A call for dialogue. Unpublished paper.

Prah, K (2017) Has Rhodes fallen? Decolonising the humanities in Africa and constructing intellectual sovereignty. Available at: http://www.assaf.org.za/files/ASSAf%20news/Has%20Rhode%20Fallen.docx%20ASSAF%20Address%202015.22017.pdf (accessed March 2017).

#RhodesMustFall (2015) #RhodesMustFall statements, *The Johannesburg Salon,* 9: 6–19.

Royzman, B, McCauley, C and Rozin, P (2005) From Plato to Putnam: Four ways to think about hate, in R Sternberg (ed.) *The Psychology of Hate.* Washington, DC: The American Psychological Association, pp. 3–35.

Rudin, J (2017) Deconstructing decolonisation: Can racial assertiveness cure imagined inferiority, *The Daily Maverick,* 22 January. Available at: http://dailymaverick.co.za/article?id=84504#WM-Mfk1MTIU (accessed March 2017).

Santos, B (ed.) (2007) *Cognitive Justice in a Global World: Prudent knowledges for a decent life.* Plymouth: Lexington Books.

SARChI Chair (2009a) About the SARChI Chair in Development Education. Undated mimeograph in the SARChI Chair Archive.

SARChI Chair (2009b) SARChI Annual Progress Report, 2009. Pretoria: UNISA.

SARChI Chair (2009c) The most challenging of all mandates: NRF Educational Development Chair, Catherine Odora Hoppers. Transcript of interview with African PhD Literature Student, Andersson (first name not provided).

Sopazi, L (2016) The black body: A playground of whiteness, in *Black Opinion,* 7 September. Available at: http://blackopinion.co.za/2016/09/07black-body-playground-whiteness/ (accessed March 2017).

Soudien, C (2017) Debates in the decolonisation movement and their relevance for curriculum renewal in South African higher education. Unpublished mimeograph.

Tabisher, A (2017) Irony of students' shallow call for decolonisation, *Cape Argus,* Wednesday, 8 March, p. 11.

Xaso, L and Pikoli, Z (2017) Black culture turned into a commodity, *The Independent,* 19 March, p. 18.

Chapter 4
Turn inwards to connect outwards: South Africa's universities in historical perspective

Ahmed Bawa

> Why is it that science in independent India, despite all the investments in it, is not the potentially creative force it threatened to be during the nationalist period?
> (Atma Ram, Chairman of India's National Committee on Science and Technology)

Is the South African university in ruins?
In his 1999 book, *The University in Ruins*, the late Bill Readings bemoaned the impact of globalisation on the future of the North American university through the erosion of its key mandates: the construction of national identity, the progressive extension of national culture and so on (Readings, 1996). In some respects, it is that debate about the purpose of universities as social institutions that was raised by student activists in South Africa between 2015 and 2017. Being knowledge-intensive institutions, at the heart of this debate are serious questions around the knowledge project of the sector, as in its research and teaching/learning. The transition and the policy process that followed it did produce serious attempts to understand the purposes of higher education as drivers of political, social and economic reconstruction, but its revisiting of the knowledge project of South Africa's universities and science councils was, at best, an incomplete project. Revisiting the knowledge project would have meant coming to grips with the historical evolution of the system, its articulation with the transition of the 1990s, its location within the geopolitics of knowledge and, perhaps most importantly, its capacity to address the projects of national reconstruction and the reintegration of its knowledge enterprise with that of the rest of Africa.

Even so, there were serious attempts to understand the shifts needed to achieve a vast realignment of the universities and science system with the transition of 1994 (Kraak, 2000). It would be a rather crude caricaturing of the university sector to imagine that the knowledge project has remained unchanged over the last 30 years or that there has not been considerable thought given to it. I shall return to this in more detail later on in this chapter. This process of realignment and engagement was drawn into a tension between the transformatory challenges of the socio-political juncture and the desire to ensure that it was properly and coherently aligned with the envisaged project of shifting South Africa towards a knowledge economy (Blankley and Booysens, 2010).

At the height of the recent student actions, during September/October 2016, there were a few days during which there was a discussion about whether the university system should be placed in a state of suspension or not. About 17 of the 26 universities were shut down and the rest were in some state of instability. Remarkably, during this period of great instability, except for the universities' leaders themselves, there was no defence of the sector; there was silence from the government, the private sector, the not-for-profit sector, civil society, parents and students. This deafening silence was a signal for the higher education sector to engage in self-reflection and introspection, an opportunity to revisit core understandings of the purpose of universities as social institutions. How did the universities become so alienated from their numerous publics? 'Is the university in ruins?'

Among the many student activist voices at the time, one heard a powerfully articulated view that the higher education system was a part of the socio-political infrastructure that produced and maintained a society of deep inequality, grinding poverty, corruption and, ultimately, the erosion of the promises of the Freedom Charter and the struggle for democracy. One has to ask whether it is time to think more specifically of a social justice agenda for higher education: broadening the access and success of students, addressing the 'decolonisation' of its knowledge project and maximising the opportunity for the intellectual, physical, social and emotional development of its students; thereby reconfiguring its relationship with its publics.

The National Commission on Higher Education (NCHE), established in 1995 by President Nelson Mandela, produced a transformatory framework for universities (National Commission on Higher Education, 1996). For all its limitations, the report of the NCHE and the subsequent Higher Education White Paper (1997) and Higher Education Act (1997) did provide the basis for some sort of social contract between higher education and government, industry, the trade unions and civil society. The construction of a National Policy Framework is not the same as the development of a social contract since much depends on the balance of forces in the negotiations in the policy development process, which depends, in turn, on the socio-political context within which it takes place. This line of thinking will be developed later in this chapter.

While South Africa's knowledge system is contained mainly within the university system, there are significant parts in the science council system, industry, various government departments, think tanks, and the not-for-profit sector. Universities, though, are special in the sense that while they too generate, apply and disseminate knowledge, their key social function lies in undergraduate and postgraduate education. They are central to the project of nation-building, to the sustainable study and development of national culture, to producing human capacity in all areas of professional work and, of course, to meeting the high-level educational needs of the economy.

As a way of understanding why the centre of gravity of the national knowledge enterprise leans so heavily towards that of the knowledge metropolises of the Global North, the conditions that gave rise to the South African higher education system are explored by taking a brief look at the conditions in Natal, now KwaZulu-Natal (KZN), at the time of the founding of the former University of Natal. An attempt is made to understand how the post-1994 policy influences produced mainly a consolidation of this existing 'colonial' knowledge project. The student activism of 2015–17, if it is seen as a moment of political disjuncture, forces a reconsideration of South Africa's knowledge project and, by extension, the purpose of our universities as social institutions. What would such a reconsideration point to? This will probably help us to address the question of whether there is a need for a new social compact between higher education and society.

Looking back at the period of colonialism and apartheid

Except for the still evolving Sol Plaatje University and Mpumalanga University, the other 24 public universities in South Africa all have their roots, in some way or other, deeply embedded in our colonial and apartheid past with their purposes and roles defined by the context within which they came into being.

Prior to the establishment of the University of Natal (UN) in 1910, now a part of the University of KwaZulu-Natal, young whites in Natal were either sent to universities in the United Kingdom or to the South African College or they were taught post-school arts and sciences at the exceptional high schools in the province (Guest, 2017). The primary purpose of establishing the university was clearly to educate the young of the white, settler community in the arts and sciences and to produce the professionals to serve the needs of that community in each metropolitan area. Programmes to produce teachers, lawyers, agriculturalists, engineers, etc, were established. The creation of the Natal Technical College in 1907 (a progenitor of the Durban University of Technology [DUT]) to produce highly trained and skilled technicians, technologists and administrative workers of many kinds required for the local industrial base, predated the formation of the UN (Durban University of Technology, 2007). The UN soon began to produce the agriculturalists, engineers, financial experts, etc, for the colonial economy.

The other role assumed by the UN was to ensure that there was a constant injection of knowledge, technologies and techniques into the industrial base of the local economy. Quite soon after its establishment, a number of research institutes were co-created by the university and the industries in its social and geographical hinterlands. For example, the South African Sugar Research Institute came into being in 1925[1] (while the UN was still a college of the University of South Africa [UNISA]); the Oceanographic Research Institute,[2] and the Institute for Commercial Forestry Research[3] in 1947; and the Sugar Milling Research Institute in 1948,[4] among others. These produced vibrant, industry-driven research enterprises in partnership with the Faculty of Agriculture in Pietermaritzburg and the Faculty of Engineering, based mainly in Durban, and with the Council for Scientific and Industrial Research (CSIR), itself established in 1945.

The interwoven connection between the UN and its community was cemented by a number of interventions. For instance, the construction of this university depended heavily on funds being set aside by the city councils of Durban and Pietermaritzburg, the investment of individuals and communities in the outlying areas of what is now KZN (Guest, 2017) and by local industry. This was further bolstered in 1954 by the intervention of the national apartheid state in providing a national university subsidy – as was the case with all the historically white universities – bringing with it concerns that the independence of this new institution would be jeopardised and its autonomy weakened. These funding streams meant that the university had to serve the needs of its communities and publics. The emergence of a consolidated colonial knowledge enterprise was entrenched by the creation of strong, multilateral and multidimensional academic and intellectual links with universities in the metropolises of the Global North, particularly the United Kingdom. This strongly shaped and reinforced the colonial knowledge project in this part of the Global South. The key engine for this was the doctoral education of the UN's lecturers and professors.

---

1   For a brief history of the South African Sugar Research Institute see http://www.sasri.org.za.
2   For a brief history of the Oceanographic Research Institute see https://www.saambr.org.za/research/.
3   For a brief history of the Institute of Commercial Forestry Research see https://www.icfr.ukzn.ac.za.
4   For a brief history of the Sugar Milling Research Institute see http://www.smri.org/history.php.

Importantly, even though the focus of this knowledge project was shaped by the intellectual traditions and innovations of the Global North, it was sharply focused on the needs of the local context. For example, the non-indigenous sugar-cane plantations and the forests of wattle, eucalyptus and pine faced local soil, climatic and pest conditions. This led to the need for the continuous development of new strains, new germ plasms, and methods and techniques to protect them against indigenous threats. This was replicated more recently in 2001 with the Rockefeller Foundation-funded African Centre for Crop Improvement at UN in an attempt to build plant-breeding capacity across the continent through a doctoral programme (PhD). While the students gathered at the UN (and later UKZN) in Pietermaritzburg for the necessary course work in theory and experimental techniques, all the experiments had to be done in the geographical context in which the plants being studied would be expected to grow (Davis, 2007). In the same way, it would not have worked for the sugar and forestry industries to have had the experimentation done in the Global North.

Interestingly, in 1947, the UN created a medical school for students of colour on a separate campus, with separate residences, libraries, lecture theatres and other facilities, attached to the King Edward VIII Hospital in downtown Durban. According to Mervyn Susser, 'the school, an initiative of the pre-apartheid government, was none the less in conformity with both the segregationist principles of apartheid, and with society's unlabelled practice of racial segregation and unequal rights' (Susser, 2006). Interestingly, it attracted an excellent faculty and it, too, produced a knowledge project driven by the context in which it found itself. In many respects, this medical school was shaped by the patient profile of the King Edward VIII Hospital and by the development of health clinics in rural Natal. Led by Dr Sidney Kark, 'widely recognised as one of the 20th century's most original, inspirational and influential leaders in social medicine', this medical school became the intellectual and scholarly home for the development of community and social medicine. It has a strong tradition of original scholarship (Brown et al, 2002: 1744).

As the political context in Natal began to shift in the 1970s, beginning with the development of the powerful student activism of the South African Students Organisation (SASO) led by Steve Biko, Strini Moodley and others, and the National Union of South African Students (NUSAS), followed by the re-emergence of the trade union movement, small cohorts of scholars at the UN, led by individuals like Rick Turner, engaged the new context both as political activists and activist scholars, producing counter-narratives to the established, traditional knowledge project. As a result of this activism, strong connections emerged between the university and community-based organisations and the trade union movement, producing small but powerful influences on the nature of the university and its knowledge project. A plethora of institutes, centres and groups emerged, each acting as a dynamic interface between the inside of the rather conservative white university and the forces of social and political change outside it (Bawden, 1992). Their dependence on donor money inevitably left them very much at the edge of the university and when, in the early 1990s, this money began to dry up, they slid into crisis and most eventually disappeared, because they were never properly integrated into the formal structures of the university. In 1995 there were about 80–90 of these dynamic interfaces at the UN. However, five years later, most of them had disappeared. They were vulnerable by design; the dominant knowledge project prevailed.

On the other hand, the historically black institutions, both rural and urban, were created with a simply defined academic project – that of producing the kinds of professionals and skilled personnel to meet the needs of apartheid's 'independent' ethnic constructions. Except for the University of Fort Hare, they were direct products of apartheid's imagination. They were not designed as places of research, for the scholarly creation of new knowledge or for the production of independent and critical scholars (see Mngomezulu, Chapter 6, in this volume). The academic emphasis was almost always on teacher education, public management, law, business sciences and management, social work, the health sciences, and so on. To serve these academic programmes, one also saw the emergence of the sciences, humanities and social sciences – but these were never conceived of as flagship academic enterprises. There is no gainsaying that the knowledge project of these institutions was also driven by the needs of an internal colonialism.

As in the case of the historically white universities, there were often interesting and important countervailing developments at these universities. The legendary role of the University of Fort Hare in producing some of Africa's outstanding leaders is well known and documented. Fort Hare and the UN's medical school produced thousands of student and academic political and scholarly activists, many of whom took up leadership positions in the post-1994 government structures. More importantly, several researchers and research groups at these institutions played key roles in shaping the new policy frameworks, such as the Reconstruction and Development Programme (RDP). Against all odds, these institutions produced some outstanding scholars in many disciplines. Did they push at the traditional intellectual boundaries? Mostly not. These institutions were tightly controlled with administrations aligned with the apartheid state. They were brutal to student and scholar activists. Where there were interesting scholarly adventures into new intellectual terrains, this happened because of the organic location of the scholars in social and political networks connected to the liberation movement.

Ultimately, all South African universities were defined and shaped by the context that gave rise to them and, for all intents and purposes, both historically white and historically black universities were instruments of the colonial and apartheid systems and their knowledge projects were designed in such a way. It is probably true to argue that 22 years after the NCHE, those dominant knowledge traditions prevail, notwithstanding the construction of a significant number of attempts to build counter-ideological, countervailing intellectual enterprises. The key question is what kind of intellectual ecosystem would allow the traction as new approaches are developed.

The higher education and science and technology policy processes

There were two national policy processes between 1995 and 1997 that impacted heavily on the higher education system – the higher education policy process and the science and technology one. The NCHE sought to develop some sort of national consensus about what was required of the higher education system as the 1994 moment played itself out. The Commission, led by Professor Jairam Reddy, former vice-chancellor of the historically black University of Durban Westville, and constituted of individuals from across the societal spectrum, created a number of task teams that worked through issues related to the size and shape of the system, the definition of a transformatory agenda, the development of a new co-operative governance framework, etc (National Commission on Higher Education, 1996). At about the same time, Dr Ben Ngubane, then Minister of the Department of Arts, Culture, Science and Technology (DACST), established a team to develop a Green Paper on Science and Technology. Both processes had far-reaching consequences for South Africa's knowledge system. Among others, one of the key findings of both processes was what was seen as a fundamental disarticulation of the teaching and research systems from the needs of a reconstructing South African political economy.

The NCHE focused on the future role of higher education in constructing the new democratic citizen, on nation-building, on deepening and strengthening democracy, on broadening access and thereby contributing to a national social mobility project, and on enhancing the civic engagement of universities. The science and technology policy processes, on the other hand, were driven predominantly by the question of how to galvanise the science and technology system to enhance the innovative capacity of South Africa's industrial base and to strengthen the reconstruction capacity defined in the RDP. The concern was that even though good-quality research was being done, it was not finding its way into the registration of new patents and new products.

This, of course, posed questions about the organisation and funding of the national science system. What was state and private-sector research funding being spent on and could this be more strategically deployed? How much basic, fundamental research was needed and could this be more strategically supported? Was consideration being given to global experiences; for instance, was the traditional linear research and innovation spectrum giving way to more complex circular, non-linear ones? Much significant work was done to understand these questions better (Kraak, 2000).

The accelerated infusion of knowledge and digital technologies into production processes in the industrialised North played a significant role in the policy process engaged in here. This shift necessarily brought about expectations of new kinds of articulation between the research and innovation enterprises at universities and production processes in industry and elsewhere. An interesting study of this phenomenon in Europe, captured in *The New Production of Knowledge* (Gibbons et al, 1994), spoke essentially of the evolution of a new mode of knowledge production, which the authors called Mode 2 knowledge production. They argued that it was fundamentally different from the traditional Newtonian linear forms of knowledge production. Without going into any detail about the nature of Mode 2 knowledge production, it represents the potential for much tighter university–industry partnerships in the research and innovation processes, all the way from the definition of the problem and the shaping of the conceptual phase of the research–innovation complex to the point of production of the outputs. The teams are transient in nature, depending on the project, and the outputs are much broader than traditional academic outputs. Following Peter Scott's dictum that the world is not so kind to divide itself up into disciplines, these Mode 2 projects are, by definition, multidisciplinary (or transdisciplinary) in nature (Scott, 1984). Perhaps most importantly, experience seems to indicate that Mode 2 projects have the potential to produce both basic science and product-related outputs. This kind of discourse framed the debates and discussions in 1995–96 on the designing of the South African science and innovation system, which potentially sought to bring the universities into much stronger collaboration with industry.

Crucially, there was no interrogation at this time of the ideological roots of the existing knowledge enterprise and of its epistemological foundations. The emphasis was on attempting to understand how South Africa at its transition would shape the organisation and prosecution of the existing science enterprise to address a rather instrumentalist purpose: how best to navigate towards a knowledge economy. The result of this policy exercise was the establishment of an organising framework, the National System of Innovation (White Paper on Science and Technology, 1996).

The other project of the 1994 moment – that of understanding the system's role in nation-building – was captured in the Education White Paper 3, *A Programme for the Transformation of Higher Education* (1997). In summary, the transformation of the higher education system and its institutions requires:

- Increased and broadened participation. Successful policy must overcome a historically determined pattern of fragmentation, inequality and inefficiency. It must increase access for black, women, disabled and mature students, and generate new curricula and flexible models of learning and teaching, including modes of delivery, to accommodate a larger and more diverse student population.

- Responsiveness to societal interests and needs. Successful policy must restructure the higher education system and its institutions to meet the needs of an increasingly technologically oriented economy. It must also deliver the requisite research, the highly trained people and the knowledge to equip a developing society with the capacity to address national needs and to participate in a rapidly changing and competitive global context.

This influential White Paper arose out of the NCHE process and was the basis for the creation of the Higher Education Act of 1997. While these particular projects for higher education were fundamental to a transforming system, one sees again the furtherance of an instrumentalist imagination, without any serious interrogation as to whether the existing knowledge enterprise at our universities was suitable for these purposes.

So, what happened? Why was the transition of 1994 not used as an opportunity to visit the more fundamental questions relating to the nature of the South African knowledge enterprise? The student actions in 2015–17 were a reminder that the knowledge project was, for all intents and purposes, an incomplete one. And perhaps this was an indication that the validity/authority of the social compact inherent in the policy processes of 1994 had run its course. By 2015, for a very small but important sector of the student population, the universities had been subsumed as an integral part of the infrastructure of a political economy that produced social injustice: continuing levels of poverty and worsening inequality, a creaking health system for the poor, etc. It was time to ask whether the colonial roots underpinning the foundations of our universities were being dismantled or evolving into something new. And to what extent 'something new' is necessary for the creation of new, more organic connections between universities and all of society.

It is important to emphasise that the universities are all deeply complex social and intellectual spaces with hugely interesting counter-ideological enterprises going on in them but the knowledge projects at their core are still significantly shaped, renewed and consolidated by their original mandates. The thesis being presented here is that this core withstood the transformatory agenda of the policy processes at the transition and that this is at the heart of the alienation of the sector from its new publics. On the other hand, that agenda was hugely successful in shifting the demographics of the system, addressing issues of effectiveness and efficiency, etc. Over a very short period, the UN went from being a 'white' university to a 'black' university in terms of student demographics, resulting in a significant alienation from its traditional public but with little if any connection to its new publics.

Development as experiment

Shiv Visvanathan, in an essay titled 'On the annals of a laboratory state', reflects on the way in which post-independence India constructed its five-year development plans to probe similar questions (Visvanathan, 1997). It is an unsettling analysis and it is a vivid reminder that the knowledge question is not just a South African phenomenon. Visvanathan argues that tracing the genealogy of modern science back to Bacon's *Novum Organum* published in 1620 and to Descartes in his *Discourse on Method* published in 1637 is incomplete and that 'the triptych is only complete with the work of Thomas Hobbes' through his monumental *Leviathan* published in 1651. Visvanathan argues that Hobbes' work provided the philosophical schema for science as society, thereby connecting science to power and hence to 'fear, death, terror, and violence'. This immediately leads to probing the relationship between knowledge and the project of development. Visvanathan continues:

> One can see the same trend in the modern discourse on development. Development should be regarded as a scientific project. It represents the contemporary rituals of the laboratory state. As a project, it is composed of four theses, ingrained in the logic of western science, of modernity as technocracy. One can call them:
>
> 1. *The Hobbesian project*, the conception of a society based on the scientific method;
> 2. *The imperatives of progress*, which legitimise the use of social engineering on all those objects defined as backward or retarded;

3. *The vivisectional mandate,* where the other becomes the object of experiment which in essence is violence and in which pain is inflicted in the name of science;
4. *The idea of triage,* combining the concepts of rational experiment, the concept of obsolescence, and of vivisection – whereby a society, a subculture or a species is labelled as obsolete and condemned to death because rational judgement has deemed it incurable.

Development as a technocratic project includes all four themes. In fact, if concepts could ever be death warrants, the above glossary could be regarded as genocidal.

Modernisation is a double whammy for countries in the Global South, he argues. After countries have been subjected to colonialism together with all of its infrastructure to maximise extraction most often through violent oppression, in the post-independence period, development strategies adopted by new political elites basically engage the same system of extraction through 'development as science' in their quest for modernity. The dependence on the colonial infrastructure and in particular on the same knowledge paradigms, without properly understanding their genealogy or sufficiently interrogating the nature and content of the science–power nexus, has the potential to cause deep socio-political and economic harm.

What can be learned from this? South African universities produced about 22 000 research papers in 2015, about 1 per cent of the world's output, and slightly more than 2 700 PhDs a year. Interestingly, some 56 per cent of its research output is in collaboration with researchers in other parts of the world. This is happening at a time when the national spending on research is in decline, especially the contribution of the private sector. While the average citation level of South African research is close to the global average, if one looks at the top 10 per cent of papers of the global output in terms of citation levels South Africa's share increases from about 6.8 per cent in the medical and health sciences, to 8.6 per cent in the natural sciences and to 9.6 per cent in the humanities and social sciences. This indicates that South Africa's research system punches above its weight in terms of these traditional metrics (Academy of Science, 2015).

Notwithstanding the rapid rise in the production of research outputs, patents and doctoral graduates, there is still deep concern that the science system has not contributed maximally to the needs of inclusive development. It may well be a right moment to turn intellectual attention to investigating new forms of knowledge, new modes of knowledge production and new relationships between science, knowledge and power in the design of development projects. Perhaps most importantly, attention must turn to generating new cohorts of passionate, courageous and talented scholars to address the rebalancing of the rather lopsided geopolitics of knowledge and bring this project to a locus at the central core of the institutions and the system as a whole.

Are universities in South Africa, South African universities?
The connection that the 26 public universities have with millions of South Africans is at best tenuous. While families and communities see universities as powerful engines for social mobility, they would be hard-pushed to think of the universities as representative institutions that may be seen as engines of cultural development, social problem-solving, language development and so on. It is an amazing fact – a failure of purpose – that 25 years after the transition, South Africa continues to fixate on apartheid's social construction of race, with very little university-based intellectualisation of this issue. The question posed in the post-1994 policy moment was to ask how our universities could best be deployed to fit the purposes of a transition marked by transformation towards a non-racial, non-sexist democracy, together with the development of a globally competitive knowledge economy. Did the sector succeed?

To address this, a starting point could be a deliberate strategy of re-engagement of the universities with their new diverse and plural publics. This would have to be through their knowledge projects so that the engagement is at their very core, so that change begins to take shape systemically. This means that they must assume the responsibility to produce all kinds of knowledge about the context in which they operate. We may discuss what we think context means. For instance, in the case of Durban, we could think of the context as a set of concentric spaces that grow out from what the Warwick Junction in the CBD is to the Durban University of Technology, to the city of Durban, to the eThekwini Municipality, to the province of KwaZulu-Natal, its coastline and so on – keeping in mind that our universities are all national universities as well as African universities and, ultimately, they are global in nature. They are fundamentally institutions of place and time.

The assumption of this responsibility of generating knowledge about the context does not predetermine a kind of isolationism. This does not mean that these universities should not work with scholars and institutions in other parts of the world to produce knowledge of this context. Neither does it mean that South African scholars should not be working on understanding other contexts, other realities. The world is much too interconnected to imagine virtual boundaries between knowledge domains. And of course, this does not mean that South African institutions should not be working on global projects. Many of the challenges facing humanity are simultaneously intensely local and global in nature – from curbing the ravages of HIV/AIDS and extensively drug-resistant tuberculosis (XDR TB), to galloping trends of consumption and unsustainable human–earth nexuses and global warming, growing socio-economic inequality, racism, gender-based violence and many other forms of grotesque violence and wars. Entering the global knowledge system on its own terms is an essential requirement for the 'decolonising' of the university's knowledge projects. What are the potential drivers of reconstructing or 'decolonising' the knowledge enterprise? Three examples are explored here.

Embedded information, techniques and knowledges

A few years ago, Mduduzi Paulus Mokoena, a young microbiologist at the Durban University of Technology, who had just completed a PhD in the area of fermentation, set about trying to understand how the process of fermentation in the preparation of food had evolved among the Qadi community in Inanda to the north of Durban (Chelule, Mokoena and Gqaleni, 2010). With a team of students, all of whom had to be proficient in isiZulu, and after much negotiation and discussion with the local chief, Mokoena and his students engaged four generations of women about the way in which they used fermentation in the preparation of food. These conversations were carefully recorded, analysed and translated into laboratory experiments. When the experiments did not work, they returned to the community and continued the engagement, which led to reshaped experiments. Soon after the work was published in an 'international' journal, the team received an e-mail from a group in north-east China who were working on a very similar study and seeking to form a collaborative project.

Mokoena's project contributed to the codification of information and techniques deeply embedded in a cultural ecology, constituted of many kinds of information and knowledge produced through decades of practice. The women that were involved, and the community more generally, experienced some sense of connection with this institution of higher learning. For the students involved, this could only have been an extremely important epistemic connection between the biotechnology they were studying and their own life experiences and traditions in similar communities. This is a way to create new conversations between universities and one of its publics; a way to build new connections and even ownership.

Reductionism and complexity

Of course, knowledge codification of this kind is one way in which paths to new research methodologies may emerge and, in time, contribute to the evolution in the dominant paradigms of science and its methods. Naresh Dadhich, a theoretical physicist – a general relativist – at the Interuniversity Centre for Astronomy and Astrophysics in Pune, India, explores ways in which deep-seated pluralism in Indian intellectual traditions and community life shapes young minds in ways that may produce tensions within the scientific enterprise – tensions between the plural and the digital, between the integrative and reductionist (Dadhich, 2014). And as we see increasingly from within the field of physics and other traditionally reductionist disciplines, the ideas of complexity are rapidly beginning to imprint themselves on new ways to study the universe (Gefter, 2014).

Considering the earlier discussion of Mode 2 knowledge production, one might ask if the shift from reductionist to integrative knowledge production is one way in which we may begin to explore the emergence of new, interesting approaches to knowledge production. It may also be important to understand the relationship between these integrative approaches and indigenous underpinnings, such as '*ubuntuism*', which may drive this trend towards more nuanced, integrative ways to deal with complexity – which, by the way, is the normal state of the universe and its contents.

The coexistence of multiple knowledge systems

Societies often have within their diversity-difference matrix, the composition of a discursive space manufactured from multiple knowledge systems. The majority of South Africans coexist simultaneously within modernism (with all of its paraphernalia), the world of traditional knowledge systems (such as traditional health systems), multiple spiritual and religious systems, and so on. While this ought to contribute towards building strong, resilient and cohesive communities, this is not necessarily the case. The implications of this reality for policy development and implementation are germane.

Adam Ashforth, for instance, described through his studies on witchcraft in Soweto the coexistence of multiple beliefs and understandings of the mechanism of HIV transmission among individuals who had a thorough understanding of the transmission of HIV through the exchange of bodily fluids (Ashforth, 2005). He describes existing beliefs in which the art of delivery (or transmission) of the virus is given to those with powers derived from witchcraft (Ashforth, 2002).

There have also been reports of the South African Police Service sometimes calling on people who are believed to be in possession of extrasensory capacities to solve crimes or find people who have disappeared. Under stressful conditions, individuals resort to incongruent systems of knowledge, giving rise to shifting belief systems. This is further complicated by the existence of a hierarchy of knowledge systems.

What are the implications of all this for policy development and for social cohesion? The challenge then is to understand the role of universities in creating discursive spaces where conversations between these partially intersecting or non-intersecting knowledge systems happen with respect and dignity (see Adesina, Chapter 11, in this volume). In an important contribution, Brenda Leibowitz captures this issue:

> This does not mean that all forms of knowledge are equal, but that the equality of knowers forms the basis of dialogue between knowledges, and that what is required for democracy is a dialogue amongst knowers and their knowledges. This dialogue is necessary because the present context where Western knowledge forms are all-powerful is problematic in two ways. It is inadequate to solve the problems of social injustice and inequality of our times (Leibowitz, 2017).

Visvanathan, reflecting on the same challenge of building the idea of cognitive justice in India, emphasises the importance of the 'plural availability of knowledges' (Visvanathan, 2009; also see Higgs, Chapter 12, in this volume).

South Africa's undergraduate graduation rate at just over 50 per cent represents a significant cost in talent and resources. There are several reasons for this, one of which is possibly the complex matter of epistemic access,[5] especially where there has been significant and rapid change in student demographics (Morrow, 2009). Universities are often designed around archetypal students with particular cultural traditions and particular preparation for university study. If the majority of students come from schools that largely fail to play this role, there is a need to understand whether there are sufficient meshes between the curriculum encountered by students and the knowledge types/platforms they bring with them – which may differ significantly from what is assumed they bring with them.

It may help to reiterate this line of thinking. In most complex societies, multiple knowledge systems coexist and interact with one another. In 'decolonising' contexts, these knowledges are embedded in value systems

---

5   Morrow, W (2009) *Bounds of Democracy: Epistemological access in higher education*. Pretoria: HRSC Press.

so that some are seen as superior and others inferior. Universities often play modern 'civilising' missions, scrubbing out the internal and the indigenous and implanting knowledge forms drawn from modernity. In such societies, people coexist in these multiple knowledge systems and will slip from one to another quite seamlessly, depending on the context. Students occupy mental spaces shaped by a number of knowledge systems. When one or more of these are deliberately and systematically excluded from the process of curriculum construction, there could be hindrances to learning. While this may not happen deliberately, it is a powerful form of exclusion.

Conclusion

South Africa's transformation to a caring, nurturing, complex and multilayered democracy depends on its capacity to produce a social imaginary deeply steeped in social justice, thereby defining a new historical epoch based on a new social compact. It has to produce the foundations for a new ontology and epistemology of a more complete liberation that the negotiated settlement of the 1990s did not produce. South Africa's 26 public universities will simultaneously be part of the process that produces these foundations and they will be depended on to craft new directions in knowledge production and dissemination.

If the student actions of the last three years are to be considered as a political disjuncture of some sort, then it is the responsibility of this society to engage the place of universities in a national reconstruction project, a rekindling of the revolutionary ethos that captured the interest and passion of the struggle generation for another kind of project. Newer generations of activists have the responsibility to take this process forward, conscious of the fact that the 'decolonising' project is global in nature. Each society has its internal mapping of power relations and its own version of internal colonialism – and especially so in the decolonising, non-aligned world.

For the university system, these fundamental shifts will have to emerge through the re-engaging of new publics, thereby reshaping their relationship with society without stripping it of any of its critical edge or its capacity to produce new generations of graduates and scholars who will bear critical skills, integrity, the capacity to engage in ethical thinking and the ability to engage complexity. At the individual level, the theologian DA Forster explores this notion:

> To be able to identify and place one's self within the world is a crucial element of one's wellbeing. Ontologically, it shapes the image we have

of ourselves, as well as our relation to others, and ultimately informs our understanding of the place we understand ourselves to occupy within the whole of the Kosmos (Forster, 2010).

Perhaps the same applies to universities. It would be a rather crude caricaturing of the university sector to imagine that there have not been changes over the last 30 years. It is necessary to revisit and document the curriculum explorations of the past, the experimental changes to the programmes of arts, social sciences and health sciences in particular, and investigate why in many cases these did not gain longer-term traction. At the heart of the new knowledge enterprise is the issue of engagement with new publics without which the construction of an ontology and epistemology of engagement will not be possible. This has the potential to be an extraordinarily exciting project.

References

Academy of Science of South Africa (2015). Unpublished study.

Ashforth, A (2002) An epidemic of witchcraft? The implications of AIDS for the post-apartheid state, *African Studies*, **61**(1): 121–43.

Ashforth, A (2005) *Witchcraft, Violence, and Democracy in South Africa*. Chicago, IL: University of Chicago Press.

Bawden, R (1992) *From Extensions to Transactions: A university in development for development*. Ottawa: International Development Centre.

Blankley, WO and Booyens, I (2010) Building a knowledge economy in South Africa, *South African Journal of Science*, **106**(11&12): 373–79.

Brown, TM and Fee, E, Kark, S and Cassel, J (2002) Social medicine pioneers and South African emigres, *American Journal of Public Health*, **92**(11): 1744–45.

Chelule, PK, Mokoena, MP and Gqaleni, N (2010) Advantages of traditional lactic acid bacteria fermentation of food in Africa, in A Méndez-Vilas (ed.) *Current Research, Technology and Education Topics in Applied Microbiology and Microbial Biotechnology*, Vol. 2. Badajoz, Spain: Formatex Research Center, pp. 1160–67.

Cloete, N, Muller, J, Makgoba, MW and Ekong, D (eds) (1997) *Knowledge, Identity and Curriculum Transformation in Africa*. Cape Town: Maskew Miller Longman.

Dadhich N (2014) The Indian plural mind, *Economic and Political Weekly*, **49**(10), 8 March.

Davis, S (2007) *African Alliance Funds Next Cohort of Crop Breeders*. Available at: https://www.scidev.net/global/food-security/news/african-alliance-funds-next-cohort-of-crop-breeder.html (accessed July 2017).

Department of Arts, Culture, Science and Technology (1996) *White Paper on Science and Technology: Preparing for the 21st Century*. Pretoria: Department of Arts, Culture, Science and Technology, 4 September.

Department of Education (1997) Education White Paper 3, *A Programme for the Transformation of Higher Education Higher Education*. Pretoria: Department of Education, July 1997.

Department of Education (1997) Higher Education Act 101 of 1997. Pretoria: Department of Education. Available at: https://www.india-seminar.com/2009/597/597_shiv_visvanathan.htm.

Durban University of Technology (2007) *Heralding the Centenary: Years of wisdom*. Durban: Corporate Affairs Department, DUT.

Forster, DA (2010) A generous ontology: Identity as a process of intersubjective discovery. An African theological contribution, *HTS Teologiese Studies/Theological* Studies, **66**(1): 731, 12 pages.

Gefter, A (2014) Theoretical physics: Complexity on the horizon, *Nature*, 29 May.

Gibbons, M, Limoges, C, Nowotny, H, Schwartzman, S, Scott, P and Trow, M (1994) *The New Production of Knowledge: The dynamics of science and research in contemporary societies.* London: Sage Publications.

Guest, B (2017) *Stella Aurorae: The history of a South African university.* Pietermaritzburg: The Natal Society Foundation.

Jansen, J and Motala, S (eds) (2017) Introduction – Part 1. *Curriculum Stasis, Funding and the 'Decolonial Turn' in Universities: Inclusion and exclusion in higher education in South Africa*, Special Edition, *Journal of Education*, **68**: 1–2.

Kraak, A (2000) *Changing Modes: New knowledge production and its implications for higher education in South Africa.* Pretoria: Human Sciences Research Council.

Leibowitz, B (2017) Cognitive justice and the higher education curriculum, in Jansen, J and Motala, S (eds) *Curriculum Stasis, Funding and the 'Decolonial Turn' in Universities: Inclusion and exclusion in higher education in South Africa*, Special Edition, *Journal of Education*, **68**: 93–111.

Morrow, W (2009) *Bounds of Democracy: Epistemological access in higher education.* Pretoria: HRSC Press.

National Commission on Higher Education (NCHE) (1996) *A Framework for Transformation.* Pretoria: Department of National Education.

Readings, W (1996) *The University in Ruins.* Cambridge, MA: Harvard University Press.

Scott, P (1984) *The Crisis of the University.* London: Croom Helm.

Susser, M (2006) A personal history: Social medicine in a South African setting, 1952–55. Part 2: Social medicine as a calling: Ups, downs and politics in Alexandra Township, *Journal of Epidemiology and Community Health*, **60**(8): 662–68.

Visvanathan, S (1997) On the annals of a laboratory state, in *A Carnival for Science: Essays on science, technology and development.* Delhi: Oxford University Press, 15–47.

Visvanathan, S (2009) The search for cognitive justice. Available at: http://www.india-seminar.com/2009/597/597_shiv_visvanathan.htm 9 (accessed 29 September 2019).

Chapter 5
Equity in higher education and education for all: Critical considerations

Shireen Motala

Introduction
Since the advent of democracy in 1994, the South African government has pursued equity in education, despite increasingly limited public finances. While discrimination in social spending has been considerably reduced, with race no longer a criterion, inequalities remain because of the high costs of achieving fiscal parity in education. In higher education, slowly growing fiscal inputs are not translating into greater efficiency and quality outcomes. Questions persist about whether the current approach to equity is adequate, and whether differential redistribution that favours the underprivileged has taken place. The slow progress towards equity has been brought into sharp focus by the widespread protests in 2015 and 2016 around affordability of higher education, not just in South Africa but also in countries like Brazil, Germany and England (Calitz and Fourie, 2016; see also chapters 7 to 9 in this volume). Students have sought to challenge current ideologies and put their concerns of accessibility of higher education, decolonisation and academic freedom firmly on the transformation agenda through the mobilisation of the #FeesMustFall movement.

This chapter begins with an overview of policy shifts in the South African higher education system, particularly in relation to education funding. It then examines four major themes in higher education: (1) fee-free education and free higher education; (2) education as a public and private good; (3) expansion, equity and quality; and (4) equitable funding models and approaches. I argue that it is necessary to affirm and embed the notion that education is a public good, and that social justice must drive educational reform.

In this chapter, equality denotes uniformity or, in public policy terms, non-discrimination (Rawls, 1972; Secada, 1989). However, the concept of equity that informs this research goes further, encompassing social justice and presupposing differential distribution to achieve its goals (Sayed, 2002)

Recently, the Oxfam report (2016) and the studies of Thomas Piketty (2014), Dani Rodrik (2016) and Kaushik Basu (2017) have put inequality into sharp and uncomfortable focus. Piketty provides detailed evidence to illustrate how inequality and inequity have increased among nations, leading to the development of plutocracy. Basu (2017: 3) notes that this rising global inequality has been accompanied by a surging sense of disenfranchisement that has fuelled alienation and anger, and even bred nationalism and xenophobia. He also points out that 'as people struggle to hold onto their shrinking share of the pie, their anxiety has created a political opening for opportunistic populists, shaking the world order in the process'.

The provision of public goods is occurring in a global context where the form of the state is changing and where inequality rather than poverty *per se* has become the defining feature of political, social and economic life. This is not to downplay the daily reality of grinding poverty for millions. However, as Tawney argued, poverty is the unacceptable face of inequality: 'What thoughtful rich people call a "problem of poverty", thoughtful poor people call with equal justice a "problem of riches"' (Tawney, 1913:10). Against this backdrop, I want to turn my attention to equity and inequality in higher education in South Africa, and ask the simple question: how far have we come?

Policy overview

While there has been progress towards equity, equality and redress in post-apartheid South Africa, the reality, noted by the National Planning Commission (2015), is that an estimated 48 per cent of the population live on less than US$2 a day, and that at 0.67, the Gini coefficient is the highest in the world (*Mail & Guardian*, 30 September 2016). The unemployment rate in South Africa increased to 27.2 per cent in the second quarter of 2018, from 26.7 per cent in the first quarter. It is the highest jobless rate since the first quarter of 2004 (Statistics South Africa, 2018).

This section presents a historical overview of the financing of higher education in South Africa from 1994 to the present. The crucial year of 1994 saw the advent of democracy accompanied by expectations created by the African National Congress (ANC) that free education would be provided for all. Concurrently, there was a rapid increase in student enrolments in higher education (Pillay, 2010)

Pressure of this kind has not relented and has led to a number of commissions being set up on higher education funding (Heher Commission of Inquiry into Higher Education and Training, 2017; Minister of Higher Education and Training's Input for Presidential Commission, 2016). These commissions resulted from the #FeesMustFall protests, which threw higher education into crisis and alerted the government to their responsibility to ensure access to education for all. The commissions explored the possibility of fee-free higher education (CHE, 2016a; CHE, 2016b; CHE, 2016c; Minister of Higher

Education and Training's Input for Presidential Commission, 2016)

In institutional terms, the structure of higher education did not change between 1994 and 2004, with 21 public universities and 15 technikons in the country (CHE, 2016a). In 2004 this was reduced to 11 traditional and six comprehensive universities and six universities of technology. Three more universities were added, one in the Northern Cape, Sol Plaatje University; one in Mpumalanga, University of Mpumalanga; and Sefako Makgatho Health Sciences University, which was developed from the former Medical University of South Africa (Medunsa) in Gauteng (HESA, 2014; CHE, 2016a).

This institutional reconfiguration was awkward as it still had to be decided which institutions were merging. Proposals were devised by a National Working Group in 2001, and the process was only concluded two years later amid much political negotiation. The main rationale for the mergers was to promote transformation and improve the efficiency of the higher education system (HESA, 2014; CHE, 2016b). Also, the merged institutions were expected to reflect diversity, as had been mandated by the 1997 White Paper on Education.

Between 1994 and 1997, the funding model was based on labour market needs and student demand. The 1997 White Paper replaced this with a planning-steering model taking labour market demands into account but also facilitating equity and redress (Pillay 2010: 156). The funding system after 2004 set out to apply one set of rules for all universities, only deviating when it came to research output. Another dimension was the allocation of earmarked funding to facilitate mergers and development (CHE, 2006a: 45).

From 1994 to 2003, the South African Post-School Education (SAPSE) funding formula, introduced in 1983, was still in place (Report of the Ministerial Committee for the Review of the Funding of Universities, 2013; CHE, 2016a). The SAPSE formula provided funding to higher education institutions based on student numbers. This increased inequity and inequality, as there were different levels of funding for students in humanities and the natural sciences (DHET, 2012; CHE, 2016a). The formula also 'contained several so-called cost components graduated partly on the basis of historical cost' (CHE 2016a: 46).

Finally, in 2004, the SAPSE funding formula was phased out and replaced with a 'state steering mechanism' (CHE 2016a), meaning that higher education financing would now be based on block and earmarked grants. Block grants had three objectives: to underpin teaching input and output, research output, and provide institutional support. These grants could only be used for the intended purposes (CHE, 2016a; CHE, 2016b; Heher Commission of Inquiry into Higher Education and Training, 2017). The largest portion of these block grants is for teaching input, in recent years amounting to 65 to 67 per cent of total allocations.

Another important mechanism is the ongoing National Student Financial Aid Scheme (NSFAS), originally the Tertiary Education Fund for South Africa (TEFSA), instituted in 1991 with annual funding of R25 million (CHE, 2016a: 48). In 1999, by the NSFAS Act, TEFSA became NSFAS. Initially, TEFSA was purely a loan scheme but in some cases its awards evolved into bursaries in the form of rebates and awards for academic performance. This evolution continued, and in 2012, 53 per cent of NSFAS funds were awarded as bursaries (CHE, 2016a; CHE, 2016c; Heher Commission of Inquiry into Higher Education and Training, 2017).

Over the past two decades, higher education has not been as well funded as basic education (Motala, 2017) and higher education funding has, in fact, decreased over time. It continues to be a relatively small part of overall education expenditure, with primary and secondary education allocated 57.9 per cent of resources and higher education 15.5 per cent (National Treasury, 2017, national and provincial databases, education components and shares in SA 2010/11–2016/17). In January 2016, then South African President, Jacob Zuma, set up a Commission of Inquiry into Higher Education and Training (the Heher Commission) to determine if fee-free higher education would be feasible in South Africa. The recommendations of the commission were far-reaching, and included the following:

- government should increase its expenditure on higher education and training to at least 1 per cent of GDP, in line with comparable economies;
- the government should adopt an affordable plan to develop more student accommodation;
- government must investigate further the viability of 'online and blended learning' to address the funding and capacity challenges facing the higher education and training sector; and
- all students at TVET (technical and vocational education and training) colleges should receive fully subsidised free education with grants covering the full cost of study and that no student should be partially funded.

Most significant is that the commission recommended that all undergraduate and postgraduate students studying at public and private universities and colleges, regardless of family background, be funded through a cost-sharing model of government-guaranteed income-contingent loans sourced from commercial banks. Through this cost-sharing model, the commission recommended that commercial banks issue government-guaranteed loans to students, repayable upon graduation and subsequent attainment of a specific income. Should a student fail to reach the required income threshold, government bears the secondary liability. The commission recommended that the existing NSFAS model be replaced by a new Income Contingency Loan System. At the lowest specified income threshold level, the interest rate is lowest, increasing in accordance with specified increases in income.

On 16 December 2017, in a historic announcement, going further than the recommendations of the Heher Commission, President Zuma announced fee-free education for all poor students. Following this, R67 billion was allocated for the programme to be phased in over the medium term (National Treasury, 2018: 54). This allocation was an attempt to address the demands for fee-free education resulting from the 2015 #FeesMustFall protests.

Whatever the political motivation may have been, this proposal, the announcement that students whose parental income is less than R350 000 per annum would receive free education, has put into sharp focus that in South Africa social equity and education equity need to be addressed simultaneously. In this manner, the low quality of education offered in poor communities will not continue to perpetuate their exclusion. In a parallel process, important progress is being made through the delivery of social grants (Bhorat and Cassim, 2013), which address poverty and inequality, and as Patel (2013) argues, there are real long-term benefits to this social investment. In line with Ball's (2003) view of interlocking inequalities, South African education policy-makers need to understand that the mobilisation of social resources is critical to the reproduction of advantage and that insufficient social resources reproduce disadvantage. Educational and social provision must be viewed as an integrated platform to address poverty and underdevelopment. I will return to this theme later.

Equity, expansion and quality in higher education

The increasing demand for higher education, due to globalisation and the rise of the knowledge economy, is reflected in fast-growing higher education enrolments in sub-Saharan Africa, with a growth of 10 per cent annually between 2000 and 2010 (Wangenge-Ouma, 2010; Rensburg, Motala and David, 2016). Higher education has been shifting from an elite system to one promoting universal access, leading to a review of education financing models. At the same time, many challenges continue. These include inadequate access (particularly at secondary and tertiary levels), poor quality of provision, inefficiency (as reflected in high dropout and repetition), and inequity in access and the distribution of resources. In sub-Saharan Africa, low expenditure on higher education is a consequence of competing pressures on the education budget, severe resource constraints and pressure from social sectors such as health and welfare and a lack of sufficient recognition by governments of the value of higher education for economic growth, social welfare and broader sustainable development (Pillay, 2010). These issues, present all over Africa, are evident in South Africa also, and they have generated similar reactions. Principles of fairness and equality of opportunity underlay student demands in 2015 and 2016 (see chapters 7 to 9 in this volume): applicants should not be excluded if they qualify in terms of admission criteria, and they should have access to institutions they choose. The latter point presents a powerful challenge to the current bifurcated tertiary education landscape (Allais, 2016).

Consider the statistics in relation to the major indicators of access, efficiency, quality and resource allocation in tertiary education. Student enrolments increased dramatically by 67 per cent between 2002 and 2016, from 450 000 to 950 000, with the major growth being in African enrolment, which reached 70 per cent of the total student population. In the same period, the growth in permanent academic staff was 20 per cent, and the staff–student ratio grew to an alarming 1:55 from an earlier 1:40 (Simkins, 2016).

Cohort studies (CHE, 2013) show that less than half of the students enter a three-year degree programme, and of those who do, up to 50 per cent take up to six years to graduate. One in four students – excluding those at the University of South Africa (UNISA) – drops out before the second year of study. Only 35 per cent of the total intake, and 48 per cent of contact students, graduate within five years. While allowance is made for students taking longer than five years to graduate and for those returning to the system after dropping out, it is estimated that some 55 per cent of an intake will never graduate. Access, success and completion rates continue to be racially skewed, with white student completion rates on average 50 per cent higher than African rates.

Government funding to universities decreased from 49 per cent of total funding in 2000 to 40 per cent in 2014 (Cloete, 2016). Fees increased in the same period by 9 per cent per annum in the context of a 5 to 6 per cent inflation rate. It is apparent that the higher education system is under considerable strain, with low throughputs, rising enrolments, high staff to student ratios, and an unsustainable funding base with poor NSFAS loan recovery. To maintain a competitive edge in a rapidly transforming knowledge economy, countries need to invest more in quality education. But, with an investment of less than 1 per cent of GDP, historically South Africa has not invested enough in higher education, nor has it reached its own target of 1 per cent on research and development, a figure that is well below international targets. As a percentage of GDP, higher education funding decreased to 0.67 per cent in 2015.

Ndelu (2018: 20) observes that as early as 1998, NSFAS was being funded inadequately and that the amounts disbursed to individual students were insufficient to cover the cost of higher education. She notes that while NSFAS funding increased rapidly, fees continued to rise faster, with concerns also about maladministration and corruption, the slow pace of payments and student selection. The NSFAS model also did not accommodate those in the 'missing middle', who do not meet the criteria for funding, but whose socio-economic status excludes them from accessing tertiary education. Significantly, the protests were most visible in the former white universities, where fees far exceeded those of former black universities. As Wangenge-Ouma (2012) notes, the calls for free higher education illustrate that our funding instruments fall short of addressing students' needs. For students there is also a lack of clarity as to whether NSFAS funds are a loan or a grant, and the dramatic reduction in loan recovery in 2015 further exacerbated the funding crises.

A key priority in relieving funding pressures is to improve the internal effectiveness and efficiency of the higher education system and, indeed, the schooling system, bringing to the fore the relationship between equity and efficiency. This requires systematic interventions to address the knowledge and skills gap between school and university through restructuring the curricula and qualifications. External and internal efficiencies can also be addressed, the former by improving the relevance of programmes and ability of graduates to meet societal and labour market needs, and the latter by improving how resources are allocated, within and across institutions, and by improving levels of degree completion.

Fee-free education for all or for the poor
Calculations of the cost of providing free higher education often draw on examples from developed countries. In Africa, early post-independence provision of free higher education was for small numbers and proved unsustainable as systems expanded. Research from Africa and Latin America indicates that free public education benefits the rich far more than the poor, because students from the wealthier classes are in a better position to compete for access to selective public universities, while all but the most gifted students from poorer backgrounds are relegated to private fee-paying institutions or public institutions of low quality. Oketch (2003) highlights distributional problems in education funding in sub-Saharan Africa with strong competition between basic and higher education; Archer (2015) argues that this situation is regressive in that the poor subsidise the rich; and Barr (2004) notes that even in OECD countries, government subsidies for higher education predominantly benefit the rich.

Davids and Waghid (2016) notes that while the ostensible intention of the #FeesMustFall movement was to benefit poor youth, only 5 per cent of South Africans aged between 15 and 34 years are university students, while 34 per cent are unemployed. A World Bank study, which examined the effect of government spending and taxation on inequality, noted that higher education was the least progressive of social expenditures, since it benefits a very small part of the population (Woodhall, 2007). In our current discourse, there is slippage between the concepts of 'fee-free education', 'free education for all' and 'free education for the poor'. In the debates that followed the recent wave of student protests, those calling for 'fee-free education for all' focused specifically on the demand for no fees for all students; 'free education for all' advocates included fees and the related full costs of education provision, involving housing and subsistence as well; and those supporting 'free education for the poor' proposed a model which differentiates students into groups or categories based on parental income.

Different concepts have different consequences. Cloete (2016) argues that in a developing country, the call should be for 'affordable higher education for all', with a clear understanding that affordable means different costs for different social groups. This can be expanded to the provision of free education for the poor, with an agreed definition of which strata of society constitute 'the poor' (Motala, 2016). Many commentators (Heher Commission, 2017: 105) make it clear that while fee remission is an important equity gain in a society characterised by high levels of inequality and poverty, considerations of social inequity also require attention to the full package of accommodation, books and subsistence. The 'full cost of study' proponents argue persuasively that subsidising tuition alone is of little practical value. Van den Berg and Raubenheimer (2015) describe lack of food and housing as a 'powerful force' that contributes to poor academic performance, an inability to participate meaningfully in campus life, and attrition. Wangenge-Ouma (2012) notes that, with the shift from an elite to a more representative student population, the needs are greater and must include the full support package for the poorest.

Proponents of 'free education for all' suggest that current models, which classify households into income groups and apply means tests, are flawed, because they lead to increased vulnerability for the poor, high levels of indebtedness, reduced savings towards retirement and a compromised standard of living (Oxfam, 2016). Instead, increasing corporate tax from 28 per cent to 30 per cent and the skills development levy from 1 per cent to 3 per cent might be considered, as well as dealing decisively with corruption. Such an approach, which concentrates on the structural aspects of inequality and uses tax revenues for higher education funding, is preferable to the idea of a differentiated approach to the 'rich' and 'poor'.

Also persuasive is the argument to make free education available to the poor, based on the available disposable income of the family, through a differentiated post-school system, with differentiated funding and fees. Teferra (2016) notes that a number of African universities, in Uganda, Malawi and Kenya, have moved from free higher education for all to cost sharing and to ensuring that university resource bases are both consolidated and diversified. Cost sharing in higher education is defined as 'a shift in the burden of higher education costs from being borne exclusively or predominantly by government, or taxpayers, to be shared with parents and students' (Johnstone, 2003: 351). This redistributive model is gaining support in South Africa, with the premise that free education must be made available to the poor and that the wealthy must pay their share. As in the South African context, where the cost-sharing model and income contingent loans (ICL) have gained currency, achieving this objective has its challenges. These include the need for substantial initial investment to launch loan schemes based on public funds and, as the South African experience is revealing, limited private capital for student loans to complement what is received from the public purse. There are also problems in recovering loan repayments from graduates. The complexity of the income contingent formula, based on a sliding scale of parental income, requires clear interpretation and explanation to assist parents to understand how the scheme would work and how it would benefit them. As an OCED report (2008) notes, for cost sharing to be compatible with equality of opportunity and access, it must be accompanied by measures that remove financial barriers to entering tertiary education, especially for more disadvantaged groups. Ndelu (2018) notes that with South Africa's currently faltering economy, free quality education as demanded by the 'fallists' is not feasible. This is also the Ugandan and Zimbabwean experience.

Higher education as private and public good

Higher education is arguably both a private and a public good, and there is a worldwide trend to expect individuals to pay more for the costs they incur in benefiting from it. As noted earlier, decreases in state expenditure on higher education meant that student fees had to be correspondingly increased. The profitability of investing in higher education can be calculated by undertaking a cost–benefit analysis, which reviews social and private returns to education.

Higher education has a major effect on economic development and private earnings. In sub-Saharan Africa, returns on tertiary education are higher than returns on schooling: South Africa has one of the highest returns on higher education in the world with considerable rewards in wages and employment opportunities. The private rate of return on education thus presents a persuasive argument for an increase in private fees, but the high social returns also indicate that investment in education is a profitable investment for the state since it impacts positively on areas such as health and welfare (De Villiers and Steyn, 2007).

Unterhalter et al (2018) raise the overarching question of who defines the public good and how. There appear to be two distinct ways in which higher education and the public good are conceptualised. Firstly, qualifications, knowledge production, innovation, development of the professional classes and expertise can be perceived as leading to particular economic, social, political or cultural manifestations of public good (Stiglitz, 1999; McMahon, 2009). Others illustrate the relationship between higher education and the public good, for instance, through reducing prejudice, democratisation, critical thinking and active citizenship (Leibowitz 2013; Calhoun, 2006; Marginson, 2011).

Higher education in sub-Saharan Africa has moved from the establishment of flagship national universities in the post-independence period, which were intended to form a state bureaucracy (Teferra, 2016), to developmental universities with a commitment to indigenising knowledge and benefiting marginalised populations, through more recent tendencies towards the marketisation of public institutions and encouragement of the private sector (Assié-Lumumba, 2006; Mamdani, 2007; McCowan 2016). This relates to current debates which closely associate calls for decolonised education with effective resource allocation and equity. As Maringira and Gukurume (2018: 38) note, the #FeesMustFall movement created a space to articulate grievances about broader social and structural transformation, as well as raise issues around being black and racial inequality. Students believed that the state has a strong interest and presence in the operation of universities in South Africa in terms of their administration, in who is admitted and who can write and speak for them.

Factors preventing the effective development of higher education are its slow growth, the credibility of parts of the post-school system, inefficiencies across the entire education sector and concomitant capacity constraints. Graduate employment tends to be well rewarded in South Africa and the resulting high tax collection could bolster the argument for low fees or no fees. But low graduation rates make its feasibility doubtful. Wangenge-Ouma and Cloete (2008) suggest that South Africa's higher education system can be characterised as low government investment and low effective participation with very high costs. It is affordable for the elite, relatively affordable for the middle class, although with loans and debt, and totally unaffordable for the poor. For development and growth, government needs to invest more in tertiary education, increase participation with improved completion rates and establish a differentiated fees structure.

Indeed, to contribute effectively to economic growth and development, a much higher participation rate, in the realm of 30 to 50 per cent, is required in higher education, well above the current rate of 20 per cent. A Council on Higher Education (CHE) report suggests that higher education needs 'between twice and three times as many well-prepared entrants as the pre-tertiary sectors [schools and colleges] are currently producing – around 100 000 additional candidates'. But neither the schooling nor the technical and vocational education and training (TVET) college systems make this achievable in the 'foreseeable future' (CHE, 2013: 25).

Modelling funding equity

Over the last five years, several ministerial task teams and commissions have examined the chronic underfunding of higher education and assessed the possibility and promise of free tertiary education. These include teams led by the then Deputy President Cyril Ramaphosa in 2012, Derrick Swartz, Vice Chancellor of Nelson Mandela Metropolitan University (NMMU) in 2013 and Sizwe Nxasana, Chairperson of NSFAS and CEO of First National Bank in 2015, as well as reports from the CHE in 2016 and, most recently, the Heher Commission in 2017.

Alongside these deliberations, independent researchers along with civil society organisations, Universities South Africa (USAf), the NSFAS and a number of tertiary institutions have built up a significant body of knowledge on higher education funding (Motala, 2016). Various models have been presented, with different scenarios, including their likely impact in a context of low economic growth with a constrained fiscus. Questions have been asked about the viability of the current funding model, and about whether, in a developing country, free higher education is affordable or even desirable. Current mechanisms for dispensing student financial aid are also under intense scrutiny, and a more equitable allocation of resources for the entire education sector, one that is viable, credible and inclusive, is being considered. The relationship between poverty, access to quality education and societal change has highlighted such systemic issues.

There seems to be unequivocal consensus that any new funding model must be based on social justice. Simply put, no academically achieving and deserving student should be excluded from university because they cannot afford it. Publicly funded tertiary education for the poorest in our society who meet academic merit criteria must be made available as soon as possible. There is also agreement on certain key principles, which has distinctly shifted the discourse: for example, that full cost provision for the neediest students must include accommodation, food and books; that the 'missing middle' students outside the NSFAS criteria must be guaranteed access through a combination of grants and loans; that funding for higher education must increase; and that an increase in the share of the GDP devoted to this sector from 0.7 to 1–1.5 per cent must be considered. Undoubtedly, the diverse skills needed by our society and economy require serious attention to the learning needs of the entire cohort of young people in the 18–24-year age group (Motala, 2017: 21).

Students have brought the inequalities in our society into sharp focus and have demonstrated their deep frustration with the numerous inconclusive funding review processes, and with poor governance, corruption and wastage. At the same time, the student movement appears fragmented and their ultimate objective is not clear. To end the impasse, proposals need to translate into firm and achievable short-, medium- and long-term commitments. The macro funding principles embedded in the above commitments are cost sharing, efficiency and quality, and education as a public good. This will go a long way to contributing to much-needed stability in our increasingly fragile higher education sector.

Conclusion

This chapter has illustrated that various strategies have been put in place to address the many seemingly intractable problems in South African higher education to realise equitable and quality education. The necessary conditions for the delivery of quality and decolonised education are adequate finance and human resources, involvement and a sense of ownership by role-players, regular monitoring and evaluation, and sustained effort. At both school and tertiary levels, the issues are strikingly similar: the education process needs to be understood as a continuum for interventions to be effective. Above all, it is essential to affirm and embed the notion that education is a public good and insist that equality and social justice must drive educational reform. In particular, differential redistribution must define our approach to equity. Widespread community mobilisation is required to ensure that the gains in access to education and participation become the foundation for learning and outcomes. These will offer real life chances for our young people in further and higher education and in the labour market, thus enabling mobility out of poverty.

There remain many questions about whether the pro-poor policy and the fee-free trajectory are genuinely on track towards fundamental transformation or whether they are merely ameliorating, without overcoming, existing funding inequities. What we need is a new model of equity, relevant to our specific context, which prioritises differential distribution. The state needs a more aggressive approach to redistributing resources, including human resources. Doing this would address poverty and disadvantage, as well as accessibility and choice.

References

Allais, S (2016) Towards measuring the economic value of higher education: Lessons from South Africa, *Comparative Education*, **53**(1): 147–63.

Archer, A (2015) Free higher education is an inequality engine, *Business Day*, 20 October.

Assié-Lumumba, NT (2006) *Higher Education in Africa: Crises, Reforms and Transformation*. Dakar: Council for the Development of Social Science Research in Africa (CODESRIA).

Ball, S (2003) The more things change... Educational research, social class and interlocking inequalities. Professorial lecture, Institute of Education, University of London.

Barr, N (2004) Higher education funding, *Oxford Review of Economic Policy*, **20**(2): 264–83.

Basu, K (2017) *The Insecurity of Inequality*. Project Syndicate: The World's Opinion Page. Available at: https://www.project-syndicate.org/commentary/rising-inequality-globalization-by-kaushik-basu-2017-04'https://www.project-syndicate.org/commentary/rising-inequality-globalization-by-kaushik-basu-2017-04 (accessed September 2019).

Bhorat, H and Cassim, A (2013) South African welfare system success story: A rapid asset delivery programme, 5 February 2014. Available at: http://www.brookings.edu/blogs/africa-in-focusposts/2014/01/24-south-africa-welfare-success-bhorat-cassim'http://www.brookings.edu/blogs/africa-in-focusposts/2014/01/24-south-africa-welfare-success-bhorat-cassim (accessed May 2018).

Calhoun, C (2006) The university and the public good, *Thesis Eleven*, **84**(1): 7-43.

Calitz, E and Fourie, J (2016) The historically high cost of tertiary education in South Africa, *Politikon*, **43**(1): 149–154.

Cloete, N (2016) University fees in South Africa: A story from evidence. Centre for Higher Education Transformation (CHET), May.

Coleman, JW (1986) Planning and Resource Allocation Management. *New Directions for Higher Education*, 55

Council on Higher Education (CHE) (2013) *A proposal for undergraduate curriculum reform in South Africa: The case for a flexible curriculum structure*. Pretoria: CHE.

Council on Higher Education (CHE) (2016) *South African higher education reviewed. Two decades of democracy*. CHE Funding Task Team. Pretoria: CHE.

Davids, N and Waghid, Y (2016) #FeesMustFall: History of South African student protests reflects inequality's grip, *Mail and Guardian*, 10 October.

Department of Education (DoE) (1997) Education White Paper 3: A programme for the transformation of higher education, July 1997

Department of Higher Education (DHET) (2012) Department of Higher Education and Training. Annual Report, 2012-2013. Pretoria, South Africa.

De Villiers, P and Steyn, G (2007) The changing face of public financing of higher education, with special reference to South Africa, *South African Journal of Economics*, **75**(1): 136–54.

Fedderke, J, De Kadt, R and Luis, J (2000) Uneducating South Africa: Government policy and the failure to address the apartheid legacy, 1910–1993, *International Review of Education*, **46**(3–4): 257–81.

Heher Commission (2017) Commission of Inquiry into Higher Education and Training. The Presidency, Pretoria, South Africa.

Higher Education South Africa (HESA) (2014) *2014 Annual Report*. Pretoria: Higher Education South Africa.

Johnstone, DB (2003) The economics and politics of cost sharing in higher education: Comparative perspectives, *Economics of Education Review*, **23**: 403–410.

Leibowitz, B (2013) Attention to student writing in postgraduate health science education: Whose task is it? or how? *Journal of Academic Writing*, **3**(1): 30-41.

Mamdani, M (2007) *Scholars in the Marketplace: The dilemmas of neo-liberal reform at Makerere University* 1989-2005. Pretoria: Human Sciences Research Council (HSRC) Press.

Marginson, S (2011) Higher Education and Public Good, *Higher Education Quarterly*, **65**(4): 411-433.
Maringira, G and Gukurume S (2018) Being Black in #FeesMustFall and #FreeDecolonisedEducation: Student Protests at the University of the Western Cape. An analysis of the #FeesMustFall Movement at South African universities. Johannesburg: Centre for the Study of Violence and Reconciliation (CSVR).
McCowan, T (2012) Is there a universal right to higher education? *British Journal of Educational Studies*, **60**(2): 111–128.
McCowan, T (2016) Universities and the post-2015 development agenda: An analytical framework, *Higher Education*, **72**(4): 505-23.
McMahon, WW (2009) *Higher Learning: Greater Good: The Private and Social Benefits of Higher Education*. Maryland: Johns Hopkins University.
Mngomezulu, S, Dhunpath, R and Munro, N (2017) Does financial assistance undermine academic success? Experiences of 'at risk' students in a South African university, *Journal of Education*, **68**. DOI: https://doi.org/10.17159/10.17159/2520-9868/i68a05
Moloi, K, Makgoba, M and Miruka, C (2017) (De)constructing the #FeesMustFall Campaign in South African Higher Education, *Contemporary Higher Education*, **14**(2): 211–23.
Motala, S (2013) Equity, quality and access in South African education: A work still very much in progress, in R Southall and P Naidoo (eds) *New South African Review*. Johannesburg: Wits University Press, pp. 221–35.
Motala, S (2013) Making rights realities: Education reform in post-apartheid South Africa, in C Harber (ed.) *Education in Southern Africa*. London: Bloomsbury, pp. 47–67.
Motala, S (2014) Equity, access and quality in basic education, in T Meywa, M Nkondo, J Chitaga-Mabugu, M Sithole and F Nyamnjoh (eds) *State of the Nation 2014: A twenty year review*. Cape Town: HSRC Press, pp. 284–99.
Motala, S (2016) Breaking the university impasse: Time to put plans and research into action, *The Conversation*, October.
Motala, S (2017) Curriculum stasis, funding and the 'decolonial turn' in universities: Inclusion and exclusion of higher education. Journal of Education Achieving 'free education' for the poor – a realisable goal in 2018?' in Jansen, J. and Motala, S. (ed.). 67.
National Planning Commission (2015) *Second Diagnostic Report*. Pretoria: Government Printer.
National Treasury (2018) *Estimates of National Expenditure*. Pretoria: Government Printer.
Ndelu, S (2018) *A rebellion of the poor: An analysis of Fees Must Fall movements in South Africa*. Johannesburg: Centre for the Study of Violence and Reconciliation (CSVR).
Oketch, MO (2003) Affording the unaffordable: Cost sharing in higher education in sub-Saharan Africa', *Peabody Journal of Education* **78**(3): 88–106.
Organisation for Economic Co-operation and Development (OECD) (2008) *Growing Unequal? Income Distribution and Poverty in OECD Countries*. Paris: OECD.
Oxfam Report (2016) Financing, not funding, mechanism needed. *ProQuest* 26, November.
Patel, L (2013) *Do social grants create more problems than they solve?* Helen Joseph Memorial Lecture, 14 October, University of Johannesburg.
Pedró, F, Leroux, G and Watanabe, M (2015) *The privatization of education in developing countries: Evidence and policy implications*. UNESCO Working Papers on Education Policy N° 2. UNESCO.
Piketty, T (2014) *Capital in the Twenty-First Century*. London: Belknap Press.
Pillay, P (2010) *Higher Education Financing in East and Southern Africa*. African Books Collective
Rawls, J (1972) *A Theory of Justice*. Oxford: Oxford University Press.
Rawls, J (2001) *Justice as Fairness: A Restatement*. Cambridge, MA: Belknap Press.
Rensburg, I, Motala, S and David, S (2016) Research Collaboration among Emerging Economies: Policy implications for BRICS nations, *International Journal of Economic Policy*

in Emerging Economies, **9**(4): 344–60.

Rodrik, D (2016) The Abdication of the Left. Project Syndicate. Available at: https://www.project-syndicate.org/commentary/anti-globalization-backlash-from-right-by-dani-rodrik-2016-07 (accessed July 2019).

Sayed, Y (2002) Democratising education in a decentralised system: South Africa policy and practice, *Compare: A Journal of Comparative and International Education*, **32**(1), 35–46.

Secada, WG (ed.) (1989) *Equity in Education*. London: Falmer.

Sen, A (1999) *Development as Freedom*. Oxford: Oxford University Press.

Simkins, C (2016) Funding. From *South African Higher Education Reviewed: Two decades of democracy*, Pretoria: Council on Higher Education (CHE).

Statistics South Africa (2017) *Quarterly Labour Force Survey* (P0211) Quarter 1, October. Available at: http://www.statssa.gov.za/publications/P0211/P02111stQuarter2017.pdf (accessed June 2018).

Statistics South Africa (2018) *Quarterly Labour Force Survey* (P0211) Quarter 1, October.

Stiglitz, J (1999) The World Bank at the Millennium, *The Economic Journal*, **109**(459): 577–97.

Tawney, R (1913) *Memoranda on the Problems of Poverty*. London: William Morris.

Teferra, D (2016) African flagship universities: Their neglected contributions, *Higher Education*, **72**(1): 79–99.

Unterhalter, E, Allais, SM, Howell, C, McCowan, T, Morley, L, Ibrahim, O, and Oketch, M (2018). Conceptualising Higher Education and the Public Good in Ghana, Kenya, Nigeria and South Africa. In: Proceedings of the CIES 2018 Annual Conference. Comparative and International Education Society (CIES), Mexico City, Mexico.

Van den Berg, L and Raubenheimer, J (2015) Food insecurity among students at the University of the Free State, *Journal of Education*, **28**(4): 160–69.

Van der Berg, S (2012) Equity in education expenditure. Unpublished manuscript.

Wangenge-Ouma, G (2010) Funding and the attainment of transformation goals in South Africa's higher education, *Oxford Review of Education*, **36**(4): 481–97.

Wangenge-Ouma, G (2012) Tuition fees and the challenge of making higher education a popular commodity in South Africa, *Higher Education*, **64**(6): 831-44.

Wangenge-Ouma, G and Cloete, N (2008) Financing higher education in South Africa: Public funding, non-government revenue and tuition fees, *South African Journal of Higher Education*, **22**(4): 906–19.

Woodhall, M (2007) *Funding Higher Education: The contribution of economic thinking to debate and policy development*. World Bank education working paper series. Number 8. Washington, D.C.: World Bank.

Chapter 6
The challenges of transforming South Africa's historically black universities

Bheki R Mngomezulu

Introduction
This chapter discusses the challenges of transforming South Africa's historically black universities (HBUs), which were created by the promulgation of a government Act, in line with the apartheid policy. Interestingly, this controversial Act was called the Extension of University Education Act (No. 45 of 1959). Section 2(1) stated that the then Minister of Education, in consultation with the Minister of Finance, could establish, maintain and conduct University Colleges for Bantu persons. Section 2(2) stated that the Minister of Education could also establish, maintain and conduct University Colleges for non-white persons other than Bantu persons. Race and ethnicity were the key variables used in this arrangement. It was envisaged that these university colleges would metamorphose to become fully-fledged universities serving different population groups in terms of race and ethnicity.

Reflecting on this issue while penning the foreword to a document titled *Transformation and Restructuring: A new institutional landscape for higher education*, the then Minister of Education, Kader Asmal, recalled: 'The origins of the current institutional structure of the higher education system can be traced back to the geo-political imagination of apartheid's planner, Hendrik Verwoerd and his reactionary ideological vision of "separate but equal development"' (Asmal, 2002: i). Commenting on the controversial Act of 1959, Asmal (2002: i) argued that the Act 'was far from extending access to higher education on the basis of the universal values intrinsic to higher education'. His argument was based on the fact that the Act was divisive.

It is within this historical context that black and white universities emerged; the establishment of black universities did not just happen by accident. It was a cogently thought through and meticulously implemented policy decision meant to sustain social *classification* and social *stratification* (Crompton, 1993; Seekings, 2003). The polarisation of the South African society in all spheres of life was to continue until the demise of apartheid in 1994.

With the advent of democracy, the transformation and reconfiguration of the education sector in general, and the higher education sector in particular, gave rise to the classifications: 'historically black universities' (HBUs) and 'historically white universities' (HWUs).[1] In line with the Constitution of the Republic of South Africa (Act 108 of 1996), the transformation of higher education became inevitable. As part of the nation-building agenda, the democratic government resolved to abolish the racially and ethnically divided universities. Both HBUs and HWUs had to undergo transformation. Studies have been carried out to establish how HWUs have transformed (or failed to transform) in terms of embracing black students (Mnguni, 2000; Goldschmidt, 2003; Bazana and Mogotsi, 2017). A focus on HBUs is important because vestiges of the old order remain conspicuous – they continue to be under-resourced compared to their HWU counterparts.

The first section of this chapter discusses two key concepts – challenges and transformation. The second part examines the history of the transformation of higher education in South Africa. It takes a closer look at important Acts passed by the Government of National Unity (GNU) in 1994[2] and some reports in this regard. It addresses this theme from a general perspective, then switches to the challenges of transforming HBUs in particular. The chapter then proffers a few ideas on how to address some of these challenges.

Challenges

As a noun, the word 'challenge' means 'that which puts you to the test'. The transitive verb 'challenge' means to arouse, stimulate or present a difficult situation. Therefore, if we talk about *challenges* to transforming HBUs, we mean those factors that impede transformation in HBUs. Some authors use the term 'challenges' interchangeably with 'life events' (Dodge et al, 2012: 228). This is because life events prompt one to think harder or to be innovative in dealing with those events. In the same vein, when there is no challenge, the need for innovation is either minimised or is rendered unnecessary. In this context, if HBUs could be transformed easily, there would be no need to devise strategies to ensure that transformation happens. Therefore, when we talk about *challenges* to the transformation of HBUs we mean impediments and hurdles that need to be overcome to ensure institutional transformation.

---

1 Others refer to these as 'historically advantaged universities' and 'historically disadvantaged universities'.

2 The Government of National Unity (GNU) was established in 1994 following the first democratic election on 27 April of that year. It included the African National Congress (ANC) and the National Party (NP). On 30 June 1996, the NP took a decision to withdraw from the GNU, resulting in its disbandment on 3 February 1997.

Transformation

Anderson and Anderson (2010) asked a dual question: 'What is transformation, and why is it hard to manage?' Implicit in this question is the notion that transformation is not an easy process to manage, even after we have managed to define 'what' transformation is. Venter and Tolmie (2012: 1) admit that transformation is a complex, open-ended concept. Venter (2015: 175) goes further to aver that this concept is 'so vague and indistinct that it is basically an unusable term'.

However, these views should not be misconstrued to mean that transformation has no value whatsoever because it is still used extensively in the literature. Du Preez, Simmonds and Verhoef (2016: 1) argue that it refers to a *change in form* and that it includes the idea of *remodelling, modification* and *restructuring*. The two key concepts associated with transformation are *change* and *evolution*. Any change associated with transformation takes one of two forms, that is, either an *internal* or an *external* process (Malabou, 2008).

In the context of the transformation of HBUs, this meant that these institutions had to undergo change or take on a new form. Whether this change was internal or external depends on one's point of view and the lens used in the analysis. Transformation should not be equated to deracialisation (of staff and student), which falls under the umbrella of transformation but has a specific focus. The reality is that in the post-1994 period, it became a necessity for the new government to transform and reconfigure the HBUs and higher education to emulate what was already happening on the political front. However, transformation has proved to be a daunting task, especially in HBUs for different reasons. Du Preez, Simmonds and Verhoef (2016: 3) state that the transformation of higher education was framed largely by two documents: the Education White Paper 3 (1997) and the 2008 report of the Ministerial Committee on Transformation and Social Cohesion and the Elimination of Discrimination in Public Higher Education Institutions. These reports are discussed later.

Social transformation

Social transformation forms a part of transformation but its focus is narrower. Khondker and Schuerkens (2014: 1) state that 'Social transformation implies a fundamental change in society, which can be contrasted with social change viewed as gradual or incremental changes over a period of time.' With regard to the HBUs, they could not dissociate themselves from the ongoing transformation in the society and they had to reflect changes. In a nutshell, transformation refers to a wide range of changes from student and staff profiles to infrastructure and resource allocation.

The transformation of higher education in South Africa after 1994

The transformation of higher education in post-apartheid South Africa went through two distinctive phases. The first phase was transformation from apartheid to the new political order. The second phase was broader and was ushered in by phenomena such as globalisation, internationalisation and technological advancements (Badat, 2010). Subsequently, new challenges have surfaced, including structural problems, the underpreparedness of students entering university, and discontinuity in terms of the knowledge gap between secondary and higher education, and between higher education and the labour market (Nzimande, 2012: 12; see also chapters 3 to 5 in this volume). South African universities have also faced an identity crisis in the post-apartheid era.

As one would expect, the transformation process was never going to be an event but rather a long-drawn-out and tedious process because of damage that was done by the demeaning and discriminatory apartheid education policies. One should not forget that other African countries also felt obligated to transform their education systems after independence in the 1960s and 1970s (Adeyemi 2000; Mukhwana and Kande 2017; see also chapters 13 to 19 in this volume), so South Africa's exceptionalism should not be overemphasised (Mamdani, 1996).

However, the case of South Africa was slightly different from the rest of the African continent. Corroborating this, Venter (2015: 176) opines that 'In South Africa's higher education, transformation has a clear primary reference, apartheid.' The rest of the African continent experienced colonialism in its general sense, whereas in South Africa apartheid was 'colonialism of a special type' (Hirson, 1992; Webster et al, 2017). This was so for two reasons. Firstly, the oppressors were once the oppressed under British domination. Secondly, they were 'resident oppressors' as opposed to what prevailed in other African countries, where the oppressors resided in the metropolis and only sent envoys to control Africa. The policy of assimilation adopted by France in West and Central Africa did not apply in South Africa. However, elements of Britain's indirect rule were incorporated, accompanied by the co-option of African traditional leaders, who were expected to implement apartheid laws or risk losing their positions as 'chief'.

Against this background, it is important to trace the transformation of higher education in South Africa sequentially to appreciate how the process unfolded, and to understand the challenges faced by the post-apartheid government in transforming the higher education sector in general. This will also place the HBUs and their characteristic peculiarities within the broader context and compare them to their HWU counterparts.

The process unfolds

By 1993, the Interim Constitution of South Africa had already given pointers to the direction the post-apartheid government would take to reconfigure the political landscape. The adoption of the new Constitution in 1996 meant that all subsequent legislation (including higher education legislation) would be guided by this document. It is safe to say that by this time the issues of equality and efficiency of South Africa's higher education system were already under scrutiny. There was general consensus that transformation within this sector was unavoidable. This decision was predicated on the understanding that since higher education is the apex of the entire education system, it could not be left untransformed as the country was entering a new political phase in its beleaguered history. Like other African countries at independence, it was envisaged that higher education institutions would play a critical role in the development and nation-building agenda through research, training of graduates and the education of society on what needed to be done under the new political dispensation.

The first step towards the transformation of higher education was ushered in by the establishment of the National Commission on Higher Education (NCHE) in 1995. This body charted a programme of transformation for the sector. Consequently, 'by 1997, key higher education policy and legislation informed by the work of the Commission was in place to enable the systematic programme for the transformation of higher education to unfold' (CHE, 2009:1). Its report, 'An Overview of a New Policy Framework for Higher Education', marked the first phase in the reconfiguration of the higher education landscape (see chapters 2 to 4 in this volume).

The Education White Paper 3 of 1997 (hereinafter the White Paper) marked the second step. This document was explicit on what needed to be done and stated that the transformation of higher education had to 'reflect the changes that are taking place in our society' (DoE, 1997: 2); in other words, higher education institutions could not be left behind while the country was pushing its transformation agenda. Furthermore, the White Paper (1997: 2) noted that '[t]he higher education system must be transformed to redress past inequalities, to serve a new social order, to meet pressing national needs and to respond to new realities and opportunities.' For transformation to happen, it had to be guided by a clearly defined framework. The White Paper stated that the higher education system had to be planned, governed and funded as a single national co-ordinated system. This was to enable those saddled with the responsibility of overseeing the envisaged transformation process to overcome the triple challenges of fragmentation, inequality and inefficiency.

It should be noted that the transformation of the higher education system did not happen in a vacuum – it was 'part of the broader process of South Africa's political, social and economic transition, which includes political democratisation, economic reconstruction and development, and redistributive social policies aimed at equity' (DoE, 1997: 29). Transformation in this sphere was a *necessity*, not an *option*, and those involved in this sector were obligated to initiate and implement changes. The wheels of transformation were grinding in the country.

The transformation of higher education took different forms, including the formation of one national higher education system, structural changes, efficiency, mergers of academic institutions and institutional compliance in terms of redressing inequality (such as accessibility, equality of race and gender, demographics of staff and students) (Du Preez, Simmonds and Verhoef, 2016: 3). Over the years, scholars have analysed each or some of these areas, for example, Soudien (2010: 882) examined 'structural transformation'. Others have analysed transformation and its implications for staff; transformation as a problematic concept; transformation and reflexivity in university teaching, research and community service; performativity in higher education transformation; to name just a few (Fourie, 1999; Bitzer and Bezuidenhout, 2001; Waghid, 2001; Van Wyk, 2005). For these reasons, transformation of higher education in South Africa should be seen as a process, not an event.

The merger of South African universities

The merger of South African universities was part of the transformation process. The idea had already been proposed in 1997 (Higher Education Act No. 101 of 1997). The institutional restructuring that occurred after 2001 'provided the opportunity to reconfigure the higher education system so that it was more suited to the needs of a developing democracy' (Moloi, Mkhwanazi and Bojabotseha, 2014: 472). But it was not until 2003/04 that this policy decision was implemented. Under the stewardship of the then Minister Kader Asmal, the number of universities was reduced from 36 to 21 but later increased slightly to 23 and then to 26. These institutions were divided into full universities and universities of technology (see Motala, Chapter 5, in this volume). The latter were tasked specifically to produce technicians and engineers.

The connections between politics and education became evident during the process of the mergers – there is a compelling view that these mergers 'were politically motivated' (Mouton, Louw and Strydom, 2013: 285–86). The process of merging institutions of higher education encountered resistance to change and low levels of trust (Eloff, 2009). This was because these universities served different racial and ethnic groups. As the political factor was brought into the equation, it further compounded the already complex merger process. In the Western Cape, it was not easy to merge the University of Cape Town (UCT), the University of the Western Cape (UWC) and Stellenbosch University (SU) because of the political history of each of these institutions. For example, UCT predominantly accommodated English-speaking whites, UWC was originally meant for the coloured population, while SU mainly served Afrikaans-speaking whites. Consequently, only the Cape Peninsula University of Technology (CPUT) emerged from this process, when the former Cape Technikon and the Peninsula Technikon merged into one institution on 1 January 2005 (see chapters 7 to 9 in this volume). The other three universities retained their identities.

General Bantu Holomisa tried to defend the former University of Transkei (UNITRA) but his efforts were fruitless and UNITRA eventually formed part of the Walter Sisulu University (WSU). Similar debates ensued in other parts of the country, either in support of or challenging these mergers. Eventually, the merger process was carried out as part of the transformation agenda. Among the new universities that emerged were the University of KwaZulu-Natal (UKZN), the University of Johannesburg (UJ) and the University of Limpopo (UL). The universities of technology were the Cape Peninsula University of Technology (CPUT), the Tshwane University of Technology (TUT), the Vaal University of Technology (VUT), the Durban University of Technology (DUT) and the Mangosuthu University of Technology (MUT). Each of these institutions was dominated by a black student population, although other racial groups were not prevented from enrolling. This state of affairs continued for many years. For example, in 2015 the student population at DUT was 27 023. In 2016 this figure increased slightly to 28 334. A racial breakdown of these students in 2016 revealed that black students accounted for 81 per cent of the entire student population. The other racial groups were Indian (15 per cent), white (3 per cent) and coloured (1 per cent) (DUT Annual Report, 2016: 40).

Therefore, it is clear that transformation worked somewhat but did not reach the expected level. In a way, this is not surprising. Enrolment figures in public higher education between 2004 and 2007 revealed that black students constituted the largest number. In 2004, black students numbered 453 640, coloureds were 46 090; Indians were 54 315; while whites were 188 687. In 2005, black students numbered 446 946; coloureds stood at 46 302; Indians numbered 54 611; and there were 185 847 white students. In the following year (2006), there were 451 106 black students and 48 588 coloured students; Indians numbered 54 859 while the number of white students stood at 184 667. In 2007 the picture remained unchanged with black students still leading the pack at 476 768; coloureds at 49 069; Indians at 52 596; and whites at 180 463 (CHE, 2009: 19).

While the merger of South African higher education institutions was part of the transformation process, it soon became clear that they would not be able to accommodate the increasing number of students. Calls for broadening university access were made. In response to this call, government gradually increased the number of universities from 21 to 26. The University of Mpumalanga (UM), which was promulgated in 2013 and accepted its first students in 2014, and the Sol Plaatje University (SPU), which also opened in 2014, became new additions. Government also established technical and vocational education and training (TVET) colleges using the Further Education and Training Colleges Act (No. 16 of 2006). The aim was to channel students towards these institutions to increase the number of technicians that would contribute to the country's economic development. Giant strides have been taken in this regard by increasing the skills base. However, there is still the challenge of getting the youth to see TVET colleges as an attractive alternative to universities.

Transformation with a focus on racism

A focus on racism is important. It is relevant to the challenges of transforming South Africa's HBUs, which are by their very nature a racial creation. In 2008, the Minister of Higher Education and Training appointed the Ministerial Committee on Transformation and Social Cohesion and the Elimination of Discrimination in Public Higher Education Institutions (MCTHE) to address racism. The need for this initiative was occasioned by a racist incident at the University of Free State (UFS) in 2007, which was commonly known as the 'Reitz saga' in subsequent media reports.

Suransky and Van der Merwe (2014: 1) aptly recall: 'The incident shook the university's institutional culture to the core and became a catalyst for change for universities across the country.' These authors noted that the Ministry of Education had already identified systemic problems within the institutional cultures of universities as one of the key obstacles to change. In their view, the honeymoon was over. They fittingly captured this view thus: 'Twenty years after Nelson Mandela became President of South Africa, it is evident that the euphoria of liberation from apartheid has made way for a more sober realization that deeply entrenched inequalities and injustices are still at the core of the country's social fabric' (Suransky and Van der Merwe, 2014: 2). Implicit in this statement was that the country had to deal with transformation and address the remaining vestiges of apartheid, which caused friction and animosity in society.

Subsequent to completing its work, the MCTHE produced the *Report of the MCTHE* (2008). What was remarkable about this report was that it deviated slightly from the 1997 White Paper. Although both documents put particular emphasis on transformation, the latter was broader and proposed that transformation had to address *all* aspects of university life and not focus only on institutional compliance. Specifically, the report stated that 'the transformation agenda includes the necessity to examine the underlying assumptions and practices that underpin the academic and intellectual projects pertaining to learning, teaching, and research' (DoE, 2008: 11).

Francis and Hemson (2010: 876) averred that one implication is that 'we need research that explores discrimination with a view to interrogating the whole system of higher education'. In the same vein, Du Preez, Simmonds and Verhoef (2016: 3) concluded that 'The MCTHE report (2008) marks a shift from research on structural transformation to a broader ideological discourse of transformation'. There is an acknowledgement of the fact that such an ideological discourse addresses people's beliefs and assumptions about transformation of higher education (Soudien, 2010). Therefore, the *Report of the MCTHE* was a step forward in advancing the transformation of South African universities.

The discourse referred to earlier explores discrimination and racism generally. In terms of the transformation of higher education, it includes epistemological change; discrimination and exclusions in terms of religion, ethnicity, sexual orientation, class and language; the Africanisation or decolonisation of the curricula; beliefs, attitudes, values and commitments of the whole system; power; diversity; and intellectual justice (Du Preez, Simmonds and Verhoef, 2016: 3).

In a nutshell, race has remained one of the key variables in any analysis of South Africa's post-apartheid higher education (see Malabela, Chapter 7, and Ndelu, Chapter 9, in this volume). Therefore, no discussion on the transformation of universities after 1994 would be complete without touching on race. After all, the HBUs and HWUs were created as a result of race (and ethnicity) – both of which are social constructs (Montagu, 1964). The deracialisation of South African academic institutions has unwittingly had a class component embedded in it. This fact has played itself out differently across the HWUs. It is against this backdrop that Leibowitz and Bozalek (2014: 96) observed that the skewed participation of students and academic staff, according to race, 'is accompanied by skewed output, also according to race.' These authors were reiterating the importance of race in the analysis, but race is not the only variable through which we can measure transformation, as the next section will show.

Challenges experienced in transforming HBUs

It is important to state two points at the outset. Firstly, the transformation of HBUs cannot be understood outside of the broader context presented earlier. Secondly, transformation was never going to be an easy process by any reckoning. Part of the problem was that the HBUs were under-resourced compared to HWUs and most were located in rural or peri-urban areas, so attracting white staff and white students was bound to be a mammoth task – almost an insurmountable challenge. This meant that the staff and student profiles would remain almost the same as under apartheid. These points are expounded later.

Transformation of the infrastructure

It is common knowledge that under apartheid black universities had very poor infrastructure. As part of the transformation agenda, the new government had to address this issue as a matter of urgency. The challenge was that if the political leadership were to inject money into these institutions, the HWUs would see it as discrimination. This meant that government had to strike a balance between up-scaling HBUs while also giving something to HWUs. On the one hand, political leaders had to acknowledge that HBUs needed more money to upgrade their poor infrastructure or put up entirely new buildings to bring them closer to HWUs. On the other hand, they had to ensure that they did not ignore HWUs entirely. With fewer resources at its disposal, the new government faced serious challenges. Under Minister Blade Nzimande, the Department of Higher Education and Training (DHET) tried its level best to support HBUs financially. Institutions like UWC, WSU, the University of Zululand (UNIZUL) and the University of Venda (UNIVEN) were some of the beneficiaries. But there was no way that the decades-old apartheid legacy could be addressed overnight. So, despite these interventions, the infrastructure of HBUs is nowhere like that of HWUs.

Transformation of student and staff profiles

Implicit in the acronym 'HBUs' is the embedded assumption (which is actually a reality) that these institutions reflected a black outlook, especially in terms of the student profile. They either had very few or no students at all from the other racial groups. Initially, white students could not enrol at these institutions due to prohibiting legislation. When this legislation was removed, the lack of resources did not make HBUs attractive to white students who were used to having all the resources they needed. This explains why, even after 25 years of democracy, the old status quo still remains. For example, institutions like the University of Zululand in KwaZulu-Natal and the University of Venda in Limpopo province still have a predominantly black student population. Where other races exist, they constitute an insignificant minority. While it cannot be denied that some of these institutions are engulfed by corrupt practices and mismanagement, it is equally true that their infrastructure cannot be equated to that of the HWUs. It was easier for black students to migrate to the HWUs due to the assumed status associated with the latter, which have better financial and material resources and better infrastructure. Inadequate resources have hindered transformation in HBUs. Proper management would enhance the HBUs' attractiveness to staff and students and possibly sponsors.

A university such as UWC, which was meant for the coloured population, attracted more black students than white students. One reason was that during the liberation struggle UWC was dubbed 'The intellectual home of the left' due to its sympathy towards the liberation cause. Many former liberation fighters returning to South Africa found a home at UWC. Some such as Kader Asmal and Jakes Gerwel later occupied senior positions in the new government. This political identity of UWC saw the university attracting more black students than white students. In the process, transformation in terms of the students' profile has not materialised. There are white students, even some international students, but these constitute an insignificant number. This has frustrated transformation efforts.

Regarding staff, the HBUs had some white staff members, albeit few. After 1994, this picture changed somewhat as more educated black lecturers joined these institutions, including those coming back from exile. At the same time, some white lecturers either resigned or moved to HWUs for different reasons. Consequently, when looking at the staff profile at the HBUs, there are very few white staff members across the board. This means that the transformation agenda in this regard has not been successful. Among other reasons is the fact that most of these HBUs are located in rural areas and thus fail to be as attractive as the urban-based HWUs.

Transformation of the curricula

On the transformation of the curricula, the picture envisaged by the White Paper in 1997 has not materialised. This is not surprising. Changing university curricula is a mammoth task. It is like moving the whole cemetery as opposed to just moving a single grave to another location – something that could be done with relative ease (Johnson, 1966; Mngomezulu, 2012). There were several reasons for this challenge. Firstly, in instances where white lecturers remained at the HBUs, they continued to teach a Westernised curriculum with which they were comfortable. Even where black lecturers joined these universities, they were either reluctant to transform the curriculum or lacked the power and confidence to do so by virtue of the fact that they occupied low-ranking positions and could not make curriculum decisions. Others had not been exposed to an Africanised curriculum themselves and, therefore, had no source of reference. The #FeesMustFall movement in 2015 and 2016 demanded the decolonisation and Africanisation of the university curriculum. This shows that transformation in this area has not happened. What is encouraging is that there are academics who have started decolonising the university curriculum. To assist those who lack the necessary knowledge to do so, some Africanist scholars, such as Mngomezulu and Hadebe (2018), are already publishing in this area. Among other things, they make proposals on how political science as an academic discipline could be Africanised. This includes using current African political issues to explain political concepts and political phenomena such as governance, lootocracy and civilisation.

Transformation of research and postgraduate supervision

Any university that is worth the name must conduct research and publish. This is how universities generate new knowledge. The transformation agenda meant that the HBUs had to revisit their research focus and methods in line with the changed and changing political environment, but this has not been easy. Firstly, given that the HBUs do not enjoy the luxury of having huge endowment funds like the HWUs, their research agenda is often dictated to them by their funders or sponsors. This issue has been discussed at length in the broader African context (Mngomezulu, 2014).

Academics at the HBUs are still at a disadvantage when it comes to publishing. There are many gatekeepers – most of whom are fixated on the old practices. This means that even if Africanist researchers want to transform research, their publications are not likely to see the light of day unless journal editors and publishers buy into the idea. The sad reality is that the HBUs find themselves having to subscribe to Western practices in order to comply and be accepted. For example, they choose topics that are alien to the African context and use Western-oriented methodologies and theories to conduct research and to teach.

This is also linked to postgraduate supervision. Postgraduate research projects at the HBUs are expected to 'meet the standards', which actually means that they must adopt the Western approach at the expense of an African focus. Consequently, very few postgraduate dissertations and theses employ African epistemologies. A student who wants to use *Ubuntu* as a theoretical approach is likely to be discouraged from doing so on the grounds that 'no thesis or dissertation has used this approach'. This author piloted this change of focus and successfully supervised a master's student who obtained her degree *cum laude*.[3] However, except for these isolated cases, transformation in student

---

3   Selela, GC (2015) Ubuntu and indigenous knowledge in relation to the elderly at KwaSani

supervision is still a serious concern. Similarly, the teaching of a transformed curriculum has not yet gained ground.

Towards finding solutions

It is true that South Africa's experience is slightly different from that of the rest of the African continent; however, there are lessons to be learnt from these when addressing some of the challenges enumerated earlier. For example, in East Africa the political and academic leadership faced similar challenges but they put their heads together to deal with these. They read and published African literature, taught students using local examples and encouraged them to appreciate African oral history (Mngomezulu, 2004; 2012).

Regarding the curriculum, research agenda and postgraduate supervision, the HBUs could use local examples to explicate concepts across academic disciplines. Books written by Africanist scholars could be prescribed for teaching. More postgraduate students could be encouraged to choose topics that speak to African issues than is currently the case. This was an implicit message during the #FeesMustFall movement. In cases where topics covering other parts of the world are chosen, locally grounded research methodologies and research frameworks could be used. Course modules could be revised. 'Africa in international perspective' is one of the relevant modules in this regard. It presents Africa as part of the global community instead of being its appendage and coming into the picture only as the supplier of raw materials to the industrialised world. Introducing oral histories into the curriculum would also go a long way towards addressing curriculum issues.

In terms of the infrastructure, the HBUs could use their alumni and local businesses to raise funds to renovate old buildings and build new ones. The same strategy could be used to raise funds to subscribe to journals and buy library books and laboratory materials. University councils, chancellors and vice-chancellors could approach other countries for donations, not loans, since the latter come with conditions. The former Vice-Chancellor of the University of Venda, Professor Peter Mbati, did exceptionally well in this regard. Following his appointment on 1 February 2008, he solicited funds from many countries and the business community nationally and internationally, so that his institution could supplement the government subsidy. He received accolades for this when his term of office ended (*Nendila*, Newsletter of the University of Venda, November–December 2017).

The transformation of the student and staff profile at the HBUs may appear

---

Municipality, KwaZulu-Natal. Master's of Social Science in Political Science, University of KwaZulu-Natal.

difficult to achieve at face value, but here, too, they could do something. For example, if they were to increase their research outputs, they would be able to generate more money, which would enhance their research productivity. With more research outputs, they would be able to improve their ratings and address their infrastructure needs. These developments would contribute to attracting the best academics and students from other racial groups. International students would also be attracted to these institutions. Another strategy, which is already underway in many of these universities, is to establish more collaboration with other reputable universities nationally, continentally and internationally. This would have a propensity to change the image of the HBUs and make them competitive and attractive. Therefore, the HBUs should establish more strategic relations with other universities across Africa and further afield.

In a nutshell, none of these challenges is impossible to address. Certainly, some challenges are more demanding than others and might take longer to resolve, but this does not mean that they are insurmountable. All that is needed is the political will to transform. Once the will is there, concerted efforts can be made to change dreams into reality. Lastly, South Africa's HBUs cannot go it alone. They must learn from the experiences of other African countries. As already mentioned, the East Africans have a lot to offer in this regard from their experience with the now defunct Federal University of East Africa. There are other examples elsewhere across Africa.

Conclusion

This chapter has discussed several issues under the banner of transformation. It has focused on the HBUs but, as demonstrated earlier, transformation cannot be discussed in isolation. The context is necessary to have a better understanding of the impediments to the transformation of the HBUs in South Africa. What is clear is that the situation we are confronted with is rooted in history. Secondly, since 1994, the South African government has been hard at work trying to reverse the wrongs of the past. The road has been long, winding and sometimes bumpy and slippery. Despite all the challenges, giant strides have been made to date. While the focus has been on the HBUs, the HWUs also have their challenges. Therefore, the country needs joint efforts by different stakeholders in order to address the challenges associated with the transformation of the higher education sector as a whole. South Africa is a unitary state guided by its Constitution, which deems race and ethnicity obsolete. So, any challenge facing the country should be tackled in its entirety as a national problem. This is one of the reminders of the ills of apartheid.

References

Adeyemi, JK (2000) Academic manpower needs of Nigerian universities, *Higher Education Review*, **32**(2): 36–44.

Anderson, D and Anderson, LA (2010) *What is Transformation, and Why is it Hard to Manage?* Durango: Being First.

Asmal, K (2002) Foreword, in *Transformation and Restructuring: A new institutional landscape for higher education* (June). Pretoria: Ministry of Education.

Badat, S (2010) *The challenges of transformation in higher education and training institutions in South Africa*. Johannesburg: Development Bank of Southern Africa.

Bazana, S and Mogotsi, OP (2017) Social identities and racial integration in historically white universities: A literature review of the experiences of black students, *Transformation in Higher Education*, **2**(0): 1–13.

Bitzer, EM and Bezuidenhout, SM (2001) 'Transformation' as a problematic concept in the realm of higher education in South Africa, *Journal for Humanities*, **41**(1): 33–40.

Council on Higher Education (CHE) (1995) *Review of Higher Education in South Africa: Selected themes*. Pretoria: CHE.

Council on Higher Education (CHE) (2009) *Higher Education Monitor No 8 (October). Enrolments (Headcount) in public higher education by race, 2004–2007*. Pretoria: CHE.

Crompton, R (1993) *Class and Stratification: An introduction to current debates*. Cambridge: Polity Press.

Dodge, R, Daly, AP, Huyton, J and Sanders, LD (2012) The challenge of defining wellbeing, *International Journal of Wellbeing*, **2**(3): 222–35.

Du Preez, P, Simmonds, S and Verhoef, AH (2016) Rethinking and researching transformation in higher education: A meta-study of South African trends, *Transformation in Higher Education*, **1**(1): 1–7.

Durban University of Technology Annual Report, 2016.

Eloff, T (2009) *Vice-Chancellor's Newsletter*. March.

Fourie, M (1999) Institutional transformation at South African universities: Implications for academic staff, *Higher Education*, **38**: 275–90.

Francis, D and Hemson, C (2010) Initiating debate: South African Journal of Higher Education issue on transformation, *South African Journal of Higher Education*, **24**(6): 875–80.

Goldschmidt, MM (2003) Identifying labels among university students in the new South Africa: A retrospective study, *Journal of Black Studies*, **34**(2): 204–21.

Hirson, B (1992) Colonialism of a special type and the permanent revolution, *Searchlight South Africa*, **2**(4) (January): 48–55.

Johnson, GM (1966) The University of Nigeria, in MG Ross, *New Universities in the Modern World*. New York: St Martin's Press.

Khondker, H and Schuerkens, U (2014) Social transformation, development and globalisation, *Sociopedia.isa*, DOI: 10.1177/205684601423

Leibowitz, B and Bozalek, V (2014) Access to higher education in South Africa: A social realist account, *Widening Participation and Lifelong Learning*, **16**(1): 91–109.

Malabou, C (2008). *What Should We Do with Our Brain?* New York: Fordham University Press.

Malabou, C (2012) *The Ontology of the Accident: An essay on destructive plasticity*. Cambridge: Polity Press.

Mamdani, M (1996) *Citizen and Subject: Contemporary Africa and the legacy of late colonialism*. Princeton, NJ: Princeton University Press.

Mngomezulu, BR (2004) A political history of higher education in East Africa: The rise and fall of the University of East Africa. PhD dissertation, Rice University, Texas.

Mngomezulu, BR (2010) *Flying to the Heights: A social and political history of Juba Primary School*. Saarbrücken, Germany: LAP Lambert Academic Publishing.

Mngomezulu, BR (2012) *Politics and Higher Education in East Africa: From the 1920s to 1970*. Bloemfontein: Sun Press.

Mngomezulu, BR (2014) The impact of government policies on the sustainability of social sciences: Lessons from Africa. Paper presented at the ACSUS 2014 Conference, KKR Hiroshima Hotel, Japan, 1–3 December 2014.

Mngomezulu, BR and Hadebe, S (2018) What would the decolonization of a Political Science curriculum entail? Lessons to be learnt from the East African experience at the Federal University of East Africa, *Politikon*, **45**(1): 66–80.

Mnguni, MM (2000) The role of black consciousness in the experience of being black in South Africa: The shaping of the identity of two members of AZAPO. Master's thesis, Rhodes University, Grahamstown.

Moloi, KC, Mkhwanazi, TS and Bojabotseha, TP (2014) Higher education in South Africa at the crossroads, *Mediterranean Journal of Social Sciences*, **5**(2): 469–77.

Montagu, A. 1964. *Man's most dangerous myth: The fallacy of race*. Cleveland, OH: World Publishing Company.

Mouton, N, Louw, GP and Strydom, GL (2013) Present-day dilemmas and challenges of the South African tertiary system, *International Business & Economics Research Journal*, **12**(3): 285–300.

Mukhwana, E and Kande, A (2017) Transforming university education in Africa: Lessons from Kenya, *Journal of Rural Development*, **2**(3): 341–52.

Nendila: Newsletter of the University of Venda, November–December 2017.

Nzimande, B (2012) Minister's Preface, *Green Paper for Post-school Education and Training*. Republic of South Africa: Department of Higher Education and Training.

Republic of South Africa (1996) *The Constitution of the Republic of South Africa (Act 108 of 1996)*.

Republic of South Africa, Department of Education (DoE) (1997) Education White Paper 3: *A Programme for the Transformation of Higher Education*. Pretoria: Government Printer.

Republic of South Africa, Department of Education (DoE) (1997) Higher Education Act (No 101 of 1997). Pretoria: Department of Education.

Republic of South Africa, Department of Education (DoE) (2006) Further Education and Training Colleges Act (No 16 of 2006). Pretoria: Department of Education.

Republic of South Africa, Department of Education (DoE) (2008) *Report of the MCTHE*. Pretoria: Department of Education.

Seekings, J (2003) *Social Stratification and Inequality in South Africa at the End of Apartheid*. Working Paper, No 31, Centre for Social Science Research, University of Cape Town.

Selela, GC (2015) Ubuntu and indigenous knowledge in relation to the elderly at KwaSani Municipality, KwaZulu-Natal. Master's of Social Science thesis in Political Science, University of KwaZulu-Natal.

Soudien, C (2010) Grasping the nettle? South African higher education and its transformative imperatives, *South African Journal of Higher Education*, **24**(5): 881–96.

Suransky, C and Van der Merwe JC (2014) Transcending apartheid in higher education: Transforming an institutional culture, *Race Ethnicity and Education*. Available at: http://dx.doi.org/10.1080/13613324.2014.946487 (accessed March 2019).

Union of South Africa (1959) Extension of University Education Act (No 45 of 1959). Pretoria: Government Printer.

Van Wyk, B (2005) Performativity in higher education transformation in South Africa, *South African Journal of Higher Education*, **19**(1): 5–19.

Venter, R (2015) Transformation, theology and the public university in South Africa, *Acta Theologica*, **35**(2): 173–203.

Venter, R and Tolmie, F (2012) *Transforming Theological Knowledge: Essay on theology and the university after apartheid*. Bloemfontein: Sun Press.

Waghid, Y (2001) Knowledge production and higher education transformation in South Africa: Towards reflexivity in university teaching, research and community service, *Higher Education*, **43**: 457–58.

Webster, E, Pampallis, K, Mawbey, J, Cronin, J, Mashilo, AM and Van Niekerk, R (2017) *Unresolved National Question in South Africa: The left thought under apartheid and beyond.* Johannesburg: Wits University Press.

Section III: Lessons from South Africa's Student Movement

Chapter 7
South Africa's student movement: A Wits perspective[1]

Musawenkosi Hemelton Malabela

Introduction

Student protests against fee increments have been happening sporadically over the years, especially at historically black universities (Badat, 2016).[2] However, 2015 witnessed a wave of renewed student protests under the banner of #FeesMustFall. At the centre of these protests were the historically white universities such as the universities of the Witwatersrand (Wits) and Cape Town (UCT) (see Ndelu, Chapter 9, in this volume). This chapter traces what led to the formation of the #FeesMustFall movement at Wits by providing a timeline of key events from 2015 to 2016, including the call for transformation within the university; the struggle for free, quality, decolonised education; and how the university management responded to these issues. Individual and group interviews were conducted with protesting and non-protesting students, as well as with academic staff, in the quest to understand the meanings behind the events that took place at Wits. These interviews were supplemented with media reports and university correspondence.[3]

#FeesMustFall 2015: Background to the struggle at Wits

The fees issue has been an ongoing struggle in universities, with students protesting yearly against rising fees. The #FeesMustFall movement symbolises the culmination of a long dissatisfaction with exorbitant university fees and insufficient state funding of higher education. Cloete notes that:

---

1 This is drawn from a longer research paper which I wrote for the Centre for the Study of Violence and Reconciliation's (CSVR): #Hashtag: An analysis of the #FeesMustFall movement in South Africa: Research report. This is the shorter version and updated since the events of the #FeesMustFall in 2015–2016.

2 The emergence of a democratic government in 1994 threw student organisations into considerable disarray. For example, the focus of student organisations in historically black institutions shifted from protest action against an illegitimate government to demands for unrestricted access to higher education, expanded financial aid to needy students and relief from personal debt to higher education institutions (Jansen, 2004).

3 As a student registered at Wits University, I also got e-mails from management to detail what was happening on campus. The e-mails served as the 'university's side of the story'.

One way of measuring the state's contribution is to consider the percentage of the Gross Domestic Product (GDP) that is allocated to higher education. The percentage increased between 2004/2005 and 2015/2016, from 0.68 per cent to 0.72 per cent, and from some R9.8 billion to R30.3 billion. However, this level of funding is low in comparison with a number of other countries: in 2012, Brazil allocated 0.95 per cent of GDP to higher education, Senegal and Ghana 1.4 per cent, Norway and Finland over 2 per cent and Cuba 4.5 per cent. If the state was to spend 1 per cent of GDP on higher education, this would amount to R41 billion – an additional R11 billion (Cloete cited in Badat, 2016: 3).

The Vice-Chancellor of Wits, Adam Habib, details this decline in subsidies in the following manner:

Famously, the portion of funding universities receive from government has declined from 49 per cent to 40 per cent over the course of the past decade, while student fees have risen from 24 per cent to 31 per cent in order to cover the shortfall. Meanwhile, tertiary education inflation is about 4 per cent higher than the regular rate of inflation, sitting now at around 6 per cent per annum (in Poplak, 2016).

Therefore, universities are left with no option but to increase fees, disadvantaging deserving students from poor backgrounds. In February 2015, the Wits Student Representative Council (SRC) launched the '1 month 1 million' campaign to raise funds for students who could not afford fees. Booysen and Bandama (2016) note that the campaign helped to raise public awareness of the problems with the funding model of higher education. Shaeera Kalla, then SRC president, felt that the campaign foregrounded the funding crisis by noting that 'The 1 Million 1 Month campaign ... once again highlighted the inadequate funding of higher education that has become normalised in South Africa... This normalisation is only a further perpetuation of the race-based inequality in South Africa inherent in our universities' (SAHO, 2016).

Despite the campaign successfully raising more than R5 million, it was not enough to cover the outstanding student fees at Wits. However, it was noted by the SRC president that this was not just a campaign but also a form of peaceful protest against the status quo. Shaeera Kalla and her colleagues argued that there was a need for 'systematic and structural change' to address funding and transformation of race-based inequalities in South Africa. Clearly, the campaign's aims were multifaceted: to raise funds for poor students; to highlight that fees were unaffordable; and to alert stakeholders to the looming crisis in higher education. Why, then, did their call for free education not capture the public imagination? Is it because the campaign was peaceful? Nothing much was said about this campaign until the violence associated with the #FeesMustFall movement, which emerged a year later. One student leader said the '1 month 1 million' campaign highlighted that students have always wanted to be part of the solution, in contrast to the manner in which the media projects them as violent and destructive. The invisibility of the initiative by students forms part of a larger economic and political problem in South African institutes of higher learning. For example, the former black universities had always experienced student protests, not only around fees, but also around poor infrastructure (insufficient computers or laboratories) and accommodation (see Malabela, 2017).

The '1 month 1 million' campaign was followed by #RhodesMustFall, which started at UCT and was centred on the notion of decolonising the university. It gained momentum and spread to other universities. At Wits it was organised by postgraduate political science students under the banner of #TransformWits. On 26 March 2015, #TransformWits met to discuss five main issues (Pilane, 2015):

1. the need for more black academic staff to be recruited within the university;
2. a more Afrocentric curriculum;
3. Adam Habib's 'cosmopolitan university' vision;
4. the university's support for poor students; and
5. broader transformation in South Africa.

The main aim of #TransformWits was to discuss transformation at Wits and 'the meeting ended with a mini march to the stairs of Great Hall, where students demonstrated solidarity with the other transformation protests and campaigns currently taking place at the UCT, Rhodes and UKZN [University of KwaZulu-Natal]' (Pilane, 2015). Worth noting is that there had already been talks between universities, especially around the issue of decolonisation, as black students rejected the alienating institutional cultures of the previously white universities. As Jansen (2004: 301) notes, 'The problem for urban institutions [predominantly white universities] ... will be the complex task of transforming institutional cultures in ways that are more inclusive and accommodating of the statistical diversity of the student populations.'

In April 2015, the #TransformWits movement launched its manifesto and resolved to deal with the following six issues:

1. Africanisation of university symbolism and institutional memory;

2. radical revision and Africanisation of all university curricula;
3. fast-track Africanisation of academic staff contingency;
4. an end to worker discrimination and outsourcing;
5. an end to financial exclusion of students;
6. revision of the departmental academic structures that impede the output of black students (Zidepa, 2015).

The transformation issues included decolonising the curriculum, support for black academics, and ending worker discrimination and financial exclusion of students. These activists defined decolonisation of the university as 'The rejection of white supremacy and hetero-patriarchal order along with other forms of prejudice that characterise the colonial project, as well as the quest to redress the socio-economic, political, and spiritual depredations of colonial history' (Chinguno et al, 2017: 18).

The #FeesMustFall at Wits was not only about the transformation of the academic programme but also about broader transformation of the university and forged an alliance with workers, especially outsourced workers. 'It presented a demand for the decolonisation and de-commodification of education and articulated this to the abolition of outsourcing of university support staff' (Chinguno et al, 2017: 24).

Satgar (2016) gives a detailed explanation of workers' and students' collaboration and critically explains how new struggles are re-emerging post-1994 in which students as the future middle class are involved in a liberatory and complicated class relationship with outsourced workers. These new protests have also recentred Black Consciousness and Africanist politics in the emancipation struggle of black people from the shackles of poverty. Vuyani Pambo, who later became a prominent leader in the #FeesMustFall movement, was quoted as saying, 'Wits had been brutal to the black students, workers and lecturers' (Booysen and Bandama, 2016: 319). His main argument was that Wits alienates black people within the university, including students, outsourced workers and even lecturers. Indeed, many students in most universities referred to the cleaners as their 'parents'. This was to embody a different kind of politics; its language depicted all those who were black or coming from historically disadvantaged backgrounds as being treated like foreigners in universities that seemed to glorify a history of conquest. Therefore, #FeesMustFall falls into a larger political contestation of the transition in South Africa, where many black people have been contesting what it means to be a citizen in South Africa. At universities, as highlighted by Poplak (2016), many black students found statues that glorified white murderers.

Current student leaders have used various forums to raise pertinent issues which staff and worker unions had failed to deal with until October 2015 when #FeesMustFall started.

> This is one of the key narratives that is missing when the protests are being spoken about that it was nothing but violence and destruction of university property. We were raising structural issues of oppression and marginalisation of poor black people at Wits (Interview, student leader, 2016, Johannesburg).

These events led to a growing class and race consciousness among students as they challenged the Wits University management on transformation, outsourcing and financial exclusion. However, those interviewed for this study felt strongly that Wits management did not appreciate their grievances as they decided to increase fees in 2015, which triggered the formation of the Wits #FeesMustFall movement. In the next section, Shaeera Kalla, the SRC president at that time, discusses the university's decision to increase fees despite students' reservations about that decision.

Wits #FeesMustFall is born

South African History Online (SAHO, 2015) narrates that Shaeera attended a Wits Council meeting on 8 October 2015 accompanied by Nompendulo Mkhatshwa (then incoming president). The issue of fee increases was discussed and the chairperson asked council members to vote for or against a fees increment. Apart from one academic, Professor David Dickinson, the SRC president and the only other student representative present, everyone else voted for an increase. Mkhatshwa reflected on this council meeting in an interview with *Destiny* magazine (December 2015: 22):

> When I arrived, I realised just how much voices of students were completely undermined by the lily-white council. We were just as good as pictures on the walls of that boardroom. Students' discussions are generally held in 20 minutes and taken to a vote very quickly.

Most student leaders interviewed shared the perception of being undermined by university council meetings. They felt that students' agenda items were quickly dispensed with by outvoting students' representatives since they were a minority in council. Student leaders felt disempowered in what they regard as their pseudo-participation. Hence, in their decolonisation agenda, students were also calling for equal representation in both council and senate. This feeling of disempowerment led students to use protest as a form of engagement and as the only bargaining tool that they have. Shaeera felt that the only option they had was to protest. 'This [was] a turning point towards protest being the only viable option left to deal with unfair exclusionary fee increases' (SAHO, 2015).

It is important to note that the 2015 protest was initiated by the SRC. The SRC led the protest under its banner and took full responsibility for it. This chapter later discusses the political power struggles that rocked #FeesMustFall at Wits, including the fall of Mkhatshwa, largely due to her interview with *Destiny* magazine and her strong association with the African National Congress (ANC).[4]

Peaceful disruption of university activities

Following the university's decision to increase fees, the SRC immediately released a communiqué expressing their unhappiness about the fee increment for 2016. A decision to shut down the university was taken by a group of students with the support of the SRC. The university entrances were blocked and Senate House was occupied and renamed Solomon Mahlangu House.[5] Council has subsequently adopted and renamed Senate House as Solomon Mahlangu House, a point the chapter returns to later when looking at the decolonisation of university spaces. The occupation of Senate House, the administrative building of Wits, was symbolic, and students demanded that management come down and address them. They demanded that the university reverse the decision to increase fees. These protests were peaceful but disruptive of university academic activities. However, the #FeesMustFall movement did employ violent tactics to achieve its goal. Also, the protest tended to alienate non-protesting students and lost the movement public sympathy. Nevertheless, Duncan (2016) contends that people often conflate protests with violence, especially the media. The peaceful disruption of university academic activities was a symbolic expression by Wits students:

> They just occupied the strategic entrances and made sure that no one comes in and there is no one going out... They then stopped everything to a standstill and it started as a symbol of saying 'we want you to feel what it means if you can't get into the university', what it means for

---

4   After her appearance on the cover of *Destiny* magazine, Mkhatshwa was rejected by #FeesMustFall at Wits and fell from glory. She was accused of wanting to steal the movement and use it for her own political ambitions; of being a populist seeking media attention; of being a sell-out; of dividing the movement and wanting to crush it; and of taking orders from Luthuli House (ANC) to kill the movement.

5   The decision to rename Senate House, as Solomon Mahlangu House, was linked to a song that students were singing about the struggle icon, who was hanged by the apartheid regime.

some of us who are excluded because we don't have funding (Interview, protesting student, 2016, Johannesburg).

The university responded to the shutdown by approaching the court to seek an interdict, which allowed the police to be at the service of the university management in that they could be called in at any time to restore order. Most interviewees argued that the university's response of calling the police onto campus was the genesis of the violence, as police used excessive force and provoked the students into retaliating violently.

The Vice-Chancellor of Wits, Habib, argued that the violence was not caused by the presence of the police and private security; rather, they were brought in as a response to the violence of the protesting students. 'They [police] were brought in as a result of the arson or disruptions of the academic programme' (Habib, 2016b).

However, the use of private security on campus was problematic because many personnel did not have any form of identification and there were allegations of sexual harassment perpetrated by private security officials. Thereafter the university insisted that each security official wear a name tag. On the whole, the students during this period continued to protest peacefully without destroying any university property. They would meet at Solomon Mahlangu House to discuss their plans for the peaceful disruption of university academic activities. On 16 October 2015, Habib left the Higher Education Summit in Durban to address the protesting students. The students insisted that he should call a council meeting with immediate effect to address students' demands. Habib describes what transpired:

> This faction, essentially taking instructions from an outside political party which called for the complete shutdown of universities, was not in a position to accede to a resolution. In fact, given that it was a very small minority (it had not won a single seat in a recent student leadership election), it served its strategic interest to effectively play a politics of spectacle. This involved insisting that all decisions were made in the mass meeting, where rational and pragmatic voices were silenced by accusing them of selling out (Habib, 2016b).

It is interesting that the Vice-Chancellor of Wits never saw the protest as that of students' frustration about the issue of financial exclusion. Instead, as the quote shows, he was attributing it to some outside political influence. The elected SRC was led by the Progressive Youth Alliance (affiliated to the ANC), and the

Economic Freedom Fighters Student Command had no SRC seat. So, Habib was arguing that there was a third force involved (ie the EFF, the political party). This is an interesting take on the situation since it denied the agency of the students and merely attributed the tension to a 'political party'. However, for students it was a symbolic victory that the Executive Committee of the Council had taken place in front of them. Habib argued, in an article in the *Daily Maverick*, that there was no democracy within the student movement and that those who opposed the dominant narrative were often called sell-outs for voicing views that were against those who were pushing for continued protests. Wits students were not prepared to go back to class without achieving their goal of free education. The prolonged struggle at Wits saw #FeesMustFall spread to other universities. The fact that the movement was now nationwide was a positive development for student leaders at Wits, especially the SRC president. She narrated how she felt when the movement spread throughout the country to other campuses and explained how the movement was coordinated:

> It was remarkably inspiring to see how quickly protests spread to other universities around the country. We were not shocked because these issues are not limited to one university – there is a fissure in the education system. There was a national communication WhatsApp group and various other groups where we kept updating each other on the developments at our various universities. The days were extremely busy; we had to be on the move. Students would come and ask us about various issues – suggest ideas; we had debates and discussions and study sessions inside Solomon Mahlangu House, formerly known as Senate House (SAHO, 2016).

The support from the students and the national coordination of the movement gave strength to the leadership of the movement, which at Wits now included Mcebo Dlamini, Nompendulo Mkhatshwa and Vuyani Pambo.

The students at Wits, joined by students from the University of Johannesburg, decided to march to Luthuli House, the headquarters of the governing ANC. Students now understood that the fight was not with the university, which was not in a position to offer free education, but rather with the ANC-led government, whose responsibility it was. Shaeera Kalla explained the significance of this march:

> Students at Wits collectively decided that we would take a memorandum to Luthuli House in preparation for the meeting at Union Buildings,

> which we had taken a decision not to attend, the reason for this being that our demands were clear, there was no need to discuss them over tea. Furthermore, we wanted to again radically change the power relationships that exist, between Council and students, for example, and the State and its people. We wanted the President to address the issues directly, with reasonable plans and timeframes given in response to our very reasonable and legitimate demands (SAHO, 2016).

The students wanted a commitment from the ANC that, as the governing party, it would take action and talk to the relevant ministers in government to respond to students' demands.

> The march was simple; we just wanted Gwede [Mantashe] to call his ministers and say 'do something maCom'. He has that power and it was also symbolic in that we [were] showing those in government that we know where the power lies. They all report to Luthuli House so we were going to their bosses before we meet them as government ministers deployed by Luthuli House (Interview, Economic Freedom Fighter Student Command [EFFSC] member, 2016, Johannesburg).

The march was an important moment in the movement in that it highlighted what the students wanted from the ANC as the ruling party. Ultimately, the announcement was made that there would be no fee increment for all universities in 2016. However, some students continued to protest at Wits, despite the announcement of a zero per cent fee increase. Many student activists argued that the zero per cent fee increment was the first step towards free education, but it did not address the issues of outsourcing, the exploitation of workers and the decolonisation of university spaces and the curriculum. It is worth noting that, from the outset, the EFFSC[6] wanted the struggle to focus on the insourcing of workers and free education, while the Progressive Youth Alliance (PYA) wanted the university management to delay the proposed fee increases. Thus, after the zero per cent increase announcement, the PYA[7] were satisfied. However, the EFFSC wanted to continue the struggle of the outsourced workers, which led to divisions within the movement. The EFFSC continued with its support of workers until the university made the decision for them to be insourced. The

---
6   The EFFSC is the student wing of the Economic Freedom Fighters (EFF).
7   The Progressive Youth Alliance (PYA) is the alliance of the ANCYL, Young Communist League and Muslim Student Association, which contests elections in institutions of high learning in South Africa.

first workers were insourced in early January 2017 and the process has now been completed as all general workers are now insourced.

Free, decolonised education
Some activists, especially those from the EFFSC, argued that their demand was not for a zero per cent fee increment but for free, quality, decolonised education. One student activist explained the importance of this call for free, decolonised education:

> This talks to some of the issue that was not resolved post the transition in 1994 and is the question around education, access and not only just about access but also around the curriculum, the decolonisation of that curriculum (Interview, protesting student, 2016, Johannesburg).

Many interviewees asserted that the current curriculum was alienating to black students as it did not include the African experience and was more about the European experience. Hence, #FeesMustFall focused not only on fees, but also on decolonising the curriculum:

> It is in a way challenging the current curriculum that in a way must accept African culture. And the African experience [must] become the centre when it comes to education because as it stands now the system is designed to alienate the African experience… (Interview, protesting student, 2016, Johannesburg).

Hence the decolonisation of education is necessary in order for the African child to 'exist' and not feel marginalised within academia. As Godsell and Chikane (2016: 60) note:

> [t]he other level is the problem of students who are now ostensibly welcomed on HWI [historically white institution] campuses, but discover that they still have no agency or identity. Their delight at getting through the gate changed to despair and anger as they realised that their outsider status and inability to change things, or even to act, remained unaltered.

It is for some of these reasons that black students at Wits challenged this colonial educational system, which requires them to assume new identities in order to be recognised by the system. Even though black students have access to these previously white universities, they cannot lay claim to them and call them home. Thus, the financial exclusion, as indicated above, was later linked to a broader claim, of the importance of having an African university instead of having a university in Africa (Ndlovu-Gatsheni, 2013; see also Motala, Chapter 5, in this volume). Ndlovu-Gatsheni (2013: 11) further notes: 'What is even more disturbing is that African children and youth begin a journey of alienation from their African context the very moment they step into the school, church, and university door.' As Mbembe (2015: 6) notes, 'when we say access, we are also talking about the creation of those conditions that will allow the black staff and student to say [about] the university: "This is my home. I am not an outsider here. I do not have to beg or to apologise to be here. I belong here."' The opposite, however, is what is happening in these universities, as blacks always have to beg and apologise to be in these spaces. They do not have a feeling of belonging because the structure has not changed.

> You have to die for you to live; you have to lose everything about yourself and learn to socialise yourself again into the culture here. Most of us who have come out tops here, we have lost ourselves as a black child because we are trying to be something we are not; we all trying to be white. We are all trying to learn another culture that is alien to us, because of the system. That is why it is easy for you to move from here to Oxford and you fit in straight away, there is no problem ... because you have now assimilated... That is how the system is like right now, that as an African child you have to lose yourself to make it (Interview, protesting student, 2016, Johannesburg).

These feelings of discrimination and alienation were shared by many of the students. The #FeesMustFall movement appears to have provided a space that is not ordinarily available for students to talk freely about their pain and suffering within former white universities. Students' renaming of Senate House to Solomon Mahlangu House was a symbolic action to decolonise university spaces to also reflect their own history:

> We have Wartenweiler Library. We have Cullen Library. We have Oliver Schreiner Library. All these places are named after white men. There is nothing African here at Wits. We decided through our meetings that we will call Senate House, Solomon Mahlangu as we see him as someone who has died for the liberation of this country (Interview, Wits SRC member, 2016, Johannesburg).

Solomon Mahlangu was an Umkhonto weSizwe soldier who was hanged by the apartheid regime when he was 22 years old. He is a symbol of struggle for protesting students at Wits and other universities across the country, along with Steve Biko and other struggle icons. The students today believe that, two decades into democracy, they are still fighting the same fight that was fought by those activists. This links with Satgar's (2016) argument that the student protesters of today are drawing on Black Consciousness and Africanist politics to make sense of their struggle post-1994.

Power struggle within #FeesMustFall at Wits

The #FeesMustFall movement was started by the Wits SRC leadership. However, some students allege that once the movement gained its momentum, there was interference from political organisations outside campus. The PYA, which included the South African Student Congress (SASCO), the ANC Youth League (ANCYL) and the Muslim Student Association, was the leading SRC student organisation at Wits. It is alleged that the PYA-led SRC was instructed by the ANC to suspend its protest after the President announced a zero per cent fee increment. However, this created tension with the EFF-aligned student movement, which wanted the protest to continue until free, quality and decolonised education was achieved. The EFF-aligned student movement also wanted the protest to continue in support of outsourced workers. One PYA leader had this to say:

> You know we went to Union Buildings if you recall quite clearly, the intention of the #FeesMustFall last year was that we are demanding a zero per cent fee increment … When we came back there was a view, from the EFF to be quite precise, to say, What about workers? Let us start a new struggle of insourcing. Actually, even that zero per cent must not be celebrated – we want free education now (Interview, Wits SRC member, 2016, Johannesburg).

It is at this point that divisions started to emerge within #FeesMustFall at Wits. The EFF-aligned student movement led by Vuyani Pambo continued to protest over outsourced workers to be insourced, and they eventually won and the process began in 2017. The PYA was accused of selling out the workers by agreeing to return to classes. Some respondents asserted that the leadership of Nompendulo Mkhatshwa started to be compromised at this point. It is further alleged that her leadership was compromised by her strong association with the ANC.

> As a student leader [it] is not wrong to be politically aligned but the moment you participate actively in active politics of governance, in ANC councils and all those things, it led to her downfall because

students started saying, 'Nompendulo is not our president' and there was nothing that we could do about that and eventually she was nowhere to be found (Interview, SRC member, 2016, Johannesburg).

Following the publication of *Destiny* magazine, in which Nompendulo was interviewed and appeared on the cover, she was accused of using the #FeesMustFall movement to advance her political ambitions, with allegations that she was hired by the ANC during this period. Was the fall of Nompendulo[8] also a result of the politics of patriarchy within the #FeesMustFall movement? It is possible that her leadership as a female disrupted the dominant script of men as leaders within student movements and politics in general. Vuyani Pambo and Mcebo Dlamini also became dominant faces of #FeesMustFall at Wits, but there were no allegations of them using the movement to advance their own political ambitions. Is it because it is the norm in politics for men to occupy positions of power? Did the gender of Nompendulo as a black female activist play a role in these allegations? It is common cause that female political leaders are often not given the same political respect as their male counterparts. This branding of the movement and interventions by political parties weakened the movement and caused divisions.

The leadership of the #FeesMustFall movement across different universities is dominated by male students. It is, therefore, important that female student leaders such as Nompendulo, Shaeera and others emerge and re-emerge to assert a politics of emancipatory black Africanist feminism.

Wits management

Most of the students interviewed believed that management had not been supportive, as evident in fees increases in 2015 and 2016. 'University management seems to be anti-poor and anti-black because these decisions to increase fees affect poor black students' (Interview, SRC member, 2016, Johannesburg).

Students said that protesting was the only option they had as the university management often did not listen to their concerns, as noted:

In our meeting with the Chief Financial Officer Linda Jarvis and Accountant Daniel Gozo, we were arrogantly dismissed when we asked for this information, with Daniel saying it would be impossible to give

---

8   She was sworn in as a member of parliament for the 6th democratic administration. Student leaders at Wits believe this was made possible by the #FeesMustFall movement at Wits, which profiled her, and this could have been the ANC rewarding her for her role in killing off this movement at Wits.

> projections. We felt that the entire consultation process was a means to keep us busy and not really engage on an intellectual level on how unsustainable these fee hikes are (SAHO, 2016).

The students added that the university management did not engage with them in 'good faith', especially when fee increments were discussed. This sense of not being heard is what prompted the formation of #FeesMustFall and other protests that have taken place since then. Another complaint raised against the university management was the use of, and overreliance on, court interdicts to silence students.

> You know as a result of this court order we could not gather in groups, nor sing or take any form of protest on campus. The protest dies, but the students continue the conversations and organise events for the movement to keep the momentum going in and outside campus (Interview, PYA member, 2016, Johannesburg).

Student leaders were suspended for violating these court interdicts. The court orders were also used by the university to justify bringing police onto campus, which led to violence. Students made numerous allegations of police brutality: 'The violence just went downhill; from there on it was just a lot because literally every 10 minutes we were getting shot at, teargassed and stun-grenaded so it was getting too much' (Interview, PYA member, 2016, Johannesburg).

In response to the police brutality, students resorted to looting and damaging property, both on and off campus, which derailed the movement because these acts cost them public sympathy, which they needed to achieve their cause. This cycle of violence affected the movement and it started shedding huge numbers as students feared police violence: 'Because you must admit that you can't defeat the state in terms of violence; they possess the monopoly of violence' (Interview, EFFSC member, 2016, Johannesburg).

During this period, Mcebo Dlamini was arrested and remanded in custody for a month before being released on bail and students claimed that his arrest was aimed at instilling fear. The arrest of the student leaders had an impact on the number of protesters. The message was clear from the state: they wanted to crush the protest and the arrest of Mcebo Dlamini was especially important and symbolic in this regard. As one student activist argued, the way they arrested him at his residence early in the morning made it even more difficult to keep the momentum of the protest going as people were generally scared and did not want to be seen in the picket lines because they did not know what could happen to them at night.

Students blamed the increased level of violence on the university management. They also spoke about the relationship between the violence on campus and the neoliberal agenda of the state and higher education sector, as well as of the collusion between the state and the university:

> There is a relationship between politics and economics, the political ideology that they subscribe to is neoliberal and doesn't accommodate anything to deal with anything free or whatever and free education. So, they do not have a solution to the demands that the students are presenting on the table so the only way is to suppress it. And how do you suppress it? You use violence (Interview, protesting student, 2016, Johannesburg).

The state ultimately succeeded in demobilising the students because the protests subsided and the university was able to reopen. Student leaders note that violence re-emerged in 2017 and that all protests at the university have been accompanied by violence, with university always responding by calling in the police and private security. The securitisation of the university has been criticised – by all stakeholders, including progressive academic staff – for inhibiting a conducive learning environment.

Conclusion

#FeesMustFall at Wits was central to the 2015 major gain of a zero per cent fee increase. It also brought to the fore the debate around free higher education, which President Zuma announced in December 2017. After the successes of 2015, during 2016 the focus moved to the decolonisation of the university and not just fees. This decolonisation project, started by the movement at Wits, is important as it highlighted some of the structural issues at the university, like the marginalisation of African experiences in the curricula. Changing the demographics of the student body alone does not mean that the university has transformed – much more needs to be done to ensure that black students feel that they are a part of the university.

Significantly, the movement has re-established the decolonisation and transformation debates in the national discourse. The rainbow nation promised by Mandela in 1994 has been questioned, given the increasing inequalities between the rich and the poor. The movement has forced South Africans to ask difficult questions about what the 1994 democratic breakthrough really meant for poor black people. It is no wonder that the issues went beyond the economic to the subjective or ontological issues faced by students and workers on campus. It is within this problematic – of a state and university that have accepted the neoliberal framework – that many began to call for insourcing and a quality, free, decolonised education. Thus, the university struggles are merely a microcosm of the realities of post-apartheid South Africa, where the cry for economic emancipation by the previously disadvantaged has been met by police brutality. The memory of those massacred in Marikana was still fresh in the minds of many students. Adam Habib has caricatured the response of the students as them desiring their own Marikana. This is a revealing statement – that sometimes those sitting in positions of power fail to see the importance of changing the exclusionary structures in society. It is reckless to see the angry response by those who are oppressed as a desire for death. As long as this cry for economic emancipation remains ignored, South Africa will continue to witness the emergence of social movements.

References

Adams, S (2015) Far from over: Interview with Nompendulo Mkhatshwa, *Destiny*, December Issue, No. 95.

Badat, S (2016) Deciphering the meanings, and explaining the South African higher education student protests of 2015–16, 1 February 2017. Available at: http://wiser.wits.ac.za/system/files/documents/Saleem%20Badat%20-%20Deciphering%20the%20Meanings,%20and%20Explaining%20the%20South%20African%20Higher%20Education%20Student%20Protests.pdf (accessed 25 July 2018).

Booysen, S and Bandama, K (2016) Annotated timeline of the #FeesMustFall revolt 2015–2016, in S Booysen (ed.) *Fees Must Fall: Student revolt, decolonisation and governance in South Africa*. Johannesburg: Wits University Press.

Chinguno, C, Kgoroba, M, Mashinini, S, Masilela, BF, Maubane, B, Moyo, N, Mthombeni, A and Ndlovu, H (2017) *Rioting and Writing: Diaries of Wits Fallists*. Johannesburg: Society, Work and Development Institute (SWOP), University of the Witwatersrand.

Duncan, J (2016) *Protest Nation: The right to protest in South Africa*. Pietermaritzburg: UKZN Press.

Godsell, G and Chikane, R (2016) The roots of the revolution, in S Booysen (ed.) *Fees Must Fall: Student revolt, decolonisation and governance in South Africa. 2016*. Johannesburg: Wits University Press.

Habib, A (2016a). An open letter to colleagues critical of campus safety and security arrangements, *Daily Maverick*, 18 January.

Habib, A (2016b) Op-ed: The politics of spectacle – reflections on the 2016 student protests, *Daily Maverick*, 5 December.

Jansen, J (2004) Changes and continuities in South Africa's higher education system, 1994 to 2004, in L Chisholm (ed.) *Changing Class: Education and social change in post-apartheid South Africa*. Cape Town: HSRC Press.

Malabela, M (2017) We are already enjoying free education: Protests at the University of Limpopo, in M Langa (ed.) *#Hashtag: An analysis of the #FeesMustFall movement at South African universities*. Johannesburg: Centre for the Study of Violence and Reconciliation (CSVR), Wits University.

Mbembe, A (2015) Decolonising knowledge and the question of the archive. Available at: http://wiser.wits.ac.za/system/files/Achille%20Mbembe%20-%20Decolonising%20Knowledge%20and%20the%20Question%20of%20the%20Archive.pdf (accessed July 2018).

Ndlovu-Gatsheni, S (2013) Why decoloniality in the 21st century? *The Thinker*, 48, February.

Pilane, P (2015) #TransformWits: What students want, *Daily Vox*, 27 March. Available at: https://www.thedailyvox.co.za/transformwits-what-students-want/ (accessed July 2018).

Poplak, R (2016) TRAINSPOTTER: Adam Habib: The rock, the hard place, and the cruel beauty of an uncaring universe, *Daily Maverick*, 4 October.

Satgar, V (2016) Bringing class back in: Against outsourcing during #FeesMustFall at Wits, in S Booysen (ed.) *Fees Must Fall: Student revolt, decolonisation and governance in South Africa*. Johannesburg: Wits University Press.

South African History Online (SAHO) (2015) *University of Witwatersrand Student Protests 2015 Timeline*. Available at: http://www.sahistory.org.za/article/university-witwatersrand-student-protests-2015-timeline (accessed August 2018).

South African History Online (SAHO) (2016) Interview with Shaeera Kalla, former SRC president at Wits University, interviewed by Kyla McNulty. Available at: http://www.sahistory.org.za/archive/interview-shaeera-kalla-former-src-president-wits-university-interviewed-kyla-mc-nulty (accessed July 2018).

Zidepa, L (2015) #TRANSFORMWITS announces manifesto, Wits Vuvuzela, 11 April. Available at: http://witsvuvuzela.com/2015/04/11/transformationwits-announces-manifesto/ (accessed July 2018).

Chapter 8
South Africa's student movement: A Rhodes[1] perspective

Corrine Knowles

Introduction

On the evening of Sunday, 10 June 2018, behind one of Rhodes University's Kimberley Hall residences, a student was attacked, possibly raped. When other students arrived to investigate the incident, a man emerged and ran off laughing, and the survivor could not be found. Ongoing investigations by the police, the Rhodes Campus Protection Unit and students themselves have at the time of writing not yielded any arrests or closure. After the attack, students urged one another on social media platforms to meet the following Tuesday morning at 7.30, to finalise a list of demands around student safety and rape culture. In the end, only a handful of students arrived, and about 10 students handed over a memorandum to the vice-chancellor on the steps of the main administration building. In the days following the attack, communications were sent from the university communications division, promising to increase safety, urging students to report instances of sexual violence, and outlining the university's stance against sexual violence of any kind (Koti, 2018).[2]

The significance of this story stems from the stark difference (in terms of student activism) in the aftermath of the attack in comparison with the protests against rape culture at the institution which took place in March and October 2015, and in particular in April 2016. These protests – and lessons learnt from them – form the basis for this chapter. Various protests, pickets, occupations, police violent action, arrests, hospitalisations, court cases and negotiations continued intermittently until the end of 2016. From my observations, internal disciplinary actions and exclusions associated with the protests seem to have come to an end in the first quarter of 2018. This chapter argues that without an

---

1 Rhodes University was renamed the University Currently Known As Rhodes (UCKAR) by protesters and allies during the 2016 student protests. In 2018, following a decision by the Rhodes University Council to halt any consultative process around renaming, and instead to keep the name, some are using the acronym USKAR – the University Still Known As Rhodes.

2 Koti (2018) provides a brief report on this story and the follow-up in the local Makhanda/Grahamstown newspaper. Available at: http://www.grocotts.co.za/2018/06/19/rhodes-steps-up-security/ (accessed November 2018).

overt political framework that permeates the teaching, working and living spaces of the institution, it will replicate neoliberal values and practices at the expense of poor black students. This has been the challenge for Rhodes, the smallest of the country's 26 public universities, and elsewhere – where the discourse around transformation has been co-opted, bureaucratised and domesticated, thereby used to service a neoliberal agenda. This chapter maps the distance between the political praxis of protest and the transformation discourse, using three ideas as lenses: embodiment, collectivism and re-centring. These will be examined against the backdrop of student protests in Rhodes over the period of 20 months. The ideas overlap, as they should, as it is their combination that could effectively dismantle and transform a colonial and apartheid past.

The student movement on the Rhodes campus was deeply affected by the university's and state's responses to various protests in 2015 and 2016, and these have had a profound impact on current student activism. During the April 2016 RU Reference List protest,[3] hundreds of students protested for days, initially spontaneously mobilising on a Sunday night, and meeting throughout the days ahead to draw up strategies and memoranda, march, negotiate, establish values and directions, interrupt lectures, attend alternative curriculum lectures and discuss what should happen next. Two years later, in June 2018, only 10 students committed themselves to a march, despite many having heard the screams of the student being attacked on that Sunday night, and many of them having written their outrage, fear and anger on social media pages following the attack. Why are students suddenly reluctant to engage when there is a collective concern? As one student put it on the popular and anonymous *Rhodes Confessions* Facebook page:

> I didn't join the march at 7:30 am on 12 June 2018. I was scared. As a g18 [a first year in 2018], you hear all these horror stories from the seniors about the dangers of protesting, your parents on the other hand warn you sternly against protesting because they don't want you to lose your degree. I honestly wanted to be part of it. But how sure was I that I was not going to get arrested, because apparently we can't protest at Rhodes.[4]

---

3 The RU Reference List protest began when a list of names, titled 'Reference list', was dropped on an anonymous Facebook page (*Rhodes queer crushes and confessions* – now removed). Within minutes, people were commenting on the post, implying that the names were of alleged rapists or sexual abusers. A protest began spontaneously, with about 400 students moving from residence to residence, calling for those on the list to come out and explain themselves.

4 #RUConfessions16352. Available at: https://www.facebook.com/rhodesuniconfessions/posts/1655719181143321 (accessed June 2018).

Muzenda (2018) reminds us that in 2015 and 2016 during the student protests on the Rhodes campus, 'People put their bodies, their mental health and their education on the line to fight an injustice, to champion something they believed in. To see their fight stomped out so swiftly is painful, but I know that this is not the end of the story' (Muzenda, 2018). Similarly, Chengeta (2018), who gives a comprehensive account of the events that unfolded in the 2016 protests, poignantly concludes that 'For many of us who remember what happened in 2016, it's "safer" to stay silent.'

There are many traumatising and teachable moments from the student movement and protests that happened on the Rhodes campus from March 2015. This chapter addresses some of the lessons from South Africa's student movement from a Rhodes University perspective, in part as a protest against some of the silencing that continues. As a microcosm of South African society, the university protests demonstrate a difficult institutional relationship with democracy and transformation. Both of these ideas are mainstreamed and embedded in policies and protocols. However, this chapter argues that we are profoundly challenged by the inequalities that are not adequately addressed in the various groups that make up the university, and in the relations of power that influence who we can be in the university space. Even though the committees that make decisions in the university have wide representation, as Hassim (2004: 19) points out, without a transformational agenda, inclusion and representation in themselves fail to achieve the transformative outcomes for which they are set up.

There are a variety of perspectives on student movement at Rhodes. My standpoint is from the position of an older, white woman who has taught for the last decade in the Rhodes University Humanities' Extended Studies (ES) programme.[5] This has shaped my relationships with ES students each year and has afforded me profound insight into their lives and concerns. All the ES students are black and many are working-class, who attended township or rural schools. It is their perspective that has fashioned my activism over the past few years and the writing of this chapter.

To remind myself and track the thinking underpinning student activism on the campus, I examined the Facebook pages of an organisation that emerged early in 2015 at Rhodes University, the Black Student Movement (BSM).[6] The issues on the table then were transformation of the curriculum, changing the name of the university, better pay for the lowest class of workers, and

---

5   My pedagogy is aligned to hooks (1994) *Teaching to Transgress: Education as the practice of freedom*. London: Routledge.
6   BSM Facebook page. Available at: https://www.facebook.com/groups/1551730468423783/ (accessed June 2018).

recognition – in the form of their usual residence accommodation during the short vacation – for the poor black child who could not afford to go home for the short vacations. Alasow, a master's student on campus when BSM came into being, described that first protest meeting in March 2015 thus:

> On Wednesday last week, a group of Rhodes University students held a meeting to show solidarity with students at UCT, whilst also discussing the name of our own university and the lack of meaningful transformation here. The meeting was closely surveyed by the Campus Protection Unit. Following the meeting, students embarked on a peaceful march to the administration building to raise their concerns. University authorities locked them out with no justification (Alasow, 2015a).

This first encounter between peaceful protesters and university security was significant and awkward. The Rhodes campus is notoriously open – while boom gates prevent cars from entering areas that are reserved for staff parking at two of the entrances to the campus, these operate only between 8.00 am and 5.00 pm on weekdays and are open in between. There are no fences or gates separating the campus from the town, and because half of the student population live in the residences on campus, many students regard the campus as their home away from home. The insourced Campus Protection Unit (CPU) monitors security on campus, and the third core objective of the unit is 'to strive to earn the respect and confidence of the Rhodes community by projecting an image of courtesy, concern and competence, and by providing a quick and knowledgeable response to emergency situations'.[7] What is clear from the video footage of the students attempting to enter at the doors of the main administration building is that the CPU were unprepared for the rights and responsibilities around peaceful protest, that they incorrectly read the situation as 'an emergency', and that students on the campus were outraged at being 'locked out' of their own campus.

Embodiment

This first encounter between students and security provides a way to speak about *embodiment*, which is the first lesson from the protests. Hooks argues:

> Any radical pedagogy must insist that everyone's presence is acknowledged. That insistence cannot be simply stated. It has to be demonstrated through pedagogical practices. To begin with, the professor must genuinely value

---

7   Available at: https://www.ru.ac.za/campusprotection/ (accessed June 2019).

everyone's presence. There must be ongoing recognition that everyone influences the classroom dynamic, that everyone contributes. These contributions are resources (hooks, 1994: 8).

hooks' ideas concern pedagogy, the practice and praxis of teaching to transform. Where teaching and learning are core functions of the university, these ideas about pedagogy speak to a way of thinking about a student that is perhaps missing from many lecture rooms and, by association, missing from the way students live their lives on Rhodes' campus. Her ideas about embodiment draw on Buddhist thinker Thích Nhât Hanh, who was concerned about a holistic approach to healing pedagogy, which requires us to think of each other as whole human beings, 'striving not just for knowledge in books, but knowledge about how to live in the world' (hooks, 1994: 15). hooks regards 'embodiment' as a significant moment of liberatory pedagogy. She goes on to argue:

> We must return ourselves to a state of embodiment in order to deconstruct the way power has been traditionally orchestrated in the classroom, denying subjectivity to some groups and according it to others. By recognising subjectivity and the limits of identity, we disrupt that objectification that is so necessary in a culture of domination (hooks, 1994: 139).

Even before the protests began, students had begun to articulate the divide between their ordinary lives and what they learn in university. In a brutally poignant piece in the local *Grocott's Mail* newspaper, Siyanda Centwa wrote of his experiences as a working-class black student who came to Rhodes from the local township. He speaks of feeling 'stuck thanks to the poor education that I got in school and stuck because township life is unforgiving and barren' (Centwa, 2013). Rhodes represented a release from this, but he goes on to say: 'Despite the fact that I feel deeply blessed to have the opportunity to study at Rhodes, my first year was extremely difficult for social more than academic reasons.' The social reasons were about the alienation he felt from other black students who were not working class and who, perhaps, were more easily absorbed into a white institutional culture. The attitude of these students affected the extent to which he felt able to participate in class. It confirms hooks' argument that a culture of domination can lead to objectification, for instance, of somebody from a different class. The experience led him to feel 'that the pressure is on for me to pretend to be who I am not' (Centwa, 2013).

Centwa was not alone. Many of these initial student protesters were in the humanities, where ideas about inequality, justice, civil obedience, legitimacy, class, gender and race are taught as abstract ideas in disciplines such as Politics, Sociology and Philosophy, drawing heavily on the canon of Western thinkers. This positions the poor black student as an object. In my experience, the actual embodied inequalities in the classroom and university in South Africa are unacknowledged in a number of these courses. The first protest was a way to raise these concerns and counter the silences around inequalities and a lack of transformation on campus. It was a contribution to the conversation, using methods (such as peaceful protest) that are protected in our Constitution, learnt in the humanities disciplines and practised all over South Africa. It was a way to disrupt the power configurations in the institution, giving voice and subjectivity where there had been silence and a sense of domination (hooks, 1994: 139).

Naicker, one of the students present at this first protest, argued at the time that while formerly white institutions have significantly increased the number of black students, 'the institutional culture and practices of the university remained decidedly white'; and speaking of student protesters at the time, 'the culture and practices of those students within the university came into direct conflict with the ways in which these elite institutions functioned' (Naicker, 2016: 57). Saleem Badat, former Vice-Chancellor of Rhodes, explains this further, claiming that 'those who are black and come from disadvantaged backgrounds experience the environments and cultures of the historically white universities as discomforting, alienating, disempowering, and exclusionary' (Badat, 2015). Jagarnath, a lecturer at Rhodes at the time, concurs and claims that in conversations about transformation, 'the discussion is framed in a way that casts the black student and the black academic, whether absent or present, as the problem. Even on the occasions when the endemic racism of the institution is identified as a central problem it is not confronted' (Jagarnath, 2015).

Furthermore, when many of the lecturers in humanities subjects are white, even if they believe in the embodiment of knowledge, their experience of whiteness limits the extent to which their black students feel recognised in the conversation. hooks explains that a black professor has a privileged position in this kind of conversation, which 'does not emerge from the "authority of experience" but rather from the *passion* of experience, the *passion* of remembrance' (emphasis added) (hooks, 1994: 90). For hooks, passion 'is a way of knowing that is often expressed through the body, what it knows, what has been deeply inscribed on it through experience' (hooks, 1994: 91). This urges us to treat students as whole people, with rich experiences, passions and memories, in order to connect these to the kinds of examples and texts we use in our curricula. If we are to take hooks' insights seriously, it means seeing our students as whole people, and to see their bodies facilitates their passions, and the memory that connects students to their histories, homes, families and communities – the knowledge we work with. As Mkhize, a lecturer at Rhodes at the time, notes about the protests: 'The students were talking about pedagogy, freedom, methodology – and they were not doing it for 100 marks; they were articulating an intellectual vision for a more humane society and critiquing our universities for paying lip service to transformation' (Mkhize, 2015).

If academics were to work in this way, we would work as a public good, recognising that students (and we) could leave our classrooms as more whole, less fragmented people, our lives orientated by the profound ideas that have found resonance in bodies and minds, affecting how we imagine and work towards our own and collective futures. Student protesters in March 2015 were teaching us this important lesson. The institutional culture that was the backdrop for the student movement at Rhodes demonstrates the ways in which the university has been unforgivingly slow to undo and reverse the racism and inequalities which are the legacy of colonialism, apartheid and capitalism, and points to a lack of recognition of their material consequences for black staff and students.

Collectivism

Collectivism provides a second lens of understanding the student movement. This is based on ideas around what is individual, what is generic, what is a political collective and what place does collective student action have in a university. In academic discourse, which the Western canon encourages as an 'unhurried, speculative, analytical, and uncommitted' voice as opposed to the everyday voice, which is 'urgent, personal, emotive, and tribal [*sic*]' (Northedge, 2003: 24), students are required to step away from their personal selves and 'become' analytical. This is a particularly Cartesian approach to knowledge work, which problematically separates the mind from the body, and which is dismissive of more holistic ways of knowing – arguably this is a challenge for the decolonising of knowledge. I argue that few students are able to do this separating of mind from body without the cost of their identities and psychological health, which have been socialised and shaped more holistically outside of academic settings. Dualism separates students from their social and political selves and turns them into what is generic, as opposed to what is a collective. A challenge we face in South African universities today is the pull towards a neoliberal approach, which sees students as generic consumers and customers. This plays down the role of the university as a public good and confines humanities knowledge to abstract ideas, which must be learnt for exams. If we are serious about universities being transformative spaces, seeking to decolonise the thinking and canon that are favoured in the colonial institution, our work with students needs to recognise who they are, and expand the possibilities of who they may become. When we fail to do this, we support an academic project that is individualistic, in that it does not translate into making a difference in how people live their lives, how they relate to each other and their communities, and how they think about their degrees in terms of the contributions they can make to a better life *for all*.

This way of thinking about knowledge – as a contribution to the collective – emphasises the idea of collectivism, which was a recurring lesson from the protests: if we recognise the bodies of the students we teach, and recognise the way that knowledge is embodied, it is a way to connect the ideas of the curriculum to the lived experience of students, but also a way to connect with each other as a collective, united in the search for relevant knowledge of and for our society. hooks reminds us that 'a feeling of community creates a sense that there is a common good that binds us' and that 'one way to build community is to recognise the value of each individual voice' (hooks, 1994: 40). And Motlafi (2015) speaks about the need to be cognisant of 'broader communal liberation' and the importance of thinking in terms of community rather than individual rights. This idea of thinking as a collective, in solidarity, in relation to each other, is an important idea that recurred in how the protests and the student movement unfolded.

In the early protests of 2015 at Rhodes, students worked collectively to bring their bodies and their bodily concerns (such as student hunger and student access to their residences during the short April vacation) to the university. It was their bodies, bearing the pains of misrecognition and exclusions, which appeared together at the doors, holding a memorandum to hand over to the vice-chancellor.

The contradiction between thinking and acting as a political collective, and the university's emphasis on a particular kind of dualistic individual, is illustrated by the ongoing story of the student movement: conversations around student accommodation during short vacations, the name change and curriculum transformation continued after this initial protest described earlier. In a circular to the university towards the end of March, published on the BSM Facebook page, the vice-chancellor urged the university community to raise their concerns in a civil and dignified manner. This perhaps undermined the level to which protesting students' passions had been ignited around these issues of student accommodation and transformation, and by the very real blocking of their access to the main administration building to hand over a memorandum of their concerns. Passion is messy and unpredictable, and requires us to be attentive and present, rather than merely abstracted. The vice-chancellor argues in this circular that 'we should use the power of rational and reasoned argument, logic and debate to forge common ground on these issues where we hold different views. We must also be open-minded and be willing to be persuaded to change our position on the matter based on the quality of the argument advanced' (VC Circular, March 2015). Dealing with the issues raised by protesting students, he carefully articulated his stance on each concern, presenting a range of contestations on the issues, and pointing to a democratic process which could take us forward. I argue though that his emphasis on 'quality of argument' and reasoned debate did not appeal to student protesters, because they felt their bodies and emotions were not recognised in the *actions* that followed these civil and intellectual engagements. It also dismissed their collective activism. Furthermore, what the university recognises as a quality argument ignores the inequalities of language. The misreading and misrecognition of the students' concerns, the focus on the manner of delivery rather than the message, represented a rupture in the relations between protesters and management.

By the time the next short vacation began in September, students had intensified their struggle. The university had responded to their request for short vacation accommodation by asking that poor black students approach the office of the Dean of Students to ask for accommodation, and that this would be dealt with in a case-by-case manner (VC circular, March 2015). But students were not happy with the idea of 'performing their poverty' by having to make a case as individuals in order to be recognised as worthy of accommodation during this period, believing that the university needed to take a more principled and systemic stance on the matter. Mobilising towards the end of August, students entered and occupied the vice-chancellor's office and senior common room, and then went on to occupy the Council Chamber where faculty, senate and council meetings take place (*Grocott's Mail*, 2015a). Describing this round of protests 'amid a flurry of online racial insensitivities', Dennet (2015) wrote that the students were protesting 'inequality at the university and injustices faced by marginalised students'. Accommodation during the short vacation was the impetus to intensify the earlier protest in March, which indicates that in those months between the two short vacations, students did not feel heard, nor that their concerns were adequately addressed Once again, they collectively brought their bodies to this encounter, and this time the response was more decisive: protesters were under the impression that they would be allowed to address a senate meeting, due to be held in the Council Chamber on Friday, 28 August 2015. At the last minute, the meeting was moved to the postgraduate village, about 1 kilometre away, demonstrating, perhaps, the way in which whiteness and privilege are able to move easily to keep themselves central in institutions such as Rhodes. Undeterred, the students marched to the new meeting place, determined to have their concerns heard. At the gates of the postgraduate village, members of CPU locked them out and the police were called – they arrived in 'at least seven vans' including a canine unit. Eventually students made their way into the grounds and the senate meeting room. The BSM statement describing the events of the day went on to say that 'many members of Senate, including the Chair, smirked at the issues raised by students. One member of Senate [a white male professor] threw water into the face of a young female BSM member. When she asked him why he disrespected her in this way, he arrogantly blew her a kiss' (BSM press statement, August 2015).

An observation from this encounter is that although there was no doubt that the students' concerns would have formed part of the agenda for that senate meeting (senate is overwhelmingly white and male – Rhodes Digest of Statistics, 2017), students did not believe that they were adequately represented or recognised.

Re-centring

The third idea that emerges as a lesson from the protests is that of *re-centring*. Drawing on Asante's work, Mkabela (2005, 179) defines the Afrocentric paradigm as one 'which deals with the question of African identity from the perspective of African people as centred, located, oriented and grounded' (Mkabela, 2005: 179). Ngũgĩ wa Thiong'o (1986: 1–139) explains that education needs to begin from the self, in Africa, and then it can 'radiate outwards' – he cautions that Africa should be 'at the centre of things, not existing as an appendix or a satellite of other countries and literatures, things must be seen from the African perspective' (Ngũgĩ wa Thiong'o, 1986: 1–139). Thus, re-centring is not a novel idea, but very much part of the post-colonial project. That universities in South Africa have in many ways failed to centre Africa comprehensively in their thinking and knowledge-making is troubling, and a legitimate concern for the protesters. If students were being introduced to African thought and thinkers, it could allow them to orientate their learning to the challenges in our communities and continent. It could inspire their own contributions to knowledge-making in a more seamless and relevant way.

To introduce the concept of re-centring as it applies to the student movement, Alasow, writing again in September of 2015, succinctly explains the position of the BSM:

> The BSM is not interested in the 'right' way of doing things. The 'right way of doing things' is only useful for people who wish to integrate those on the peripheries into the centre. It is of no use to those who wish to eradicate the very categories of 'periphery' and 'centre'. Most fundamentally: a movement which seeks to move society away from an oppressive status quo and towards an emancipated future, cannot adopt the liberal 'methodology' of participation in oppressive structures. Lorde poetically pointed out that 'the master's tools will never dismantle the master's house'. The moment the custodians of the status quo approve of the BSM's way of doing things, it will be perpetuating that which it seeks to resist. The BSM must continue occupying, protesting and disrupting. It must challenge the status quo – and its custodians. The means to attain the South Africa of tomorrow cannot rely on the approval of the beneficiaries of the South Africa of today (Alasow, 2015b).

Alasow's reflection is important because it reveals the way in which student protests are positioned in relation to university management as the 'custodians of the status quo'. That students mobilised in order to present themselves and their concerns to the decision-making bodies in the university demonstrated their understanding of their own marginality, and a desire to re-centre the poor black student in the thinking and resolutions of the custodians of power. This was, in itself, a transformative act. hooks argues that transformation is 'that historical moment when one begins to think critically about the self and identity in relation to one's political circumstance' (hooks, 1994: 47). Ngcobozi, a student at Rhodes at the time, and initiator of the #RhodesSoWhite campaign, explains that the issues that were being raised by student protesters 'are all entry points into broader concepts of transformation and black students laying claim to space, and the right for their space to be reflective of a transforming institution' (Ngcobozi, 2015). And Erskog, also a student at Rhodes at the time, explains the protests at Rhodes thus:

> The university currently known as Rhodes is known for its apolitical student body. Have students, in the 20 years of 'democracy', collectively voiced dissident political opinions with such force? Have students openly and collectively discussed and challenged the politics of oppression? Is it not then transformational to see a black student movement gathering in public to discuss the institutional racism and its effects on those worst off in society? When the apolitical shifts to political, that is in itself transformative (Erskog, 2015).

Erskog's observations remind us of the way in which it was the coming together of students around a shared belief in social justice and freedom from oppression that was transformational – thinking beyond the individual to the collective was a way to locate the struggle in the systems of oppression. So, the mobilisation on campus during 2015 was an awakening, recognition by the BSM students, of their political location in the institution. By bringing their bodies, their memoranda, their songs, their concerns, they were re-centring the black student in the university imagination. As Badat argued, 'Blacks, women, gay and lesbians, and other historically disadvantaged or marginalised groups are expected to accept, integrate and assimilate into the discomforting institutional cultural norms' (Badat, 2015). Student protesters disrupted this positioning to place themselves physically in the centre of the power constructs of the institution. If, as a public good, the university is to make any contribution to the social, political and economic challenges in our country, it is, surely, to address inequality. We are the most unequal country in the world. To change this comprehensively means to put the poor in the centre – as a subject – of our deliberations. It is to provide historically disadvantaged people with a platform to show us the world, the challenges, the resilience, the opportunities and the dreams of the majority, who will remain stuck in poverty if we do not reconfigure our arrangements of whose ideas and dreams matter.

The BSM's work to embody and re-centre the concerns of poor black students as a collective in the university in the April and August mobilisations set up, in many ways, a much broader, more inclusive set of fees protests that happened in October 2015. The national call to shut down universities to protest fee increases inspired many students and staff who were not part of the earlier protests. Roads were barricaded and students were mobilised, and the university was shut down for a week. These led to an organised march through the town which included the vice-chancellor and senior management on Wednesday, 20 October, and a live feed of President Zuma's announcement on Friday afternoon that there would be no fee increase for 2016 (*Grocott's Mail*, 2015b). Although these protests seem, in retrospect, to be contained and cohesive, they were not without internal complications, particularly regarding leadership of the movement.

During the April and August/September BSM protests and occupations, leadership was shared and fluid, emphasising the idea of collectivity, which does not seek to empower one at the expense of others, but to recognise that there are different kinds of contributions that are valuable. A detailed analysis is needed to track the voices that emerged and shone at various moments of this process. There were strong black women who found their voice during that time – many of them have been referenced earlier and were active on social media and in interviews in national media, as well as in student gatherings on campus. However, working in the context of a society and a university – which did not adequately dismantle race, class and gender inequalities, and which failed to challenge problematic configurations of power in its staff and student groups, in its power hierarchies, or with its pedagogy, sharing power in a rotational way – became challenging for some who were used to a patriarchal power that was uncontested in other arenas. A BSM statement in October provides this message – after an extremely volatile and difficult night – that some in the movement had used patriarchal privileges to undermine the kinds of leadership that had been practised by the group since its inception:

> During the mobilisation, there were many women in the group of protestors who felt attacked and threatened by some of the men in the group who questioned the role of women in the protest. As an intersectional movement, the BSM condemns any form of patriarchy and acts that might put the lives of women in danger. We value and appreciate solidarity and support from the men at Rhodes during this National Shut Down, but we feel strongly that those who join the protest be respectful of the work black women have been doing for transformation on this campus since the beginning of the year. We condemn this conduct by these men last night. We also condemn students participating in the protest while intoxicated, thereby aggravating an already volatile situation. The forcible removal of students from residences is an example of this (BSM statement, 22 October 2015).

This demonstration of patriarchy was dangerous and would emerge as an issue again in 2016.

On the Rhodes campus in 2015, apart from police presence at the postgraduate village described earlier, and some instances during the October protests,[8] direct contact between protesters and police on campus was restrained. This is in harsh contrast to what happened on campus in the #RUReferenceList rape-culture protests in April 2016. Not only was there a stark difference in the confrontations between police and students during these protests, but also in the university's response – 'forcible removal of students from residences' (BSM statement, 22 October 2015). The #RUReferenceList protests revealed a shift in the university management's response to student protests, and the absence of protection of student protesters from police. The

---

8   During these protests, the police arrived a few times, but were persuaded by the vice-chancellor to remain on the outskirts of the campus.

university issued an interdict, banned any disruption of lectures, called police, and gave little support to around 40 students who were arrested, and at least as many who were injured in various eruptions of chaos when police shot at students using stun grenades and rubber bullets.

While the 2015 protests were challenging in many ways, the protests that transpired in 2016 ruptured relations on campus in a way that has silenced dissent and increased the divide between management and other groups on campus that supported students' concerns. The BSM's statement above highlights that the organisation is intersectional, condemning 'any form of patriarchy and acts that might put the lives of women in danger'. Hassim argues that 'the task of feminism is to examine the particular ways in which power operates within and between the political, social and economic spheres of specific societies – in effect, this is a political project of transformation' (Hassim, 2004: 3). This fits the context of this chapter. The 2016 #RUReferenceList protests began in April:

> On 11 April 2016, the campaign 'Chapter 2.12' was established to raise awareness on institutional rape culture and to question the University Currently Known As Rhodes' (UCKAR) response to sexual assaults. The aim was to pressure management to amend their policies pertaining to this issue and the procedures which are used to deal with cases of sexual assault. UCKAR management shut down the campaign by removing posters which were aimed at raising awareness about the rape culture in the institution, and further aimed at putting management to task on issues of sexual assault. Management claimed that they removed these posters in order to conduct a private investigation (RUReferenceList statement, 2016).

The protest escalated quickly. Some of the posters reflected statements that were made to survivors who reported their rapes, such as 'you will ruin his life'; 'concentrate on your school work'; 'there is not enough evidence'. Posters had been removed, put back, removed again, and then on Sunday, 17 April, an anonymous post was shared to the Rhodes SRC Facebook page, titled 'Reference List', with nothing but 11 names and 'et al' at the end of it. Within minutes, students began to comment that these were men who were guilty of sexual harassment, assault or rape. The post and comments have since been removed, but hundreds of comments indicated that these were known offenders. Students began to mobilise spontaneously, going from residence to residence, calling for those on the list to come out. Three of these alleged rapists accompanied the protesters to what became known as 'Purple Square', an entrance to the campus outside the Drama Department, where protesters spent the night talking, strategising and planning a shutdown in order to deal with the issue of the rape culture on the campus (Chengeta, 2018, gives a comprehensive description of the protest). As Gqola points out in her difficult and seminal book on rape: 'Ending the rape epidemic in South Africa is going to require that many more people think critically about how seemingly benign behaviour enables rape to thrive.' She explains that 'Rape is not about sex. It is about power' (Gqola, 2015: 144).

The response to this protest was a swift and brutal display of power (see Dorfling's [2015] film, *Disrupt*, which follows this protest; and Chengeta [2018] especially to compare this to the protests of the previous year). As mentioned, at one stage in the October 2015 FeesMustFall protests, some men entered women's residences and forced women out on a cold night to join the protests, some of them without shoes and in their pyjamas. As volatile and terrifying as this situation was, no police were called, and the situation was resolved despite the trauma that many felt at the time. In contrast to this, two of the women student leaders from the Reference List protests have been excluded for life from the university, in part for the alleged 'kidnapping' of the three men who accompanied the protesters to Purple Square on the night of the protests. In the April 2016 protests, the vice-chancellor, the registrar and the police were at Purple Square early on Monday morning, 19 April, to try to break up the protests and remove the barricades. In the messy chaos that ensued at several of the university entrances, stun grenades and rubber bullets were fired, students and staff were hurt, and protesters were arrested. This escalated violence continued over the following weeks; an interdict was taken out against students and Public Order Police (POP) came out of town to patrol the streets of Rhodes in numbers and in full riot gear. Writing on the police violence during the student protest, Duncan observes:

> Sociologists have argued that political violence by protesters is rarely ever adopted overnight or consciously. Rather, in the early stages of the protest cycle, such violence is generally unplanned, small in scale and limited in scope. It often occurs as a spontaneous reaction to an escalation of force by the police or a more general closure of democratic space (Duncan, 2016).

Conclusion

The kinds of physical and emotional violence that became the hallmark of the 2016 protests on the Rhodes campus (including the life-time exclusions for women leaders of the 2016 rape protests) are the subject of further research.

For now, this chapter concludes with two fundamental observations. Firstly, the protests of 2015 presented political awakening of students on a campus that had seemed, for decades, apolitical. During this time, students brought their bodies collectively to what had merely been intellectual ideas and policy frameworks around transformation, in order to re-centre the poor black student in the university's imagination. Although the response was awkward at times, and there were numerous extremely difficult moments, police were kept out. Instead, various groups of students, staff and management worked to resolve differences through demanding and challenging negotiation processes. Looking back, it would seem that the lessons that students were teaching us at the time were about the gap between the *word*, in policies, speeches and lectures around transformation and democracy, and the *substance* and *actions* that failed to live up to them. Because Rhodes is a small campus, it is hard to turn away from these clear messages, and I believe that this could have contributed to a far more vigorous engagement with race, class and gender inequalities and transformations. The 2015 protests and engagements set the tone for a deepened democratic process, which would require the principles of embodiment and re-centring to work. Speaking as one of the lecturers 'positioned as allies to the students', kaCanham observes that 'we believe that the stone throwing and fires would not happen if we threw everything we have at transforming this historic dream to reality. *We need each other for this to happen*' (kaCanham, 2016) (emphasis added). Negotiations between management and protesters throughout the 2015 and 2016 protests taught us about the power of the collective: the way in which the students' voices and concerns could be articulated because they were a collective, however complicated this was; the way the university, made up of different groupings, was forced to sit around a table and consider how to move forward as a collective – these were special moments, difficult but important.

The second observation is that we missed this important opportunity; that the violence that transpired – by police whose presence was sanctioned on campus by management in 2016 protests; and the violence of non-recognition of the bodies that were shot at, arrested, chased, surveilled and excluded in these protests and their aftermath – has broken the spirit of many. Some will argue that Rhodes is transforming; that the comprehensive Sexual Violence Task Team report and its 90 or so recommendations (Chengeta, 2018) devised over months of hard work following the #RUReferenceList# protests, are being implemented slowly; that students are still encouraged to question and to critique; that the university is doing its best to shift rape culture, patriarchy, racial inequalities and curriculum transformation. But others look at the way in which the university responded to legitimate concerns and wonder if there is any redemption, any way back from the horror of what happened on campus during and after the 2016 protests. There are some who believe that people have been silenced from speaking out; that young black staff have even more reason to leave (and have done so); that the student body has reverted to being apolitical, compliant and complicit; that we have failed as an institution to take students seriously when they raised the issues; and that we have failed as an institution to shift, despite transformation imbizos and task teams. We missed important lessons, and I wonder if we can find our way forward from here. What can and must keep going is the embodied, re-centring, collective-thinking scholarship and activism of young Africans that continue to counter a Western, patriarchal, capitalist and individualistic trend. However, as Ndlovu-Gatsheni says, 'What is promising though in the domain of struggles for epistemic freedom is that younger African scholars have not given up the liberatory agenda of rethinking, thinking, and even unthinking some ideas introduced on Africa by colonialism and hegemonic Eurocentric thinking' (Ndlovu-Gatsheni, 2013). This is our inspiration and hope.

References

Alasow, JG (2015a) What about Rhodes University must fall? *Daily Maverick*, 23 March Available at: https://www.dailymaverick.co.za/opinionista/2015-03-23-what-about-rhodes-university-must-fall/#.WyEYS0iFPIV (accessed June 2018).

Alasow, JG (2015b) Policing student politics: is there a right way to protest? *Daily Maverick*, 8 September. Available at: https://www.dailymaverick.co.za/opinionista/2015-09-08-policing-student-politics-is-there-a-right-way-to-protest/#.WyIbW0iFPIX (accessed June 2018).

Badat, S (2015) University turmoil: The beginning of a social movement, *The Journalist*. Available at: http://www.thejournalist.org.za/spotlight/university-turmoil-beginning-of-a-social-movement (accessed June 2018).

BSM Press Statement regarding events of Friday, 28 August. Available at: https://www.facebook.com/lerato.mohale.90/posts/10207487264476759https://www.facebook.com/lerato.mohale.90/posts/10207487264476759 (accessed June 2018).

Centwa, S (2013) Tales of a divided city: Not a place for peasants, *Grocott's Mail*. Available at: http://grocotts.pl-dev.co.za/2014/03/10/tales-of-a-divided-city-not-a-place-for-peasants/

Chengeta, G (2018) #RUReferenceList: The fear of repercussions still lingers, *Mail & Guardian*, 6 July. Available at: https://mg.co.za/article/2018-07-06-00-rureferencelist-the-fear-of-repercussions-still-lingers.

Dennet, B (2015) Rhodes University: A demand for transformation, *Mail & Guardian*, 9 September. Available at: https://mg.co.za/article/2015-09-09-rhodes-university-a-demand-for-transformation#.VfEpEy9jQDg.facebook (accessed June 2018).

Dorfling, M (2015) *Disrupt*. Available at: https://www.youtube.com/watch?v=YZqQdMhitgY (accessed June 2018).

Duncan, J (2016) Why student protests in South Africa have turned violent, *The Conversation*. Available at: https://theconversation.com/why-student-protests-in-south-africa-have-turned-violent-66288 (accessed June 2018).

Erskog, M (2015) Transformation in action, *Daily Dispatch*, 14 April. Available at: https://www.dispatchlive.co.za/news/opinion/2015-04-14-transformation-in-action/ (accessed June 2018).

Grocott's Mail (2015a) Students sleep-in over vac lodging. Available at: http://www.grocotts.co.za/2015/08/27/students-sleep-in-over-vac-lodgings/ (accessed June 2018).

Grocott's Mail (2015b) Students celebrate Fee Victory. Available at: http://www.grocotts.co.za/2015/10/23/students-celebrate-fees-victory/ (accessed June 2018).

Gqola, P (2015) *Rape: A South African nightmare.* Johannesburg: Jacana

Hassim, S (2004) Voices, hierarchies and spaces: Reconfiguring the women's movement in democratic South Africa. A case study for the UKZN project entitled Globalisation, Marginalisation and New Social Movements in Post-Apartheid South Africa.

hooks, b (1994) *Teaching to Transgress. Education as the practice of freedom.* London: Routledge.

Jagarnath, V (2015) Working while black at Rhodes, *Daily Maverick*, 14 April. Available at: https://www.dailymaverick.co.za/opinionista/2015-04-14-working-while-black-at-rhodes/#.WyChxUiFPIX (accessed June 2018).

kaCanham, H (2016) Ceasefire. WordPress blog. Available at: https://hugokacanham.wordpress.com/2016/10/23/cease-fire/ (accessed June 2018).

Mkabela, Q (2005) Using the Afrocentric method in researching indigenous African culture, *The Qualitative Report*, **10**(1): 178–89.

Mkhize, N (2015) Tenacious belief in the ideal of the university, *Business Day*, 5 May. Available at: https://www.businesslive.co.za/bd/opinion/columnists/2015-05-05-tenacious-belief-in-the-ideal-of-the-university/ (accessed June 2018).

Motlafi, N (2015) Why black women in South Africa don't fully embrace the feminist discourse, *The Conversation*. Available at: https://theconversation.com/why-black-women-in-south-africa-dont-fully-embrace-the-feminist-discourse-45116 (accessed June 2018).

Muzenda, M (2018) South Africa: Why has Rhodes University silenced student activism? *This is Africa*, 21 June. Available at: https://thisisafrica.me/rhodes-university-silenced-student-activism/ (accessed June 2018).

Naicker, C (2016) From Marikana to #FeesMustFall: The praxis of popular politics in South Africa, *Urbanisation*, **1**(1): 57.

Ndlovu-Gatsheni, S (2013) The dynamics of epistemological decolonisation in the 21st century: Towards epistemic freedom, *Strategic Review for Southern Africa*, **40**(1): 34.

Ngcobozi, L (2015) RhodesSoWhite: An insight, *The Conmag*, 27 March. Available at: http://www.theconmag.co.za/2015/03/27/rhodessowhite-an-insight/ (accessed June 2018).

Northedge, A (2003) Rethinking teaching in the context of diversity, *Teaching in Higher Education*, **8**(1): 17–32.

#RUConfessions16352. Available at: https://www.facebook.com/rhodesuniconfessions/posts/1655719181143321 (accessed June 2018).

VC circular (2015) March. Available at: https://www.facebook.com/groups/1551730468423783/permalink/1555948164668680/ (accessed June 2018).

Chapter 9
South Africa's student movement: A UCT perspective

Sandile Ndelu

Introduction

The University of Cape Town (UCT) is often perceived as having a dual identity. On the one hand, it is a university whose leading research output and cutting-edge facilities place it in the position to create knowledge and to train a competent (elite) workforce for the top tier of the South African economy. Thus, it is not rare to come across the rhetoric that UCT admits and employs only top-performing students and leading academics, respectively, and that its graduates are 'highly sought after' (Moore, 2017). On the other hand, it is a university that often emphasises its supposed progressive and transformative identity. It often notes its history of opposing injustice by referencing that it began admitting women and black students in the 1880s and 1920s, respectively. Moreover, the enrolment of the latter population group increased significantly in the 1980s and 1990s, 'when the institution, reading and welcoming the signs of change in the country, committed itself to a deliberate and planned process of internal transformation' (UCT, n.d.).

Globally, the university has earned its prestige through its consistent ranking as the best on the African continent.[1] The university takes these international university rankings seriously. This status highlights two key issues. First, it allows the university to continue marketing itself as being globally competitive: by notionally distancing itself from the African universities that generally perform poorly in these rankings and by benchmarking itself against Anglo-Saxon universities and intellectual traditions (Dlamini, 2016). This has earned

---

1 See, for example: 2019 *Times Higher Education* (THE) World University Rankings. Available at: https://www.news.uct.ac.za/article/-2018-09-27-uct-leapfrogs-up-through-world-rankings; 2019 *Times Higher Education* (THE) Emerging Economies University Rankings. Available at: https://www.news.uct.ac.za/article/-2019-01-16-uct-remains-top-university-in-africa; *Quacquarelli Symonds (QS) World University Rankings*. Available at: https://www.news.uct.ac.za/article/-2018-06-07-uct-in-the-qs-top-200 https://www.news.uct.ac.za/article/-2018-05-28-the-top-university-in-africa; *Financial Times* Executive Education Customised Rankings 2018. Available at: https://www.news.uct.ac.za/article/-2018-05-16-gsb-in-the-financial-times-top-90; *QS World University Rankings by Subject*. Available at: https://www.news.uct.ac.za/article/-2018-03-02-uct-performs-in-2018-subject-rankings (accessed September 2018).

UCT the status of 'gateway to Africa', primarily for the West and Global North. Second, the rankings create an imperative for the university to focus its resources on looking outwards to fit into the global, which ought to be read as white, Western and Eurocentric, paradigm, rather than looking inwards in order to build its relevance within the local, which is a post-colonial, post-apartheid settler colony (Dlamini, 2016; see also Bawa, Chapter 4, and Higgs, Chapter 12, in this volume).

What is often left unarticulated in UCT's local and global branding is that the institution remains, much like its roots as the South African College (a school where young white men were prepared to take their places as elites in South Africa's fast-expanding industrial economies), a space that reproduces South Africa's racial and class inequality problem by entrenching the technocratic elite through shoring up what Bourdieu would describe as 'academic capital' (Castells, 2001: 207; Naidoo, 2004: 458). As a result, UCT is a place where scores of international students and visiting academics come to access and consume Africa under the guise of 'internationalisation' and where local students come to be assimilated into Western standards of success, or what UCT Cameroonian Professor of Social Anthropology Francis Nyamnjoh (2016) terms 'whitening up'. The university does this by essentially being a Western university that just happens to be located on the African continent. Nyamnjoh argues that this process of whitening up is most illustrated by the curricula offered by the university. He asserts that 'the resilience of colonial education in Africa sacrifices local relevance for international recognition' (Nyamnjoh, 2016: 67). Nyamnjoh (2016: 70) continues by stating:

Education in Africa has been and mostly remains a journey fuelled by an exogenously induced and internalized sense of inadequacy in Africans, and one endowed with the mission of devaluation or annihilation of African creativity, agency and value systems.

Thus, the demand for a decolonised curriculum at UCT ought to be located within black students pushing back against the university as a place where almost half of its student population comes to whiten up and the enduring feelings of marginalisation and epistemic violence among those who, for various reasons, cannot or refuse to whiten up. This pushback directly led to the first iteration of the Fallist student movement, which emerged at UCT as the #RhodesMustFall (#RMF) campaign in 2015. #RMF's initial concern was lobbying for the indefinite removal of a bronze statue of colonial-era British businessman and politician, Cecil John Rhodes, from the university's main campus. In addition to the physical removal of the Rhodes statue, #RMF put forward a list of long-term demands as a means of purging Rhodes and his contemporaries' colonial legacies from the university (#RMF, 2015). This list of demands included the call for the decolonisation of the university's curricula. Through periodic interventions since 2015, #RMF and its associates have raised questions and forced the university community along a path of reassessing and reconstructing what the university teaches, who teaches it and how it is taught. This chapter offers a critical reflection on the journey that the UCT community has travelled towards responding to the #RMF demand for decolonised curricula. The chapter begins by providing an exposition of the #RMF vision for decolonised university curricula by making specific reference to the movement's archive of speeches, interviews, advocacy materials and publications. This will be followed by a critical reflection on some of the programmes, interventions and initiatives that are emerging at UCT and to what extent they advance the #RMF vision for a decolonised curriculum.

'Next, the invisible statue': #RhodesMustFall and the demand for a decolonised curriculum

With the Rhodes statue having been removed from the university on 9 April 2015, #RMF directed its focus towards 'the invisible statutes' – its medium to long-term demands. One such demand was the call for 'free, decolonised education'. This section attempts to explain and organise the movement's vision of a decolonised curriculum, as codified in the movement's mission statement published on 25 March 2015. Although #RMF's demands for the decolonisation of the curriculum are listed as separate and distinct in the movement's mission statement, in practice they have been much more interwoven and fluid. A decolonised curriculum requires relevant and rigorously conducted research. This research in turn requires people who have a combination of the skills and lived experiences to conduct and disseminate it through the practice of teaching. In addition, the pursuit of the #RMF demands for decolonised curricula has not been linear – some of the demands were rigorously pursued by the movement as a collective, others were pursued by individuals within the collective. Some of the demands have changed or developed over time, while others have been wholly abandoned by the movement; some demands have been sharpened, while others have been diluted (Ndelu, 2017).

Content, languages and methodologies

From its inception, #RMF insisted on the use of 'decolonisation' rather than 'transformation' (which was oft preferred by the university and its administrators) when referring to the movement's demands. #RMF (2015) explained that:

> we have begun to understand the need for a new language that challenges the pacifying logic of liberalism. This logic presents itself to us in these ideas of 'reform' and 'transformation', which are legitimised by the Constitution – a document which violently preserves the status quo. Transformation is the maintenance and perpetuation of oppression, hidden within meaningless surface-level change. We have recognised that what is needed instead is the radical decolonisation of this institution, which is necessarily linked to the black condition, both nationally and internationally. Our existence as black people is defined by a violent system of power. The University's processes and language naturalise that colonial system. Therefore, if we wish to get rid of that system of power, we have to destroy the processes altogether. Decolonisation is this very destruction.

Nadira Omarjee (2018: 83), a research associate at UCT's Centre for African Studies, argues that #RMF's insistence on a decolonised rather than transformed curriculum stems from the desire to determine a future built on self-determination and self-reliance, while being in a position to remember the past and engage with the present. Prolific decolonial scholar Ngũgĩ wa Thiong'o (1986) rationalises this by explaining that it is only 'after we have examined ourselves, [that we are able to] radiate outwards and discover peoples and worlds around us. With Africa at the centre of things, not existing as an appendix or a satellite of other countries and literatures, things must be seen from the African perspective'. #RMF (2015) frames these principles clearly in their demands for a decolonised curriculum. In their view, the university ought to

> implement a curriculum which critically centres Africa and the subaltern. By this we mean treating African discourses as the point of departure – through addressing not only content but languages and methodologies of education and learning and only examining Western traditions in so far as they are relevant to our own experience.

The implementation of decolonised curricula, as understood by #RMF, varies from discipline to discipline. Yanisha Teelock-Lallah, a Mauritian graduate of the French section of UCT's School of Languages and Literatures, estimates that decolonisation of the curriculum in her discipline would require a deliberate elevation of literature authored by black women authors. Teelock-Lallah (Interview, 2016) asserts that:

> We need to stop using white literature. In French it's called negritude – it comes from an oppressed position. We need black female authors – we need to be studying them instead of white female authors all the time. In French arts and culture, we need more and need to encourage more black females to be writing on black cultures and stop representing Western cultures as being the mainstream ones.

Dr Lauren Paremoer, who at the time was a senior lecturer in the UCT Department of Political Science, takes Teelock-Lallah's understanding of a decolonised curriculum further by noting that a decolonised curriculum in political science is a curriculum that destabilises and critically deconstructs the foundational assumptions, logics and inheritances of the canon. Paremoer (Interview, 2016) further notes:

> I have always tried to design a curriculum that is informed by black feminist principles. What I mean by that is a curriculum that makes visible the invisible intersecting axes of discrimination and oppression that people face, particularly black women. A curriculum that takes seriously the principle that the personal is political – things that we experience as private are actually integral to building a particular kind of public life that excludes certain claims and certain types of people to being seen as equal... I have [also] tried always to include critiques of conventional political sciences. By 'conventional political sciences' I mean North American and even more specifically US political science as it is the canon that dominates. Particularly to question the assumptions that that canon makes about which experiences are normal, typical and generalizable – which are usually the experiences of modernity, so called Western societies, and the pathologisation of so-called third world or other societies that goes with that.

Moreover, Paremoer also introduces continuous self-critique and reflection as a key element of a decolonised curriculum. She describes decolonising the curriculum as a labour that is never complete, that is always continuing and that requires sustained effort and ingenuity in order to be sustained. She reflects (Interview, 2016):

I have mostly focused on African-American feminist critiques and not so much coming out of South Asia and Latin America. I would like to focus much more on Latin American and the feminist critiques of capitalism. The problem is the language. And I like those critiques because I also think it's also connected to a different way of understanding the world. To a different ontology, where to be alive is not just to be a person but to be imbedded in a world of living things, which includes nature, and which includes acknowledging that people have spiritual lives. And that's an equal way of seeing the world. In terms of African scholarship: scholarship on conviviality, openness. These are modes of engagement and social relations that don't assume that one group of people will know everything. There is a kind of incompleteness that we all have and that's necessary if we want to be people that truly want to understand the world from someone else's perspective.

Although talking from different perspectives, as a student and as a teacher, both Teelock-Lallah and Paremoer reveal that the practice of centring those voices, stories, experiences and theories – which have been marginalised by the epistemic hegemony of the Global North – is critical to decolonising the curriculum.

Pedagogy

There is increasingly growing commercial concern in today's university, including UCT. Its operations are premised on what Mbembe (2015) terms the 'quantifiable subject', where quantity supersedes quality and where 'excellence itself has been reduced to statistical accountancy', particularly when it comes to teaching. University administrators are primarily concerned with the number of students that are accepted, the number of students that are taught, and the number of students that have progressed from one level to the next. UCT Professor of Media Studies Adam Haupt similarly bemoans how 'a lot of us are so obsessed with producing the next monograph, the next international journal. That's going to get us through probation, keep us in our jobs, we must always publish' (Interview, 2016). Indeed, numbers are an important indicator of the success of a university's role as both a creator and disseminator of knowledge. However, quantitative indicators must be triangulated with other equally important indicators, such as quality and social impact.

In order to counter the university's preoccupation with quantity at the expense of quality, #RMF demanded the elevation of a Freirean pedagogy – that is, a teaching culture that destabilises the power disparity between the educator and learner, as well as placing equal value on formal and informal curricula, which may or may not be shared within the classroom (Omarjee, 2018). Thuli Gamedze, a master's student at the Michaelis School of Fine Art who was intimately involved in #RMF and describes it as an 'intense political education', suggests that part of decolonising the curriculum for her would require destabilising the arrogance of the academe, assuming that it is the ultimate and most authoritative repository of knowledge and enlightenment (Interview, 2016). To this end, her 'Master's project in a way tries to look at the occupation at Bremner and tries to take pieces of that, that were useful to think about how we can form spaces outside of university for learning more creatively, more relevant curriculum but also spaces that are not so violent' (Gamedze interview, 2016).

Inside the classroom, the movement demanded that the university 'improve academic support programmes' (#RMF 2015). A key frontier in this regard is the question of language. Luckett (2016) explores the angst that is often experienced by black students entering a historically white university like UCT, where English is the only language of instruction. She explains that there is often a mismatch between the university's continuously steadfast work of equitably admitting a more diverse cohort of black students and the same university investing little to nothing in linguistically and culturally accommodating these large numbers of socio-economically, geopolitically and culturally diverse black students that they are admitting (Luckett, 2016: 421). Moreover, Haupt agrees with Ngũgĩ wa Thiong'o, paraphrased in Mbembe (2015), that 'the African university of tomorrow will be multilingual'. Furthermore, Haupt (Interview, 2016) questions:

> How do you develop critical and academic literacy without stigmatising a people along racial lines? Whether they teach physics or media, how does critical literacy affect what they teach and how they teach? The historical approach has been assimilation. To say: 'oh, so you speak 5 languages, but do you speak English well. We must pull you from where you are into the system' – assimilation. And it's easier to do that than to advance multilingualism as an asset rather than a deficit.

Furthermore, Haupt (Interview, 2016) notes that in addition to the undervaluing of multilingualism among students, multilingualism among educators is underutilised:

> As educators, a lot of us are not multilingual. And if we are, we suppress it. We do not utilise it as an asset in the classroom because in order to do

that (a) a lot of people would have to learn more languages than just the two that they know and (b) they would have to upskill, 'how do I say this in my mother tongue' is quite difficult. We need to fundamentally rethink what we do as educators.

But the deepening of the public discourse on multilingualism within South African universities has been stunted by the debate around the continued use of Afrikaans as a language of instruction at historically Afrikaans universities. This debate has been nestled between the acknowledged benefits of having students being taught in their home language, on the one hand, and the constitutional imperatives to reverse apartheid-era patterns of racial discrimination. This has taken South Africa along the trajectory of what Haupt (Interview, 2016) describes as 'assimilation' by making English the universal language of university instruction, rather than along a trajectory of asking what it would take to develop all South Africa's official languages into languages of instruction and, most importantly, what it would take for all South African universities to embrace multilingualism within their pedagogical practices. For example, in the recent South African Constitutional Court case of *Afriforum and Another v University of the Free State*, Chief Justice Mogoeng Mogoeng, noted:

> Effective access to the right to be instructed in an official language of choice must be given effect to, but without undermining equitable access, preserving exclusivity or perpetuating racial supremacy. It would be unreasonable to wittingly or inadvertently allow some of our people to have unimpeded access to education and success at the expense of others as a direct consequence of a blind pursuit of the enjoyment of the right to education in a language of choice. This, in circumstances where all could properly be educated in one common language.

In this sense, English as a language of instruction is viewed not only as a unifier within universities, which are becoming increasingly more diverse, but also as a gateway to global competitiveness, both for the university and the student. Mogoeng notes that at the University of the Free State, 'many Afrikaner students prefer English which they see as a tool of communication that would enhance their prospects of being global players'. This is echoed by Teferra and Altbach (2004: 46) who assert that:

> In the age of the Internet, globalization, and expanding knowledge systems, which are all driven by a few Western languages, no country can afford to remain shielded in a cocoon of isolation brought about

by language limitations. Such isolation would prove both disastrous and, likely, impossible to achieve.

However, these arguments are defeatist in that they overemphasise the 'impracticability' of achieving multilingualism within the university, and underestimate the opportunities that exist for the pursuit of a deliberate policy of multilingualism within universities. The project may be time- and resource-intensive, but it is by no mean impractical nor impossible. The academic development of Afrikaans, albeit in the furtherance of a white supremacist and Afrikaner nationalist ideal, provides important lessons in this regard.

Research

The #RhodesMustFall movement placed the need for decolonised curricula side by side with a decolonised research agenda. The reason for this is that if the curricula were to be decolonised, the production of the knowledge from which it is sampled would have to be decolonised as well (Luckett, 2016: 424). Haupt (Interview, 2016) explains that 'a lot of my research speaks to what is happening and has always featured prominently in the media curriculum'. This is largely due to the nature of his discipline:

> In media studies, a big part of what we are about is political economy, interrelational politics, engagement with current affairs. We tune in [to the socio-politics of the day]. Ironically, before the shutdown, I was about to teach a block for Media, Power and Culture starting with race as a social construction and relating that to intersectionality and making that speak to media and cultural studies.

Unfortunately, much of this still remains on the margins of the mainstream curricula. Thus, when Haupt asserts that his discipline, Media and Cultural Studies, 'tunes in' it becomes necessary to probe deeper into where the media studies discipline opts to fixate its gaze; through whose eyes and to what end. Importantly, it ought to ask the more interesting question of how the discipline and its technocratic armoury *ought* to 'tune in' in order to move the subaltern into the centre. Thus, the student activists demanded that the university 'introduce a curriculum and research scholarship linked to social justice and the experiences of black people' (#RMF, 2015). Through this, they display an understanding of the intimate exchange between what is taught inside lecture theatres and what is researched outside them.

Importantly, #RMF also understood that the socio-political context within which academic research is conducted is to be critically engaged if the university's curricula and research agenda are to be Afrocentric. This would require problematising curricula that are intended to meet the needs of colonialism and apartheid. It would require problematising the role that political and economic elites – both of whom have been in the pockets of industries that are largely controlled by white men located in the Global North – play in directing universities' research agendas. It is not enough to claim that academic freedom allows academics to pursue their academic interest when the lack of funds to undertake such research makes it structurally difficult to do so. The influence of big capital can be seen in the number of industry-sponsored research chairs and grants being directed towards securing the interests of the political and economic elites. When big capital is involved, the principle of academic freedom is the first casualty. Paremoer agrees and notes that a university being conducted as a for-profit business enterprise, which produces technocrats for industry, distorts its role of producing knowledge for the public good. Paremoer (Interview, 2016) asserts that:

> The fact that [UCT] is historically an institution that produces elites and that in the post-apartheid era it was continuing this function by creating more black elites. The institution upholds capitalism but is also rooted in and has a deep history of the minerals and resources complex. This is continued through sponsoring of centres and buildings at universities [by large corporates].

This has been in sync with the global trend away from the 'social knowledge university' and towards the 'market university', which, as Cooper (1997) notes, is 'now under much more pressure by both their governments and the business community to supply products (graduates and research) to enhance international competitiveness of the national economy'.[2]

The result has been that 'less lucrative' development-based disciplines and their research agendas are neglected, while disciplines that stand to benefit big corporates, such as science, technology, engineering and mathematics (STEM), are well resourced and maintained. At UCT, the Centre for African Studies, the African Gender Institute and the Department of Linguistics remain some of the smallest disciplines within the Humanities Faculty, to the extent that they have been truncated into a single department.[3] Prior to 2017 and the advocacy

---

2   Dave Cooper presented data and posed interesting questions about the future of research at UCT in the context of the commodification of the functions of the university as far back as the late 1990s.

3   Mahmood Mamdani, Amina Mama and Neville Alexander played critical roles in

of #RMF, African Studies did not offer any course at the undergraduate level, continuing to deprive students of access to the discipline. Instead of being disciplines that are central to the curriculum, African Studies, Gender Studies and Linguistics have been set aside as specialist and fringe disciplines. It is against this backdrop of the ghettoisation of disciplines which ought to be the bedrock of a decolonised curriculum that #RMF (2015) also demanded that the university 'provides financial and research support to black academics and staff' and that it 're-evaluates the standards by which research areas are decided – from areas that are lucrative and centre whiteness, to areas that are relevant to the lives of black people, locally and on the continent'.

Academics

The University of Cape Town is faced with an anomaly: whereas the majority of the student body is black and female, the majority of the teaching staff is white and male. But this anomaly is no coincidence. The university seems to have a problem with retaining black faculty and promoting them. Nyamnjoh (2016), citing UCT Law Professor Evance Kalula, writes:

> Kalula notes that newly recruited promising women and black staff are often 'thrown into the deep end, to sink or swim'. In the Law Faculty where he taught from 1992–2012, the result is that there has been very little effective transformation for twenty years. Black members of staff who have left in frustration have often cited among their reasons for leaving 'a non-supportive environment which at best ignored, undervalued or marginalised them, and in some respects was hostile'.

This is not, however, peculiar to the Law Faculty. Nyamnjoh (2016) further notes that the issue of black academics is a problem that is acute across all faculties and all disciplines, negatively affecting black students across the university. Thus, at the centre of the demand for decolonised curricula has been the vexed issue of black academics. #RMF (2015) demanded that the university 'radically change the representation of black lecturers across faculties'. This call has been alongside the ongoing advocacy of the UCT Black Academic Caucus (BAC), which has sustained momentum on the question of academic appointments and promotions. This has been coloured by #RMF's (2015) demands that the university: (1) 'revise the limitations on access to senior positions for black

---

establishing and developing the Centre for African Studies, the African Gender Institute and the discipline of social linguistics, respectively, at UCT. Although none of them remains at UCT, their legacies continue to be instructive for the aforementioned disciplines within the university.

academics. This includes interrogating the notion of "academic excellence" which is used to limit black academics' and students' progression within the university'; and (2) 'increase the representation of black academics on the currently predominantly white, male decision-making bodies which perpetuate institutional racism'. As Cornell and Kessi (2017) argue, being thin on black faculty or having black faculty that is disillusioned and unmotivated has an adverse effect on the educational outcomes for both black and white students. The result is that black students' sense of exclusion and alienation is amplified, while white students are deprived of the richness of a diverse teaching staff (Cornell and Kessi, 2017: 1887).

Programmes, projects and interventions for curriculum change

The emergence of the Fallist student movement and its demands inspired an almost knee-jerk reaction from the university's management. Behind these prominent responses of denials, negotiations and the criminalisation of protesters, university communities, including management, faculty and students, also began formulating co-ordinated interventions as a direct response to the #RhodesMustFall demands for decolonised curricula. These have emerged from the highest level of university administration to the most grassroots level of student collaborations. At the institutional level, the centre of UCT's attempts to begin the process of decolonising its curriculum has been the Curriculum Change Working Group (CCWG). The group, co-chaired by UCT professors Elewani Ramugondo (Occupational Therapy) and Harry Garuba (African Studies), was a multi-sectoral group of experts commissioned by the former vice-chancellor, Max Price, in January 2016. The CCWG was mandated to engage with faculties, departments, academics and students in order to 'initiate deep curriculum conversations in relation to the challenges of transformation, as well as opportunities and debates that the call for decolonisation brought to the University' (CCWG, 2018: 8). The objective was to ensure that the entire university was working towards decolonising the curriculum and pedagogies together rather than in 'patchy' silos (CCWG, 2018: 8). To assist the university on this journey, the CCWG solicited the assistance of experts in the field of decoloniality, among them prolific scholars such as Ngũgĩ wa Thiong'o, Nelson Maldonado-Torres and Gayatri Spivak. The biggest deliverable of the CCWG (2018) is the Curriculum Change Framework, which gives a broad guideline to the direction that ought to be taken by the university community as a whole in order to substantively meet the demands of the student movement for a decolonised curriculum. However, this framework is still subject to the approval of the university's statutory bodies, including the senate, which is overwhelmingly dominated by UCT's majority-white, male professoriate.

The framework also does not deal with: (1) whether it would be binding on all faculties, departments and academics; (2) how the university plans on monitoring and enforcing compliance; and (3) how a binding framework might impact on the principle of academic freedom, which the university so jealously guards. Already, there are signs of cleavages within the university. Ramugondo was not appointed to the position of Deputy Vice-Chancellor for Teaching and Learning – a decision which she has approached the courts to review. Her argument is that she was 'deemed unappointable', despite being the most qualified, in terms of both academic credentials and experience, of the shortlisted candidates. Her case, supported by the BAC, echoes the #RMF demand that black academics and black students ought to be at the forefront of reimagining what an African university with decolonised curricula ought to look and feel like. Moreover, it seems that the framework has not received general legitimacy within the university academic community, with some faculty members making public pronouncements against it.[4]

Inside the lecture theatre, faculty members have also begun doing the hard work of decolonising what is taught and how they teach it. Key to this has been an emphasis on collaboration – horizontally between faculty and faculty and vertically between faculty and student. An example of the former is the establishment of a multidisciplinary major in African Studies in 2017, thanks to the tireless lobbying of Mamdani's successor, Lungisile Ntsebeza (2015). Located within the Centre for African Studies, the major offers courses for all levels of the general undergraduate humanities degree, covering topics such as African Political Thought, Representations of Africa, and Language, Power and Freedom. Some of the courses, such as Africa: Culture, Identity and Globalisation, are targeted specifically at students registered in other faculties, including Engineering and the Built Environment and Health Sciences. Examples of the latter include the establishment of research institutes such as the Hub for Decolonial Feminist Psychologies in Africa, where senior students and academics co-create and pedagogically deliver what they have conceptualised to be a decolonised curriculum (Anon, 2018). Additionally, others have opted

---

4   For example, note the unfavourable comments on the Curriculum Change Framework by the following academics: Philosophy Professor Bernhard Weiss (http://www.news.uct.ac.za/downloads/reports/ccwg/2019-01-11_CCF_Comment_BernhardWeiss.pdf); Philosophy lecturer, Dr George Hull (http://www.news.uct.ac.za/downloads/reports/ccwg/2018-12-11_CCF_Comment_GeorgeHull.pdf); Emeritus Professor of Mathematics George Ellis (http://www.news.uct.ac.za/downloads/reports/ccwg/2018-10-10_CCF_Comment_EProfGeorgeEllis.pdf); and Professor Rebekka Sandmeier of the South African College of Music (http://www.news.uct.ac.za/images/userfiles/downloads/media/2018-07-31_CurriculumChangeFramework_SACM.pdf), among others.

to collaborate with their students by inviting them to be an active part of creating the curriculum for a particular course. However, this only works if the students are treated as equals in the classroom space, if information goes back and forth and if the invitation is genuine and not simply a means of laying claim to being responsive to the Fallist discourse, without being completely open to what decolonising an academic discipline means in practical terms. Simply writing an essay may not necessarily be enough to transform the curriculum and pedagogy, as has been the case in a few courses, including the Commercial Transactions Law course where students were given the option to 'write an essay titled "The Decolonisation of the South African Law of Sale"' in 2017, even though nothing in the coursework for that year vaguely engaged the topic. This type of co-option of the language of decolonisation to mask a deep lack of transformational imagination can be seen as a move to further entrench a neoliberal curriculum agenda.

While some faculty members can be seen to be co-opting the language of decolonisation, others have faced alienation and victimisation for pursuing the teaching of what they perceive as a decolonised curriculum. This is particularly the case for those academics who have adopted disorientation as a strategy for surfacing the coloniality of their various disciplines with the objective of inspiring a process of decolonisation. One example is that of Lwazi Lushaba, who at the time was still serving probation as a lecturer in the Political Studies Department when he was served with a written warning by the Head of Department, Professor Anthony Butler, for inviting Fallist student leaders into his classroom to teach a section of the coursework. The HoD was moved to action by having received complaints from students and parents who felt that their class had been 'disrupted' and that Lushaba had involved himself in 'political mobilisation rather than lectur[ing]'. Lushaba's (2016) response not only puts on record his version, but also provides a lesson on how theory can be brought to life through first-person accounts of voices that are otherwise on the margins of the academe:

[It was the] lecture of the 15th August 2016, which supposedly triggered the HoD's letter to me. In the week prior to the 15th I had diligently taken students through the compound thematic of colonialism, coloniality and decolonisation. Later in the week of the 15th I was to take students through Political Culture and Political Socialisation. I had reasoned, in my black mind, that one of the defining features of South Africa's political culture is the culture of protest. So, in order to breathe life to these themes, viz. culture of political protest and decolonisation, I decided to invite #RMF activists to class. They enlightened us through political songs of protest and in turn gave political speeches on how #RMF began, on what decolonising the university means to/for them, mapped for us how the protest last year unfolded, told us of their experience of state violence, criminalisation and suspension by the university. These were not secondary accounts from a lecturer who has never been part of the historic student protest at UCT. Rather they came from key #RMF dramatis personae. I found them revealing – of course I also encountered new struggle songs, which revealed a complex that was at once of political meaning-making as well as making of a collective black political subject of emancipation. The activists were nothing but walking archives of the struggle to both Africanise and decolonise knowledge in a supposedly South African university in 2015. Their speeches made vivid their genuine love for themselves, for black people and for the country. History at an appropriate moment shall thank them most profoundly for their selflessness and sacred love for the land.

Some students have opted to seek answers to the question of how to decolonise the university's curriculum from outside the confines of the university and its lecture theatres. These interventions have been aimed to destabilise how knowledge is created and disseminated. One such intervention was Umhlangano – which emerged from the shutdown of the university's Hiddingh Campus which houses the departments of Fine Art and Drama – during the 2016 iteration of the Fallist student movement. Gamedze (Interview, 2016) asserts that Umhlangano was an exploration of protest as a form of knowledge and meaning-making. Gamedze (Interview, 2016) explains the motivation behind Umhlangano thus:

> For me, what the general frustration felt like at our campus was that UCT and Hiddingh campus had somehow depoliticised art practice and had liberalised it into something that feeds into a specific white market. And kind of just denies what's happening in the country. For me largely it was around how do we continue the trajectory of politicised art practice in South Africa and how do we break out of this very white mode of art practice that is directly informed by capitalism and which uses the experience of the other (being someone who is not a white cishet able-bodied man) only for capitalist gains ... so I think that Umhlangano was trying to address that and the violence that that inflicts on bodies on the campus. Thus, the main aim was not a shutdown – the campus was shut down but it was more about appropriating the campus.

The student and staff members that were involved in Umhlangano used their various artistic crafts to create meaning and to open up discursive space in ways that they had not experienced within their lecture theatres. Their 'artivism' also involved publics that are not ordinarily part of the university community. Umhlangano's barricades were art pieces within themselves, giving the public a chance to engage with what was happening within that university campus without necessarily entering it.

Conclusion

The conversation on a decolonised curriculum at UCT is an ongoing one that has recently been reinvigorated by the #RhodesMustFall movement. This chapter has examined the #RhodesMustFall movement's bundle of demands, punctuated with the musings of people within the movement, as well as people looking into the movement. Although the labour of decolonising the curriculum at UCT is by no means near completion, the years succeeding the emergence of the movement have inspired engagement and action, both within and outside the university's lecture theatres. However, much remains to be done to translate the many ideas on how to decolonise the curriculum into tangible actions yielding concrete results. UCT's journey presents at least two dangers that ought to be guarded against. First, there is the danger of the discourse of decolonisation and its radical potential being hollowed out by neoliberal forces co-opting it for their narrow objectives. Second, there is the danger of complacency as university office administrators and student activists, who are central to keeping the issue firmly on the table, move out of the university or grow disillusioned with the perceived slowness of the process. Finally, it is crucial that while consultation, collaboration and integration are deepened in order to achieve meaningful curriculum transformation in South Africa, the gaze remains firmly affixed on the university and the project of reimagining its ownership, inner workings and role within civil society. As Morrison (2001: 278) cautions:

> If the university does not take seriously and rigorously its role as guardian of wider civic freedoms, as interrogator of more complex ethical problems, as servant and preserver of deeper democratic practices, then some other regime or ménage of regimes will do it for us, in spite of us, and without us.

References

Anon (2018) UCT launches Hub for Decolonial Feminist Psychologies in Africa, *UCT News*. Available at: http://www.humanities.uct.ac.za/news/uct-launches-hub-decolonial-feminist-psychologies-africa (accessed September 2018).

Castells, M (2001) Universities as dynamic systems of contradictory functions, in J Muller, N Cloete and S Badat (eds) *Challenges of Globalisation: South African debates with Manuel Castells*. Cape Town: Maskew Miller Longman.

Curriculum Change Working Group (CCWG) (2018) Curriculum Change Framework. Available at: https://www.news.uct.ac.za/images/userfiles/downloads/media/UCT-Curriculum-Change-Framework.pdf (accessed September 2019).

Cooper, D (1997) Introduction: Comments on the 'market' and/or 'development' university with respect to UCT discussions on 'changing research cultures', *Social Dynamics*, **23**(1): 23–41.

Cornell, J and Kessi, S (2017) Black students' experiences of transformation at a previously 'white only' South Africa university: A photovoice study, *Ethnic and Racial Studies*, **40**(11): 1882–99.

Dlamini, R (2016) The global ranking tournament: A dialectic analysis of higher education in South Africa, *South African Journal of Higher Education*, **30**(2): 53–72.

Luckett, K (2016) Curriculum contestations in a post-colonial context: A view from the South, *Teaching in Higher Education*, **21**(4): 415–28.

Lushaba, L (2016) An open letter to Professor Anthony Butler: HOD Politics Department, *Black Opinion*, 1 September. Available at: https://blackopinion.co.za/2016/09/01/whose-skin-colour-evidence-moral-depravity-cultural-decrepitly-sexual-permissiveness-whose-brown-bodies-modern-rational-knowledge-inscri/ (accessed October 2018)

Mbembe, A (2015) Decolonizing knowledge and the question of the archive, *Aula magistral proferida*. Available at: https://wiser.wits.ac.za/system/files/Achille%20Mbembe%20-%20Decolonizing%20Knowledge%20and%20the%20Question%20of%20the%20Archive.pdf (accessed September 2019).

Moore, K (2017) UCT graduates a cut above the rest, *UCT News*, 21 June. Available at: https://www.news.uct.ac.za/article/-2017-06-21-uct-graduates-a-cut-above-the-rest (accessed August 2018).

Morrison, T (2001) How can values be taught in this university, *Michigan Quarterly Review* **XL**(2): 278. Available at: http://hdl.handle.net/2027/spo.act2080.0040.201 (accessed September 2019).

Naidoo, R (2004) Fields and institutional strategy: Bourdieu on the relationship between higher education, inequality and society, *British Journal of Sociology of Education*, **25**(4): 457–71.

Ndelu, S (2017) 'Liberation is a Falsehood': Fallism at the University of Cape Town, in M Langa (ed.) *An Analysis of the #FeesMustFall Movement at South African Universities*. Johannesburg: Centre for the Study of Violence and Reconciliation.

Ngũgĩ wa Thiong'o (1986) *Decolonising the Mind: The politics of language in African literature*. London: Heinemann Educational.

Ntsebeza, L (2015) A vision for a three-year undergrad degree in African Studies, *The Monday Paper*, 5 January. Available at: https://www.news.uct.ac.za/publications/mondaymonthly/archive/-edition/2015-05-25-edition-04/-article/2015-01-05-a-vision-for-a-three-year-undergrad-degree-in-african-studies (accessed July 2018).

Nyamnjoh, FB (2016) *#RhodesMustFall: #Nibbling at resilient colonialism in South Africa*. Bamenda: Langa Research and Publishing Common Initiative Group.

Omarjee, N (2018) *Reimagining the Dream. Decolonising academia by putting the last first*. Leiden: African Studies Centre, Leiden University.

#RhodesMustFall (2015a) UCT RhodesMustFall: Mission Statement, 25 March 2015.

Available at: https://jwtc.org.za/resources/docs/salon-volume-9/RMF_Combined.pdf (accessed October 2019).

#RhodesMustFall (2015b) The RhodesMustFall statement read out at today's mass meeting and before the removal of the statue, 9 April 2015 (online document).

Teferra, D and Altbach, PG (2004) African higher education: Challenges for the 21st century, *Higher Education*, **47**(1): 21–50.

University of Cape Town (n.d.) History introduction. Available at: uct.ac.za (accessed September 2019).

Interviews

Interview with Adam Haupt, Professor of Media Studies, 2016, Cape Town.

Interview with Lauren Paremoer, Senior Lecturer in Political Studies, 2016, Cape Town.

Interview with Thuli Gamedze, Master's of Philosophy in Art History student, 2016, Cape Town.

Interview with Yanisha Teelock-Lallah, Graduate student of French Language and Literatures, 2016, Cape Town.

Section IV: Transforming South Africa's Humanities Curriculum

Chapter 10

The aporias of 'decolonisation' in the South African academy

Joel Modiri

Introduction

The terms 'decolonisation', 'decolonising' and their Latin American cousin, 'decoloniality', now travel with unprecedented ubiquity and promiscuity throughout higher education and public discourse. As a successor and rival to the worn projects of 'transformation' and to a lesser extent 'Africanisation', 'decolonisation' has risen to prominence as the supervening motif and buzzword employed by South African academics and universities struggling to respond to the accumulated contradictions of South Africa's colonial and apartheid history, thrown into sharper relief by the world-historical student protests of 2015–17. A cursory review of recent books, edited collections, journal articles, lecture series, summer schools and conference programmes in the South African academe leaves one hard pressed not to find academics engaged in the project of 'decolonising' this or that discipline and concept, or positing a 'decolonial' critique or reading of some text or phenomenon. This excessive proliferation of 'decolonisation' as a trendy noun and verb in the academic and institutional life of the South African university raises inescapable questions about its integrity and value as an intellectual method, scholarly mode of inquiry, political practice and emancipatory ideal. Indeed, the almost ritualistic invocation of the notion of decolonisation situates it nervously between a critical zeitgeist, which discloses productive, radical and disruptive directions for knowledge production, and a gratuitous referent for potentially platitudinous and vacuous scholarship.

The discourse of decolonisation in South Africa takes place in a context shaped by both a demographic and conceptual overrepresentation of whiteness in academic disciplines, the media and other avenues of knowledge production. As the upper echelons of the South African academy (particularly in the highly resourced and research-intensive historically white universities) remain disproportionately white (see Breetzke and Hedding, 2018), and as whiteness is inseparable from the historical unfoldment of colonialism, imperialism and racism, the demand for decolonised spaces and curricula must struggle for legibility and validation within an antagonistic and indifferent institutional, socio-cultural and epistemic field. The endless harangues and complaints by white academics depicting calls for 'decolonised' curricula as vague, nativist, atavistic, unscholarly, identitarian, racist and a constraint on academic freedom are symptomatic of an 'orthodox dismissiveness' that Charles Mills has named 'white ignorance' (see Mills, 1997: 9–19; Mills, 2007; 2015). In his famous account of white epistemologies of ignorance, Mills tracks the ways in which the historical installation of systems of colonial conquest and white supremacy was accompanied by a 'particular optic, a prism of perception and interpretation and worldview' tied to whiteness. This, in turn, produces a 'particular cognitive orientation to the world' grounded in the acceptance of Eurocentric cultural assumptions and generating a specific pattern of knowing and seeing – or rather *not* knowing and *not* seeing (Mills, 2007: 218). 'White ignorance', in other words, is the name for the differential epistemic standpoint causally tied to white people's socialisation, racist beliefs and material group interests, which then manifests as 'structured blindness' to historical injustice – that is, amnesia, denial and overall skewed inferential patterns and a deficient conceptual apparatus in relation to the workings and effects of colonialism and racial injustice. 'White ignorance' is also what sustains the belief in the self-evident universality and superiority of Western over African thought and also conditions the doubt concerning the scientific and philosophical value of black scholarship more generally. As the call for decolonisation raises not only intellectual but also specific existential questions for white South African academics, it poses a challenge likely to face substantial resistance and misconception. There are probably more difficult questions here about the stakes and dangers involved in surrendering the struggle for intellectual sovereignty (Prah, 2016) to beneficiaries of colonialism and apartheid. What I wish to highlight for the moment is the problem that, as a result of its imbrication in a northbound and socially white gaze, the Westernised South African university houses a large cadre of academics – from all racial groups – who have neither the training, the will nor the imagination to radically reconfigure the knowledge archive in a way that would initiate a conceptual decolonisation of the disciplines and, hence, of the university.

Working in a largely theoretical and speculative vein, this chapter seeks to apprehend the deeper roots of the widespread depoliticisation, attenuation and commodification of decolonisation as an epistemological signifier and political imaginary. This concerns the problem of institutionalising unstable and contested political histories, subjectivities and locations into the curricular objects and analytic methods of the Westernised neoliberal university. Put another way, this is a problem that transpires when the devastatingly radical critiques of the racism and Eurocentrism of university institutional cultures, academic research, curricula, canons and pedagogies migrate from the margin and the underground to the hegemonic centre. In particular, I will trace three troubling effects of this institutionalisation: (1) 'decolonisation' falls captive to the ongoing neoliberal remaking of the university; (2) it undergoes subjection to disciplinary normalisation and policing; and (3) it atrophies into a metaphor for intellectual and pedagogical transformations to the complete neglect of the material and concrete reality of continuing settler-colonial white supremacy and racial capitalism in post-1994 South Africa.

The purpose of this chapter is, thus, not to give a definition of decolonisation or an account of what a decolonised curriculum in any particular discipline or area of study entails. Rather, it aims to consider the possible conditions for a project of decolonising knowledge in the South African university. The discussion will, therefore, assume to treat decolonisation as a radical and multivalent signifier, enacted and elaborated on by multiple traditions of anti-colonial, post-colonial and decolonial thinking and practice. In the main, the term principally evokes struggles to overcome colonial power and violence; seeking fundamental change through dismantling white supremacy; critically interrogating, provincialising and de-privileging Western epistemologies and concepts; seeking out alternative and *new* African and Global South knowledges and ways of being; excavating lost and silenced histories and centring African culture and experience; exposing neocolonial continuities; refusing assimilation into alien and oppressive orders and reclaiming liberation, dignity and sovereignty – and more. It reaches beyond the political and economic structures of society and into the social, cultural, psychological, spatial and onto-epistemic domains. Decolonisation speaks not only to the past but is also a gesture of openness to what is to come – a different knowledge, different ethical relations and a different world.

The underlying theme of my argument is that any movement to enact the decolonisation of the curricula and the university will remain abortive if it is not immediately tied to the struggle for a decolonised world. The invocation of decolonisation in academic, political and popular discourse entails a deep and direct reckoning with the historical specificity of settler-colonialism in the making of South Africa. Insofar as such an invocation works critically against the founding myths of post-1994 South Africa (reconciliation, liberal non-racialism, 'born-frees', white innocence, historic closure, etc), this chapter also underscores the discomforting, incommensurable and even aporetic character of decolonisation, and argues that the source of the aporetic within decolonisation today pertains to the irreversible, irreparable, unforgivable horrors of colonial conquest and its afterlives.

The neoliberal undoing of decolonisation

But the South African university is not only the Westernised university of colonial modernity but also the neoliberal university of late global capital – a troubling combination that shapes the cultures and practices of knowledge production, teaching and learning, and university life in very specific ways (see Baatjies, 2005). We understand neoliberalism, following Wendy Brown, as a governing rationality and order of reason that directs all human activity – including every feature of academic life – towards the supervening aims of capital appreciation, maximised return-on-investment, increased competitive positioning, brand enhancement and career advancement (Brown, 2015: 9–10). In this way, neoliberalism has produced an ongoing deformation of the *academic* character of the university by transforming its activities, subjects and overall mission in accordance with market-oriented economistic and instrumental logic. As Brown (2015: 9–10) explains, neoliberal reason

> transmogrifies every human domain and endeavor, along with humans themselves, according to a specific image of the economic. All conduct is economic conduct; all spheres of existence are framed by economic terms and metrics, even when those spheres are not directly monetised.

Because neoliberalism is construed here not only as an economic system but also a set of socio-cultural norms that extend the model of the market and its schemes of valuation to all spheres of human activity (Brown, 2015: 31), it shapes not only the governance of institutions but also the values and desires of human subjects. In particular, neoliberalism both imagines and transforms human beings into 'human capital tasked with improving its competitive position and with enhancing its (monetary and non-monetary) portfolio value' (Brown, 2015: 10). Neoliberal rationality thus involves the economisation of non-economic spheres and practices, which in turn involves 'remaking the knowledge, form, content, and conduct appropriate to these spheres' (Brown, 2015: 31). Neoliberal rationality, in other words, 'literally *marketises* all spheres' and interpellates human subjects to 'think and act like contemporary market subjects', even in cases where monetary wealth is not at issue (Brown, 2015: 31). When this form of reason filters into the university, all subjects and activities of the university come to be 'construed on the model of the contemporary firm', governed by business-oriented and corporatist idioms and modes of management and conduct (Brown, 2015: 22). Exorbitant tuition fees, due to decreased state funding, the push for online education and for-profit short courses, managerialism and business culture, professionalisation of academe and the pressure for the teaching of academic disciplines to take an increasingly vocational character, are now all routine and defining features of university life (see Soudien, Chapter 3, Bawa, Chapter 4, and Malabela, Chapter 7, in this volume). Academic teaching and research are now also increasingly tied to marketised metrics of academic productivity that measure knowledge according to publication units, impact factors and Global North appeal (coded as 'international') and learning is measured in accordance with throughput rates, student evaluations, course enrolments and job preparation (Brown, 2015: 175–200).

One of the more damaging effects of this transmogrification of the university through neoliberalism is that academics themselves are impelled to approach intellectual work in a market-oriented fashion. And herein lie the conditions for the neoliberal capture and commodification of the project of decolonisation. Under the pressure of the neoliberal encomium to 'generate, accumulate or invest', academics themselves become heavily concerned with advancing their careers, seeking promotion and gaining prestige through self-promotion on social media, networking, National Research Foundation (NRF) ratings, key performance indicators, citation indexes, grants, fellowships and prizes. Publications are prized, not primarily for their intellectual value but for their profitability in terms of subsidy, immediate marketability and applicability – especially to a public hungry for slogans, quick solutions and common sense – and the venue of their publication. Also notable here is that the neoliberal remaking of the university, and its central tropes of excellence and productivity, not only ignore but also intensify existing hierarchies and disorders within the university, principal among them being institutional racism and sexism, bureaucracy, deteriorating mental health and well-being of staff and students, and mediocrity owing to rushed and underdeveloped scholarship.

In such a context, many universities and scholars may be turning to the discourse of decolonisation, not necessarily out of a deep-rooted fidelity or searching inquisitiveness about its intellectual, cultural and political richness but because – as the latest trendy buzzword of the 'academic market' – it presents a lucrative avenue for the Academic as Self-Investing Entrepreneur to maximise their capital value. This is most apparent in the proliferation of academic seminars, conference panels, journal special issues, and books and articles that carry the title of decolonisation, but which end up being unrelated to, or even antithetical to, the intellectual and political traditions associated with it. This is apparent as well in those who approach decolonisation in purely descriptive terms (regurgitating trite and superficial understandings of the concept or producing a laundry list of non-Western intellectuals) and those purporting to provide a 'practical' blueprint for *how to* decolonise a particular discipline, concept or object of study.

So, in the deluge of academic work travelling under the banner of decolonisation and decoloniality, it is not uncommon to hear references to ours as 'the time of decoloniality' or 'the age of decolonisation' – a time that is also heavy with many ironies. Universities in South Africa now regularly parachute in academics from the Global North to pontificate on the meaning of decolonisation; scholars publish books and journal articles on decolonisation with American and European publishers that charge exorbitant prices; and academics model themselves as 'experts' on decolonisation to acquire speaking engagements, postgraduate students and institutional recognition. The bona fides and intentions of these universities and scholars are not what is at issue here. Rather, it is the apparent lack of tension, the almost neat cohesion and harmony, between the aims of the neoliberal university and the activities of those engaged in decolonising it, that is of concern. Indeed, it appears that neoliberalism is literally the condition for the legion of incantations of decolonisation across today's academic landscape. If the socio-economic exclusions and historical disorientations of the neoliberal university are what incited the calls for epistemic and institutional decolonisation in the first place, it has been the metrics and mechanisms of that same university that have elevated and repackaged – and thus truncated – decolonisation into a brand-new niche industry to be ploughed for reward and recognition. Spectacularly, that which historically promised a fundamental challenge to the university has now become its most legitimating property.

Institutionalising decolonisation?

Given how thoroughly saturated and deformed the university is by a neoliberal ethos and logic, what perils trail its seeming privileged status as the nerve centre for the work of decolonisation globally? Mahmood Mamdani makes the case that the present models of the university in South Africa and Africa were inspired by the colonial modern (Mamdani, 2016: 70). In other words, the university as we know it – its institutional form (discipline-based, exclusive and hierarchical) and its curricular content (Western knowledge) – has its genesis in a particular European time, space and experience. The central mission of the university in this modern conception was essentially the study of the 'undifferentiated human' (Mamdani, 2016: 70). It was based on a singular vision of the human which, although formed by the (particular) European experience, was presented as universal. In this vision, only the European was imagined as human, with colonised peoples falling into different species of sub- and non-human. The original inability of the colonial modern to acknowledge the plurality of human experience emanated from the imperial ambitions of

Europe – the fact that it sought to expand into, and conquer, the world and to civilise others in its own image (Mamdani, 2016: 70). The arrival of Western civilisation on African shores through colonial conquest was as systematic as it was violent, and the modern university as we still know it was central to this process: deepening the erasure of precolonial African epistemologies and ontologies, as well as arming the settler population with the knowledge, skills and values necessary to rule over the indigenous African population (see also Adebajo, Chapter 2, and Bawa, Chapter 4, in this volume). The blood-soaked historical dynamics of racial domination, coloniality, capitalism and global Empire are thus embedded in the primordial structure of the university. In our context especially, this means that the South African university is fundamentally imbricated in the very problems – Eurocentrism, racism and hierarchy – it is being called upon to resolve. This is further complicated by David Scott's (2004) reminder that colonial modernity has not only left its mark on the material and symbolic world as an order of oppression, violence and dehumanisation, but has also produced the very subjects called to resist and overthrow it.

From the perspective of the Black Radical Tradition and its figuration of decolonisation as the critique and negation of Western civilisation (Robinson, 1983), the university remains an unredeemed object of radical questioning. Hence Fred Moten and Stefano Harney declare that the path of the subversive intellectual is 'to be *in* but not *of*' the university (Moten and Harney, 2013: 26). Against injunctions to restore and reform the university, they appear to suggest that the work of decolonisation can only take place in the 'underground … the *undercommons of enlightenment* … where the revolution is still black, still strong' (Moten and Harney, 2013: 26). To be *in* but not *of* the university – an injunction to continually decentre and resist its claims to authority and its monopoly over knowledge and pedagogy. This is an injunction that stands in stark contrast to contemporary struggles for belonging to the university – demanding greater staff diversity, transformed curricula, emotionally supportive spaces, renamed buildings, and affordable tuition fees and accommodation. Does such a request not signal an investment in the university's regimes of accounting, professionalisation and instrumentalisation? How does a critique of the university as fundamentally colonial metamorphose into a *plea* to be seen, heard and represented within the university's structures of recognition and knowledge validation? The answer to these questions is not as simple as rehearsing the old reform versus revolution debate, nor can it be adequately captured by invoking the resubordinating, dehumanising and conservative effects of assimilation as a form of change. (I want to bracket away two further layers to the problem: first, how demands for the transformation or decolonisation of the university require academics to provide not only a deep and broad academic education in the disciplines but also to provide job training and guaranteed employment, emotional safety and hospitality, cultural and personal affirmation, as well as politicisation and consciousness-raising; and second, how this has also introduced a peculiar burden on black and women academics to perform duties of pastoral care for students and junior colleagues.)

Rather, I would contend the demand for spatial, institutional and epistemic decolonisation in higher education today deepens the university's monopoly on knowledge production and discourse, and thereby imposes strictures on how we think about and enact possibilities for decolonisation today. The most obvious of these strictures relate to the pre-eminence of the English language (and thus, Western culture) as the medium of academic discourse, the idealisation of secular reason, logic and method over myth, spirituality and the supernatural, as well as the preference for textuality over orality – the latter an effect of what Oyèronké Oyewumi identified as the privileging of sight and the visual as a mode of understanding and describing reality in Western culture (Oyewumi, 1997: 3). As noted earlier, Mamdani highlights the university's roots in both colonialism and European *modernity*, meaning that rationalisation, coherence, singularity, linearity, order, mastery and individualism are also defining features of the university. This adds the additional problem of attempting to incorporate oppositional and subversive knowledges into the formal structures of academic institutionality and ceremony, resulting in the regulation and reification of those knowledges.

For Robin Kelley, the desire to comprehensively incorporate anti-racist, anti-colonial, socialist and feminist literatures in the formal university curriculum extends the regulatory power of the university over our political and intellectual lives and reading choices (Kelley, 2016). This has the principal effect of closing down and foreclosing other spaces and modalities of intellectual and political engagement outside of the university. He invokes the example of black radical and socialist study groups as instances of alternative sites for political reflection, community and self-cultivation (Kelley, 2016). The need for a public culture of critical literacy beyond the university cannot be overstated. In an essay suggestively entitled 'Freedom's silences', Brown also reminds us that silenced and subjugated discourses contain an element of resistance insofar as they are unregulated and outside of the dominant episteme. Consequently, their excavation – that is, their exposure to the institutional gaze – risks eroding precisely their emancipatory potential (Brown, 2005: 89–90). The disappearance of the productive tension between the inside and outside of the university could likely result in radical texts becoming sterile and orthodox – no longer the provocative, life-changing and eye-opening discoveries they were to earlier generations of activist intellectuals, but simply and only part of the laborious routine system of homework, assignments and exams.

The institutionalisation of a radical political concept (such as decolonisation) through curricula and university policies harbours a deeper conservatism. As a claim for hegemonic representation within the framework of disciplines, curricula and syllabi, the conceptualisation of decolonisation adopted in any given context must constantly police the boundaries of what constitutes and does not constitute a decolonising or decolonised curriculum. This includes repressing or expelling objections directed towards it. We see these in the critique offered by feminist, queer and trans activists and intellectuals regarding what they view as an overtly masculine, 'cishet' and phallocentric vision of decolonisation (which centres male intellectuals); or the refrain by working-class students of the still elitist and middle-class character of 'decolonial' intellectual spaces. There are also Africanist repudiations of critical theories and categories imported from Europe, North America and Latin America, and even ecological critiques of anthropocentric visions of decolonisation in which humans still wield a violent mastery over nature and non-human animals. This is not to even mention historiographical and philosophical debates concerning the colonial construction and representation of Africa, blackness, indigeneity/nativity and the nation-state, which at least undermine an absolute certainty about their ability to found an ethics, theory and praxis of decolonisation (Fanon, 1967; Mudimbe, 1988; Mafeje, 1990; Mamdani, 2012; Ramose, 2017). Contestations internal to African, postcolonial, black radical and decolonial thinking have long tutored us in the pitfalls of a programme of asserting racial and cultural alterity that merely inverts colonial stereotypes, re-inscribes Manichean logics, and falls into the trap of vindicationism.[1] The crisis of any formal curriculum, including a putatively decolonised one, is that the institutional pressures placed on it within higher education institutions concerned with credits, notional hours, learning outcomes and assessment, require knowledge to be represented in disciplined and formulaic terms, thereby minimising the complexity, open-endedness and mystery of the world such knowledge is meant to represent and understand.

There is yet one more thread to the problem that will lead us into the next section. As calls for the decolonisation of the university are delivered through

---

[1] 'Vindicationism' refers to the political and intellectual practice undertaken by anti-colonial and anti-racist movements of making a case for the inherent civilisational value and equal humanity of colonised and oppressed peoples in response to dehumanisation. This often takes the form of documenting and valorising important cultural, political and scientific achievements and characteristics of those peoples as a way of refuting and correcting historical distortions and degrading stereotypes. For all its virtue as a way of reclaiming dignity and humanity, the oft-noted limitation of vindicationism has been its acceptance of the moral and epistemological framework of the colonial, racist and oppressive order which it contests.

and intertwined with the language of trauma, pain, vulnerability and invisibility, we see the development of primarily emotional and sentimental attachments and aversions to particular intellectual traditions. On the one hand, texts coded as 'Western' or 'masculine' are indiscriminately vilified and those marked as 'decolonial' or 'intersectional' are uncritically venerated. The point is not that vilification and veneration are inappropriate responses to texts, theories and thinkers. It is rather that either response should preferably be preceded by informed judgement of the literature in question. The point is also not that affect, or politics suffused with affect, has no place in pedagogy and intellectual life. On the contrary, they are essential to it, but must be wedded to practices of metacritique and autocritique to avoid collapsing into moralism and narcissism.

The turn to affect and (personal) lived experience in the political culture of academic protest again exceeds the classical concern with the ways this individualises and psychologises what are deeply political, collective and structural phenomena. It has rather to do with the fact that the historical moment in which universities are having to grapple with radical transformation and decolonisation is one in which we are all reeling, not from the aftermath of history but its accumulation. This is a historical moment, in other words, where the failures and falsities of the liberal-democratic promise are ever more apparent; where the workings of white supremacy and racial capitalism have not only endured but also intensified; where the ontological gulf between humanity and blackness has not yet been fully bridged. In a moment of such profound historical disappointment and powerlessness, university curricula and scholarship stand in as substitutes for an unfulfilled historical confrontation with the founding antagonism and come to be a site of compensation for a haunting and unredeemed past – a past that is emphatically not past.

The dead ends of decolonisation? Decolonisation as metaphor

If the Eurocentrism and racism of the South African university, as well as its alienated relationship to the continent, the black experience and the Global South, are the historical outcome of its rootedness in the settler-colonial foundations of South Africa itself, what does it mean to ask the university to disavow its very possibility condition? A kind of cul-de-sac emerges here when one tries to resolve the most foundational historico-political problem in South Africa – the very legitimacy and coherence of 'South Africa' as an artefact of white supremacy and imperial violence – through public higher education institutions and curricula, which are mere symptoms and drivers of that problem. The call for decolonisation of South African universities, public spaces and socio-cultural practices, and values more generally, is principally a reaction to the deep and enduring fault lines and contradictions of South Africa's colonial and apartheid history – and the failure to redress and resolve these in the making of the new constitutional dispensation (see Bawa, Chapter 4, Mngomezulu, Chapter 6, and Higgs, Chapter 12, in this volume). In other words, the challenges of epistemic justice are bound up with larger unresolved historical injustices. This implies that the decolonisation of the university is politically and ethically unthinkable outside of the decolonisation of South Africa itself.

In this regard, the distinction developed by Mogobe Ramose between democratisation and decolonisation as distinct modes of post-colonial reconstruction is crucial (Ramose, 2001). Democratisation concerns the inclusion of the racially oppressed and conquered peoples into the existing arrangements of power and knowledge created through colonial conquest. Since the injustice is seen to lie in the exclusionary excesses of those arrangements rather than in their very foundation, democratisation preserves the dominant colonial order through extending equal rights of access and participation to those it had formerly excluded and violated. The democratisation paradigm takes the history of legal apartheid, racial discrimination and segregation as its starting points, and thus presumes to redress this history through integration (enfranchisement) and cohesion. Conversely, the decolonisation paradigm takes the *longue durée* of colonial conquest, land dispossession and epistemicide as its starting points. As such, it seeks the dissolution of the world of the conqueror and its epistemological and ontological frameworks. Decolonisation seeks to abolish the power relations and epistemologies of the dominant colonial order through a process of restoration and repair that recentres the dignity and sovereignty of the colonised indigenous peoples. Ramose mobilises this distinction not only to highlight the radical opposition between democratisation and decolonisation but also to specifically illustrate that post-conflict democratisation in South Africa marked a retreat from the exigency of fundamental change and genuine liberation.

Similarly, Veracini (2007) suggests that most settler-colonial polities have followed processes of social transformation that seek to evade and undermine the exigency of decolonisation by displacing rather than addressing the settler-colonial 'past'. Accordingly:

> the determinations of a settler colonial present avoided rather than decolonised. In the end, an emphasis on alternative traditions of settler-Indigenous partnership has been easier than insisting on the need to decolonise settler colonial sovereignties, and a widespread disinclination to enact substantive decolonising ruptures resulted in a tendency to avoid disturbing the foundational determinants of settler colonial polities. Foundational settler narratives were ultimately resilient…

Thus, the turn to liberal modes of post-conflict democratisation as the dominant modalities of post-colonial reconstruction has not been primarily about enacting genuine post-settler and post-conquest passages of transition and reharmonisation, but rather about expanding the definition of 'who can claim belonging to the settler body politic that leaves the settler-colonial structures unchallenged'. Democratisation, in other words, preserves that which decolonisation aims to destabilise and undo and, in turn, deepens the historical antagonisms and social disharmony engendered by settler-colonial white supremacy. To sharpen the point further: 'South Africa' (as a territory, polity and idea) is an artefact of colonial sovereignty created by its two European conquering powers in the 'racial contract' that gave rise to the Union of South Africa (Magubane, 1996; Mills, 1997). While the South African university takes shape in this historical process as a central instrument of social reproduction, it is South Africa itself that remains the proper historical target of the unsettling drive of decolonisation.[2]

Dominant figurations of decolonisation in South African academic and public discourse have primarily taken two forms, which I argue have involved mocking and heckling – but never dismantling – white supremacy at the socio-economic, psychic, cultural and epistemic levels:

- *Diversity and multiculturalism* (primarily involving accommodation of 'subaltern' voices and empathy with the racial 'Others' of white people; treatment of non-Eurocentric knowledges and experiences as supplementary and complementary to the normative Western archive; negotiation and reconciliation of differences through pedagogy; and exoticisation and infantilisation of non-Western epistemologies and cosmologies).

- *Symbolic and aesthetic change* (which entails redesigning and renaming institutional spaces and buildings; performing gestures of acknowledgement and recognition; promoting accession of black people to positions of power and authority; and decorative and ceremonial use of African languages and symbols).

In these two forms, the failure to interrogate the colonial construction of South Africa results in a struggle for *decolonisation in South Africa*, which does not at the same time *decolonise South Africa*. In taking 'South Africa' for granted, the movement for decolonisation is in actuality adopting a grammar and project of democratisation, of fortifying and extending rather than terminating the

---

2   This view is central to the vision of decolonisation espoused by the Azanian (Pan-Africanist Black Consciousness) political tradition in South Africa in its dissent against the multiracial Charterism of the African National Congress. See Madlingozi (2017) and Modiri (2018).

interlocutory life of South Africa and its foundational coloniality and anti-blackness. Much of the disorientation, rancour, viscerality, discord, anxiety, recrimination, incoherence, rage, performativity, dissent and reaction that characterise the state of higher education on the question of decolonisation may lie somewhere in this disarticulation or interval between seeking decolonisation *in* South Africa and imagining a *decolonised South Africa*, which is to say the end of 'South Africa' (Dube, 1983). Whereas the former is intelligible to our schemas and frameworks of possibility (and is thus unthreatening in the final instance), the latter stands disturbingly at the threshold of our imagination. At any rate, it is becoming increasingly clear that no 'easy victories' or reforms are possible in a settler-colonial society as racially bifurcated and unequal as post-1994 South Africa. We take from settler-colonial studies the understanding of settler-colonialism as a 'structure and not an event', undergirded by a 'logic of elimination' in which the settler invasion instantiates a violent and permanent interdiction of indigenous life in order to create on its ruins a new polity and world (Wolfe, 2016). As such, any attempts at change must be directed towards a fundamental reckoning with the settler-colonial present and with the unlivable conditions and relations it has engendered through its nearly four centuries on these shores.

For this reason, the conversion of decolonisation into a metaphor for critical pedagogy, deconstruction of knowledge, social justice and/or curriculum transformation is untenable. This is to affirm Eve Tuck and K Wayne Yang's rightly famous injunction in their article of the same title that 'decolonisation is not a metaphor'. In their article, Tuck and Yang underscore 'what is unsettling about decolonisation' (Tuck and Yang, 2012: 1). They insist that decolonisation 'brings about the repatriation of indigenous land and life' and should not be conflated with 'other things we want to do to improve our societies' (and, we could add here, our universities) (Tuck and Yang, 2012: 1). They write to register their concern about the 'ease with which the language of decolonisation has been superficially adopted' and metaphorised into a critical methodology, especially within the educational sphere. This metaphorisation of decolonisation is also what enables many, especially white scholars – with little evidence of indigenous, African and Global South literature and politics in their previous scholarship – to draw on the language of decolonisation without any serious commitment to abolishing their own racialised subject position and complicity in maintaining the whiteness of the academy. As Tuck and Yang (2012: 3) write:

> When metaphor invades decolonization, it kills the very possibility of decolonization; it recenters whiteness, it resettles theory, it extends

innocence to the settler, it entertains a settler future. Decolonise (a verb) and decolonization (a noun) cannot easily be grafted onto pre-existing discourses/frameworks, even if they are critical, even if they are anti-racist, even if they are justice frameworks.

Decolonisation in Tuck and Yang's formulation is an unsettled and unsettling notion that neither promises a seamless reconciliation of present divisions nor forecloses future struggles. It cannot be subsumed under or absorbed by discourses of human rights, constitutional democracy and transitional justice, and it cannot be circumscribed within the site of the university alone. The all-too-easy adoption of decolonising frameworks, discourses and theories in settler-colonial societies continues the trend of privileging 'settler fantasies of easier paths to reconciliation' and enacting 'moves to innocence', which problematically seek to alleviate settler guilt and complicity and rescue settler normalcy and futurity. One of these 'moves to innocence' – which they see as ultimately sustaining the settler-colonial order – is the excessive focus on decolonising the mind or cultivating critical consciousness as if that were the sole task and meaning of decolonisation (Tuck and Yang, 2012: 19). While conscientisation is indispensable for any revolutionary transformation of the social order, it cannot act as a substitute for the much more uncomfortable task of facing up to the unspeakable horrors of colonial-apartheid, restoring conquered lands, materially dislodging white social, economic and cultural power, and ultimately rebuilding a new society on the basis of African history, knowledge, and experience. Following Aimé Césaire and Frantz Fanon, Tuck and Yang position decolonisation as material and not metaphor – involving a break, however uneven, with the violent determinations of the colonial order and holding out a non-teleological future of unresolved possibilities (Tuck and Yang, 2012: 20, 31). Decolonisation urges an embrace of an 'ethic of incommensurability', of those elements of decolonisation that destabilise and unsettle the certainties of the status quo, bringing no neat closure to the concerns of all involved (Tuck and Yang, 2012: 30). Incommensurability is a recognition that decolonisation will 'require a change in the order of the world', which does not entail a mere reversal or replication of colonial power relations, but a radical break with those relations. 'A break', write Tuck and Yang, 'and not a compromise' (Tuck and Yang, 2012: 31).

The reduction of decolonisation, first, into a solely conceptual and epistemic exercise and then into a 'proper object' of the university's academic and institutional operations amounts to a resettlement that negates the incommensurable, unstable, incalculable and aporetic moments within the dense history and future of the struggles and visions that the term encompasses.

Even well-meaning attempts to make decolonisation legible and practical – read: palatable – through the curriculum erode precisely the unsettling force of decolonisation inherited from the ongoing struggles of colonised peoples across the globe. The university must continually account for its deeply entrenched epistemic violence, Eurocentrism and racism. But this alone will not be enough if we continue to follow a path of 'friendly understanding', which once again exonerates whites from historical responsibility, manufactures false social cohesion and, ultimately, maintains the overall political ontology and economy of conquest – its hierarchies of power, knowledge and being. Tuck and Yang instead propose an embrace of 'dangerous understanding' linked to an ethic of incommensurability (Tuck and Yang, 2012: 35). 'Dangerous understanding' performs a refusal of all hegemonic settlements: both settler-colonialism and the negotiated settlement. This extends to a refusal of a settler future, of safe and easy answers and of reconciliation in the midst of unresolved historical injustices and unclaimed responsibilities. Whereas dangerous understanding affirms the 'unwritten possibilities' of decolonisation, friendly understanding is the dead end of decolonisation.

Conclusion

The signifier 'decolonisation' carries with it the unbearable weight and intransigence of history. As an ongoing resistance to this history, it also registers the disturbing persistence of the structural and epistemological dynamics of colonial conquest into the post-1994 period. How is it that more than two decades after the formal end of apartheid, black students and academics are having to contend with curricula that brazenly privilege Global North and socially white perspectives and knowledges in a black-majority African country that declares itself free, equal and non-racial? How can it be that, despite voluminous literature exposing the situatedness (and hence particularity) of all knowledges, the intellectual productions, cultures and languages of white Europeans and Americans continue to be presented as universal and authoritative? And why does it appear as though our desires, imaginations and horizons of possibility show no signs of a truly decolonised future? There are many answers to these questions, but the most pertinent for this chapter relate to how the anomalous overrepresentation of whites in the academy, and the immense power they wield over the production and dissemination of knowledge and discourse in the academy and beyond, are symptomatic of our failure to reckon with South Africa's settler-colonial and racist history. This is a failure that itself must be reckoned with, rather than sublimated at the site of the university.

The attempt to decolonise the university in a still colonial and white supremacist society such as South Africa, and within an imperial capitalist global order, surfaces not only dilemmas but aporias. The purpose of this chapter was to chart three of these aporetic predicaments, which, taken together, raise the danger of converting a political struggle for the remaking of society and the world into a curricular object of the neoliberal, Westernised and white-dominated university. Of course, none of this suggests that the work of decolonising knowledge and spaces in the universities is insignificant. On the contrary, the increasing adoption of different decolonising frameworks in the study and critique of academic disciplines and public discourse represents a historic opening for the emancipatory knowledges we need to understand and resolve the problems and challenges produced by our history. This chapter highlights that the contemporary South African university is organised by neoliberal logics that threaten to commodify and, hence, depoliticise those emancipatory knowledges and institutionalise them within its largely conservative disciplinary structures. The meaning and possibilities of decolonisation would be severely eroded if it is reduced to a metaphor for the merely conceptual exercise of revising curricula, diversifying the professoriate and redesigning spaces. In the result, decolonisation would wither into a demand to belong to the universities but not yet for the universities to belong to us, and we would be interpellated into adopting minoritarian vocabularies and sensibilities at odds with the liberatory impulse of decolonisation in our context.

To maintain fidelity to the great ideals of the anti-colonial wars of resistance and the revolutionary political and intellectual traditions of anti-colonialism and anti-racism, which have followed in their wake, we must hold on to the aporetic promises of decolonisation – its most combative and most capacious imaginings. Decolonisation is an insatiable reparatory demand, an insurrectionary utterance that always exceeds the temporality and scene of its enunciation. It entails nothing less than an endless fracturing of the world colonialism created.

References

Baatjies, IG (2005) Neo-liberal fatalism and the corporatisation of higher education in South Africa, *Quarterly Review of Education and Training in South Africa*, 1(12): 25–33.

Breetzke, GD and Hedding, DW (2018) The changing demography of academic staff at higher education institutions (HEIs) in South Africa, *Higher Education*, **76**: 145–61.

Brown, W (2005) *Edgework: Critical essays on knowledge and politics*. Princeton, NJ: Princeton University Press.

Brown, W (2015) *Undoing the Demos: Neo-liberalism's stealth revolution*. New York: Zone Books.

Dube, D (1983) *The Rise of Azania, the Fall of South Africa*. Lusaka: Daystar.

Fanon, F (1967) *Black Skins, White Masks*. New York: Grove Press.

Kelley, RDG (2016) Black study, black struggle, *Boston Review*, 7 March 2016. Available at: http://bostonreview.net/forum/robin-d-g-kelley-black-study-black-struggle (accessed July 2018).

Madlingozi, T (2017) Social justice in a time of neo-apartheid constitutionalism: Critiquing the anti-black economy of recognition, incorporation and distribution, *Stellenbosch Law Review*, **28**: 123–47;

Mafeje, A (1990) The 'Africanist' heritage and its antinomies, *Africa Development*, **15**: 159–83.

Magubane, BM (1996) *The Making of a Racist State: British Imperialism and the Union of South Africa 1875–1910*. Trenton, NJ: Africa World Press.

Mamdani, M (2012) *Define and Rule: Native as Political Identity*. Cambridge, MA: Harvard University Press.

Mamdani, M (2016) Between the public intellectual and the scholar: Decolonization and post-independence initiatives in African higher education, *Inter-Asia Cultural Studies*, **17**: 68–83.

Mills, C (1997) *The Racial Contract*. Ithaca, NY: Cornell University Press.

Mills, C (2007) 'White Ignorance,' in S Sullivan and N Tuana (eds) *Race and Epistemologies of Ignorance*. New York: SUNY Press, pp. 11–38.

Mills, C (2015) Global White Ignorance, in M Goss and L Mcgoey (eds) *Routledge Handbook of Ignorance Studies*. Abingdon UK: Routledge, pp. 217–27.

Modiri, J (2018) The Jurisprudence of Steve Biko: A study in race, law and power in the 'afterlife' of colonial-apartheid, PhD thesis, University of Pretoria.

Morse, C (1999) Capitalism, Marxism, and the Black Radical Tradition: An interview with Cedric Robinson, *Perspectives on Anarchist Theory*, 3 (Spring). Available at: http://perspectives.anarchist-studies.org/5robinsoninterview.htm (accessed July 2018).

Moten, F and Harney, S (2013) *The Undercommons: Fugitive planning and black study*. New York: Minor Compositions.

Mudimbe, VY (1988) *The Invention of Africa: Gnosis, philosophy and the order of knowledge*. Indianapolis: Indiana University Press.

Ndumiso D (2012) Decolonising the university: A precondition for justice, in AISA (ed.) *Peace and Security for African Development*. Pretoria: HSRC, pp. 160–174.

Oyewumi, O (1997) *Invention of Woman: Making an African Sense of Western Gender Discourses*. Minneapolis: University of Minnesota Press.

Prah, K (2016) Has Rhodes Fallen? Decolonising the Humanities in Africa and Constructing Intellectual Sovereignty, 20 October 2016, *The Academy of Science of South Africa (ASSAf) Inaugural Humanities Lecture*. Pretoria: HSRC.

Ramose, M (2001) An African perspective on justice and race, *Polylog*. Available at: http://them.polylog.org/3/frm-en.htm.

Ramose, M (2017) Wiping away the tears of the ocean/Ukusulaizinyembezizolwandle, *Theoria*, **152**: 22–57.

Robinson, CJ (1983) *Black Marxism: The making of the black radical tradition*. Chapel Hill, NC: University of North Carolina Press.

Santos, Boaventura de Sousa (2017). *Decolonising the University: The challenge of deep cognitive justice*. Newcastle: Cambridge Scholars Publishing.

Scott, D (2004) *Conscripts of Modernity: The tragedy of colonial enlightenment*. Durham, NC: Duke University Press.

Tuck, E and Yang, KW (2012) Decolonisation is not a metaphor, *Indigeneity, Education & Society*, **1**: 1–40.

Veracini, L (2007) Settler colonialism and decolonisation, *Borderlands*, 6. Available at: http://www.borderlands.net.au/vol6no2_2007/veracini_settler.htm (accessed July 2018).

Wolfe, P (2016) Settler colonialism and the elimination of the native, *Journal of Genocide Research*, **8**: 387–409.

Chapter 11
Going to Sokoto to look for something in the pocket of your ṣòkòtò: The curious case of African sociology and decolonisation[1]

Jimi Adesina

Introduction

This chapter addresses the odd questions of African sociology and the demands for 'decolonisation'. Long before the demand for 'free, decolonised education', I opted for 'endogeneity' in describing what the project should entail. I chose as the subtitle the 'curious case of African sociology and decolonisation', for two reasons. It would seem that the persistent bemoaning of the absence of African sociological reflections on human sociality arises for two primary reasons. They relate to ignorance and ignoring. First, ignorance of the African social science scholarship manifests in bemoaning its absence. Second, there is the wilful neglect of what exists. When there is engagement, it can be so facile that it results in distortion. The title is a Yorùbá adage – *oun ti a n wa lọ si Sokoto wa l'ápò ṣòkòtò*. Literally, going to a distant place (Sokoto in Northern Nigeria) in search of an item that is in your trouser pocket.

Twenty-one years after the transition from racist minority rule in South Africa, it took the angry and disruptive protests from students to get everyone's attention that pedagogy is not merely technical. Effective pedagogy involves the validation of the collective memories that students bring into the classrooms – a case made in a 2005 presidential address to the South African Sociological Association (Adesina, 2006a) and the theme of a 2006 inaugural lecture at Rhodes University (Adesina, 2006b). The revolt started in the university where, 20 years earlier, the so-called 'Mamdani Affair' played out.[2] A lesson of the 'affair' is that contestation over curriculum is not merely about contents – it is primarily about power: the power to determine what constitutes knowledge, who are the legitimate knowledge-makers and which knowledge gets disseminated. Knowledge is a primary determinant of the human constitution.

---

1   Part of the work presented here was supported by a research grant (Grant Number 64984) received from South Africa's National Research Foundation.
2   The 'Mamdani Affair' at the University of Cape Town (UCT) occurred between 1997 and 1998, around the design and teaching of a foundation course on Africa in the Faculty of Social Sciences and Humanities. See *Social Dynamics*, **24**(2) of 1998 for further details.

If you are taught that people like you do not produce valid knowledge, you would likely take received knowledge from others as valid for your context and as the basis of social practice. This breeds self-loathing. As Bernard Magubane once noted, 'if you control people's mind, you control a lot'.[3] As Mamdani notes, 'the South African academy, even when it was opposed to apartheid politically, was deeply affected by it epistemologically' (Mamdani, 1998: 64), an epistemology that denies the capacity of Africans to produce knowledge.

In the following section, I provide a conceptual clarification of the key terms used in this chapter. I then argue that the project of decolonisation (or endogeneity) must pass the 'Aimé Césaire Challenge', before highlighting three constitutive aspects of the African sociological project and some of the materials that should be reflected in a transformed sociology curriculum.

Terms of the debate: Some conceptual clarification

It is important to clarify the use of three core ideas in this chapter. First, 'African sociology' denotes critical intellectual reflections on human sociational dynamics by Africans, not simply works of professional sociologists. By 'Africans', I refer to people who are self-referentially African and/or owe their origin to the African continent, including the African diaspora. Second, endogeneity connotes critical reflections that draw on 'the kind of knowledge [identifiable] as an internal product drawn from a given cultural background' (Hountondji, 1997: 17). Endogeneity concerns intellectual efforts that take their locales as the basis for critical reflections and theoretical elucidation.

Third, I make a distinction between 'Eurocentric' and 'Eurologos' discourses. Eurocentric discourses involve implicit or explicit hierarchies of being that place Europe and its diaspora (EAiD)[4] at the apex, and as the exemplar of human achievement to which other regions and people relate in degrees of inferiority and which they should emulate. By contrast, 'Eurologos' discourses and scholarship take Europe as the reference point of analysis. They need not construct a hierarchy or see EAiD as the exemplar of human history. As Raewyn Connell (2007; 2010; 2011) noted, much of the early writings in European sociology are Eurocentric in this sense and implicated in the project of empire. Weber's *The Protestant Ethic and the Spirit of Capitalism* (1985) would fall into this category, as would Durkheim's (1915) *The Elementary Forms of the Religious Life*. Each of these works inheres an explicit rendering of the world in an order of hierarchy, with Europe at the apex. By contrast, works such

---

3   This section draws on 'Mahmood Mamdani: Meeting the challenge of decolonisation'. Available at: https://www.mbeki.org/2017/05/27/mahmood-mamdani-meeting-the-challenge-of-decolonisation.

4   EAiD will include Europe, North America, Australia and New Zealand.

as Bourdieu's (1984) *Distinction* and Esping-Andersen's (1990) *Three Worlds of Welfare Capitalism* or his *Social Foundations of Post-industrial Economies* (Esping-Andersen, 1999) are Eurologos. Indeed, these are examples of European endogeny.

Finally, I differentiate between Eurocentric works and the problem of mimicry that results from 'epistemic dependence' (Adesina, 2006a; 2006b), 'captive minds' (Alatas, 1977) or 'extraversion' (Hountondji, 1995; 1996; 1997). If (South) African scholars decide to mimic Weber or Bourdieu, one can hardly blame Weber or Bourdieu.

The Aimé Césaire Challenge and epistemic reclamation

The epistemic reclamation of sociology that should infuse the contents of the new curriculum should pass the Aimé Césaire Challenge. At the end of his October 1956 letter of resignation from the Communist Party of France, Aimé Césaire proclaimed:

> There are two ways to lose oneself: walled segregation in the particular or dilution in the 'universal'. My conception of the universal is that of a universal enriched by all that is particular, a universal enriched by every particular: the deepening and coexistence of all particulars (Césaire, 2010 [1956]: 152).

A transformed curriculum should avoid being walled off in the particular and being diluted in the universal. Césaire's letter also offers an important insight into how we engage with the calls for 'One Sociology' (Sztompka, 2010), the 'internationalisation' of European ideographic sociology, or anxieties over how little Africans feature in the 'canons' of international sociology (Sitas, 2014). In an age where Césaire is drafted into projects at odds with his intent, an elaboration is required. 'We are convinced,' Césaire argued,

> Our question (or if you prefer, the colonial question) cannot be treated as a part of a more important whole, a part over which others can negotiate or come to whatever compromise seems appropriate in light of a general situation, of which they alone have a right to take stock (Césaire, 2010 [1956]: 147)

Reflecting on the relationship with many in the metropole, Césaire (2010 [1956]: 149) further notes:

> We are indeed dealing with a brother, a big brother who, full of his

own superiority and sure of his experience, takes you by the hand (alas, sometimes roughly) to lead you along the path where he knows Reason and Progress can be found. Well, that is exactly what we do not want ... we cannot delegate anyone else to think for us, or to make our discoveries for us ... we cannot allow anyone else, even if they are the best of our friends, to vouch for us.

In a different context, Césaire (2017) argued that 'we have never regarded our specificity as the opposite or antithesis of universality... *We want to have roots and at the same time communicate...* I believe in the importance of exchange, and exchange can only take place on *the basis of mutual respect*' (italics mine).

Transforming the sociology curriculum needs to be wary of the demands for 'one sociology', internationalisation of sociology or the more 'friendly' efforts at inducing epistemic dependence. There have been two waves of the demand for transcending the Eurocentrism of Western sociology. The first wave was from the late 1980s to the early 1990s; the second was in the first decade of the 21st century. Responses to these demands vary. Archer (1991) and Sztompka (2010) represent the 'soft' and 'hard' responses to these calls, respectively. Archer's response called for 'a single Sociology, whose ultimate unity rests on acknowledging the universality of human reasoning' (Archer, 1991: 131). Sztompka's response was more hard-edged. Drawing inspiration from Beck (2006), Sztompka acknowledged the 'methodological nationalism' of a variety of Western sociologies. He then tagged onto Beck's call for methodological 'cosmopolitanism' in staking his appeal for 'one sociology':

> Doing sociology in accordance with universalistic global standards, using uniform conceptual frameworks, models, orientations, theories and methods – detached from any local genealogy, and accountable before worldwide sociological community – does not stand in the way of emphasizing particular local problems, studying and solving them and in this way contributing original results to the global pool of sociological wisdom (Sztompka, 2010: 27).

Sztompka seems unaware of the irony of his argument. The 'conceptual framework, models, orientations, theories and methods' that he offers for 'one sociology' are precisely those developed in the ideographically European national traditions. This turnkey approach to reflecting on sociality in non-European contexts is what Hountondji (1996; 1997; 2002) calls 'extraversion'. Hardly anything qualifies more for Césaire's notion of others seeking 'to think for us'. Sztompka's references to Africa in his paper drip with imperial condescension. Archer's appeal to 'universality of human reasoning' does not travel well either. What you reason about is the lived experiences and meaningfulness of life; these differ depending on your geographical and socio-economic location. It is not enough to appeal to a common human capacity to reason; the object of sociology is reasoning about specific dimensions and specificities of human sociality.

There are less intrusive, seemingly more 'solidaristic' efforts. Elsewhere, I have flagged Michael Burawoy's (2004a; 2004b; 2005a; 2005b; 2005c) ventures in propagating his (specific) public sociology as 'inducing epistemic dependence'. Between the launch of the idea and its presentation – the presidential address – to the American Sociological Association (ASA), the contents and meaning of 'public sociology' changed markedly. It became difficult to determine what public sociology entails – other than that sociology has diverse audiences or publics. The version that Burawoy put forward as his presidential address had lost the 'radical' edge of the version presented in Durban, South Africa, in 2003. A contrast is Ben Agger's (2000) earlier, but largely unacknowledged, exposition of 'public sociology'. A central point for Agger's 'public sociology' is that 'all intellectual work is always already political' (Agger, 2007: 269). This is against Burawoy's taxonomy, which Agger (2007: 272) notes is Parsonian, and gives concession to 'professional sociology' as if it were devoid of political commitments. Even in its best version, Burawoy's public sociology, Agger (2007: 272) notes, is suffused with 'latter-day messianism'.

More relevant to the issue of epistemic dependence and the project of turnkey theories is Burawoy's effort at the global propagation of his version of 'public sociology'. For an idea that has its origin in getting the American sociological community to resist the cold climate of George W Bush's presidency, the tradition of ASA presidents circulating their pet ideas within the US sociological community took a global turn. From Latin America to the Middle East, Europe and South Africa, the concept of public sociology was put forward as a global panacea for rejuvenating the sociological enterprise. An American ideographical idea became a global solution.

Public sociology was offered as a framework for interpreting data. In the South African case, the work of sociologists engaged with the labour movement in the 1980s was offered as a quintessential way of doing public sociology. For a time, many South African sociologists rushed to embrace Burawoy's ideas as analytically valid; a way of helping us to think about our context. It is from the taxonomy of sociology – of policy sociology, professional sociology, critical sociology and public sociology – that he offers that Burawoy's public sociology derives its specificities. Policy sociology is akin to 'dirty sociology'. By contrast, public sociology is emancipatory – it engages with subalterns and at the behest of the downtrodden. As with all taxonomies, Burawoy's version hides more than it reveals, almost to the point of distortion. The question that I raised in 2006 at a seminar in Johannesburg was whether the South African sociologists that engaged with the labour movement in the 1980s felt they were doing 'public sociology' or 'policy sociology'? First, only if you think policy is the exclusive domain of the state (or the corporate world) is it possible to disregard the trade union policy works of South African academics. Was that work policy or public sociology? Even more directly, is Karl von Holt's work on South Africa's National Planning Commission dirty sociology? Only when you turn your back on the state and fail to acknowledge the feasibility of progressive, even emancipatory projects by the state, does any engagement with the state translate into dirty sociology. In the name of solidaristic engagement, we were handed a turnkey concept with little or no traction for helping us to make sense of our context. The effect is to promote epistemic dependence.

A final example seeks to edify theorising in the Global South: Raewyn Connell's (2007) *Southern Theory*. Like Burawoy's, Connell's thesis witnessed a rapid take-up. Yet, what the work demonstrates is the author's lack of familiarity with the African social science community. Theorising in the African context is reduced to Akìwọwọ and Hountondji. Like Keim (2010:108), Connell averred the 'absence of female outlooks and voices'. It is hard to comprehend how the works of Amadiume (1987; 1997; 2000), Oyěwùmí (1997; 1998a; 1998b; 2003; 2005) and Nzegwu (2006), among many other scholars, could have gone unnoticed. When Connell (2014) finally acknowledged Oyěwùmí (but not Amadiume or Nkiru) in reference to her first book (Oyěwùmí, 1997), it was to dismiss her as siding with 'powerful men in postcolonial regimes... [who] fend off demands for gender equality by branding feminism as a neo-colonial intrusion' (Connell, 2014: 555). She anchored her dismissal of Oyěwùmí on Bakare-Yusuf's profound misreading of Oyěwùmí (Adesina, 2010). It is difficult to imagine that Connell read Oyěwùmí's book, much less engaged with the wider body of her works. Otherwise, it is hard to understand how Connell could embrace other scholars in the South, who point to the limited traction of Western gender discourse in many communities of the Global South and how colonialism distorted relations between males and females in the colonies, but fail to recognise these very same arguments in Oyěwùmí's oeuvre. Even in seeming acts of solidarity, the necessity for us to tell our stories, unperturbed by the gaze of others, is a primary task in the African teaching and practice of sociology.

Critical African reflection on sociation dynamics: Exploring the contents of our ṣòkòtò

In this section, I return to African works of critical reflection on human sociality. The first part of this section concerns materials stretching into African antiquity. The second involves more contemporary critical reflections. The third concerns efforts at mining African ontological narratives for source codes for doing sociology. The last is offered as illustrative of what is possible when we take African ontological narratives seriously as the basis of our scholarship. The focus is on logic and sense-making or epistemology. I discard Giddens' idea that sociology 'concerns itself above all with modernity' (Giddens, 1996: 3). If that were the case, a sociology of Medieval Europe would be impossible (Adesina, 2006b).

African sociological reflection: From antiquity to recent times
By now there is little doubt that the works of Ibn Khaldūn (1332–1406), the 14th-century Berber scholar, qualify as serious critical reflections on human sociality (Schmidt, 1930; Dhaouadi, 1990; 2008; Adesina, 2006b; Alatas, 2013, 2014). His magnum opus, *Kitāb al -Ibar,* (Ibn Khaldūn, 1355), offered 'a new science of human organisation and society'. The work articulated the concept of *asabiyyah* to explain group cohesion, its erosion and reconstitution, 515 years before Emile Durkheim's (1893) idea of social norms (Adesina, 2006b).

Much of Du Bois' (1868–1963) scholarship was produced as academic sociology. *The Souls of Black Folk* (Du Bois, 1903) is arguably the most famous collection of his essays, but Du Bois' works stretch widely. His field research outputs from 1898 are extensive,[5] but so are his writings as a public intellectual and an activist. Du Bois' sociological contributions ranged from the sociology of race to crime, housing and social structure. A contemporary of Émile Durkheim, Du Bois was written out of the history of sociology – something Rabaka (2010a) characterised as 'epistemic apartheid'. Happily, the re-affirmation of Du Bois' sociological contributions is taking place (Rabaka, 2007, 2008, 2009, 2010a, 2010b; Wortham, 2005; 2009; Du Bois and Wortham, 2011). A reconstitution of the sociology curriculum in South Africa cannot ignore Du Bois or Ibn Khaldūn.

Diop (1974; 1987; 1991), as Mamdani reminds us, has a distinct resonance for continental African scholars. The significance of Diop is in the feasibility of African social history 500 years before European colonial encounter. It is an intellectual venture that offers documentary insights into everyday life in the Sahel and a negation of the idea that Africa is primarily about orality (see Mboup, Chapter 15, in this volume). The matriarchal foundation of most African social formations, offered by Diop, animated Amadiume's (1997) *Re-*

---

5 For a sample of Du Bois' outputs, see https://www.loc.gov/rr/program/bib/dubois/.

inventing Africa. Bala Usman (1981; 2006) provides a similar documentary on social history of the precolonial Northern Nigeria that Mamdani (2012) held up as an antidote to colonial historiography. However, it is in the access to human sociational dynamics that Usman and Diop provide the basis for engaging with African sociological discourses.

Other works that can be considered under the theme would range from Fadipe (1970 [1939]) to Cabral (1966; 1969; 1970a; 1970b; 1972; 1973; 1974; 1979), Kwame Nkrumah (1964; 1965), Julius Nyerere (1967a; 1967b; 1968; 1971), and Govan Mbeki (1939; 1944; 1964). Fanon, Césaire and others are candidates for inclusion. From the mantra that 'the history of all hitherto known societies is the history of class struggle', Cabral begged to differ. He poses the question:

> Does history begin only with the development of the phenomenon of 'class', and consequently of class struggle? To reply in the affirmative would be to place outside history the whole period of life of human groups... It would be to consider – and this we refuse to accept – that various human groups in Africa, Asia, and Latin America were living without history, or outside of history, at the time when they were subjected to the yoke of imperialism (Cabral, 1966: 5).

It is an affirmation of the epistemic privileging of one's locale. Cabral's (1970a) 'National liberation and culture' is a highly textured engagement with the cultural dynamics of imperial oppression, its intended epistemicide and the centrality of culture in national liberation.

Nkrumah's many writings offer a critical engagement with the multifaceted dimensions of imperial domination, including epistemic ones, even after formal independence. Nyerere's works are relevant to a sociology of education and rural development. The works of Awolowo (1953; 1955; 1958; 1960) and Nyerere and their policies in government offer the conceptual underpinnings for our work as incumbent of the South African Research Chair in Social Policy.[6] Govan Mbeki (1939; 1964) is important in a new sociology curriculum considering the attention that he paid to rural conditions and political resistance.

Critical reflections on human sociality: An African scholarly community
The shift from a broad intellectual reflection on sociality to scholarly works throws up a large body of works within the African context. In the South

---

6   The work at the South African Research Chair in Social Policy is concerned with rethinking social policy in Africa, which is transformative of the economy, social institutions and social relations, and human capability. The author is the holder of this Chair.

African context, I have been preoccupied with the works of Bernard Magubane, Archie Mafeje, Ruth First, and later Fatima Meer — missing voices in many of our sociology classes and curriculum. Keim (2008; 2011) has drawn attention to the vibrancy of the labour studies section of sociology in South Africa. However, against the general focus on industrial, formal employment, Jacklyn Cock's (1980) *Maids and Madams* offers compelling insight into domestic work and the social reproduction of white families. Fatima Meer's (1976) *Race and Suicide in South Africa* is an elegant and empirically rigorous study that remains largely neglected.

Focusing on some of the works that offer analytical concepts, Mamdani (1996) coined the idea of 'decentralised despotism' in making sense of the governmentality of late colonialism. Thandika Mkandawire offers concepts such as 'choiceless democracy'; 'disempowered democracies' (Mkandawire, 2005a); the 'maladjustment' of African economies (Mkandawire, 2005b); and the distinction between 'Merchant State' and 'Rentier State' (Mkandawire, 1995) in understanding the fiscal bases of state conduct in Africa. These are important concepts for political sociology and economic sociology. It is perhaps in the area of social policy and social development that Mkandawire's analytical creativity shines best. The concept of 'Transformative Social Policy' (Mkandawire and UNRISD, 2006; Mkandawire, 2007) allows us a handle to transcend the EAiD bias in social policy. Mhone's (1982) 'enclavity' illuminates the sociological dynamics of mineral-led African economies. Samir Amin's (1972) taxonomy of different socio-economic regimes in Africa remains important, even today. The artisanal rigour of Mafeje (1991) is a benchmark for scholarly works in endogeny.

It is perhaps in the field of 'gender studies' that the most significant works of epistemic rupture have emerged. The works of Amadiume, Oyěwùmí and Nzegwu are grounded in Oyěwùmí's (2004: 8) aphorism: 'the analyses and interpretation of Africa must start with Africa'. In 'Reappropriating matrifocality', Adesina (2010) sets out critical areas in which these works enacted epistemic ruptures in gender discourses. Underpinning Western gender discourse are three core themes: the treatment of women as minors, the exclusion of women from the public space, and the mapping of social roles on biological bodies. These markers, Amadiume, Oyěwùmí and Nzegwu demonstrate, do not travel well. Second, there is the impact of the colonial encounter, and encounters with the Abrahamic faiths, in androcentring the cultures. Even so, the markers of these non-gender binaries in these societies survive. Amadiume's (1987) *Male Daughters, Female Husbands,* demonstrates forms of sociality that would confound Western gender discourse. Matriarchy – as modes of women's power in Amadiume's Nnobi – stretched from the lineage to the political system: a dual-sex system of social, economic and political regulations. Oyěwùmí demonstrates how social roles often do not coincide with anatomical bodies, and gender binaries are not particularly helpful: 'rather, the primary principle of social organization was seniority defined by relative age' (Oyěwùmí, 1997: 31). If we were to follow the gender discourse and its binaries, the question she posed in her most recent book is 'what gender is motherhood?' (Oyěwùmí, 2016).

Contrary to the gross misrepresentation of their works, when they are not being ignored, all three are painfully aware of the extensive subversion of the position of women since the colonial period. Amadiume's (1993) account of her fieldwork shows how female Christian converts in the community considered pre-Christianisation female political orders and positions as heathenish. Oyěwùmí (2016) recaps her earlier works that reveal patriarchal intrusion in the Yorùbá context. Nzegwu's (2006) painful personal experience is placed against testimonies of how colonialism subverted women's socio-economic and political power.

Bakare-Yusuf (2004) enacted a troubling instance of condemning a scholar with a poor reading of her text. As Adesina (2010) demonstrates, Bakare-Yusuf accused Oyěwùmí of claiming what she did not. For example, Oyěwùmí did not claim that the Oyo Yorùbá culture has 'remained pure across time without discontinuities or paradigm shift in collective self-understanding' (Bakare-Yusuf, 2004: 61). Indeed, this is the precise opposite of Oyěwùmí's argument – Chapter 4 of *Invention* alone should clarify this. For the counter-claims that Bakare-Yusuf made, she offered no ethnographic data. In following Bakare-Yusuf down the rabbit hole, Connell (2014) enacted her ontological disconnect from the cultural context of Oyěwùmí's ethnography. If there is something to learn from Amadiume, Oyěwùmí and Nzegwu, it is that the demand for the decolonisation of thought must embrace the decolonisation of relations between males and females. The reappropriation of matrifocality is an important contribution of these scholars (Adesina, 2010).

Epistemic exploration in the House of Ọrúnmìlá: Source codes for doing sociology

The third dimension of sociological scholarship takes the question of endogeneity beyond 'letting our local ethnographic data drive our analyses' to matters of logic and epistemology. What I offer here is illustrative; it rests on the corpus of Ifá texts (a body of Yorùbá sacred texts). Akínṣọlá Akìwọwọ's plea for indigenous sociology (underpinned by Ifá texts) was part of a larger intellectual movement at the University of Ife in the 1970s. His Aṣùwàdà Principle is a derivative of *Ayajọ Alasuwada* – a segment of Ifá texts invoked at the establishment of a new village or residence. Rather than just a critique of Akìwọwọ (Keim, 2008), Adesina's (2001; 2002) intervention was to push Akìwọwọ's work towards its potential for epistemic rupture. Akìwọwọ's initial efforts involved 'doing Sociology in the vernacular' without transcending the functionalist paradigm. This is not to diminish Akìwọwọ's tremendous achievement. In Akìwọwọ's (1999) response to Lawuyi and Taiwo (1990), he introduced Bart Kosko's (1993) fuzzy logic, as the epistemic underpinning of the Aṣùwàdà Principle. Adesina (2001; 2002) argued, however, that Òrúnmìlà[7] is not a fuzzy logician. Rather, the idea of 'T'ibi T'ire Logic' (more recently, Òrúnmìlà logic) was suggested to capture Yorùbá sense-making, which suffused Ifá texts. It derives from the Yorùbá saying: t'ibi t'ire la dá'lé ayé – the world was formed in the cohering of 'contradictory' things. This is referred to as the 'mutual embeddedness of (seemingly) contradictory things' (Adesina, 2001; 2002; 2006a; 2006b: 141).

If Aristotelian logic abhors indeterminate middle-ground (and something is 'either this or not this') and fuzzy logic inhabits the indeterminate middle-ground (and things are this or that to a degree), Òrúnmìlà logic rests on the interpenetration of seemingly contradictory things. To the Hegelian–Marxian idea of thesis and antithesis, Òrúnmìlà logic suggests that thesis and antithesis are mutually embedded and codeterminate. One is not this or that; one is often this *and* that – and many things embedded in one. Death is not the opposite of life – life and death are mutually constitutive.

The method of knowing and sources of knowledge that emerge from Ifá texts and Yorùbá ontological narratives do not ask us to choose between sense, reason and inspiration/faith. Rather they affirm the coexistence of sense, reason and illumination. They do not occasion Sorokin's idea of 'faith' as the basis of knowing since the Orisa religion, which Ifá inhabits, is not a faith-based religion; it is what Abímbólá (2006) calls a 'practical religion'. Ifá divination does not depend on spirit medium – it is a system subject to external adjudication and involves co-creation by the diviner and her client. Its curative therapies are products of the power of observation, drawing inferences and illumination. Kayọde Adeṣọgan (1973a; 1973b; 1979) and others have demonstrated its pharmacognosy.

The epistemological underpinning of Ifá texts and Yorùbá ontological narratives invites fidelity to contingency, complexity and mutual embeddedness of seemingly contradictory things. Òrúnmìlà logic invites us to transcend epistemic orientation to dualism and teleology. It invites fidelity to nuanced

---

[7] Òrúnmìlà is the Yorùbá deity of wisdom, believed to have inspired the Ifá divination system.

narratives rather than categorical exclusions or binaries. This logic, and the metatheory it suggests, offer an exciting prospect for a distinct mode of reasoning about human sociality. The greater task that awaits (South) African sociologists is to mine the diversity of endogenous knowledge systems for the source codes for doing and teaching sociology. It is a venture that requires immense ontological density and proficiency in local languages and sense-making.

It is often said that the Akìwọwọ Project was a confounding dead end (Connell, 2007; Sitas, 2006); a project and debate that went nowhere. It is a conclusion based on a curious idea of visibility confined to the two journals of the International Sociological Association. Seemingly, if your works do not exist there, they do not exist. The debate and the extension of the Akìwọwọ Project have continued on three fronts. First is the iteration of Akìwọwọ's Asuwada Principle in the vein of Mákindé (Omobowale, 2010; Omobowale and Akanle, 2017). The second involves joining the philosophical debate initiated by Lawuyi and Taiwo (Ademoyo, 2009). The third concerns efforts to drill for deeper epistemological materials (Adesina, 2001; 2002; 2006a; 2006b). Ademoyo's (2009) realist intervention in defence of Akìwọwọ derives from the works of Dipọ Fáshínà, a philosopher at the Obafemi Awolowo University. Taiwo (2004) continues to explore the philosophical treasures of the Ifá text. The scholarship around the Ifá text continues to grow; an excellent recent example is by Adegbindin (2014).

Conclusion

I opened this chapter by noting how we often go searching for what is not lost. Through acts of wilful ignorance and sordid neglect, a whole library of scholarly works is closed off. Ignorance is then projected as absence. In the quest for a decolonised education, it is important that those who are so richly endowed should not proclaim poverty. For those, staff and students, who understand the imperative of decolonisation, the resources for enacting it are within reach. Transforming sociology would require embracing the works produced by the African intellectual community and exposing students to these works.

An interesting insight for curriculum reform is evident in how Mamdani (1998) originally designed a first-year course around specific debates within the African social science community. This has several advantages. Students are introduced to, and get to read, works of individual scholars. However, because the course is framed by debates, students get to have a sense of intellectual engagements within the community, and they focus on the flow of ideas within the community rather than deify individual scholars. The students avoid the idea that the community thinks in mono-epistemic terms. It may also help to avoid the prevailing tendency to speak of Africa in the singular. Education becomes more about situated critical reading rather than memorising contents.

A transformed curriculum should not wall (South) African sociologists in the particular. It should expose the students to diverse ideas from different parts of the globe, without privileging the EAiD. Further, it does not involve ignoring Weber, Marx or Bourdieu, but teaching them in their contexts – ideographically.

For the students, while it is important to rail against a colonial, extraverted curriculum, this is only an initial step: a necessary anger that needs to be expressed. The real task lies in study groups that read, debate and exhaustively consider existing works. Inspired by what already exists, the crucial task is to produce new waves of endogenously grounded knowledge.

References

Abímbólá, K (2006) *Yorùbá Culture: A philosophical account*. Birmingham: Iroko Academic Publishers.

Adegbindin, O (2014) *Ifá in Yorùbá Thought System*. Durham, NC: Carolina Academic Press.

Ademoyo, A (2009) Purpose, human sociality and nature in Akiwowo's sociology of knowledge: A realist interpretation, *African Sociological Review/Revue Africaine de Sociologie*, **13**(2): 16–28.

Adesina, JO (2001) Sociology and Yorùbá Studies: Epistemic intervention or doing sociology in the vernacular [expanded version], *Annals of the Social Science Academy of Nigeria*, **13**: 57–91.

Adesina, JO (2002) Sociology and Yorùbá Studies: epistemic intervention or doing sociology in the vernacular, *African Sociological Review*, **6**(1): 91–114.

Adesina, JO (2006a) Sociology beyond despair: Recovery of nerve, endogeneity, and epistemic intervention, *South Africa Review of Sociology*, **37**(2): 241–59.

Adesina, JO (2006b) Sociology, endogeneity and the challenge of transformation, *African Sociological Review*, **10**(2): 133–50.

Adesina, JO (2008) African sociology, in WA Darity, Jr (ed.) *International Encyclopedia of the Social Sciences*. New York: Macmillan Reference.

Adesina, JO (2010) Reappropriating matrifocality: Endogeneity and African gender scholarship, *African Sociological Review*, **14**(2): 2–19.

Adesogan, EK (1973a) Anthraquinones and anthraquinols from Morinda lucida: The biogenetic significance of oruwal and oruwalol, *Tetrahedron*, **29**(24): 4099–102.

Adesogan, EK (1973b) Coumarins and other components of Afraegle paniculata. *Phytochemistry*, **12**(9): 2310–12.

Adesogan, EK (1979) Oruwacin, a new iridoid ferulate from Morinda lucida, *Phytochemistry*, **18**(1):175–76.

Agger, B (2000) *Public Sociology: From social facts to literary acts*. Lanham, MD: Rowman and Littlefield.

Agger, B (2007) *Public Sociology: From social facts to literary acts*, 2nd edition. Lanham, MD: Rowman & Littlefield.

Akiwowo, A (1999) Indigenous sociologies: Extending the scope of the argument, *International Sociology*, **14**(2):115–38.

Alatas, F (2013) *Ibn Khaldun: Makers of Islamic civilization*, 1st edition. New Delhi: Oxford University Press.

Alatas, F (2014) *Applying Ibn Khaldūn: The recovery of a lost tradition in sociology*, in Routledge Advances in Sociology. London: Routledge.

Alatas, H (1977) *Intellectuals in Developing Societies*. London: Cass.

Amadiume, I (1987) *Male Daughters, Female Husbands: Gender and sex in an African society*. London; Atlantic Highlands, NJ: Zed Books.

Amadiume, I (1993) The mouth that spoke a falsehood will later speak the truth: going home to the field in Eastern Nigeria, in D Bell, P Caplan and W Jaham Karim (eds) *Gendered Fields: Women, men and ethnography*. London: Routledge, pp. 182–98.

Amadiume, I (1997) *Re-inventing Africa: Matriarchy, religion, and culture*. London: Zed Books.

Amadiume, I (2000) *Daughters of the Goddess, Daughters of Imperialism: African women struggle for culture, power, and democracy*. London: Zed Books; distributed in the USA by Palgrave.

Amin, S (1972) Underdevelopment and dependence in black Africa: Origins and contemporary forms, *Journal of Modern African Studies*, **10**(4): 503–24.

Archer, M (1991) Sociology for One World: Unity and diversity (ISA Presidential Address), *International Sociology*, **6**(2): 131–47.

Awolowo, O (1953) *The Price of Progress*. Ibadan: Regional Public Relations Officer.

Awolowo, O (1955) Some aspects of our economic problem. Address to the Lagos Chamber of Commerce, Nigeria.

Awolowo, O (1958) *Freedom and Independence for Nigeria: A statement of policy*. Ibadan: s.n.

Awolowo, O (1960) *Awo: The autobiography of Chief Obafemi Awolowo*. Cambridge: Cambridge University Press.

Bakare-Yusuf, B (2004) 'Yorubas don't do gender': A critical review of Oyeronke Oyewumi's *The Invention of Women: Making an African sense of Western gender discourse*, in S Arnfred, B Bakare-Yusuf, E Waswa Kisiang'ani, D Lewis and O Oyewumi (eds) *African Gender Scholarship: Concepts, methodologies and paradigms*. Dakar: CODESRIA Books, pp. 61–81.

Beck, U (2006) *The Cosmopolitan Vision*. Cambridge: Polity Press.

Bell, D (1947) Adjusting men to machines: Social scientists explore the work of the factory, *Commentary*, **37**: 79–88.

Bourdieu, P (1984) *Distinction: A social critique of the judgement of taste*. Cambridge, MA: Harvard University Press.

Burawoy, M (2004a) Public sociologies: Contradictions, dilemmas and possibilities, *Social Forces*, **82**(4): 1603–18.

Burawoy, M (2004b) Public sociology: South African dilemmas in a global context, *Society in Transition*, **35**(1): 11–26.

Burawoy, M (2005a) 2004 American Sociological Association Presidential address: For public sociology, *British Journal of Sociology*, **56**(2): 259–94.

Burawoy, M (2005b) The critical turn to public sociology, *Critical Sociology*, **31**(3): 313–26.

Burawoy, M (2005c) The return of the repressed: Recovering the public face of US sociology, one hundred years on, *Annals of the American Academy of Political and Social Science*, **600**: 68–85.

Cabral, A (1966) The weapon of theory. Paper presented at the First Tricontinental Conference of the Peoples of Asia, Africa and Latin America, Havana, Cuba, January 1966.

Cabral, A (1969) *The Struggle in Guinea*, Reprint – Africa Research Group, 1. Cambridge, MA: Africa Research Group.

Cabral, A (1970a) National liberation and culture: 1st Eduardo Mondlane Memorial Lecture (20 February 1970). In *Eduardo Mondlane Memorial Lecture Series*. Syracuse, NY: Syracuse University.

Cabral, A (1970b) *Revolution in Guinea: Selected texts*. New York: Monthly Review Press.

Cabral, A (1972) *Our People are our Mountains: Amilcar Cabral on the Guinean Revolution*. London: Committee for Freedom in Mozambique, Angola & Guiné.

Cabral, A (1973) Identity and dignity in the context of the national liberation struggle, in A Cabral (ed.) *Return to the Source: Selected speeches of Amilcar Cabral*. New York: Monthly Review Press.

Cabral, A (1974) *Return to the Source: Selected speeches*. New York: Monthly Review Press.
Cabral, A (1979) *Unity and Struggle: Speeches and writings*. New York: Monthly Review Press.
Césaire, A (2010) [1956] Letter to Maurice Thorez, *Social Text*, **28**(2): 145–52.
Césaire, A (2017) Cultural diversity as a factor in development. UNESCO. Available at: http://www.unesco.org/culture/aic/echoingvoices/aime-cesaire.php (accessed August 2017).
Cock, J (1980) *Maids & Madams: A study in the politics of exploitation*. Johannesburg: Ravan Press.
Connell, R (2007) *Southern Theory: The global dynamics of knowledge in social science*. Cambridge: Polity Press.
Connell, R (2010) Learning from each other: Sociology on a world scale, in S Patel (ed.) *The ISA Handbook of Diverse Sociological Traditions*. Thousand Oaks, CA: SAGE Publications, pp. 40–51.
Connell, R (2011) Sociology for the whole world, *International Sociology*, **26**(3): 288–91.
Connell, R (2014) The sociology of gender in southern perspective, *Current Sociology*, **62**(4): 550–67.
Dhaouadi, M (1990) Ibn Khaldun – the founding-father of Eastern sociology, *International Sociology*, **5**(3): 319–35. doi: Doi 10.1177/026858090005003007.
Dhaouadi, M (2008) The forgotten concept of human nature in Khaldunian Studies, *Asian Journal of Social Science*, **36**(3–4): 571–89. doi: 10.1163/156853108x327083.
Diop, CA (1974) *The African Origin of Civilization: Myth or reality*, 1st edition. Chicago, IL: Lawrence Hill Books.
Diop, CA (1987) *Precolonial Black Africa: A comparative study of the political and social systems of Europe and Black Africa, from antiquity to the formation of modern states*. Chicago, IL: Lawrence Hill Books.
Diop, CA (1991) *Civilization or Barbarism: An authentic anthropology*, 1st edition. Chicago, IL: Lawrence Hill Books.
Du Bois, WEB (1903) *The Souls of Black Folk: Essays and sketches*. Chicago, IL: AC McClurg & Co.
Du Bois, WEB and Wortham, RA (2011) *The Sociological Souls of Black folk: Essays by W.E.B Du Bois*. Lanham, MD: Lexington Books.
Durkheim, É (1915) *The Elementary Forms of the Religious Life: A study in religious sociology*. London: George Allen & Unwin.
Esping-Andersen, G (1990) *The Three Worlds of Welfare Capitalism*. Cambridge: Polity Press.
Esping-Andersen, G (1999) *Social Foundations of Post-industrial Economies*. Oxford: Oxford University Press.
Fadipẹ, NA (1970) [1939]. *The Sociology of the Yorùbá*. Ibadan: Ibadan University Press.
Giddens, A (1971) *Capitalism and Modern Social Theory: An analysis of the writings of Marx, Durkheim and Max Weber*. Cambridge: Cambridge University Press.
Giddens, A (1996) *In Defence of Sociology: Essays, interpretations and rejoinders*. Cambridge: Polity Press.
Go, J (2016) Globalizing sociology, turning south. Perspectival realism and the southern standpoint, *Sociologica*, 2/2016. doi: 10.2383/85279.
Hountondji, PJ (1995) Producing knowledge in Africa today: The second Bashorun MKO Abiola Distinguished Lecture, *African Studies Review*, **38**(3):1–10.
Hountondji, PJ (1996) *African Philosophy: Myth and reality*, 2nd edition. Bloomington, IN: Indiana University Press.
Hountondji, PJ (1997) Introduction, in PJ Hountondji (ed.) *Endogenous Knowledge: Research trails*. Dakar: CODESRIA Books, pp. 1–39.
Hountondji, PJ (2002) *The Struggle for Meaning: Reflections on philosophy, culture, and democracy in Africa*, Research in International Studies Africa Series. Athens, OH: University Center for International Studies.

Ibn Khaldūn, AA (1355) *Kitāb al-'ibar wa-dīwān al-mubtada' wa-al-khabar: fī ayyām al-'Arab wa-al-'Ajam wa-al-barbar wa-man 'āṣarahum min dhawī al-ṣulṭān al-akbar : al-Juz' 7. [i.e. al-Juz' 1.].* Fez: al-Maktabah al-Tijāriyyah al-Kubrā.

Keim, W (2008) Social sciences internationally: The problem of marginalisation and its consequences for the discipline of sociology, *African Sociological Review/Revue Africaine de Sociologie,* **12**(2): 22–48.

Keim, W (2010) Review: Raewyn Connell's (2007) *Southern Theory: The global dynamics of knowledge in social science* (Polity Press), *Transcience,* **1**(1): 106–08.

Keim, W (2011) Counterhegemonic currents and internationalization of sociology: Theoretical reflections and an empirical example, *International Sociology,* **26**(1): 123–45.

Kosko, B (1993) *Fuzzy Thinking: The new science of fuzzy logic,* vol 1. New York: Hyperion.

Lawuyi, OB and Olufemi, T (1990) Towards an African sociological tradition: A rejoinder to Akiwowo and Makinde, *International Sociology,* **5**(1): 57–73.

Mafeje, A (1991) *The Theory and Ethnography of African Social Formations: The case of the interlacustrine kingdoms,* Codesria Book Series. London: CODESRIA.

Mamdani, M (1996) *Citizen and Subject: Contemporary Africa and the legacy of late colonialism,* Princeton Studies in Culture/Power/History. Princeton, NJ: Princeton University Press.

Mamdani, M (1998) Is African studies to be turned into a new home for Bantu education at UCT? *Social Dynamics,* **24**(2): 63–75.

Mamdani, M (2012). *Define and Rule: Native as political identity, The W.E.B. Du Bois lectures.* Cambridge, MA: Harvard University Press.

Mbeki, G (1939) *Transkei in the making.* Verulam.

Mbeki, G (1944) *Let's do it together: What cooperative societies are and do,* Sixpenny Library. Cape Town: African Bookman.

Mbeki, G (1964) *South Africa: The peasants' revolt.* London: International Defence and Aid Fund for Southern Africa.

Meer, F (1976) *Race and Suicide in South Africa,* International Library of Sociology. London: Routledge and Kegan Paul.

Mhone, GCZ (1982) *The Political Economy of a Dual Labor Market in Africa: The copper industry and dependency in Zambia, 1929–1969.* Rutherford: Fairleigh Dickinson University Press.

Mkandawire, T (1995) Fiscal structure, state construction and political responses in Africa, in T Mkandawire and AO Olukoshi (eds) *Between Liberalisation and Oppression: The politics of structural adjustment in Africa.* Dakar, Senegal: CODESRIA Books, pp. 20–51.

Mkandawire, T (2005a) Disempowering new democracies and the persistence of poverty, in M Spoor (ed.) *Globalisation, Poverty and Conflict.* Dordrecht: Kluwer Academic Publishers, pp. 117–53.

Mkandawire, T (2005b) Maladjusted African economies and globalisation, *Africa Development,* **XXX**(1&2): 1–33.

Mkandawire, T (2007) Transformative social policy and innovation in developing countries, *European Journal of Development Research,* **19**(1):13–29.

Mkandawire, T and UNRISD (2006) *Transformative Social Policy: Lessons from UNRISD research.* Geneva: United Nations Research Institute for Social Development, pp. 1–6.

Nkrumah, K (1964) *Consciencism: Philosophy and ideology for decolonization and development with particular reference to the African revolution.* London: Heinemann.

Nkrumah, K (1965) *Neo-colonialism : The last stage of imperialism.* London: Nelson.

Nyerere, JK (1967a) *Education for Self-reliance.* Dar es Salaam: Government Printer.

Nyerere, JK (1967b) *Socialism and Rural Development.* Dar es Salaam: Government Printer.

Nyerere, JK (1968) *Freedom and Socialism = Uhuru na ujamaa: A selection from writings and speeches, 1965–1967.* Dar es Salaam: Oxford University Press.

Nyerere, JK (1971) The role of an African university, *Journal of Modern African Studies,* **9**(1):107–14.

Nzegwu, N (2006). *Family Matters: Feminist concepts in African philosophy of culture*, SUNY Series, Feminist Philosophy. Albany, NY: State University of New York Press.

Omobowale, AO (2010) Academic dependency and sociological theorizing in the Third World: A case study of Akiwowo's Asuwada Theory of Sociation, in K Sinha-Kerkhoff and SF Alatas (eds) *Academic Dependency in the Social Sciences: Structural reality and intellectual challenges*. New Delhi: Manoha, pp. 133–56.

Omobowale, AO and Akanle, O (2017) Asuwada epistemology and globalised sociology: Challenges of the South, *Sociology*, **51**(1): 43–59.

Oyěwùmí, O (1997) *The Invention of Women: Making an African sense of Western gender discourses*. Minneapolis, MN: University of Minnesota Press.

Oyěwùmí, O (1998a) De-confounding gender: Feminist theorizing and Western culture, a comment on Hawkesworth's 'Confounding Gender', *Signs*, **23**(4): 1062.

Oyěwùmí, O (1998b) Making history, creating gender: Some methodological and interpretive questions in the writing of Oyo oral traditions, *History in Africa*, **25**: 305.

Oyěwùmí, O (2003) *African Women and Feminism: Reflecting on the politics of sisterhood*. Trenton, NJ: Africa World Press, p. 267.

Oyěwùmí, O (2004) Conceptualising gender: Eurocentric foundations of feminist concepts and the challenge of African epistemologies, in S Arnfred, B Bakare-Yusuf, E Waswa Kisiang'ani, D Lewis and O Oyěwùmí (eds) *African Gender Scholarship: Concepts, methodologies, and paradigms*. Dakar: CODESRIA Books, pp. 1–8.

Oyěwùmí, O (2005) *African Gender Studies: Theoretical questions and conceptual issues*. Houndmills, Basingstoke: Palgrave Macmillan.

Oyěwùmí, O (2016) *What Gender is Motherhood? Changing Yorùbá ideals of power, procreation and identity in the Age of Modernity*. New York: Palgrave Macmillan.

Rabaka, R (2007) *W.E.B. Du Bois and the Problems of the Twenty-first Century: An essay on Africana critical theory*. Lanham, MD: Lexington Books.

Rabaka, R (2008) *Du Bois' Dialectics: Black radical politics and the reconstruction of critical social theory*. Lanham, MD: Lexington Books.

Rabaka, R (2009) *Africana Critical Theory: Reconstructing the black radical tradition, from W.E.B. Du Bois and C.L.R. James to Frantz Fanon and Amilcar Cabral*. Lanham, MD: Lexington Books.

Rabaka, R (2010a) *Against Epistemic Apartheid: W.E.B. Du Bois and the disciplinary decadence of sociology*. Lanham, MD: Lexington Books.

Rabaka, R (ed.) (2010b) *W.E.B. Du Bois: A critical reader*, International Library of Essays in Classical Sociology, xlvii. Burlington, VT: Ashgate.

Schmidt, N (1930) *Ibn Khaldun: Historian, sociologist and philosopher*. New York: Columbia University press.

Simpson, IH (1989) The sociology of work: Where have the workers gone? *Social Forces*, **67**(3): 563–81.

Sitas, A (2006) The African Renaissance challenge and sociological reclamations in the south, *Current Sociology*, **54**(3): 357–80.

Sitas, A (2014) Rethinking Africa's sociological project, *Current Sociology*, **62**(4): 457–71. doi: 10.1177/0011392114524505.

Sztompka, P (2010) One sociology or many? In S Patel (ed.) *The ISA Handbook of Diverse Sociological Traditions*. Thousand Oaks, CA: SAGE Publications, pp. 21–8

Taiwo, O (2004) Ifá: An account of a divination system and some concluding epistemological questions, in Ki Wiredu (ed.) *A Companion to African Philosophy*. Oxford: Blackwell Publishing, pp. 304–12.

Usman, YB (1981) *The Transformation of Katsina, 1400–1883: The emergence and overthrow of the sarauta system and the establishment of the emirate*. Zaria, Nigeria: Ahmadu Bello University Press.

Usman, YB (2006) *Beyond Fairy Tales: Selected historical writing of Yusufu Bala Usman*, 1st edition.

Zaria, Nigeria: Abdullahi Smith Centre for Historical Research.

Washington, BT and Du Bois, WEB (1907) *The Negro in the South, his Economic Progress in Relation to his Moral and Religious Development: Being the William Levi Bull Lectures for the year 1907.* Philadelphia, PA: GW Jacobs & Company.

Weber, M (1985) *The Protestant Ethic and the Spirit of Capitalism.* London: Unwin Paperbacks.

Wortham, RA (2005) Du Bois and the sociology of religion: Rediscovering a founding figure, *Sociological Inquiry,* **75**(4): 433–52.

Wortham, RA (2009) *W.E.B. Du Bois and the Sociological Imagination: A reader, 1897–1914.* Waco, TX: Baylor University Press.

Chapter 12
Transforming South Africa's curricula through African philosophy

Philip Higgs

Introduction

Ramose (2004: 138) reminds us:

> [F]or at least three centuries since the conquest of the indigenous people in the unjust wars of colonization, the education curriculum in South Africa did not include African philosophy. For the colonial conqueror and the successor in title thereto the indigenous conquered peoples had neither an epistemology nor a philosophy worth including in any educational curriculum.

Education in Africa in the 21st century operates in both a post-colonial and globalising context. However, the curricula in post-colonial Africa are still, to a large extent, confronted by the legacy of colonial education, which remained in place decades after political decolonisation. Despite the advent of decolonisation, African education systems mirror colonial education paradigms inherited from former colonial education systems and, as a result, the voices of African indigenous populations are negated. Colonial education was hegemonic and disruptive to African cultural practices, indigenous epistemologies and ways of knowing. The centuries-old subjugation of Africa to colonial exploitation, ranging from slavery to the creation of socio-economic structures during the colonial era, which were designed to achieve maximum extraction and exportation of raw materials, wreaked serious damage that remains palpable years after the demise of colonial rule. This was accomplished, as Nkomo (2000: 4) notes, by a whole range of arrangements including educational philosophies, curricula and practices whose context corresponded with that of the respective colonial powers. This meant that with the advent of colonisation, traditional African epistemologies started disappearing due to cultural repression, misrepresentations and devaluation (Ramose, 2001; 2004; Higgs, 2016). Colonialism in Africa thus provided the framework for the organised subjugation of the cultural, scientific and economic life of many on the African continent. This subjugation ignored indigenous African knowledge systems and impacted on African people's way of seeing and acting in the world. In fact, African identity, to all intents and purposes, became an inverted mirror of Western identity (see Modiri, Chapter 10, Owusu-Ansah, Chapter 17, and Wanjala, Chapter 19, in this volume). This gave rise to numerous attempts to reassert the significance of indigenous African knowledges in the face of hegemonic Western forms of knowledge, which have determined the discourse on education in Africa from the onset of colonial occupation. Such a discourse on the transformation of education in South Africa has emphasised the ideas of an African essence, culture and identity, as well as indigenous African knowledge systems.

Consequently, there is an existential and humane need today to decolonise the curriculum in South Africa by means of a post-colonial education system that reclaims indigenous African voices through curriculum reforms and the transformation of education discourses (Ramose, 2004; Higgs, 2008). In this chapter, I argue for the reclamation of indigenous African knowledges in educational discourses which are directed at the transformation of the curriculum in South Africa, whereby Africans can reclaim their voices in the education spaces of South Africa. This reclamation should, however, not exclude and negate Western forms of knowledge but should rather be directed at what I refer to as *a fusion of epistemologies*, which seeks to integrate both indigenous African knowledges and Western forms of knowledge in education. Such a *fusion of epistemologies* would provide the epistemological framework for transforming South Africa's education curriculum and would be enacted by what I call a *postmodern dis-position*.

African indigenous knowledges and the hegemony of Western knowledge

African societies have experienced various forms of domination in their histories, such as the slave trade, colonialism, neo-colonialism and globalisation. Central to this domination is the problem concerned with the negation and devaluation of indigenous African knowledges and the hegemony of Western forms of knowledge (Akena, 2012; Kodirekkala, 2016). Although each African state has its own experience of this domination, Sefa Dei (1998: 510) notes that there is 'a shared history of colonial and imperial imposition of external ideas and knowledges over much of the continent'.

One of the consequences of the hegemony of the Western episteme for indigenous African knowledges was the fundamental erasure of the rich knowledge legacy of the African people. Western sentiment often locates authentic knowledge only within its own political and cultural boundaries, while at the same time concluding that knowledges derived from African people are non-scientific.

The West uses this hegemonic discourse as an apparatus of control to sustain an unequal relationship between what they would call 'developed' and 'underdeveloped' countries. Central to the Western development model stand the notions of 'progress' and 'science'. The resulting Western discourse universalises the material and economic aspects of human life. The acquisition of certain material things, or lack thereof, determines whether people are progressive or non-progressive, and thus the development of concepts such as 'First World' and 'Third World'. Maher (2000: 64–65) observes that the First World serves as a model of progress – the desirable way of living – while the Third World represents 'a degenerate enclave of people who cannot manage their own lives'. Progress – in the hegemonic discourse of the West – is only achieved through the advancement of science, whose findings are regarded as universal, value-free and objective. As a result, Maher (2000: 65) argues that this scientific way of understanding the universe became the only way of knowing and pursuing progress, and meant that indigenous knowledges in non-Western societies, including Africa, were relegated to an inferior status. According to Le Grange (2000: 115), non-Westerners have, consequently, been kept ignorant of their culture's scientific and technological achievements, because of the strong position of Western science and technology. As a result, to date, indigenous African knowledge systems including an African episteme, have not been included in any significant way in the curricula of education institutions and they have not been allowed into public domains (see Bawa, Chapter 4, in this volume). Only the Western episteme – which includes heritages, cultures, institutions, norms and idiosyncrasies – is important in education institutions and the public domain. In the light of this, Odora Hoppers (2001: 74) observes that Africans lost all self-confidence to participate in a conversation that marginalised all the heritage and legacy enshrined in an indigenous African episteme.

The era of colonialism and slavery thus influenced Africans negatively – it was a time of self-alienation, during which, as Okolo (1985: 6) argues, Africa's true values and modes of being were distorted and attuned to Western values. As a result, Africans lived and acted inauthentically, untrue to their nature and their world. In short, the being of Africans was negated, removed from history as an active participant through creative freedom and initiative.

However, during the postcolonial era, Africans have become more and more interested in asserting the truth about themselves and their world. Since their independence from colonial rule, they see their mission as being human as well as African. Kwame Nkrumah (in Okolo, 1985: 6) argues that 'the desire of the African people themselves to unite and to assert their personality in the context of the African community has made itself felt everywhere'.

However, when it comes to reasserting the cultural heritage of indigenous African people, the controversial issue of regaining and affirming a distinctive African identity – as opposed to a predominantly Western identity – is still very present. Snyman (2002) addressed this issue when he asked whether 'Africa's otherness' did not result from the West's and, in this case, he refers to Europe's attempt to constitute and maintain its self-image and identity by fashioning, as a precondition, a 'deserving enemy'. He argued that modernity was born when Europe posed itself against 'an-other'. In this context, attempts at affirming a distinctive African identity were said to be aimed against what Snyman (2002: 65) called 'the trap of Eurocentricity', namely the claim of cultural universalism that can easily become a variation of cultural imperialism or ethnocentrism.

Dussel (1993: 66) refers to this Eurocentric problematic as 'the myth of modernity'. In terms of this myth, modernity or Europe, Dussel (1993: 68–70) argues, understands itself as the most developed and superior civilisation in the world. This sense of superiority, he believes, obliges Europe to develop the rest of the world's underdeveloped nations, even by violent means if necessary. Modernity was thus born in a period, he maintains, when Europe was to align itself against 'an-other'. Europe could only, therefore, he claims, accomplish this by conquering and colonising an alterity that gave back its image to itself. Subsequently, the affirmation of Afrocentricity vis-à-vis Eurocentricity, Dussel (1993: 73) concludes, is a reminder to Europeans that they cannot think for themselves without Africa. To do that is to suppress the conflicts that shaped modern Europe and continue to shape postmodern Europe.

Dussel (1993: 76) offers a significant insight into this problematic, by arguing that the binary opposition of Eurocentricity and Afrocentricity should be seen as part of a process that moves towards transmodernity, that is, beyond the 'myth of modernity'. He (1993: 76) refers to transmodernity as 'a project of political, economic, ecological, pedagogical and religious liberation that constitutes a co-realisation of that which modernity is incapable of accomplishing, namely an incorporative solidarity between the centre (Europe) and the periphery (Africa)'.

Transmodernity, therefore, attempts to establish an integrated form of knowledge that acknowledges both indigenous African knowledge systems and Western forms of knowledge. Consequently, attempts at decolonising colonised forms of knowledge in Africa should be seen to locate indigenous African knowledges within a holistic epistemology, which includes Western forms of knowledge. This means that attempts at reclaiming an African epistemic should not in any way strive for an epistemology of exclusion. In short, such attempts at reclamation should acknowledge both indigenous African knowledge systems and Western knowledge systems as constituting necessary components of a holistic framework of knowledge systems, which benefit each other.

The danger in not acknowledging such a mutual compromise is that, just as a Western or Eurocentric approach to identity and knowledge can be perceived to be imperialistic and universal, there is also the potential for the ideological nature of an African-centred approach to identity and knowledge to become as universal and exploitative, especially in the image of an ethnic fundamental understanding of Afrocentricity, which champions the tragic victims of socio-political conditions for which there is no way out.

African indigenous knowledge systems and education

Heleta (2018:5) asserts that education must be free from Western epistemological domination, Eurocentrism, epistemic violence and world-views that were designed to degrade, exploit and subjugate people in Africa and other parts of the formerly colonised world, and that decolonised people should not accept anything from the Global North in an uncritical manner.

However, I would argue that the interaction between a Western approach to what counts as valid knowledge and an African approach to valid knowledge needs continual displacement to ensure that neither obtains a dominant position in any form of educational discourse in Africa (Abah, Mahebe and Denuga, 2015; Mawere, 2015). The ideal, I would argue, represents what I call a *fusion of epistemologies* of both indigenous African knowledges and Western forms of knowledge in education. What this means is that a core strategy should be adopted, which seeks the best of both indigenous African and Western epistemologies because, as Odora Hoppers (2002:15) states, 'the local contextual expertise that indigenous knowledge frames can offer, can complement some of the mechanical, technical, and scientific precision capabilities of Western knowledge systems to generate forms of creativity that benefit and empower everyone'. The potential impact of such an epistemological arrangement, or *fusion of epistemologies*, on education in South Africa is outlined below.

In the first instance, it will ensure that indigenous African knowledges are acknowledged in education curricula in South Africa. To date this has not happened in any real sense because these knowledges have been marginalised by the continued presence of Western epistemological frames of reference (see Adesina, Chapter 11, in this volume). What is required is that the educational project of transforming education in South Africa be redirected. This does not mean doing away with Western epistemological frames of reference, but rather involves an attempt at the creative integration of a diversity of epistemological frames of reference in education curricula, including indigenous African knowledges.

Secondly, such a fusion of epistemologies will encourage critical questions being directed at the knowledge content that is included in education curricula in South Africa, and how this knowledge is integrated in various subject programmes. This will require, Odora Hoppers (2002: 20–21) claims, a critical or reflexive *praxis* and an ongoing willingness towards reflexivity. She goes on to state that such a self-reflexive praxis directed at an educational sphere, which advocates the rediscovery of an African *gnosis* (way of knowing), will be concerned with, among other things:

- critiquing conceptual systems that depend exclusively on a Western epistemological order;
- establishing parameters of rationality, and ethically sound and ecologically constituted ways of thinking;
- paying attention to the originality of African contributions and the foregrounding of African indigenous knowledge systems; and
- monitoring and evaluating cultural and gender bias in curricula.

Thirdly, such a *fusion of epistemologies* will address issues of alienation and dominance. By means of critical inquiry, any oppressive situation will be unveiled, analysed and changed. This idea has been echoed by Freire (1970: 36) in his notion of 'reflection and action', and by Newsum (1990: 85) in his reference to 'reflection with positive and active participation'. Any form of education will in such an instance, McLaren (1989: 189) notes, be primarily involved with processes of inquiry that do not see the oppressive situation as a closed world from which there is no exit, but rather as a process of constructing and building possibilities through imagination and hope. Hence, any form of education in South Africa that seeks to integrate indigenous African knowledges and Western forms of knowledge will be concerned mainly with empowering learners in order to gain increasing confidence in their own abilities, while at the same time acquiring a sense of pride in their own ways of being and acting in the world. This means that these forms of education will provide learners with an acknowledgement of the legitimacy of their own voices after they have grappled with the education content offered to them. In so doing, learners will be encouraged to seek out the significant connections between the knowledge contents offered in education curricula and their own life experiences.

Finally, a fusion of epistemologies, which seeks to integrate both indigenous African knowledges and Western forms of knowledge in education, will see knowledge development as a holistic journey that includes process, content and the socio-cultural context in which learning is being modelled (see Higgs, 2016). According to Odora Hoppers (2002: 15), the view that sees knowledge simply as information, mediated by schooling, should be challenged because this removes learners from knowledge as wisdom and, consequently, draws attention from those who hold the responsibility for the transmission of such knowledge. Ramose (2001: 2) reminds us, furthermore, that wisdom is an openness to unfolding practices, which also acclaims cooperation rather than conquest and competition. The golden rule of wisdom, he argues, is that 'reductionism, absolutism, universalism, and dogmatism are an injury to the complexity of life as a holistic phenomenon'.

According to these insights, a fusion of epistemologies in education in South Africa, which incorporates indigenous African knowledges with Western forms of knowledge, should, therefore, perceive learning as cooperation and not primarily competition, in its endeavour to construct knowledge that empowers local communities to embark on their own educational practice and development. Embracing a fusion of epistemologies in the transformation of the curricula in South Africa will, in turn, be undergirded by a perspective on African philosophy that adopts what I refer to as a *postmodern dis-position* (Higgs, 2017).

The transformation of the curriculum in South Africa and a postmodern dis-position

There is a growing literature on attempts to critically understand and apply the concept of postmodernism in African philosophy and, by extension, the analysis of the postcolonial African predicament (Ciaffa, 2008; Afolayan, 2012; Araia, 2014; Etieyibo, 2014; Mungwini, 2014).

In embracing a postmodern turn for African philosophy in its efforts to transform South Africa's curricula, I have assumed a critical standpoint regarding modernity and the philosophies of the Enlightenment that underpinned it. This postmodern turn is aptly captured by West (1990: 93) as a drive

> to trash the monolithic and homogeneous in the name of diversity, multiplicity, and heterogeneity; to reject the abstract, general, and universal in light of the concrete, specific, and particular; and to historicize, contextualize, and pluralize by highlighting the contingent, provisional, variable, tentative, shifting, and changing.

Postmodernism, therefore, emerges, as Sim (2001) notes, as 'a rejection of many, if not most, of the cultural certainties on which life (particularly) in the West has been structured over the last couple of centuries'.

But when it comes to African culture, some scholars, Mungwini (2014: 19) observes, have expressed scepticism about postmodernism and its relevance to cultures outside the West, such as Africa (see Ekpo, 1995). However, Sim (2001) asserts that if by postmodernism we refer to the deployment of philosophy to question and possibly overturn the grand narratives and universalising theories in culture, both at the theoretical and political level, then there cannot be any question concerning its relevance to postcolonial Africa. In fact, it is in formerly colonised cultures more than anywhere else that the power and promise of postmodernism as a critical theory of society is seriously required.

Mungwini (2014: 19) claims that we would do well to learn from Outlaw's (1991) famous article 'African philosophy: Deconstructive and reconstructive challenges', in which he appropriates the theory of deconstruction from within the Western academy to make effective use of it in unmasking and undoing the Eurocentric residues inherited from colonialism, which continue to influence discourses in African philosophy. In the light of this, it may be that 'the antidote is always located in the poison', as Serequeberhan phrases it (1994: 11), while acknowledging the difficulty of avoiding recourse to Western forms of knowledge in the process of redeeming Africa. It is therefore important for African philosophy to be able to appropriate Western forms of knowledge for its own positive development and as effective tools for the critical rejection of colonial discourses.

I believe this is how postmodernism can and should be utilised in African philosophy in attempting to transform the South African curriculum because postmodernism provides, in the words of Kenzo (2002: 323), an opportunity for African scholars 'to think differently and otherwise about Africa'. Kenzo (2002: 323) argues strongly that

> it is legitimate to think of Africa in terms of postmodernism because the current postcolonial situation calls for it and it is beneficial to think about Africa in terms of postmodernism because postmodernism clears free space at the margins of Enlightenment reason where true alterity can be sought and expressed.

In the light of this, Mungwini (2014: 19) is convinced that, given the extent to which modernity and its Enlightenment project conspired against Africa, it seems reasonable that any philosophy which attempts to question modernity or to review its normative framework and rules of engagement should out of necessity also take root in Africa. In fact, it is only when modernity acknowledges, through critical self-introspection, the existence of different ways of interpreting reality, that new spaces for the emergence of what he (2014: 20) refers to as a 'polycentric global epistemology' can be created and that consequently

> There is no doubt that the postmodern turn holds promise for Africa going forward. Through its radical, uncanny unmasking of the principles and ruses of Western culture, power and history, the postmodern turn is opening the way for non-Westerners in general and Africans in particular, to radically re-think the fundamental categories through which they have hitherto perceived, received or rejected the West (Mungwini, 2014: 20).

And herein is to be found, I believe, the philosophical and educational mandate for the transformation of South Africa's curricula through African philosophy. In advocating such a mandate, I argue for the adoption of what I call *a postmodern dis-position* in the transformation of the curricula through African philosophy. In this instance, I argue that African philosophy should be opposed to that formulation of knowledge espoused by modern Western/European thought, where rationality is closely connected to knowledge. Such a re-vision of Western/European rationality is fundamentally directed at the process by which African philosophy attempts, as Appiah (1992: 105) claims, 'to become modern within the framework of its own peculiar context'.

However, we should be careful not to overlook the fact that knowledge is not only local but also intersubjective. Alongside many indigenous African knowledge cultures, there are also many different knowledge cultures on the African continent, which testifies to its fundamentally plural composition. If this is overlooked, we might be confronted with the danger of a renewed fundamentalism in African philosophy that is founded on the view of a particular African knowledge culture. It is, therefore, important that those who advocate the transformation of the South African curriculum through African philosophy ensure that African philosophy take cognisance of an African knowledge culture that does not only include the idea of what I refer to as plural conversations in an inter-African context, but also includes a cross-cultural epistemic which facilitates cross-cultural dialogue and understanding. The merits of such an African knowledge culture include:

- its acknowledgment of alternative forms of knowing and their accompanying cultural expressions in both an inter-African context and in a cross-cultural context;
- its insistence that knowledge production is not independent of moral and

political value in its grounding of rationality in social relations; and
- its recognition of the role of commitment, caring and feeling in rationality.

In the light of this, I am proposing an orientation to African philosophy that has cultural relevance insofar as it is mounted on concepts peculiar to an inter-African context, as well as in the larger context of a continuing cross-cultural dialogue. Such an orientation to African philosophy acknowledges the necessity to develop the ability to grasp the fundamentals of indigenous African cultures and other cultures by way of adopting and living out what I call a *postmodern dis-position*. Such a postmodern dis-position would perceive an African knowledge culture not only as an inter-cultural African philosophy of personal intent, but also as the practice of cross-cultural dialogue, where culture takes on the form of a consensual or social epistemology, that is, an epistemology deliberately situated in a cultural context and sensitive to the need for cross-cultural dialogue.

Such cross-cultural dialogue is based on what I refer to as *plural conversations*, in which the process of reason is revealed in a movement towards an agreed consensus, arising from careful deliberation and the exercise of choice in reaching a conclusion. If, at a later stage, the conclusion is found to be incorrect, which it may well be, then it can be recognised as such and rectified through an extension of the same process. In arguing that plural conversations are necessary for the intersubjective negotiation of knowledge, I would argue for the enactment of a consensual or social rationality that reflects a sense of solidarity in the experience of shared plural conversations.

This constitutes the exercise of reason in a postmodern moment that pauses to reflect on the limits of our understanding, while at the same time respecting diversity and unassimilated otherness in the experience of finding the space to listen and converse. All this is manifested in an age that Lyotard (1979: 278) claims can no longer talk about a totalising idea of reason, because 'there is no reason, only reasons'. Such a discourse on rationality does not limit itself to the following of formal rules and procedures of thought in making sense of the world, but reveals itself in the intersubjective engagement of what I call a *postmodern dis-position*. By a *postmodern dis-position*, I mean that fundamental reorientation that we adopt in relation to our intersubjective engagement with the world. Here we have to deal with a deep personal transformation, which impacts on the way we engage with others in our practical everyday experiences in thinking and acting.

In developing my argument, I propose that such a personal transformation, when it comes to African philosophy, is taken up in a postmodern dis-position that is marked by certain moments which are manifestations of something much more fundamental about us as individuals. Here I draw on a seminal contribution by Burbules (1995) in identifying such moments as being constituted by a sense of plurality, fallibilism, pragmatism and judiciousness.

A *sense of plurality* is fostered partly by having been exposed to a range of different perspectives, but also by engaging them in a way that enables one to consider seriously the merits of each. This means that in teaching African philosophy, we reveal a capacity to regard alternative positions without a 'rush to judgement' in that we can withhold our own opinions in an engagement with other points of view. This capacity is fostered primarily not by the exercise of certain intellectual skills, but by the exercise of a disposition and capacity for restraint. Such a capacity for restraint reveals that we recognise what our own prejudices might be, while acknowledging the limits of our own capacity to appreciate fully the viewpoints of others, and while caring enough about others to exert the effort necessary to hear and comprehend what they are saying. A sense of plurality, therefore, has to do with commitment, caring and feeling. It is clearly not a purely rational and cognitive endeavour.

Burbules (1995) maintains that such a sense of plurality is supported, not by a position of holding no view, but by the position of having regarded other views thoughtfully and sympathetically enough to realise that each has something to be said for it, so that one is distanced somewhat from the attitude that there is or can be one best way of all. We would, therefore, in teaching African philosophy, acknowledge the fact of difference – perhaps irreconcilable difference – as a condition of the social world and take our direction not from an ethnocentric presumption of superiority, or the erasure of difference in the name of presumed consensus around a unified truth, but in a thoughtful and sensitive engagement across differences, while even at times leaving some of those differences in place.

One of the great insights of modern philosophy of science is Popper's (1972) reminder not to be afraid of making mistakes, because it is only through the discovery of error, through some process of falsification, that we are driven to change. Indeed, Popper's recommendation seems to extend far beyond the confines of scientific hypothesis testing (where it is typically applied) to a broader vision and attitude to life. In a variety of contexts, both personal and professional, and intellectual and emotional, we all have experienced failure, error, frustration and disappointment. If we can live with this – as we must – it is usually with the understanding that these experiences have formed us, taught us something and strengthened our capacity to endure change. In this broader sense, what Burbules (1995) refers to as *a sense of fallibilism* is also distinctive of a postmodern dis-position.

What is involved in a sense of fallibilism when it comes to teaching African philosophy? First, it requires certain commitments, or certain risks, that run the possibility of error. Purposely hiding behind obscurantism, withholding commitment, or playing it safe by only conforming to the conventional and obvious, are all ways of avoiding mistakes and hence, ultimately, of avoiding learning and change. Second, it requires a capacity to recognise that one is wrong, which is fundamentally linked with the capacity to admit, to oneself and to others, that one was wrong. This includes our capacity to hear and respond thoughtfully to the criticisms of others. Third, it involves a capacity for reflection, as we ponder not only that we have made a mistake, but also why it happened and how we can change to avoid repeating it in the future.

A sense of fallibilism, in teaching African philosophy, therefore speaks of a capacity for change – change prompted by one's own recognition and acknowledgement of error, but also supported by a social environment in which the process is regarded with favour and not disdain. This, of course, means that we must exist in contexts that support and encourage difference, but also that we must have the capacity and willingness to engage others in plural conversations that make the meaningful juxtaposition of different views possible. A sense of fallibilism also implies a particular view of learning, namely, that we gain new understandings, not only by the accumulation of novel information, but also by the active reconstruction of our frameworks of understanding. This sort of change requires that we encounter and interact with radically different points of view from our own.

Then there is what Burbules (1995) refers to as a *pragmatic sense*, which I believe also distinguishes a postmodern dis-position. Here reference is not being made to a specific school of thought – such as that found in Dewey, James or Pierce – but rather a deeper attitude that underlies a general worldview, namely a belief in the importance of practical problems in driving the process of intellectual, moral and political development. Such an outlook is sensitive to the particulars of given contexts and the variety of human needs and purposes.

What a sense of pragmatism means for the teaching of African philosophy is that it should reflect a tolerance for uncertainty, imperfection and incompleteness as the existential conditions of human thought and action. Yet, it should also recognise the need for persistence in confronting such difficulties with intelligence, care and flexibility. The central lesson of fallibilism in philosophy, from Socrates to Popper, is that we proceed not towards truth but away from error. It is much easier to know when we are wrong than when we are right. The philosophical consequence of this insight is distrust in obtaining sought-after results. Certain approaches to inquiry are relied on – including 'conversational' ones – not because they will yield a convergence around truth or agreement, but because experience has shown them to be reliable ways of avoiding certain kinds of egregious mistakes. There is no guarantee built into them to produce what we seek. We merely expect that whatever they yield is more likely to be dependable than what we might have received from other approaches. Such a commitment to a process of inquiry or negotiation in African philosophy, without certainty of results, is what describes a pragmatic sense, which is also a primary feature of a postmodern dis-position.

Supportive of such a pragmatic sense in African philosophy are social contexts in which an emphasis on success is not exaggerated, and in which failure and frustration are accepted as inevitable conditions of growth. In such a social context, the offering of cooperative assistance and constructive suggestions, or asking for them, forms socially and personally acceptable options.

But in African philosophy, we also need to recognise our own limitations. This would mean that we know when not to try to work out certain things in a rational way, while at the same time regarding the skills of rationality and the assessment of reasons as simply heuristics in the much more complex process of trying to decide what to believe and what to do. In recognising that it is not reasonable to try to apply the analysis of logic or the strict rules of evidence or the critique of informal fallacies to every situation, we reveal what Burbules (1995) calls a sense of judiciousness. A sense of judiciousness implies a capacity for prudence and moderation, even in the exercise of reason itself. We are not always reasonable. We occasionally fail to act upon our own best inclinations. We frequently fall short of our aspirations. Acknowledging and accepting this in ourselves and in those around us, and asking others to accept it in us, are related to the acceptance of a sense of fallibilism and the willingness to embrace imperfection and incompleteness, which is part of the pragmatic sense of reasonableness.

There is often more than one reasonable thing to believe, to say or to do; and it is part of the fallacy of Cartesian conceptions of rationality that they seek a determinative calculus that will converge on the one best or right answer. A sense of judiciousness in African philosophy will reveal that we are discerning about when and how to follow the dictates of argument in the strict sense of the term, and are receptive to the influence of other kinds of persuasion as well. In the actual practice of communicative interaction, strict and conclusive arguments are very rare. Alongside this form of argumentation is a vast range of interlocutory styles, including questions, allusions, unsubstantiated suggestions, metaphors and other tropes, as well as an even broader range of expressions, gestures, touches, tonal utterances and other kinds of communication. To participate in plural conversations in African philosophy, therefore, entails a sense of judiciousness regarding the influences of other avenues of mutual exploration, negotiation and the pursuit of understanding.

A sense of judiciousness, as is the case with a sense of plurality, fallibilism and pragmatism, therefore speaks of a certain disposition that governs the ways in which we engage with others in our practical everyday experiences in thought and action, and how we perceive the world in relation to ourselves and others. The nature of our intersubjective engagements should, therefore, lie at the heart of how we think and act, even in relation to our endeavours in African philosophy when it comes to transforming the curricula in South Africa.

Conclusion

In this chapter, I reflected critically on the need for the veracity of indigenous African knowledges to be recognised in education discourses in South Africa because of the hegemony of Western forms of knowledge on the African continent, especially when it comes to the transformation of South Africa's curricula. In so doing, I argued for the reclamation of indigenous African knowledges in educational discourses that are directed at the transformation of the curriculum, whereby Africans can reclaim their voices in the education spaces of South Africa. Such a reclamation should, however, not exclude and negate Western forms of knowledge but should rather be directed at what I referred to as a fusion of epistemologies, which seeks to integrate both indigenous African knowledges and Western forms of knowledge in education. This implies that decolonising the curriculum in no way means that decolonisation will lead to localisation, isolation or only the Africanisation of the curriculum; rather a decolonised curriculum will not neglect other knowledge systems and the global context because graduates need to function competently in a complex and connected world. To do this successfully, South Africa's universities will have to develop graduates that possess knowledge about the world and all its complexity. The call for the decolonisation of the curricula is, therefore, neither an advocacy to be anti-West, nor is it discouragement to learn from the West and the rest of the world. Such an epistemic integration would provide the framework for transforming South Africa's education curricula that would be enacted by what I called a postmodern dis-position.

African philosophy, in adopting such a postmodern dis-position in transforming South Africa's curriculum, would be seen to acknowledge the necessity for an intercultural philosophy of intent, where rationality takes on the form of a consensual or social knowledge culture that has room for passionate commitment, as well as open-mindedness, emotion and intellect, in addition to intellectual rupture and consensus.

African philosophy in adopting a postmodern dis-position would, I believe, enact a wisdom that will allow it to contribute to making the curriculum relevant to the material, historical and social realities of the various communities in South Africa in which it functions, as a directive framework for education.

Such a sense of wisdom Ramose (1998: 13) reminds us is

an openness to unfolding practices, which also acclaim co-operation, rather than conquest and competition. The golden rule of wisdom is that reductionism, absolutism, and dogmatism are an injury to the complexity of life as a holistic phenomenon.

References

Abah, J, Mashebe, P and Denuga, DD (2015) Prospects of integrating African indigenous knowledge systems into the teaching of science in Africa, *American Journal of Education*, **3**(6): 668–73.

Afolayan, A (2012) We are all Postmodernists Now! African philosophy and the postmodern agenda, *Wisdom and Philosophy*, **5**(2): 53–78.

Akena, FA (2012) Critical analysis of the production of Western knowledge and its implications for indigenous knowledge and decolonisation, *Journal of Black Studies*, **43**: 599–619.

Appiah (1992) Appiah, KA (1992) *In My Father's House: Africa in the Philosophy of Culture.* Oxford: Oxford University Press.

Araia, G (2014) *Modernism, Postmodernism and Afrocentrism: Meanings for Ethiopia.* Oakland, CA: Institute of Development and Education (IDEA), Inc. Sunday, 12 October.

Burbules, NC (1995) Reasonable doubt: Towards a postmodern defence of reason as an educational aim, in W Kohli (ed.) *Critical Conversations in Philosophy of Education.* New York: Routledge.

Ciaffa, JK (2008) Tradition and modernity in post-colonial African philosophy, *Humanitas*, **12**(1&2): 121–45.

Dussel, E (1993) Eurocentrism and modernity, *Boundary*, **2**(20): 65–76.

Ekpo, D (1995) Towards a post-Africanism: Contemporary African thought and postmodernism, *Textual Practice*, **9**(1): 121–35.

Etieyibo, E (2014) Postmodern thinking and African philosophy, *Filosofia Theoretica: Journal of African Philosophy, Culture and Religion*, **3**(1): 67–82.

Freire, P (1970) *Pedagogy of the Oppressed.* New York: Herder and Herder.

Heleta, S (2018) Decolonisation of higher education: Dismantling epistemic violence and Eurocentrism in South Africa, *Transformation of Higher Education*, **1**(8): 1–8.

Higgs, P (2008) Towards an indigenous African educational discourse: A philosophical reflection, *International Review of Education*, **54**(3–4): 89–108.

Higgs, P (2016) The African Renaissance and the transformation of the higher education curriculum in South Africa, *African Education Review*, **13**(1): 89–103.

Higgs, P (2017) Teaching African philosophy and a *postmodern dis-position*, in A Afolayan and T Falola (eds) *The Palgrave Handbook of African Philosophy.* London: Palgrave Macmillan.

Kenzo, MJR (2002) Thinking otherwise about Africa: Postcolonialism, postmodernism and the future of African philosophy, *Exchange*, **31**(4): 323–41.

Kodirekkala, KR (2016) Cultural ecology in the erosion of local knowledge: Folklore among Konda Reddis of South India, *Journal of Asian Anthropology*, **15**(1): 21–35.

Le Grange, L (2000) Is there space for enabling disparate knowledge traditions to work together?

Challenges for science (education) in an African context, *South African Journal of Education*, **20**(2): 114–17.

Lyotard, JF (1979) *The Postmodern Condition: A report on knowledge*. Manchester: Manchester University Press.

Maher, A (2000) Marginalizing African indigenous knowledges in education and its impact on development: The case of Somalia, *Education and Society*, **18**(2): 61–73.

Mawere, M (2015) Indigenous knowledge and public education in sub-Saharan Africa, *Africa Spectrum*, **2**: 57–71.

McLaren, P (1989) *Life in Schools: An introduction to critical pedagogy in the foundations of education*. New York: Longman.

Mungwini, P (2014) Post ethnophilosophy: Discourses of modernity and the future of African philosophy, *Phronimon*, **15**(1): 16–31.

Newsum, HE (1990) *Class, Language and Education*. Trenton, NJ: Africa World Press

Nkomo, M (2000) Educational research in the African development context, in P Higgs, N Vakalisa, T Mda and N'D Assie-Lumumba (eds) *African Voices in Education*. Cape Town: Juta.

Odora Hoppers, CA (2001) Indigenous knowledge systems and academic institutions in South Africa, *Perspectives in Education*, **19**(1): 73–85.

Odora Hoppers, CA (2002) *Indigenous Knowledge and the Integration of Knowledge Systems: Towards a philosophy of articulation*. Cape Town: New Africa Books.

Okolo, CB (1985) African philosophy and social reconstruction, *Journal of African Studies*, **12**(1): 4–9.

Outlaw, L (1991) African philosophy: Deconstructive and reconstructive challenges, in OH Oruka (ed.) *Sage philosophy: Indigenous thinkers and modern debate on African philosophy*. Nairobi: ACTS Press.

Popper, K (1972) *The Logic of Scientific Discovery*. London: Routledge.

Ramose, MB (1998) Foreword, in S Seepe (ed.) *Black Perspectives on Tertiary Institutional Transformation*. Johannesburg: Vivlia Publishers and University of Venda.

Ramose, MB (2001) Foreword, in S Seepe (ed.) *Black Perspectives on Tertiary Institutional Transformation*. Johannesburg: Vivlia Publishers and University of Venda.

Ramose, MB (2004) In search of an African philosophy of education, *South African Journal of Higher Education*, **18**(3): 138–160.

Sefa Dei, GJ (1998) Education for development: Relevance and implications for the South African context, *Canadian Journal of Development Studies*, **19**(3): 509–27.

Serequeberhan, T (1994) *The Hermeneutics of African Philosophy*. London: Routledge.

Shizha, E (2013) Reclaiming our indigenous voices: The problem with postcolonial sub-Saharan African school curriculum, *Journal of Indigenous Social Development*, **2**(1): 1–18.

Sim, S (2001) Postmodernism and philosophy, in S Sim (ed.) *The Routledge Companion to Postmodernism*. London: Routledge.

Snyman, G (2002) Eurocentrism and Afrocentrism: What is Western/African research? in CW du Toit (ed.) *Research, Identity and Rationalism: Thinking about theological research in Africa*. Pretoria: UNISA Press.

West, C (1990) The new cultural politics of difference, *The Humanities as Social Technology*, **53**: 93–109.

Section V: African Schools of Thought

Chapter 13
The Ibadan School of History

Toyin Falola

Introduction

Kenneth Dike was regarded as the founder of the Ibadan School of History that emerged in the 1950s. Other prominent members of the school included AE Afigbo, JFA Ajayi and Obaro Ikime. In 1953, Kenneth Onwuka Dike was a new academic in the Department of History at University College, Ibadan. He engaged the Eurocentric racism and prejudice that had coloured almost all of Africa's written history from the 15th to the 20th century: 'Because of the myth that the African has no culture and no history, colonial policies – political, social, economic – are all directed to the transformation of the African into an inferior white man' (Dike, 1953).

European colonialists and historians alike had written about an 'age of darkness' that allegedly shrouded African history, declaring that the entire continent was without any noteworthy history prior to contact with the Europeans (Trevor-Roper, 1968: 9). Academic coverage of the African continent started with European contact in the 15th century, and it described Europe's great privilege, bringing 'civilisation' to the continent[1] along with the European heroes who made it all come to pass.[2] To modern eyes, this seems quite one-sided, and it was exactly that.

Rather than an African history, it was an amalgamation of various European perspectives – involving Germany, France, Portugal, Great Britain and Italy, among others – that did not consider the perspectives of the conquered. They assumed that the conquered were anarchic savages (Perham and Simmons, 1962: 16). Progressing through this 'history', amateurs, officials and others wrote of the transatlantic slave trade that started in the 15th century. Between the 15th and 19th centuries, the slave trade was the sole focus of these writers, because this was all that mattered to them.

The focus shifted from human trade to raw materials by the 19th century,

---

1 See, for instance, Batten, TR (1939) *Tropical Africa in World History*. London: Oxford University Press.
2 See, for example, Flint, J (1960) *Taubman Goldie and the Making of Modern Nigeria*. London: Oxford University Press.

when slavery was abolished. These new commercial relationships between the continent and the West led to another 'slavery' of sorts, through territorial domination. Naturally, European historians never described it as such. Control of the continent led to the development of new colonial powers in the 20th century, mostly under Great Britain's supervision. This was, once again, considered a tremendous victory for the Europeans and the only thing worth discussing in academic and official settings.

This was it. All that was deemed worth mentioning was grandiose white saviours dominating the African continent, justified by biblical interpretations that validated the conversion of the continent and the superiority of the white man. These views and interpretations presented the European presence as a blessing for the African people. They had become more 'civilised', according to European standards.[3] This was written in papers, books, and even textbooks for university students taking history courses.

Kenneth Dike and the rise of the Ibadan School of History

At University College, Ibadan, founded in 1948, its pioneering history department did not include African studies programmes because the subject of 'African Studies' was not believed to be necessary, or even important. It was guided by the University of London, which infused the curricula with British values and praise for imperialism. The faculty was entirely British and none among them had any experience with African-centred history[4] (see Rugumamu, Chapter 14, in this volume). Kenneth Onwuka Dike was an exception to this trend. He was considered to be the founder of the Ibadan School of History and a major force that led the fight against a Eurocentric historical view and academic suppression of Africa.[5] He joined the University of Ibadan's History Department in 1950, and his academic interests were unlike the others. That same year, he had completed his doctoral thesis, titled *Trade*

---

3 See, for instance, Bosman, W (1967) [1705] *A New and Accurate Description of the Coast of Guinea: Divided into the Gold, the Slave and the Ivory Coasts*. London: Ballantyne and Company; Houston, J (1725) *Some New and Accurate Observations of the Coast of Guinea*. London: J Peele; and Barbort, J (1732) *A Description of the Coasts of North and South Guinea* (London).

4 See, for instance, Omolewa, M (1980) The education factor in the emergence of the modern profession of historians in Nigeria, 1926–1956, *Journal of the Historical Society of Nigeria*, **10**(3)(December); Batten, TR (1939) *Tropical Africa in World History*. London: Oxford University Press; and Flint, J (1960) *Taubman Goldie and the Making of Modern Nigeria*. London: Oxford University Press.

5 The singular attention to Dike in this essay, dictated by space limitation, is to focus on (1) the evolution of an African agency in a more intense manner; and (2) to highlight a crucial aspect of leadership, which is needed to accomplish transformation. Of course, I have written on other members of the school in three books and various essays.

and Politics in the Niger Delta, 1830–1885, which would be published in 1956 by the Clarendon Press in London. It presented an Afrocentric perspective on imperialism. Its main source of data came from archival materials, which was unprecedented. Arguably, the more ground-breaking body of evidence used in his research was both the exploration of a new archive and African oral tradition – a vital contribution that allowed the nature of the African identity to shine through (Dike, 1956). Throughout the rest of his scholarship, Dike used similar materials and similar tactics, allowing 'Africanity' to be represented properly in African history. Because of this work, Dike was hailed as the 'father of modern African historiography' (Ifemesia, 1984: 3).

He directed his attention toward nationalism, and he felt that the African people could be revitalised, allowing them to reclaim their own identity, if they studied their history through a lens that erased racism and provided clear signs of African achievement. In his own words:

> Every nation builds its future on its past; so the African must not only instinctively have faith in his own inheritance, but must also satisfy himself by scientific inquiry that it exists… For young and emergent nations there is no study as important as that of history; the reasons are clear enough. Our past is very much a part of our present, and as we comprehend that past so will the problems of the present be illuminated. Most great and far-reaching movements have begun with a romantic appeal to the past (Dike, 1953: 31).

Dike's views, and his passion for reclaiming African history on Africans' own terms, made him the face of what came to be called 'nationalist historiography' for the African people. Based on this vision, his new curriculum for the Department of History at University College, Ibadan, allowed for the rise of the 'Ibadan School'. This term would be used by outsiders to describe the revolutionary route that the university was taking under Dike's leadership.

While Dike was definitely radical for taking great strides in 'Africanising' the continent's history and authenticating African studies, this model had been quietly festering ever since European imperialists had invaded the continent. Africans had resisted the European invasion and struggled for their own independence, resulting in powerful expressions of nationalistic pride. After their experiences with conversion, slavery and European dominance, African intellectuals began to piece together their own timeline of history:

- When Europeans invaded the African continent, they considered local history to be negligible, because it was not recorded in writing. The people's civilisations were not in the same style as European nations. The Europeans saw these differences as inferior, viewing Africans as in need of conversion and civilising. The slave trade exacerbated and heightened feelings of racism and white superiority over Africans. Europeans considered Africans to be subhuman and worthy of reproach.

- European racism, empowered by the slave trade, fuelled the imperialism that ultimately marginalised Africans from their own societies.
- Europeans justified imperialism in many ways, which included the Eurocentric history they created. It was known to nationalist historiographers as a 'colonial library'. The library was a combination of prejudice and egotism, which ensured the ongoing relegation of Africa.
- An African educated elite arose. They used their education as a tool, inspiring nationalistic pride that confronted the injustices inflicted on the African people. These elites chose to look back to the past, struggling to assert themselves so that their voices could be heard. They realised that Africans must fight to establish their own interpretation of the past, affirm their cultural views and create a hopeful resurgence for themselves.
- With the Ibadan School's help, academic writing about African history began to challenge the colonial library. Nationalism had become not just a cultural movement at this point, but also an academic movement. Thus, African historiography was born, talking about the great institutions, such as kingship, invented by Africans to manage themselves in the long centuries before the colonial conquest. It pointed to great leaders of the past, such as Mansa Musa; affirmed the rights and talents of Africans for self-governance in the modern era, citing Marcus Garvey and Herbert Macaulay; and it highlighted monumental physical accomplishments, such as the Great Zimbabwe city and the pyramids.

By definition, African nationalist historiography is an academic and cultural movement seeking to redefine the African identity by fiercely defending Africa's past and looking to it as inspiration for future progress. African nationalist historiography is about the authority of Africans calling out the racism and wrongs accumulated against them. For this reason, it is also about resistance. Rather than cowering before the oppressor, African nationalist historiographers fight against the oppressor, as their ancestors did when they fought for their own independence. To clarify: African nationalist historiographers do not want to eliminate Europeans from history altogether. That would rewrite history completely, which is not their aim. They aim to focus not on the Europeans' impact, but rather on the African response to it. African nationalist historiographers want to use their pride, passion and enthusiasm to show how Africans had a brilliant past – they knew how to maintain their traditions while adapting to unstoppable changes.

Curriculum transformation efforts of the Ibadan School of History

The creation of the Ibadan School certainly was and is pivotal, making much-needed changes to African scholarship and history on continental and global levels. However, Dike's mission to change the curriculum was not always easy. At the beginning of his career, the University of Ibadan's curriculum was still under British supervision. The British opposed Dike's changes, because they saw them as 'unacademic'. Happily, Dike was able to make changes elsewhere; he briefly transferred to the West African Institute for Social and Economic Research (WAISER) in 1952. There, he created the National Archives of Nigeria.

When Dike returned to the University of Ibadan, he had more power and prestige, allowing him to do what he wanted in shaping the Ibadan School. His prestige increased further when he became vice-chancellor of the university – and the first indigenous one, at that. He used his position to make the history department essential for his mission of nationalism. When the British finally agreed to let the university become more Nigerianised, he was able to recruit other Nigerians to become members of the faculty.[6]

With Nigerians on the faculty, the African voice could be heard clearly. These new faculty members used their own work, usually through their theses, as 'textbooks' for new history curricula that were, for the first time, Africa-centred. At last, Africans were gaining respect in the academic community. They were seen as vocal, and no longer as passive and yielding, as past historians made them out to be. Africans were presented as heroes of their own kind and the agents of their own destiny. Like Dike, these faculty members used oral sources in their theses, thus validating oral tradition as legitimate historical material.

With this new – distinctly African – voice, the Ibadan School allowed African students to gain a new perspective on their own history. It was no longer white-washed. Ultimately, nationalist historiography was the backbone of the history curricula. Courses indicted colonialism as an oppressive force that failed to consider or adapt to Africa's traditions. They also made Africans, not

---

6   To learn more about the courses and the college in its early stages, see Mellanby, K (1958) *The Birth of Nigeria's University*. Ibadan: Ibadan University Press; and Ajayi, JFA and Tamuno, TN (eds) (1973) *The University of Ibadan, 1948–73: A History of the first twenty-five years*. Ibadan: Ibadan University Press.

Europeans, the heroes – something quite unimaginable in academia at the time.

No longer was Taubman Goldie the heroic face, and a white heroic face at that, of Nigeria's conqueror. In Dike's work, for example, Goldie was described merely as a founder of the Royal Niger Company, not the father of the entire country. Europeans had presented Jaja of Opobo as a backward, uncivilised Nigerian chief who resisted the 'greatness' of European free trade. Because of Dike and his colleagues, Jaja was rewritten as a patriot and a resistance hero.

The innovation from these first Nigerian professors at the Ibadan School created a new legacy and wave of notable academic scholarship based on nationalist historiography. By the mid-1950s, Dike and other pioneering academics created the Historical Society of Nigeria. Dike served as its first president from 1955 to 1969 (Ifemesia, 1984: 5). The society held annual conferences, adding to the burgeoning collection of African academic voices. It also held regular seminars with graduate students, inspiring future African academic voices. In 1956, the society published its first major academic journal, *Journal of the Historical Society of Nigeria*, which received international praise for generating new and engaging scholarship. Another journal, titled *Tarikh*, was published in the mid-1960s, bringing history to high schools and general readers. In 1980, the society released its most prestigious work, a book edited by Obaro Ikime, titled the *Groundwork of Nigerian History*, which provides a detailed history of Nigeria (Ikime, 1980).

Around this time period, Dike and his colleagues maintained their nationalistic spirit by founding Historical Research Schemes. These were designed to resurrect the African past by separating Nigeria into multiple regions, each of which acquired local academic funding for research. Scholars in these regions gathered local data to be accumulated into an amalgamation of credible, scholarly accounts of the country. A 'scheme' was established at the University of Ibadan, known as the Institute of African Studies. This institution was used to document and research Nigerian scholarship and data, and it served as a centre of cultural activity, promoting Nigerian artists.

In 1955, in the western region of Nigeria, the Yorùbá Research Historical Scheme received a five-year grant for conducting 'cultural research'. This scheme, with the help of anthropologists, historians and archaeologists, studied the inception of the Yorùbá. Archaeological excavations and oral sources provided evidence of the Yorùbá's rich talents, culture and history (Biobaku, 1956). The Ibadan School – with grants from the Colonial Development and Welfare Fund and the Carnegie Trust of America, as well as financial support from the Federal Government of Nigeria – then created three more schemes for Northern Nigeria, Benin and Arochukwu.[7]

The main result of these efforts changed the methodologies of historians studying Africa, particularly because of the increased use of oral sources.[8] Using oral sources was a rebellious defiance of the dominant Western academy. Academics like SO Biobaku, Ajayi and Banji Akintoye wanted to ensure that the African voice was not forgotten in history; they felt that the best way to do this was to keep African oral sources alive in research. To this end, Ajayi suggested that Africans 'have to reclaim and package the past, set appropriate boundaries to contain and curtail the West [and] reorganise the creation and presentation of knowledge' (Falola, 2003: 306).

Dike knew that 'when Europe occupied Africa, her scholars did not attempt to understand or to build on the historical traditions in existence there'. Europeans did not find much written African history, so it was not considered as valid as the European histories that had been written for centuries. However, Dike had some reassuring thoughts for the nationalist historiography movement. He favoured a shift in methodologies towards authentic, African oral sources that were 'fairly accurate' in genre (Dike, 1953: 251).

> Fortunately for the historian of today, African historical consciousness remained alive throughout the period of colonial rule; that tradition was too much a part of [the] African way of life to succumb to the attacks of the European scholar. Even in the heyday of white supremacy some educated Africans of the period were sufficiently dominated by their past to feel impelled to commit to writing the laws, customs, proverbs, sayings and historical traditions of their own communities.[9]

The Ibadan School was integral in adding Africa back to the voice of Africa. Arguably, this contribution is the school's most enduring legacy. Many

---

7   See, for example, Omer-Cooper, JD (1980) The contribution of the University of Ibadan to the spread of the study and teaching of African history, *Journal of the Historical Society of Nigeria*, **10**(3): 23–31.

8   The achievements are always embellished by historians. For its potential and limitations, see the following: Alagoa, EJ (1975) The interdisciplinary approach to African history in Nigeria, *Présence Africaine*, **94**: 171–83; Alagoa, EJ (1978) The relationship between history and the other disciplines, *Tarikh*, **6**(1): 12–20. To learn more about the use of oral sources, see the following: Biobaku, SO (1956) The problem of traditional history, with special reference to Yorùbá traditions, *Journal of the Historical Society of Nigeria*, **1**(1): 43–47; Alagoa, EJ (1966) Oral tradition among the Ijo of the Niger Delta, *Journal of African History*, **7**(3): 405–419; Afigbo, AE (1966) Oral tradition and history in Eastern Nigeria: An essay in historical methodology, Part 1, *African Notes*, **3**(3): 12–20; and Part 2, *African Notes*, **4**(1): 17–27.

9   Dike, KO. Introduction to the Ibadan History Series, reprinted in a number of titles in the series published by Longman.

prominent scholars emerged as members of the Ibadan School, such as Adiele Afigbo, Omoniyi Adewoye, Obaro Ikime, Tekena Tamuno, RA Adeleye, Emmanuel Ayandele, JA Atanda, Bolanle Awe, Anthony Asiwaju, and EJ Alagoa. They wrote on various subjects, including indirect rule, the 19th century, leadership and institutions (Falola and Aderinto, 2010).

The reverberations of African voices were felt beyond the university level, making changes at the secondary education level. The Ibadan School influenced the curricula of African history in secondary schools and the textbooks used in the curricula. The textbooks were certainly a reflection of nationalist historiography; they no longer described Africans as a vague 'tribal' collective. Instead, Africans were individualised and nuanced. They were discussed in the greater context of region, culture and trade among other Africans. In the end, the textbooks fed the desires of African students who had been asking for a more inclusive history since the 1940s.

Fortunately, the strengthened curricula from the Ibadan School inspired generations of future African academics who used methodologies that were similar to their predecessors (Ajayi, 1973: 153). The Ibadan School started a revolution that instilled great nationalistic pride in its academics and in the general African public. The reassurance that Africans are an empowered, intelligent people is an accomplishment that is impossible to overstate. People were always empowered and intelligent in a sense, but they were never able to fully express themselves – through no fault of their own. Dike and the Ibadan School gave them a chance to combat Western powers with the written, academic word. They no longer needed to allow others to characterise them. They could properly demonstrate their will, not just surviving, but thriving and lifting up their own ancestors' legacy.

Criticisms of the Ibadan School of History

Despite the Ibadan School's achievements, it had its limitations. The Ibadan School has received criticism over the decades, and much of it is warranted. In the latter half of the 20th century, the main criticism was that the Ibadan School's ideology of nationalist historiography was not relevant for Africa's present. Critics argued that, although history was a way to inspire nationalistic pride and to learn from past mistakes, they asked the Ibadan School: 'Why be consumed with past societies when the focus should be on the country's current state, especially when the situation on the entire continent is so fragile and uncertain? Why see past African societies as something glorified when the current societies derived from them are falling apart?' These questions arose after the 1970s, along with the failures of the civil war, military commands and government. Such failures indicated a weak nation-state, which completely contradicted the nationalist historiographers' goals of promoting the nation-state as something strong and good. This criticism caused JFA Ajayi, who became the Dean of Nigerian History after Dike, to poignantly note that 'of all the branches of African Studies, African history is the most useless of all the disciplines [because of its] failure to relate research to the practical problems of Africa' (Ajayi, 1980: 296).

The idea of relevance applied to another question: how much do modern Africans relate to Africans of the past? Even if they feel pride, is that enough to identify with their people that were characterised on modern Africa's behalf? This calls for a re-evaluation of how history is studied and written so that it resonates with a modern audience. Critics have recommended more syntheses of history and fewer monographs.

National histories can be more motivating and relevant than local histories. For example, AI Asiwaju argues that historians should focus less on regional schemes and more on the entire nation.[10] Some recommend broadening the focus even more, presenting a Pan-Africanist perspective with themes that relate to all black and all African people. With a broader focus, scholars do not want Africans to be blurred together into one vague unit – scholars want to find a sense of harmony in all Africans. Simply put, modern scholars have wanted to make history not only relevant but also a tool for unification. It can give all Africans the same sense of purpose, and the same mission, to help rebuild the continent. A common theme that could achieve this aim might be a historical account of ethnicity, and how ethnicity affected interactions between various African peoples.

Obaro Ikime, a leading representative of the Ibadan School, responded to these concerns with consent and grace in his 1979 inaugural lecture. He advocated a link between historical studies and modern problems, in the hopes that all Africans could integrate. He advised historians to explain how their research revealed the origins of modern problems. History, in his view, was only useful if it directly helped nation-building. Ultimately, Ikime believed that history should be in service to the present nation-state, rather than the other way around – a drastic shift for the original nationalist historiography movement (Ikime, 1979). Ikime strongly emphasised that history should not be studied for its own sake. History must have a reason for being:

---

10 For example, Asiwaju, AI (1984) History and national awareness in Nigeria, in OE Erim and OE Uya (eds) *Perspectives and Methods of Studying African History*, pp. 77–83.

Our country is seeking to forge a true nation, that demands the instinctive loyalty of its citizenry. This is a worthy goal after which all nations of the world have striven. In the achievement of that goal, every nation has used history as one instrument. All that has varied is the way and the degree to which history has been used. The Nigerian historian need not be ashamed of playing a role that historians all over the world have unashamedly played and continue to play. It is my view that a historian can play this role by the kind of history he writes, his choice of words, his turn of phrase... Increasingly, our researchers must take into consideration national problems of political and social relations, of government and governmental systems and the ends which society seeks to attain. Only in this way can we ensure that the Nigerian history that we write ... makes some definite contribution to the national effort in its varying ramifications.

Another criticism related to issues of relevance was that the Ibadan School and nationalist historiography resisted change – something necessary for any improvement in the nation-state – and that their claims had striking inconsistencies. For instance, nationalist historiographers said that the continent did not need European contact in order to be considered a collection of advanced, intelligent civilisations; meanwhile, these historiographers also wanted Africa to be placed in the same league as European models with historical writing and academia. The Ibadan School's message suggested that Africa could be like Europe if given enough time – even though the Ibadan School also encouraged Africa to reject Europe. The Ibadan School's curricula promoted progress and the renovation of ideas, but it also said that students should always admiringly turn to the past for inspiration.

Marxists – who later developed alternative schools at the University of Dar es Salaam and Ahmadu Bello University in Zaria – saw the school as too intellectually and politically conservative (see Rugumamu, Chapter 14, in this volume). The school was accused of ignoring class analysis, women and gender studies, labour and the peasantry, and, in general, history from below. Prominent members of the school were accused of being obsessed with power, using their elitism and connections to become vice-chancellors of major universities (Dike, Ajayi, Ayandele, Tamuno and Biobaku), federal ministers (Adewoye, and Adeleye), and state commissioners (Afigbo, Awe and Atanda). These obsessions were enabled by the range of opportunities provided by institutions and governments that were just taking shape; the opportunism of a historical moment was combined with the opportunism of aggressive pathfinders. In the process, scholars defined the nation-state even as they became implicated in the crises of a new nation, contributing to the causes of the Nigerian Civil War, the rise of the military and the mismanagement of the country.

Despite these criticisms, the African nationalist historiography movement had noble, well-meaning intentions. There is a happy medium between fostering nationalistic pride and addressing complicated civic issues. Various academic workshops, during and throughout the 1970s, looked for this compromise, seeking to merge nationalist historiography's original mission with more modern goals. Academics knew that not all universities could implement a common curriculum, but they advised universities to follow some important common principles:

- Mandate that national and continental African history be taught.
- Ensure that African historical perspectives be at the centre of all history courses.
- Make sure that other regions of the world are not excluded from curricula, so that African students and citizens are not isolated on their continent. However, information about other regions should be delivered in a manner that relates to African problems.
- Allow the history of economics, science, industrialisation, philosophical thought and technology to be taught in such a way that African students specifically may grasp a better understanding of the complex modern world (Alagoa, 1977: 123).
- Create epistemologies based on organic African ideas, using non-archival-based sources to generate new ontologies that culminate in a pluriversalist way of thinking, instead of the universalist one. This moves from the task of decolonisation, the exit of European powers in Africa to that of decoloniality, the full assertions of African agencies in intellectual and practical spaces.[11]

Conclusion

If the virtues of the original nationalist historiography were to survive, the movement itself had to undergo modernisation and evolution. There had to be more of a focus on nationalism's ability to address African problems at large. There also had to be more of a focus on history at the national and continental levels. Nationalist historiographers that had previously made such changes ended up vastly reducing contradictions and complications. Nevertheless, scholars in the 20th century and today have argued that there can be regionalism in the curricula of schools, where the change is warranted.

---

11 This position and the arguments around it are fully developed in Falola, T. (2016) *The Humanities in Africa: Knowledge production, universities, and transformation of society*. Austin, TX: Pan-African University Press.

In North Africa, where Islam is dominant, there should be implementation of curricula with greater inquiry into Islam; these questions relate to how a North African university fits into its surrounding location. And it does not have to be a dividing factor, but rather a tool of unification. Rather than separating regions like the Middle East, North Africa and sub-Saharan Africa, the curricula could reinforce the idea that all are joined by the commonality of Islam – again, as a tool of unification that looks at how places are similar rather than what makes them different. Many universities in North Africa have already taken this approach, with much success. Some courses at these universities have even constructed courses on Pan-Arabism as a cultural history.[12]

However, even with some individualisation based on location or specific regional relevance, nationalist historiography curricula must prioritise African unification. Luckily, the original nationalist historiography movement that was sparked in the 1950s set the African academy on the right track. History courses at universities and the secondary level no longer recognise Africans solely in the context of European history. Courses now explain how Africans responded to changes that were thrust upon them, and how they took the initiative to fight back against European oppressors. We have the Ibadan School to thank for this.

Bringing back the African voice to Africa is no small feat. Even though the nationalist historiography movement has undergone changes, these changes were necessary. They still promote the good intentions of the original movement. As long as African history continues to be Africanised, and ultimately relevant to nation-building, the Ibadan School's legacy will never die. As long as it is clear how Africanised history serves as the backbone of the modern African identity, and a major contribution to progress, the African voice itself will never die. An African agency has emerged – this agency must not only work for the rewriting of history, but also for the entire decoloniality of spaces and minds.

---

12   Some of the courses include: The Modern History of the Arabs; Liberation Movements in the Arab World in the 19th and 20th Centuries; Geography of Islamic Philosophy; Arab Community, Early Islam and the Umayyad State; Relations Between the Muslim World and Europe during the Crusades; The History of the Umayyads and the Mamluks; Arab Socialism; The Abbasid Empire; Arab Historiography; The History of Alexandria in Islamic Times; The History of Islam in Africa South of the Sahara; Islamic Civilisation; A Survey of Islamic History and Medieval Europe; The Arab State; and Islamic Egypt up to the End of the Mamluk Times.

An appendix on the leading light of Ibadan School of History: The life and endeavours of Kenneth O Dike

Early life and education of Dike

Kenneth Onwuka Dike, was one of the most renowned Nigerian historians of the 20th century. Although born and raised in Southern Nigeria, he obtained his bachelor's degree from Durham University in England, his Master's degree from the University of Aberdeen in Scotland, and his PhD from King's College London (Olulana, 2017). His undergraduate and graduate education informed his life's work as an African historian. He focused primarily on ridding European influence and Eurocentric ideas from African history in a way that centred on the narratives, experiences and voices of African people.

As a student abroad, he was heavily involved in student organisations, such as the West African Students Union (WASU) which engaged in political activities that put them in the midst of Africa's post-World War II cultural and social revolution. Alex Animalu, Kenneth Dike's personal biographer, stated that students would go to Dike for consultation regarding the political, social and economic issues plaguing their countries. He aided them in drafting and editing papers and pamphlets for their causes (Nwauwa, 2009). Whether he knew it or not, Dike's role in revolutionising Africa had already begun.

Written work and activism

In 1954, Dike founded the Nigerian National Archives to address the country's problem with national record storage and preservation (National Archives of Nigeria, 2007). This project allowed Nigerians to control their own historical documents, preventing the loss or erasure of important events and cultural practices from pre-colonial through post-colonial eras. Professor Dike also helped found the Historical Society of Nigeria in 1955 at University College, Ibadan, to preserve and promote historical scholarship, especially regarding Nigerian history.[13]

Dike delved into historical research as Nigeria was preparing for independence in the 1950s. By 1956, he had written a book titled *Trade and Politics in the Niger Delta, 1830–1885*. He purposely wrote about the relationship with the British Crown from a Nigerian perspective, rather than a British one. The book explored the ways in which British colonial rule undermined indigenous government structures in the Niger Delta during that time, while

---

13 The Historical Society of Nigeria was established in 1955 at the University College Ibadan. The founding fathers include distinguished scholars like Kenneth O Dike and Abdullahi Smith. *Historical Society of Nigeria*, 2009. Available at: historicalsocietynigeria.org/aboutus.htm (accessed September 2019).

simultaneously discussing the complexities of Euro-African relations. The book gained immediate fame, inspiring a handful of other books regarding the Niger Delta during the colonial era (Alagoa, 1998: 9).

What was so revolutionary about Dike's reclamation of historical narratives? Under European rule and influence, African history was heavily biased. It refused to acknowledge significant African leaders, empires and events, erasing history and skewing the perception of African people. While studying abroad in the United Kingdom, Dike discovered an Africa he did not recognise and did not grow up with. This realisation propelled him to take an active role in preserving African, specifically Nigerian history in a way that had never been done before. The bulk of Dike's research took place during and towards the end of British colonial rule. His work came on the heels of a paradigm shift, divorcing African history and scholarship from the colonial, racist traditions that it had been tied to for so long.

Kenneth Dike's intellect was not confined to books or research; it was also practical and applied throughout his life. He held various administrative positions. In 1962, he became the first African Vice-Chancellor of Ibadan University and continued his scholarship in African history there (Nwauwa, 2009). He wanted to make the institution's curriculum more relevant and reflective of Africans themselves, rather than reflective of European narratives of Africa and its people. Dike's commitment to promote scholarship done for and by Africans allowed him to become the chief organiser at the First International Congress of Africanists in Ghana in December 1962. His opening statement focused on the importance of African studies, publications and research, specifically done by African scholars, in a non-colonial context. This was uncommon in the newly independent Nigeria.

In addition to Dike's academic endeavours, he was also involved in the Biafra independence movement which was active in the south-eastern region of Nigeria. Political instability, religious and socio-ethnic tensions, and overall deteriorating conditions between the Igbo and Hausa people were frameworks through which this conflict was frequently analysed. Kenneth Dike's call to the independence movement was bolstered by the extrajudicial killing of Igbo people (Animalu, 1997). In 1966, he stepped down from his position as vice-chancellor to focus his efforts on Biafra. Dike's Igbo background and his passion for Nigerian affairs spurred his active role in the movement; from 1967 to 1970, he acted as a mobile ambassador for Biafra, which included duties such as promoting the Biafran right to state sovereignty throughout Nigeria, West Africa and – due to Dike's status – internationally as well.

Later life and legacy

Later in life, Dike found himself pioneering African studies halfway across the world, at Harvard University. In the 1970s, he established the first courses on sub-Saharan Africa and laid foundations for years of serious African scholarship at the university (Laurknck, 1983).

Kenneth Dike's administrative and academic accomplishments are surpassed by the ideology that he embodied. His call for African-sponsored scholarship, free from biased Eurocentric influence, inspired many within the continent and those in the diaspora. Upon receiving an Honorary Doctor of Law degree from the University of Michigan in 1979, he was compared to Copernicus, the acclaimed thinker, because he had examined Nigeria in a way that revolutionised the way in which historiography is conducted on the continent.[14]

Dike's research technique was heavily focused on oral traditions, while European scholarship depended on written documents to preserve and dictate history. An outstanding amount of African history had been lost by ignoring oral narratives – European historians thought that undocumented events were not worthy of study, but, as Dike said, 'whether records are written or embodied in folklore and tradition, behind them lies [the] real human history recorded in cultural patterns, industry, religion and art' (Chuku, 2013).

KO Dike's work is world-renowned and well respected in Africa and across the globe. His written work and activism continue to inspire many African historians and scholars to centre the African perspective in their techniques, rather than following the foreign, colonial traditions that saturate history curricula worldwide.

References

Afigbo, AE (1966) Oral tradition and history in Eastern Nigeria: An essay in historical methodology, Part 1, *African Notes*, 3(3): 12–20; and Part 2, *African Notes*, 4(1): 17–27.

Ajayi, JFA (1973) Post-graduate studies and staff development, *The University of Ibadan 1948–73: A history of the first twenty-five years*. Ibadan: Ibadan University Press, p. 153.

Ajayi, JFA (1980) Canada provides food for thought, *West Africa*, 26 May, p. 296.

Ajayi, JFA and Tamuno, TN (eds) (1973) *The University of Ibadan, 1948–73: A history of the first twenty-five years*. Ibadan: Ibadan University Press. Alagoa, EJ (1975) The interdisciplinary approach to African history in Nigeria, *Présence Africaine*, 94: 171–83;

Alagoa, EJ (ed.) (1977) *The Teaching of History in African Universities*. The Proceedings of a Workshop Sponsored by the Association of African Universities at the University of Lagos, Lagos, Nigeria, mimeograph, 14–21 September.

Alagoa, EJ (1978) The relationship between history and the other disciplines, *Tarikh*, 6(1): 12–20.

Alagoa, EJ (1998) Of days, bread, and mushrooms: The historian as hero, in EJ Alagoa (ed.)

---

14 Citation by the University of Michigan on the occasion of the conferment of Honorary Doctor of Laws on Professor Kenneth Onwuka Dike in 1979, as cited in Animalu, AOE (1997) *Life and Thoughts of Professor Kenneth Onwuka Dike*. Nsukka, Nigeria: Ucheakonam Foundation, p. 200.

Dike Remembered: African reflections on history. Port Harcourt, Nigeria: University of Port Harcourt Press, p. 9.

Animalu, AOE (1997). *Life and Thoughts of Professor Kenneth Onwuka Dike*. Nsukka, Nigeria: Ucheakonam Foundation.

Anon. (1983) Kenneth O Dike dies in a Nigerian hospital, *The New York Times*, 13 November. Available at: www.nytimes.com/1983/11/13/obituaries/kenneth-o-dike-dies-in-a-nigerian-hospital.html (accessed November 2018).

Asiwaju, AI (1984) History and National Awareness in Nigeria, in OE Erim and OE Uya (eds) *Perspectives and Methods of Studying African History*. Enugu, Nigeria: Fourth Dimension Publishing Company, pp. 77–83.

Barbort, J (1732) *A Description of the Coasts of North and South Guinea; and of Ethiopia Inferior, vulgarly Angola*. In six books. Available from Duke University Libraries.

Batten, TR (1939) *Tropical Africa in World History*. London: Oxford University Press.

Biobaku, SO (1956) The Yorùbá Historical Research Scheme, *Journal of the Historical Society of Nigeria*, **1**(1): 59–60.

Bosman, W (1967) [1705] *A New and Accurate Description of the Coast of Guinea: Divided into the Gold, the Slave and the Ivory Coasts*. Original edition, London: Ballantyne and Company.

Chuku, G (ed.) (2013) *Igbo Intellectual Tradition: Creative conflict in African and African diasporic thought*. New York, NY: Palgrave Macmillan.

Dike, KO (n.d.) Introduction to the Ibadan History Series, reprinted in a number of titles in the series published by Longman.

Dike, KO (1953) African history and self-government, *West Africa*, **37**; reprinted in C Ifemesia (ed.) (1988) *Issues in African Studies and National Education: Selected works of Kenneth Onwuka Dike* Awka. Nigeria: KO Dike Centre, pp. 71–79.

Dike, KO (1956) *Trade and Politics in the Niger Delta, 1830–1885: An introduction to the economic and political history of Nigeria*. Oxford: Clarendon Press.

Falola, T (2003) The Ade Ajayi's cumulative: Reformulating the humanities in Africa, in A Oyebade (ed.) *The Foundations of Nigeria: Essays in honour of Toyin Falola*. Trenton: NJ: Africa World Press, p. 306.

Falola, T (2016) *The Humanities in Africa: Knowledge Production, Universities, and Transformation of Society*. Austin, TX: Pan-African University Press.

Falola, T and Aderinto, S (2010) *Nigeria, Nationalism, and Writing History*. Rochester, NY: University of Rochester Press.

Flint, J (1960) *Taubman Goldie and the Making of Modern Nigeria*. London: Oxford University Press.

Houston, J (1725) *Some New and Accurate Observations of the Coast of Guinea: Geographical, natural and historical*. London: J Peele.

Ifemesia, CC (1984) Funeral Orations, *Bulletin of the Historical Society of Nigeria*, Special Number Announcing the Death of Professor K Onwuka Dike, p. 3.

Ikime, O (1979) *Through Changing Scenes: Nigerian history yesterday, today and tomorrow*. Ibadan: University of Ibadan, Inaugural Lecture.

Ikime, O (ed.) (1980) *Groundwork of Nigerian History*. Ibadan: Heinemann.

Laurknck, M (1983) Former History Professor dies: Was African Studies pioneer, *The Harvard Crimson*, 14 November. Available at: www.thecrimson.com/article/1983/11/14/former-history-professor-dies-was-african/ (accessed August 2018).

Mellanby, K (1958) *The Birth of Nigeria's University*. Ibadan: Ibadan University Press.

National Archives of Nigeria (2007). *National Archives of Nigeria*. www.nigerianarchives.gov.ng/

Nwauwa, AO (2009) KO Dike and the new African Nationalist historiography, in T Falola and A Paddock (eds) *Emergent Themes and Methods in African Studies: Essays in Honor of Adiele E. Afigbo*. Trenton, NJ: African World Press.

Olulana, D (2017) Kenneth Dike. PR2J3C4 – Nigeria @ Her Best, 3 January. Available at: the234project.com/people/nigeria/kenneth-dike/ (accessed August 2018).

Omer-Cooper, JD (1980) The contribution of the University of Ibadan to the spread of the study and teaching of African history, *Journal of the Historical Society of Nigeria*, **10**(3): 23–31.

Omolewa, M (1980) The education factor in the emergence of the modern profession of historians in Nigeria, 1926–1956, *Journal of the Historical Society of Nigeria*, **10**(3) (December). Available at: https://www.jstor.org/stable/i40092349 (accessed 15 October 2019).

Perham, M and Simmons, J (1962) *African Discovery*. London: Faber and Faber, p. 16.

Trevor-Roper H (1968) *The Rise of Christian Europe*. New York: Harcourt, Brace, p. 9.

Chapter 14
The Dar es Salaam School of Political Economy

Severine M Rugumamu

Introduction
The fame and stature of the 'Great Debates' of the University of Dar es Salaam School of Political Economy lasted for about two-and-a-half decades, from the late 1960s through to the 1980s, defined by the articulation and disarticulation of contending ideological and knowledge positions, in the narrowest Gramscian tradition. In the 'war of positions', intellectual defenders of the hegemonic knowledge system variously seek to kill, repress, ignore or otherwise marginalise contending ones.[1] During the euphoria of decolonisation and the rise of national liberation movements, it became incumbent upon nationalist historians and their liberal expatriate colleagues to rewrite previously suppressed Africa's historical past. They sought to demystify colonial racial arrogance and stereotypes, and expose mythologies, while articulating and celebrating the struggles of the 'fathers of nations' and their nation-building endeavours. By the mid-1960s, the glamour of the nationalist school of knowledge production and representation had worn out. It was superseded by the political economy analyses of dependency, Marxist-Leninist and world systems schools, all using variants of the Marxist political economy tools of analysis. It attributed Africa's underdevelopment and its global marginality to the system of capitalist imperialism and exploitation, tracing asymmetrical relationships between Africa and Europe from 15th-century slavery to formal colonialism and later to contemporary neocolonialism and globalisation. The political economy scholarship generated a set of ideas that had parallels with liberatory theory discourse in Latin America, ostensibly seeking to change and transform social injustices and inequity.

However, the crisis in the capitalist accumulation system from the mid-1970s, the disintegration of the global socialist system and miraculous development experiences of countries in East Asia from the early 1908s witnessed a gradual but discernible decline of the Marxist political economy school at the University of Dar es Salaam. It saw the rise of the counter-hegemonic ideology of neoliberalism. The collapse of global socialist experiments led to the strong

---
1 On the role of organic and traditional intellectuals and 'war of position' in knowledge production, circulation and use, see Antonio Gramsci (1971: 10–15).

belief in the power of the free market to fix any African economic and political problems. Like the two previously disgraced schools of dependency and Marxism-Leninism, neoliberalism was enthusiastically adopted by the University of Dar es Salaam academy, lock, stock and barrel. Strangely enough, I shall later argue, social science scholarship at the University of Dar es Salaam seems to have gone full circle, from liberalism during the 1950s and 1960s to Marxism in the 1960s and 1970s and back to neoliberalism since the late 1980s.

This chapter begins by outlining the changing contexts and dynamics of knowledge production and dissemination in the pre- and post-independence Tanzania, then looks at the rise and decline of the Dar es Salaam school of nationalist historiography. After a detailed discussion of the School of Political Economy at the University of Dar es Salaam and its influence on knowledge production, dissemination and use, it then examines the rise of neoliberalism and the gradual decline of this school. The final section concludes by teasing out lessons that can be drawn from the Tanzanian experience of knowledge production and dissemination.

Tanzanian context of knowledge production

The rise and fall of the Dar es Salaam School of Political Economy is better understood when properly situated in its historical and political contexts. Arguably, the social production of any knowledge, its dissemination and use hardly take place in a vacuum. The changing hegemonic visions of dominant social groups are created and recreated in response to changing circumstances and struggles. In turn, those visions are circulated until they assume a 'common sense' status for the rest of society in guiding their everyday understanding of the world around them. Historically, knowledge dominance, censorship and struggles have been an integral part of North–South relations. Religious and racial doctrines were used by major Western powers to justify conquest and the enslavement of the African people, while dominated subaltern knowledge systems were institutionally 'silenced', to use historian Jacques Depelchin's (2004) very apt book title, *Silences in African History*. Later, notions of 'civilising missions' were used to justify colonial political control, economic exploitation and social domination. Education and religion were used as colonial ideological instruments to promote Western culture, values and tastes as being superior, while debasing the colonised culture and values for being 'inferior', 'primitive', 'barbarian' and 'inhuman'. This has parallels with the contemporary capitalist globalisation dispensation, where neoliberal theory is paraded as unassailable in justifying market-led and corporate-dominated globalisation. Its hegemony is constructed, reproduced and extended on the basis of its superior access to the dominant social groups and to their economic, political and cultural power over resources. It could be said that in the era of global capitalist hegemony, Marxian political economy has long been viewed as a form of knowledge production and distribution that sought to produce counter-hegemonic knowledge systems, which are both transformative and liberatory in nature and scope. No wonder, Tanzania's intellectuals – as well as overall African-dominated subaltern knowledge systems – tended to draw heavily on Marxian political economy paradigms.

However, the hegemonic knowledge systems under capitalism have always been in a permanent contestation with the subaltern knowledge systems of the dominated working classes and other social groups, whose well-being is fundamentally insecure and held hostage to capital needs and drives. In this sense, the explicit objective of the much-maligned but activist Marxian political economy is to seek not only to explain, critique and challenge capitalist globalisation, but, unlike contending theories of development, its ultimate objective is also to create specific knowledge systems and strategies that can effectively foster a full and complete human emancipation. As a subaltern knowledge system, Marxism is fundamentally about knowing and changing the world. This occurs when the subaltern groups realise their own capacity to become philosophers of their daily experiences; they come to understand the hegemonic common sense that they otherwise take for granted. This is perhaps what Karl Marx (1977: 158) was referring to when he said that 'the philosophers have only interpreted the world, in various ways; the point is to change it'. A brief history of the University of Dar es Salaam illustrates that the knowledge production and distribution of an institution may traverse parallel paths, with twists and turns in the fortunes of contending social forces seeking to influence its methods and outputs.

The University of Dar es Salaam was established as an affiliate College of the University of London in 1961, a few months before independence. In 1963, it became an affiliate College of the then newly established University of East Africa. Later in 1970, the University of East Africa split into three independent national universities: Makerere University, Uganda; Nairobi University, Kenya; and the University of Dar es Salaam, Tanzania. Like its counterpart colleges of Makerere and Nairobi, the University of Dar es Salaam was essentially a bourgeois academic institution fashioned on Western norms, values and paraphernalia. The degrees that were granted during the colonial period by Makerere, Legon and Ibadan colleges strictly followed the structure, curricula and language of the 'mother' metropolitan institution, namely the University of London. They were also wholly staffed with faculty members recruited mainly from the United Kingdom. As Paul Zeleza aptly notes, 'concepts and models were eagerly imported, tested, and accepted or rejected according to prevailing academic fashions in the global North' (Zeleza, 1997: 33) In short, the colonial education system, its paradigms and the hegemony of Western thought remained largely sacrosanct. And African knowledge systems and the voices of the indigenous population were ignored at best and silenced at worst.

In various ways, however, the Tanzanian political experience was essentially unique. Firstly, unlike its counterparts, the University of Dar es Salaam implemented rapid 'nationalisation' of the teaching and research faculty and employed visiting lecturers from the Socialist bloc and accepted graduate training offers from the Soviet Union and East European governments.[2] Not surprisingly, young nationalist scholars, together with some liberal expatriate colleagues, felt obligated to develop university curricula and research programmes that gradually moved away from Eurocentric epistemology to reflect the aspiration, cultures and history of the African people. Moreover, right from its very inception, the intellectual thrust at the university benefited profoundly from comradely interactions with members of the African Liberation Movements and southern African exiles living in Tanzania. Dar es Salaam headquartered the Organisation of African Unity's Liberation Committee.[3] Most exiles, refugees and liberation movement combatants had been thoroughly inspired by works on African and Latin American political economy by such writers as Amilcar Cabral, Frantz Fanon and Che Guevara on the notion of total liberation of the continent.

Second, thanks to Tanzania's relative political stability, serious intellectual debates and discussions went on uninterruptedly for well over three decades. The university became a place for fresh insights and visions, and an arena where fundamental social ideas were pronounced, challenged, clarified or disputed in a relatively dignified manner. Even a few Marxist scholars, local and foreign, who claimed the socialist policies pursued by Tanzania were not leftist enough, were often tolerated. Sadly, in most other African countries on the continent, producers of anti-statist ideologies found themselves at loggerheads with the political leadership; they were either construed as subversives to be silenced or they quickly sought refuge elsewhere. The situation at the University of Dar es Salaam was different from the realities at universities in apartheid South Africa

---

2 One of the ground-breaking publications at the university was by a Hungarian scholar, then head of the Economics Department, Tamás Szentes (1972).

3 Tanzania offered itself as a rear base for fighting for liberation, hosting the forces of many movements, including the African National Congress (ANC) and the Pan Africanist Congress (PAC) from South Africa; the Mozambique Liberation Front (FRELIMO); the People's Movement for the Liberation of Angola (MPLA); the Zimbabwe African National Union (ZANU); the Zimbabwe African People's Union (ZAPU); and the South West Africa People's Organisation (SWAPO) from Namibia.

and Chancellor College, Malawi, where, for example, the teaching of politics and library acquisition of what was perceived as 'subversive literature' were either outrightly forbidden or strictly censored. Not surprisingly, hundreds of thousands of valuable books, journals and magazines produced by, for example, Progressive Publishers from Moscow; Académiai Kiadó from Budapest, Hungary; Leipzig Borsenvere from East Germany; and Foreign Languages Press, Beijing, were selling at almost give-away prices at the University of Dar es Salaam Bookshop in the 1960s, 1970s and 1980s. Students, lecturers and the general public acquired them easily as reference learning and research materials or even as a way of building up a serious home library.

Third, the East–West rivalry and Cold War ideological struggles provided non-aligned countries like Tanzania with ample space for independent thinking, intellectual innovation and practice. Radical scholarship and critical Marxist perspectives became popular and influenced many scholars on the African continent. As is well known, several important theoretical attempts were made in the Global South to challenge entrenched liberal orthodoxies.[4] Those intellectual innovations, it will be argued, filtered uninterruptedly into Tanzania's ideological debates. Furthermore, exemplars of successful socialist construction in Eastern Europe, Asia, Latin America and, particularly, the Cuban revolution, as well as the successes by oppressed peoples in the Indo-China wars of imperialist aggression, served as reference points to socialist-leaning scholarship. The latter demonstrated both the extent to which a global superpower would seek to impose its will over a poor developing country and the actual possibility that such a nation, under a correct class and ideological leadership, could defy and defeat imperialism. These experiences helped to radicalise not only African liberation movements but also many youths on university campuses on the African continent. Amilcar Cabral's theoretical formulation of history, class and national liberation became important reference points for scholars and student activists at the University of Dar es Salaam, who were ideologically eager to transcend the conservative politics of modernisation, stability and development paraded by bourgeois scholarship.

Fourth, unlike most post-colonial African countries, Tanzania offered a relatively more enabling environment for intellectual debates and discourse. Julius Nyerere, the first and long-serving Tanzanian post-independence leader,

---

4   Raul Prebisch's centre-periphery model of the world economy and his explanation of the declining terms of trade provided intellectual justification for policies of import-substitution industrialisation. Arthur Lewis's dual economy model of economic development with unlimited supplies of labour justified policies of industrialisation and agricultural revolution. Similar independent thinkers drawn from Latin America and Africa achieved international academic standing during this period. For details on thinking space provided by the Cold War, see Girvan (2007).

provided almost whatever it took to promote relatively free intellectual discourses. As the publisher – Pambazuka Press – of *Africa's Liberation: The legacy of Nyerere* put it in its back-page summary, 'Nyerere was not simply a player on the national terrain, he was a pan-Africanist and internationalist – in thought, writings and, crucially, in practice'.[5] He welcomed the tradition of free speech and critical inquiry, and he actively participated in most of those debates. This intellectualism was amply vindicated by his own ideological stamp on the social theory of African Socialism without class struggles and by his on-the-mark interpretation of the neocolonial nature and character of African neocolonial states (Nyerere, 1968). Later on, in his Convocation Address at Ibadan University, Nigeria, in 1976, in his typical Fanonian candour, President Julius Nyerere exposed the 'false decolonisation' of African countries thus:

> The reality of neo-colonialism quickly becomes obvious to a new African government which tries to act on economic matters in the interest of national development and for the betterment of its masses. For such government immediately discovers that it inherited the power to make laws, to direct the civil service, to treat with foreign governments and so on, but it did not inherit effective power over economic development in its own country. Indeed, it often discovers that there is no such a thing as national economy at all (Nyerere 1978: 9).

A rich tradition of open and robust discussion, consensus and even dissent was gradually established, nurtured and often tolerated at the University of Dar es Salaam. Little wonder, then, that President Nyerere came to enjoy the unparalleled adulation across the world and was variously described as Africa's 'philosopher-king', or the 'greatest thinker-president' by various writers. Issa Shivji (2011:1) describes him aptly as 'the most articulate, intense, and militant of the first generation of African nationalists ... he stood head and shoulders above many of his political contemporaries. He was a radical nationalist, progressive, pan-Africanist, and broadly anti-imperialist.' Goran Hyden and Donald Williams (1993) shared similar sentiments. They opine, among other things, that Nyerere's presidency was the most symbolic in all of Africa, carefully framing the nation-building project with the goal of remaking the entire nation into a super-community. They add further that 'Nyerere's own rationale for communitarian, one-party democracy became a source of inspiration for many other political leaders in the region... Tanzania had much greater influence in African than its

---

5   See, for example, Chachage and Cassar (2010).

otherwise modest accomplishments might suggest' (1993: 92–93). In addition, Ali Mazrui (1967: 22) writes that 'Of all the top political figures in English-speaking Africa as a whole, Nyerere is perhaps the most original thinker of them all'. Arguably, such unparalleled intellectual qualities distinguished him for his guarded tolerance of controversial ideological positions.

Fifth, the ruling party in Tanzania, TANU, adopted the policy of 'socialism and self-reliance' in February 1967, famously called the Arusha Declaration. It was widely acknowledged as a bold national and anti-imperialist statement and development strategy, outlining an alternative, left-leaning vision of African socialism. In attempting to chart a new course for development and transformation of the economy and the society, the Arusha Declaration did not mince words about its grand vision of development:

> We have been oppressed a great deal, we have been exploited a great deal and we have been disregarded a great deal. It is our weakness that has led to our being oppressed, exploited and disregarded. Now we want a revolution – a revolution which brings an end to our weakness, so that we are never again exploited, oppressed or humiliated (Nyerere, 1968: 235).

Scholars of left ideological leanings trekked to Tanzania to study, research, write and participate in the on-going revolution. Tanzanian scholars, student activists and political cadres, as well as Tanzania-based Marxist-Leninist African liberation movements, collectively established a very rare critical mass of organic intellectuals. As observed earlier, Dar es Salaam was the headquarters of the Organisation of African Unity's Liberation Coordinating Committee, and this meant that it was a home and a rear-base to refugees and liberation movement personalities from all over Africa. Together they constituted a critical mass of public intellectuals popularly known as the 'Dar es Salaam School of Political Economy'. With the onset of the global economic crisis in the early 1970s, the rise of conservative governments in major capitalist countries, the failure of socialist experiments in the former Soviet Union and Eastern Europe, and the so-called economic development miracles of Southeast Asia that were capitalist-leaning, neoliberal ideology became, *de facto*, the hegemonic ideology on a global scale. The failure of the model originally formulated by Marx and his followers to work similar miracles provided ready-made ammunition for those inclined to demolish Marxian political economy. This short backdrop provides the historical origins of the University of Dar es Salaam's 'Great Debates', starting from nationalist historiography and methodological debates in the social sciences.

Nationalist historiography and beyond

Political independence created propitious conditions for nationalists to write and reinterpret African history, society, culture and development. The colonial knowledge system had hitherto portrayed African societies as exotic, intellectually retarded, governmentally despotic, culturally passive and politically penetrable. Based on a hierarchical classification of races, peoples and cultures, colonial historiography placed its own at the top to justify its world dominance. It was officially interpreted as the history of the invaders, namely, the Phoenicians, the Hamites and later Europeans, with self-appointed missions to civilise static and unchanging primitive natives.[6] Subsequent modernisation economic theories of Walt Rostow and Talcott Parsons' sociological attributes of modernity presented Africa-type societies as backward and lacking in agency. The teaching and inculcation of 'modern European ideas' and the establishment of 'modern institutions', it was claimed, would provide the impetus for guiding primitive societies to break 'traditional' barriers to modernity. The nationalist narratives, on the other hand, sought to shift the parameters of knowledge production and dissemination in Africa. This was a counter-colonial resistance project, drawing on hybrid processes of representation, self-determination and self-writing, as well as dismantling assertions of cultural superiority of imperial Europe against African societies.[7] Understood in the above sense, the nationalist scholarship sought to reinterpret pre-colonial and post-colonial Africa, showing the vibrancy in society, culture and institutions. They, in fact, were not passive objects of colonial rule, unable to influence their own fate or prone to respond irrationally to situations, as claimed by racist colonial orthodoxies. The History Department at the University of Dar es Salaam went the extra mile to design transformative knowledge production and dissemination programmes, and establish research programmes, novel research methodologies, interpretations and criteria for scientific acceptability without looking over colonial shoulders.[8]

---

6   In his *Philosophy of History*, GW Hegel (1956: 91–99) categorically stated that African societies had no history before European colonisation. He further laments that 'perhaps in the future, there will be some African history to teach. But at present, there is none: there is only the history of Europeans in Africa.'

7   For details on the reconstruction of African history and society see, among others, Temu and Swai (1981) and Falola (2004).

8   According to Isaria Kimambo (1991) research in the Department of History included seven priorities, namely: (1) massive programme of collecting oral traditions; (2) serious experimentation with agrarian history; (3) political studies at area level; (4) make research findings readily available in print; (5) extension of oral research into earlier colonial period in order to cover response to invasion and early colonial rule; (6) greater concern for intellectual in addition to politico-economic history; and (7) continuation on coastal settlements and societies.

From the outset, even long before the launch of the Sunday Morning Ideological Classes, the Department of History was one of the centres of intellectual debates at the University of Dar es Salaam. It established its academic professional association, the Historical Association of Tanzania, in 1966, its own publication outlet, namely *Tanzania Zamani: A journal of historical research and writing*, and a weekly history seminar. The history seminar attracted participants across disciplines such as political science, sociology and economics. The first book-length publication from the department, *A History of Tanzania*, formally inaugurated the nationalist historiography, by explicitly breaking with the dominant themes of imperial history (Kimambo and Temu, 1969). As would be expected, it largely examined the evolution of political institutions during the pre-colonial period, colonial institutions and capitalist economic relations, as well as the rise and triumph of nationalism.[9]

Unlike colonial knowledge production that exclusively relied on archives left behind by missionaries, explorers and anthropologists, nationalist historiographers ventured into novel methodologies by exploring oral traditions, historical linguistics and archaeology, as well as undertaking interdisciplinary research and publication activities. The scope and coverage of research and publication expanded to cover such themes as labour and labour migration, the environment, medicine, identity, diplomacy, the military and cultural heritage and tourism. Above all, in an effort to decolonise the discipline, the department promoted the introduction of new history syllabi and resource materials for secondary schools and colleges.[10]

As documented by the premier Tanzanian historian, Isaria Kimambo, the Department of History embarked on rewriting histories of different ethnic groups in Tanzania before colonialism. These included, among many others, B Brock among the Nyika; S Feierman among the Shambaa; I Kimambo among the Pare; A Redmayne on the Hehe; R Roberts among the Nyamezi; A Shorter among the Kiambu; and R Wills on the Fipa. They all appeared in an edited collection under the title of *Tanzania before 1900* (Roberts, 1968). As Kimambo (1991: 12) has observed, from there onwards the 'department was recognised as a distinct school of historiography'. This early nationalist rewriting of African history was dubbed by European peer reviewers as the 'Dar es Salaam School of Historiography'. Viewed retrospectively, the nationalist historiography scholarship at the University of Dar es Salaam played the critical intellectual and ideological role of deliberately and courageously demystifying colonial

---

9   On colonial institution structures and African reactions against colonial domination see, among others, Kimambo and Temu (1969) and Kaniki (1980).

10 The new areas of historical knowledge production at the University of Dar es Salaam are discussed by Masebo (2017) and Lawi and Mapunda (2005).

history, its racist policies, silences and its institutions.

Shortly thereafter, however, the Dar es Salaam School of Historiography came under intense intellectual fire and rebuttals. The scholarship was accused on several fronts, including its overconcentration on the role of post-colonial political leaders at the expense of their subjects; its exaggeration of the efficacy of the African initiative; its lack of concern for internal differentiation and class conflicts, as well as its unquestioned legitimisation of the post-colonial state governance styles. Above all, the scholarship was serially faulted for devoting too little space to the history-making role of the masses under both the colonial and post-colonial dispensations.[11] Others, including Ali Mazrui (1984), argued that the scholarship was too empirical, not theoretical enough, and that it tended to promote elitist history from above. Still others vehemently ridiculed and castigated it for cherry-picking research topics and issues while silencing others, such as the dilemma of Africa's persistent exploitation and underdevelopment, false decolonisation processes, political repression and tyranny on an unprecedented scale. As Donald Denoon and Adam Kuper claim:

> [T]he new historiography has adopted the political philosophy of the current African nationalism, has used it to inform the study of African history. That commitment inclines the school toward rhetoric in defence of narrowly selected themes and interpretations, and the stereotyping and total rejection of other views... In short, it is ideological history (1970: 348).

Frantz Fanon's (1976) biting critique of the national bourgeoisie in new states in his famous book, *Wretched of the Earth*, was increasingly becoming intellectually valid. Although the national petty bourgeoisie had managed to articulate the popular demands of the masses during the independence struggles, it had no clear ideological direction capable of stirring neocolonial nations and territories out of the lethargy of underdevelopment; nor did it realise its structural capacity and limitations of operating under the yoke of imperialism. Arguably, after several decades of underdevelopment and marginalisation, the much-vaunted Kwame Nkrumah's 'seek ye first the political kingdom' began to lose some of its glitter and its ideological hegemony dwindled in the social knowledge production industry. Very quickly thereafter, the material poverty of the broad masses of the people was understood as underdevelopment, using the materialist conception of history. Together with Fanon, Andre Gunder Frank (1969) was discovered in Latin America and imported into Africa. The Marxist

---

11 On the critique of nationalist historiography see, for example, Mafeje (1976), Zeleza (1997) and Temu and Swai (1981).

school of political economy gradually assumed hegemony as liberalism and modernisation theories were fast eclipsed.

The Dar es Salaam School of Political Economy

The social and ideological context for the rise, sustenance and, later, the fall from grace of the Dar es Salaam School of (Marxian) Political Economy was a confluence of several historical conjunctures. First, conventional modernisation theories, policies and practice together with massive Western development aid, know-how, technology and investment had had disappointing results across the continent in general and Tanzania in particular. Similarly, the income and wealth differential between a small but growing section of well-to-do citizens vis-à-vis the rest was widely interpreted as a bad omen for a stable and peaceful nation. A serious and in-depth rethink of alternative emancipatory development strategies became imperative. Coincidentally, variants of socialism were being mooted and put into practice in several African countries by the mid-1960s.[12]

It was against this backdrop that the famous Arusha Declaration was promulgated in February 1967 (Nyerere, 1967). The Arusha Declaration of intent committed the Government of Tanzania and people to a policy of 'socialism and self-reliance'. As pointed out earlier, this was anti-imperialist development strategy, promising to construct a socialist economy, democratic politics and an egalitarian society. Similarly, at the level of knowledge reproduction, this declaration sought to usher in, in a bold departure from conventional bourgeois thought and practice, a radical socialist orientation in social science research, teaching, and even praxis in the country. Not surprisingly, one month after the promulgation of the Arusha Declaration, the University of Dar es Salaam's top management, faculty, and representatives from the ruling party and its mass organisations as well as senior government officers met to discuss the 'Role of the University College, Dar es Salaam in a Socialist Tanzania'. The report on the conference emphasised that the university had an obligation 'to produce committed intellectuals, men and women, who share a distinctive and unified world outlook, a particular way of perceiving, comprehending and understanding man's social universe' (University College, 1967: 117). In short, the university was officially mandated to produce and disseminate relevant knowledge to address the social, political and economic problems of Tanzania, supporting the construction of socialism and self-reliance. From then onwards, Marxist theories of capitalism and imperialism, their various offshoots such as

---

12 They include Algeria, the Republic of Guinea, the People's Republic of Congo, Benin, Somalia, the Democratic Republic of Congo and Ethiopia.

theories of development and underdevelopment, became popular subjects of study, debate and discussion.

In 1969, barring the Faculty of Social Science, which offered a course called East African Society and Environment, a common interdisciplinary course of Development Studies was introduced to all undergraduate degree programmes at the University of Dar es Salaam. The latter was initially a two-year compulsory course offered by the Department of Development Studies in the Faculty of Arts and Sciences and, later, by the Institute of Development Studies. This institute was mandated to generate and impart knowledge to undergraduate and graduate students on Tanzania's problems and challenges of constructing a socialist society, economy and politics by deploying Marxist-inspired tools of analysis. In the first year, the course broadly covered development in a historical perspective. Specific topics included the Theory of Social Development, the Political Economy of Capitalism, the System of Colonialism, and the System of Underdevelopment and Anti-Imperialist Struggles. Socialism as an Alternative System of Development was offered in the second year. Specific topics covered included the Development of Socialist Thought; Political Economy of Socialism; and Socialism as a System of Production and Social Services. Besides the acquisition of knowledge *qua* knowledge, of developing critical thinking, the compulsory programme in development studies at the University of Dar es Salaam sought to deliberately inculcate the spirit of nationalism and, above all, socialist consciousness among the youth. At the graduate level, similar methods of knowledge production and dissemination were employed. Political economy perspectives and thematic issues were covered. Besides a common course in methodology, other relevant courses included Political Economy; Socialist Transformation in Tanzania; Socialist Planning and Management; and Utilisation of Science and Technology. I should hasten to emphasise that the teaching of development studies in the University of Dar es Salaam dates back to October 1966, when university students demonstrated in the streets of Dar es Salaam to protest against legislation that aimed at instituting a compulsory 'National Service' scheme for all secondary school leavers and fresh university graduates.

As already alluded to, the imperative of interrogating the paradigm informing development in general, and that of the nature and character of education on offer, became increasingly obvious and urgent. Moreover, all academic units at the University of Dar es Salaam, and especially those in the faculties of Social Sciences and Law, were mandated to restructure their teaching and research programmes to respond to the imperative of building socialism and self-reliance in Tanzania. Depending on the academic training and ideological orientations of faculty members, responses to government directive were many, varied and mixed. Some bourgeois-trained and ideologically conservative academics tended to drag their feet, questioning the rationale for watering down what they considered to be internationally accepted golden norms and standards. It is important to emphasise that units with strong conservative ideologies and dispositions, such as Political Science and Law, tended to drag their feet and ended up failing to develop coherent theoretical frameworks with the necessary internal coherence, consistency and logic.[13] Other traditional disciplines, such as history and economics, responded enthusiastically and with a sense of urgency.

As already pointed out, the Department of History emerged once again as one of the leading centres of radical ideological debates, teaching, reflection and writing at the University of Dar es Salaam. It was no coincidence that it housed prominent and well-established Marxist scholars such as Walter Rodney, Jacques Depelchin, Dan O'Meara, Henry Slater, Bonaventura Swai, Ernest Wamba-dia-Wamba, Gershom Mishambi, and many others. These scholars succeeded in redesigning undergraduate and graduate teaching and research programmes, giving them a heavy dose of Marxian political economy orientation. Additional new political economy-related courses included Capitalism and Imperialism in World History; Colonialism and Nationalism; Neocolonialism and Revolutionary Movements; Revolutions and Socialist Transformations; Imperialism and Transformation; and a colloquium on the Political Economy of Tanzania. The restructured teaching programme also generated research projects by students and members of the faculty (Wamba-dia-Wamba, 1993: 10).

Slowly, but discernibly, other departments within the university borrowed a leaf from the History Department. The Economics Department introduced new courses in its undergraduate programmes: Political Economy of Underdevelopment and Planning; Economic Policy and Planning; Programming and Planning; Socialist Agricultural Systems; and Regional Planning. Similarly, the Department of Sociology introduced new courses in its programmes: Introduction to Political Economy; Industrial Society and the Rise of the Working Class; and Comparative Socialist Development. Finally, the Department of Political Science came up with the following political economy-related courses: Introduction to Political Economy; Political Economy of Underdevelopment Areas; Tanzanian Socialism and African Political Thought; Imperialism and Liberation; Issues in the Management of Public Enterprises;

---

13 The struggles to introduce the Marxian Political Economy perspective in teaching and research in the Faculty of Law remained inconclusive. The debate revolved around the dilemma of producing lawyers with a lot of non-legal knowledge and not proficient in law. For insights into this debate, see a collection of essays written by members of the Law Faculty, edited by Shivji (1986).

and Socialist Theories of Development. As Hyden and Williams observe in a think-piece, 'Political Science in Post-Independence Africa', 'virtually all courses on "transition to socialism", "socialist construction" or "socialist management" borrowed texts from China, Cuba or the Soviet Union to demonstrate that socialism is possible in Africa' (Hyden and Williams, 1989: 21). One should hasten to ask: where else would they have turned to?

Although the Marxian political economy tradition is diverse and heterogeneous, it is possible to identify some common tenets. Marxism-Leninism is the scientific approach to the study of social development. As developed by its principal founders, Marx, Engels and Lenin, scientific socialism is the ideology of the only class that can bring an end to capitalism and initiate the construction of society transitioning to communism. Generally, Marxian political economy comprises an integrative analysis of the economy, society and politics. These three aspects are considered not in isolation but as dynamically interdependent structures that have evolved historically. Traditionally, the Marxian political economy analysis seeks to analyse complex and long-term social and economic processes instead of the conventional descriptions of isolated economic and political events. It emphasises the need to examine the material conditions of people's lives by searching processes of class formation and class struggles not only to uncover the underlying exploitation and alienation of labour but also to formulate relevant liberation strategies. In more recent times, the methodology has concentrated on the socio-economic consequences of neoliberal globalisation, the financialisation of the world economy and the power of transnational capital. The methodology has had the explicit aim of not only critiquing and challenging the global capitalist system and its social organisations, but, equally importantly, also producing social knowledge for constructing a more just society beyond capitalism.

The adoption of open-to-all Sunday Morning Ideological Classes from the militant student activists institutionalised a novel collective method of knowledge production, distribution and learning at the University of Dar es Salaam. The auditorium was always fully packed. The process of knowledge production and learning included presentations of research findings, seminars, debates and colloquia. Participants included lecturers, student activists and members of the general public, including political activists, cadres of African liberation movements and foreign researchers interested in the political economy of Africa in general and Tanzania in particular. Questions relating to underdevelopment, blocked growth, dependence, political retrogression and socialist construction were mooted. Leading luminaries included Walter Rodney, Terence Ranger, Issa Shivji, Dan Nabudere, Mahmood Mamdani, Archie Mafeje, John Saul, Jacques Depelchin and Lionel Cliffe. Gradually, the

University of Dar es Salaam shed some of the paraphernalia of a standard ivory tower institution.

Following Rodney's (1972) ground-breaking work, *How Europe Underdeveloped Africa*, other left-leaning books and monographs were published. Major works that were produced included Tamás Szentes (1972); Lionel Cliffe and John Saul (1973); Justinian Rweyemamu (1973); Clive Thomas (1974); Shivji (1976); Kwan Kim et al (1979); Yash Tandon (1982); Dan Nabudere (1977); Henry Bernstein (1976); Jacques Depelchin (2004) and Ernest Wamba-dia-Wamba (1993). These works, and many others, attempted to offer alternative conceptions to the modernisation theories of development. Issa Shivji (1993), one of the leading organic intellectuals at the time, described the 1970s and early 1980s as the 'Golden Age' of a Marxist Political Economy at the University of Dar es Salaam. Participants at the Sunday Morning Ideological Classes were exposed to some of the leading progressive works and classic texts. Issa Shivji later noted:

> I have already indicated the intellectual ferment, the Golden Age, so to speak, of intellectualism at the Hill. It was all pervasive as we read profusely. Every publication was an event; every return from a field trip was an occasion for reflection, every seminar was a forum for ideological struggle, which, admittedly, we sometimes overdid it... Nonetheless, I believe it was a great period imbued with unfaltering commitment to the cause of the *Wretched of the Earth*. And that was its greatest strength (Shivji, 2002: 286).

Whatever the theoretical, ideological and political weaknesses of those debates, they did establish a new conceptual framework for teaching, research and reflection. They sharpened the division between those 'progressive scholars' who wanted to re-examine the purpose, structure and content of university education, and 'establishment scholars' who saw education as part of the process of civilising Africans and reproducing a compliant middle-class cadre. The University of Dar es Salaam political economy debates and resulting writings had an enormous impact, not only on teaching and learning among its keen participants but it was also equally influential in the raising of a revolutionary consciousness among the youth at the university and beyond. Modernisation orthodoxies became easy intellectual punching bags for their progressive counterparts.

The unique role played by the University Students' African Revolutionary Front (USARF), founded in the wake of the Arusha Declaration, is noteworthy. It was founded in September 1968 by a small group of militant pan-Africanist students drawn from Tanzania, Uganda, Sudan, Malawi and Ethiopia. Yoweri

Museveni, the President of Uganda, was elected its founding chairman. It was a student-only initiative. Dr Walter Rodney, the leading Marxian theoretician, was one of the few young faculty members who was involved, but purely in a relationship of equality. Members of the USARF tended to believe that the Arusha Declaration constituted a socialist revolution and that the task ahead was to create the necessary conditions for socialist construction and transformation. Until it was deregistered by the state, the USARF had three primary objectives. First, according to President Yoweri Museveni's autobiography, *Sowing the Mustard Seed* (1997: 26–30), through its regular leaflets, handouts and official magazine, *CHECHE*, it sought to disseminate Marxist-Leninist ideas among students and raise their ideological consciousness and enthusiasm. Second, it sought to contribute positively to the ideas of African revolution and people's struggles elsewhere. In the university setting, the USARF was always on the look-out to expose reactionary lecturers, popularly tagged as 'imperialist agents'. Outside the university, the USARF sought to establish comradely relationship with various liberation movements based in Tanzania. In 1968, for example, it organised a seven-person learning trip to the Mozambique Liberation Front's (Frelimo) liberated zones in northern Mozambique. They discussed and shared experiences with combatants and political leaders and the organisational structures in liberated zones, raising consciousness among citizens and military preparedness among citizens. Finally, the USARF aimed to get students to identify with the causes of the toiling masses in Tanzania, Africa and elsewhere by extending a helping hand to various Ujamaa villages in rural Tanzania.[14] In short, as Issa Shivji (1986) has concluded, its activities helped enormously to stimulate the revolutionary spirit and activism among students, and later among the labour unions.

In his professorial inaugural lecture, Isaria Kimambo, one of the leading members of the Dar es Salaam school of nationalist historiographers, highlighted congratulatory remarks from the external examiner's report to the Department of History, noting:

> The Department is to be congratulated for having successfully instilled a sense of history in the students. They clearly have a specific orientation – a materialist one. They also are confronting concepts and internalising them, which is always a difficult task for undergraduates. Above all, they have a world view of history. So the Department is doing a good job (Kimambo, 1991: 28).

---

14 On the role of USARF in raising revolutionary consciousness among the youth, see Museveni, Y (1997) *Sowing the Mustard Seed: The struggle for freedom and democracy in Uganda*. London: Macmillan, pp. 26–30.

Moreover, the intellectual impact of the University of Dar es Salaam's political economy debate also went far beyond the confines of the university corridors into the public domain, as evidenced by popular debates in the pages of the *Daily News*, the main government English-language newspaper. The indirect intellectual reach of the school in East Africa was further enhanced by annual East African Universities' Social Science Conferences.[15] As Dan Nabudere notes, the appearance of his own work, *The Political Economy of Imperialism* drew heated debate and, ultimately, necessitated the editor of the paper in an editorial to call a halt to it.

The University of Dar es Salaam's 'Great Debate' centred essentially on how to understand, explain and engage imperialism in the neocolonial formations of East Africa. It originated in response to the publication of three very important books around the mid-1970s. These include Issa Shivji's (1976) *Class Struggles in Tanzania,* Dan Nabudere's (1977) *The Political Economy of Imperialism*, and Mahmood Mamdani's (1976) *Politics and Class Formation in Uganda.* As noted earlier, each sought to undertake rigorous analysis of concrete political economy conditions in order to provide strategies and tactics for fighting against imperialism. The debate was largely cast in terms of who rules in the neocolonial formations and what class interests they serve. Who was the principal enemy of the exploited and oppressed people of East Africa? Who is the immediate enemy? What were the manifestations of international class struggle on the national scene? What strategies and tactics were to be deployed in the struggle against imperialism? What was the role and capacity of the working class and their vanguard parties? In addressing these questions, two major contending positions emerged: those considered progressives and those considered reactionaries. Name-calling and caricaturing among comrades in seminars and in written rebuttals were not uncommon. In Tandon's edited volume (1982) *University of Dar es Salaam Debate on Class, State and Imperialism,* the publisher notes (in the cover blurb):

> In the Marxist-Leninist tradition, the exchanges were sharp and uninhibited by bourgeois politeness or hypocritical applauses ... that debate was not only important to Marxists in Tanzania but also to Marxists elsewhere in Africa and outside in their study of imperialism and the struggle against it.

On the one hand, there was a group of scholars led by Shivji (1972) and

---

15 In addition to participants from Uganda, Kenya and Tanzania, others came from Zambia, Malawi, Nigeria, Sierra Leone, the United Kingdom and the United States.

Mamdani (1976) who claimed that the social strata that exercised economic and political control – that is, the bureaucratic and economic bourgeoisie – were tactically the immediate enemy of the people. Although imperialism was identified as the principal enemy, it remained an external force. Arguably, the struggle against imperialism was to be carried out on two fronts: at the local and international levels. Such delineation was considered analytically important in order to identify the internal forces that oppress and exploit the people on behalf of the external forces, namely imperialism. To do otherwise, it was claimed, would disarm the working class ideologically and allow their oppressors to shelter in the camp of the people. At a national level, a united anti-imperialist front, led by the proletarian mass party, was proposed, composed of workers, peasants, progressive and petit-bourgeois elements in order to capture state power. At the international level, upon capture of state power, the proletarian-led state institutions were expected to undertake deliberate economic measures to initiate the implementation of economic and political disengagement from imperialism.[16] To that effect, economic and diplomatic strategies of equal measure were suggested to establish mutual co-operation relations with the more advanced socialist countries of Europe.

The Great Debate faulted the Shivji–Mamdani line of argumentation on several grounds. Firstly, it was fiercely criticised for abstracting class formations and class struggles from the totality of imperialism, the global system within which they were but a part. Casting those social classes that hold state power in neocolonies as a full-fledged 'bureaucratic bourgeoisie', and those with substantial national capital outlays as a full-fledged 'commercial bourgeoisie', was found to be not only analytically inelegant but also factually inaccurate. The debaters ridiculed the Shivji–Mamdani line for misrepresenting Fanon's Chapter Three on 'The pitfalls of the national consciousness'. Secondly, they were criticised for their inability to conceptualise how the international financial oligarchy could actually rule on a global scale without formal global state structures and bureaucracies. Under capitalist globalisation, class formation had become less and less tied to a particular nation-state or territory. The transnational capitalist class was the global ruling class because it owned the leading worldwide means of production and controlled the levels of global decision-making. It was a hegemonic block of various economic and political actors from both the Global North and the Global South (Robinson and Harris,

---

16 On the question of disengagement, Rodney (1972: 350) argues that 'It was not meant total isolation, but a reduction of economic dependency, elimination of surplus outflows, utilisation of this surplus for construction of nationally integrated economies, equitable cooperation with friendly socialist countries and mobilisation of the masses for rapid development and defense.'

2000: 11–12).[17] Thirdly, there was the question of the national bourgeoisies – bureaucratic and commercial – who were incorrectly cast as fully fledged, articulated and autonomous social classes from the global financial oligarchy. In fact, they remained structurally petty and subordinate partners. Worse still, they were cast purely in racial and national territorial terms. Fourthly, it was argued that some strategic issues remained poorly problematised:

- Was the national proletariat ideologically developed enough to become the veritable political force capable of leading the struggle for the national democratic revolution?
- Other than the alliance of workers and peasants, which other social forces would be included or excluded, and why?
- Finally, upon seizure of state power, what were the institutional foundations for anchoring a national democratic state and a planned national economy?

On the other hand, there was a group of scholars led by Rodney (1972), Nabudere (1977) and Tandon (1982) who claimed to define imperialism in strict Leninist terms as worldwide capitalism, in which finance capital and the financial oligarchy had acquired control over basic industries and the credit system, and, on the basis of this control, exported finance capital for the exploitation of cheap labour and other resources in backward countries. The financial oligarchy was, *ipso facto,* cast as the global ruling class. By the same token, it was further argued that the global expansion of capital had plausibly negated the very basis for a full-fledged national bourgeoisie to emerge in the oppressed and dominated socio-formations. In its stead, it produced a petty bourgeoisie of every definition. The ideological task of the radical intellectual, it was argued, was to recognise and expose the exact nature of imperialist contradictions at different stages of the struggle in order to determine the content of the united front under the leadership of the working class – contradictions between imperialist and socialist countries; contradictions between imperialist capital and those between imperialist countries; and contradictions between imperialist countries and dominated countries. For neocolonial formations, the principal contradiction was cast as one between imperialism and local comprarorial agents, on the one hand, and the oppressed and exploited people, on the other. Consequently, the struggle was essentially an anti-imperialist

---

17 According to William Robinson and Jerry Harris (2000: 15) the indicators of a transnational capitalist class include worldwide spread of transnational corporations and private financial institutions, the proliferation of mergers and acquisitions across national borders, and the increased interlocking of positions within the global corporate structure. They express their interests in global rather than local capital through free-market neoliberal ideologies and the culture-ideology of consumerism.

struggle and not exclusively a class struggle confined to each country or nation. The national bourgeoisie and petty bourgeoisie were equally oppressed by imperialism and, therefore, had a chance of joining the popular united front against imperialism during the phase of the 'new democratic revolution'.

Like the Shivji–Mamdani camp, the latter group of analysts tended to offer almost a similar strategy against imperialism. They only differed on the details. The eventual overthrow of the neocolonial state and the establishment of a national democratic revolution were suggested as the first order of intervention toward building socialism in any progressive neocolonial state in the Global South. Depending on ideological inclinations, it was argued that sections of the national bourgeois and petit bourgeois classes would tactically be mobilised to join the broad alliance of the working class and peasants in the struggle to seize power from imperialism and its national bourgeois allies.

However, critical strategic issues remained inadequately problematised. To start with, there was the question of who and how to mobilise a broad national alliance of progressive forces for the completion of the national democratic revolution against the backdrop of a pervasive false consciousness among the working classes and their inability to play a vanguard role. This broad alliance would reflect both political and ideological compromises in each concrete national condition. The alliance would include not only the usual middle strata, radical sections of the intelligentsia, students, the rural and urban petty bourgeoisie, but also sections of the bourgeoisie itself. Moreover, upon seizure of state power, what would be the institutional foundations to anchor and nurture a national democratic state, able and willing to create organs of people's power as an effective weapon of the struggle? What would be the nature and character of the transition from democratic to socialist revolution and relations with a world system of socialist political economies? Finally, theoretical questions of the possibility of constructing socialism in neocolonial countries in the Global South, by-passing a stage of full-grown capitalism, remained contentious and largely unresolved.

Ultimately, it was agreed among comrades that unresolved questions were to be handled by in-depth and critical studies dealing with the concrete political struggles of each African country. In the introductory chapter in the *University of Dar es Salaam Debate* edited by Tandon (1982), Abdul-Rahman Mohammed Babu, former Tanzanian veteran politician, aptly summarises the ultimate objective of the book:

> The purpose of these essays is obvious: Marxists do not engage in debates just for the fun of it as in school debates. The principal task is to change the world. Their debates are about the correct understanding

of the world around us. Once this world is understood, then the task is to outline policies, which will guide their struggle – to draw up the general line. This is arrived at by concrete analysis of a concrete situation in any given area. To do this they use the dialectical methodology, which is universally applicable, and they relate it to their concrete situation (Babu, 1982: 10).

The rise of neoliberalism

Until the publication of Bill Warren's (1973) trenchant article, 'Imperialism and capitalist industrialisation' in the *New Left Review* and, subsequently, his much-celebrated full-length book, *Imperialism: Pioneer of Capitalism* (1980), variants of the Marxian school held unchallenged sway and dominated the analytic and policy frameworks on the political left in Tanzania. Following in the footsteps of Karl Marx's trenchant observations on the future impact of colonialism in India,[18] Warren's work sharply and discernibly shifted the contours of the development studies discourse. He broke with the traditional outlook, arguing that the old theory of imperialism was being contradicted repeatedly by experiences of successful variants of capitalism after World War II. On the contrary, Warren forcefully argued that direct colonialism had powerfully impelled socio-economic changes by laying the foundations for development of the productive forces and initiating capitalist industrialisation, indigenously rooted capitalism and, ultimately, world socialism. By dissolving most of the pre-capitalist socio-economic systems, imposing primary commodity production for export, and introducing Western education values and institutions, colonialism provided the necessary development framework for modernisation and development in most non-European countries. State-

---

18 Karl Marx (1853) foresaw the double mission of British imperialism in India. One, the destructive mission, and, two, the regenerative mission – the annihilation of a developmentally retrogressive Asiatic society – and the laying of the material foundations of Western society in Asia. More specifically he adds:
I know that the English millocracy intend to endow India with railways with the exclusive view of extracting at diminishing expense, the cotton and other raw materials for their manufactures. But when you have once introduced machinery into the locomotion of a country, which possesses iron and coals, you are unable to withhold it from its fabrication. You cannot maintain a net of railways over an immense country without introducing all those industrial processes necessary to meet the immediate and current wants of the railway locomotion, and out of which these must grow the application of machinery to those branches of industry connected with the railways. The railway system will therefore become in India, truly a forerunner of modern industry… Modern industry resulting from the railways system will dissolve the hereditary division of labour upon which rest the Indian castes, those decisive impediments to Indian progress and Indian power. Marx, K (1853) The future of British rule in India, *New York Daily Tribune*, 8 August.

led development accumulated institutional capacity to mobilise domestic resources and successfully planned and executed policies designed to promote and protect domestic accumulation, as well as implement a phased integration into the global capitalist system. He concluded that the dependency theory of underdevelopment cannot explain the impressive development performances of first-tier, newly industrialised countries (NICs), second-tier NICs and, later, that of China and India. These cumulative experiences, together with the mass failure of socialist construction experiences in the former Soviet Union and Eastern Europe, directly challenged the theoretical tenets of Marxian political economy. It became increasingly fashionable to posit that under certain historical contexts, imperialism might be a progressive force for development.

Perhaps not surprisingly, some prominent and hardcore dependentistas, such as Colin Leys (1980), Ferdinando Cardoso and Enzo Faletto (1979), John Senders and Sheila Smith (1986) and others, had to retract their earlier firmly held ideological positions and resurrected the ideas of the developmental state and nationalist bourgeoisie as potential institutional agencies for an escape from the scourges of underdevelopment. Later, when President Ferdinando Cardoso of Brazil dismissed the idea that periphery countries were developing in 'distorted ways', he noted:

> [T]oday we know that this is not true. Countries which were able to manage their economies sensibly to the transformation of the modes of production within capitalism as well as social issues have had more favourable trajectories than others. The case of Asian Tigers is well known. What remains of determinism ... certainly must be fundamentally reformulated (cited in Estefania, 1995: 283).

Similarly, addressing the obsolescence of dependency theory, Alice Amsden (1979: 342) argues:

> [The] major thesis of dependency theory is that the rise of foreign trade and the arrival of foreign capital from the 'core' lie at the heart of the underdevelopment of the 'periphery'. Taiwan, however, presents dependency with the paradox. It is both more integrated in world capitalism than other poor market economies and more dependent on foreign trade.

It was against these theoretical reversals, recantations and empirical insights that the dependency paradigm and policies of disengagement seem to have temporarily stumbled, then fallen from grace.

More poignantly – and in measured prose and great detail – Samir Amin (1990: 68) powerfully concluded that the opportunity costs of autarky were simply too great to constitute a viable developmental path in the Global South. He admonishes us that 'the peoples of the periphery are not equally ripe for the beginning of the socialist delinking'. In the meantime, he further counsels that 'this set of countries must cope with capitalist worldwide expansion and should struggle to ensure that its modalities are the least damaging to the eventual ripening of the liberation'. This observation was widely considered as the final nail in the coffin of the Marxian political economy school. International development policy came to be dominated broadly by the Washington Consensus, advocating privatisation, free trade, export-led growth, financial capital mobility, macro-economic austerity and liberal democracy.

Conclusion

The University of Dar es Salaam's School of Political Economy, like other paradigms before and after it, has temporarily fallen from grace. However, if neoliberal development policies and strategies have failed to deliver on capitalist promises of growth and prosperity to the majority of world citizens, then a paradigm shift would be well ordered. Frequent and periodic capitalist crises and accompanying devastating impacts, particularly on poor economies and societies, continue to highlight the relevance, urgency and imperative of Marxian political economy. From the earlier discussions, at least three lessons of best practice can be gleaned from the experiences of the University of Dar es Salaam School of Political Economy. First, for African intelligentsia and activists to assume the role and stature of organic intellectual, they may wish to consider, at least as a first step, unapologetically embracing the Marxian political economy perspective as was the case at the University of Dar es Salaam. As a critique of bourgeois scholarship, the Marxian political economy perspective satisfactorily facilitates the interrogation of historically handed-down knowledge systems in order to radically shift the very parameters of the establishment debate. Furthermore, the framework provides a philosophical outlook and a revolutionary theory of explaining the world around us and how to change it, as well as drawing up a programme of revolutionary action to address the systemic crises of capitalism. This is the only currently available analytical perspective that ably lays bare the scourges of capitalist domination, exploitation and oppression of the working masses, and provides a relevant road map for revolutionary practice against the system, putting, at front and centre, the power structures, class interests and the struggles of competing groups in society. Above all, as a normative intellectual enterprise, the Marxian political economy framework takes the side of the poor and powerless and sees the system of capitalism as the primary and strategic enemy of the poor working masses.

Secondly, at its peak, the Dar es Salaam School of Political Economy debate critically interrogated the extent to which the national policies, strategies and institutions engendered by the Arusha Declaration would resolve Africa's perennial problems of poverty, ignorance and disease. The open-to-all Sunday Ideological Classes were an innovative collective pedagogy of knowledge production, dissemination and use. These Sunday classes helped participants to challenge each other in addressing common intellectual questions and contestations, thus facilitating the stimulation of sharper political consciousness and exploration of alternative development strategies. The Sunday seminars endorsed and practised Paulo Freire's (1993: 100–1) incontrovertible philosophical concept that 'all men [sic] are philosophers'.[19] Accordingly, a democratic and non-hierarchical discourse setting, comprising interdisciplinary professors, lecturers, students and members of civil society, defined the University of Dar es Salaam School of Political Economy pedagogy. The back-and-forth debates, discussions and in-print rebuttals produced a critical mass of what Antonio Gramsci refers to as 'organic intellectuals' – those who were ready and willing to carry with them the 'organic' values, interests and aspirations of the oppressed social classes, by which they sought to influence and shape the intellectual climate and perspectives of the whole social collective. The University of Dar es Salaam's organic intellectuals took it upon themselves to produce transformative knowledge for social action in the interests of the marginalised classes and social groups, as well as, ultimately, speaking truth to power without fear or favour, as vindicated by curriculum review debates. As already discussed, one of the lasting testaments of the Dar es Salaam period was Yash Tandon's (1982) publication, *The University of Dar es Salaam Debate on Class, State and Imperialism*.

The final lesson to be carefully examined from the Dar es Salaam School of Political Economy would be how best to implement state-sanctioned directives of defining and redesigning education curricula at all levels to reflect the imperatives of building a democratic society, politics and economy. Once again, competing roles of the establishment and organic intellectuals came to the fore. The unsettled question was always about how best to integrate the Marxist world-view in teaching, research and outreach activities within ideologically compromised conventional programmes. On the one hand, departmental units

---

19 The central plank of Paulo Freire's argument is that humans, as beings of praxis, are endowed with the capacity for interrelated theory and action, mutually reinforcing action and reflection in order to continually transform our social and physical reality.

that housed a critical mass of Marxist-inspired scholars and plentiful other resources, such as History and Economics, organised themselves democratically and managed to arrive at a consensus on innovative political economy-related programmes and methodologies for teaching, research and extension services. On the other hand, units with strong conservative ideologies and dispositions, such as Political Science and Law, tended to drag their feet and ended up failing to develop theoretical frameworks with the necessary internal coherence, consistency and logic. In this regard, a co-ordinating body, with powers to vet proposed new teaching, research and outreach programmes, may be considered to effectively rein in the overwhelming influence of establishment scholarship. As noted earlier, they have superior access to the neocolonial state and dominant social groups with economic, political and cultural power to make resources available to intellectuals of their choice. These apparent advantages could effectively be counterbalanced by the intimate engagements of organic intellectuals with the exploited and oppressive classes, as well as undertaking basic and action research in every critical area of concern, in collaboration with enlightened sections of the state.

References

Amin, S (1990) Colonialism and the rise of capital: A comment, *Science and Society*, **54**(1): 67–72.

Amsden, A (1979) Taiwan's economic history: A case of Etatism and a challenge to dependency theory, *Modern China*, **5**(2): 341–80.

Babu, A-R (1982) Introduction, in Y Tandon (ed.) *University of Dar es Salaam Debate on Class, State and Imperialism*. Dar es Salaam: Tanzania Publishing House.

Bernstein, H (1976) Underdevelopment and the Law of Value: A critique of Kay, *Review of African Political Economy*, **6**: 60–73.

Cardoso, FH and Faletto, E (1979) *Dependency and Development in Latin America*. Berkeley, CA, University of California Press.

Chachage, C and Cassam A (eds) (2010) *Africa Liberation: The legacy of Nyerere*. Oxford: Pambazuka Press.

Cliffe, L and John, S (1973) *Socialism in Tanzania*, vols 1 & 2. Nairobi: East African Publishing House.

Denoon, D and Kuper, A (1970) Nationalist historians in search of a nation: The new historiography in Dar salaam, *African Affairs*, **69**(277): 329–49.

Depelchin, J (2004) *Silences in African History: Between the syndromes of discovery and abolition*. Dar es Salaam: Mkuki na Nyota Publishers.

Estefania, J (1995) Desenvolvimento: Maais politico dos temas economicos, *Revista de Economia Politica*, **15**(4): 147–68.

Falola, T (2004) *Nationalism and African Intellectuals*. New York: University of Rochester.

Fanon, F (1976) *The Wretched of the Earth*. Harmondsworth: Penguin Books.

Frank, A (1969) *Latin America: Underdevelopment or revolution?* New York: Monthly Review Press.

Freire, P (1993) *Pedagogy of the Oppressed*. New York: Continuum Book.

Girvan, N (2007) *Power Imbalances and Development Knowledge*, North–South Institute Papers, Toronto, September.

Gramsci, A (1971) *Selections from the Prison Notebooks*. New York: International Publishers.

Hatch, J (1976) *Two African Statesmen: Kaunda of Zambia and Nyerere of Tanzania*. Mishawaka, IN: NTC Contemporary Publishing.

Hegel, G (1956) *Philosophy of History*. New York: Dover Publications.

Hyden, G and Williams, D (1989) Political Science in post-independence Africa, in W Oyugi (ed.) *The Teaching and Research of Political Science in East Africa*. Addis Ababa: OSSREA: pp. 3–32.

Hyden, G and Williams, D (1993) Community model of African politics: Illustrations from Nigeria and Tanzania, *Comparative Studies in Society*, **36**(1): 68–96.

Kaniki, M (1980) *Tanzania under Colonial Rule*. London: Longman.

Kim, K, Mabele, R and Schultheis, M (eds) (1979) *Papers on the Political Economy of Tanzania*. Nairobi: Heinemann Education Books.

Kimambo, IN (1991) Three decades of production of historical knowledge at Dar es Salaam. Professorial Inaugural Lecture. Dar es Salaam: University of Dar es Salaam.

Kimambo, I and Temu, AJ (1969) A History of Tanzania. Nairobi: East African Publishing House for Historical Association of Tanzania.

Lawi, Y and Mapunda B (eds) (2005) *History of Disease and Healing in Africa*. GEGVA-NUFU Publication, No 7, Dar es Salaam.

Leys, C (1980) Challenging development concepts, *IDS Bulletin*, **11**(3): 21–24.

Mafeje, A (1976) The problem of Anthropology in historical perspective: An inquiry into growth of Social Sciences, *Canadian Journal of African Studies*, **1**: 307–33.

Mamdani, M (1976) *Politics and Class Formation in Uganda*. New York: Monthly Review Press.

Marx, K (1853) The future of the British rule in India, *New York Daily Tribune*, 8 August.

Marx, K (1977) "Theses on Feuerbach XI". In D McLellan (ed), *Karl Marx: Selected Writings*. Oxford: Oxford University Press.

Masebo, O (2017) New thematic directions in History at the University of Dar es Salaam, 1990s to 2017, *Tanzania Zamani: A Journal of Historical Research and Writing*, 9(2): 1–92.

Mazrui, A (1967) Tanzaphilia: A diagnosis, *Transition*, **31**(June–July): 20–26.

Mazrui, A (1984) *Nationalism and the New States in Africa*. London: Heinemann.

McLellan, D (ed.) (1977) *Karl Marx: Selected Writings. Theses on Feuerbach XI*. Oxford: Oxford University Press, pp. 171–74.

Museveni, Y (1997) *Sowing the Mustard Seed: The struggle for freedom and democracy in Uganda*. Oxford: Macmillan Publishers.

Nabudere, D (1977) *Political Economy of Imperialism*. Dar es Salaam: Tanzania Publishing House.

Nyerere, J (1967) *Freedom and Socialism*. Nairobi: Oxford University Press.

Nyerere, J (1968) *Ujamaa: Essays on Socialism*. New York: Oxford University Press.

Nyerere, J (1978) The University of Ibadan Convocation Address, *University Echo*, May, University of Dar es Salaam.

Pratt, C (1976) *The Critical Phase in Tanzania, 1945–1968: Nyerere and the emergence of a socialist strategy*. New York: Cambridge University Press.

Roberts, A (ed.) (1968) *Tanzania Before 1900*. Nairobi: East African Publishing House.

Robinson, W and Harris, J (2000) Toward a global ruling class? Globalisation and a transnational capitalist class, *Science and Society*, **64**(1): 11–54.

Rodney, W (1972) *How Europe Underdeveloped Africa*. London: Bogle-L'Overture Publications.

Rweyemamu, J (1973) *Underdevelopment and Industrialisation in Tanzania*. Nairobi: Oxford University Press.

Senders, J and Smith, S (1986) *The Development of Capitalism in Africa*. London and New York: Methuen.

Shivji, I (1976) *Class Struggles in Tanzania*. London: Heinemann.

Shivji, I (ed) (1986) *The State and the Working People in Tanzania*. Dakar: CODESRIA Books.

Shivji, I (1993) *Intellectuals at the Hill*. Dar es Salaam: Dar es Salaam University Press.

Shivji, I (2002) From liberation to liberalism: Intellectual discourses at the University of Dar es

Salaam, *Austrian Journal of Development Studies*, **3**: 281–94.

Shivji, I (2011) Nyerere, Nationalism and Pan-Africanism, *Pambazuka News*, 17 March. Available at: www.pampazuka.org/panafricanisms/nyerere/nationalism/and/pan/africanism (accessed September 2018).

Shivji, I (2012) Walter A Rodney, in C Chang (ed.) *Walter A Rodney: A promise of revolution*. New York: Monthly Review Press, pp. 83–94.

Szentes, T (1972) *The Political Economy of Underdevelopment*. Budapest: Académiai Kiadó.

Tandon, Y (ed.) (1982) *University of Dar es Salaam Debate on Class, State and Imperialism*. Dar es Salaam: Tanzania Publishing House.

Temu, A and Swai, B (1981) *Historians and Africanist History: A critique of post-colonial history examined*. London: Zed Press.

Thomas, C (1974) *Dependency and Transformation: The economics of transition to socialism*. New York: Monthly Review Press.

University College, Dar es Salaam (1967) *Report on the Conference on the Role of the University College, Dar es Salaam in a Socialist Tanzania*. Mimeo. Dar es Salaam: University of Dar es Salaam.

Wamba-dia-Wamba, E (1993) African history and teaching history in Dar es Salaam, *Tanzania Zamani: A Journal of Historical Research and Writing*, **1**(3)(April): 1–19.

Warren, B (1973) Imperialism and capitalist industrialisation, *New Left Review*, **1**(81): 3–44.

Warren, B (1980) *Imperialism: Pioneer of capitalism*. London: Verso.

Zeleza, P (1997) *Manufacturing African Studies and Crises*. Dakar: CODESRIA Books.

Chapter 15
The Dakar School of Culture

Samba Buri Mboup

Introduction

As a natural gateway to Africa, Dakar, the capital city of Senegal, is positioned as an intellectual and cultural capital that has hosted and continues to host world cultural events such as the 1966 and 2010 editions of the World Festival of Black Arts (FESMAN) and the Dak'Art Biennale. The Senegalese capital has also pioneered African institutions of learning and culture such as the University of Dakar (now University Cheikh Anta Diop/UCAD), the former École Normale William Ponty and the Museum of Black Civilisations, established in 2019. Such examples testify to the country's commitment to Pan-Africanism and openness to the world. It is within this context that the establishment of the Dakar School of Culture, Scholarship and Thought (the Dakar School) can be located. The school's intellectual legacy is derived from the seminal contributions of two towering contemporary figures in the area of knowledge generation and application: Senegal's Cheikh Anta Diop, a scientist with specialisation in nuclear physics, history, Egyptology and cultural studies; and the Egyptian-Frenchman Samir Amin, an economist and political scientist.

Over the past decades, many private tertiary institutions have blossomed near Dakar and these have attracted cohorts of students from Africa and elsewhere to the Senegalese shores, including distinguished Pan-Africanist figures such as Ghana's Ayi Kwei Armah and Haitian Gerard Chenet. Various cultural institutions such as Per-Ankh in Popenguine, Sobo Bade in Toubab Dialaw and the Pan-African Culture and Research Centre in Yène have been created on the Petite Côte. On a daily basis, the impact of the activities in such institutions, the sociability of their founders, and their rootedness in their respective locations have contributed to perpetuating and consolidating a commonly shared Pan-Africanist spirit in the areas of culture, research, scholarship, thought and community outreach. This occurs in an environment marked by the development of other platforms of intense intellectual activity and debate, such as the 'Saturdays of Economics' organised by the German Rosa Luxemburg Foundation.

Both Cheikh Anta Diop and Samir Amin were path-finders who distinguished themselves through their contributions to progressive scholarship for the transformation of society. They were both thought leaders, revolutionary thinkers and committed Pan-Africanists. In a variety of ways, Diop and Amin epitomise the African *organic intellectual* figure. Other Marxist and Pan-Africanist scholars who have made valuable contributions to the disciplines of economics and political science at the Dakar School include Abdoulaye Ly, Baïdy Ly (the 'Old Lion'), Amadou Aly Dieng, Chérif Salif Sy, Moustapha Kassé, Jacques Bonjawo, Youssouph Mbargane Guissé and Bernard Founou-Tchuigoua. Cheikh Anta Diop's disciples include Ayi Kwei Armah, Pathé Diagne, Babacar Diop, Aboubacry Moussa Lam, Moustapha Diop, Yoporeka Somet and Cheikh Mbacké Diop.

There are a cohort of organic intellectuals like Samba Diabare Samb, Mame Mbenda Mboup, Ibou Mbengue and Guilé Mboup. The pre-colonial space of indigenous knowledge systems and the Islamic and Ajami traditions are represented by other towering figures such as Thierno Souleymane Bale, Cheikhou Oumar Tall, Cheikh Ahmadou Bamba, el-Hadj Malick Sy, Cheikh Moussa Camara, Cheikh Ady Touré and Moussa Ka. Although Cheikh Anta Diop and Samir Amin are associated with the Dakar School, their perspectives and the epistemic fields of their respective research have travelled far beyond the confines of Dakar. Indeed, their contributions were made from a broader Pan-African, even global, perspective. Samir Amin's seminal contributions have been acknowledged by the Dakar-based Council for the Development of Social Science Research in Africa (CODESRIA).

This chapter takes stock of the irreplaceable role of indigenous knowledge and educational systems and of important works written in Arabic or Ajami. However, the main focus is on Cheikh Anta Diop's contribution to Afrikology as an alternative paradigm for knowledge generation and application, with specific implications for the transformation of perspectives and research methodologies in the humanities and the social sciences, as well as for curriculum reform and the search for an alternative pedagogy.

Cheikh Anta Diop and Afrikology
Political and intellectual profile
Born in Senegal on 29 December 1923, Cheikh Anta Diop was a tireless defender of the cause of Africans and oppressed peoples. A committed Pan-Africanist, he was one of the first of his generation to articulate the need for Africa's political independence and unity. From the early 1950s he also put forward a proposal for the intensive reforestation of the continent, within the framework of a global strategy, to combat drought and promote environmental preservation. In the 1960s, Diop also tried to alert African people and the

international community to the nuclear threat posed by the then apartheid regime in Tshwane (Pretoria), who were attempting to build a nuclear arsenal with the capacity to target any part of Africa.

The Senegalese scholar was trained in various disciplines of the humanities and social sciences, including history, linguistics, anthropology, Egyptology and philosophy, as well as exact sciences like physics. Diop established a radio-carbon laboratory for dating archaeological and palaeontological artefacts, which made it possible to achieve accurate chronologies. He was Chair of the Association of Black Researchers and Scientists and a Professor of History at the then University of Dakar (now renamed after him). During the World Festival of Black Arts and Cultures in Dakar in 1966, he shared, together with African-American W.E.B. Du Bois (see Morris, Chapter 21, in this volume), the award to the black scholar whose work impacted most positively on the education of black people in the 20th century. Diop, together with Théophile Obenga from the Republic of Congo, made an outstanding contribution to the 1974 UNESCO Symposium on the Peopling of Ancient Egypt in Cairo.

Diop's work reflects a careful scrutiny and profound knowledge of Africa, its history and the realities of its peoples, their cultures, lifestyles, value systems and other systems of representation stemming from their relationship with their own habitats and environment. He contributed to historiography by establishing two key ideas: first, Africa is the Cradle of Humankind and of human civilisation; and second, there is a profound historical, linguistic, anthropological and cultural unity among African peoples. Diop's research themes included the genetic relatedness of African languages; the origin and nature of the Semitic world; Africa's invaluable contributions to world civilisation and wealth; the characterisation of African pre-colonial socio-economic formations; and the convergence of African languages in conducting scientific inquiry.

According to José Do-Nascimento (1987), the main purpose of Diop's work was to lay the scientific foundations for the consolidation of an all-African political and historical consciousness and the creation of the necessary conditions for Africa's Renaissance. Diop put his superior intellect to work on some of the main challenges for Africa's future: the continent's global security; gender equity and women's empowerment; the need for organic intellectuals; a continental policy and doctrine on energy and industrialisation; the development of an African economic market and the management of African national resources for Africa's development; and the need for an organic reconnection with the African diaspora.

Diop's political strategy (1964; 1974) is based on a vision of the future and on high political ethics and principles. Such a vision is anchored, first, on the need for 'a reflection to articulate in a rational, coherent, operational way', the problems confronted by Africans and to find viable, durable solutions to these. In this regard, the challenges to be addressed include the need to restore an all-African consciousness; re-establishing historical continuity in Africa; and the edification of an alternative paradigm for a new global civilisation and an African Renaissance (Diop, 2003: 227–33).

Before and beyond Nicolescu's Manifesto of Transdisciplinarity

For Ugandan scholar Dan Nabudere, as early as the 1950s, Diop was grappling with the creation of a value-laden knowledge reflecting the African worldview, which led him to 'move between Egyptology, anthropology, linguistics, nuclear physics, bio-chemistry and palaeontology' (2007: 6–34). As a result, Diop created 14 dating methods that are still used today, thus providing scientific evidence previously unattainable within disciplines such as Egyptology and anthropology.[1] 'What Diop did here was to move between History (Egyptology), Anthropology and the Physics laboratory, [thus] occupying all the empty spaces between them in order to bring facts to life to support the writing of an indigenous, authentic history of Africa' (Spady, 1986: 98, cited in Nabudere, 2007). Diop's intellectual journey started before and extended beyond Romanian Basarab Nicolescu's (2002) *Manifesto of Transdisciplinarity*, in order to embrace 'a vision of the future' as stressed by Nabudere. This journey led Diop to establish the operational concept of 'logical availability of the mind', to overcome the 'crisis of reason' and embark on a new logic built on the basis of modern physics, as manifested in microphysics and astrophysics (Diop, 1991a: 370–71).

A living legacy

Diop's work has become a living legacy and is being perpetuated, completed and expanded, but also critically reassessed, by his disciples, including the team of the *Journal of Egyptology and African Civilizations*. The first issue of the journal – regularly published since February 1992 – included a presentation of the laser AmonFont (n.d.: 105–21) invented by Cheikh Mbacké Diop and Samory Candace Diop; this is a computer software program for the composition of hieroglyphic texts on Macintosh computers. The same issue featured a summary by young Cameroonian nuclear physicist Jean-Paul Mbelek of his book published in 1991, under the title of *Photons and Gravitons: Incompleteness of the Equations of Electro-dynamics and Gravitation*. Mbelek proposes a

---

1 An example is the melanin dosage test: a method that enables a researcher to identify the skin colour of a mummy through analysis of the residual quantity of melanin contained in its skin and body parts.

reformulation of the Rutherford–Soddy axiomatic law on the disintegration of radioactive nuclei, with important implications for the fields of nuclear physics, radioactivity theory and cosmochronology, particularly for the determination of the age of the solar system and the study of nucleosynthesis processes in the stars. The author also succeeded in recapturing and reintroducing the African concept of *Nun* (the original *materia prima*), as an operational concept in the area of cosmology.

The Dakar School's relevance to South African higher education
South African higher education could learn from Senegal's best educational practices and the work done at the Dakar School of Culture and other institutions. For example, from the work of Ahmadou Bamba to contemporary African institutions like Per Ankh (House of Life), education was and remains a comprehensive endeavour, ruled by the principles of learner-centredness and *Shemsu* (a corporate approach to learning as a collective journey). Not only was the purpose of these education systems to convey a rational knowledge from the point of view of both the *logos* (science or theoretical knowledge) and *technê* (instrumental or applied knowledge), it was also about the development of the human spirit, mind, body and character through the acquisition or reinforcement of fundamental qualities and values, as well as the customs and social and cultural codes relevant to people's lives and communities (socialisation).

Secondly, there should be an option for mother-tongue-based multilingual education, as advocated by a group of academics from 14 tertiary institutions who met in Stellenbosch in August 2010 for a seminar on multilingualism in higher education. Diop (1954: 1975) was an advocate for mother-tongue, multilingual education and he translated Albert Einstein's Principle of Relativity as well as other advanced concepts in quantum physics, chemistry, and modern and tensor algebra, into Wolof for greater pedagogic value. Moreover, the scientific establishment of the genetic relatedness of all African languages was propounded by Diop. Théophile Obenga and others also had significant ideas for the teaching and learning of mathematics and science and for the production of didactic materials in South African languages.

In conformity with an integrated (national, sub-regional and pan-Africanist) approach to teaching and learning put forward by the University of South Africa's (UNISA) Academy of African Languages and Science (AALS) in 2010, textbooks and readers produced in Lesotho or Botswana could, with a few adjustments, serve the learning purposes of South African learners speaking any form of Sesotho or Setswana, and vice versa. It would also be possible to customise materials in isiZulu at a relatively low cost, in order to teach any subject, including maths and science, to learners and speakers of isiXhosa or, to a lesser extent, isiNdebele, even siSwati or Shangaan.

Thirdly, the use of the nine volumes of the *General History of Africa*, to which Diop and many other African scholars made seminal contributions, must be institutionalised in South African universities, to help transform the epistemology of the humanities and social sciences, with implications for curricula reform, enhanced pedagogy and the production of relevant and quality didactic materials. Special attention must also be paid to areas such as language planning and early childhood education and development. A holistic approach to education, consistent with an alternative pedagogy project, is key to the Africanisation of curricula. This entails policies aimed at boosting interdisciplinary research, coordinated teaching and peer-learning (*Shemsu*).

The paradigm shift that was advocated in South Africa responded to the need to craft or consolidate an institutional space in academia for the promotion of an alternative paradigm for the study of the country's African indigenous languages and knowledge systems, as well as in other areas of the humanities and social sciences. This process was expected to signal the end of a dominant trend of relative epistemological and intellectual insularity, as a result of the combined legacies of apartheid and post-apartheid scholarship. South Africa's intellectual tradition is still marked by the pervasive influence of Eurocentric epistemologies and orthodoxies, despite their questionable value in the areas of knowledge production and application (see chapters 10 to 12 in this volume.)

For Théophile Obenga (1985), intentional sciences provide a more holistic approach to research and scholarship that are more relevant to societal challenges, such as the management of linguistic and cultural diversity, social integration and citizenship, and viable statehood and nation-building. Other tasks of the Dakar School's apostles included fast-tracking the implementation of mother tongue-based multilingual education policies; assessing the relevance of Marxist epistemology; consolidating platforms of constructive debate on scholarly matters to ameliorate the impact of a pervasive culture of entrenched academic territoriality; and producing case studies and monographs in African scholarship. For example, besides producing monographs in the area of theoretical and descriptive linguistics, and linguistic and cultural anthropology, there is a need to produce theoretical models that will bridge the prevailing epistemic gaps in the description, documentation and classification of South Africa's indigenous languages and knowledge systems.

Mainstreaming the legacy of Cheikh Anta Diop

The challenges that confront knowledge production, dissemination and application in South Africa cannot be successfully addressed without an effort to mainstream Diop's important contributions to scholarship. This entails the constitution of pluri- and interdisciplinary research teams to respond to threats to sound scholarship, emanating from conservative white gatekeepers in South Africa, supported by their black proxies.

Diop's legacy has important methodological implications. First, given the fundamental unity of African societies and peoples, it is impossible to understand, let alone explain, any part of Africa in its own respect, out of its continental and global contexts. Secondly, from a diachronic perspective, a permanent dialectical movement is necessary between contemporary Africa and Egyptian antiquity, as the intellectual journey back to Egypt and the Nile Valley civilisations makes it possible to understand many aspects of African contemporary societies. At the same time, the nature of contemporary Africa provides conceptual tools to make an accurate assessment of ancient Egyptian realities, reframing them back into their own African contexts. Only then will it be possible to overcome what Obenga has termed the 'anarchic dispersal of contents', and the state of relative underdevelopment of African scholarship, which, despite progress made, is still dominated by case studies and monographic perspectives, without historical depth or cultural consistency.

Conclusion

Swiss linguist Ferdinand de Saussure, in his 1916 *Course in General Linguistics*, reveals that linguistic evidence of a genetic nature is the 'most indisputable method to show the existence of cultural ties between two or many peoples' (De Saussure, 1916). Indeed, the genetic relatedness between Egyptian (Pharaonic and Coptic) and other modern African languages was scientifically demonstrated on the diachronic scale by Obenga (1973; 1985; 1993; 2004) and Diop (1974; 1977; 1988), as well as the genetic relatedness of current African languages (on the synchronic scale) by C Meinhof (1899); M Guthrie (1948, 1967); J Greenberg (1966) and G Ngom (1996). This has contributed to reinforcing the notion of a profound linguistic and cultural, but also historical and anthropological, unity among African populations.

Diop's and Obenga's work owes a lot to Greenberg's (1966) *Languages of Africa*. However, it is Diop who first applied himself to filling the methodological gaps in Greenberg's classification of African languages in his 1977 study, *Parenté génétique de l'égyptien pharaonique et des langues négro-africaines*. Having demonstrated the historical and cultural unity of all Africans in his previous work, Diop resorted to the rule of phonological, morphological and semantic correspondences to show the structural unity and genetic relatedness between Pharaonic Egyptian and African languages. Obenga (1973; 1985a; 1985b; 1993) strengthened Diop's thesis through scientific demonstration, notably in a paper presented at the UNESCO Symposium on the Peopling of Ancient Egypt held in Cairo in 1974.

For Obenga and Diop, Greenberg's so-called 'Afro-Asiatic' family is either the result of a methodological oversimplification or a linguistic ghost. Yet Greenberg's model of classification is still followed by many South African linguists, including highly respected colleagues who have made seminal contributions to African scholarship. Therefore, there is a need to develop historical and comparative linguistics and studies in onomastics in South Africa, to revisit the Southern Bantu linguistic and cultural maps, as designed by scholars such as Greenberg and Guthrie.

As ancestors of humankind and human civilisation, African peoples have also built institutions and produced discourses around their own practices. Hence, the need to discover, recapture and reactualise the gnoseologic and theoretical principles underlying their own 'discourses on God, the being, society, politics, as well as on economics or the nature of power' (Diagne, 1981: 91). For example, it is widely agreed that dialectics are nothing but 'the theory of change and of the specific' (Sine, 1983: 14). One would only need to go back to the solar theory of power and creation in Khemetic (ancient Egyptian) thought, to understand the complex relationship between the concepts of *Nun* or original *materia prima* and those of *RoMut* – consciousness coming out of matter in its transformational phase – and *Neter* – an active principle of change and categorial transformation. African people did not wait for Marx – let alone African Marxists – to discover and scientifically formulate some of the basic principles and laws that govern the relationships between matter and consciousness.

As demonstrated by the Senegalese scholar Pathé Diagne, Africa is home to a history of knowledge as old as time. Its uniqueness should be emphasised not through a racial phenomenon, but in purely cultural and historical terms. Obviously, the specificities of this intellectual context, particularly its varied discourses and orders of discourses, 'could escape neither the mark of time and history nor diversity, nor even contradictions or conflicting interests' (Diagne, 1981: 88). Nevertheless, it is possible today to retrace – through space and time – and to recreate the continuity and coherence of African intellectual thought, separating it from Indo-European and Semitic epistemological forms. Therefore, to build a theory of liberation and development, of democracy and social progress, while ignoring such African national thought and knowledge, would be – in Diagne's opinion – the same as 'digging under our own feet, a vacuum' of several millennia, which could be filled by no political or scientific dissertation, as learned and brilliant as such a dissertation might be (Diagne, 1981).

In concluding, South African educationists and curricula developers should take advantage of Africa's rich legacies in the area of socio-political governance, institution-building and knowledge production in a variety of areas to reform curricula contents, together with the generic images of Self and Other, as shaped through scholarship and the media. The goal is to refocus the hearts, mind-sets and outlooks of South African students and youth back into self-knowledge, self-love and self-respect, by creating conditions for a Cultural Renaissance. This would need to be synonymous with psychological healing, rebuilding self-esteem, moral regeneration and spiritual upliftment so as to better prepare them to tackle societal and structural challenges, in particular, those encountered in South Africa's higher education in the area of knowledge generation, sharing and application. Lessons from the Dakar School of Culture could be helpful in this regard.

References

Ajayi, JFA (1986) L'Education dans l'Afrique contemporaine: Historique et perspectives. Communication au colloque organisé par l'UNESCO à Dakar (25–29 Janv 1982), sur le thème: Le Processus d'Education et l'Historiographie en Afrique. Editions de l'UNESCO, Coll. Etudes et Documents.

Diagne, P (1981) L'Europhilosophie face à la pensée du Négro-Africain. Dakar: Editions Sankoré.

Diop, CA (1954, 1964, 1979) *Nations Nègres et Culture*. Paris: Présence Africaine.

Diop, CA (1974) *The African Origin of Civilization: Myth or reality?* Chicago, IL: Lawrence Hill Books.

Diop, CA (1975) Comment enraciner la science en Afrique: exemples Walaf (Sénégal), *Bulletin de l'IFAN, série B*, **37**(1): 154–233.

Diop, CA (1977) *Parenté génétique de l'égyptien pharaonique et des langues négro-africaines: Processus de sémitisation*. Dakar: IFAN-NEA.

Diop, CA (1988) *Nouvelles recherches sur l'égyptien ancien et les langues négro-africaines modernes*. Paris: Présence Africaine.

Diop, CA (1990) [1959] *The Cultural Unity of Black Africa: The domains of matriarchy and of patriarchy in classical antiquity*. Chicago, IL: Third World Press.

Diop, CA (1991a) [1981] *Civilization or Barbarism*. Chicago, IL: Lawrence Hill Books (Original in French, 1981. Paris: Présence Africaine.)

Diop, CA (1991b) *Precolonial Black Africa* (trans. H Salemson). Chicago, IL: Lawrence Hill Books.

Diop, C M'backé (2003) *Cheikh Anta Diop, l'homme et l'oeuvre*. Paris: Présence Africaine.

Do-Nascimento, J (ed.) (2008) *La Renaissance Africaine comme alternative au développement*. Paris: Editions L'Harmattan.

Do-Nascimento, J (1987) Sur la portée opératoire de l'oeuvre de Cheikh Anta Diop, in *Revue Nomade*, 1/2, Paris.

Greenberg, J (1966) *Languages of Africa*. Bloomington, IN: Indiana University Press.

Guthrie, M (1948) *The Classification of the Bantu Languages*. London: Oxford University Press, published for the International Languages Institute.

Guthrie, M (1967–71) *Comparative Bantu: An introduction to the comparative linguistics and prehistory of the Bantu languages*, vols 1–4. Farnborough: Gregg International Publishers.

Hountondji, PJ (1998) La Cooptation: Sur quelques aspects du savoir Mondialisé. Texte d'abord présenté sous forme de communication au Colloque Mondialisation et Sciences Sociales en Afrique. CODESRIA/Graduate School of Humanities and Social Science, University of Witwatersrand, Johannesburg, 14–18 September.

Karenga, M (1996) *Reconstructing Kemetic Culture*. Los Angeles, CA: University of Sankore Press.

Mazrui, A and Wagaw, T (1982) Towards de-colonisation of modernity: Education and cultural conflicts in East Africa. Paper presented at the Dakar Colloquium on Process of Education and Historiography in Africa, UNESCO, pp. 36.

Mbelek, J (1991) Interaction entre photons et gravitons – limitations imposées aux méthodes radiométriques de datation, *ANKH Review of Egyptology and African Civilizations*, 1:89-103.

Mboup, SB (2008) Linguistic decolonization and African Renaissance, in DE Mutasa and E Etieno Ogutu (eds) *Teaching and Administering in African Languages: A road map to African Renaissance*. Pretoria: Simba Guru Publishers, pp. 60–130.

Mboup, SB (2014) 21ème Siècle: Colloque International Francophonie et Langues Nationales/ Commémoration du Cinquantenaire du CLAD, UCAD II, 21/22 Nov. 2014. Dakar: Presses Universitaires de Dakar.

Mboup, SB (ed.) (2014) African Heritage Research Study, MINDS, Johannesburg. Challenges and stakes in the Africanisation process of research, scholarship and university curricula in the context of African Renaissance. Public lecture, University of the West Indies, Kingston, September 2007. (First published in Pan-African Journal *Waar-Wi*, 2, Dakar-Senegal, Aug./Sept. 2006.)

Mboup, SB (2015) Propos d'un Africophone sur la Francophonie et les conditions pour un nouveau partenariat au 21ème siècle. A paper presented at the International Colloquium Francophonie et Langues Nationales, Université Cheikh Anta Diop, Dakar, in November 2014.

Meinhof, C (1899) Introduction to the phonology of the Bantu languages. Berlin: Reimer.

Nabudere, D (2006) Towards an Afrikology of knowledge production and African regeneration, *International Journal of African Renaissance Studies,* 1(1): 7–32.

Nabudere, D (2007) Diop C.A. The social sciences, humanities, physical sciences and transdisciplinarity, *International Journal of African Studies*, 2(1) (July).

Ndlovu-Gatsheni, SJ (2012) Archie Mafeje: The Rethinking of Knowledge in and on Africa: Past, Present and Future. A Proceedings Report of the launch of the Archie Mafeje Research Institute (AMRI) at UNISA, Africa Institute of South Africa.

Ngom, G (1996) Egypte ancienne-Afrique noire: Pensées et légendes, *Ankh*, 4/5(July): 102.

Nicolescu, B (2002) *Manifesto of Transdisciplinarity*. New York: State University of New York.

Nkuhlu, W (2005) The role of African higher education at the dawn of the 21st century. Paper presented at the launch of the Southern African Universities Vice-Chancellors Association.

Obenga, T (1973) *L'Afrique dans l'Antiquité: Egypte ancienne/Afrique noire*. Paris: Présence Africaine.

Obenga, T (1985a) *Histoire et conscience. Historique en Afrique: l'Egypte et le reste de l'Afrique noire*. Conférence prononcée à Niamey, 3 March 1982, et publiée dans les Cahiers du CELTHO, 02/12.

Obenga, T (1985b) *Les Bantu*. Paris: Présence Africaine.

Obenga, T (1993) *Origine commune de l'Égyptien ancien, du Copte et des langues Négro-Africaines modernes*. Paris: L'Harmattan.

Obenga, T (2004a) Africa in the 21st Century: Integration and Renaissance. Paper presented at the First Conference of Intellectuals from Africa and the Diaspora. Organised by the

African Union, Dakar, 6–9 October 2004.

Obenga, T (2004b) African Philosophy: The Pharaonic Period, *Per Ankh*: 2780–330.

Olukoshi, A and T-Zeleza, P (2004) *African Universities in the 21st Century*, vol 1: *Liberalisation and Internationalisation*. Illinois and Dakar: CODESRIA Books.

Sine, B (1983) *Le Marxisme devant les sociétés africaines contemporaines*. Paris: Présence Africaine.

Sithole, MP (2009) *Unequal Peers: The politics of discourse management in the social sciences*. Pretoria: Africa Institute of South Africa.

Spady, JG (1986) The changing perception of CA Diop and his work: The pre-eminence of a scientific spirit, in *Great African Thinkers*, vol. 1, *Cheikh Anta Diop*. New Brunswick and Oxford: Transaction Publishers.

UNESCO (1974) Le peuplement de l'Egypte ancienne et le déchiffrement de l'écriture méroïtique': Actes du colloque du Caire, Jan/Feb. 1974, Histoire Générale de l'Afrique, Collection 'Etudes et Documents', No 1, 1978.

Section VI: African Transformation Initiatives

Chapter 16
Decolonisation, the Heinemann African Writers Series and the making of a transnational, Pan-African literary audience

Harry Garuba

Introduction

In a speech entitled 'Birth of a Literature: Heinemann, African Writers Series and I', delivered by the Kenyan writer Ngũgĩ wa Thiong'o to mark the 40th anniversary of the Heinemann African Writers Series (AWS) in April 2002, he remarked:

> I have sometimes been accused of being a living contradiction for publishing with Heinemann in the African Writers Series. How can you, while denouncing imperialism, make a deal with a London-based publishing house that manufactures words harvested from Africa and African hands and then sells the finished product, the book, back to Africa for a profit? In what way is this different from the similar process of gold, diamonds, copper, coffee, tea, all mined or grown in Africa, processed in the West and sold back to Africa, the price of both the raw material and the finished product determined by the West? (Ngũgĩ wa Thiong'o, 2013: 1–2).

The speech was a complex reflection on his literary career, his relationship with the Heinemann AWS from its beginnings to 2002, and the birth of modern African literature (see Wanjala, Chapter 19, in this volume). Paradoxically, less than a year after Ngũgĩ wa Thiong'o's celebratory speech, Heinemann announced that it was discontinuing the series and that it would not be publishing any new titles. This is duly noted in the publisher's bibliographic note appended to the published version of Ngũgĩ's speech (2013: 10).

Ngũgĩ wa Thiong'o was not alone in his unease about the relationship of Africa and African writers to Heinemann, which was to become the biggest and most influential publisher of African writing in the first three decades following the political independence of many African countries in the 1960s. Many writers and intellectuals voiced this dissatisfaction in myriad ways. This chapter will engage these critiques later.

However, in this chapter, I argue that in spite of the many critiques and contestations of the Heinemann AWS and its role in the making of modern African literature and its canon, there are lessons to be learnt from it at this time in South African higher education, when the clamour for decolonisation has reached a new pitch as a result of the student protests of the past few years. Beginning in 2015 with the #RhodesMustFall protests at the University of Cape Town, which targeted the Rhodes statue in front of the university's Jameson Hall, the protests developed into a broad contestation of colonial and apartheid-era symbols that dotted the landscape of the institution and the country as a whole (see chapter 7 to 9 in this volume). This movement spread to other campuses and, in no time, the call for the decolonisation of institutions of higher learning in general enveloped the entire country. The movement specifically focused on the curriculum and the pedagogical practices within these institutions, which the students claimed were unabashedly Eurocentric and, therefore, unfit for the post-apartheid era.

In making the argument that there are lessons to be learnt from the Heinemann AWS, this chapter acknowledges the legitimacy and validity of several of these critiques, centring in the main, as they did, on issues of cultural imperialism, hegemony and dependency, just like the current student movement. However, I highlight several of the practices set in motion by the AWS, which would be hugely beneficial to the South African decolonisation imperative. These include, but are not limited to, accessibility, the production of low-cost paperbacks, the republishing and reprinting of old/classic texts and titles, translations, the mining of the school market, and the promotion of a pedagogic imaginary or what elsewhere I have referred to as 'teacherly texts' (Garuba, 2017) in the making of the canon of modern African literature. Furthermore, it is important to note, by way of a temporal, historical conjuncture, that the AWS was inaugurated at the moment of post-independence decolonisation in Africa; it therefore fulfilled a significant need, both for the new nations that were coming into being and for the construction of new 'national', pan-African subjects out of a medley of colonial subjects dispersed across unstable geographies of belonging. Learning the lessons of the AWS could help to realise similar objectives in South Africa.

In making this argument, I begin by outlining the context of the emergence of the AWS and then go on to enumerate some of these critiques and some of the more recent responses to them by others, before finally laying out some of the legacies of the series and the lessons that can be learnt from them at the present moment of South African decolonisation.

Context: The story of the Heinemann Education Books AWS

The story of the establishment of the Heinemann Education Books (HEB) AWS has become something of a legend in African letters. This legendary status belies its modest, almost fortuitous beginnings. After a journey through Ghana and Nigeria, Alan Hill discovered that

> the big British publishers regarded West Africa as a place where you sold books, not where you published them: and these books were overwhelmingly school books. Moreover, they were almost all written by British authors, and produced in Britain. The idea that you could publish books by African authors, and especially creative writers, had not yet occurred to these great houses, whose only concern was to make money out of the expanding school market. They were taking their profits out of West Africa, and putting nothing back in the way of investment in local publishing and encouragement of local authors (Hill, 1988: 122–23).

We may be sceptical about the purely altruistic sentiment expressed here about publishers who give nothing back and emphasise the underlying profit motive behind Hill's pursuit of African publishing, not explicitly stated here. Surely, in addition to the altruism, it is important to note that the expanding book market he identifies, a result of the post-independence expansion in education, also made his decision to establish the series a sound economic and commercial proposition. Hill persuaded Chinua Achebe, a young writer, whose 1958 book, *Things Fall Apart*, had been favourably reviewed in the London press and received attention in its literary circles, to become general editor of the series. Achebe accepted and the AWS was launched in 1962 with four titles: reprints of Achebe's *Things Fall Apart* and *No Longer at Ease,* and publication of Cyprian Ekwensi's *Burning Grass* and Kenneth Kaunda's *Zambia Shall Be Free.* Hill noted:

> His [Achebe's] role was crucial. Not only did he read every MS, in some cases undertaking editorial work, but he would identify good new authors for the Series. His very presence was a magnet for would-be writers during the ten years of his editorship. That wonderfully fruitful decade in which we published one hundred titles in the AWS (Hill, 1988: 123).

The rest, as they say, is history.

The story of the Heinemann AWS has been told many times over by the key players and writers – Allan Hill, James Currey, Chinua Achebe, Ngũgĩ wa Thiong'o, etc. – so that it hardly bears retelling. However, a few highlights need to be noted. The first is the editorial decision-making process, which, as the series grew, became dispersed over three locations – Ibadan, London and Nairobi – with editors in each location having a say in which books were published, translated or reprinted. Since the series – contrary to stories about it being oriented towards a Western audience – was largely sold in Africa and needed the buy-in of local examination boards, which prescribed curricula and selected books for schools, it was only wise to depend on this kind of triangular decision-making; in other words, people on the ground recommending manuscripts that they believed would get the nod from local or regional examination boards. With Aig Higo at the Ibadan office, and Henry Chakava and later Simon Gikandi at the Nairobi offices, they had eminently well-qualified and -positioned individuals in charge of these African offices. Despite this triangular structure, it was not really decision-making by committee – it all depended on the support and enthusiasm of the editors recommending the titles. By all accounts, about 80 per cent of the books were sold in Africa, 10 per cent in Britain, and 10 per cent in North America (Currey, 2003: 581). This is why the series ran into trouble during the foreign currency squeeze of the 1980s and the structural adjustments programmes that heightened the crisis in many African countries, including Nigeria, which accounted for a large percentage of these sales. It was also at about this time of this crisis that the North American market began to feature more prominently in the editorial decision-making process. According to Currey:

> A total of 270 titles appeared during the years from 1962 to 1984, including books by all three African winners of the Nobel Prize for Literature – Naguib Mahfouz, Nadine Gordimer and Wole Soyinka. Output peaked at 22 titles in one year, and for years, 15 or more were published annually: not many for a continent, but unmatched in the history of British and American publishing (2003: 582).

A second point worth noting is that the AWS took on translations with a zeal that conventional educational publishers, respecting the discipline of literature, would not normally do. By going full-scale into translations, the AWS created a climate in which translated texts could be found among recommended titles in English departments and among titles recommended by school and examination boards in English literature syllabi and examinations. These days, when reading and analysing translation has become fairly common with the rise of postcolonial studies and lately World Literature, it is easy to forget how innovative (or simply different) this was from conventional approaches to literary study at that time. Within the first decade of its existence, the AWS had published translations of Ferdinand Oyono's *House Boy* and Ousmane Sembène's *God's Bits of Wood,* among others. Clive Barnett, in his article 'Disseminating Africa: Burdens of representation and the African Writers Series', says:

> In fact, the HEB archives show that the *AWS's* editors were very active in pioneering the translation of works from Gikuyu, Kiswahili, Ndebele, Shona, Yoruba, and Amharic. And furthermore, in the mid-1970s, they made significant efforts to develop a Series of Kiswahili translations of *AWS* originals (Barnett, 2005: 79).

This investment in translation may simply have been a result of the fact that many more African writers had been published in French and there was the need to bring this material to English-speaking African countries. There was also the insistence by many African writers that, although their works were written in English, they were first conceived in their indigenous languages and then 'translated' into English; and this may also have helped to propel this investment in translations. All the same, the study of translated texts did create a disciplinary 'promiscuity', which may not have been immediately apparent to teachers and boards who were simply looking for African material to include on their reading and prescribed lists.

In addition, it is also noteworthy to recall that, at the time, the usual publication practice was to publish books first in hardback and later produce the paperback edition. By publishing directly into paperback editions, the series met the need for accessibility and low cost at the same time. While Heinemann may have 'stolen' this idea and its orange cover design from Penguin, it helped to establish a market and to brand the series. With the books selling for as little as 25 pence, they were affordable for the markets they were designed to serve. (There may be a lesson for South African publishers and book retailers here!) The branding also made them easily recognisable.

Furthermore, for an educational publisher with an eye to the school market, the publication of texts such as Oyono's *Houseboy* and Tayeb Salih's *Season of Migration to the North* shows that the editors were also capable of taking risks, although with some reluctance, with regard to what may be considered sexually explicit material – this at a time when British publishers were still careful about such matters. They were also not averse to publishing texts that showed formal experimentation beyond the usual fare of social realistic narratives. The publication of Dambudzo Marechera's *The House of Hunger* and Bessie Head's *A Question of Power* testify to this.

These points are worth noting because they often get lost in minutiae of the narratives that detail the phenomenal rise of the series and the role of the various editors in this process, along with the criticism that the series was merely a cultural arm of the imperial project.

Critiques of the African Writers Series

Though this chapter focuses on the lessons that can be learnt from the HEB AWS, we would be remiss if we did not outline some of the many critiques of the series. Criticism of the AWS has taken many forms. The Nigerian cultural critic Odia Ofeimun, for example, accused the series of the 'ghettoisation' of African writers and that it was a means of exerting imperialistic control over African writers. In the 40th anniversary speech, with which this chapter began, Ngũgĩ wa Thiong'o responds to this criticism by asserting:

> The African Writers Series has published writers from virtually every African country thus enabling dialogue among readers and writers from the three main colonial traditions: Portuguese, French and English... Rightly or wrongly, the Series may be accused of ghettoisation, of being part of a neo-colonial enterprise, and its foundation does indeed coincide with Africa's transition from a colonial to neo-colonial relationship with the West (2013: 8–9).

In addition to these cultural traditions anchored on colonial languages, Ngũgĩ wa Thiong'o may well have mentioned writers and readers from other language traditions such as Yorùbá, Arabic, Swahili, and so on.

But the accusation of cultural imperialism could not be so easily dismissed. Writing on 'The challenges of the AWS' in *West Africa* magazine in January 1993, Ofeimun argues:

> The view began to take root in many African circles that the AWS was part of a general imperialistic structure for controlling African possibilities. The view was part of a general battle to indigenise African political economies as well as decolonise the African mind (1993: 56).

This accusation was echoed in Gareth Griffiths book, *African Literature in English: East and West*, where he claims that rather than publishing existing contemporary African English, the African Writers Series aimed to create it (2000). He in fact suggests in another essay, 'Writing, literacy and history in Africa', that Heinemann's AWS project was as 'directive and invasive as that of missionary presses and the colonial publishing institutions' (Griffiths, 1997: 157). While it is all well and fine to draw this line of continuity between colonial and missionary institutions and a largely postcolonial market-oriented enterprise like the AWS, the forcefulness of the allegation does disturbingly seem to deny agency to African writers in any meaningful manner. In fact, much of Olabode Ibironke's work, using material from the Heinemann archive at the University of Reading, focuses on the manner in which many postcolonial writers, notably Wole Soyinka and Chinua Achebe, confront and challenge the structures of colonial and postcolonial (publishing) domination and craft their own unique messages and identities out of these structures. His essays, such as 'African writers challenge conventions of postcolonial literary history' and 'Reinventing the nation in Africa', explore the forging of this agency among African writers. This may appear to be simply a question of perspective but it is much more than this; many forms of this dependency perspective almost completely discount the subversive work that African writers located within these structures perform.

Another critique of the 'Orange Series', as the AWS came to be known, is the accusation that it has largely supported and promoted writers from certain parts of the continent. Phaswane Mpe (1999), for instance, in 'The role of the African Writers Series in the promotion and development of African literature' suggests that Chinua Achebe promoted Igbo, Nigerian and West African writers during his tenure and that James Currey helped to bring South African writers into the series. Currey responded to this in this manner:

> It seems to be held that Chinua Achebe went out of his way to support West African, Nigerian, and Igbo writers. Of course, we all have our networks. Thank goodness the Series managed to get off to a flying start with many good writers from Nigeria. There is no doubt that Ngũgĩ's presence in Nairobi brought in East African writers, though he had the competition from the East African Publishing House's Modern African Writers Series. Alan Hill has over-emphasised my own role in bringing in South African writers. What I am certain of is that Chinua Achebe, the editors in Africa and I myself were delighted by good writing wherever it came from (Currey, 2003: 582).

Rebecca Clarke, who was to be the last commissioning editor of the series before it stopped issuing new titles, brings a gender dimension to these critiques. In an argument about the absence of women writers from discussions of Africa and the relative absence of African women publishers in African publishing in general, she slips in this question: 'It is interesting to note, that from its inception to date, all the editors who have been involved with the African Writers Series have been male – is this just a co-incidence?' (Clarke, 2001: 52).

She continues in the same vein:

> One of the striking features of post-independence writing from Africa is that it was characterized by the scarcity of women writers. For example, when Heinemann's African Writers Series was launched, there was not a single female writer included. This omission is indicative of the lack of serious and sensitive critical attention from which African women writers suffered in the late 1950s and 1960s, although there were in fact, several important novels written by women like Adelaide Casely-Hayford and Mabel Danquah who had pioneered fiction writing by women long before the 1960s in West Africa (Clarke, 2001: 52).

The gender dimension she brings to these debates was typical of the titles published under the AWS and of African literature in its formative years and well worth drawing attention to.

Another common accusation was that the flourishing of the AWS hampered the development of local publishing by its market dominance and its cultural power. While there is some truth to this allegation, it needs to be noted that local publishing enterprises in East Africa, Zimbabwe and Nigeria often signed on important local writers, whom they later sub-leased to international publishing houses. A good example is Okot p'Bitek's *Song of Lawino*, which was first published by the East African Publishing House and was only sub-licensed to Heinemann in the 1980s. The AWS also developed partnerships with local publishing houses, a notable example being the East African Publishing House, referred to earlier.

Perhaps the most enduring critique of the AWS has been the accusation that it created a literature that was outward-looking, a literature oriented towards the West rather than being directed at its national or continental audience. This accusation has been made by African writers themselves, who have spoken of literary agents and scouts representing publishing houses asking them to make their writing more 'African'. Critics such as Graham Huggan (2001) have also noted the overwhelming ethnographic and anthropological focus of many of the novels published by the AWS. Arguably the most theoretically sophisticated elaboration of this idea is Eileen Julien's (2006) essay, 'The extroverted African novel'. In this essay, she details the various indices of extroversion in African novels that constitute the canonical texts taught in schools, universities and other educational institutions in Africa and across the world. In addition to detailed descriptions of cultural practices and ways of life, they make copious use of African idioms and expressions, even when they do not serve any artistic purpose in the novels; she includes the explanations and glossaries that are appended to these novels. She labels these practices as 'ornamentalism', which she sees as indicative of the extroversion she theorises.

While it is undeniable that these writing practices are dominant in many of the novels, it is less easy to directly conclude that these are solely the result of an orientation towards the West. They could conceivably be directed at other African audiences unfamiliar with the local objects and local cultural practices described. I can testify to the fact that I have taught students in South African universities who have no idea what a yam is or what kola nuts are. The Kenyan critic Simon Gikandi has spoken of his fascination with the yams described in Achebe's novels. There are also audiences within the nation itself who do not know what these objects are and what the cultural practices signify. It may not be entirely ungenerous to suggest that what is at play here is what the philosopher Paulin Hountondji has described as the myth of African unanimity. As he argues, the idea that Africa is one large homogeneous cultural group, where people outside a specific cultural or ethnic group completely understand and share the cultural practices of other groups, is a colonial myth (Houtondji, 1983).

Graham Huggan's assertion that the AWS promoted an 'anthropological exotic' in the novels they published is a variant of the extroversion argument, asserted from the perspective of exoticism (Huggan, 2001). Although Huggan is unambiguous about his claim of an anthropological exotic, he does, however, argue that the more accomplished African writers such as Chinua Achebe produced auto-ethnographies that simultaneously used and subverted the display/exhibition complex, which this form was meant to serve. All the same, the notion of the AWS promoting extroversion and self-exoticisation has stuck and the image it has created of certain forms of African writing has been difficult to shake off. I will return to this later.

There can be little doubt that the few critiques I have used as illustrations focus, on the one hand, on the question of cultural power and dependency in relation to the ideological work the AWS is seen to have done and the political economy of publishing on the continent. Arguably, the most sustained reflection on and rebuttal of many of these arguments is made in Olabode Ibironke's study of the Heinemann AWS and the writers it published in his book titled *Remapping African Literature* (2018). Ibironke's argument is basically that the critiques are overwhelmingly made from a position of structural determinism, which completely ignores the agency of the writers themselves. By insistently focusing on the metropolitan location of the apparatus of production and the constraining influence it exerts on African writers, the agency of the writers in the process is sidelined. He begins the concluding chapter of the book in this manner:

> Accounts on the question of whether intellectual autonomy from colonial culture is desirable or even possible have tended to a pessimism, which we need not accept if we consider … the material agency of writers in exerting genuinely decolonizing counter-pressures to the forces of an apparatus that seeks to confine them. Because the discourse of African literary criticism has focused on colonial and structural determinism, it misses what I term *auto-heteronomy* and especially how that is more defined by a universal regime of production (Ibironke, 2018: 305).

I believe that Ngũgĩ wa Thiong'o's biographical reflections on his own writing and his relationship with Heinemann and the AWS, mentioned at the beginning of this chapter, speak to this agency and redirect the unidirectional discourse of the writer's dependency and the publisher's absolute control.

Heinemann, the AWS and lessons for decolonisation in South African higher education

In the context of the clamour for decolonisation in South African higher education, within which this essay is embedded, it is apt to begin with an important observation about the link between the imperative of education and decolonisation (see chapters 3 to 5 in this volume). Decolonisation as conceived in the immediate postcolonial moment of the 1950s and 1960s was – at its core – a matter of education and re-education. And education was seen as an iterative, interrogative and dialogic enterprise, in the manner in which Paolo Freire (1968) had imagined in his seminal book titled *Pedagogy of the Oppressed*. This approach was what drove the decolonising moment of those days. It was anchored in the understanding that the people lived their knowledge, no matter how imperfectly. That lived experience became the basis of the texts that scholars and intellectuals struggled to name in the conceptual and categorical language of academic work. It often surprises me that when critics quote a proverb from Achebe's novels, they often attribute it to the 'transcriber': instead of quoting the Igbo people, we quote Chinua Achebe. As Chinua Achebe says, so we enthuse, 'Proverbs are the palm oil with which words are eaten'; even when we know that this is clearly an Igbo proverb and Achebe acknowledges it as such. But our citational protocols insist that we erase the people and name an individual; we need a theory that individualises the collective to deal with issues such as this; and these issues take on a particularly important dimension when it comes to intellectual property rights. The lessons that we can take away from the AWS and the earlier moment of decolonisation are both practical and conceptual/theoretical.

In the article, 'Teacherly texts: Imagining futures in Nuruddin Farah's past imperfect trilogy', I assert:

> [F]or most postcolonial literatures or literatures from emergent literary spaces (to use Pascale Casanova's term [2004: 35]), literary value inheres as much in the *teacherliness of the text* as it does in whatever other aesthetic values it may possess: that is, the text's ability to illustrate, rework, or represent some theme or issue considered to be of major significance and to open it up for *teaching* – about empire, nation, and identity, or post nation, diaspora and globalization, for instance – is as much a source of value as any of its other formal qualities (Garuba, 2017: 17).

In making this assertion, I am not espousing a crude didacticism; I am only following in the footsteps of Chinua Achebe's often cited essay 'The novelist as teacher', in which he says:

> The writer cannot expect to be excused from the task of re-education and regeneration that must be done. In fact, he should march right in front… I for one would not wish to be excused. I will be quite satisfied if my novels (especially the ones I set in the past) did no more than teach my readers that their past – with all its imperfections – was not one long night of savagery from which the first Europeans acting on God's behalf delivered them (1989: 45).

The centrality of the 'teacherly' task was asserted by nationalist leaders across the board in the immediate years of post-independence reconstruction. This is how Dipesh Chakrabarty puts it in a discussion of what he refers to as the 'pedagogic style' of the leaders of that period:

> Just as the emergent nations demanded equality with the Euro-American nations while trying to catch up with them on the economic front, similarly their leaders thought of their peasants and workers simultaneously as people who were already full citizens – in that they had the associated rights – but also as people who were not-quite full citizens in that they needed to be educated in the habit and manners of citizens. This produced a style of politics on the part of their leaders

that could only be called pedagogical. From Nasser and Nyerere to Sukarno and Nehru, decolonization produced a crop of leaders who saw themselves, fundamentally, as teachers to their nations (Chakrabarty, 2005: 4814–15).

This decolonising moment was what really created the AWS and produced its crop of writers. The success of the moment lay in the ability to convene a transnational, pan-African public and literary audience, and this was precisely what the AWS and its writers tapped into. Ibironke aptly captures this problematic of this moment when he claims that:

[T]he ultimate problem of classification of African literature today as African, Postcolonial, and World Literature rather than as National literatures, the more conventional classification, poses the question of how the history of the literature addresses the experience of cosmopolitan production, which is becoming the single most important philosophical topic of the moment (Ibironke, 2018: 26).

It is important to understand the significance of this moment, both in terms of displacing conventional disciplinary distinctions and boundaries, and creating a pan-African audience for a set of literary texts anchored on a pedagogical imaginary that authorised many of the literary and artistic practices of the writers, along with the publishing protocols adopted and the choices made by publishers.

Having said this, let us return to the legacies of this era and the lessons that can be learnt from it. There are the practical issues such as accessibility: the AWS made low-cost paperbacks available to a large school audience at prices which were affordable: reprints of old classics, translations, etc, which we have already mentioned. One of the perennial complaints of teachers of African, postcolonial and minority literatures has been that not only do they have to construct a syllabus and reading list every time they have to teach a course, they also have to source the texts for the students, as many of them are often unavailable or out of print. The unavailability of texts in print, which was a major problem in those days, remains as acute in these days of the internet as it was then. Tejumola Olaniyan and Ato Quayson's more recent anthology of African literary criticism makes this point again in its introduction.

There is no need to elaborate any further on these practical issues from which lessons can definitely be learnt. But these practical lessons will pale into insignificance if they are not combined with the ideological work of imagining a transnational, pan-African literature that subverts the colonial geographies of patchwork nation states to which we have become increasingly beholden, even in these times of transnationalism and globalisation. It may be argued that the time of pan-Africanism is long past but the decolonial turn in intellectual work in the Global South may be thought of as producing a similar – though not identical – moment to which the pedagogic imaginary on which decolonisation was anchored has become even more urgent and important. The student movement and the call for decolonising the curriculum and creating 'pluriversities' rather than consolidating the monolithic university (which has absorbed the very worst tendencies of the neoliberal, corporate university) tell us that the moment to learn these lessons is now. The ideological work that the Heinemann AWS did in their time and the epistemological counter-pressures exerted by the writers need to be brought together again and reformulated, not simply as resistance to the cultural hegemony of empire but also as a struggle against epistemic violence of a more pernicious kind, cloaked as incontrovertible knowledge, to which there is no alternative.

References

Achebe, C (1989) The novelist as teacher, in *Hopes and Impediments: Selected essays*. New York: Doubleday, pp. 40–46.

Barnett, C (2005) Disseminating Africa: Burdens of representation and the African Writers Series, *New Formations*, **57**(1): 74–94.

Chakrabarty, D (2005) Legacies of Bandung: Decolonisation and the politics of culture, *Economic and Political Weekly*, **40**(46): 4812–18.

Clarke, R (2001) Women publishers in Africa and the North, in CR Veney and PT Zeleza (eds) *Women in African Studies Scholarly Publishing*. Trenton, NJ: Africa World Press, pp. 45–64.

Currey, J (2003) Chinua Achebe, the African Writers Series and the establishment of African literature, *African Affairs*, **102**(409): 575–85.

Currey, J (2008) *Africa Writes Back: The African Writers Series and the launch of African literature*. Oxford: James Currey.

Freire, P (1972) [1968] *Pedagogy of the Oppressed*. Harmondsworth: Penguin.

Garuba, H (2017) Teacherly texts: Imagining futures in Nuruddin Farah's past imperfect trilogy, *Boundary*, **244**(2): 15–30.

Griffiths, G (1996) Documentation and communication in post-colonial societies: The politics of control, in A Gurr (ed.) *Year's Work in English Studies*, **27**: 21–37.

Griffiths, G (1997) Writing, literacy and history in Africa, in MH Msiska and P Hyland (eds) *Writing and Africa*. London: Routledge, pp 139–58.

Griffiths, G (2000) *African Literatures in English: East and West*. Harlow: Longman.

Hill, A (1988) *In Pursuit of Publishing*. London: John Murray.

Hountondji, PJ (1983) *African Philosophy: Myth or Reality*. Bloomington, IN: Indiana University Press.

Huggan, G (2001) *The Postcolonial Exotic: Marketing the margins*. London: Routledge.

Ibironke, O (2015) African writers challenge conventions of postcolonial literary history, in F Ekotto and KW Harrow (eds) *Rethinking African Cultural Production*. Bloomington, IN: Indiana University Press.

Ibironke, O (2017) Reinventing the nation in Africa: The political writings of Chinua Achebe and Wole Soyinka, in T Falola and C Hoyer (eds) *Global Africans: Race, ethnicity and shifting*

identities. New York: Routledge.
Ibironke, O (2018) *Remapping Africa Literatures*. London: Palgrave Macmillan.
Julien, E (2006) The extroverted African novel, in F Moretti (ed.) *The Novel*, vol 1: *History, Geography and Culture*. Princeton, NJ: Princeton University Press.
Mpe, P (1999) The role of the African Writers Series in the development and promotion of African literature, *African Studies*, **58**(1): 105–22.
Ngũgĩ wa Thiong'o, N (2013) Birth of a literature: Heinemann, African Writers Series and I, in *In the Name of the Mother: Reflections on writers and empire*. Woodbridge, Suffolk: James Currey, pp. 1–10.
Okot p' Bitek (1984) *Song of Lawino and Song of Ocol*. Oxford: Heinemann.
Ofeimun, O (1993) Challenges to the AWS, *West Africa*, 18–24 January.
Olaniyan, T and Quayson, A (eds) (2007) Introduction, in *African Literature: An anthology of criticism and theory*. Malden, MA: Blackwell Publishers.
Warner, M (2002) *Publics and Counterpublics*. New York: Zone Books.

Chapter 17
Ghanaian transformation efforts

David Owusu-Ansah

Introduction

This chapter examines the post-independence policies of successive Ghanaian national governments in terms of the formulation and implementation of education policies that are deemed relevant for national development.

In 2003, at the University of Nairobi in Kenya, Professor Ali Mazrui delivered a public lecture on the re-Africanisation of African universities. The eminent scholar asked a very pertinent question: 'How can a university help to develop the society to which it belongs?' He aptly observed that 'no university is ever able to help develop a society unless the society is first ready to help develop the university' (Mazrui, 2003: 135).

The discourse that has made the contributions in this volume necessary is the view that pre-apartheid goals and content of education helped to develop the society to which the institution of higher learning belonged in South Africa. In other words, there was a symbiotic relationship between the apartheid state and knowledge production within the universities for the purpose of sustaining the state of affairs. Several years ago, I had the privilege of reviewing a book by Dickson A Mungazi (1991) titled *Colonial Education for Africans: George Stark's policy in Zimbabwe*. Mungazi, a Zimbabwean scholar, examined the country's education policies that spanned the period from the passing of the 1899 Education Ordinance in South Rhodesia until the outbreak of the nationalist war in 1961. Mungazi noted that the controversial education official George Stark and the country's Prime Minister Godfrey Huggins developed policies for the natives that were racist and exclusive. Those policies, he observed, were borrowed from South Africa, which also has white settler communities. The Gold Coast (Ghana) and other British West African colonies present a parallel experience as they were non-settler colonies. This chapter is cognisant of these historic differences that shaped the school systems and the experiences and challenges that confronted those who sought change.

It is instructive to note that since 2015 there has been a burgeoning number of academic and media articles on radical educational reforms in South Africa (Horsthemke, 2004; Prinsloo, 2010; Heleta, 2016). The dominant voices in favour of change call for a transformed tertiary education system that is more

'Africanised' and decolonised. It is further argued that an Africanised curriculum would contribute to opening access to liberal education and validate local knowledge and African knowledge production (Garuba, 2015; Heleta, 2016).

South African scholars Jansen and Motala speak about 'the remarkable curriculum reforms across universities in South Africa in recent times led by African scholars often in partnership with colleagues in universities across the world' (Jansen and Motala, 2017: 9; see also Motala, Chapter 5, in this volume). The authors further bemoan the term 'decolonisation' and the manner in which some have used it to describe the kind of change that is ultimately needed in South African higher education (see also Modiri, Chapter 10, in this volume). Jansen and Motala examine its possible consequence:

> The very language of decolonisation of curriculum is therefore inappropriate and even misleading in 21st century South Africa. Unless of course White South Africans are colonialists who should be driven into the sea and whose outsized influence on the public curriculum holds us hostage in a black majority country under black governance for two decades (2017: 10).

In other words, Jansen sees the challenges to education reforms in South Africa to be broader than that implied by the term 'decolonisation'[1] and he is worried that the possible consequence of such a decolonised curriculum – if it ever were to be successful – 'would trap already disadvantaged children and youth in a curriculum cul-de-sac when we reduce essential and powerful disciplinary knowledge to the everyday experiences of students, with all the chauvinism that entails' (Jansen and Motala, 2017: 10–11).

Garuba (2015) engages Africanised education reforms in an opinion piece titled, 'What is an African curriculum?' The author notes the fear expressed

---

1   The history of 'decolonisation' is linked to the effort of previously colonised peoples to dismantle the apparatus of the colonial state and its impact. Frantz Fanon's (1965) *A Dying Colonialism* suggested a revolutionary path to destroying the system that subjugated the people. With regard to the content of schooling, the colonial administration endeavoured to establish an education system that was deemed appropriate for Africans. It is clear then that the decolonisation process of education is aimed at adjusting the content of education to suit national developments in the post-colonial era and not necessarily ditching every aspect of acquired learning. Africanisation is only part of the process of decolonisation. For a deeper conversation on the subject, see Kwame Nkrumah (1965b) *Neo-colonialism: The last stage of imperialism*. New York: International Publishers; VY Mudimbe (1988) *The invention of Africa: Gnosis, philosophy, and the order of knowledge*. Bloomington, IN: Indiana University Press. See also Ngũgĩ wa Thiong'o (1994) *Decolonising the Mind: The politics of language in African literature*. Portsmouth, NH: Heinemann.

by some educated individuals 'that they [the public and radical students] do not have the competence to discuss curriculum [but to] merely call attention to its necessity'. However, Garuba highlights the changes in the post-colonial Kenyan education system in the 1960s and the push for multicultural curricula in Western countries in the 1980s, which were triggered by public debates and engagements (see Wanjala, Chapter 19, in this volume).

The debate for change has generated several questions that do not yield consensus. Some of these include: Are white faculty members, who were trained in the respective disciplines to teach and research at the apartheid-era institutions or at institutions of higher learning during the colonial era in Africa, capable of leading curriculum changes to suit the educational needs of post-independent African states? If the answer is negative, then what are the challenges and 'strategies for the universities to increase faculty of colour and the underrepresented in the academy as part of the transforming process?' (Hull, 2015; Govender, 2016). Furthermore, how can curriculum changes be made in a manner that guarantees academic quality and standards to retain the international competitiveness of post-colonial universities? These concerns, as pertaining to South Africa, were also reflected upon in Suellen Shay's essay in the *Mail & Guardian* (Shay, 2016). In other words, there are those who continue to wonder whether previously colonised people can think in the manner that would make the incorporation of African thoughts and experiences into the curriculum relevant for the education of subsequent generations (Dabashi, 2015).

To be sure, as Melber (2018) observed in the essay 'Knowledge production and decolonisation', the questions being asked in the South African situation are not unique. In societies where higher education has been the domain of the privileged few, calls for fair access to and inclusion in the process of educating the broader population are usually challenged. But as Mazrui (2003) noted, the symbiotic relations between educational institutions and the societies to which they belong must, at best, be shaped in a manner that allows societal concerns and problems to be addressed through appropriate knowledge production. The question then is, what has been Ghana's post-colonial challenges and how have issues such as access, curriculum and knowledge production been engaged at its institutions of learning?

Education in Ghana: The early years

In 1994, the new South African majority government inherited 36 universities, technical and vocational institutions (technikons) from the erstwhile apartheid state (see Adebajo, Chapter 2, in this volume). Ghana at independence in 1957 inherited the University College of Gold Coast (now the University of Ghana) in Accra, which was established in 1948 as one of the tertiary institutions the British colonial government proposed for its West African territories to 'promote higher education, learning and research' (Hussey, 1945: 165–70; Daniel, 1997/98: 649). In 1952, the Technology College (now the Kwame Nkrumah University of Science and Technology) was established in Kumasi as the country's second institute of higher learning. Ghana's third university was established in 1962. The University of Cape Coast was founded to train teachers to staff secondary schools and teacher training colleges. In other words, while the focus of South Africa's reform movement is directed at curricula transformation at its well-established ivory towers, in Ghana the focus was on building from scratch an educational system that was appropriate for post-independence national development. But, one cannot analyse tertiary education in Ghana without a synopsis of the history of schooling in the country.

The history of Western education in Ghana is linked to the arrival of European merchants on the Gold Coast of West Africa to trade in gold and later in slaves. At their permanent trade posts, which were ultimately fortified castles, the denominational priests who ministered to the castle population also ran schools for a small group of other children. According to the historian CK Graham (1971), some children of wealthy Africans and even local chiefs received instruction at the castle schools, but the majority of pupils were mixed-race children of the European staff and their African women. The primary purpose of the schools was to prepare the children to participate in the European trading enterprise. Christian denominational education was a major part of the curriculum. Prominent students of castle schools included Anton Wilhelm Amo (d. 1753), who pursued further education and received a doctorate degree in Germany, Jacobus Capitein (d. 1747), who studied at the University of Leiden in Holland and was ordained the first African Protestant priest in 1737, and Philip Quaque (d. 1816), who received further education in Great Britain and was also ordained an Anglican priest in 1756. Despite the efforts of Philip Quaque to expand and sustain the school at Cape Coast castle, funding presented a challenge and it was not until the mid-19th century that concerted attempts to provide education for the general population took a significant turn.

Various Christian denominations, who were competing to propagate the gospel in Ghana, established the first schools that guaranteed access to children from poor background (Bartels, 1965; Church of the Province of West Africa, 1974; O'Connor 2000). Denominational schools spread mostly to the southern part of the country. Typically, such schools provided basic primary education in religious subjects and tutoring in the English language. Spreading the gospel also informed the efforts of European missionaries – such as Johann Gottlieb

Christaller (d. 1895) of the Basel mission – to translate the Bible and other devotional materials into the local Akuapem language. The mission schools therefore formalised local language literacy (Christaller, 1933; 1964). Basic arithmetic was also taught.

Control of the schools, the selection of teachers and the determination of subjects to emphasise the pedagogy were the church's prerogatives until 1882, when the colonial government of the Gold Coast engaged the mission schools, established board of inspectors to supervise the schools, and called for curriculum improvement. Those mission schools that followed the guidelines established in the government's Educational Ordinance of 1882 received grants-in-aid and became classified as 'government-assisted' programmes. However, the large part of school funding came from the missions and private sources.

Despite efforts to standardise the curriculum, as a result of the 1882 education ordinance, education for children remained at the elementary level. Those seeking post-basic school learning and who could afford the cost or received sponsorship travelled to Europe or attended the Church Missionary Society Anglican school, established in 1827 as Fourah Bay College in Sierra Leone. It was at such overseas schools that prominent persons such as John Mensah Sarbah, David Asante, James Kwegyir Aggrey and JE Casely-Hayford, all from the Gold Coast, were educated. In 1927, in the colony itself, during Gordon Guggisberg's administration, the first public-funded primary and secondary comprehensive programme was founded at Achimota and admitted students from across the country. Guggisberg's role in developing the potentials of Gold Coast Africans is often celebrated (Wraith, 1967; Coe, 2002; Brukum, 2005). He had served as the railway surveyor in Nigeria and the Gold Coast and worked with Africans before the Great War, so he was cognisant of their capabilities. Most importantly, the governor envisioned that local people would manage their own affairs in the future and, therefore, needed to be trained for such endeavours. In fact, the vision of the school was summed up as follows:

> Achimota hopes to produce a type of student who is 'Western' [modern] in his intellectual attitudes toward life, with respect for science and capacity for systematic thought, but who remains African in sympathy and desirous of preserving and developing what is deserving of respect in tribal life, customs, rules and law (Gold Coast, 1932; Fraser, 1965; Agbodeka, 1977).

It can be observed that Achimota intended to produce what Nkrumah would later label the 'New African'. But, despite the remarkable progress usually associated with the Guggisberg administration, by the early 1950s, when Kwame Nkrumah became Leader of Government Business and headed the majority African party in the National Assembly, only a small percentage of the nation's population of school-going age had any formal learning. This was particularly evident in the northern part of the colony, where the colonial government had restricted Christian missionary work because of the dominant Muslim population (Bening, 1990). The Christian denominational institutions were still the main sponsors of formal Western education so 'schooling' became synonymous with conversion to Christianity, and the colonial government placed impediments that hindered church groups from spreading schools among Muslim populations. Missionary work in Muslim communities was once described in a colonial document as 'a little short of calamity' (Communication from Acting CCNT to Colonial Secretary, 1913), and when French missionaries tried to enter the northern region to open schools, the British colonial government set English certification as a prerequisite for French teachers (Der, 1983). Economic historian Roger Thomas (1973) believes that the reluctance to spread formal education to the northern region was linked to government policies that intended to preserve the northern territories for the recruitment of manual labour. Sociologist Christine Oppong (1966) observed that even after formal basic education spread to the region in the 1960s, the number of girls that attended school was infinitesimal (see also Owusu-Ansah, Abdulai and Sey, 2013). As a result, the problem of education in the wake of independence and the immediate post-independence period was one of access to basic schooling for all. There was also the need for formal learning to be relevant to the development of the new nation.

Improvements and access to education and the Africanisation of knowledge production in the post-colonial era in Ghana

The 1882 Education Ordinance was the first government education policy in the history of the Gold Coast. The limitations of mission education for Africans, associated with developments from the 1880s, were observed in the post-First World War period when the Foreign Mission Conference of North America appealed to the Phelps-Stokes Fund to sponsor a review of education in sub-Saharan Africa. The Commission Reports of 1922 and 1925, which covered several countries including the Gold Coast, called for appropriate native education that addressed the socio-economic needs of the indigenous populations. Programmes at Tuskegee and Hampton Institute in the United States, which focused on character training, agricultural education and 'mechanical operations necessary for the improvement of the condition of the mass majority of the people', were deemed appropriate for Africans (Thomas, 1922). Similarly, in the United Kingdom, the Education Committee of the Conference of Missionary Societies in Great Britain and Ireland submitted a statement to the Secretary of States for the Colonies regarding appropriate education for Africans. This resulted in the establishment of the Advisory Committee on Native Education in British Tropical Africa in 1923, which in the same year, and again in 1948, offered recommendations and provided guidelines for the improvement of education (Great Britain, 1935). Among other things, the committee called for greater government engagement with the provision of formal education in the territories. However, it was only in 1951, when an all-African National Legislative Assembly of the colony was elected, that a more aggressive and forward-looking education policy to tackle the problem of access to basic education for all would materialise (Gold Coast Education Department, 1951; Owusu-Ansah, 2010; Yeboa-Afari, 2017).

The 1951 Accelerated Education Plan, which the all-African legislature approved, made provision for access to basic education for all children of school-going age. Unlike previous colonial government commission recommendations that lingered, the majority all-African National Legislative Assembly was ready to implement the plan. The scheme envisioned adult mass education through radio programming, but, most importantly, the plan endorsed public funding of a six-year primary education for all children. Middle schooling was naturally to follow and it was also anticipated that the more able students would seek admission to the now tuition-free – but guardian-paying boarding and lodging – secondary schools.

It is important to note that members of the all-African Assembly, including Kwame Nkrumah, were educated at church-affiliated schools and, therefore, their decision to direct all national funding for education away from mission schools was due to the fact that the majority of school-aged children did not have access to such institutions during the colonial era. In the end, however, Article 6 was modified in a manner that granted the churches continued funding, but the government trained all teachers and determined the school curriculum for all schools in the country. Subsequently, the church and any group that adopted the Education Ministry-approved curriculum and received funding from the government became recognised as 'stakeholders'. In fact, the leadership of the church in Ghana has, over the decades, demonstrated its commitment to supporting academic excellence. These churches have a history of not only supporting basic education but they were also pioneers in establishing the first teacher training colleges in the country to train the church-affiliated schools' staff (Nkansa-Kyeremateng, 1995; Boahen, 1996; Essamuah, 2010). Today, many have transitioned to become private university campuses to meet the increasing need for tertiary education in the country.

As noted earlier, the nation's premier university at Legon, the University of Ghana, was established in 1948 in the last decade of colonial rule 'to produce men and women who have the standards of public service and capacity for leadership which the progress of self-government demands and to assist in satisfying the need for persons with a professional qualification required for the economic and social development of the colonies' (Daniel, 1997/98: 649). In anticipation of the future modernisation of the country, the University of Science and Technology was officially opened in Kumasi in 1952. In 1962, the University of Cape Coast was established specifically to focus on the preparation of teachers to staff the increasing number of secondary institutions (Dwarko and Kwarteng, 2003). Still cognisant of the issue of access for all, the Government of the First Republic declared that 'University Education in Ghana is free and will continue to be free. It will be accessible to all those who are capable of higher learning' (Nkrumah, 1965a). But free university education for all did not mean an open admissions policy. Because of the limited faculties and facilities at the universities, many capable applicants, instead, attended one of the several specialist colleges (in sports, music, languages and other) that operated in the country. Today, even though there are over a dozen public universities across the nation, the very high demand for tertiary education has resulted in the founding of many private fee-paying universities in the country. But, again, one should raise the question: In what manner can knowledge production at these institutions be said to have been Africanised?

Pan-Africanism and Africanisation were favourite political and educational visions for higher education in the period immediately after independence. In 1962, when the University of Cape Coast was opened and with the establishment of the Nkrumah Ideological Institute at Winneba in Ghana (now part of the University of Education at Winneba), students from African colonies were allowed admission (Frehiwot, 2015). Nkrumah articulated his views on knowledge production at the nation's tertiary institutions in his 25 October 1963 speech to inaugurate the Institute of African Studies at the University of Ghana, Legon. President Nkrumah believed that 'the university has a clear duty to the community which maintains it, and which has the right to expect concern for its oppressing needs' (Haizel, 1993: 68). Thus, the Institute of African Studies was charged with a more specific obligation to conduct research and

> to study the history, culture, languages and arts of Ghana and of Africa in a new Africa-centred way – in entire freedom from the propositions and presuppositions of the colonial epoch and from the definitions of

those professors and lecturers who continue to make European studies of Africa the basis of this assessment. By the work of this Institute, we must reassess and assert the glories and achievements of our African past and inspire our generation and succeeding generations with a vision of a better future (Nkrumah, 1963).

For Nkrumah, relevant research on Africa contributed to the humanities and raised the consciousness of Ghanaian citizens. 'African music, dancing and sculpture' that had been labelled as 'primitive' and 'reinforce[d] in pictures as something grotesque, as a curious, mysterious human backwater, which helped to retard social progress in Africa and prolonged colonial domination', needed to be researched and reinterpreted. He also envisioned the Institute of African Studies as an international centre of excellence and research for knowledge production. Thus, this institute needed to be a welcoming multinational and multicultural environment for the critical exchange of ideas. He added: 'non-Ghanaian and non-African professors and lecturers are welcome'. However, he asserted that those whose 'mental makeup has been largely influenced by their [European] system of education and the facts of their society and environment … must endeavour to adjust and reorient their attitudes and thought to our African conditions and aspirations' (Nkrumah, 1963: 3).

The Institute of African Studies at the University of Ghana started its operation in 1960, three years before its official inauguration. Dr Thomas Hodgkin, 'best known for his historical writings on Africa … and having helped to initiate extra-mural education in the Gold Coast and Nigeria in 1947' (Allman, 2013: 185–88), was appointed the first director of the institute and Professor Ivor Wilks was the institute's deputy director. The institute focused on offering research and postgraduate degrees in the areas of African historical and social studies, modern African states and African arts. It was also assigned the unique responsibility of offering lectures in African studies to all first-year students admitted to the University of Ghana (Allman, 2013: 189; Zeleza, 2003: 149–94).

International scholars who frequented and were affiliated with the Institute of African Studies, and whose research influenced the field of African history, include Peter Shinnie and Merrick Posnansky in the field of archaeology, Nehemia Levtzion and John Hunwick in Islamic studies, René Bravman in Islamic art history, Sinclair Drake in sociology, Ray Kea in Danish and local histories, and Ivor Wilks who produced excellent works on the history of the Asante and its Muslim neighbours. Allman was right to have observed that the predominant presence of international scholars at the institute did not mirror the recolonisation of knowledge production. Rather, it presented an environment in which international scholars fairly and critically participated in the evaluation of local resources, which was precisely what Nkrumah envisioned. For example, at the inauguration of the Institute of African Studies in 1963, President Nkrumah commended the work that Ivor Wilks and his senior research assistant, al-Hajj Ishaq Boyo, had begun – collecting and documenting Arabic manuscripts across Côte d'Ivoire and the northern parts of Ghana. Wilks and Boyo's field interviews with Muslim leaders became important resources, not only for the former's publications, and are now also available to students of Islamic studies in Ghana and West Africa. In other words, this was an 'Africanisation' project that provided validity for oral traditions and interviews as relevant sources for the writing of history. Wilks and his colleagues engaged in the systematic and comprehensive organisation of sources that allowed for the reinterpretation of history in the context of Africa's encounters with Europe and the Islamic world. Indeed, my dissertation and subsequent publications benefited from Wilks' projects.[2] The remarkable archaeological excavation that scholars affiliated to the institute conducted across the country significantly contributed to knowledge production (Schildkrout, 1987).

Basil Davidson arrived at the institute in February 1964 to participate in another endeavour that was dear to the heart of President Nkrumah – the writing of history textbooks on Africa and the African diaspora designed for secondary and post-secondary institutions (Davidson, 1969; Allman, 2013). While the publications of international scholars who became affiliated with the institute are often highlighted in academic journals and conferences, for Ghanaian students the works of historian Professor A Adu Boahen and musicologist Nana Kwabena Nketia defined the African character of the University of Ghana and its Institute of African Studies. Educated at the Methodist Mfantsipim Secondary School in Cape Coast, Boahen attended the University of Ghana and later received his doctoral degree in history from the School of Oriental and African Studies in London. He commenced teaching at the University of Ghana in 1959 and Wilks was one of his contemporaries. The older Professor JHK Nketia attended Presbyterian Teachers' College at Akuapem-Akuropong prior to attending the University of London and the Julliard School of Music in the United States. Both Nketia and Boahen were faculty members at the University of Ghana in 1963. Professor Nketia is credited with the introduction of African music certification at the institute,

---

2   The Wilks field interviews and the Arabic documentation project materials are now part of the institute's collections, as well as at Northwestern University Africana Library in Evanston, Illinois. The 'Asante Biographical Project' is also deposited at the African Library at Northwestern University.

where he later became its director. Products of the institute's music, drumming and dancing programmes now teach at secondary schools. Others perform internationally and are, therefore, important cultural ambassadors. Cultural productions, written and produced by the institute's graduates and performed at the National Theatre or televised, are now commonplace. Indeed, this is what Nkrumah envisioned when he called on 'the gown to come to town' (Nkrumah, 1963; Kwami, 1994).

For his part, Professor A Adu Boahen is remembered for several books he wrote on the history of colonial rule in Africa, especially for students at the secondary school level. Boahen's *Topics in West African History* became a prescribed book because it was well-organised, well-written and concise. He raised no question that he did not immediately address, logically and accurately. He argued that the civilisation of West Africa was historically African. The glory and structures of pre-colonial African kingdoms, such as Asante, Dahomey and Benin, were all critically examined. He assessed colonial rule fairly by engaging the pros and cons of the encounters. A great intellectual in the Gramscian sense, Professor Boahen exemplified fully the life of the scholar-politician-activist, who commented on national developments in a manner that did not always please those in political power. He demonstrated the point that the Africanised university must be conscious of and concerned with developments in the society within which it operates. For Professor Boahen and his Ghanaian colleagues, such as philosophers Kwasi Wiredu and Kwame Gyekye, as well as historical anthropologist Professor Kwame Arhin, the appropriate content of humanities education was foundational in producing a conscious, confident and engaged student. This is consistent with Harry Garuba's (2015) observation that 'every curriculum in every discipline – be it in geology or medicine, history or chemistry – assigns value to its objects of study and withdraws it from others, which could be thought of as belonging to the same domain'. And, that 'in addition to assigning value, a curriculum also determines the academic formation of a new generation. That is, it helps to create people who think in a particular way about particular subjects and talk about them in a particular language and idioms' (see also Ugwuanyi, 2007; Baker, 2013).

Reflections

Successive Ghanaian governments since independence have viewed the provision of formal education as critical to the economic development of the country. In fact, as Haizel observed, Ghanaians perceive access to education as their right as citizens. He further commented on the prevalence of the view among Ghanaians that education is intended to prepare students for job-seeking rather than self-employment or entrepreneurship. Accordingly, those who have successfully completed the school system but remain unemployed deem their education worthless (Haizel, 1993: 78). If Haizel's assessment were applied to the current debate around graduate unemployment in Ghana, one would conclude that the curriculum of the school system in the country needs further Africanised review. In this context, 'Africanisation' would be defined not only in terms of access to schools, but also curriculum design in the sciences, engineering and the humanities to make them seamless and suitable for national development. Thus, Ali Mazrui was right to have argued that the discussion around Africanisation should encompass all levels of learning. Aptly, he concluded that 'no university can be a first-class institution of higher learning if the secondary schools that feed into it are all mediocre.' Furthermore, the 'quality of education at the primary and secondary levels need to be sustained [better], if the final candidates for possible admission to the universities are to be of high standard' (Mazrui, 2003: 6).

The establishment of universities for teacher education, science and technology, medicine, agriculture and pharmaceutical sciences, to mention but a few, reflects the national efforts to link training to development. Even though the number of Ghanaian instructional faculty and staff at the universities is in the upper 90th percentile – another Africanisation indicator – great concerns regarding pre-tertiary education still confront policy-makers. The conversations around access, quality and structure of pre-tertiary schools persist (Quist, 2003; Adu-Gyamfi, Donkor and Addo, 2016). In response to criticisms on quality and content, the government announced in June 2018 that, effective from September 2018, teacher training colleges in the country would become University Colleges to ensure that all pre-university schools are staffed in the future with bachelor degree holders (Myjoyonline.com, 17 June 2018). Also, the government implemented a free secondary education policy for all students entering the first year of secondary school, effective from September 2018. This was in fulfilment of a 2016 election campaign promise that a free secondary education policy would eliminate fees, including admission, utility use, library and computer, meals and boarding fees. Students attending non-boarding secondary schools receive free lunch (Ghana News Agency, 2017).

Prior to these recent developments, the major education reforms in the history of the country since 1951 were those recommended in 1975 by the Dzobo Commission and reviewed and implemented a decade later during Jerry Rawlings's military administration in 1987 (Boateng, 1995; Buah, 2002; Osei, 2010). The Dzobo Commission called for a new type of pre-university education that was consistent with national development. It advocated the incorporation of vocational education, sciences and agriculture at the junior secondary level. The emphasis on science and vocational education does not imply that humanities' subjects were not considered important. Rather, it was meant to identify and stimulate students with a propensity for practical education. For this to happen, the commission advocated a restructuring of the pre-university educational system that Ghana inherited from European missionaries. The inherited educational system required six years of primary schooling, followed by four years at the middle schools, which was usually the end of formal learning for many pupils. The secondary education was a five-year (O-level) programme, after which the highly qualified students pursued two years of advanced learning (A-levels) to prepare them for the competitive university entrance selection. The 1987 education reforms retained the old six-year basic primary programme but abridged the four-year middle school into a three-year junior secondary school. The former seven years of secondary education was also reduced to three years. Overall, the new system compressed the old 17 years of pre-tertiary curriculum to 12 years (Adu-Gyamfi, Donkor and Addo, 2016).

The 1987 reforms led to the creation of an Islamic Education Unit (IEU) within the Ghana Education Service. Staffed with professional Muslim officials educated at the nation's universities, the IEU was created to introduce national secular subjects to the curriculum of the Islamic religious schools that opted to come under the Ministry of Education's supervision. Similar to the Christian denominational institutions that the government had partnered with from 1951, proprietors of Islamic schools who joined the Islamic Education Unit became 'stakeholders'. The government provided and paid secular subject instructors, provided school inspections, and paid the salary of one Arabic language teacher for each participating school. In February 2018, the government expressed its intention to hire 3 000 additional Arabic language teachers for the Islamic Education Unit schools and even to develop Islamic teacher colleges across the country (Armiyawo, 2002; Boniface, 2018). In my co-edited book on *Islamic Learning, the State and Secular Education in Ghana*, we provided the long narrative of a history that goes as far back as colonial times to assess the progression of Muslim relations to secular learning in Ghana. We reviewed the challenges that the modern government faced at independence and thereafter to attract Muslim children to public-secular schools. The innovative approach of working with Islamic religious school proprietors to become stakeholders in the provision of secular learning is indicative that the 'Africanisation' process of providing access is one that must be persistent. Indeed, by 2006, over 260 000 Muslim children had opted for the Islamic-cum-secular schools (k-junior secondary schools) and about 45 per cent of the students were girls (Owusu-Ansah, Abdulai and Sey, 2013).

Despite the progress made with the incorporation of Islamic schools into the formal secular system, the 1987 Education Act, which aimed to implement the recommendations of the Dzobo Commission Report of 1974/75, had its challenges, which subsequent administrations have tried to address. Questions are still being raised about the quality of school facilities at rural locations compared to those in urban and affluent neighbourhoods. And despite the commitment of the state to providing educational access through the tertiary level, adequate funding remains a challenge (Thompson and Casely-Hayford, 2018). In fact, in an essay on '"The Public Good" in African higher education: Select issues for policy' (2002), a former Vice-Chancellor of the University of Ghana and later the Secretary-General of the Association of African Universities, Professor Akilagpa Sawyerr, observed that the term 'Africanisation' in its broadest context implies appropriate nation-building. From such a perspective, the lessons from Ghana demonstrate that there are no quick fixes to address the challenges that face national educational systems. Rather, there is the need for continued and deliberate assessment of the national vision for education and serious efforts need to be made to address them systematically and in a timely fashion. In the case of Ghana, it is already obvious to the majority of citizens and politicians that quality pre-tertiary schooling is necessary to prepare students properly for tertiary programmes. At the post-secondary level of education, even though great progress has been made since independence in the spread of such institutions, new problems have emerged (Sawyerr, 2004). The obvious ones include the challenge of providing adequate physical facilities, the need to recruit highly qualified instructors to replace aging faculty members, and the imperative to address the financial challenges faced by economically deprived students and parents to foot the cost of post-secondary education. Additionally, there is the need to provide appropriate technical skills and humanities education for the changing market, and to introduce or expand the curriculum to contribute to knowledge production that is culturally appropriate. According to Professor Sawyerr, all these challenges fall within the broader effort to Africanise the education system. To address these challenges, Sawyerr pointed to the need for the state to provide full support to education at all levels to ensure the quality and social relevance of learning (Sawyerr, 2004: 26–53). It is also important that institutes and centres, such as the Institute for Pan-African Thought and Conversation (IPATC) at the University of Johannesburg in South Africa and the Institute of African Studies (IAS) at the University of Ghana, in partnership with other education-oriented agencies, continue to sensitise citizens through their research and public engagement.

References

Adu-Gyamfi, S, Donkor, WJ and Addo, AA (2016) Educational reforms in Ghana: Past and present, *Journal of Education and Human Development*, **5**(3): 158–72.

Agbodeka, F (1977) *Achimota in the National Setting: A unique educational experience in West Africa.* Accra, Ghana: Afram Publications.

Allman, JM (2013) Kwame Nkrumah, African studies, and the politics of knowledge production in the Black Star of Africa, *The International Journal of African Historical Studies*, **46**(2): 181–203.

Arhin, K (1979) *West African Traders in Ghana in the Nineteenth and Twentieth Centuries.* London and New York: Longman.

Arhin, K (1980) Asante military institutions, *Journal of African Studies*, **20**(77–78): 49–62.

Arhin, K (1985) The role of the Presbyterian Church in the economic development of Ghana, *Research Review*, **1**(2): 152–65.

Armiyawo, S (2002) An overview of the Islamic Education Unit Council. Accra, Ghana: Unpublished.

Armiyawo, S (n.d.) Islamic Education Unit in the Greater Accra region: An overview. Accra: Unpublished.

Baker, RA (2013) The British Model, 'Africanization' of the curriculum and other issues: The influence of Professor DW Ewer (1913–2009) on university teaching in Ghana and on biological education in Africa, *Journal of Higher Education in Africa*, **11**(1–2): 143–59.

Bartels, F (1965) *The Roots of Methodism.* London: Cambridge University Press.

Bening, B (1990) *History of Education in Northern Ghana, 1907–1976.* Accra: Ghana Universities Press.

Boahen, AA (1996) *Mfantsipim and the Making of Ghana: A centenary history, 1876–1967.* Accra, Ghana: Sankofa Educational Publishers.

Boateng, EA (1995) Crisis, change, and revolution in Ghanaian education, 14–16 November. Paper delivered at the First Series of the Armstrong-Amissah Memorial Lectures.

Boniface, Hon AS (2018) More Islamic Teacher Training Schools to be established across the country, 12 February. Available at: ghanaguardian.com.

Brukum, NJK (2005) Sir Gordon Guggisberg and socio-economic development of Northern Ghana, 1919–1927, *Historical Society of Ghana*, **9**: 1–15.

Buah, FK (2002) The place of history in the reformed education, *Transactions of the Historical Society of Ghana*, **6**: 139–46.

Christaller, JG (1933) *Dictionary of the Asante and Fante Language called Tshi (Twi).* Basel, Switzerland: Printed for the Basel Evangelical Missionary Society.

Christaller, JG (1964) *A Grammar of the Asante and Fante Language, called Tshi (Chwee, Twi) based on the Akuapem Dialect with Reference to the other (Akan and Fante Dialects).* Farnborough, Hants: Gregg Press.

Church of the Province of West Africa (1974) *Anglican Church of Ghana, 1752–1974.* Accra, Ghana: Diocese of Accra.

Coe, C (2002) Educating an African leadership: Achimota and the teaching of African culture in the Gold Coast, *Africa Today*, **49**(3): 23–44.

Communication from Ag. CCNT to Colonial Secretary, 10 February 1913. ADM 56/1/139.

Dabashi, H (2015) *Can Non-Europeans Think? Essays on overcoming postcoloniality.* London: Zed Books.

Daniel, G.F (1997-98) *The University of Ghana: The Commonwealth Universities Year Book.* London: Association of Commonwealth Universities.

Davidson, B (1969) *The African Genius: An introduction to African cultural and social history.* Boston, MA: Little, Brown.

Der, BG (1983) Missionary enterprise in Northern Ghana, 1906–1975: A study of impact.

Unpublished thesis from the University of Ghana.
Dwarko, D.A and Osei Kwarteng, K (2003) *A History of the University of Cape Coast: Forty Years of Resilience, 1962-2002.* Accra: Woeli Press.
Education Department (1952) *Annual Report of the Education Department for the Year 1952.* Accra, Ghana: Government Printer.
Essamuah, CB (2010) *Genuinely Ghanaian: A history of the Methodist Church Ghana, 1961–2000.* Trenton, NJ: Africa World Press.
Fanon, F (1965) *A Dying Colonialism.* New York: Grove Press.
Fisch, R (1894/1911) *Girls' Boarding School Aburi.* University of Southern California Libraries.
Fraser, P (1965) *Education and Social Change in Ghana.* Chicago, IL: University of Chicago Press.
Frehiwot, N (2015) Pan-African education: A case study of the Kwame Nkrumah Ideological Institute, print media and the Ghana Young Pioneer Movement, in C Quist-Adade and V Dodoo (eds) *Africa's Many Divides and Africa's Future: Pursuing Nkrumah's vision of Pan-Africanism in the era of globalization.* Newcastle upon Tyne: Cambridge Scholars Publishing, pp. 296–322.
Garuba, H (2015) What is an African curriculum? *Mail & Guardian,* 17 April. Johannesburg, South Africa.
Ghana News Agency (2017) Free SHS to Commence September 2017. Accra: Government of Ghana.
Gold Coast (1932) Achimota College Report of the Committee appointed by the Governor of the Gold Coast to Inspect the Prince of Wales' College and School. London: Crown Agents of the Colonies on behalf of the Government of the Gold Coast.
Gold Coast Education Department (1951) *Accelerated Development Plan for Education, 1951.* Accra: Government Printing Department.
Govender, P (2016) Strategies for the universities to increase faculty of colour and underrepresented in the academy as part of the transforming process, *Mail & Guardian,* 12 July. Johannesburg, South Africa.
Graham, CK (1971) *History of Education in Ghana from the Earliest Times to the Declaration of Independence.* London: Frank Cass.
Great Britain (1935) Memorandum on the Education of African Communities, Advisory Committee on Education in the Colonies. London: H.M. Stationery Office.
Haizel, EA (1993) Education in Ghana, 1951–1966, in K Arhin (ed.) *The Life and Work of Kwame Nkrumah.* Trenton, NJU: Africa World Press.
Hawkins, S (2002) *Writing and Colonialism in Northern Ghana.* Toronto: University of Toronto Press.
Heleta, S (2016) Decolonisation of higher education: Dismantling epistemic violence and eurocentrism in South Africa, *The Journal* 1(1). Available at: https://TheJournal.org.za/index.php (accessed September 2019).
Horsthemke, K (2004) Knowledge, education and the limits of Africanisation, *Journal of Philosophy of Education,* **38**(4): 571–87. Available at: https://doi.org/10.1111/j.0309-8249.2004.00405.x (accessed September 2019).
Hull, G (2015) So white you've got to wear shades, *Mail & Guardian.* 26 August. Johannesburg, South Africa.
Hussey, ERJ (1945) Higher Education in West Africa, *African Affairs,* **44**(177): 165-170.
Institute for Pan-African Thought and Conversation (IPATC) (2018) Transforming Ivory Tower to Ebony Towers: Lessons from South Africa's curriculum transformation in the humanities from Africa and African-American Studies. Concept Paper. Johannesburg: University of Johannesburg, South Africa.
Jansen, J and Motala, S (eds) (2017) Curriculum stasis, funding and the 'decolonial turn' in universities: Inclusion and exclusion in higher education in South Africa, in Special

Edition, *Journal of Education*, **68**: 10–15.

Kwami, R (1994) Music education in Ghana and Nigeria: A brief survey, *Africa: Journal of the International African Institute*, **64**(4): 544–60.

Mazrui, AA (2003) Toward re-Africanising African universities: Who killed intellectualism in the post-colonial era, *Alternatives: Turkish Journal of International Relations*, **2**(3&4): 135–63.

McCaskie, T (2000) *Asante Identities: History and modernity in an African village, 1850–1950*. Edinburgh: Edinburgh University Press.

Melber, H (2018) Knowledge production and decolonisation – not only African, *Strategic Review for Southern Africa*, **40**(1): 4–15.

Mudimbe, VY (1988) *The Invention of Africa: Gnosis, philosophy and the order of knowledge*. Bloomington, IN: Indiana University Press.

Mungazi, DA (1991) *Colonial Education for Africans: George Stark's policy in Zimbabwe*. New York: Praeger.

Myjoyonlin.com. (2018) New 4-year BEd programme to start in September.

Ngũgĩ wa Thiong'o (1994 *Decolonising the Mind: The politics of language in African literature*. Portsmouth, NH: Heinemann.

Nkansa-Kyeremateng, K (1995) *The Presbyterian Church of Ghana and National Development*. Accra, Ghana: Sebewie Publishers.

Nkrumah, K (1963) Speech at the opening of the Institute of African Studies, 25 October. Accra: Legon.

Nkrumah, K (1965a) Sessional Address to Parliament. Accra: Government Printer.

Nkrumah, K (1965b) *Neo-colonialism: The last stage of imperialism*. New York: International Publishers.

O'Connor, D (2000) *Three Centuries of Mission: The United Society for the Propagation of the Gospel, 1701–2000*. London and New York: Continuum.

Oppong, CF (1966) Dagomba responses to the introduction of schools, *Ghana Journal of Sociology*, **2**: 17–25.

Osei, GM (2010) *Education Reforms in Ghana: Curriculum in junior secondary school*. New York: Nova Science Publishers.

Owusu-Ansah, D (2010) History of the education system of Ghana, in R Marlow-Ferguson (ed.) *World Education Encyclopedia: A survey of education systems worldwide*. Detroit, MI: Gale Group.

Owusu-Ansah, D (2014) *Historical Dictionary of Ghana*, 4th edition. New York: Rowman & Littlefield.

Owusu-Ansah, D, Abdulai, I and Sey, M (2013) *Islamic Learning, the State and the Challenges of Education in Ghana*. Lewiston, ME: Edwin Mellen Press.

Porter, His Grace Archbishop WT (1951) Catholics and the revised education plan: An authoritative statement, *The Gold Coast Observer*, **XII**(18), 7 September.

Prinsloo, P (2010) Some reflections on the Africanisation of higher education curricula: A South African case study, *Africanus*, **40**(1): 19–31.

Quist, HO (2003) Secondary education. A 'tool' for national development in Ghana: A critical appraisal of the post-colonial context, *Africa Development*, **28**(3–4): 186–210.

Sawyerr, A (2002) 'The public good' in African higher education: Select issues for policy, *Newsletter of the Social Science Academy of Nigeria*, **5**(1): 25–30.

Sawyerr, A (2004) Challenges facing African universities: Selected issues, *African Studies Review*, **47**(1): 1–59.

Schildkrout, E (ed.) (1987) *The Gold Stool: Studies of the Asante center and periphery*. New York: The American Museum of Natural History.

Shay, S (2016) Urgent strategy needed to decolonise university curricula, *Mail & Guardian*, 20 June. Johannesburg, South Africa.

Thomas, JJ (1922) *Education in Africa: A Study of West, South, and Equatorial Africa by the Education Commission, under the auspices of the Phelps-Stokes Fund and Foreign Mission Societies of North America and Europe*. New York: Phelps-Stokes Fund.

Thomas, R (1973) Forced labour in British West Africa: The case of the Gold Coast, *Journal of African History*, **14**: 427–67.

Thompson, NM and Casely-Hayford, L (2018) *The Financing and Outcomes of Education in Ghana: Research Consortium on Education Outcomes and Poverty*. Department for International Development, Recoup Working Paper, March, No 16.

Ugwuanyi, O (2007) Decolonisation and the quest for mental freedom in Africa: An appraisal of Wiredu, *Eastern Africa Journal of Humanities and Sciences*, **7**(1): 35–49.

UNESCO (1999) *Statistical Yearbook*. Paris: UNESCO.

Wraith, R (1967) *Frederick Gordon Guggisberg, Myth and mystery*. Oxford: Oxford University Press.

Yeboah-Afari, A (2017) *Conversations with My Father: A Biography of B. Yeboah-Afari, Ghana's First Minister of Agriculture and Brong-Ahafo's First Regional Commissioner*. Tema, Ghana: DigiBooks.

Zeleza, PT (2003) Academic freedom in the neo-liberal order: Governments, globalization, governance, and gender, *Journal of Higher Education in Africa*, **1**: 149–94.

Chapter 18
Ugandan transformation efforts

Pamela Khanakwa

Introduction

While university colleges affiliated to the University of London had been established in West and East Africa in the immediate post-war era, it was not until the 1960s that some of them experienced a renaissance of African culture that began to shape their administration, curricula and research. During this decade of decolonisation, African universities were inspired 'by a new spirit of pride and interest in Africa' (Rimmington, 1965: 109). Emerging African leaders and academics were preoccupied not only with political independence but also the decolonisation of knowledge and Africanisation of the university. As Sicherman (2003: 254) observed, many of those who called for Africanisation during the 1960s imagined that 'an African focus in both curriculum and staff would suffice to produce an African university'. South African academic Bheki Mngomezulu posited that Africanisation meant 'giving the university an African flavour and outlook', which was to be reflected in, among others, 'student profile, staff profile, curriculum and syllabus and research and teaching methods' (2003: 98). Thus, common denominators of Africanisation included curricula transformation, recruitment of African staff and promoting African-oriented research.

Emerging African politicians and academics would play a central role in the process of Africanising the university. For example, the government of independent Ghana under Kwame Nkrumah undertook some radical measures to Africanise the University College of Gold Coast at Legon (see Owusu-Ansah, Chapter 17, in this volume). The college was able to delink from the University of London and become an independent degree-granting institution (University of Ghana) in 1961 with Nkrumah as its first chancellor. As a further step towards Africanisation, the administration emphasised recruitment of African staff. The existing predominantly European staff were dismissed, and individuals had to seek reappointment on different terms under which, among others, Europeans were not eligible for permanent and pensionable appointments (Rimmington, 1965: 109). Malawian scholar Paul Zeleza has observed that Ghana's independence and subsequent Africanisation of the University of Ghana constituted important landmarks in Africa's determination 'to decolonise its political and knowledge economies' (Zeleza, 2009: 111). The Nkrumah administration's actions influenced the leadership of other African universities of the epoch.

In contrast, the process of Africanisation at Makerere College in Kampala, Uganda, was rather gradual. Established in 1922 as a government technical school offering largely technical education and professional training in medicine and engineering, Makerere began to offer academic courses leading to Cambridge school certificates in 1933. Following the 1944 recommendations of the Asquith Commission, Makerere was elevated to university college status and affiliated to the University of London in 1949. The University of London determined the curriculum, examinations and staff until 1963, when the University of East Africa (UEA) was inaugurated. The new university consisted of three constituent colleges: Nairobi, Dar es Salaam and Makerere (see Rugumamu, Chapter 14, and Wanjala, Chapter 19, in this volume). This resulted in the end of Makerere's affiliation with the University of London (Makerere University College Report for the year 1962–63). The UEA introduced East African degrees and sought to symbolise and promote the idea of being an East African university. Subsequently, authorities at Makerere University College focused on East Africanisation. The focus shifted to indigenisation and Ugandanisation following the transition to an autonomous national university in 1970.

Africanisation at Makerere

Although Makerere only became an autonomous national university in 1970, deliberate institutional efforts to promote Africanisation date back to the immediate post-independence period, when the UEA was inaugurated and the special relationship between Makerere and the University of London was subsequently terminated. As a step towards becoming truly East African, authorities at the three sister colleges (Makerere, Nairobi and Dar es Salaam) focused on the Africanisation of staff. In his introduction to the Makerere University College Report of 1962–63, the principal, Bernard Bunsen, underscored the need to adapt the standards of UEA to the cultural and social needs of the three East African countries. He further appealed for both 'cultural and intellectual East Africanisation' which, he argued, would only be realised with 'significant increase in the proportion of East African staff' (Makerere University College Report for the year 1962–63: 2). To this end, Bunsen called upon 'more East-African minds' to apply for positions at Makerere (Makerere University College Report for the year 1962–63: 2). He deliberately focused on East Africanisation as a strategy to give the university an African outlook (see Wanjala, Chapter 19, in this volume). The principal also clarified that

'East-Africanisation' would be done 'on purely academic grounds' in order to maintain standards. In Bunsen's view, the University College needed 'first and foremost, the lively, independent and enquiring mind; the mind of the researcher and teacher' (Makerere University College Report for the year 1962–63: 2). These were key aspects that required attention in recruitment processes.

During the 1960s and 1970s, there was gradual progress in the Africanisation of academic staff. Prior to the inauguration of the UEA and the subsequent emphasis on East Africanisation, Africans constituted a smaller percentage of the academic staff, although this gradually increased over the years. For instance, in the academic year 1960–61, there were 91 expatriates and six East Africans who constituted only 6.2 per cent of the staff. During the 1961–62 academic year, there were 93 expatriates and nine East Africans, who constituted 8.8 per cent of the staff. And in the academic year 1962–63 there were 110 expatriates and 16 East Africans constituting 12.7 per cent. During the 1963–64 academic session, there were 111 expatriates and 23 East Africans constituting 17.1 per cent (Makerere University College Report for the year 1963–64: 2). It should be noted that despite the fact that Makerere University College emphasised East Africanisation in this period, recruitment of expatriate staff was not banned, as the increase in the recruitment of East Africans was followed by a concurrent increase in numbers of expatriates.

The academic year 1964/65 equally recorded success in terms of East Africanisation. With a generous grant from the Rockefeller Foundation, Makerere established a Special Lectureship Scheme that provided for the appointment of lecturers. This enabled the college authorities to appoint more African staff. In addition, East Africans were elected to positions of directors or chairs of academic units. Notably, S Kajubi was appointed as the Director of the Institute of Education, while Kenyan Ali Mazrui was offered the Chair of Political Science, and Joseph Lutwama was appointed Chair of Preventive Medicine (Makerere University College Report for the year 1964–65: 4). The appointment of such Africans to leadership positions in their various academic units was a significant step towards Africanisation.

Recruitment of local staff continued during the academic year 1965/66. In Arts, out of the 22 established academic positions, East Africans held six positions, accounting for 27.3 per cent; in the Social Sciences, out of 17 established positions, six were occupied by East Africans constituting 35.3 per cent (Makerere University College Report for the year 1965–66: 4). By 1968/69 the number of East Africans appointed to established posts in the college had significantly increased: '114 East Africans occupying established posts, special lectureships and tutorial fellowships' (Makerere University College Report for the year 1968–69). There were also nine members of staff from different African countries. At the same time, four East Africans who had distinguished themselves in their fields were elected to chairs and professorships. In total, 'the number of East Africans holding professorships and Headships of Departments was about fifteen' (Makerere University College Report for the year 1968–69). Towards the end of 1969, Mr A Wandira, who had served as secretary and registrar of the college, was appointed Professor and Dean of Education. Makerere University College was certainly making some progress in building capacity of permanent African staff at the most senior levels.

In 1970, Makerere became an autonomous national university and, henceforth, the Government of Uganda and other donor agencies offered fellowships to postgraduate students in an effort to make Ugandanisation possible. Increasing concerns about indigenisation of academic staff preoccupied university administrators in the academic year 1971/72. By the end of this session, Ugandans held 145 positions out of the total academic establishment of 438. This was just a little over 30 per cent, which was still on the lower side and not satisfactory. It was clear that Makerere University needed to 're-double efforts in training many more Ugandans for academic careers' (Makerere University, Kampala Report July 1971–June 1972). In this regard, university authorities appealed to the Government of Uganda to increase the number of fellowships for Ugandan students at least threefold and to provide more generous support for staff development programmes. It was hoped that the government would seriously invest in and undertake Ugandanisation of the university as part of nation-building.

The Africanisation initiative was not limited to academic staff. It was extended to the administrative staff as well. In the 1962–63 College Report, the principal had observed with concern that 'I myself, and my senior colleagues in administration have been keenly feeling the lack of senior African colleagues, and in 1963/64 we very much hope to see some progress in this direction.' The principal invited African graduates of 'standing and the right experience' to apply for any administrative position at Makerere (Makerere University College Report for the year 1962–63: 2). Emphasis on qualification was important to keep up the quality and standard. Within a year, the call yielded results. In his introduction to the 1963/64 College Report, the first Ugandan principal, Yusuf Lule, observed that there was significant progress in the Africanisation of administrative staff. While there had been eight expatriates and two East Africans in 1962–63, it was envisaged that in the 1964–65 academic year, there would be four expatriates and seven East Africans (Makerere University College Report for the year 1963–64: 3). With the exception of the vice-chancellorship, the rest of the senior positions, namely Chair of Council, Principal, Vice Principal as well as Secretary and Registrar, were filled by Africans (Makerere University College Report for the year 1963–64: 1). During the academic year 1965–66, 10 out of 12 established positions in the central administration were held by East Africans, accounting for 83.3 per cent (Makerere University College Report for the year 1965–66: 4). It is clear that the Africanisation of administrative staff progressed at a much faster pace in comparison to academic staff.

Department of History
Early efforts to Africanise, 1952–62

Attempts at Africanising the curriculum in the Department of History began in the early 1950s, when Makerere College was still affiliated to the University of London. Established in 1949, the Department of History focused on European-oriented courses during its initial three years. However, a component of African history was introduced following the recruitment of Kenneth Ingham as a lecturer in 1951. Ingham was a war veteran with a PhD in Indian Colonial History from Oxford and hardly knew anything about African history. Nonetheless, he laid the foundation for the Africanisation of both the curriculum and staff in the department (Ogot, 2002; Sicherman, 2003). In 1952, Ingham revised the curriculum of the department and introduced the first course on African history titled 'History of Tropical Africa'. This was taught alongside 'History of the British Empire' and 'Social and Economic Development in Great Britain since 1783'. While the course on 'History of Tropical Africa' was criticised for focusing more on the activities of Arabs, American slave traders and Europeans in Africa, and less on Africans, its introduction was key to the future of African history in the department (Ogot, 2002).

By 1957, when he was appointed Chair of the Department of History, Ingham had established a fairly strong team of professional historians (including RW Beachey, DA Low, JEM Khabaza and OW Furley) at Makerere and enhanced the academic profile of African history. More African-oriented courses were introduced and undergraduate students were required to take between one and three African-oriented courses. Students pursuing Honours in History had to take 10 courses, three of which had to be African-oriented (Ogot, 2002), while those pursuing a Bachelor of Arts degree were required to take three history courses, one of which had to be African-oriented. Although some staff felt that the African component of the history curriculum was not entirely progressive, the effort towards Africanisation of the curriculum under Ingham's leadership cannot be denied.

Ingham hired the first African historian in the department, Bethwell A Ogot, a former student of the college who was recruited to assist in the department from September to December 1959. Ogot would later be appointed as an assistant lecturer in the department in January 1962 (Department of History Annual Reports, 1959–60 and 1961–62). Prior to Ogot's appointment, the department had relied solely on expatriate staff, partly because there were no qualified Africans to teach at university level. No doubt, Ogot's appointment demonstrated the will of the department's leadership to train and develop African capacity.

All criticism notwithstanding, Ingham was progressive and, with the colonial government's support, he was able to make progress with promoting African history. Relying on the support of Sir Andrew Cohen, who was Governor of Uganda from 1952–57, Ingham and DA Low set out to promote research and production of African history. As a member of the Legislative Council himself, Ingham had a special relationship with Governor Cohen, who at that time had been tasked with preparing Uganda for independence. Among other things, Cohen had to reorganise the Legislative Council to include African representatives. Taking advantage of his position, both as Professor of History and member of the Legislative Council, Ingham was able to make a case for African history. During an East African Governors' Conference in 1952, the then governments of Uganda and Tanganyika and that of the Colonial Science Research Council proposed to publish the History of East Africa series.

Henceforth, with Colonial Development and Welfare funds, members of the Department of History at Makerere carried out research on different aspects of East African history, which later led to the publication of two volumes of *History of East Africa* in 1963 and 1965 (Harlow, Chilver and Smith, 1965; Makerere College, the University College of East Africa Report for the Year 1956–57 and 1957–58). In 1958, Ingham himself published a book titled *The Making of Modern Uganda* in which he examined the effects of the British administration in Uganda since the proclamation of the Protectorate. And, in 1963, he published yet another book, *A History of East Africa*. In a context where European historians were still dominated by the Hegelian notion of the essential darkness of the African past, Ingham and Low demonstrated that it was possible to study and produce African history in Uganda during the late colonial period.

Ingham also promoted outreach activities. During his tenure, members of the History Department delivered lectures on the history of Uganda and workings of government, not only to students but also individuals working with the government, including police cadets. In addition, Ingham addressed the Uganda Cultural Society and the Kampala Rotary Club on historical topics (Makerere College, The University College of East Africa, Report for the year 1957–58). Some members of staff in the department also delivered lectures to secondary school students (Makerere College, The University College of East Africa, Report for the year 1958–59). And, in July 1959, when the Ugandan branch of the Historical Association was formed, Ingham became its first president (Makerere College, The University College of East Africa, Report for the year 1959–60). Ingham's contribution to Africanising history at Makerere cannot be overemphasised. By the eve of Independence, the study of African history began to take shape as a serious field of inquiry at Makerere and, by the time Ingham left East Africa in 1962, African history was already recognised in government circles. With his departure, the pace of Africanising the department nearly stalled. Even those who had criticised his curriculum innovations and demanded a more radical African-centred syllabus lamented that with his departure in 1962, the future of the department looked bleak (Ogot, 2002).

East Africanisation to Ugandanisation: 1963 to 1972

As it turned out, the fears that members of the Department of History expressed in 1962, following Ingham's departure, were well founded. While the departments of history across the region promoted the study of African history in the immediate post-Independence period, at Makerere Africanisation of the curricula stalled, resulting in a decrease in African courses. Beachey, who succeeded Ingham and hired two Ugandan historians, Phares Mutibwa and Semakula-Kiwanuka in 1965 and 1967, respectively, produced a far less African-centred syllabus between 1963 and 1967 (Sicherman, 2003). In spite of having Ugandan historians in the department, there was no corresponding increase in African courses. In contrast to Ingham's tenure, students pursuing general BA degrees did not study any African-oriented history, while those studying towards an honours degree were offered only two African-centred courses out of eight. This sharply contrasted with the emphasis on the promotion of African courses during Ingham's leadership in the years before Independence.

Margery Perham has observed that the 1960s generation of African historians engaged the African continent from a new angle. Following attainment of independence, Africans 'desire[d] to see their history rewritten, or rather, for the first time fully written'. This was important because they regarded their history 'as part of the basis of their self-respect and self-identification, both as a race and also as members of the new nations which are struggling to find internal unity and external status' (Perham, 1965: 13). However, in the case of Uganda, most of the initial works on East Africa's history were written by non-Africans. This was partly because there were not many qualified Ugandans conducting research. To address this gap, during the 1960s many African/ Ugandan graduates of history embarked on further degree programmes at the School of Oriental and African Studies (SOAS), London, and Oxford University in England, McMaster in Canada, the State University of New York in the United States, University College Dar es Salaam in Tanzania and the University of Ghana at Legon. During these years, the Department of History heavily relied on foreign training.

The late 1960s was an exceptional moment in Uganda's intellectual life. Africanisation in the Department of History was revived following the appointment of Professor JB Webster, a Canadian, who came to Makerere from Ibadan in late 1968. Webster took over the leadership of the department from a Ugandan historian, Semakula-Kiwanuka, who until then was acting Head of Department. Webster 'was surprised to find that the spirit of African nationalism that he had absorbed at Ibadan was largely absent at Makerere' (Sicherman, 2003: 263). The Ibadan School of History had emerged in the 1950s and was very vibrant in the production of Africa's pre-colonial history and the forging of a Nigerian identity (see Falola, Chapter 13, in this volume). Influenced by what he had seen at Ibadan and, in the spirit of making the department relevant, as well as identifying with the project of nation-building, Webster launched the 'History of Uganda Project' in 1969. This project was envisioned to lead to the production of two volumes on the history of Uganda. Webster also used the 'History of Uganda Project' to Africanise staff and curriculum. The main objective of this was to generate 'a new history of Uganda which will bring East African history more closely in line with the modern historiographical standards' (Sicherman, 2003: 271). The project emphasised precolonial history and the use of African sources. In this way, the project respected African agency and sought to demonstrate that 'African history and history of European activities in Africa are two different themes'. It also set out to debunk the colonial supposition that Africa had no history (Sicherman, 2003: 271). This project was funded by the Makerere Research and Publications Grants Committee, the Rockefeller Foundation (1969–71) and the Ford Foundation.

The History of Uganda Project further enhanced Africanisation by involving students in conducting empirical research under supervision; equipping them with techniques of historical research and writing; underscoring the importance of bonding with their societies as well as encouraging them to appreciate the knowledge of the elders (Sicherman, 2003: 271). The project brought on board undergraduate and graduate students in historical research throughout Uganda. It was expected that research from the project would lead to a two-volume history of Uganda. Despite the challenges encountered, both staff and students produced considerable publications. The most prominent was Uzoigwe's *Uganda: The Dilemma of Nationhood*, which was published in 1982.

In 1971, in an effort to further Africanise the History of Uganda Project, Dr Donald Denoon organised research seminars in the department with the primary aim of bringing together graduate students and staff to reflect on and synthesise research and fieldwork for the previous three years (Makerere University, Kampala Report, July 1970–June 1971). It was hoped that the seminars would continue during the 1971/72 academic year and contribute to the production of a new history of Uganda. Unfortunately, the progress in the department was shattered and the History of Uganda Project abandoned prematurely following Idi Amin's overthrow of Milton Obote's regime in a military coup in 1971. Under the new regime, 'Amin forbade research of any kind which involved fieldwork' (Sicherman, 2003: 280).[1] This ban heavily hit the Department of History. Like the rest of the university, the Department of History suffered a mass exodus of staff during Amin's regime. The few professional Ugandan historians went into exile and some of the expatriate staff abandoned ongoing research projects.

It is important to note that Webster's History of Uganda Project either coincided with or was informed by the broader university research agenda, as well as the wider nation-building project. During the academic year 1969/70, a Visitation Committee to Makerere University College appointed by the then President of Uganda (Milton Obote) to inquire into the affairs of the National University of Uganda – which Makerere was to become on 1 July 1970 – had recommended the following:

> Makerere must become part and parcel of the Uganda nation. The University must totally identify itself with the aims of society and must play its full part in meeting these goals. The University must not sit on the fence or hold itself aloof as a disinterested observer. It must throw in its lot with the aspirations of society and work hand in hand with the Government to build a united and prosperous country. This is only logical since it is the Ugandan people who created and are going to sustain this University (Makerere University College Report for the year 1969–70: 2).

Clearly, the Obote-appointed Visitation Committee underscored the role of Makerere University in nation-building and, interestingly, Webster's 'History of Uganda Project' seemed to blend in well with this recommendation. Webster certainly had a good relationship with President Obote. Sicherman (2003) reveals that Obote approved Webster's proposed curricular review

---

1   Sicherman quotes directly from Webster's memoir.

amidst objections from the entire Faculty of Arts and Social Sciences. Webster successfully lobbied for a Kenyan, Joseph Ouma, to become Dean of Arts and Social Sciences at Makerere in 1969. Ouma became the only black dean at Makerere. However, in 1970, following recommendations of the Visitation Committee, Obote replaced Ouma with Webster. This upset some of the African staff at Makerere who henceforth tagged Webster as 'Obote's dean' (Sicherman, 2003: 267).

Webster further promoted Africanisation of the department by introducing an inter-university exchange of staff between Makerere and the University of Ibadan in 1970. With financial assistance from the Rockefeller Foundation, Dr Denoon, then staff at Makerere, spent a year at Ibadan and, in exchange, Mr AC Unomah went to Makerere. Dr Denoon would later go to the University of Toronto, Canada, as a visiting Professor of African History (Makerere University College Report for the year 1969–70).

To make the department visible and contribute to nation-building, members of staff engaged in community outreach activities by going out to deliver lectures to both government departments and secondary schools. Together with the Ministry of Education, the department sponsored two conferences for secondary school teachers in 1971. The purpose of the conferences was primarily 'to acquaint school teachers with the latest interpretations in African history' (Makerere University, Kampala Report, July 1970–June 1971: 63). This was yet another mechanism through which the department was seen to contribute to nation-building.

Webster also used his contacts to secure postgraduate fellowships for African students in the department and, within two years, it had the highest number of graduate students who were eager to participate in knowledge creation. The department had staff who were 'well equipped to supervise postgraduate work in most East African subjects' (Sicherman, 2003: 277). In 1970/71, the Department of History recorded 17 Ugandans pursuing graduate studies in different parts of the world, including Ibadan, SOAS, Michigan, Santa Barbara, Princeton, Moscow, Oxford, Wisconsin, Dalhousie and Makerere. Out of the 17, five were enrolled at Makerere (Makerere University, Kampala Report, July 1970–June 1971: 63), a confirmation of the promotion of graduate studies. In the 1970/71 annual report the university noted: 'We are grateful here to the Government of Uganda, other friendly governments, Foundations and Agencies which offer fellowship to our postgraduate students to make Ugandanisation possible' (Makerere University, Kampala Report, July 1970–June 1971: 2). In the same year, the Department of History appointed six new staff to lecturer positions, including both Ugandans and non-Ugandans. In addition, four Ugandan graduate students were hired as teaching assistants

(Makerere University, Kampala Report, July 1970–June 1971: 2).

It is important to point out that the process of Africanising the African universities was not always smooth. One of the major problems, as Rimmington (1965: 110) pointed out, was 'the defining of the relationship between state and university, between politician and professor'. It turned out that 'African politicians are often extremely sensitive to research findings and opinions suggesting adverse criticism of themselves, and there are not yet sufficient safeguards for those with highly developed critical ability, either African or expatriate'. Right from the immediate post-independence period, there were governments that 'interfered with the freedom of both universities and individual members of staff'. The case of Idi Amin's restrictions on research in the early 1970s provides a good example. So, does Milton Obote's attack on Ali Mazrui when he tried to Africanise the political science curriculum at Makerere. Obote feared that Mazrui 'was becoming a politician, and not a political scientist' (Mngomezulu, 2003: 107).

Lessons from Makerere's experience

Africanisation of staff, curricula and research at Makerere has a long history dating back to the late colonial period when some units like the Department of History gradually introduced African-oriented courses into the syllabus and also hired African academic staff.

Both colonial and postcolonial governments influenced the Africanisation process. During the 1950s, Ingham was able to influence curricula development in the Department of History and promote research in East African history, in part because he had the support of Governor Andrew Cohen. Similarly, Webster made some significant impact in the same department in the period 1969–70 because he enjoyed the support of President Milton Obote.

Africanisation of the university is a political project that fits within specific historical contexts. In the 1960s, the constituent colleges of the UEA underscored East Africanisation, but when Makerere University College became Makerere University in 1970, the focus switched to Ugandanisation. The major point here is that Makerere had to identify itself with, and reflect the aspirations of, the Ugandan nation. The Department of History participated in this process in different ways, including conducting research, delivering lectures and promoting staff development.

Makerere relied on foreign funding for both training and research. Research from the late colonial and early postcolonial periods relied heavily on donor agencies, including the Rockefeller Foundation. In the 1950s, research on the history of East Africa was made possible by Colonial Development and Welfare funds, while the History of Uganda Project was funded by the Rockefeller Foundation and the Ford Foundation, as well as the Makerere Research and Publications Grants Committee.

Africanising the curriculum in the Department of History at Makerere was initiated and, for the most part, led by non-Africans. Despite his limited knowledge of African history, Ingham introduced African history into the department's curriculum in 1952. From the late 1960s into the 1970s, Webster spearheaded the changes in the department, most notably the 'History of Uganda Project' which was key in the Africanisation of the department.

When Makerere ended its special relationship with the University of London in 1963, the focus was devoted to East Africanisation of both administrative and academic staff. Africanisation of administrative staff happened much faster than that of academic staff. Despite the emphasis on the recruitment of African staff, expatriate staff were still recruited.

Africanisation and transformation of the curriculum require qualified, experienced and committed staff. This calls for capacity building, which can be achieved through the promotion of postgraduate studies and the recruitment of teaching assistants – but there must be funding for this to succeed. The late 1960s into the early 1970s marked the peak of progress in the Department of History, in part because of visionary leadership and government support.

Mere Africanisation of staff might not necessarily translate into curriculum transformation. Some Ugandan staff in the Department of History preferred and emphasised European-oriented courses at the expense of African courses. Paradoxically, non-African heads of department contributed significantly to curriculum transform.

References

Harlow, V and Chilver, EM (eds) assisted by Smith, A (1965) *History of East Africa*, vol II. Oxford: Clarendon Press.
Ingham, K (1958) *The Making of Modern Uganda*. London George Allen and Unwin.
Ingham, K (1963) *A History of East Africa*. London: Longman.
Makerere College, the University College of East Africa Report for the Year 1956–57.
Makerere College, the University College of East Africa Report for the Year 1957–58.
Makerere College, The University College of East Africa, Report for the year 1958–59
Makerere University College Report for the year 1962–63, Principal's Introduction, Makerere University Library Archives.
Makerere University College Report for the year 1963–64, Makerere University Library Archives.
Makerere University College Report for the year 1964–65, Makerere University Library Archives.
Makerere University College Report for the year 1965–66, Makerere University Library Archives.
Makerere University College Report for the year 1968–69, Makerere University Library Archives.

Makerere University College Report for the year 1969–70, Makerere University Library Archives.

Mngomezulu, RB (2003) What does the Africanisation of a university entail? Lessons from East Africa, *Affrika: Journal of Politics, Economics and Society*, **3**:(1–2), 97–113.

Ogot, AB (2002) Three decades of historical studies in East Africa, 1949–77, in T Falola and ES Atieno Odhiambo (eds) *The Challenges of History and Leadership in Africa*. Trenton, NJ: Africa World Press, pp. 493–510.

Perham, M (1965) Introduction, in V Harlow and EM Chilver (eds) assisted by A Smith, *History of East Africa*, vol II. Oxford: Clarendon Press.

Rimmington, TG (1965) The development of universities in Africa, *Comparative Education*, **1**(2): 105–12.

Sicherman, C (2003) Building an African Department at Makerere, 1950–72, *History in Africa*, **30**: 253–82.

Uzoigwe, GN (1982) *Uganda: The Dilemma of Nationhood*. Studies in East African Society and History. New York: Nok Publishing International.

Zeleza, PT (2009) African studies and universities since independence: Looking ahead, *Transition*, **101**: 110–35.

Chapter 19
The development of contemporary literature in East Africa[1]

Chris Wanjala

Introduction

The concern for a literary tradition in East Africa is an old one. It is tied to the attempts by East African 'men of letters' to liberate the African aesthetic. For a long time, what held sway in this sub-region was the 'Great Tradition' – a literary culture based on English. African children were introduced to the English language when they first went to school so their literary education was thus more imitative than creative. The African school was based on the English school, with a debating society, a Sunday school, a school magazine and the open school speech day. These institutions shaped the first experiences of the African child: the school debates were conducted in the English language; the school magazine accepted short stories and poems in the English language; and the subjects debated and written about revolved around career roles and the adjustment of the African child to the Western world. This English literary culture was reinforced when the African child joined the University College and manifested itself in the English Department magazines available to students in Kampala, Nairobi and Dar es Salaam. These included *Transition, East Africa Journal* and its literary supplements, *Ghala* and *Zuka*.

New schools of literature have emerged at the universities of Nairobi and Dar es Salaam, forged by writers who grew up outside of the university 'English Lit' culture. These included Okot p'Bitek and Okello Oculi from Uganda, Taban Lo Liyong from South Sudan and Kenya's Ali A Mazrui. These writers worked with other East Africans, including Pio Zirimu, Peter Nazareth, Grant Kamenju, Ngũgĩ wa Thiong'o, Micere Githae Mugo and Chris L Wanjala, to sever East African literary culture from the English-based 'Great Tradition'. East African men and women of culture have redefined their literature. They have consciously based their writings on the oral tradition, while keeping

---

1 This chapter is based on the author's inaugural lecture and a paper titled 'Lessons from Kenya', presented at the Institute for Pan-African Thought and Conversation conference – 'Transforming Ivory Towers to Ebony Towers: Lessons for South Africa's Curriculum Transformation in the Humanities from Africa and Africa-American Studies' in Johannesburg in August 2018.

their literary practice within the circles of the global debate. The rumbles in the United States and the United Kingdom over canon revision affected us here in East Af+rica in a very direct way. The departments of Literature and English in these two Anglo-Saxon countries stole our idea of literature and its relevance to history and society, and resold it to the whole world. But East African writers have built on their oral traditions, which have become the bases for their creativity and literary criticism. This foundation is becoming stronger by the day.

Curriculum transformation efforts in Kenyan universities

I have the notoriety of having advocated in the Kenyan newspaper *Daily Nation* in May 1990, the scrapping of the then public universities' undergraduate literature syllabus that was originally prepared by the Department of Literature at the University of Nairobi in the 1973/74 academic year. Literature and linguistics are taught separately on the main campus of the University of Nairobi but at the College of Education and External Studies, linguistics – especially English – and literature are taught in one department.

Moi, Egerton and Kenyatta universities have followed the example of the main campus of the University of Nairobi. Kenyan academic KE Senanu noted in 1997:

> At Moi University, the department of literature is located in the school of social cultural and development studies, an interdisciplinary institute whose challenge consists in raising questions about the value and the contribution of our various disciplines of knowledge to the transformation of our society (Senanu, 1997).

There seem to be two emphases in the teaching of literature, in both Kenyan universities and secondary schools. First, there is the emphasis on content and, second, a focus on form and the language of literature. These put us on the horns of a dilemma: we have to choose either a generic approach or a thematic one to the study and the teaching of literature. Eddah Gachukia – then a part-time lecturer in the Department of Literature at the University of Nairobi – propagated the generic or structural approach in the early 1970s. In her paper for a staff meeting on 28 June 1973, Gachukia addressed the issue of 'The effective handling of language by students of literature'. She challenged the department to initiate a programme to improve literature students' use of language. She then went on to offer a big cautionary remark about the literary revolution of the 1970s:

It is an apparent fact that with our enthusiasm over the Africanisation and the broadening of the literature programme, both here at the University and in the East African Secondary Schools, we have lost the emphasis that used to be placed on the teaching of the English language through the study of English Literature. There is a general feeling that the standard of expression, both oral and written, is not what it should be and that something ought to be done about it. For besides attempting to train students in the arts of critical judgement and enjoyment of literature, it is also our duty to train them for practical life (for the teaching profession, journalism, editing, etc.) (Gachukia, 28 June 1973).

Indeed, on the strength of Gachukia's recommendations, a course called 'Language Use and Description' was initiated and taught until 2018. She wanted the University of Nairobi to maintain its language laboratories and teach translation techniques to students of oral literature (Gachukia, 28 June 1973). There is the view that literature is 'first and foremost the art of words', while another view holds that literature is an expression of cultural values (Senanu, 1997: 9). This latter view was propounded by Ngũgĩ wa Thiong'o in his two papers, 'Discussion paper No. 2' and 'Literature and society'.[2] While presenting the new literature syllabus at the University of Nairobi, Ngũgĩ came up with the following eight hypotheses:

1. Academic staff in the Department of Literature at the University of Nairobi were at war 'with a tradition of scholarship, with a category of thinking, with a way of looking at the world fashioned within a historical framework of Western Europeanism'. Literature arises from individual societies – it is best expressed by the genius of that society. Human alienation is the subject of much European literature because Europe was dead, dehumanised by capitalism. Europe celebrates art for art's sake. Africa – by implication – could not afford to do so.

2. All Western education and the philosophy of Europe's and America's great thinkers and philosophers support oppression. They oppress and suppress voices of dissent and liberation.

3. African departments of literature in the 1960s and early 1970s perpetuated oppression because they taught Western literary values and exalted decadent literary traditions like Romanticism, Critical Realism and Modernism. This was done mostly by expatriate literary experts.

---

2   A paper that was published later in Gachukia, EW and Akivaga, SK (eds) (1978) *Teaching Literature in Kenya Schools*. Nairobi: Kenya Literature Bureau.

4. African literary scholars want to liberate the study of literature and promote aesthetic theories based on oral literature, and use them to analyse their own indigenous literature.
5. Literature arises from individual societies. It is best expressed by the genius of those societies.
6. The University of Nairobi's Department of Literature is more progressive than most. It must revise its syllabus.
7. At the centre of our study must be our people – their poverty, their ignorance and their diseases. This project must be people-specific.
8. The revolution in the teaching of literature started by the University of Nairobi must gain more momentum and percolate through Kenya's secondary schools.

Subsumed under this debate was the question 'Should Africans study the literature of North America, Europe and Japan at their universities?' In the 1990s, the Kenyan University literature syllabus needed to be reformed. The issues I raised then about the syllabus were still with us in 2018. The teaching of literature in Kenya's public universities is so important that universities elsewhere in Africa often look to the University of Nairobi as a model.

James Ogude is one of the products of the University of Nairobi's Department of Literature. In 2019, he was the Director of the Centre for the Advancement of Scholarship at the University of Pretoria in South Africa. Ogude draws from the views of Socialist Realism, which we trained him to embrace at the University of Nairobi in the 1970s. Before Ogude relocated to South Africa, he helped to establish the Department of Literature at Moi University in Kenya. He is one of the Kenyan scholars abroad who have helped in the promotion of teaching and research on Kenyan literature. He has popularised authors like Grace Ogot, Ngũgĩ wa Thiong'o and Meja Mwangi in South Africa and he has introduced a course titled 'Fiction and Ideology in Kenya', dealing with Euro-Kenyan literature, the canonical writers and the post-colonial experience after the 1960s.

The literature syllabi in Kenyan public and private universities do require a review, however. We have been re-examining the curriculum for many years and many adjustments have been made to give the syllabus a practical face and to give the students the orientation they did not get in their secondary schools. There are problems posed by divorcing language from literature. Some universities train teachers of literature and language in schools so that they should be able to handle all the linguistic and literary aspects of the Kenyan secondary certificate syllabus.

It would be wrong to say that things began going wrong with the abolition of the Department of English at the University of Nairobi in 1970. We should rather talk of the separation of literature from language departments in Kenyan universities as a 'practice which began at the University of Nairobi in the early seventies and as a result of a literary revolution launched by the triumvirate of Ngũgĩ wa Thiong'o, Okot p'Bitek and Taban Lo Liyong' (Senanu, 1997: 8).

The centre of operation in our literary studies has shifted. We do not only put African literature as the centre – both oral and written – but we must also write in our local languages. Learning the literature of the African peoples should also be compulsory. The approach to African literature is both thematic and stylistic: we go beyond language use to 'Stylistics', a course that runs through all four years of undergraduate study at Nairobi University. We teach 'Practical Criticism', in which students learn how to go about reading a novel, poem or play. We also teach them how to take notes and how to write an essay or a term paper.

Literary transformation in East Africa

The problem of grounding our studies in the African soil has been solved by creating programmes that put oral literature at their centre. The history of African political thought teaches us that African leaders had to return to their traditions to explain their world-view vis-à-vis Western ideas of governance. Those writers who stress content in African literature have taken the ideas of African politicians, philosophers and historians into consideration. But to talk about the growth of an East African literary tradition is to explain the development of an East African literary consciousness, which defines our post-coloniality. In order to discuss the post-coloniality of our literature, we must concern ourselves with the way literature has shaped our Tanzanianness, our Ugandanness, our Kenyanness or, in a word, our East Africanness. Since the publications of Ngũgĩ wa Thiong'o's *Weep Not, Child* (1964) and Okot p'Bitek's *Song of Lawino* (1966), we have developed a literature in East Africa that has stopped us from looking at European and North American literature as our cultural yardstick. In other words, we concern ourselves with the literature that has separated us from Europe and North America. There are many master's and PhD dissertations in our public universities that deal with post-coloniality in East Africa. These theses demonstrate how East African literature enacts a new history that separates us from our colonial past and connects us with our democratic future. Our present realities provide us with a second chance as a human race after our first chance was disastrously ruined by a century of European colonial rule.

The story of individualism in the post-colonial context is one in which African children do not want to conform to a Westernised society. Parents of these children want them to study the local situation and appreciate it before they study the foreign situation. It is in this respect that the concept of alienation – in relation to literature – is discussed in the West Indies (Caribbean Literature), African-American and African literature (see chapters 20 to 22 in this volume). Colonial and independent African situations of alienation have been engaged for six decades by creative writers.

East African literature forms part of the global aesthetics. It is important that its development and critical climate are evaluated in order to bridge the gap between East African and global debates on literature. East African literature has been developed not only by East African writers – it has also been influenced by Western scholars. Foreigners who have worked in East Africa have had an impact on the East African scene. The growth of the University of East Africa, which emerged in 1963, is synonymous with the growth of East African literature.

Some professors of literature in East Africa subscribe to the approach that stresses language use and description in the study of literature. But how different are their methods from those of the expatriate literary experts who were condemnatory and talked dismissively about East African literature and culture?

In the post-colonial era, literature has been explained by the 'natives' themselves. To their voices were added the voices of female critics. Mikhail Bakhtin and Ngũgĩ wa Thiong'o now drive us to the communities that produce the literature for meaning. Society and the language give us a set of abstract norms and rules that we carry around in our heads. The conflicts and contradictions in our thinking are reflected in language as we express it. In the study of literature, we first need to classify literature at the level of words and then proceed to see different texts for what they are. In our literature courses in the Nairobi Department of Linguistics and Literature, we introduce students to the nature and function of literature. We ask the question 'What is literature?' We go into the relationship of literature with other disciplines and discuss its aesthetic values.

During the nationalist period in the 1950s, African literary scholars had high regard for literature and culture. The perpetrators of English culture like David Cook (Makerere University), James Stewart (University College, Nairobi) and Robert Green (University College, Dar es Salaam) understood literature to be a carrier of values. The English novel, which Ngũgĩ wa Thiong'o and his contemporaries studied at Makerere (and Chinua Achebe's contemporaries studied at Ibadan University), came with English values (see Garuba, Chapter

16, in this volume). In any event, the students who joined the University College in Nairobi came from their own literary background and traditions. Before I came to the University of Nairobi, for example, I had been exposed to oral forms (spoken, recited, declaimed or sung). These compositions and performances exhibited an appreciable degree of literary validity. They came from the folk imagination, beliefs and customs, lessons in the arts and crafts, and the history and literary creations of my people; they came from an oral and non-literate society in which practically everything was communicated by word of mouth.

The functions of Western and African literature may be the same in terms of the creation of moral and aesthetic awareness. In the 1970s, we were critical of the use of the English language because it created an East African elite that was distant from the masses. It was also widely believed that the competent use of English had a remarkable effect on the onward or upward mobility of the learner. English opened avenues to the Commonwealth and North American world for the East African. These are not the writers who wrote the literature, but the white male lecturers in English who taught at the universities of East Africa in Kampala, Nairobi and Dar es Salaam (see Rugumamu, Chapter 14, and Khankwa, Chapter 18, in this volume). They traversed the entire literary scene and offered advice to the East African reading elite. They wrote books, articles and literary essays for people like themselves in South Africa, West Africa, Europe, North America, Australia and New Zealand.

The critics still exist but have moved from East Africa to North America, South Africa and Europe. They network through organisations like the Association for Commonwealth Literature and Language Studies (ACLALS), the Afro-Asian Writers Association and the African Literature Association. Between the 1950s and the 1970s, these were white males. From the 1970s to the 1990s, they were indigenous African males. These individuals now write books and articles on fiction, poetry and drama, and attend meetings at the university, in the department, in the faculty, in the senate and even in the council. They were chairs of their departments, deans or directors of institutes, principals, deputy vice-chancellors or vice-chancellors. They travel to conferences, workshops, summits and symposia, and regularly appear on television. They give advice to undergraduate students and their younger colleagues.

The business of these men and women is literary appreciation. They select great works for study and point out faults and weaknesses in these works. They see themselves as intermediaries between the creative writers and the young and untutored readers. The great writers of the time speak through them. They shape the literary tastes and the cultural values of their time. They direct readers to good writers, both past and present. The literary critics of the industrialised world – North America, Europe and Japan – are pro-establishment critics. They reflect the bias of their societies. This bias became apparent when some of them operated in Africa between the 1950s and the 1970s. They masqueraded as democrats and liberals but, in essence, they defended the dictatorship of the bourgeoisie.

British academic David Cook is an example of a leading literary scholar in East Africa during this epoch of the 1950s. He edited *Origin, East Africa; Poems from East Africa; Short East African Plays*, and *In Black and White*. His studies included broad perspectives of African literature. Some of the texts he studied included those of his students and their contemporaries. They included Ngũgĩ wa Thiong'o's *A Grain of Wheat* (1967), Peter Palangyo's *Dying in the Sun* (1968), and Okello Oculi's *Prostitute* (1968). Cook studied the art of persuasion in East Africa. He studied Jomo Kenyatta's 1938 *Facing Mount Kenya*, among other East African texts.

He belongs to a group of European and North American scholars who devoted themselves to the promotion of African literature. His counterpart in West Africa was the German academic Ulli Beier, who often was heavily criticised for romanticising traditional Africa. In his obvious admiration for African society, Cook was blind to its complexity and flaws. He was unwilling to commit himself and unable to express a point of view on any controversial matter. Cook was a typical liberal white male who was in Africa to apologise for Europe. His contemporary was Margaret MacPherson who wrote a book, *They Built for the Future: A chronicle for Makerere University College 1922–1962*, published in 1964.

The European imperialists were responsible for many of the changes in cultural and material life in contemporary Africa. The shattering experience of the Mau Mau Uprising and the emergency of the 1950s provided much fodder for creative writing by Europeans and Africans in Kenya. Europeans changed the cultural, socio-economic and political lives of Africans by planting churches in Africa, bringing their education system to Kenya, which was ill-suited to the African, and settling on the best land. Land alienation from Africans to Europeans – whether farmers or missionaries – created emotional turmoil in African lives. Institutions established by the Europeans have continued to unleash alienation on Africa. Alienation of the writer is clear in the idyllic picture drawn of the past by the African. It is also evident in the way that some African writers romanticise not only the African past, but also African leaders. Here, we argue with Taban Lo Liyong and say, 'we can no longer trust an African just because he is an African' (Taban Lo Liyong in Helen Tiffin, 1979: 18). The over-romanticisation of Africa and the African past is symptomatic of the writer's alienation from the realities of oppression and economic deprivation. We sometimes accuse Okot p'Bitek and Senegalese Leopold Sedar Senghor of this form of alienation.

The literature that we teach in East Africa is about societies in transition. It is German playwright Bertolt Brecht's poetry and drama, Russian writer Tolstoy's fiction and essays, and South African Athol Fugard's drama. The literature deals with where we have been and where we are headed. Masheti Masinjila was one of the officials of the Kenya Oral Literature Association (KOLA) in the 1990s. KOLA has done much to promote theories and methods of studying oral literature in East Africa. If members of this association had been Americans or Nigerians, the world would have known about what they were doing.

East African literary scholars have moved beyond answering the question 'What is literature?' Local ideas about literature have been canonised. These writers have entrenched ideas on the study of literature in East Africa popularised by Ngũgĩ wa Thiong'o, Okot p'Bitek and Taban Lo Liyong. Okot p'Bitek saw the need for relevance and commitment in research. Literary theory in East Africa had to incorporate the study of oral literature. Masinjila argued that Kenyan researchers have shown a degree of theoretical awareness evident in their consistency as to what they regard as pertinent literature. Since oral literature was conceived of within historical and pedagogical needs, which were outlined by pioneer scholars such as Ngũgĩ, Okot p'Bitek, Henry Owuar-Anyumba and Lo Liyong, there already exists a conceptual framework within which researchers have tended to operate. Strictly speaking, there may not be a harmonious, well-articulated theoretical construct that Kenyan scholars follow. Yet, its absence does not necessarily preclude the identification of trends that are theoretically unique and significant to East African literature (in Okoth-Okombo and Nandwa, 1992: 17).

The quest for 'popular literature' in East Africa

The term 'popular literature' entered into the criticism of African literature in the mid-1940s when the colonial British Governors of East Africa met to examine the dearth of reading materials for Africans. They then sought to provide literature and textbooks for Africans and Asians. In October 1945, Directors of Education met in Kampala, Uganda, and resolved that an interterritorial organisation was required to advise colonial governments in East Africa on the kind of literature that should be produced to cater for the needs of textbooks, language books and books for the general reader. Later in the same month, they invited British author Elspeth Huxley to look into the needs of East African countries with regard to popular literature, and to make proposals on how these needs could be met. She submitted a report which, inter alia, recommended the setting up of an East African Literature Bureau to publish books for East African countries including Kenya, Tanzania and Uganda.

Huxley made recommendations for the printing and distribution of books, and for setting up a lending library service throughout East Africa. In 1947, CG Richards worked Huxley's recommendations into a detailed scheme. He became the first Director of the East African Literature Bureau (EALB) in 1948 and set out to promote popular literature and its total flow, especially the flow of 'desirable literature' to encourage research. The bureau was to act as a literary agency and edit and put into publishable shape materials for textbooks in English and in the four languages of the East African community, namely Swahili, Luganda, Kikuyu and Dholuo-Gang. The bureau would run a fortnightly magazine in the four languages, and disseminate books for popular readership through sales and libraries. It would also encourage literary creativity by offering prizes and other awards to notable and aspiring talents.

Popular literature, in this case, included adapted novels, and original stories and plays, written in simple English by Africans, with an African setting. The Bureau published a series of books on the achievements of European explorers, missionaries and administrators, reflecting the bias of its originators. Books in indigenous languages covered a multitude of subjects: agriculture, civics, family welfare, economics, commerce, biographies of famous people, geography, language, law, literacy, history, health, medicine, poetry, politics, religion, science and sociology.

Richards retired in 1963 and Noah Sempira, the Book Production Officer in the Uganda branch of the EALB, became the director. With the demise of the East African Community (EAC) (incorporating Kenya, Tanzania and Uganda) after barely a decade, the EALB was split on territorial lines, giving way to the Kenya Literature Bureau in July 1977. This bureau still enjoys parastatal status in Kenya's Ministry of Education, and carries on the functions of the defunct EALB. It assisted in the development and dissemination of Swahili culture by making available in print major works of Swahili which were in manuscript form. The writing of the books in Swahili and other indigenous languages was encouraged by the East African Inter-territorial Language Committee which consisted of Europeans and Africans. Members of this group re-wrote the manuscripts, and polished them so much that the final editions of the publications often read like translations from works written originally by Europeans. Creative works in indigenous languages were too short to engage readers for a long time. Those African authors who wrote in their indigenous languages did not expect to have a large market. They were themselves often so alienated from the cultural traditions of their people that their modes of composition were alien to African styles of narrative.

The East African Publishing House was launched with the publication of the Swahili edition of Kenyan nationalist hero JM Kariuki's (1963) book, *The Mau Mau Detainee*, and later thrived on titles on the Mau Mau Uprising. These included Kenyan Godwin Wachira's *Ordeal in the Forest* and Kenyan Charity Waciuma's *Daughter of Mumbi*. From 1966, the East African Publishing House published a series of books, including the novels of Kenyan Grace EA Ogot such as *The Promised Land* (1966) and the works of Ugandan Okello Oculi, *Orphan* and *Prostitute* (1968).

The launching of the African Writers Series by British publisher Heinemann, on the other hand, brought East Africa into the limelight, by publishing Ngũgĩ wa Thiong'o's *Weep Not, Child* in 1964 (see Garuba, Chapter 16, in this volume). This was the first novel to be published by an East African writer and it won a special award at the Festival of Negro Arts in Dakar, in 1965. This novel was followed by Ngũgĩ's *The River Between* and then *A Grain of Wheat* (1967). Ngũgĩ's books published between 1964 and 1968 were imbued with historical realism, which we find in novels by other African writers. They talk about what might have happened during the African independence struggle. *The River Between* is a novel of conflict, set in pre-independence Kenya. The European characters in his books are detestable. Ngũgĩ wa Thiong'o is not a Christian novelist so European missionaries occupy a limited space in his books.

Ngũgĩ's *Weep Not, Child* (1964) is situated in the context of an African revolution. One of the main characters in the novel is Ngotho, an African worker on a European farm owned by Mr Howlands. Many members of Ngũgĩ's family had participated in Kenya's struggle for independence and were arrested by the colonial police. What the author recounts in his four books is based on what actually took place during his childhood between 1938 and 1953 – the years preceding the Mau Mau Uprising and its repression – and later during the Emergency of 1950 to 1960. Ngũgĩ's novels, like those of Nigeria's Chinua Achebe, Senegal's Ousmane Sembène, and South Africa's Alex La Guma, were among the first novels that engaged the African struggle for political independence.

Conclusion

This chapter has demonstrated how Kenyan and East African writers exploited the rich tradition of oral literature.

But, it must not be forgotten that East Africa's popular literature of the 1970s emerged at a time when the world capitalist system was undergoing a series of major crises, with international monetary instability and America's removal of the dollar from the gold standard. Inflation and unemployment were major problems and sources of increased antagonism. In the United States itself, there was considerable opposition to racism and foreign aggression (see chapters 20 to 22 in this volume). In the peripheral African capitalist societies, the comprador classes resorted to the mobilisation of 'tribe' for class purposes in order to control the tensions and opposition generated by underdevelopment and inequality.

Popular literature thus found a ready market – it provided a mirror of society for readers who wanted people of their kind portrayed in literature. Readers looked to popular books as a therapeutic drug, for escapism from their stark realities, and also as a basis for self-criticism and restraint. Authors were seen as family psychiatrists, moral philosophers and youth advisers. For the first time, East Africans were worried about the pernicious role of literature, the destructive influence of sex in novels and films, and commercialised art. East African literature had, however, finally emerged from the dark shadows of European colonialism.

References

Bangura, A (2015) *Toyin Falola and African Epistemologies*. New York: Palgrave Macmillan.
Chege, M (2009) The politics of education in Kenyan universities: A call for a paradigm shift, *African Studies Review*, **52**(3): 55–71.
Cook, D (ed.) (1965) *Origin, East Africa: a Makerere Anthology*. London: Heinemann.
Cook, D (ed.) (1976) *In Black and White: Writings from East Africa with Broadcast Discussions and Commentary*. Nairobi: Kenya Literature Bureau.
Cook, D and Lee, M (eds.) (1968) *Short East African Plays in English*. London: Heinemann
Cook, D and Rubadiri, D (eds.) (1971) *Poems from East Africa*. London: Heinemann.
Eliot, TS (1982) Tradition and the individual talent, *Perspecta*, **19**: 36–42.
Gachukia, E (1973) Staff Meeting Presentation in the Department of Literature at the University of Nairobi, Kenya.
Kariuki, JM (1963) *The Mau Mau Detainee*. Nairobi: East African Publishing House.
Kenyatta, J (1938) *Facing Mount Kenya: The Tribal Life of the Gikuyu*. London: Secker and Warburg.
Lathem, L (2005) Bringing old and young people together: An interview project, in D Pollock (ed.) *Remembering: Oral history performance*. New York: Palgrave Macmillan, pp. 67–84.
MacPherson, M (1964) *They Built for the Future: A chronicle for Makerere University College 1922–1962*.
Mavia, D (2005) Shifting visions: Of English language usage in Kenya, *Kunapipi*, **27**(1): 14.
Mazrui, A (1995) African languages and European linguistic imperialism, in S Frederici (ed.) *Enduring Western Civilization: The construction of the concept of Western Civilization and its 'others'*. Santa Barbara, CA: Praeger, pp. 161–74.
Mazrui, AA (2003) Towards re-Africanizing African universities: Who killed intellectualism in the post-colonial era? *Alternatives: Turkish Journal of International Relations*, **2**(3&4): 135–63.
Ngũgĩ wa Thiong'o (1964) *Weep Not, Child*. London: Heinemann Educational Books.
Ngũgĩ wa Thiong'o (1966) *The River Between*. London: Heinemann Educational Books.
Ngũgĩ wa Thiong'o, (1967) *A Grain of Wheat*. London: Heinemann Educational Books.

Ngũgĩ wa Thiong'o (1974) Literature & Society: Paper presented to the Conference on the Teaching of African Literature in Schools, Nairobi, unpublished.

Ngũgĩ wa Thiong'o, (1978) Literature and society, in EW Gachukia and SK Akivaga (eds) (1978) *Teaching Literature in Kenya Schools*. Nairobi: Kenya Literature Bureau.

Ngũgĩ wa Thiong'o, (1980) *Devil on the Cross*. London: Penguin.

Ngũgĩ wa Thiong'o, (1981) *Writers in Politics: Essays*. London: Heinemann Educational Books.

Oculi, O (1968) *Orphan* and *Prostitute*. Nairobi: East African Publishing House.

Ogot, GEA (1966) *The Promised Land*. Nairobi: East African Publishing House.

Okot p'Bitek (1984) *Song of Lawino & Song of Ocol* (No. 266). London: Heinemann Educational Books.

Okoth-Okombo, D and Nandwa, J (eds) (1992) *Reflections on Theories and Methods in Oral Literature*. Nairobi: Kenya Oral Literature Association.

Oruka, HO (ed.) (1990) *Sage Philosophy: Indigenous thinkers and modern debate on African philosophy*, vol 4. Leiden: Brill Academic Publishers.

Palangyo, P (1968) *Dying in the Sun*. Heinemann Educational Books.

Senanu, KE (1997) *Utafiti wa Kiswahili*. Nairobi: Kenya Publishers Association.

Situma, J (1999) *Mpuonzi's Dream*. Nairobi: Africawide Network.

Situma, J (2001) *The Mysterious Killer*. Nairobi: Africawide Network.

Terdiman, R (2001) The marginality of Michel de Certeau, *The South Atlantic Quarterly*, **100**(2): 399–421.

Tiffin, H (1979) *The Empire Writes Back: Theory and Practice in Post-Colonial Literature is a 1989 non-fiction book on post colonialism*. London: Routledge.

Tutuola, A (2014) *Feather Woman of the Jungle*. London: Faber & Faber.

Wachira, G (1968) *Ordeal in the Forest*. Nairobi: East African Publishing House.

Waciuma, C (1969) *Daughter of Mumbi*, Nairobi: East African Publishing House.

Wasamba, P (2014) Oral literature scholarship in Kenya: Achievements, challenges and prospects, in *International Conference on the Preservation of Ethiopian Cultural and Literary Heritage*, Debre Markos University, Debre Markos, Ethiopia, March, p. 1.

Section VII: Lessons from African-American Studies

Chapter 20

De-colonising the 'pre-history' of African and African-American studies: Confronting racism in the American episteme

Zine Magubane

Introduction

In 1996, on the occasion of his suspension from the course 'Problematising Africa', which he had been asked to design, Professor Mahmood Mamdani wrote an essay, 'Is African Studies at UCT to be turned into a new home for Bantu Education?' In this essay, Mamdani revealed how the orientation of African Studies at the University of Cape Town (UCT) was inadequate to a post-apartheid academy because it was developed outside Africa by non-Africans, and within the context of colonialism, the Cold War and apartheid. It thus reflected a colonial episteme wherein an imagined 'division of labour' existed between the disciplines and area studies.

> The disciplines studied the white experience as a universal, human experience; area studies studied the experience of people of colour as an ethnic experience. African Studies focused mainly on Bantu administration, customary law, Bantu languages, and anthropology. This orientation was as true of African Studies at the University of Cape Town as it was of other area study centres (Mamdani, n.d.).

In this chapter, I shall historicise the conceptual divide that Mamdani identifies by locating its emergence in a specific setting – the close of the Civil War through the early 20th century – and place it in the context of the era's most pressing political issue: the 'Negro Problem'. The work and careers of two of the founders of American sociology – W.E.B. Du Bois and Robert Ezra Park – will be my focus as they were strongly influenced by their engagements and conflicts with Booker T Washington, the most important black politician in the world between 1888 and 1915 (see Morris, Chapter 21, in this volume). As such, by default, Washington set the terms for how the 'Negro Problem' would be defined – first as a site for political intervention and later as a recognised target of academic inquiry. Sociology is a particularly interesting discipline from which to probe the origins of the discipline–area studies conceptual divide because sociology, like African and African Diaspora Studies (AADS), has roots in what was then called 'applied philanthropy' on the 'Negro Problem'. As will be discussed in the next section, long before the 'science of society' found an institutional home in the university with three defined objects of theoretical attention – society, the social process and social control – sociology was the branch of 'applied philanthropy' that 'owned' the 'Negro Problem'. One of the Southern Sociological Society's stated aims was to 'solve the race question' (McCulloch, 1912: 3). Many people who later became prominent sociologists – Robert Park being the most notable example – began in the world of 'applied philanthropy' (ie colonial management) of the 'Negro Problem', thus making AADS' institutional positioning vis-à-vis the discipline of sociology not only more curious but also uniquely illuminating. Since the founding generation of sociologists (with the exception of Du Bois) felt it was necessary to put the discipline's historical imbrication in the praxis of the Negro Problem 'under erasure' – to make the claim that they were, indeed, producing universal truths about the 'white experience as universal, human experience' – closer investigation of why they felt this was necessary and how this erasure was accomplished helps us understand the conceptual soil in which the area studies centres and AADS programmes that proliferated after the Cold War took root.

'Educating the Negro to work': The 'Negro Problem' as 'applied philanthropy'

Mamdani's comments underscore two assumptions that bring the separating of area studies from the disciplines into sharp focus. First, because area studies involve 'applied' work, it is seen as preoccupied with that which is particular rather than universal. Second, area studies are seen as focused on gathering raw material (ie data), while the disciplines are seen as oriented towards theoretical generalisation and abstraction. Mamdani specifically mentions 'Bantu administration' and 'customary law'– two examples of 'applied' research. I see 'Bantu administration' and 'applied philanthropy' as being parallel concepts. As sites of political action and fields of academic investigation, they ultimately refer back to the legal architecture and set of institutions that arose to facilitate the coercion of black labourers. When Booker T Washington defined the 'Negro Problem' as working towards 'fitting the native peoples to meet the new demands of the world's industry and commerce', he defined a problem for which 'industrial education' like 'Bantu administration' was the solution (Washington, 1906; Harland and Smock, 1982: 551). Better still was the fact that the 'Negro Problem' knew no national boundaries. Although 'the Negro

Problem in South Africa [was] entirely different from what it [was] in Central or West Africa [and] Barbados and Jamaica in the West Indies present still different conditions', all of them called for 'a type of education similar to that worked out at Hampton and Tuskegee' (Washington, 1906 [1982]: 551).

America, like all post-emancipation societies, struggled with the fact that, given the chance, emancipated slaves never voluntarily returned to the fields; nor did they embrace the idea of being wage labourers or, as the parlance of the time held it, 'wage slaves'. They wanted the independence that only landholding could provide (see Chapter 21 in this volume). Garrison Frazier, an emancipated slave, put it best when he said, 'the way we can best take care of ourselves is to have land, and turn it and till it by our own labour' (Smith, 1996: 28). In other words, in the absence of land, they preferred work arrangements that gave them the maximum possible autonomy. Black freedmen from New Orleans, Louisiana, drew up a manifesto wherein they protested and denounced the attempts of the former slaveholders to 'transform the boon of liberty into a disguised bondage' by unfair labour contracts that restricted the workers' right to move or debt peonage whereby employers advanced food and seeds at inflated prices that drove workers into assuming debts that could never be repaid (Smith, 1996: 68). In the face of concerted and global working-class black resistance, the former plantation owners in the American South, the newly emerging plantation owners in colonial Africa, and the newly minted industrial classes in the Global North devised a range of 'applied philanthropic' and 'reform' strategies to deal with what they uncharitably called the 'Negro Problem'.

The institutional response to black workers' preference for self-provisioning and independence over wage labour and submission to a boss was the 'Negro Industrial and Agricultural College'. Booker T Washington, who graduated from one such institution (Hampton Institute) and went on to found another (Tuskegee Institute), described these schools as educating blacks for 'humble service – service of the hand, service of the head, and service of the heart' (Washington, 1903: 497). Wealthy industrialists, aware of the fact that the American South stood in a colonial relation to both the northern American states and the Global North, because it supplied raw materials and cheap labour, took a keen interest in these schools – sitting on their boards of directors and providing generous financial support. When Andrew Carnegie visited Tuskegee Institute on the occasion of its 25th anniversary celebration, it was noted that his interest 'was that of a man who looks after his investment' (Park, 1906: 351). Speaking before the Armstrong Institute of New York on the topic 'The American Negro vs the future of the American Republic', Carnegie asked the audience: 'Do you ever stop to think what Great Britain would give for those 9 000 000 Negroes to work the vast territories of South Africa? Why, without the Negro the world would have very little cotton, and the Southern states would be a poverty-stricken nation' (Anon, 1906: 1).

The Negro Industrial College linked the colonial oppression of Africans in America and Africans on the Continent by providing the infrastructure and workers through which 'intelligent Negro labour from America' (that is, workers who had already been disciplined to meet the demands of world industry and commerce) would carry out the work of 'applied philanthropy' on the Continent (Anon, 1903: 5). Applied philanthropy in this case was 'teaching the natives to grow cotton' (Robinson, 1906: 355). Park and Washington organised a conference in 1912, 'The International Conference on the Negro', which brought together colonial officials, missionaries, industrial elites, academics and representatives from 18 foreign countries to discuss applied philanthropy on the Negro Problem and to develop strategies whereby industrial education could be diffused to 'all parts of the world in which the Negroes constitute any large portion' (Park, 1912: 117).

Industrial schools also led Washington and Park to speculate about what implications this new political ordering of the world potentially had for thinking about 'race' and 'culture' as social forces in a more 'abstract' or, what we might think of as, 'academic' sense. Park and Washington were aware of how the work of Franz Boas had revolutionised the emerging 'sciences of man'. In *The Story of the Negro*, a product of their many years of collaboration, Park and Washington hypothesised as to how the social forces working to 'bind the American Negro to the African Negro' might best be understood (Washington, 1909: 31). Their belief in the existence of a 'racial tie' connecting people in Africa to the diaspora lent powerful institutional support to the ideas, first developed by independent scholars like George Washington Williams (*History of the Negro Race* [1882]) and Edward Wilmot Blyden (*Christianity, Islam, and the Negro Race* [1887]), that AADS constituted an autonomous field of inquiry. It also served, however, to deradicalise these ideas. Blyden and Williams had been much more critical of racism and imperialism than Washington and Park ultimately were. Their analysis of the ties uniting Africans at home and in the diaspora was also far more rigorous. For example, in a 1919 essay, 'The conflict and fusion of cultures with special reference to the Negro', which appeared (by no accident) in *The Journal of Negro History*, Park speculated as to how much tradition enslaved Africans brought to America, what elements persisted and how they shaped African-American culture. In contrast to Du Bois, who believed that a considerable fund of African tradition and cultural practices survived the middle passage, Park and Washington believed that 'the amount of African tradition which the Negro brought to the United States was very small' (Park, 1919: 116). Park concluded, on the basis of very thin evidence, that nothing had survived the middle passage save the 'Negro temperament' — a quasi-biological construct that located certain 'racial traits' like sensuality, humour, passion, and loyalty in Africans' ancestral nature. Du Bois, on the other hand, spent a career searching for the social mechanisms that connected people of African descent and produced work like *Black Folk Then and Now: An Essay in the History and Sociology of the Negro Race* (1939) and *The Gift of Black Folk* (1924), which examined phenomena like revolutionary action, folklore, political organisation and religion with the aim of teasing out the commonalities, differences and sources of connection (see Morris, Chapter 21, and Allen, Jones and Regassa, Chapter 23, in this volume).

The first generation of American sociologists were heavily involved in 'applied philanthropy' on the 'Negro Problem'. Booker T Washington enthusiastically endorsed the Southern Sociological Congress and delivered an address, 'The Southern Sociological Congress as a factor for social welfare', at the 1914 annual meeting. Robert Ezra Park (who later went on to found the famed 'Chicago School' of sociology) also endorsed the congress and its work. Because the Southern Sociological Congress explicitly named 'solving the race question' as one of its chief aims, several sections of the meeting were always devoted to presenting research on the 'Negro Problem'. Papers were delivered on subjects like 'Negro crime', 'Negro home life and standards of living', 'Infectious disease in the Negro community', 'Industrial schools in Africa', and 'The Negro and the New South' (McCulloch, 1914: 9). These sections of the congress always drew the largest number of delegates and the biggest audiences — sometimes up to 400 people attended a single talk.

The Southern Sociological Congress was strictly interested in applied work for the purpose of better and more efficient administration. The papers that were presented at the various meetings were always overflowing with empirical data of various sorts — statistics on birth rates, death rates, crime, disease and employment were always on offer. However, researchers also tried to collect data that could potentially shed more nuanced light on the texture of their informants' day-to-day lives. Thus, papers on folklore, song, artistic practices and religion were not uncommon. Although these researchers had no interest in what Du Bois and Park would later call 'putting science into sociology' — by developing reliable methods of observation and measurement and some objective means of systematising and arranging data — nevertheless, their applied work yielded the data without which the 'systematisers' (that is, theoretical sociologists) would have had nothing to arrange.

The fact that this data consisted chiefly of facts about the lives of people of African descent around the world would eventually pose a unique set of contradictions for the pioneers of 'scientific' sociology. It would pose parallel problems for the first generation of scholars who charged themselves with the task of studying, writing and analysing the histories, cultures and lives of people in Africa and the diaspora, who entered a terrain whose terms had been set by the self-proclaimed 'theoretical' sociologists.

'The story of the Negro': From applied philanthropy to an empiricist epistemology

Booker T Washington and W.E.B. Du Bois disagreed on many things – industrial education chief among them. Du Bois decried industrial education as indicative of Washington's acceptance of 'the alleged inferiority of the Negro races' (Du Bois, 1989 [1903]: 39). Washington most likely would have vehemently disagreed. He often spoke about how 'proud' he was of 'his race'. 'I had rather be what I am, a member of the Negro race, than to be able to claim membership in any other race', he wrote in *Up from Slavery* (Washington, 1995 [1901]: 19). Indeed, he claimed it was this pride that led him to write (together with Robert Park) *The Story of the Negro*, which 'aimed to sketch the history of the Negro people' (Washington, 1909: 3). Indeed, it would appear, on the surface at least, that Washington and Du Bois shared a belief that racism had made it necessary for blacks to understand 'the life of [their] people in Africa and America to which [they] might point with pride and think about with satisfaction' (Washington, 1909: 5). The same point that Washington made in *The Story of the Negro* was made by Du Bois in *The World and Africa* wherein he called for an 'interpretation of Negro history [to] contradict the theory of the natural and eternal inferiority of black folk' (Du Bois, 1996 [1906]: 117). Both Du Bois and Washington told of their shame at seeing Africa and Africans depicted as savages in schoolbooks. Washington recalled his horror at seeing 'George Washington placed side by side with a naked African, having a ring in his nose and a dagger in his hand' (Washington, 1909: 9). Du Bois had a similar experience, noting that in the geography books that he encountered in school, the most 'uncivilised' and 'bizarre' personages represented Africans, while whites were depicted as kindly and distinguished philanthropists (Du Bois, 2007 [1940]: 49). In addition to feeling that Africans and African Americans deserved an autonomous field of study devoted to challenging these stereotypes, they also agreed that black people in Africa and America had enough self-consciousness to reflect somewhat objectively on their own experience in order to abstract from and transcend what was particular to it.

Park and Washington located the genesis of this self-consciousness in the ending of slavery, which enabled 'the Negro people to think of themselves as having a past and a future separate and distinct from the white race'

(Washington, 1909: 8). A lot of what Park and Washington claimed to know about the culture and traditions of people of African descent on the Continent and in the diaspora stemmed from three sources. First, there were the students enrolled at Tuskegee. In addition to African Americans, there were students from the West Indies, East Africa, Central Africa and southern Africa. In *The Story of the Negro*, Washington recounted how a student of the 'Bushman race' not only spoke up to correct some misinformation that was being disseminated in a geography lesson, but also enthralled his fellow students with pictures and artifacts from home. Second, there was research carried out by Tuskegee researchers at home and abroad. Washington noted that much of what was known about African people was 'gathered from reports of missionaries and travelers and from the experiments of Tuskegee students in Togo and other parts of Africa in cotton culture' (Washington, 1906: 550). *The Southern Workman*, the official organ of Hampton Institute, ran a feature on 'The work of primitive peoples', as part of a series on 'primitive' art that aimed at creating respect for the creative genius of Africans by demonstrating that the household utensils and implements of warfare had 'real artistic merit' (Anon, 1911: 199). *The Coloured American Magazine* carried a half-page picture of Togo expedition leader John Robinson outfitted in 'the royal robe of a West African king' and surrounded by 'the interesting and beautiful design of the fabric woven by native weavers' (Robinson, 1906: 356).

Third, there were the institutions developed by Washington to provide practical forms of assistance to defined segments of the African-American community. Park often said that his work at Tuskegee allowed him to get close to black people and gather data under conditions of proximity that exceeded his wildest dreams. When he was sent by Washington to inspect rural schools, he got a sense of life in rural communities. When Washington hosted the Negro Farmers Conference, which brought together farmers from all over the South to talk about their affairs, he learnt still more about the 'human aspects of Negro life' delivered in the 'eloquent language of the people themselves' (Park, 1941: 43). At these gatherings, Park heard hymns sung and folktales told that were original creations. Washington also founded a Negro Business League, which yielded information about and contact with the lives of middle-class African Americans. A mountain of statistics was gathered and disseminated every year as part of Tuskegee's *Negro Year Book*.

All of this holds relevance for thinking about Mamdani's critique of the disjuncture between applied and theoretical knowledges. Since Washington was 'essentially pragmatic' and thus 'allergic to theories of any kind', he did not concern himself, as Du Bois and Park did, with thinking through the implications of the fact that although 'applied knowledge' was held to be subordinate to 'theoretical abstraction', abstract concepts were not necessarily antecedent to research. In other words, there is a continuous and dynamic interplay between empirical observation and abstract conceptualisation that poses questions of the 'chicken-and-egg' variety. 'Applied philanthropy' supplied the raw material upon which sociologists' empiricist methodologies were built. Empiricism, in turn, was the foundation for conceptual abstraction, theorisation, generalisation and, ultimately, universalisation. Facts were the foundation of everything. As Park explained, it was imperative that scientific sociologists be able to 'describe the kinds of facts that sociology must look for to answer the questions that sociology asks' (Park, 1921a: 170).

From empiricism to science: The Negro Problem and the 'logical character' of facts

One of the cardinal tenets of scientific sociology is that, without a conceptual apparatus, useful observation is impossible. What the researcher 'sees' is dependent upon the concepts she employs. However, abstract concepts are also the by-products of research. Park, for example, argued that sociology 'explained' – that is, theorised – the 'concrete records of human nature and experience' (Park, 1921b: 21). He included ethnology, folklore, applied philanthropy, social surveys and government commissions under the general heading of these 'concrete records'. As late as 1921, Park was still concerned that sociology had not become properly scientific and he located the problem in the data that provided the building blocks for concept formation. Du Bois had made a similar point many years prior, in 1904, when he said that sociologists were still 'groping after a science' because they had no way to make theoretical sense of the tremendous mass of accumulated material – he called it a 'tangled mass of facts' – that had been produced from applied philanthropy (Du Bois, 1978: 53). Thus, Du Bois called for 'verifiable facts' which he defined as facts that were ascertained by observation and measurement (Du Bois, 1978: 54). Park made a similar argument when he said that the most important factor separating science from philanthropy lay in the '*logical character of facts*' that provided the foundation for the two endeavours (Park, 1921c: 406).

In strictly applied work, like that which was done on the 'Negro Problem', investigation wasn't guided by theory. Rather, practical political aims drove what problems were deemed worthy of investigation and what aspects of the problem drove data collection. That data, however, was the raw material for concept formation – an essential part of the process of theoretical abstraction. This was a problem for Park. He tried to get around it by a somewhat convoluted discussion about the 'logical character' of facts. In actuality, however, he didn't interrogate the character of the facts at all. Whereas Du Bois was highly critical of the ways in which sociological investigation as 'applied philanthropy' had produced distorted facts about black people at every turn, Park asserted that facts could be given a different 'logical character' if the investigator adopted a different stance. In other words, the investigator should change his orientation from collecting information 'merely for the purpose of determining what to do in a given case' and, instead, collect his facts with the aim of 'checking social theories' (Park, 1921a: 170). Park termed the former 'investigation' and the latter 'research' and placed the burden of change not so much on the arena in which facts were collected or the political imperatives that drove research, but rather on the investigator who would overcome these problems by approaching the data from the angle of hypothesis testing. In this way, theoretical sociology would reorient itself away from 'social problems' (the main arena for applied work) in favour of a focus on 'social processes' about which general theories could be promulgated and universal proclamations made.

Because the attitude of the researcher made the difference for Park, he could readily admit that Booker T Washington was the teacher from whom he learnt the most and that Tuskegee was the place where he gained access to the data that piqued his interest in social processes, which he later deemed the 'central problems' around which theoretical sociology should be oriented without worrying so much about the circumstances that made data collection possible. For example, he maintained that anyone wishing to understand the 'acculturation process' would do well to examine African-American history, because no other race had been in such a prolonged and close relationship with Europeans while still retaining their 'racial identity' (Park, 1919: 115). It was in the context of seeking to understand African Americans as a rural folk culture that he developed ideas as to the 'value of a human document as datum', which could bring the 'object of observation closer to the observer' (Park, 1967: 27). Anything could be a human document – casual remarks, conversations, comments and surveys – and Park insisted he could generalise from whatever aspects of the human document struck his fancy.

Two decades before, in 1898, Du Bois had suggested something similar, although he did so much more boldly, directly and creatively. Du Bois had suggested that sociology could become 'scientific' – that is, develop natural laws and generalisations, through careful study of the forces, conditions and contradictions of African Americans as they struggled to realise their 'group ideals' (Du Bois, 1898: 2; also see Morris, Chapter 21, in this volume). Du Bois did not advocate simply a change in the orientation of the researcher, but rather a wholly new approach that started simply, yet radically: 'Let us approach the question of the scientific study of a great race with open-mindedness and simple-hearted desire for truth' (Du Bois, 1978: 56). The new base assumptions were that peoples of African descent were members of the great human family; that they were capable of advancement and development; that 'race mixture' did not produce degenerate species; that it was possible for people in Africa and the diaspora to become leaders, rather than followers, in the march of civilisation.

Hence, both Park and Du Bois agreed that sociology should turn from advocacy to research; should move from speculation to hypothesis testing; should focus less on metaphysics and more on concrete evidence; and should be moving towards developing conceptual and theoretical abstractions. They also shared an awareness that the 'Negro Problem' – in all its particularity – had left its mark on the concepts and frames of reference that were the forerunners of universalisation. The two men were destined to part ways, however. Park never really engaged with the fact that the processes of abstraction, concept formation and theoretical generalisation that were so central to sociology becoming a science were built on a foundation that his contemporary, Du Bois, had described as 'uncritical' – in the selection and weighting of evidence; in the point of view from which problems were studied; and in its acceptance of 'distinct bias in the minds of so many writers' (Du Bois, 1898: 13). While acknowledging that 'there exists today no sufficient material of proven reliability upon which any scientist can base definite and final conclusions', Du Bois did aver that a start (albeit an insufficient one) had been made with the material gathered as part of the colonial encounter (Du Bois, 1898: 15). He notes:

> The material at hand for historical research is rich and abundant. There are colonial statutes and records, the partially accessible archives of Great Britain, France, and Spain, the collections of historical societies, the vast number of executive and congressional reports and documents, … the reports of institutions and societies (Du Bois, 1898: 18).

Park and Du Bois differed profoundly, however, in the way in which they imagined how the previous era of reform would be brought into the scientific enterprise. Du Bois never imagined that the political and economic conditions that led to the collection of these particular pieces of data in these particular ways would ever be buried or forgotten when sociology (or any other discipline) finally found an institutional home in the university. And, as will be discussed in the final section, because Du Bois was explicit about both the possibilities and limitations that its roots in the 'Negro Problem' had created for sociology, he pioneered a way of thinking about African and African diaspora studies that connected AADS to sociology, without reifying the 'universal–particular' or 'discipline–area studies' conceptual divide.

Conclusion: From 'The Negro problems' to 'The future of world democracy'

The basic premise of *The Story of the Negro* is that histories are not only separate, but they are also isomorphic with racial/ethnic/national categories.

> The Negro boy or girl should have an opportunity to learn something in school about his own race. The Negro boy should study Negro history just as the Japanese boy studies Japanese history and the German boy studies German history (Washington, 1909: 17).

Du Bois, in contrast, offered a relational perspective or 'connected histories' approach that didn't deny that groups travelled along different paths but also looked for instances of inter-penetration and mutual dependence. In 1915, Du Bois published *The Negro*. In this book he set out to think about the future relation of people from Africa and the diaspora to the rest of the world (Du Bois, 1915). Although he would appear, in this, to share certain conceptual affinities with Park and Washington, he is offering something that exceeds their vision. The text is his inaugural attempt to write from the perspective of connected histories, in two senses of the term. On the one hand, he is challenging the veracity of the ontology of race offered by Park and Washington in *The Story of the Negro*. There is, he states, no scientific criterion by which to divide races. Therefore, there could be no centralising thought or unified opinion that could be said to express the culture or ethos of a people. Second, he started to think and see the world through the prism of pan-Africanism, which focuses on the ties connecting workers across space and time. Crucially, he notes that most people in the world share the broad designation of 'people of colour' (he used the phrase 'coloured men'); and, therefore, a belief in the world's efficacy and promise of the world's people – a belief in humanity – was tantamount to a belief in their active agency to make and change history. Du Bois developed these ideas further in *Black Folk Then and Now*, published in 1939. *The Saturday Review* called the book an 'effective assault on the parochialism of historic and sociological writing' and praised it for having demonstrated that 'all human progress was bound up with the destiny of the Negro' (Seligman, 1939: 19). A marked difference between *Black Folk Then and Now* and *The Negro* stems from Du Bois' use of historical materialism as a method of analysis. Marxism enabled him to engage sociology and AADS in the manner he had first imagined at the beginning of his career in essays like 'The Atlanta Conferences' and 'The study of Negro problems'. Since the 1939 text was an expanded and revised version of the 1915 text, a number of chapters share the same name. However, there is a crucial difference in the penultimate chapter. In *The Negro*, the book's closing chapter was entitled 'The Negro problems'. In *Black Folk Then and Now*, the final chapter was renamed 'The future of world democracy'. Through examining the problems of democracy, he necessarily has to think through problems like world-wide industrial dislocation, as well as deal critically with the failure of socialists and communists to fully understand the problems facing labourers in Asia, Africa, South America and the West Indies. The universalising prescriptions of Karl Marx, he pointed out, were being challenged by the realities of the 'relations of white Europe to darker Asia and darkest Africa' (Du Bois, 1939: 382).

Du Bois thus challenged the ways in which sociology's origin in 'applied philanthropy' and the 'Negro Problem' overdetermined not only the place of African and African diaspora peoples within sociological study, but also conceptually positioned them as incapable of achieving the status of universality. The mutual imbrication of sociology, AADS, and 'Negro Problem' social science placed a set of constraints on the space that AADS as 'area studies' could occupy. The 'division of labour' that currently governs the separation between the disciplines and area studies is a phenomenon, therefore, that must be approached historically; with careful attention being paid to exploring how unique disciplinary histories give rise to historically specific outcomes. Washington, Park and Du Bois were all implicated in this history and came out of it holding a different view of whether, and to what extent, AADS was something particular that one ultimately needed to transcend in order to achieve universality. Du Bois, although he never wavered in his belief in the epistemological priority of theoretical abstraction and the value of searching for and then generalising about the limits of change in human action, recognised that the 'science of human action' (as sociology came to be called) held too limited a view of who it included in the category 'human'. As a corrective, he offered a way of approaching black political and social life that not only studied its various manifestations seriously, but also assumed that they were capable of providing the bases for making unverbalisable claims.

References

Anon (1903) Opposition to industrial education, *The Southern Workman*, **32**(1): 5.
Anon (1906) The way of the world: Carnegie testifies, *The Coloured American Magazine*, **10**(1): 1.
Anon (1911) The work of primitive peoples, *The Southern Workman*, **XL**(4): 199.
Du Bois, WEB (1898) The study of Negro problems, *The Annals of the American Academy of Political and Social Science*, **11**: 13–18.

Du Bois, WEB (1915) *The Negro*. New York: Henry Holt.

Du Bois, WEB (1924) *The Gift of Black Folk: The Negroes in the making of America*. Boston, MA: The Stratford Company.

Du Bois, WEB (1939) *Black Folk Then and Now: An essay in the history and sociology of the Negro race*. New York: Henry Holt.

Du Bois, WEB (1978) The Atlanta Conferences, *Voice of the Negro*, March 1904, pp. 85–89. Reprinted in DS Green and ED Driver (eds) (1978) *W.E.B. Du Bois: On sociology and the black community*. Chicago, IL: University of Chicago Press, p. 53.

Du Bois, WEB (1989) [1903] *The Souls of Black Folk*. New York: Penguin.

Du Bois, WEB (1996) [1906] *The World and Africa*. New York: International Publishers.

Du Bois, WEB (2007) [1940] *Dusk of Dawn: An essay towards an autobiography of a race concept*. Oxford: Oxford University Press.

Harland, LR and Smock, RW (eds) (1982) *The Booker T Washington Papers*. Chicago, IL: University of Illinois Press, pp. 550–51.

Mamdani, M (n.d.) Is African Studies at UCT a new home for Bantu Education? Available at: www.http//ccs.ukzn.ac.za/files/mamdani.pdf (accessed August 2018).

McCulloch, JE (1912) The call of the New South. Address delivered at the Southern Sociological Congress, Nashville, Tennessee.

McCulloch, JE (1914) Battling for social betterment. Address delivered at the Southern Sociological Congress, Nashville, Tennessee.

Park, RE (1906) Tuskegee and its mission, *The Coloured American Magazine*, **14**(5): 351.

Park, RE (1912) Tuskegee International Conference on the Negro, *The Journal of Race Development*, **3**(1): 117.

Park, RE (1919) The conflict and fusion of cultures with special reference to the Negro, *The Journal of Negro History*, **4**(2): 115–16.

Park, RE (1921a) Sociology and the social sciences: The group concept and social research, *The American Journal of Sociology*, **27**(2): 170.

Park, RE (1921b) Sociology and the social sciences: The social organism and the collective mind, *The American Journal of Sociology*, **27**(1): 21.

Park, RE (1921c) Sociology and the social sciences, *The American Journal of Sociology*, **26**(4): 406.

Park, RE (1941) Methods of teaching: Impressions and a verdict, *Social Forces*, **20**(1): 43.

Park, RE (1967) *On Social Control and Collective Behaviour: Selected papers*, Chicago, IL: University of Chicago Press.

Robinson, JW (1906) A Tuskegee graduate in West Africa, *The Coloured American Magazine*, **10**(5): 355–56.

Seligman, HJ (1939) Negro destinies, *The Saturday Review*, 20 July, p. 19.

Smith, JD (1996) *Black Voices from Reconstruction, 1865–1877*. Brookfield, CT: The Millbrook Press.

Washington, BT (1903) Some charges against the Negro race, *The Southern Workman*, **32**(10): 497.

Washington, BT (1906) Industrial education in Africa, *The Independent*, 15 March. Reprinted in LR Harland and RW Smock (eds) (1982) *The Booker T Washington Papers*. Chicago, IL: University of Illinois Press, pp. 550–51.

Washington, BT (1909) *The Story of the Negro*. New York: Doubleday Page & Co.

Washington, BT (1995) [1901] *Up from Slavery*. New York: Dover Publications.

Chapter 21
The Atlanta School of Sociology

Aldon Morris

Introduction

Material resources are required to maintain oppression. To ensure domination, the oppressed are usually denied all but basic resources necessary for subsistence. Because systemic oppression is a contentious risky business, it requires brute power backed by guns, violence, money and surveillance. When faced with overwhelming means of violence and starvation, the oppressed find themselves trapped in a state of relative powerlessness.

Ideological resources are also required to maintain oppression. Indeed, ignorance imposed on the dominated constitutes a critical link in the chain of oppression. History has proven that while violence and material deprivation are necessary conditions for maintaining systems of human domination, they are not sufficient. The oppressed often revolt even though before them lies the open grave. Oppressors, therefore, seek to control the ideas of the dominated to ensure mental chains as crippling as physical shackles bind them. Otherwise, it is difficult to oppress people when they possess mental resources enabling critical analysis of the sources of their degradation (Morris and Braine, 2001). Thus, attitudes supporting submission are required among the subordinated to sustain oppression. Rulers need subordinates to adjust to oppression by embracing a world-view that teaches them that their unfortunate circumstances are natural and inevitable. In this mental fog, the oppressed tend to view their wretchedness as a reality outside their control, as if willed by God or the devil. Attitudes of obedience lead oppressed groups to succumb to cultures of submission that produce resignation. Indeed, passivity is the handmaiden of oppression.

This chapter has several goals organised around four sections. The first section discusses the role that education plays in the domination and liberation of oppressed people. The second explores the nature of the education used to oppress African Americans during the slavery and Jim Crow regimes. The third section analyses the Du Bois Atlanta School of Sociology, demonstrating how it provided an education of liberation, which enabled African Americans to discover and utilise their agency to overcome white domination. Finally, the chapter concludes with the importance of liberation education for contemporary freedom struggles.

Liberation education versus mis-education

Liberation education is the enemy of passivity. For freedom to become possible, overcoming passivism is essential. Paraphrasing Karl Marx, submissive attitudes of all dead generations of the oppressed weigh like a nightmare on the brains of those living under conditions of oppression. As Paulo Freire (1970) has argued, to become free, the oppressed have to develop an indigenous pedagogy that is ideologically enlightening. Thus, during bondage, slaveholders developed a pedagogy of rulers, which stipulated that slaves were not to learn to read, write or think for themselves. The masters understood that an enlightened education would enable slaves to experience a mental liberation despite the physical chains that bound them. Harriet Tubman, the great leader of the American Underground Railroad, concluded she could have freed far more slaves if only they had realised that they were slaves.

Indeed, an education that liberates is a necessary tool enabling the oppressed to free themselves. However, not all education liberates. Education for the dominated fashioned by oppressors serves as the opiate of the masses because it teaches obedience to rulers. This is the education oppressors champion as appropriate and fitting for the oppressed. The pioneer of African-American history, Carter G Woodson, labelled this education as mis-education:

> If you can control a man's thinking you do not have to worry about his action. When you determine what a man shall think you do not have to concern yourself about what he will do. If you make a man feel that he is inferior, you do not have to compel him to accept an inferior status, for he will seek it himself. If you make a man think that he is justly an outcast, you do not have to order him to the back door. He will go without being told; and if there is no back door, his very nature will demand one (Woodson, 1933: 13).

Liberation education, on the other hand, causes the oppressed to become bad-tempered, harbouring attitudes of disobedience. Oppressors stringently oppose liberation education. Throughout American slavery and the Jim Crow period, which was a regime that required legally imposed racial segregation backed by state violence, white oppressors struggled endlessly to prevent the oppressed from becoming educated. During slavery, slave states implemented harsh legal penalties against slaves learning to read or write. Thus, in North Carolina, Jay notes:

> [T]o teach a slave to read or write, or sell or give him any book [Bible

not excepted] or pamphlet, is punished with thirty-nine lashes, or imprisonment, if the offender be a free negro; but if a white, then with a fine of $200. The reason for this law, ... is that teaching slaves to read and write tends to dissatisfaction in their minds, and to produce insurrection and rebellion. (Jay, 1840: 136).

Prohibition against educating black people was evident during the oppressive Jim Crow regime. Tonea Stewart, an American actress and university professor, related a tragic event that fully captures the dangers blacks encountered when they sought to educate themselves during the Jim Crow regime:

> When I was a little girl about five or six years old, I used to sit on the front porch ... in the Mississippi Delta. I listened to my Papa Dallas. He was blind and had these ugly scars around his eyes. One day, I asked Papa Dallas what happened to his eyes. Well Daughter, he answered, when I was mighty young, just about your age, I used to steal away under a big oak tree and I tried to learn my alphabets so that I could learn to read my Bible. But one day the overseer caught me and he drug me out on the plantation and he called out for all the field hands. And he turned to em and said, Let this be a lesson to all of you darkies. You ain't got no right to learn to read! And then daughter, he whooped me, and he whooped me, and he whooped me. And daughter, as if that wasn't enough, he turned around and he burned my eyes out! (Franklin, 2007: 179).

Therefore, oppressors understood that an educated captive is a dangerous phenomenon threatening the entire enterprise of domination.

By the turn of the 20th century, the American federal government mandated that all children, irrespective of race, had to attend school to acquire an education. White Southerners responded by creating special schools for blacks: the Jim Crow segregated schools (Anderson, 1988). Black segregated schools contained poor facilities, inadequate intellectual materials, including books, and poorly paid, less educated teachers (see chapters 22 and 23 in this volume). Black students in segregated schools tended to be extremely poor. Because of poverty, many of them attained little formal education because at young ages they dropped out of school to work in the fields to help their families survive. Moreover, when it was possible for black students to attend school, they received a white supremacy education that required them to embrace their own oppression. Routinely they saluted federal and state flags, and internalised messages stressing the heroism of southern white Civil War heroes who fought to maintain slavery. In fact, black students received an education consistent with submission to white rule; lessons of black inferiority abounded, which seeped into the impressionable minds of young, black students as they read torn books, handed down from white students, and attended dilapidated schools that contrasted sharply with the portly structures where white children received their education.

To be sure, at young ages, blacks learnt they were inferior because the enforcement of the ideology of black inferiority was crucial to white rule. Martin Luther King Jr explained how this ideology justified and sustained racial inequality:

> Black people have been kept in oppression and deprivation by a poisonous fog of lies… The twisted logic ran, if the black man was inferior he was not oppressed – his place in society was appropriate to his meager talent and intellect. The keystone in the arch of oppression was the myth of inferiority (King, 1968).

A different type of education was required if blacks were to break free of Jim Crow oppression. A radical insurgent education was necessary for the mental liberation of black people. Such an education would need to teach African Americans their actual history during slavery and Jim Crow. It would instil self-confidence and disprove the black inferiority thesis. Moreover, liberation education would promote critical thinking and, through examples, teach black people that they were fully capable of digesting big ideas and producing great intellectual achievements. The teachers of this education would need to be highly skilled black scholars who served as role models embodying intellectual excellence. Additionally, substantial resources from the oppressed community would be essential to fuel this liberation education, because, as the title of Audre Lorde's (1984) piece on racism and homophobia reveals, 'The master's tools will never dismantle the master's house'.

Social context: The Atlanta School of Sociology

W.E.B. Du Bois' Atlanta School of Sociology, founded in the late 19th century in a black school at Atlanta University, provides a foundational example of how liberation education took root among the oppressed. This exemplar demonstrated that even during the darkest years of domination, oppressed people possessed the ingenuity and agency to generate conditions for their own mental liberation. An examination of the context out of which Du Bois' insurgent School of Sociology emerged is crucial to understanding the radical nature of this innovative educational enterprise. The American Civil War wrecked the empires of the southern white aristocracy. Two-and-a-half centuries of unpaid, black, slave labour enabled slave-based empires to flourish as they bestowed economic and symbolic riches upon white plantation owners. This economy thrived because it relied on an enslaved people who, through force, constituted a relatively passive and illiterate labour force. It needs emphasising that force is necessary to guarantee domination because oppressed people are seldom subdued completely, despite ideological and mental violence, as well as physical coercion. Indeed, American slavery endured for over two centuries because, as Aptheker (1974: 67) argued, 'Behind the owner, and his personal agents, stood an elaborate and complex system of military control ... practically all adult white men were liable for patrol service'.

Nevertheless, the former slave owners desperately needed free black labour to restore their agriculturally based aristocracy that collapsed with the fall of the Confederacy. The aristocracy faced a thorny question: how were they to obtain next-to-free black labour given that ex-slaves were now free? This was a daunting situation, given that blacks now had access to formal schooling, which increased the possibility of black mental liberation? In 1896, in the case of *Plessy v. Ferguson*, 163 U.S. 537 (1896), the US Supreme Court handed the plantation owners and white supremacy a wonderful gift: it ruled that segregated facilities were constitutional so long as they were separate but equal. As a result, racially segregated accommodations came into being, including schools that would be separate and unequivocally unequal. The dethroned southern aristocracy immediately realised that through such an educational arrangement, the prospects of rebuilding their empire increased exponentially.

To reiterate, dominant whites deliberately constructed inferior, segregated black schools. While white schools produced generations of whites with intellectual skills to rule over blacks, Negro schools taught blacks to be subservient by supplying them with intellectual habits conducive to serving white masters. This curriculum triumphed because salaries for teachers and administrators, as well as educational resources, rested with state budgets controlled by white rulers. Black educators had little choice but to obey the dictates of white supremacy and prepare black youth to yield to the demands of white supremacy, which required them to learn manual labour skills and prevented them from acquiring those skills conducive to dismantling the master's house.

There was a yearning among black people for ex-slaves to receive higher education. These realities were especially apparent at the collegiate level. Few black colleges and universities existed during the Jim Crow period, because whites considered blacks to be inferior and unfit for higher education. Most of these institutions of higher learning were poorly equipped (Du Bois, 1903). The majority did not have graduate programmes and they specialised in industrial education because white rulers sought a passive industrially skilled labour force to rebuild their fiefdoms after the overthrow of slavery (see Chapter 23 in this volume). A liberal arts education was not appropriate for producing submissive peasants who were to mindlessly construct white empires. Thus, at the turn of the century, African Americans had few opportunities to acquire a broad education stressing citizenship and political enfranchisement. As a result, white scholars working in elite white universities developed scientific racism declaring blacks inferior while promulgating a black education that reinforced doctrines of black inferiority.

White rulers were not the only barrier for ex-slaves desiring a liberal arts education and the establishment of universities equipped to provide it. A central issue emerged within the black community regarding the type of education that would lead to full citizenship and social equality. This issue became paramount when the Reconstruction period failed in the closing decades of the 19th century and the Jim Crow regime came into force, which determined black life chances and overall well-being throughout the 20th century. The debate centred on whether an industrial or a liberal arts education would provide the solution or whether a combination of both was the best route to black liberation. This debate was decisive for both whites and blacks, especially Southerners. White plantation owners were clear regarding their need for docile cheap workers across race lines, while the white working class, for the first time, feared direct competition from recently freed black people. As Du Bois (1935) demonstrated, the white aristocracy concocted a winning strategy to realise their interests: divide the black and white working classes by compensating white workers with slightly better wages and social status, while paying black workers wages that were barely more than free slave labour and conferring upon them a slave-like status. In other words, according to Du Bois, the planters enabled white workers to enjoy a 'psychological wage' rooted in the idea that, no matter their economic degradation, they were better than Niggers!

For black people, this white compromise ensured that once again their fate was to endure brutal oppression. Besides the lynch rope, intimidation by mob violence, economic exploitation and political disenfranchisement, black people were to remain under a mental control inconsistent with the ethos of freedom they embraced while fighting in the Civil War to overthrow slavery. Thus, for white planters, it was proper that black people receive an education that generated docility rooted in deep feelings of inferiority. Thus, black people desiring a liberal arts education were confronted by the wrath of both the white aristocracy and insecure white workers drenched in racial prejudice.

Rising as an accommodating leader in 1995, Booker T Washington charted a course to black liberation that fully embraced industrial training as the only viable avenue to black liberation. He argued that economic independence was the key to eventual social equality. To reach this goal, black people needed to learn skills associated with manual labour, enabling them to become economically independent by acquiring property, growing their own food and establishing independent black businesses. Moreover, Washington correctly argued that white elites would embrace this educational strategy because it would produce a docile work force with skills needed to restore their empires. Following Washington's lead, they agreed that such an education would postpone indefinitely black demands for social equality and the agitation driving such aspirations. This plan tacitly accepted the black inferiority thesis.

Highly educated blacks steeped in the liberal arts agreed with the goal of attaining black economic independence and the need for industrial education to achieve it. However, they sharply disagreed that industrial education was the *only* route to liberation. Additionally, these radicals argued vociferously against any strategy downplaying black enfranchisement and full social equality. Thus, they rejected the black inferiority thesis and replaced it with demands for full civil rights based on the argument that their Creator endowed them with all the attributes possessed by human beings.

Washington dismissed as ineffective any strategy outside industrial education to achieve black liberation and castigated those who advocated other strategies, claiming that they were

> another class of coloured people who make a business of keeping the troubles, the wrongs, and the hardships of the Negro race before the public. Having learned that they are able to make a living out of their troubles, they have grown into the settled habit of advertising their wrongs – partly because they want sympathy and partly because it pays. Some of these people do not want the Negro to lose his grievances, because they do not want to lose their jobs (Washington, 1901: 118).

Washington's personal rebuke and argument that neither empowerment nor social equality could be gained through a liberal arts education angered and energised radical blacks. Nevertheless, they faced the intractable problem of Washington's power, which was buttressed by support and sponsorship from powerful whites and admiring blacks, who embraced his unprecedented power as the premier black leader. Because of his accommodating economic and political stances, white elites installed Washington as the gatekeeper who determined which black institutions received funding and which blacks were hired, especially in powerful positions. Thus, Washington not only rebuked black 'agitators' but he also blocked their endeavours – including the availability of a liberal arts education – by directing funds to institutions promoting industrial education and to 'Bookerites' who propagated Washington's principles.

Despite Washington's power, black radicals launched a targeted attack on his polices and educational philosophy. In his 1903 ground-breaking book, *The Souls of Black Folk*, Du Bois spearheaded the opposition, arguing that if black people were to be liberated they would need the leadership of black intellectuals with big ideas and ideals born of a liberal arts training. While praising Washington's efforts to achieve economic independence through industrial education, Du Bois sent out a clarion call for black people to reject Washington's tacit embrace of black inferiority and his counsel that blacks postpone struggles to achieve political and social rights. The radicals put organisational and political muscle behind their attack when, in 1905, they formed the Niagara Movement to pursue black civil rights. Even though the power of the intellectuals was minuscule compared to Washington's, they issued a challenge: the black inferiority thesis was false and could not withstand evidence to the contrary derived from scholars steeped in liberation education.

Atlanta School of Sociology

At the turn of the 20th century, an educational enterprise that pursued a radically different education from that used to oppress blacks emerged on the periphery of elite white academies. Developed in a black university embedded in a large, urban black community, the insurgent Atlanta School of Sociology was born. It persevered because of its anchor in and support from Atlanta's black community (Morris, 2015). Its professors and researchers were overwhelmingly black. Poorly compensated relative to white professors, Atlanta University's professors had few resources to conduct and publish research. Underfunded by the university because of the unavailability of adequate resources, its graduate students struggled to survive materially and intellectually given the meagre resources available for their training and subsistence.

The Atlanta School relied heavily on volunteer intellectual labour, largely provided by black professors, undergraduate and graduate students, alumni and community leaders, including school teachers and clergymen. Therefore, the researchers and scholars of this black intellectual school of thought differed sharply from its elite white counterparts, who relied on well-paid professors and elite-trained graduate students. Moreover, research funds from rich foundations and philanthropists were readily available to scholars at the prestigious white universities, such as the University of Chicago, that counted on the rich Rockefeller Foundation to replenish its coffers. White scholars received lavish funds to conduct research and accessed prestigious presses to publish it. They taught few courses, thus leaving adequate time for research and writing. Unlike the role Booker T Washington played, no white elites stood in their way, blocking funds needed to produce their scholarship. In the white mainstream, a liberal arts education, rather than industrial education, was the norm and it justified white supremacy and scientific racism.

Yet, as I will demonstrate, an intellectually independent Atlanta School of Sociology emerged at the turn of the 20th century, which challenged white supremacy and refuted the core intellectual pillars on which scientific racism stood. How such an intellectual enterprise could develop in the womb of Southern, Jim Crow racism is a wondrous mystery. The very possibility of such an enterprise seemed unthinkable because, on the one side of its development, there was vicious white racism while, on the other, stood a powerful, accommodating black leader.

However, these black professors, student researchers, teachers and clergymen constituted a melded professional and amateur team of researchers who produced innovative, original scholarship that challenged white social science's foundational claims about the nature of race and racism (Morris, 2015; Wright, 2016). They developed a counter social scientific narrative of the causes and consequences of racism, revealing the role of white oppression in relegating blacks to the bottom of the racial hierarchy. As important, they identified and dissected black agency and its role in struggles to seize black liberation. Such efforts required extensive training of researchers on how to conduct fieldwork and participant observation, and construct surveys and ethnographies. They also had to acquire the skills associated with executing tedious research, presenting it in scholarly papers in seminars and conferences, and writing and publishing articles and books to disseminate the intellectual products to scholarly communities and the public.

While the intellectual labour of members of the insurgent Atlanta School received little material compensation, their motivation derived from their devotion to a noble calling. They were convinced that rigorous, objective and bottom-up scholarship would reveal the real causes of the inequality of American blacks and people of colour throughout the black diaspora. To achieve this goal, they were compensated by liberation capital:

> Liberation capital is a form of capital used by oppressed and resource-starved scholars to initiate and sustain the research program of a nonhegemonic scientific school. Liberation capital consists of volunteer or nominally paid labours in research and other scholarly activities that are provided by a self-conscious group of professionals and amateur

intellectual workers for a subaltern school of thought that seeks to challenge the intellectual foundations of oppression... The promise of ultimately reaching the collective goal of group liberation serves as the compensation motivating this cadre of largely unremunerated intellectual workers even when they are faced with professional sanctions for their work (Morris, 2015: 188).

A foundational intellectual principle guided the Atlanta School: accurate scholarship would prove black people were not inferior, thus laying the grounds for black activism and the building of a liberation movement. The Atlanta School's intellectual leader was the Harvard University- and University of Berlin-trained W.E.B. Du Bois, who fully embraced and promoted the guiding principle of the insurgent school. From a young age, Du Bois embodied the principle that black people were not inferior and committed himself to scholarship and activism to dismantle the oppression of black people:

When I entered college in 1885, I was supposed to learn there was a new reason for the degradation of the coloured people that was because they had inferior brains to whites. This I immediately challenged. I knew by experience that my own brains and body were not inferior to the average of my white fellow students. Moreover, I grew suspicious when it became clear that treating Negroes as inferior, whether they were or not, was profitable to the people who hired their labour. I early, therefore, started on a personal life crusade to prove Negro equality and to induce Negroes to demand it (Du Bois, 1958: 1).

Given its guiding principle, the Atlanta School embraced scholarship as an intellectual weapon in the service of emancipation and liberation. In this respect, it differed fundamentally from white schools of thought who portrayed their mission as purely scientific, standing above societal power and group interest.

Another distinctive characteristic of Du Bois' Atlanta School of Sociology was its pioneering of empirical methodologies by using quantitative and qualitative methods to study black people and the oppression they endured. The school's data collection and analysis involved systematic surveys, field interviews, ethnography, archival work and census analysis. Du Boisian professional and amateur researchers resided in the communities they studied, literally interviewing and surveying thousands of black people to understand their lives, institutions and social environment.

The research and scholarship of the Du Boisian School of Sociology produced findings at variance with the mainstream. As an analyst of modernity, Du Bois and his school examined a foundational structure of capitalism and modernity, which his contemporaries Emile Durkheim and Max Weber and his predecessor Karl Marx missed: the exploitative global colour line. Analysing this global line was an intellectual hallmark of the Atlanta School, leading Du Bois to correct prophesy that 'the problem of the twentieth century is the problem of the colour-line – the relation of the darker to the lighter races of men in Asia and Africa, in America and the islands of the sea' (Du Bois, 1903: 13). Because the Atlanta School explored relationships between racism, colonialism, slavery, capitalist development and modernity, it was able to produce key insights on the social conditions of people of colour throughout the world and inspire struggles to overthrow the colour line, including the Pan-African and the American Civil Rights movements.

Another major theoretical contribution of the Atlanta School was its exploration of the lived experiences of the oppressed. Du Bois sought to understand the intersubjective worlds of people forced to toil and struggle behind the veil of racism. Seeking this understanding, Du Bois developed the theory of 'double consciousness', which has become an enduring contribution to understanding the inner lives of black people and oppressed peoples across the world (Itzigsohn and Brown, 2015). Du Bois' theory of double consciousness differed from the later sociological conception of the human self-stressing, the dominant role that communication and social interactions play in developing the identities of social actors. Anticipating later theories of the self, Du Bois viewed the self as a socially created product arising from communication and social interactions. However, Du Bois went beyond these conceptions by connecting the self to the social environment out of which it was born and shaped. He theorised that the self is fashioned in the crucibles of power arrangements, social inequality and racism. Thus, different social locations generate different selves, depending on whether one belongs to the dominant or subordinate group.

An additional distinction of the Atlanta School was its formulation of analyses from the perspective of the oppressed. Du Bois' analysis of black people proceeded from a profound question: how does it feel to be a problem? From this perspective (Morris, 2017), the school developed a distinct sociology of black Americans, which demonstrated four major conclusions.

First, African Americans were equals to other races because racial oppression, rather than biological traits, relegated blacks to the bottom of the racial hierarchy. In fact, Du Bois was among the first to argue that race is a social construct and that dominant groups, for purposes of exploitation, construct racial hierarchies.

Second, 'black crime' did not exist because social conditions, and not racial traits, produced crime. This argument flew in the face of white social scientists who argued that black people constituted a criminal class of people because of their moral degeneracy. These scholars predicted that blacks would become extinct in the near future because of inherent crime and degeneracy. The Atlanta School, by comparing blacks to European peasants and immigrants, demonstrated that, like black people, their crime rates varied according to social conditions and not race or ethnicity. Therefore, the Atlanta School demonstrated that there was no evidence to confirm the black extinction hypothesis.

Third, the black community was heterogeneous, consisting of various social classes and diverse experiences. Du Bois explicated the class structure of the black community, showing that the black experience and life chances differed across that structure. He also analysed the urbanisation of blacks as they migrated from rural agriculture in the South to cities in both the South and the North. In this manner, Du Bois identified how regional differences created different slices of black life. These arguments contrasted sharply with those of white social scientists, who portrayed black people as an undifferentiated mass.

Fourth, the black church was the dominant institution housing the organisational and cultural resources of the community. Long before the modern Civil Rights Movement, Du Bois broke with contemporaries by correctly predicting that a black movement, situated in the mass-based black church, would arise to overthrow racial inequality. White social scientists were incapable of predicting the Civil Rights and Black Power movements because their frameworks stressed black inferiority, which led them to believe that black people did not possess the intelligence, leadership, culture or organisational capacity to organise and sustain social movements for their own liberation. From the white social scientific perspective, only Caucasians were endowed with history-making agency. Thus, Du Bois' school emerged as the first intellectual enterprise to articulate the agency of the oppressed worldwide, especially the agency existing within European colonies in Africa, Asia and the islands of the seas.

In summary, the Atlanta School laid the foundation for a unique political and cultural sociology of black Americans and provided analyses of global colour lines belting the modern world that produced global racial stratification. The school's pioneering work established the intellectual and methodological foundations on which much contemporary sociology and social science are based.

Conclusion

An education of liberation is required for the oppressed to break free of mental chains and construct movements to achieve their freedom dreams (Kelley, 2002). For this to happen, subaltern communities need to develop insurgent schools of thought. This is so because, as Lorde argued, 'the master's tools will never dismantle the master's house'. Elite hegemonic schools are incapable of accurately analysing and theorising the nature of oppression confronted by the dominated. Nor can they grasp the intricate lived experiences of people who live and die behind the veil of oppression. Frederick Douglass' (1863) political declaration that 'Who would be free themselves must strike the blow' applies to the intellectual and theoretical battles that must be waged if systems of domination are to be overthrown. Lessons for the oppressed regarding mental slavery can be learnt from the Atlanta School of Sociology that emerged at the beginning of the 20th century and struck an intellectual blow to guide freedom struggles.

First, the theoretical and methodological tools formulated by outside elites cannot guide freedom struggles effectively, if at all. Insurgent intellectual schools must interrogate the core intellectual principles advanced by mainstream scholars and the dominant society of which they are a part. When the Atlanta School emerged, the mainstream argument about black people was that as a race they were inferior and incapable of changing their oppressed position because they lacked agency. The Atlanta School, through theoretical imagination and elaboration coupled with empirical ingenuity, produced data and argumentation that dismantled the mainstream dogma brick by brick. It produced a counter-narrative based on evidence that discredited the claims of scientific racism and revealed the agency existing within the black community. In so doing, it was able to hold an intellectual mirror up to the oppressed that reflected their lives and social conditions, thus enabling them to build a freedom struggle congruent with the realities they faced on the ground.

Second, the Atlanta School revealed that an insurgent school could not rely exclusively on resources provided by outside elites, whether those resources were intellectual or material. It is not in the interest of hegemonic schools and societal elites to sponsor intellectual activities to bring down their houses of power. Thus, insurgent schools are challenged to generate indigenous resources to support their intellectual innovations. To achieve this goal, the Atlanta School relied on liberation capital consisting of professional and amateur intellectual labourers willing to accept meagre wages and to provide volunteer labour to accomplish the mission of the insurgent enterprise. This approach of going outside the traditional academy revealed that there are people – liberator scientists – intellectually capable of conducting scholarly activities largely compensated by the promise of ultimately reaching the collective goal of group liberation. Insurgent schools are challenged to look beyond the traditional academy and identify what Gramsci called organic intellectuals and utilise their services to cover the deficits that develop when an enterprise pursues non-traditional radical goals. Non-establishment goals cannot be achieved through established status quo-oriented schools of thought.

Third, the Atlanta School demonstrated that ideas generated by insurgent thinkers, organised into a collective enterprise, could produce intellectual resources that are critically useful for liberation struggles. Indeed, the Atlanta School provided potent ideas for the American black freedom struggle and Pan-African movements, both locally and internationally. Thus, Dr Martin Luther King (1968) revealed that Du Bois' 1935 *Black Reconstruction in America* uncovered sources of historical black agency that were crucial for civil rights activists. King confirmed that Du Bois 'virtually, before anyone else and more than anyone else, demolished the lies about Negroes in their most important and creative period of history. The truths he revealed are not yet the property of all Americans but they have been recorded and arm us for our contemporary battles.' The Atlanta School demonstrated that scientifically sound intellectual pursuits are consistent with politically engaged scholarship.

Finally, those who would dare construct liberation education for the oppressed must not doubt that the feat is accomplishable because historic precedents, including the Atlanta School of Sociology, proved such endeavours can and did materialise. As I concluded elsewhere, if an innovative scientific school could take root in the worst of times, amid the terrorism of lynch mobs, attacks from elites within the community it sought to liberate, and discrimination from a racist society that withheld crucial resources, then maybe there is hope for all who work to produce knowledge for the purpose of understanding and transforming humanity (Morris, 2015).

References

Anderson, J (1988) *The Education of Blacks in the South, 1860–1935*. Chapel Hill, NC: University of North Carolina Press.
Aptheker, H (1974). *American Negro Slave Revolts*. New York: International Publishers.
Douglass, F (1863) Men of colour, to arms! Now or never, *The North Star*, 2.
Du Bois, WEB (1903) *The Souls of Black Folk*. Chicago, IL: A.C. McClurg and Company.
Du Bois, WEB (1935) *Black Reconstruction in America, 1860–1880*. New York: Henry Holt.
Du Bois, WEB (1958) The early beginnings of the Pan-African Movement, W.E.B. Du Bois Papers (MS 312). Special Collection and University Archive, University Libraries. Amherst, MA: University of Massachusetts.
Franklin, RM (2007) *Crisis in the Village: Restoring hope in African-American communities*. Minneapolis, MN: Fortress Press.
Freire, P (1970) *Pedagogy of the Oppressed*. New York: Herder and Herder.

Itzigsohn, J and Brown, K (2015) Sociology and the theory of double consciousness: W.E.B. Du Bois' phenomenology of racialised subjectivity, *Du Bois Review*, **12**(2): 231–48.

Jay, W (1840) *Inquiry into the Character and Tendency of the American Colonisation and American Anti-Slavery Societies*. New York: The American Anti-Slavery Society.

Kelley, RDG (2002) *Freedom Dreams: The black radical imagination*. Boston, MA: Beacon Press.

King, ML, Jr (1968) Honoring Dr Du Bois. Speech delivered at Carnegie Hall in New York City, 23 February 1968.

Lorde, A (1984) The master's tools will never dismantle the master's house, in *Sister Outsider: Essays and Speeches*. Berkeley, CA: The Crossing Press, pp. 110–14.

Morris, A (1984) *Origins of the Civil Rights Movement: Black communities organising for change*. New York: The Free Press.

Morris, A (2015) *The Scholar Denied: W.E.B. Du Bois and the birth of modern sociology*. Oakland, CA: University of California Press.

Morris, A (2017) W.E.B. Du Bois at the center: From science, civil rights movement, to Black Lives Matter, *The British Journal of Sociology*, **68**(1): 3–16.

Morris, A and Braine, N (2001) Social movements and oppositional consciousness, in JJ Mansbridge and A Morris (eds) *Oppositional Consciousness: The subjective roots of social protest*. Chicago, IL: University of Chicago Press.

Washington, BT (1901) *Up from Slavery*. Garden City, New York: Doubleday.

Woodson, CG (1933) *The Mis-education of the Negro*. Washington, DC: Associated Publishers.

Wright, E, II (2016) *The First American School of Sociology*. New York: Routledge Publishing.

Chapter 22
The Howard School of International Affairs

Krista Johnson

Introduction

This chapter focuses on Howard University and a distinguished group of its scholars who, in the 1930s through the 1950s across various fields of social science, broke away both from the mainstream American disciplinary approaches of the time and from the institutional limitations of black universities to engage in transformative scholarship and intellectual theorising on race and empire in the United States and around the world. These 'race men and women' were scholar–activists and public intellectuals who shaped public discussion about race, built a vibrant intellectual community, and participated in an animated interwar Black Atlantic world that included figures like W.E.B. Du Bois, George Padmore and CLR James, among others. In areas like politics, international relations, history and philosophy, this group of black scholars at Howard University expressed ideas and theories that had in common the foregrounding of the black experience in the United States and the world more generally. These scholars did so in a way that did not isolate their work within intellectual ghettoes, but rather demanded that their arguments be placed and contested within the broader, mainstream intellectual community (see Magubane, Chapter 20, and Morris, Chapter 21, in this volume).

This chapter also describes the work of a number of these scholars. Among the distinguished faculty at Howard during this time were philosopher Alain L Locke, the first African-American Rhodes Scholar at Oxford University and a leader of the Harlem Renaissance; Sterling A Brown, English professor, author, poet and critic; historians Rayford Logan and Charles Wesley; Merze Tate, historian and specialist on disarmament; Charles Thompson, founder of the *Journal of Negro Education*; William Leo Hansberry, a pioneer in African history; economist Abram Harris; sociologist E Franklin Frazier; Eric Williams, political scientist and first Prime Minister of independent Trinidad and Tobago; and Ralph Bunche, political scientist, United Nations (UN) Undersecretary-General and Nobel Prize winner.[1]

---

1   Howard's distinguished faculty at the time also included Ernest Everett Just, an internationally known biologist; Law School Dean William H Hastie, the first black governor of the Virgin Islands and the first black federal judge; Charles H Houston, vice dean of the Law

Despite some intellectual and political differences among them, Charles Henry (1995) and Robert Vitalis (2015) refer to this constellation of black intellectual leaders as 'the Howard School'. Henry focuses on the contributions of E Franklin Frazier, Abram Harris and Ralph Bunche, in forging a new, albeit transitional, paradigm on race and race relations. Vitalis focuses on the Howard scholars' work on world politics and international relations, and their evolving ideas about racism and imperialism (Vitalis, 2015).[2]

This chapter links this intellectual history to current debates about decolonisation, Africanisation and intersectionality, as exemplified by student movements such as #RhodesMustFall and #BlackLivesMatter in South Africa and the United States, respectively. The Howard scholars, their decolonial methodology and scholarly research agenda should be foregrounded and become part of the consciousness of contemporary scholars and activists in a world where the issues that animated these black scholars have by no means been resolved.

As a model of decoloniality, the work of the Howard scholars incorporates the following strategies: first, problematising hegemonic paradigms, theories and schools of thought; second, demythologising history; and third, decolonising knowledge production. Perhaps the area for which the Howard scholars are most known is theorising race relations paradigms (Rutazibwa, 2018). However, their work in the field of international relations, and in theorising hierarchy as a primary organising principle of the world system, is equally

---

School and architect of the NAACP legal strategy; surgeon Charles R Drew, the pioneer developer of blood plasma; linguist and sociologist Lorenzo Turner; chemist Percy Julian; W Mercer Cook, a professor of Romance Languages and later ambassador to Senegal and Gambia; and theologian and university president, Mordecai W Johnson.

2   Robert Vitalis, in his recent book, offers a revised intellectual history of the discipline of American International Relations, in which he lays bare the fact that the discipline was centrally concerned with race relations, defined as the relationship of the supposedly superior white race with the darker peoples around the world. He argues that in building a new science of international relations, which in effect was a science of imperial administration, the biological division of the world mattered much more for theory building than a territorial division (Vitalis (2015) *White World Order, Black Power Politics*, p. 20). Equally notable are the formative contributions of South African Jan Smuts and Professor Charles Manning to the discourse and discipline of international relations globally. Jan Smuts' work in promoting international institutions such as the League of Nations was part of his call for an imperial internationalism aimed at maintaining the British Empire and other white-led dominions (see Edgar and Houser (2016). 'The most patient of animals, next to the ass': Jan Smuts, Howard University and African American leadership, 1930, *Safundi: Journal of South African and American Studies*). Suganami recounts Manning's considerable influence on the discipline through his teaching, but also his role in selecting the second generation of IR teachers in Britain. Writing at the time of the Howard scholars, Manning wrote on the 'beneficence of the mandates system', and gained notoriety as a defender of South African apartheid (see Suganami, H (2001) C.A.W. Manning and the study of international relations, *Review of International Studies*, **27**(1): 91–107).

relevant to the current project of decolonial transformation. Their epistemic and methodological commitment to the colonised and subaltern, and their treatment of slavery and colonialism as constitutive of the contemporary world system, served to centre the experiences and knowledges of the non-European in historical narratives. In addition, their emphasis on relational research, which binds the differential fortunes of the people of the metropole with those at the periphery, provides a necessary counter to the tendency to fragment history into different and presumably unrelated parts. Finally, the Howard scholars were cognisant of their role as public intellectuals, and of the place of knowledge production in the conscientisation of the masses (Freire, 1972). They used education for critical consciousness, as even a cursory review of their syllabi demonstrates their commitment to the idea of a critical pedagogy of teaching on race and empire. The following sections provide a brief outline of their strategies.

American racism, Howard University and the Negro scholar in historical perspective

The history of historically black colleges and universities (HBCUs) and the historical lessons from the fields of African and Afro-American studies in the United States (see Chapter 23 in this volume) highlight how the evolution of American universities and American intellectual thought over time has replicated the racial attitudes of the broader society and actively propagated racist views and disciplinary frameworks aimed at supporting the proposition that blacks are innately inferior. In the post-Civil War era after 1865, the first two generations of black scholars confronted a hostile environment, saturated by racist thought. The first generation of black PhDs was small, and included W.E.B. Du Bois and Carter G Woodson, who were the most productive researchers and activists countering anti-black scholarship at the time.[3]

By the 1930s, while white schools still excluded black scholars, the increased number of black PhDs (and in more diverse fields), combined with policy changes by philanthropic foundations, which significantly improved the fortunes of several black institutions – including Howard University – produced the first real opportunity for blacks to pursue highly productive scholarly agendas in an albeit second-class university environment. When the second generation of black scholars came on the scene in the late 1920s and early 1930s, Atlanta, Fisk and in particular Howard benefited overwhelmingly from this influx of new talent, attracting more than 80 per cent of all black PhDs in 1936. At the time, Howard University boasted by far the largest

---

3   Between 1876 and 1914, only 14 blacks earned a PhD (Winston, 1971: 689)

concentration of black PhDs anywhere in the United States – and the world – leading some scholars to describe this period as 'the golden age' of scholarship for the institution (Greene, 1971: 695).

Under the leadership of the university's first black president appointed in 1926, Mordecai W Johnson, Howard successfully positioned itself to become the leading centre of black scholarship in the humanities and social sciences. Johnson first (re)hired Alain Locke, who had received his PhD from Harvard in 1918, won a Rhodes Scholarship to Oxford in 1907, and was a primary challenger of the central tenets of race development theory. Locke sought funding for the study of the African mandate system and aspired to create an African Studies Programme at Howard.[4] He was instrumental in bringing together the network of scholars to theorise race and imperialism. In 1928, Locke and his Howard colleagues hired the 25-year-old Ralph Bunche to teach political science. He had an MA in political theory from Harvard, and went on to receive his PhD in government from the same university in 1934, with a specialisation in comparative colonial administration. Bunche forged close ties with fellow Howard faculty member E Franklin Frazier, who received his PhD in sociology in 1931. Together, they lured Trinidadian-born Eric Williams to join the Department of Political Science. Williams, who received his DPhil from Oxford in 1938, revised his dissertation into the seminal book *Capitalism and Slavery* (1944). A Marxist, Abram Harris, arrived at Howard in 1927 and received his PhD in economics from Columbia University in 1930. In the Department of History, Rayford Logan, who received his PhD from Harvard in 1936, joined Howard's faculty in 1938. He invited Vernie Merze Tate, the first black woman to receive a doctorate in international relations, from Radcliffe College in 1941, to join the History Department, after she was turned down by Bunche and Williams in the Department of Political Science (Vitalis, 2015).

The problems of colonial policies, imperialism and the changing status of the darker peoples of the world were the main elements of the emerging Howard School paradigm, which was greatly influenced by the singular brand of the Afro-diasporan internationalism of the Howard scholars. Howard University in the 1930s fostered a unique, cosmopolitan environment in which many of its leading academics engaged in research overseas. Ralph Bunche's dissertation research took him to Paris, London, Geneva and West Africa.[5] Alain Locke studied at Oxford and in Germany, and made frequent trips to Europe throughout his career; Frazier researched folk high schools and the cooperative movement in Denmark; Harris completed a post-doctoral

---

4   Alain Locke to Rayford Logan, 13 November 1928, box 166, folder 15, Logan Papers MSRC.

5   Later he would conduct research in South Africa and Kenya (see Robinson, 2010).

fellowship at Oxford; Williams studied capitalism and slavery at Oxford; and Logan conducted primary research on the mandate system in Geneva, at the League of Nations headquarters. Merze Tate was probably the most well-travelled of all the Howard scholars. She completed a Fulbright in India, and conducted fieldwork in Indonesia, Africa and throughout the Pacific.

Overseas, Howard scholars had the opportunity to engage with African and Afro-diasporan students and intellectuals. Alain Locke, for example, would form a lifelong friendship with Pixley Seme, the founder of the African National Congress in South Africa, while at Oxford.[6] He was also a member of the London-based International Institute of African Languages and Cultures (Robinson, 2010: 75). Bunche's interactions in Britain with Eric Williams, CLR James, George Padmore – who was one of Bunche's students at Howard – and Paul and Eslanda Robeson were formative in his intellectual development (Skinner, 2010: 58).

Howard's campus was also a 'black mecca' of sorts for international visitors, particularly from Africa, the diaspora and non-European territories such as India and China, given its location in the nation's capital. The critical mass of African and Caribbean students had a definite influence on the university culture and curriculum. They also connected campus intellectual and political life with the emerging tide of anticolonial nationalism (Robinson, 2010: 75).

Problematising paradigms, theories and schools of thought

The utility of revisiting the work of the Howard School lies in the fact that it provides a rich and venerable episteme that centres race and its interlocking modalities of capitalism and imperialism in its interrogation of international relations and the international system. Howard scholars broke sharply with the preceding generation of race scholars, who embraced a biological/genetic paradigm on race, influenced by the work of Charles Darwin. They were pioneers in conceptualising race as a social construct, rejecting both biological and anthropological renderings of race.[7]

---

6   The links between South Africa and the United States, and specifically between Alain Locke and Pixley ka Isaka Seme, are well discussed in two recent books: Bongani Ngqulunga (2017) *The Man who Founded the ANC: A biography of Pixley ka Isaka Seme* and Tembeka Ngcukaitobi (2018) *The Land is Ours*.

7   Franz Boas (1911) is generally credited with evolving the academic discourse of race away from biology and towards anthropology. However, Morris (2015) argues that Du Bois is perhaps the true reference point for contemporary social constructivist theories of race. Less known are the arguments of Alain Locke, presented in a series of five lectures at Howard University in 1916, entitled 'The theoretical and scientific conceptions of race'. He argued, 'when the modern man talks about race, he is not talking about the anthropological or biological idea at all. He is really talking about the historical record of success or failure of an ethnic group ... even the anthropological factors are variable, and

Yet, it is their analysis of racism in world politics that has been largely ignored or erased, and which is most relevant today. Ralph Bunche, in his longest and most valued work, *A World View of Race*, offered a dense and detailed falsification of the claims of racial 'science' and argued that class often proved more salient in ostensibly 'racial' conflicts.

> The theory of race, endowed with a false dignity by pseudo-scientific treatment, thus serves to justify economic policies, to bolster up political ambitions, to foment class prejudices and many other types of social antagonism among both groups and nations. In this way the concept of race plays an increasingly dominant role in the political and economic affairs of our modern world (Bunche, 1936: 3).

Bunche traces the origins of the term race in the English language to the 16th century, and then demonstrates that all attempts at racial classification since then have been conceptually incoherent, arbitrary, subjective and devoid of scientific meaning.

> The term 'race', when applied in the biological sense to groups, has no scientific validity today. It is a convenient tool for the anthropologist, who employs it as a more or less artificial and arbitrary means of classifying peoples. On the other hand, it is an increasingly vicious weapon in the hands of fanatical rulers and irresponsible demagogues who wield it ruthlessly to flatter national egos and to carry out sinister political and economic policies (Bunche, 1936: 10).

Bunche's thinking on race was clearly influenced by his close colleagues and fellow Howard scholars Abram Harris and E Franklin Frazier, and assumed a decidedly Marxist posture. For Bunche, the real causes of racial conflict are social, political and economic.

> Thus social, economic and political systems, by determining the financial resources, educational and all other opportunities in the society, are intimately tied up with the physical and psychological character which the individual or group will develop. And social race becomes as important a factor as physical race or biological heredity (Bunche, 1936: 13).

---

pseudo-scientific, except for purposes of descriptive classification' (Locke 1992 cited in Henderson (2015) Hidden in plain sight: racism in international relations theory).

The conceptualisation of race as sociological, a social race, allowed Bunche and his colleagues to define race in expansive terms, but also focus on its role in enshrining and reifying exclusionary and oppressive practices throughout the world. In fact, the true conceptual innovation initiated by Bunche in *A World View of Race*, as Vitalis (2015) notes, was his theorisation of ascriptive hierarchy as the *modus operandi* of international relations.

> The vital issues involved in the practices of our contemporary political and economic life more and more imply the inequality of peoples. One of the rocks on which the noble philosophy of human equality has run afoul takes shape as the frightful bogey, race. No other subject can so well illustrate the insincerity of our doctrines of human equality and the great disparity between our political theory and our social practice as that of race.

> In a world such as ours some such creed of inequality is both inevitable and indispensable. For it furnishes a rational justification for our coveted doctrines of blind nationalism, imperialism and the cruel exploitation of millions of our fellow-men. How else can our treatment of the so-called 'inferior races' and 'backward peoples' be explained and rationalised? (Bunche, 1936: 2).

This theorisation of the international system differs markedly from the dominant approaches of the time, and those that have become hegemonic in international relations theory, that privilege anarchy or power politics as the primary ordering principle in the international system and side-line questions of race and racism. In contrast, the Howard scholars conceptualised racism as an international institution or, as Vitalis puts it, 'a set of practices and rules that sustain a particular kind of ascriptive hierarchy or system of privilege and inequality' (Vitalis, 2000). Their work offers insights into how the institution of racism has proven so resilient in the face of decades of resistance, and offers a frame for analysing how such ascriptive hierarchies get reconstituted in various temporal and geographical settings.

Merze Tate, perhaps the least known of the Howard scholars, but also the most prolific writer of the group, spent a lifetime writing and teaching on an expansive list of topics, including the disarmament movement, mechanisms of empire, mineral railways in Africa, imperialism, colonialism and the Hawaiian monarchy. Given the volume and quality of Tate's scholarly output over five decades, her work offers a rich methodological and epistemic framework for understanding race and empire in the international system, and how it shapes and impacts on knowledge and its production. Furthermore, Tate's work highlights the import of relational analysis in theorising questions of race ordering, hierarchy and exclusion.

One of Tate's earlier works, 'The war aims of World War I and World War II and their relation to the darker peoples of the world', published in 1943 in a special 'Yearbook' issue of the *Journal of Negro Education*,[8] offers a direct and passionate rebuke of her white contemporaries writing on global peace, including EH Carr, Harold Butler and JB Conliffe (Tate, 1943: 523). In contrast, Tate asserts that the dangers to world peace lie in the European powers perpetuating the 'imperialist mentality' of 'master and subject peoples'.

Her definition of 'darker peoples of the world' is expansive, and includes people of African descent in the United States, the Caribbean, Central and South America, as well as the inhabitants of Africa, India, Burma, Malaysia, China and Japan, and people of colour in the Pacific. She progresses from region to region, and outlines a series of abuses of empire, including land seizures, wage and labour exploitation, anti-democratic and authoritarian political practices, the denial of self-government, exploitative tax systems and a master–servant economy. She relates the experience of fascism in Europe to elements in the United States that she says 'today dominate the Federal Government, and the Army and Navy' (Tate, 1943: 529). Tate, along with other black internationalists at the time (see Featherstone, 2013), diverged sharply with mainstream political thinking and theorising on fascism by engaging seriously with the racialised politics of fascism, and connecting anti-fascism to anti-colonialism and struggles against racial oppression in the United States: 'The way the United States behaves toward its coloured citizens and the way Great Britain behaves toward India and Africa represent the criteria by which Anglo-American war aims must be judged' (Tate, 1943: 531).

Tate's analysis of the World War II era is one of transnational and transatlantic connections, in which she homes in on three processes that have historically undergirded the unequal global order – theft of land, theft of labour, and

---

8   The 1943 special 'Yearbook' edition of the *Journal of Negro Education* included articles by W.E.B. Du Bois, Charles Hamilton Houston and Merze Tate. From its inception, the *Journal* took an expansive approach to the topic of Negro education, and covered numerous global topics, and offered a publication site for the Howard scholars' work on race and imperialism. In his editorial remarks, Charles Thompson, the editor and founder of the *Journal*, explains the purpose and significance of this particular Yearbook. 'This Yearbook is based upon the assumption that Negro youth and their elders need to view their special disabilities in broader perspective historically and geographically… I am particularly concerned that, as Negro youth go forth to fight or otherwise help to win this war, they fight for the freedom of oppressed peoples everywhere, at home and abroad; whether they are black or brown, yellow or white – whether it is the Jew in Poland, the untouchable in India, the Hottentot in Africa, the peasant in China, or the sharecropper in Mississippi. For only by establishing freedom for all peoples can we assure it for ourselves' (Thompson [1943]: 267).

violence – and thus relates, and in fact binds, the experiences of darker peoples throughout the world (Krishna, 2001). Tate ably moves back and forth between interrogating both national and global contexts, offering a warning for white imperialists, but also speaking to a constituency of brown masses, in particular in the United States. Anticipating decolonisation movements and referencing all 'peoples of colour', Tate warned:

> They are no longer willing to accept the white man's exalted view of trusteeship; they no longer quake at the teachings of the white man's missionaries, who bring them the white man's God but a God in whom the white man does not believe; no longer are glass beads and trinkets marvelous to them; they are much more interested in the marvels of the white man's guns (Tate, 1943: 529).

Also, during the war years, Tate produced two books on disarmament that were very well received at the time, and offered a novel social movement analysis of the topic by placing emphasis on the role of non-state actors, including civil society groups and religious groups, as well as state actors. Her second book foreshadowed the rise of the 'military industrial complex' in its cautionary climax.

> Tomorrow time will be measured in the twinkle of an eye. Stratospheric projectiles and jet-propelled superbombers carrying atomic bombs at supersonic speeds will become the competitive weapon of prearmed nations against which there is no defense, except to use them first. Therefore, we argue that our security lies in keeping our research going, regardless of cost and effort, so that we can maintain the lead and stay ahead of the world in the development of atomic energy. Thus a competition in a new and awesome field threatens to supersede the old race in armaments (Tate, 1948: 273–74).

As Tate's biographer, Barbara Savage, notes, a hallmark of Tate's work was her fascination with the technological aspects and tools that nation states employed to establish and maintain power with their colonies and imperial territories, and with one another. These were subjects she explored in great detail later in her writings on missionaries in Hawaii and railroads in Africa (Savage, 2014). Her vast body of work on the Pacific Islands reflects her expansive interests, and included two books on the annexation of Hawaii by the United States. She used a detailed historical approach, which relied on records kept by the British Government, and paid equal attention to Hawaiian leaders and royals as she did to key public officials from the United States.

She portrays the 'bloodless coup d'etat' that deposed Queen Lili'uokalani, the last ruling monarch of Hawaii, in 1893 as a pivotal moment that paved the way for the eventual successful annexation. But Tate believed these events also held broader significance. 'The Hawaiian controversy was more than a partisan issue … it actually initiated the great debate in American history over the merits of imperialism' (Tate, 1965). Tate's account of Hawaiian annexation is cast as the genesis of American imperialism over people of colour abroad. Most strikingly, she provides painstaking details of the role that New England missionaries unwittingly played in this process, by learning the language and converting the Bible and educational texts into a written Hawaiian language, and establishing schools that taught, trained and converted teachers (Savage, 2014). Using an innovative generational approach that reveals the links between missionary families and subsequent generations of landowners and the ruling business class, she also demonstrates how hierarchies and systems of privilege were exported to the periphery. Part of her explanation details how the children of the missionaries were not educated alongside the children native to the islands, but were sent instead to a new network of private schools, modelled after New England preparatory schools. These schools educated members of the business and professional class but eventually included some of the children of native Christianised families.[9]

Tate's work on Hawaii is also instructive in that she clearly details the intersection of fiery domestic political debates and the two-way flow of information and ideas that was occurring between the United States and Hawaii. She examined the questions of whether slavery would be instituted in Hawaii after annexation, if free Southern 'coloured labour' could be shipped in to meet the growing demands of the sugar industry, and demonstrated that annexation debates were entangled in the ongoing political feuds on the mainland over slavery and its extension or abolition. Tate also highlights that the educational system the missionaries established for the island's people served as a model for the vocational training model employed at Hampton Institute and, later, through its graduate Booker T Washington, at Tuskegee (Tate, 1965: 12–13, 317–18).

Demythologising history and whiteness

The toppling of Rhodes' statue on the campus of the University of Cape Town (UCT) in 2015 served, not to erase history, but to demythologise that history that

---

9   The descendants of those private preparatory schools still exist; Barack Obama graduated from one of the oldest of them, the Punahou School, which was founded in 1841 (Savage, 2014).

glorifies Cecil Rhodes as a visionary, an entrepreneur and philanthropist, while obscuring the fact that he stole his wealth, he was a racist, and his political and economic exploits in southern Africa brought considerable suffering to black people (see Mbembe, 2015: 2; and Adebajo, Chapter 2, and Ndelu, Chapter 9, in this volume). As we look to forge a sustained and more robust agenda of demythologising history, the recovery of alternative, oppositional histories of domination and struggle becomes critical. Demythologising difficult themes of history, which reveal uncomfortable truths and expose social contradictions and fault lines of the past, is urgently relevant in the academy today given society's complacency and complicity with the status quo.

The Howard scholars were committed to challenging colonial and Eurocentric interpretations of peripheral societies, and did so through a deliberate epistemological and methodological commitment to privilege the perspectives of the colonised, the marginalised and the excluded. By recognising that the histories and trajectories of the metropole and the periphery are intimately entangled, their work offers a counterpoint to normative histories that separate, for example, capitalist industrialisation from the practice of slavery. In this regard, the work of a group of Afro-Caribbean scholars, including CLR James, Eric Williams and George Padmore, is particularly instructive in bringing the relationship between slavery and capitalism onto centre stage.[10]

In his seminal 1944 book, *Capitalism and Slavery*, Eric Williams develops two arguments: first, the triangular, transatlantic slave trade was central to Britain's commercial expansion and prosperity in the 17th and 18th centuries, and the development of industry; and second, the economic logics and interests of industrialisation were the primary reasons for Britain moving to abolish the slave trade, not humanitarian concerns. A major theme in Williams' book is the role that profits from the plantation economies in the Caribbean played in stimulating the development of technological innovation, manufacturing and industry in Britain, including the production of export commodities, the development of shipping services and the shipbuilding industry, and the development of coal and iron production.

Williams' analysis was based on a meticulous collection of detailed primary sources. After coming to Howard, he conducted research in Cuba, Haiti, the Dominican Republic and Puerto Rico to supplement his Oxford dissertation research. His study foregrounds a novel methodology and offers an innovative 'form of post-colonial history writing that works back and forth between the periphery and the metropole', connecting African labour on the West Indian plantations to the enormous generation of wealth for planters in the West

---

10   Williams also published *Education in the British West Indies* in 1946.

Indies and the absentee landlords back in England (McCarthy and Sealey-Ruiz, 2010).

> Britain was accumulating great wealth from the triangular trade. The increase of consumption goods called forth by that trade inevitably drew in its train the development of the productive power of the country. The industrial expansion required finance. What man in the first three quarters of the eighteenth century was better able to afford the ready capital than a West Indian sugar planter or a Liverpool slave trader? (Williams, 1944: 98).

Williams' study not only foregrounds the sugar plantations, it centres the Caribbean, geographically and figuratively located in the periphery, in the economic development of England and the world. For Williams, far from being an insignificant outpost, the West Indian colonies were central economic powerhouses. He demonstrates these relations in banking, in heavy industry and in insurance.

> The amazing value of these West Indian colonies can be presented by comparing individual West Indian islands with individual mainland colonies. In 1697 British imports from Barbados were five times the combined imports from the bread colonies; the exports to Barbados were slightly larger. Little Barbados, with its 166 square miles, was worth more to British capitalism than New England, New York, and Pennsylvania combined. In 1773 imports from Jamaica were more than five times the imports from the bread colonies; British exports to Jamaica were nearly one-third larger than those to New England and only slightly less than those of New York and Pennsylvania combined. For the years 1714–1773 British imports from Montserrat were three times the imports from Pennsylvania, imports from Nevis were over three times those from New England (Williams, 1944).

Equally significant, Williams offers extraordinary insight into the agency of the slaves, their ability to read the political climate not just in the colony but in the metropole. The Trinidadian scholar successfully reads the emancipatory current both historically and in the moment in which he was writing. His depiction of the slaves is that of nascent organic intellectuals articulating their need for change as collective subjects. He identifies a key transformative current of history, initiating a narrative of liberation theology that fellow Trinidadian CLR James elaborates on in *The Black Jacobins* (McCarthy and Sealey-Ruiz, 2010).

It was a rude shock for the Barbadian planters who flattered themselves that their good treatment of the slaves would 'have prevented their resorting to violence to establish a claim of natural right which by long custom sanctioned by law has been hitherto refused to be acknowledged'. The rebels, when questioned, explicitly denied ill-treatment was the cause. 'They stoutly maintained however,' so the commander of the troops wrote to the governor, 'that the island belonged to them, and not to the white man, whom they proposed to destroy, reserving the females.' (Williams, 1944: 204).

Williams gives us a people's history and an approach that is indigenising and relational. In sum, *Capitalism and Slavery* is a precursor to current post-colonial scholarship, and offers tools to contest and redraw Western conceptual and epistemological topography, which privileges scientific rationality and abstract theorising over historical analysis. As Sankaran Krishna contends in the case of the discipline of international relations, such dominant methodological and epistemological orientations constitute a strategy of abstraction, and serve to white-wash the historical content of global affairs (Krishna, 2001). Questions of slavery, theft of land and violence are bracketed from the analysis, while state sovereignty assumes a primary conceptual role. However, as Grovogui (2001), Henderson (2015), and others have demonstrated, the argument must be taken further to illuminate the role of race and racism in the white-wash of the discipline's conceptual and methodological lexicon.[11]

Williams and the other Howard scholars confronted this head-on in their efforts to get their work published. In Williams' case, historian Colin Palmer (1994) calls our attention to the fact that his indictment of capitalism ruffled more than the feathers of some of the prominent American historians at the time. As a result, Williams had a difficult time bringing his manuscript to publication. Palmer writes that one of the reviewers for the University of North Carolina Press stated, 'I told him [Eric Williams] that he [should] soften a somewhat caustic racial bias against capitalism'.[12] Of course, the assumption

---

11 These scholars highlight the need to rewrite the conceptual building blocks of IR, including sovereignty, territoriality, security and the nation-state, and its major figures (Errol Henderson, 2015 and Siba Grovogui, 2001).

12 Quoted in McCarthy and Sealey-Ruiz (2010) Teaching difficult history, p. 77. Merze Tate experienced difficulties publishing her work on African railways, and was told explicitly that there was no interest in the notion of imperialism. Bunche modified a funding proposal to fall in line with donor interests on race and people of colour. 'Concerning the statement made by Dr Locke, I think we ought to devote some attention to actual possibilities for the publication of articles on the Negro utilising present available media. In some fields this is relatively easy. Anthropologists deal with the Negro as a respectable topic, and the journals of anthropology take such articles without hesitation. In respect to my own field, which

here is that capitalism is non-racial, above race, has no racial bias itself – a position Williams was explicitly arguing against.

Clearly, one arena of struggle in which the Howard scholars were engaged was challenging the domain of Eurocentric disciplines and the politics of knowledge in a segregated academy. A second site of struggle in which the Howard scholars were passionately engaged concerns their opposition to the prevailing power–knowledge nexus, and their efforts to forge oppositional criticisms of power blocs, which they defined primarily as imperialist states and the capitalist class. For example, in the Caribbean, Williams makes explicit the point that repressive historical accounts that mask the inequities and injustices of plantation society are bolstered by the power of the planter–mercantile class and British and US imperial supremacy in the region. A critical component in this equation is the use of racist discourse and, indeed, the racialisation of international knowledge, which constitutes part of the operation of power that perpetuates the status quo.

Recognising that knowledge and discourse are created to serve (colonial, imperial) power, an anti-colonial politics prevails in their writings. As oppositional intellectuals, they resisted power–knowledge tyrannies, viewed education as vital for critical consciousness and the practice of liberation, and developed strategies for social change. The Howard scholars' role as public intellectuals and scholar–activists will be cursorily covered in the next section.

Decolonising knowledge through public policy research and activism

An important element in any decolonising transformation of knowledge production is the need to be explicit about the purpose of knowledge and to connect it to the material consequences of coloniality. This is the work of the organic intellectual, or what W.E.B. Du Bois referred to as the Talented Tenth (see Morris, Chapter 21, in this volume). Defining them largely by their educational training, Du Bois envisioned this critical segment of African Americans would provide the necessary leadership for racial progress. The Howard scholars were, indeed, part of the Talented Tenth and took it as their duty to work for racial uplift. In a letter to Du Bois in 1927, the young Ralph Bunche, who had just graduated with his undergraduate degree from University of California, Los Angeles (UCLA), explains his future intentions:

> Since I have been sufficiently old to think rationally and to appreciate

---

concerns the political status of the Negro, except in so far as papers having to do with colonial problems and the like are involved, there isn't a very cordial reception for papers dealing with the Negro.' – Ralph Johnson Bunche, 1940 (Herskovits, 1941: 108).

that there was a 'race problem' in America ... I have set as the goal of my ambition service to my group... I am even now fulfilling that ambition... But I have long felt the need of coming in closer contact with the leaders of our Race, so that I may better learn their methods of approach, their psychology and benefit in my own development by their influence.[13]

Indeed, much has been written that connects Howard University and its scholars during these early years with the Talented Tenth.[14] These scholars advanced a public intellectual model by linking their scholarship and teaching with intellectual activism. This cohort of radical black scholar–activists engaged the national and global black public around a variety of salient issues of the day, and forged meaningful personal and professional networks cemented in the community. Michael Winston references the Howard scholars as a 'policy research nucleus', which not only criticised public policy, but also boldly proposed innovative strategies and prescriptions designed to counteract systemic challenges around race nationally and globally (Winston, 1971).

One of the notable arenas for this kind of engagement was the numerous conferences, events and meetings held on Howard's campus at this time. In particular, the Division of Social Sciences held annual conferences that drew stellar line-ups, including Du Bois and First Lady Eleanor Roosevelt, and addressed the pressing issues of the day. These conferences were always very well attended, and included not only academics, but also labour leaders, industrialists, government officials and other professionals. These should be seen as strategic policy interventions that used their professional position and their location in the nation's capital as a bully pulpit for a range of ideas that represented a commitment to political change in the service of social justice.

The Howard scholars were also apt to use a variety of public vehicles, including commentaries in the black press, articles, speeches, books and other forms of expression such as poetry and artistic writing, to change the terms of the political debate and advance a paradigm shift in thinking on race, imperialism and hierarchy. Of note here is the remarkable role played by the *Journal of Negro Education* under the founding editorship of Charles Thompson.

---

13 Ralph Bunche, Letter to Dr William E.B. Du Bois, repr. in Robinson (2010).
14 Zachary Williams (2009) *In Search of the Talented Tenth: Howard University, Public Intellectuals and the Dilemmas of Race*; Charles Henry (1999) *Ralph Bunche: Model Negro or American Other?*; Jonathan Scott Holloway (2002) *Confronting the Veil: Abram Harris Jr, E. Franklin Frazier, and Ralph Bunche, 1914–1941*. While many scholars use Talented Tenth and public intellectual interchangeably when referring to the Howard scholars and this era, in the contemporary context the notion of the Talented Tenth is frequently used to uncritically celebrate black middle-class advancement.

As Michael Winston notes, the journal provided a 'ready and sympathetic outlet' for publications of research by the Howard scholars, and offered a potent continuing critique of the policy of racial segregation, including colonialism and imperialism (Winston, 1971: 697). In particular, the publication of the annual Yearbook of the journal provided comprehensive studies of a wide range of problems, many broader than the journal's name would suggest. For example, the 1946 edition of the Journal Yearbook was titled *The Problem of Education in Dependent Territories*, and included articles by Ralph Turner on imperialism, Rayford Logan on international trusteeship, and Du Bois on colonies and moral responsibility. Read by a wide audience, especially of black educators, the journal was instrumental in disseminating a world-view of race.

Without romanticising racial segregation, of course it is important to note that the Howard scholars' political philosophies, communal life and personae as scholar–activists were necessitated by the social realities of the world in which they lived. Another way of conceptualising the unique intellectual possibilities and challenges that black scholars faced at the time is through Aldon Morris' notion of 'liberation capital', which he defines as 'a form of capital used by oppressed and resource-starved scholars to initiate and sustain the research programme of a non-hegemonic scientific school' (Morris, 2015: 188). Morris emphasises the considerable deficit of financial resources that black scholars were forced to confront and the mobilisation of insurgent intellectual networks to overcome this challenge. However, in the long run, none of the historically black schools became even modest centres of research. Confronted with grossly inequitable resources, historically black institutions committed most of their resources to teaching and very little to research (see Chapter 23 in this volume).

In fact, Winston chides administrators for their part in not supporting research. He quotes E Franklin Frazier, who lambasts the 'ignorant administration of Negro schools which have refused the intelligent proposals of Negro scholars' (Winston, 1971: 707). Similarly, the short-sightedness of these institutions, particularly Howard University, in not supporting a university press, Winston finds startling. 'In the period of Howard's greatest research productivity, white university presses or private publishers had to be relied upon for publication opportunities' (Winston, 1971: 707).

Desegregation in the mid-1950s brought opportunities for black scholars on white campuses, and greater social upliftment for blacks in general, but also led to a decline in community. The erosion of the politics of collectivity also occurred as race and difference were reformed into individualistic terms. As African-American public intellectual Cornel West laments, the role of the black intellectual today is one of self-imposed marginality. For sociologist Patricia Hill Collins, black public intellectuals today lack the necessary spatial and cultural groundedness in communities beyond the ivory tower – the kind of groundedness that members of the Howard community maintained, for a time, even post-*Brown v. Board of Education* (West, 1985).

Conclusion

The post-colonial and post-civil rights era has transformed the grammar and syntax of racism, racialisation and white supremacy. Yet, the problem of the 21st century remains – as Du Bois had presciently predicted about the 20th century – the problem of the colour line, albeit in shifting social constellations and physical geographies. Despite the black studies revolution of the 1960s and the proliferation of siloed African-American studies, multicultural and ethnic studies programmes on US campuses, the decolonisation of the academy remains partial at best. With the embrace of multiculturalism and diversity in liberal academies, race has become domesticated. Culture and ethnicity have been introduced as a means of ostensibly conceptualising human diversity in non-hierarchical terms, but they have now been essentialised and racialised in less obvious but more insidious ways (Mohanty, 1989–90). In this liberal academic climate, as Chandra Mohanty warns, these educational practices not only transmit already codified ideas of difference, they often produce, codify and even rewrite histories of race and colonialism in the name of difference (Mohanty, 1989–90).

Decolonising educational practices requires transformations at a number of levels, both within and outside the academy. The Howard scholars' model, and surely their writings, must become part of our critical, post-colonial pedagogy that links knowledge, social responsibility and collective struggle, so that education becomes the practice of liberation. As educators, we need to mainstream our imperial legacies, and expose our students to counter-narratives that challenge the normative discourses and ideas they are exposed to on a daily basis. The writing of the Howard School offers a rich archive from which to draw in our efforts to foreground the complex issues of slavery, imperialism, race and hierarchy. Consider the transformative possibilities if a critical mass of International Relations 101 courses began with Buncheian or Howard School perspectives on the hierarchisation of the international political system, rather than the storied lessons of the Peloponnesian War.

We need to redefine learning in the context of emerging conditions of global connectivity and develop a cosmopolitan concept of learning, à la Merze Tate, that is more diverse and extensive and cannot be contained within the nation-state. This requires us to blur the lines between African, African American, and Black Studies, while also recognising our diverse experiences. Our teaching and scholarship must emphasise the relational analyses of the

Howard scholars, so that, as Ampofo argues, 'the erasure of Black lives by police shootings of Black people in the US would be read as related to the erasure of African lives crossing the desert to Europe, will be read as related to the beating of one of Africa's leading writers Binyavanga Wainaina in Berlin last month, will be read as related to the absence of a single African author in several texts on Africa' (Ampofo, 2016).

Such perspectives highlight the persistence of racial logics, not only in capitalist and nation-state modernity as analysed by the Howard scholars, but also in contemporary liberal humanitarian intervention, the war on terror, the racialisation of immigrants and Muslims, and global practices of boundary-making and border controls. In this regard, race is less of a biological or descriptive category and more of a 'floating signifier' or 'marker of subordination' (Johnson, 2012), which can be made to include a range of signified features depending on the way it is articulated with different elements in varying discourses.[15] The emergence of a new racism suggests the continued explanatory value of substantive analyses of race and hierarchy, and affirms the need to revisit and critically extend the work of the Howard School to places like South Africa and the wider continent.

References

Ampofo, A (2016) #BlackLivesMatter, #RhodesMustFall and Afro Knowledge, 10 June. Available at: http://www.cihablog.com/black-lives-matter-rhodes-must-fall-afro-knowledge/ (accessed December 2018).

Anievas, A, Manchanda, N and Shilliam, R (eds) (2015) *Race and Racism in International Relations.* New York: Routledge.

Binay, S (2011) Colouring the lines through culture? Race and racialisation in international relations. Prepared for MIRC, 28 February.

Bunche, R (1936) *A World View of Race.* Washington, DC: Associates in Negro Folk Education.

Edgar, R and Houser, MA (2016) 'The most patient of animals, next to the ass': Jan Smuts, Howard University, and African American leadership, 1930. *Safundi: The Journal of South African and American Studies.* Available at: http://dx.doi.org/10.1080/17533171.2016.1252168 (accessed 20 October 2019).

Featherstone, D (2013) Black internationalism, subaltern cosmopolitanism, and the spatial politics of antifascism, *Annals of the Association of American Geographers*, **103**(6): 1406–20.

Freire, P (1972) *Pedagogy of the Oppressed.* London: Penguin Books.

Greene, HW (1971) Sixty years of doctorates conferred upon Negroes, *The Journal of Negro Education*, **6**(1): 30–37.

Grovogui, S (2001) Come to Africa: A hermeneutic of race in international theory, *Alternatives: Global, Local, Political*, **26**(4): 425–48.

Henderson, E (2015) Hidden in plain sight: Racism in International Relations theory, in A Anievas, N Manchanda and R Shilliam (eds) *Race and Racism in International Relations.* New York: Routledge.

---

15 The notion of a new racism has become prevalent across national and disciplinary boundaries (Binay, 2011).

Henry, C (1995) Abram Harris, E. Franklin Frazier and Ralph Bunche: The Howard School of Thought on the problem of race, *The National Political Science Review*, **5**.

Henry, C (1999) *Ralph Bunche: Model Negro or American Other?* New York: New York University Press.

Henry, C (2004) The legacy of Ralph J. Bunche and education: Celebrating the centenary year of his birth, *The Journal of Negro Education*, **73**(2): 137–46.

Herskovits, M (1941) The Interdisciplinary Aspects of Negro Studies, *American Council of Learned Societies Bulletin* **32**: 101–11.

Holloway, J (2002) *Confronting the Veil: Abram Harris Jr, E. Franklin Frazier, and Ralph Bunche, 1914–1941*. Chapel Hill, NC: University of North Carolina Press.

Johnson, W (2012) Dismantling Africana Studies at Rutgers University, Commission on Race and Racism in Anthropology and the American Anthropological Association, February.

Krishna, S (2001) Race, amnesia and the education of international relations, *Alternatives: Global, Local, Political*, **26**: 401–24.

Mbembe, A (2015) Decolonising knowledge and the question of the archive. Available at: https://wiser.wits.ac.za/system/files/Achille%20Mbembe%20-%20Decolonising%20 Knowledge%20and%20the%20Question%20of%20the%20Archive.pdf (accessed November 2018).

McCarthy, C and Sealey-Ruiz, Y (2010) Teaching difficult history: Eric Williams' *Capitalism and Slavery* and the challenge of critical pedagogy in the contemporary classroom, *Power and Education*, **2**(1).

Mohanty, C (1989–90) On race and voice: Challenges for liberal education in the 1990s, *Cultural Critique*, **14**, Winter: 79–208.

Morris, A (2015) *The Scholar Denied: W.E.B. DuBois and the birth of modern sociology*. Oakland, CA: University of California Press.

Robinson, P (2010) Ralph Bunche the Africanist: Revisiting paradigms, *Trustee for the Human Community: Ralph J. Bunche, the United Nations and the Decolonisation of Africa*. Athens, OH: Ohio University Press.

Rutazibwa, O (2018) Understanding Epistemic Diversity: Decoloniality as research strategy, 4 July. Available at: https://issblog.nl/2018/07/04/epistemic-diversity-understanding-epistemic-diversity-decoloniality-as-research-strategy/ (accessed December 2018).

Savage, B (2014) Professor Merze Tate: Diplomatic Historian, Cosmopolitan Woman, American Political Science Association Meeting, August.

Skinner, E (2010) Ralph Bunche and the decolonisation of African Studies: The paradox of power, morality and scholarship, *Trustee for the Human Community: Ralph J. Bunche, the United Nations and the decolonisation of Africa*. Athens, OH: Ohio University Press.

Suganami, H (2001) C.A.W. Manning and the study of International Relations, *Review of International Studies*, **27**(1): 91–107.

Tate, M (1943) The war aims of World War I and World War II and their relation to the darker peoples of the world, *Journal of Negro Education*, **12**(3): 523–31.

Tate, M (1948) *The United States and Armaments*. Cambridge, MA: Harvard University Press.

Tate, M (1965) *The United States and the Hawaiian Kingdom: A Political History*. New Haven, CT: Yale University Press.

Thompson, C (1943) Editorial note: The American Negro in World War I and World War II, *Journal of Negro Education*, **12**: 3.

Vitalis, R (2000) The graceful and generous liberal gesture: Making racism invisible in American International Relations, *Millennium: Journal of International Studies*, **29**(2): 331–56.

Vitalis, R (2015) *White World Order, Black Power Politics: The birth of American International Relations*. Ithaca, NY, Cornell University Press.

West, C (1985) The dilemma of the black intellectual, *Cultural Critique*, **1**: 109–24.

Williams, E (1944) *Capitalism and Slavery*. Chapel Hill, NC: University of North Carolina Press.

Williams, E (1946) *Education in the British West Indies*. Port of Spain: People's National Movement Co.

Williams, Z (2009) *In Search of the Talented Tenth: Howard University, public intellectuals and the dilemmas of race*. Columbia, MO: University of Missouri Press.

Winston, M (1971) Through the back door: Academic racism and the Negro scholar in historical perspective, *Daedalus*, **100**(3): 678–719.

Chapter 23

Righteous struggle: Historically black colleges and universities in the United States

Walter R Allen, Chantal Jones and Gadise Regassa

Introduction

Historically black colleges and universities (HBCUs) have been instrumental in the social, political and economic mobility of blacks in the United States. Many high-achieving black Americans have links with HBCUs. Oprah Winfrey graduated from Tennessee State University; former president and former first lady Barack and Michelle Obama were members in Trinity United Church pastored by Reverend Jeremiah Wright, a graduate of Howard University; Rosalind Brewer, Chief Operating Officer for Starbucks, graduated from Spelman College; the list is endless. HBCUs produce the overwhelming majority of black teachers, physicians, social workers, attorneys, bankers, architects, engineers, business executives, technicians and other professionals who serve our communities. Shaped in the fiery furnace of American slavery, racism and oppression, HBCUs have emerged triumphant as an 'engine in producing black scholars, leaders for the civil rights movement, and research to highlight racist issues', as well as a place for black life making (Mustaffa, 2017: 719).

HBCUs grew out of the enduring black struggle for freedom and equality. Enslaved black people saw the transformative power and possibility of education in accessing the American dream and improving their lives (Anderson, 1988; Allen and Jewell, 2002). HBCUs have been crucial in sustaining black culture, educating black professionals who contributed to improving the overall social and economic circumstances of black people in America (Jewell, 2002; Allen and Jewell, 2002). The purpose and mission of HBCUs in the American landscape has been a point of contention for many (Allen et al, 2007). Research on HBCUs has been primarily concerned with the role of education in both the black community and American society as it relates to race and class and, more currently, their relevance in a post-civil rights society (Allen et al, 2007). Moreover, literature has engaged HBCUs and their impact on black political ideology, their role in the political advancement of educational access for black people, and how black institutions were effectively training black leaders and workers, despite challenging economic, social and political times.

Brief history of historically black colleges and universities

To understand the contribution of HBCUs to black education in America, one has to explore the history and establishment of American higher education. Since the inception of America's first colleges, it had been a common practice to limit the educational access, attainment and even literacy of enslaved blacks (Allen et al, 2007; Brown, 2013; Anderson, 1988). Prior to Emancipation, blacks were forbidden by slaveholding states to read and write (Jewell, 2002). Although the majority of enslaved black people were unable to benefit from early American colleges, Wilder (2013) reveals that slaves and the slave economy were instrumental in the establishment of America's most revered educational institutions. The purchase and sale of black people funded the establishment of campuses like Harvard, Princeton, Georgetown, Virginia and Yale universities. College founders also often used slaves as construction workers and to wait on students and faculty members. Moreover, early colonial colleges perpetuated white supremacist ideologies of black intellectual and cultural inferiority, which legitimised the dispossession of Native Americans and the enslavement of black peoples. The racism and oppression on which American higher education was founded provides the backdrop to the emergence and importance of HBCUs in the American educational landscape.

Prior to the Civil War, black people were mostly denied access to institutions of higher learning, largely because of their threat to white supremacy (Brown, 2013). However, after Emancipation, freed blacks invested in formal educational systems to secure newly gained rights and increase social and economic capital (Allen and Jewell, 2002). As black folks became emancipated, the nation began to imagine a modern public educational system (Anderson, 1988). However, due to extralegal methods and tactics, black people were ushered into a redesigned form of repression that replicated slave conditions in emancipated America (Alexander, 2010). Black education was birthed within a context of oppressive policies and practices that repressed black people's ability to be economically, socially and politically free. Anderson argues that former slaves were the first among Southerners to advocate for universal, state-supported public education. This ideology was unusual for the South, as Southern planters widely believed that the state had no role in education. Although the contribution of white northerners to the education of black people in the South is noted in the literature, it is not commonly understood that the idea of a universal education at the public expense was the brainchild of freed slaves in the postbellum South (Anderson, 1988).

For the most part, black schools in the South were staffed and run by both literate and semi-literate black community members, which came as a surprise for many white, northern missionaries who travelled to the South to help newly freed slaves (Allen et al, 2007; Anderson, 1988). As slavery in its original form became outlawed, it was widely believed by whites that newly freed slaves must be 'civilised' through education in this new post-emancipated America (Allen and Jewell, 2002; Anderson, 1988). Due to the lack of state funding, in the late 1800s HBCUs had to rely on white philanthropic organisations, missionary societies and churches, like the American Missionary Association, the Disciples of Christ and the African Methodist Episcopal Church, to fund and run their schools (Anderson, 1988; Allen et al, 2007; Jewell, 2007; Brown, 2013).

In addition to funding these black institutions, white missionaries had control over the curricula and educational goals. While there were some HBCUs funded by African-American organisations that maintained a classical liberal arts curriculum, most HBCUs focused primarily on basic skill development like etiquette and dress, labour and religious education (Allen et al, 2007). As these institutions became more established over time, they evolved into two general categories: vocational/instructional training and liberal arts. This evolution ushered in the debate between black leaders and white missionaries about the purpose of education for blacks. Woodson noted that white people were more likely to be supportive of vocational education because a liberal arts education was seen as being too intellectually rigorous for black students and it had the potential of breeding ideas of revolution and freedom (Allen et al, 2007).

This curricular debate was dominated by black thought leaders Booker T Washington and W.E.B. Du Bois, who personified the vocational/industrial model and liberal arts education, respectively (see Morris, Chapter 21, in this volume). As a graduate of Hampton University and founder of the Tuskegee Institute, Washington argued that the vocational/industrial model would be key to black economic advancement and self-reliance. Washington's conservative stance coddled white insecurity about a diminishing labour force, arguing that vocational education works to increase the morality of black students, lessen the probability of conflict between races and foster white values (Allen and Jewell, 2002; Allen and Esters, 2007). On the other hand, Du Bois, a beneficiary of a liberal arts education as a Fisk University and Harvard University graduate, argued that vocational education was too restrictive and called for a liberal arts education to meet black intellectual ability and build the next generation of black leadership (Allen et al, 2007), who could continually challenge white political and social dominance (Allen and Jewell, 2002). Washington's support for vocational education was further advanced by the Second Morrill Act of 1890, which secured state-supported technical and industrial colleges for black students.

Since inception, HBCUs have been pioneers of educational access in America. With an open-enrolment policy, HBCUs were among the first institutions to open their doors to all students, regardless of their social identities, which allowed for a diverse class across academic ability, socio-economic status, and racial and ethnic identities (Jewell, 2002; Allen and Jewel, 2002; Allen et al, 2007). In attendance were a mix of former enslaved black people, who were poor and illiterate, and a small number of students who had obtained class privilege (Jewell, 2002; Allen et al, 2007). Thus, there was a need for a wide range of curricula at the secondary and college-preparatory levels to meet the diverse needs of students (Allen et al, 2007). In the early 1900s, a considerable number of HBCUs, 41 out of 99 institutions, did not offer college-level curricula and the majority of HBCU campuses comprised pre-college students (Allen et al, 2007).

Although black students made up most of the HBCU student population, the non-black American student enrolment included 'children of white missionaries, Native Americans, poor whites, and international students from Asia, Africa, Latin America, and the Caribbean', as well as white and Jewish female students who enrolled in professional programmes (Allen et al, 2007: 268). Although gendered differences in educational access existed on these campuses, 'black women were often able to attend college in more significant numbers than their white female peers because of the open access mission of HBCUs' (Allen et al, 2007: 269). Even though black men made up most of the HBCUs' composition in 1900, as HBCUs started to expand, black women started to outnumber black men by 1935. By 1890, there were over 200 HBCUs founded in the aftermath of the Civil War (Brown, 2013). After the Second Morrill Act, HBCU enrolment grew exponentially throughout the late 19th to the 20th century (Allen et al, 2007). Anderson (1988) documents black college and professional student enrolment in Southern institutions between 1900 and 1935 grew exponentially from 3 880 in 1900 to 29 000 by 1935.

The issue of white control over black colleges persisted through the 1920s and during the 'New Negro' movement alumni and students wanted more black ownership and freedom on HBCU campuses. Previously, white leadership in black colleges enforced draconian moral and social codes that restricted black social life and non-Western curricula. Historically, American higher education institutions existed to meet societal needs – from the socialisation of its citizens, to the stratification of economic and political participation, or the allotment of resources. For instance, while white instructors were refusing to teach black students, private normal schools, secondary schools and colleges were preparing black graduates to fill the increasing demand for black teachers (Anderson, 1988). In meeting the needs, however, higher education has reflected the interests of the powerful class in controlling resources, providing opportunities for social mobility, and advancing political ideology (Jewell, 2002).

The current higher education landscape for black students

It is important to provide an overview of the enrolment and degree completion trends of black students in the United States before focusing on the HBCUs. Data from the National Center for Education Statistics show that by 2015, black students accounted for approximately 2.7 million (13.4 per cent) of the total higher education landscape (approximately 20 million students), with 2.3 million undergraduates (13.6 per cent) and 364 300 graduates (12.4 per cent) (Snyder, De Brey and Dillow, 2018a). In terms of degree types in the same year, black students were conferred 137 892 or approximately 13.6 per cent of associate's degrees (Snyder et al, 2018b); 192 715 or 10.2 per cent of bachelor's degrees (Snyder et al, 2018c); and 87 265 or 11.5 per cent of master's degrees (Snyder et al, 2018d). Among doctoral degrees conferred, 13 278 or 7.4 per cent were awarded to black students (Snyder et al, 2018e).

Black students largely attend public institutions and comprise 1.8 million or 12.2 per cent of the public total, with 854 000 students (or 13.7 per cent) at public two-year institutions and 916 500 students (or 11 per cent) at public four-year institutions (Snyder et al, 2018f). Black student enrolment has increased dramatically at for-profit institutions, although such institutions are known for higher costs, resulting in high debt and frequent loan defaults (Iloh and Toldson, 2013).

Flagships and black-serving institutions

Revisiting the 1968 Kerner Report,[1] Allen et al (2018) examined black student enrolment and degree completion between 1976 and 2015. Data for their analysis were provided through the Integrated Postsecondary Education Data System (IPEDS) and the US government statistics. They selected the top 20 states with the largest black populations and focused on three public four-year institutional types: the state flagship, the black-serving institution (BSI) and the HBCU (where present). They noted:

> Flagships have designated leadership roles and emphasis in state public higher education systems. BSIs – traditionally white institutions with a high representation of African American students, such as Georgia State University and Chicago State University – are prominent in the

---

[1] In 1968, during the civil rights movement, the National Advisory Commission on Civil Disorders – the Kerner Report – authored by the US Riot Commission, found rampant inequities and violence in areas including employment, housing and education. The Kerner Report was commissioned by US President Lyndon Johnson and is famed for stating 'our nation is moving toward two societies, one black, one white – separate and unequal', as well as naming white racism.

production of African American college graduates. Finally, HBCUs such as Morgan State University or Savannah State University, once legally segregated by race, continue to play significant roles in contemporary African American higher education (Allen et al, 2018: 45).

The states included in the analysis are especially noteworthy due to several historically important desegregation and affirmative action cases. The authors considered full-time, undergraduate, graduate and professional black women and men. Examining gender differences and similarities within race provides a nuanced view of black women's relative status in US higher education.

At flagships, black student presence has been consistently restricted to low levels over time. Allen et al describe:

> African American undergraduate enrolment at the University of California, Berkeley; University of California, Los Angeles; University of Michigan, Ann Arbor; and the University of Texas, Austin, was approximately 4.5 per cent or lower in 2015 ([table in original] table 2). This, despite the fact that the African American population is 7.1 per cent in California, 15.2 per cent in Michigan, and 12.8 per cent in Texas ([table in original] table 1) (Allen et al, 2018: 48).

Comparing flagship enrolment and state population shows that despite the varied contexts of states and institutions, similar patterns emerge, influenced by widespread rhetoric, ideology and legislation (for instance, anti-affirmative action sentiment, colour-blindness). The findings for flagships are especially problematic considering their higher academic prestige and institutional resources compared to BSIs and HBCUs. These institutional disparities result from a history of racist policies and practices (Mustaffa, 2017).

Overall, BSIs are more successful in the enrolment and graduation of black students than the flagships. However, BSIs also had fluctuating trends with both large increases and stark declines. On average, BSIs receive lower per-student funding than flagships, which are research-intensive institutions. This reflects a higher education hierarchy, which privileges selectivity (exclusion), rewarding institutions that restrict black student enrolment (Allen et al, 2018).

Historically black colleges and universities

HBCUs play critical roles in the education of black college students. Only 3 per cent of all US higher education institutions are HBCUs, yet a quarter or more of all black graduates attended HBCUs (Allen and Jewell, 2002). In

2015, HBCUs awarded approximately 14 per cent of bachelor's degrees, 6 per cent of master's degrees, and 12 per cent of doctoral degrees earned by black students (Snyder et al, 2018c; 2018d; 2018e; 2018g). Comparing historically black land-grant universities (HBLGUs)[2] and historically white land-grant universities (HWLGUs),[3] Allen and Esters (2018) show that 60 per cent of those who attend a Southern land-grant university attended a HBLGU. As expected, HBCUs have larger proportions of black students than the flagships and BSIs.

Demographic changes are apparent across HBCUs. In 2015, black students represented around three-quarters of the total HBCU enrolment (Snyder et al, 2018h). By contrast, in 1950, nearly 100 per cent of HBCU students were black. In the mid-1970s, most black students attended HWIs (Allen, 1992; Allen et al, 2007). The majority of HBCUs have experienced decreased black undergraduate enrolment and degree completion since 1976 (Allen et al, 2018). However, graduate and professional student enrolment increased at several HBCUs, with examples of both increases and declines in degree completion.[4] Our discussion of HBCU origins and missions, coupled with their place in the national higher education landscape, represents, first, an affirmation of the critical role of HBCUs in the education of black students, especially as a space for black life making (Mustaffa, 2017), and second, a call to dismantle the systemic inequities facing HBCUs, especially in the areas of funding and legislation.

Federal and state disinvestment in HBCUs

Minor (2008a) describes severely limited federal funding to HBCUs, beginning with the Higher Education Act of 1965. Ironically, despite claiming to expand HBCU infrastructures and academic resources, the average grant is around US$2 million. As the following sections show, this relatively small amount fails to adequately address the longstanding economic disparity between HBCUs and flagships and HWIs.

---

2   Historically black land-grant universities specifically refer to the 21 institutions established after the passage of the second Morrill Act in 1890. Allen and Esters' (2018) definition of HBLGUs includes the 18 institutions recognised as 1890 land-grant universities, in addition to Central State University which received land-grant status in 2014, and the University of the District of Columbia and the University of the Virgin Islands which received 1862 status.

3   Historically white land-grant universities refer to institutions funded through the Morrill Act of 1862 and provided 30 000 acres of land.

4   For information on the exact states, institutions, per cent enrolment and degree completion of black women and men across institutions, as well as a discussion of per cent changes between 1976 and 2015, see the original publication by Allen et al (2018).

There have been significant differences in how historically white and historically black land-grant institutions were funded by state and federal government. The funding model for land-grant universities requires the state to match federal funds on a dollar-to-dollar basis. Although states have consistently complied for historically white land-grant institutions, the majority of land-grant HBCUs did not receive matching state funds, resulting in the loss of millions of funding dollars (Lee and Keys, 2013; Allen and Esters, 2018). Disputing attempts to justify racial disparities in funding based on institutional differences, like context or size, Minor (2008a) reveals that on a per-student basis, funding to HWIs was double that to HBCUs within the same state (North Carolina).

Looking deeper into economic inequity between Morrill Act institutions by comparing endowments, indicators of institutional wealth and security, Allen and Esters (2018) report:

> The combined total endowment for all 21 HBLGUs was just over $740 million in 2016. Of the 18 HWLGUs that share a state with one of the 21 HBLGUs, 15 had endowments larger than all 21 HBLGUs combined, including 10 with endowments greater than $1 billion. Further, the lowest endowment of an HWLGU in the South boasts an amount of just over $500 million. By comparison, only one HBLGU has an endowment greater than $100 million (Florida A&M University = $113 million) (Allen and Esters, 2018: 4).

The origin of federal and state disinvestment in HBCUs is visible in the Morrill Act of 1890, which failed to provide equitable resources to HBCUs, compared to the institutions created from the passage of the first Morrill Act. Allen and Esters explain that 'the 1890 legislation only mandated that funding for education be distributed annually on a "just and equitable basis" as deemed by the state' (2018: 1). Yet, 'HBLGUs would receive only a single digit percentage of the funding allowed under the Morrill Act' (Allen and Esters, 2018: 4).

In contrast to narratives that the Morrill Act of 1890 was born of lofty democratic ideals, shared public interest and cooperation, Mustaffa states that it legislated white supremacy, '[supporting] the view that blacks were inferior – [and committed] cultural violence reminiscent of the 1857 Dred Scott court decision and confirmed the 1896 *Plessy* decision that followed' (2017: 716). Allen describes the long history of white supremacist decisions by the US Supreme Court, including *Dred Scott v. Sandford* (1857),[5] which continued

---

5 The opinion of the Supreme Court was issued by Chief Justice Taney. Available at: https://

slavery based on the lie that black people were 'beings of an inferior order' and 'had no rights which the white man was bound to respect' (Allen, 2005: 407). Similarly, *Plessy v. Ferguson* (1896) institutionalised the 'separate but equal' doctrine that legalised 'Jim Crow' racial segregation.

The legal landscape: Desegregation and affirmative action

The US legislature and courts have historically preserved white supremacy. Clear examples are seen in the Morrill, *Dred Scott*, and *Plessy* cases. Therefore, to re-envision and transform higher education we must recognise the intersections between higher education and the law. It is essential to reject any notion that either system is neutral in origin or practice. Patton (2016) identifies how US higher education is rooted in white supremacy. For example, the very institution responsible for legal training often fails to problematise both the law and the training (Moore, 2008). Legal education has been critiqued for marginalising the values, experiences and perspectives of 'people of colour' and/or women through the dominant narratives of legal objectivity and neutrality (Crenshaw, 1988; Guinier, Fine and Balin, 1994).

School and higher education desegregation cases

Plessy and the anti-black, 'separate but equal' doctrine show that the United States has a long history of actively pursuing black exclusion. *Brown v. Board of Education of Topeka* (1954) is held as a landmark desegregation case, overturning *Plessy*. Allen (2005) describes the depths to which those committed to white supremacy mobilised after *Brown*:

> The resistance was especially fierce across the Deep South, where white citizens, governors and state legislatures in Arkansas, Mississippi, Alabama, and Georgia defied federal law. In the wake of riots and bloodshed, federal troops had to be mobilised. Congress, the president, and federal agencies passed legislation, issued orders, and enforced laws to overturn the entrenched customs and practices of racial discrimination in education. Even with active federal intervention, progress toward educational desegregation and expanded educational opportunities for blacks in K–12 and in higher education was excruciatingly slow (Allen, 2005: 19).

Adams v. Richardson (1973) reveals especially notable examples of resistance.

---

www.law.cornell.edu/supremecourt/text/60/393#writing-USSC_CR_0060_0393_ZO (accessed November 2018).

The history of events in the declaratory judgment[6] identifies states including Louisiana, Mississippi, Oklahoma, North Carolina, Florida, Arkansas, Pennsylvania, Georgia, Maryland and Virginia that continued to operate racially segregated systems of higher education. The federal government ordered these states to submit desegregation plans, yet they submitted plans late, unacceptable plans or no plans at all. Nevertheless, the US Department of Health, Education and Welfare continued to provide advance federal funding to these states.

Mississippi's failure to desegregate higher education systems was central in various key cases, including *United States v. Fordice* (1992) and *Ayers v. Fordice* (1995; 1999) and in Alabama, *Knight v. State of Alabama* (1995). Analysis of these states and cases shows the challenges resulted from years of inequitable funding and marginalisation (Minor, 2008b; Harper, Patton and Wooden, 2009).

The present

Recently the state of Maryland was charged with continued operation of a racially segregated higher education system which disadvantages HBCUs. The court sided with the plaintiffs, ordering Maryland to remedy unequal investment (Maryland was also included in *Adams*) and establish new programmes at the HBCUs (Douglas-Gabriel, 2017). This year, Maryland offered US$100 million in settlement funding to expand academic programmes at Morgan State University, Coppin State University, Bowie State University and the University of Maryland Eastern Shore (Douglas-Gabriel, 2018). Given determined resistance to funding HBCUs, it remains to be seen whether efforts to eliminate racial segregation in the Maryland public higher education system will be successful.

Higher education affirmative-action cases

The black student higher education landscape across the United States is also deeply affected by affirmative-action bans. The persistently low enrolment of black students in elite public universities in states like California and Michigan is not surprising given systemic racism. Despite demonstrated racial inequities in educational opportunities, both states banned affirmative action programmes (Proposition 209 and Proposal 2). We cannot stress enough the tremendously negative impacts on black participation in higher education of ideologies like 'reverse discrimination', 'colour-blindness' or 'meritocracy' – frequently employed by affirmative-action opponents (Bonilla-Silva, 2017; Tatum, 2017).

---

6   See the Declaratory Judgement by District Judge John H Pratt in *Adams v. Richardson*, 356 F. Supp. (DDC 1973) at https://law.justia.com/cases/federal/district-courts/FSupp/356/92/1892620/.

Key Supreme Court cases in the long history of affirmative action challenges include *Regents of the University of California v. Bakke* (1978), *Gratz v. Bollinger* (2003) at the University of Michigan, *Grutter v. Bollinger* (2003) at the University of Michigan Law School, and *Fisher v. University of Texas at Austin* (2013; 2016). These cases narrowly tailor or strike down the use of race in admission decisions. Cheryl Harris (1993) identifies *Bakke* as an example of the legal maintenance of white property interests. The *Bakke* case enshrined 'reverse discrimination', built on the analysis that Bakke was better qualified – as defined by merit (test scores and grade point averages [GPA]) – than some minority candidates. This is a prevailing example of the Supreme Court's reliance on colour-blindness. Harris argues whiteness and property are linked by the 'right to exclude', further noting:

> Whiteness as property has taken on more subtle forms, but retains its core characteristic – the legal legitimation of expectations of power and control that enshrine the status quo as a neutral baseline, while masking that maintenance of white privilege and domination (1993: 1715).

The attack on affirmative action continued in *Grutter*, where the University of Michigan Law School affirmative-action practices were upheld. However, the Supreme Court proposed an arbitrary timeline of 25 years before ending or 'sun-setting' these programmes. Bonilla-Silva illuminates its effect, stating the programme deadline 'encourages a monumental case-by-case analysis for admitting students that is likely to create chaos and push institutions into making admission decisions based on test scores' (2017: 190). Test scores, like high school GPAs, are seen as neutral measures that reinforce conceptions of merit. In fact, these measures ignore the many systemic factors that disadvantage black students long before they even begin their college applications.

Interest convergence theory requires us to look beyond legislation at face value and rather investigate underlying motives. Critical race theory (CRT) scholar Derrick Bell (1980; 2003) critiqued *Brown* and *Grutter* by asking how a nation deeply committed to racial injustice would deliver *Brown* and uphold race-conscious admissions in *Grutter*. He offers that *Brown* was due to the alignment of black and white interests, where the United States was less committed to racial justice and more concerned with upholding political and economic advantages related to its global image as a just, fair society. This positive, idealistic image of the United States was tainted by global news showing police dogs attacking peaceful civil rights demonstrators in the South advocating for black rights.

In *Grutter*, Bell (2003) shows that the swing vote cast by Justice O'Connor, who traditionally voted against race-conscious policies, relied on rationales for enhanced learning outcomes and the workplace benefits of diversity underscored in *amici* briefs from corporations and the military. Bell (2003) states that 'When [O'Connor] perceived in the Michigan Law School's admissions programme an affirmative action plan that minimises the importance of race while offering maximum protection to whites and those aspects of society with which she identifies, she supported it' (Bell, 2003: 1625). These court cases underscore the position that racism is not a vestige of the past, rather it continues to be a defining feature of US institutions (Ladson-Billings, 2013).

Higher education barriers
In this non-exhaustive section, we highlight several systemic barriers to higher education for black students. Our aim is to pinpoint deeply rooted inequities that continue to enact violence upon black students. These findings are not novel rather they are commonplace and reflective of how 'a host of barriers calculated to insure the perpetuation of a status quo rooted in an unfair system of racial stratification is reproduced within the university' (Allen, 1992: 42). Adding to this inequity are issues of ballooning student debt, campus hostility, federal and state higher education disinvestment, and aversion to naming white supremacy in US society.

It is important to specify anti-black oppression in educational research and settings. Dumas describes how 'education must grapple with cultural disregard for and disgust with blackness' (2016: 12). One cannot properly identify the barriers to higher education for black students without the theorisation of anti-blackness. Reflecting on the work of W.E.B. Du Bois, Dumas offers: 'One can read Du Bois as seeking an education for black people that creates spaces to disrupt the exclusion of the black from the cultural and political regard extended to those who are presumed Human' (2016: 17). Furthermore, Dumas states that racialised educational policy incorporates 'a concern with the bodies of black people, the significance of (their) blackness, and the threat posed by the black to the educational well-being of other students' (Dumas, 2016: 12). Higher education as a site of anti-blackness can be seen in the examples of black student exclusion (Allen et al, 2018) and attempts to control and undercut HBCUs as spaces of black life making (Allen and Jewell, 2002; Mustaffa, 2017). The following discussion underscores this position and the importance of lived experiences.

Debt
Earlier we mentioned high costs and student loan debt, and although our

chapter is not focused on this issue, we would be remiss not to underscore it as a *huge* barrier in US higher education. As Bishop states, 'student debt from college enrolment is now an edifice of racialised poverty' (2018: 6). In the United States, the majority of black students borrow, many at extreme amounts. In 2012, data from the National Center for Education Statistics Postsecondary Student Aid Study show that only 14 per cent of black bachelor's degree recipients did not incur debt (the lowest among represented racial and ethnic groups), but one-third incurred $40 000 or more in student debt (the highest among those represented) (Baum et al, 2015).

In 2012, black students had the highest rates of loans overall, at 52.3 per cent, and both subsidised and unsubsidised loans, at 48 and 44 per cent, respectively (Goldrick-Rab, Kelchen and Houle, 2014). Black students had the second-highest rates of both private and PLUS loans, at 6 and 4.3 per cent, respectively. Also, in 2012, looking to institutional type, '73 per cent of students at for-profit colleges took federal loans, compared to 65 per cent of students attending HBCUs, 63 per cent of students at non-HBCU four-year private non-profit colleges, 50 per cent of students at four-year public colleges, and 17 per cent of students at community colleges' (Goldrick-Rab, Kelchen and Houle 2014: 19). They point especially to the growth in unsubsidised loans at for-profit HBCUs and community colleges. Allen reminds educators, policy-makers, legislators and administrators that 'where adequate financial aid is readily available, more black students matriculate and graduate' (1992: 41). Put simply, this economic disenfranchisement of black students and HBCUs is not by accident.

Campus hostility

In examining higher education spaces, critical scholarship has problèmatised campus hostility for black students at HWIs and identified stereotypes, messages of being 'out-of-place', hyper-surveillance, lack of support, policing and institutionalised gendered racism (Smith et al, 2016; Corbin, Smith and Garcia, 2018; Green et al, 2018).

Hurtado et al (1998) propose a framework and key recommendations for understanding campus climate at HWIs, centring race and ethnicity and racism. They explain several reasons for the lack of a common framework for campus racial climate (for example, role ambiguity, histories of neglect, marginalisation of critical theories and research). Their proposed framework consists of policy and practice recommendations within four areas to address campus climate including: (1) the institutional context and the historical legacy of inclusion or exclusion, (2) structural diversity, (3) the psychological dimension, and (4) the behavioural dimension. These domains importantly centre perceptions and experiences.

Looking to the White House

Throughout this work we have shown the severe federal and state disinvestment in HBCUs – an example of systemic racism. Minimal federal investment is coupled with increased accountability pressures from the White House Initiative on HBCUs, described as largely ineffective and dwindling in support to HBCUs (Minor, 2008a). The Donald Trump administration created the White House Initiative on HBCUs to focus on increasing the role of the private sector and philanthropic organisations within HBCUs (Trump, 2017). This announcement threatens to diminish federal investment and ignore the long history of private-sector, white missionary involvement and white positional power over HBCUs, resulting in curricula based on the notion of black inferiority (Allen and Jewel, 2002; Mustaffa, 2017).

Naming white supremacy/racism

Scholarship has critiqued 'racelessness' in US higher education, the aversion to naming white supremacy/racism and the failure to centre race and racism in analyses (Harper, 2012; Patton, 2016). For example, Patton et al (2007) critique a key area of higher education scholarship, student identity development, for the failure to centre race in theorising about student experiences and meaning-making processes.

We must recognise the ways racism, power and oppression intersect and are ingrained within the United States (Harris, 2015). CRT scholars boldly underline the centrality of racism. Ladson-Billings cautioned 20 years earlier that 'adopting and adapting CRT as a framework for educational equity means that we will have to expose racism in education *and* propose radical solutions for addressing it. We will have to take bold and sometimes unpopular positions' (1998: 22).

Recommendations

The harsh history of racism in the United States has plagued HBCUs, but despite seemingly insurmountable challenges, they continue to produce black graduates. While some landmark court cases and federal policies have contractually paved the way for educational equity for the black community, there are discrepancies between policy formulation and implementation. Slow governmental action to desegregate and discriminatory funding allocation by the state exacerbate many challenges that continue to undermine HBCUs today. In addition, mainstream media unfairly portray HBCUs as corrupt and ill-managed. Confusion over the issues that plague contemporary HBCUs creates challenges to supporting the case for their ongoing relevance in the current higher educational system in the United States.

The future direction of the HBCUs is a point of confusion for the higher education community for two reasons (Minor, 2008b). The contextual understanding of race and education is absent among public and higher educational professionals and scholars, and is essential for recommending sound solutions via scholarship, practice and policy. This knowledge gap is exaggerated by the diverse context, demographics and institutional types of the HBCUs. Second, public HBCUs are stuck between their historical mission and their continued evolution and relevance amidst increasing race/ethnic diversity in the United States. Furthermore, Minor (2008b) argues that although scholars understand the contribution HBCUs have made in the American educational landscape, very few are able to articulate their place and purpose in this generation and the future. Instead of reminiscing about their past, he argues, HBCUs must be better understood in the contemporary context.

To make HBCUs relevant and competitive in this current landscape, there needs to be a clear articulation and realisation of their vital role in the higher education milieu in the midst of overlapping challenges across institution types. Current challenges include, but are not limited to, demographic shifts in college enrolment, accountability and assessment, legal mandates, decreasing endowment, and changes to the curriculum and pedagogical demands (Minor, 2008b; Andrews et al, 2016). It has been difficult for HBCU leaders to secure support in this particular political and economic context. Andrews et al (2016) argue that an entrepreneurial approach to current issues could alleviate reliance on inconsistent and absent government funding, help find new strategic ways to secure external funding and community partnerships, more clearly articulate purpose in the form of branding, streamline services in more cost-effective ways and improve student recruitment.

The push to diversify HBCU enrolment sparks questions about how to be marketable to a wide range of students and competitive in the higher education market without losing the commitment to the black community. Minor (2008b) suggests that although HBCUs should not become white institutions, they should rethink how they market to students of all demographics. On the other hand, Nichols (2004) states that HBCU leadership must be adept at dealing with these issues while keeping its mission to serve the black community intact. Similarly, Freeman and Cohen (2001) argue that, in this generation, it is vital for HBCUs to strategically enhance the economic and cultural empowerment of African Americans in three ways:

> (a) playing [a] greater role in knowledge production as it specifically relates to African Americans, (b) being involved to a much greater

extent in urban development, and (c) having more leaders with vision and an understanding of the need to bridge the gap between cultural empowerment and economic development (Freeman and Cohen, 2001: 592).

Committing to the economic and cultural empowerment of African-American students will allow HBCUs to compete in an increasingly global economy while also making the curricula and campus culture culturally relevant to their core constituency.

References

Alexander, M (2010) *The New Jim Crow: Mass incarceration in the age of colour blindness*. New York: New Press.

Allen, BCM and Esters, LT (2018) Historically black land-grant universities: Overcoming barriers and achieving success. Center for Minority Serving Institutions, University of Pennsylvania. Available at: https://cmsi.gse.upenn.edu/content/historically-black-land-grant-universities-overcoming-barriers-and-achieving-success (accessed October 2018).

Allen, WR (1992) The colour of success: African-American college student outcomes at predominantly white and historically black public colleges and universities, *Harvard Educational Review*, **62**(1): 26–44.

Allen, WR (2005) A forward glance in a mirror: Diversity challenged – access, equity, and success in higher education, *Educational Researcher*, **34**(7): 18–23.

Allen, WR and Jewell, JO (2002) A backward glance forward: Past, present, and future perspectives on historically black colleges and universities, *The Review of Higher Education*, **25**: 241–61.

Allen, WR, Jewell, JO, Griffin, KA and Wolf, DS (2007) Historically black colleges and universities: Honoring the past, engaging the present, touching the future, *The Journal of Negro Education*, **76**(3): 263–80.

Allen, WR, McLewis, C, Jones, C and Harris, D (2018) From *Bakke* to *Fisher*: Black students in US higher education over forty years, in ST Gooden and SL Myers Jr (eds) *The Fiftieth Anniversary of the Kerner Commission Report*. New York: Russell Sage Foundation, pp. 41–72.

Anderson, JD (1988) *The Education of Blacks in the South, 1860–1935*. Chapel Hill, NC: University of North Carolina Press.

Andrews, DR, No, S, Powell, KK, Rey, MP and Yigletu, A (2016) Historically black colleges and universities' institutional survival and sustainability: A view from the HBCU Business Deans' perspective, *Journal of Black Studies*, **47**(2): 150–68.

Baum, S, Ma, J, Pender, M and Bell, DW (2015) *Trends in Student Aid, 2015*. Trends in Higher Education Series. New York: College Board. Available at: https://trends.collegeboard.org/sites/default/files/trends-student-aid-web-final-508-2.pdf (accessed 20 October 2019).

Bell, D (1980) *Brown v. Board of Education* and the interest-convergence dilemma, *Harvard Law Review*, **93**(3): 518–33.

Bell, D (2003) Diversity's distractions, *Columbia Law Review*, **103**(6): 1622–33.

Bishop, JM (2018) A critical case study on (anti)blackness, geography and education pathways in Twinsburg Heights, Ohio. PhD dissertation, University of California Los Angeles, Los Angeles.

Bonilla-Silva, E (2017) *Racism without Racists: Colour-blind racism and the persistence of racial inequality in America*, 5th edition. Lanham, MD: Rowman & Littlefield.

Brown, MC (2013) The declining significance of historically black colleges and universities:

Relevance, reputation and reality in Obamamerica, *The Journal of Negro Education*, **82**(1): 3–19.

Corbin, NA, Smith, W and Garcia, JG (2018) Trapped between justified anger and being the strong black woman: Black college women coping with racial battle fatigue at historically and predominantly white institutions, *International Journal of Qualitative Studies in Education*, **31**(7): 626–43.

Crenshaw, KW (1988) Toward a race-conscious pedagogy in legal education, *National Black Law Journal*, **11**(1): 1–14.

Douglas-Gabriel, D (2017) Courts side with Maryland HBCUs in long-standing case over disparities in state higher education, *The Washington Post*, 9 November. Available at: https://www.washingtonpost.com/news/grade-point/wp/2017/11/09/courts-side-with-maryland-hbcus-in-longstanding-case-over-disparities-in-state-higher-education/?utm_term=.08425e851017 (accessed November 2018).

Douglas-Gabriel, D (2018) Maryland offers $100 million to settle decade-long case involving historically Black schools, *The Washington Post*, 7 February. Available at: https://www.washingtonpost.com/news/grade-point/wp/2018/02/07/maryland-offers-100-million-to-settle-decade-long-case-involving-historically-black-schools/?utm_term=.0be761b60470 (accessed November 2018).

Dumas, MJ (2016) Against the dark: Anti-blackness in education policy and discourse, *Theory into Practice*, **55**(1): 11–19.

Freeman, KR and Cohen, T (2001) Bridging the gap between economic development and cultural empowerment: HBCUs' challenges for the future, *Urban Education*, **36**(5): 585–96.

Goldrick-Rab, S, Kelchen, R and Houle, J (2014) *The Colour of Student Debt: Implications of Federal Loan Programme reforms for black students and historically black colleges and universities.* Wisconsin HOPE Lab. Available at: https://news.education.wisc.edu/docs/WebDispenser/news-connections-pdf/thecolorofstudentdebt-draft.pdf?sfvrsn=4 (accessed November 2018).

Green, D, Pulley, T, Jackson, M, Martin, LL and Fasching-Varner, KJ (2018) Mapping the margins and searching for higher ground: Examining the marginalisation of black female graduate students at PWIs, *Gender and Education*, **30**(3): 295–309.

Guinier, L, Fine, M and Balin, J (1994) Becoming gentlemen: Women's experiences at one Ivy League Law School, *University of Pennsylvania Law Review*, **143**(1): 1–110.

Harper, SR (2012) Race without racism: How higher education researchers minimise racist institutional norms, *The Review of Higher Education*, **36**(1): 9–29.

Harper, SR, Patton, LD and Wooden, OS (2009) Access and equity for African American students in higher education: A critical race historical analysis of policy efforts, *The Journal of Higher Education*, **80**(4): 389–414.

Harris, AP (2015) Critical race theory, in JD Wright (ed.) *International Encyclopedia of the Social & Behavioral Sciences.* Amsterdam: Elsevier, pp. 266–70.

Harris, CI (1993) Whiteness as property, *Harvard Law Review*, **106**(8): 1707–91.

Hurtado, S, Clayton-Pedersen, AR, Allen, WR and Milem, JF (1998) Enhancing campus climates for racial/ethnic diversity: Educational policy and practice, *The Review of Higher Education*, **21**(3). 279–302.

Iloh, C and Toldson, IA (2013) Black students in 21st century higher education: A closer look at for-profit and community colleges (Editor's commentary), *The Journal of Negro Education*, **82**(3): 205–12.

Jewell, JO (2002) To set an example: The tradition of diversity at historically black colleges and universities, *Urban Education*, **37**(1): 7–21.

Jewell, JO (2007) *Race, Social Reform and the Making of a Middle Class: The American Missionary Association and Black Atlanta.* Lanham, MD: Rowman & Littlefield.

Ladson-Billings, G (1998) Just what is critical race theory and what's it doing in a nice field like education? *Qualitative Studies in Education*, **11**(1): 7–24.

Ladson-Billings, G (2013) Critical race theory: What it is not! In M Lynn and AD Dixson (eds) *Handbook of Critical Race Theory in Education*. New York: Routledge, pp. 54–67.

Lee, JM, Jr and Keys, SW (2013) Land-grant but unequal: State one-to-one match funding for 1890 land-grant universities. The Office for Access and Success Policy Brief: Association of Public and Land-Grant Universities. Available at: http://www.aplu.org/library/land-grant-but-unequal-state-one-to-one-match-funding-for-1890-land-grant-universities/file (accessed July 2018).

Minor, JT (2008a) Contemporary HBCUs: Considering institutional capacity and state priorities. Michigan State University, College of Education, Department of Educational Administration. Available at: https://steinhardt.nyu.edu/scmsAdmin/uploads/002/151/MINOR_Contemporary_HBCU_Report_2008.pdf (accessed July 2018).

Minor, JT (2008b) A contemporary perspective on the role of public HBCUs: Perspicacity from Mississippi, *The Journal of Negro Education*, **77**(4): 323–35.

Moore, WL (2008) *Reproducing Racism: White space, elite law schools, and racial inequality*. Lanham, MD: Rowman & Littlefield Publishers.

Mustaffa, JB (2017) Mapping violence, naming life: A history of anti-black oppression in the higher education system, *International Journal of Qualitative Studies in Education*, **30**(8): 711–27.

Nichols, JC (2004) Unique characteristics, leadership styles and management of historically black colleges and universities, *Innovative Higher Education*, **28**(3): 219–29.

Patton, LD (2016) Disrupting post-secondary prose: Toward a critical race theory of higher education, *Urban Education*, **5**(3): 315–42.

Patton, LD, McEwen, M, Rendón, L and Howard-Hamilton, MF (2007) Critical race perspectives on theory in student affairs, *New Directions for Student Services*, **120** (Special issue: *Responding to the Realities of Race on Campus*): 39–53.

Smith, WA, Mustaffa, JB, Jones, CM, Curry, TJ and Allen, WR (2016) 'You make me wanna holler and throw up both my hands!' Campus culture, black misandric microaggressions, and racial battle fatigue, *International Journal of Qualitative Studies in Education*, **29**(9): 1189–209.

Snyder, TD, De Brey, C and Dillow, SA (2018a) Total fall enrolment in degree-granting postsecondary institutions, by level of enrolment, sex, attendance status, and race/ethnicity of student: Selected years, 1976 through 2015. Table 306.10. *Digest of Education Statistics 2016*, 52nd edition, NCES 2017-094. Washington, DC: US Department of Education, National Center for Education Statistics. Available at: https://eric.ed.gov/?id=ED580954 (accessed July 2019).

Snyder, TD, De Brey, C and Dillow, SA (2018b) Associate's degrees conferred by postsecondary institutions, by race/ethnicity and sex of student: Selected years, 1976–77 through 2014-15. Table 321.20. Washington, DC: US Department of Education, National Center for Education Statistics. Available at: https://eric.ed.gov/?id=ED580954 (accessed July 2019).

Snyder, TD, De Brey, C and Dillow, SA (2018c) Bachelor's degrees conferred by postsecondary institutions, by race/ethnicity and sex of student: Selected years, 1976-77 through 2014-15. Table 322.20. Washington, DC: US Department of Education, National Center for Education Statistics. Available at: https://eric.ed.gov/?id=ED580954 (accessed July 2019).

Snyder, TD, De Brey, C and Dillow, SA (2018d) Master's degrees conferred by postsecondary institutions, by race/ethnicity and sex of student: Selected years, 1976–77 through 2014–15. Table 323.20. Washington, DC: US Department of Education, National Center for Education Statistics. Available at: https://eric.ed.gov/?id=ED580954 (accessed July 2019).

Snyder, TD, De Brey, C and Dillow, SA (2018e) Doctor's degrees conferred by postsecondary institutions, by race/ethnicity and sex of student: Selected years, 1976–77 through 2014–

15. Table 324.20. Washington, DC: US Department of Education, National Center for Education Statistics. Available at: https://eric.ed.gov/?id=ED580954 (accessed July 2019).

Snyder, TD, De Brey, C and Dillow, SA (2018f) Total fall enrolment in degree-granting postsecondary institutions, by level and control of institution and race/ethnicity of student: Selected years, 1976 through 2015. Table 306.20. Washington, DC: US Department of Education, National Center for Education Statistics. Available at: https://eric.ed.gov/?id=ED580954 (accessed July 2019).

Snyder, TD, De Brey, C and Dillow, SA (2018g) Selected statistics on degree-granting historically Black colleges and universities, by control and level of institution: Selected years, 1990 through 2015. Table 313.30. Washington, DC: US Department of Education, National Center for Education Statistics. Available at: https://eric.ed.gov/?id=ED580954 (accessed July 2019).

Snyder, TD, De Brey, C and Dillow, SA (2018h) Fall enrolment in degree-granting historically Black colleges and universities, by sex of student and level and control of institution: Selected years, 1976 through 2015. Table 313.20. Washington, DC: US Department of Education, National Center for Education Statistics. Available at: https://eric.ed.gov/?id=ED580954 (accessed July 2019).

Tatum, BD (2017) *Why Are All the Black Kids Sitting Together in the Cafeteria? And other conversations about race*. New York: Basic Books.

Trump, D (2017) Presidential Executive Order on the White House Initiative to Promote Excellence and Innovation at Historically Black Colleges and Universities. Available at: https://www.whitehouse.gov/presidential-actions/presidential-executive-order-white-house-initiative-promote-excellence-innovation-historically-black-colleges-universities/ (accessed July 2018).

Wilder, CS (2013) *Ebony and Ivy: Race, slavery, and the troubled history of America's universities*. New York: Bloomsbury Press.

Supreme Court Cases

Adams v. Richardson, 356 F. Supp. 92 (D.D.C. 1973).
Ayers v. Fordice, 879 F. Supp. 1419 (ND Miss. 1995).
Ayers v. Fordice, 40 F. Supp. 2d 382 (ND Miss. 1999).
Brown v. Board of Education of Topeka, 347 US 483 (1954).
Dred Scott v. Sandford, 60 US 393 (1857).
Fisher v. University of Texas, 570 US ____ (2013).
Fisher v. University of Texas, 579 US ____ (2016).
Gratz v. Bollinger, 539 US 244 (2003).
Grutter v. Bollinger, 539 US 306 (2003).
Knight v. State of Alabama, 900 F. Supp. 272 (ND Ala. 1995).
Plessy v. Ferguson, 163 US 537 (1896).
Regents of the University of California v. Bakke, 438 US 265 (1978).
Sweatt v. Painter, 339 US 629 (1950).
United States v. Fordice, 505 US 717 (1992).

Section VIII: Conclusion

Chapter 24
Conclusion: Key lessons for South Africa's curriculum transformation in the humanities from Africa and African-American studies

Shireen Motala

This book has provided a set of overarching themes and cases from the South African, African and African-American contexts. The volume has highlighted the fact that transformation efforts within higher education are part of ongoing struggles between civil society and political formations, which have different interests and negotiate change in the context of often contradictory relations, different values and conflicting perspectives over redistribution of resources, power and knowledge generation.

As the book has illustrated, the conditions and strategic directions in higher education were established without a deep understanding of the post-independence state in Africa and its constraints. While the purpose of the transformation project was to replace the colonial policies, structures, values and practices, these goals were difficult to achieve within a framework of compromises and concessions determined by Africa's post-independence politics and South Africa's political transition between 1990 and 1994 (Rensburg, 2017). In South Africa, the knowledge project remained largely untouched and colonial legacies persisted, as convincingly argued by several authors in this book. In other parts of Africa, schools of thought emerged challenging colonial paradigms: the Ibadan School of History, the Dakar School of Culture, the Dar es Salaam School of Political Economy, as well as curricula transformation projects in Ghana, Kenya and Uganda. As in South Africa, in the United States the approach was to assimilate into the dominant knowledge frameworks, with little regard for indigenous knowledge systems, oral traditions, culture and difference. The response was one of a struggle for agency around ideology, the form of knowledge creation and generation, and the purpose of education for national development. This gave voice to African and African-American scholarship, as seen in the Howard and Atlanta schools, with the focus beyond education transformation to include societal change.

Struggle is a dominant theme of this book, through political praxis, contestation around ideas and transition. While there is a vast literature on Western epistemological, theoretical and methodological orientations in higher education research, this book makes an important and original contribution to the development of African and African-American scholarship, its creativity and originality, and the fusion of indigenous knowledge systems with new forms of knowledge. Disciplinary, interdisciplinary and transdisciplinary bases of higher education are foregrounded in the African and African-American scholarship so richly described in this publication. In the post-independence era, Africa's tertiary institutions were caught in the tension between global and national priorities. The national priorities included redress, equity, access and efficiency. The global priorities included global competitiveness, high skills and the demands of a knowledge economy. The various discourses on curricula reform have resulted in diverse content and pedagogic practices (Lange, 2017). The insights that emerged from this book may be summarised under five headings: (1) transformation, (2) developing agency, (3) decolonising the curriculum, (4) the role of African scholarship in making knowledge accessible, and (5) implementing change in African-American studies.

The overarching themes reflect the cross-continental strands of inquiry and represent the major contribution of this book. It is, therefore, by way of conclusion, important to attempt to consider how the themes speak to one another, as a way of synthesising the lessons for South African higher education. The value of this volume is evident in the richness of cross-continental analyses, and the implications for local and global development of higher education. The interrelatedness of these broad themes is illustrated in, for example, the meanings and interpretations of transformation and how in many instances it was in fact reforms that took place. Given the dominance of the Western episteme and its hegemonic and stronghold nature, the extent to which it can provide a platform to engage in genuine transformation is constrained.

South African author Brenda Leibowitz notes that this does not imply that all forms of knowledge are equal, but that the equality of knowers forms the basis of dialogue between knowledges, and what is required for democracy to function is a dialogue among knowers and their knowledges (Leibowitz, 2017). The imperative is thus to rethink the constitutive rules for the university–society nexus; the purpose of universities; and who owns the knowledge that they generate (Odora Hoppers and Richards, 2012). Efforts towards curriculum transformation ignite questions around whose and what knowledge is privileged, and whether having African voices is a sufficient condition for transformation. As Knowles observes, we are profoundly challenged by inequalities that are not adequately addressed by the various groups that make up the university, evident in the power relations that can influence one's status in a university space (see Knowles, Chapter 8, in this volume). In this regard, the Gramscian notion of organic intellectuals is relevant to South Africa and across Africa. Stakeholders need to engage with the constitutive roles of all intellectuals in society and restore the role of knowledge holders outside the university (Visvanathan, 2011; Odora Hoppers, 2013). It is critical to redefine knowledge as a process of societal change, and not knowledge for itself.

Portuguese scholar Bonaventura de Sousa Santos (2007) labels this cognitive crisis in higher education as abyssal thinking; Argentinian academic Carlos Torres (1998) describes it as a need for knowledge democracy; Indian scholar Shiv Visvanathan (1998; 2006) dubs it as the practice in the academy of museumising knowledge which communities develop for livelihoods; while Ugandan academic Catherine Odora Hoppers (2013) describes it as the decades/centuries of cognitive injustices and subjugation.

Transformation imperatives in higher education

The first theme – transformation – is arguably the most dominant theme in the South African context. The transformation challenges in South Africa include resource scarcity and its impact on especially historically disadvantaged institutions (HDIs), rethinking knowledge industry and curriculum revisions. Resource scarcity of funding, infrastructure, IT access and food security for students affect research and teaching (see Mngomezulu, Chapter 6, in this volume). In Chapter 5, Shireen Motala focused on the policies of successive post-apartheid governments around education funding and access to higher education. Some of the authors in this volume have noted how the knowledge project in post-apartheid South Africa continues to be characterised by the persistence of Eurocentric curricula in higher education and a heavy reliance on 'knowledge metropolises of the Global North' (see Tella, Chapter 1, Adebajo, Chapter 2, and Bawa, Chapter 4). A recurring theme is of universities as social institutions and whether there is a need for a new social compact between higher education and societal formations. While issues around epistemology (Motala, 2014) seem to have been adequately engaged, questions of ontology and worldview – especially on issues such as racism and Western institutional cultures – have received little attention in South Africa (see Soudien, Chapter 3, in this volume).

The meaning, impact and effects of transformation in higher education in the global context have been limited. In a number of contexts, the emphasis has been on transformation instead of reform; however, what has often taken place is reform; as these two processes are inextricably linked. Southern African academics Michael Cross and Amasa Ndofirepi (2017) note that transformation in higher education consists of a process that involves new knowledge production and reflexive action, implying the exploration of new problems while at the same time being innovative in dealing with the old ones. These are essential for the continuous deconstruction and reconstruction of social reality, as well as social reintegration to respond innovatively, creatively and responsively to the present and future needs of society. All of which raises a final and troubling question for radical change in our universities. If in fact the curriculum problem is one in which African-centred knowledge displaces Western forms of knowledge, where are the new intellectual authorities to displace resident powers? South African academic Philip Higgs explains this by suggesting that the hegemony of the Western episteme eroded the rich knowledge legacy of the African people. Transmodernity then attempts to establish an integrated form of knowledge, which acknowledges both indigenous African knowledge systems and Western forms of knowledge (see Chapter 12 in this volume). This means that attempts at reclaiming an African episteme should not in any way strive for an epistemology of exclusion.

Key to the global challenges in higher education development is the distinction between reform and transformation, with reform denoting incremental and smaller changes, and transformation implying drastic and often radical changes (Van der Westhuizen, 2007). Transformative changes in higher education need 'rethinking thinking', which implies going beyond regulative changes to reconsider the historical and philosophical bases of education for the sake of constitutive changes (Odora Hoppers and Richards, 2012).

The response: Developing agency
A second theme is that this publication has provided a platform for the leadership of student movements across South African universities. Reminiscent of the apartheid era, the sense of a lack of agency surfaced in the South African academy between 2015 and 2017. Embarking on widespread protests, students took to campuses and the streets to demand free, decolonised and equitable education. Linking politics and protest, by using a qualitative approach, South African former student activist Musawenkosi Malabela reflected on the political climate during the student protests at the University of the Witwatersrand. He also engaged the polarised discourse between stakeholders, management and students, and their intergenerational differences (Chapter 7). South African-Zambian scholar Corrine Knowles, who wrote on Rhodes University in this volume, has argued that, without a political framework that permeates teaching, working and research, transformation will replicate neoliberal values and practices, highlighting the gap between the political praxis of protest and the transformation discourse. South African former student activist Sandile Ndelu eloquently presented in her chapter on the University of Cape Town (UCT)

how the repertoire of tactics and strategies, embodied by 'the very presence of bodies on the picket line', brought to the fore the discourses of decolonisation, decommodification and transformation in the #FeesMustFall campaign.

In Chapter 16, the Nigerian scholar Harry Garuba noted the critiques of the Heinemann African Writers series, while highlighting several practices set in motion by the series that could be potentially beneficial to the South African decolonisation imperative. These include the publication of low-cost paperbacks, republishing and reprinting classic texts and titles, translating books from French into English, and promoting a pedagogic 'imaginary' in the making of the canon of contemporary African literature.

A point made by South African educationist Ahmed Bawa is whether there could be a possibility of the 2018 generation of universities engaging with their new diverse and plural publics. This would be through their knowledge projects and the way in which they are involved in systematic and systemic change. As South African scholar Crain Soudien argued, this has to produce the foundations of a new ontology and epistemology of a more complete liberation, which South Africa's negotiated settlement did not produce. This is a critical learning opportunity from the United States and Africa. The university–society nexus and the issue of relevance thus need to be engaged.

Transformation and decolonising the curricula

In Chapter 10, South African academic Joel Modiri considered the possible conditions for a project to decolonise knowledge – the third theme – arguing that any movement that aims to implement the decolonisation of the curricula and the university itself must be linked to the struggle for a decolonised world. Using the disciplinary lens of sociology, Nigerian scholar Jimi Adesina argued that while sociological scholarship is grounded in its specific setting, there is a continued reliance on received modes of reasoning, and Western theories are often taught out of context. There continues to be a tendency to work in the familiar terrain of sociological knowledge, with an absence of African scholarly texts and scholarship, including African diaspora scholarship. This has resulted in an ongoing problem of 'status anxiety' in relation to global and local contexts.

South African academic Philip Higgs suggested in Chapter 12 that curriculum transformation should not exclude and negate Western forms of knowledge, but should rather be directed at what he refers to as a 'fusion of epistemologies', which seeks to integrate both indigenous African knowledges and Western forms of knowledge. He argued that such a fusion can provide the epistemological framework for transforming South Africa's education curricula.

Different authors have addressed the decolonial turn in South Africa in diverse ways. Crain Soudien has pointed out that it has brought to the fore the urgency to address the politics of our contemporary knowledge affordances. He argued that it has not developed a significant discursive framework and set of analytical procedures for understanding the complexity of racism. What is clear, though, is that the '#FeesMustFall' student protests highlighted some of the structural issues in South African universities, such as the marginalisation of African experiences in the curricula. Significantly, the movement has restored decolonisation and transformation debates into the national discourse – but this is not the same as a decolonial curriculum. In broad terms, it is a critical theory of education, that, through knowledge transaction across the disciplines, history, race, class, gender and power are recognised in ways that advance social justice in the classroom. Such teaching is incredibly difficult, even for those who subscribe to critical perspectives in the social, natural and biomedical sciences. It is even more challenging for those who do not buy into this particular perspective on the curriculum, knowledge and society. This, of course, raises the ethical question: since this is one view of curriculum, can it be required of those who teach in open institutions called universities and in democratic societies such as South Africa?

Making knowledge accessible, and the role of African scholarship

The fourth overarching theme in this book deals with the dilemmas of the immediate post-independence phase in Africa in the 1960s, when contestations over whose knowledge is taught, what knowledge was developed and the role of ideology took centre stage against a backdrop of domestic socio-economic and political realities and the global decline of socialism. The role of public intellectuals and public scholarship was debated as academics moved between scholarship and activism (Mamdani, 2007). This led to the emergence of centres of excellence across Africa. The Ibadan School of History offered a bold initiative that used a variety of different sources to offer an African perspective on the pre-colonial and colonial periods. It was a bold and important initiative, making much-needed changes to African scholarship and history at continental and global levels. However, there were criticisms, including whether the Ibadan School's ideology of nationalist historiography was relevant for Africa's present. Other concerns with methodology and theory emerged, about its relevance and whether in fact the school was intellectually and politically conservative (see Falola, Chapter 13).

Focusing on the Dar es Salaam School of Political Economy, Tanzanian scholar Severine Rugumamu analysed Africa's underdevelopment from a systemic perspective. The crisis in the capitalist accumulation system from the mid-1970s, the disintegration of the global socialist system and the successful development experiences of countries in East Asia led to the decline of the Marxist political economy school at the University of Dar es Salaam. This resulted in the rise of the ideology of neoliberalism. Rugumamu also highlighted the changing societal needs, as education shifted from an elite system to embrace greater access and inclusion imperatives, which required vast changes in the post-colonial era, especially in curricula transformation and knowledge production. Reminding us of Gramsci's view of 'organic intellectuals', as those who support the interests and aspirations of the oppressed social classes, he suggested that the African intelligentsia embrace this Marxian political economy perspective. Related to this is how best to implement state-sanctioned directives of defining and redesigning the education curricula at all levels to reflect the imperatives of building a democratic society, politics and economy.

The Dakar School of Culture marked a decisive epistemological break in colonial historiography, also introducing a multinational and multidisciplinary emphasis to this work. According to the Senegalese scholar Samba Mboup, the central figures were Senegal's Cheikh Anta Diop and Abdoulaye Ly and Egypt's Samir Amin. He highlights, in particular, the contribution to Afrikology as an alternative paradigm for knowledge generation and application, noting the implications of this for curricula reform and alternative pedagogies. He also considers Samir Amin's work on the important role of indigenous knowledge and educational systems and of work written in Arabic. One of the most important contributions of the Dakar School was to highlight the significance of mother-tongue-based multilingual education in a way that it could acquire greater pedagogic value, a specific contribution of Congo's Théophile Obenga.

An unresolved aspect of South Africa's democratic transition, which surfaced powerfully in the student protests in 2015–17, is the extent to which languages have been superficially adopted by universities in an attempt to improve communication. Several scholars are pointing to the need to develop African languages as academic, research and knowledge-making instruments. New concepts of language for learning include multilingual development, trans-languaging, and linguistic and cultural pluralism – as well as accepting the *Ubuntu* principle that one language is incomplete without the other (Makalela, 2019).

Following on this theme, in Chapter 18 Ugandan academic Pamela Khanakwa, tracking the process of Africanisation at Makerere University in Uganda, highlighted the importance of capacity-building and changes in staff profile, which were deliberately and carefully implemented between 1963 and 1972. The concern with the development of an African professoriate continues to be of great concern, even in South Africa today. Khanakwa made the important observation that Africanisation of staff does not necessarily translate into curriculum transformation. As she noted, some of the Ugandan staff preferred European-oriented courses at the expense of African courses, and non-African heads of department contributed significantly to curriculum transformation. In Chapter 19, Kenyan scholar Chris Wanjala examined East Africa's post-independence experience, illustrating how new knowledge was created incorporating local knowledge. The Nairobi School of Literature emerged in the 1970s with scholars such as Kenya's Ngũgĩ wa Thiong'o and Ugandan Taban Lo Liyong, and set out to promote 'aesthetic theories based on oral literature', centred on African people, society and history. This led to the development of a popular literature, which provided a mirror of the society in which people lived. Within these issues are important lessons about what constitutes curriculum transformation, issues that are especially relevant for South Africa.

Ghanaian scholar David Owusu-Ansah illustrated in his chapter, through an extensive historical review of Ghana, that there are no 'quick fixes' in addressing the challenges to reforming national education systems. There is an urgent need to expand the curricula to engage in knowledge production that is culturally appropriate. Owusu-Ansah's views resonate with those of Motala (Chapter 5) about the need for quality post-secondary education to create an effective pipeline to tertiary education, and the challenges faced by 'economically deprived students' and their parents' ability to meet these costs.

Political praxis: Implementing change in African-American studies

The fifth and final overarching theme deals with implementing change in African-American studies. American scholars Walter Allen, Chantal Jones and Gadise Regassa, in their co-authored chapter, highlighted the racism and oppression on which American higher education was founded. The authors provided the backdrop to the emergence of 'historically black colleges and universities' (HBCUs) in the United States. These institutions have been crucial in sustaining black culture and educating black professionals, who have contributed enormously to improving the overall socio-economic circumstances of black people in America. The authors presented the picture of economic inequality, and how HBCUs and 'historically white institutions' (HWIs) were differentially funded, reminiscent of apartheid. They argued that despite legislative changes, student debt, racial stratification within the university and an anti-black institutional culture persist. They therefore critiqued how scholarship sees itself as 'raceless'. Again, this standpoint resonates with the

South African context, where race, class and culture remain dominant sites of struggle as universities try to create inclusive and anti-racist institutions. The project of decolonising African and African-American studies highlights the depth of methodological inquiry evident in the extensive research of the Atlanta School, by African-American scholar Aldon Morris. Provocatively, he proposed that theoretical and methodological tools formulated by outside elites cannot guide freedom struggles effectively. The hegemony of these outside elites, their knowledge and power must be challenged, and 'insurgent scholars must interrogate the core intellectual principles advanced by mainstream scholars of which they are a part'.

In Chapter 20, South African-American scholar Zine Magubane investigated American 'social particularities' that set the terms for the histories, practices and cultures of people of African descent to be made into objects of scholarly inquiry in the period before African and African-American studies emerged in American universities. Acknowledging the need for radical curricula and institutional transformation within the academy, African-American scholar Krista Johnson's chapter examined black intellectual thinking – focused on the Howard School of International Studies – on race and empire in the United States during the era of widespread racial segregation in the 1930s and 1940s. The role of leadership is foregrounded, and the chapter demonstrates how this shaped public discussion about race, building a vibrant intellectual community in the process. Johnson noted, however, the resonance of these debates with the present, and how this intellectual history links to current debates about decolonisation, Africanisation and intersectionality, as exemplified by student movements such as #RhodesMustFall and #BlackLivesMatter in South Africa and the United States, respectively.

As the 23 far-ranging chapters in this volume have illustrated, it is clear that each society has its own internal mapping of power relations, and that decolonisiation efforts took place in different contexts. Transformation to complex, multi-layered democracies in Africa and the United States has defined a new historical epoch. An important contribution of the book is looking forward by looking back. South African educationist Ahmed Bawa argued in Chapter 4 that tertiary institutions have to produce the foundations for a new ontology and epistemology for a more complete liberation in African and American societies, which post-colonial settings have not yet produced. These renewed foundations can craft potentially new directions in knowledge production and dissemination in Africa and its diaspora. Newer generations of activists have the responsibility of moving this process forward, taking into account that the 'decolonising' project is both local and global. This book is a watershed text. It captures the problems associated with higher education in South Africa, Africa and the United States, and demonstrates that there is no turning back – decolonisation and transformation need to enter a new era of building the solutions narrative for higher education.

References

Cross, M and Ndofirepi, A (2017) Critical scholarship in South Africa: Considerations of epistemology, theory and method, in M Cross and A Ndofirepi (eds) *Knowledge and Change in African Universities: Re-imagining the terrain*. Rotterdam: Sense Publishers, pp. 85–86.

Lange, L (2017) 20 years of higher education curriculum policy in South Africa, *Journal of Education*, **68**: 92–124.

Leibowitz, B (2017) Language teacher identity in troubled times, in G Barkhuizen (ed.) *Reflections on Language Teacher Identity*. New York: Routledge, pp. 74–79.

Makalela, L (2019) Decolonization, epistemic access and language curriculum transformation. Paper presented at UMALUSI Colloquium, 23 July, University of the Witwatersrand.

Mamdani, M (2007) *Scholars in the Marketplace. The dilemmas of neo-liberal reform at Makerere University, 1989–2000*. Dakar: CODESRIA Books.

Motala, S (2014) Making rights realities: Education reform in post-apartheid South Africa, in C Harber (ed.) *Education in Southern Africa*. London: Bloomsbury Press, pp. 47–67

Motala, S, Sayed, Y and Hoffmann, N (2017) Decolonising initial teacher education in South Africa: More than an event, *Journal of Education*, **68**: 59–90.

Odora Hoppers, C (2013) Community engagement, globalisation and restorative action: Approaching systems and research in the universities, *Journal of Adult and Continuing Education*, **19**: 94–102.

Odora Hoppers, C and Richards, H (2012) *Rethinking Thinking: Modernity's 'other' and the transformation of the university*. Pretoria: University of South Africa.

Rensburg, I (2017) Mandela Education Legacy Lecture, 17 September.

Santos, B de Sousa (2007) *Cognitive Justice in a Global World: Prudent knowledges for a decent life*. Lanham, MD: Lexington Books.

Santos, B de Sousa (2015) *Epistemologies of the South: Justice against epistemicide*. New York: Routledge.

Torres, CA (1998) Democracy, education and multiculturalism: Dilemmas of citizenship in a global world, *Comparative Education Review*, **42**(4): 421–47.

Umalusi Seminar Series (2019) Conceptual exploration of decolonisation of language pedagogy, learning and assessment. Pretoria.

Van der Westhuizen, GJ (2007) An analysis of evaluations of higher education transformation in South Africa, *South African Journal of Higher Education*, **21**(3): 552–69.

Visvanathan, S (1998) A celebration of difference: Science and democracy in India, *Science*, **280**(5360): 42–43.

Visvanathan, S (2006) Alternative science, *Theory, Culture & Society*, **23**(2–3), 164–69.

Visvanathan, S (2011) The search for cognitive justice. Paper presented at the Knowledge in Question: A Symposium on Interrogating Knowledge and Questioning Science, Seminar.

Index

The letter 'n' after a page number indicates a note.

academic capacity building 18, 304, 312
academic freedom 4, 145, 148, 158
academic staff (SA)
 calls for Africanisation of 103, 104
 and embodiment of knowledge 123–124
 and exposure of mediocrity/ignorance of 21
 impact of neoliberal agenda on 161
 and staff–student ratios 71
 and transformation of HBUs 91, 92
 white academics 91, 146, 147–148, 157–158, 171
 see also black academic staff: in South Africa; white academic staff: in South Africa
academic support programmes 142
academy
 destabilising the arrogance of 142
 maintaining whiteness of 157–158, 169
 as space of debate 43
access to higher education
 calls in SA to broaden 88
 as citizens' right 293
 and issues around equity 70–71
accommodation for students 121, 125, 126
Achebe, Chinua
 battle against Western epistemological dominance 4
 and Heinemann AWS 271, 275
 misrepresentation of Africa by Western authors 24
 and novelist as teacher 279
 and quotations from 278–279
Adams v. Richardson (US) 385–386, 386
Adeleye, RA 218, 220
Adesina, JO 182, 184
Adewoye, Omoniyi 218, 220
administrative staff (Makerere University) 304–305
affirmative action (US) 386–388
Afigbo, AE 9, 23, 211, 218, 220
Africa
 African writers' over-romanticisation of 321–322
 colonial education deemed 'appropriate' for 283, 284n1, 288–289, 290
 colonial writings about 165, 211–212, 235, 235n6, 236, 334, 335, 338
 curricula as tool of unification 222
 and Diop's Afrikology 256–259, 261
 and knowledge production, as ancestors of humankind 262–263
 and knowledge production, denial of capacity to produce 175
 and myth of African unanimity 277
 rejection of marginalisation/objectification of 34
 Southern Africa 18, 335, 367
 tendency to speak of in the singular 186
 in terms of postmodernism 199
 see also East Africa; entries under 'black'; Pan-Africanism; Sub-Saharan Africa
African-American students *see* black students (US); historically black colleges and universities (US); United States of America
African American Studies Reader (Norment) 25
African and African Diaspora Studies (AADS) 330, 332, 338–339, 340
African culture
 accusation of 'cultural imperialism' against Heinemann 274–275
 centring of 35, 127, 139, 159
 colonial debasement as 'primitive' 229
 and cross-cultural dialogues 201
 decolonial renaissance of 301
 and relevance of postmodernism to 199
 see also culture
African Gender Institute (UCT) 145, 145n3, 146
African historiography
 desire to fully write Africa's history 307
 Dike as 'father of' 213
 Diop's contributions to 257
 historical timeline by African intellectuals 213–214
 as redefinition of African identity 214
 in Tanzania 235–238
 see also Ibadan School of History (Nigeria); University of Dar es Salaam: School of Historiography
African identity 15, 127, 193, 194–195, 214
African indigenous knowledge systems
 coexistence with other systems 61
 cohort of Senegalese organic intellectuals 256
 derived from African sociology 184
 and fusion of epistemologies 196–198
 and hegemony of Western knowledge 193–196
 ignorance/neglect of 174–175, 185
 need to integrate into transformed curricula 3, 193
 negated under colonialism 192–193, 194, 231

409

plural composition of 200–201
  see also knowledge systems; Western/
  Eurocentric scholarship
African languages
  alternative paradigm for study of 260
  genetic relatedness of 257, 259, 261–262
  and integrated approach to learning 259–260
  as language of instruction 3
  publication of literature in 323, 323–324
  and translations by Heinemann AWS 272–273
  see also language
African liberation movements 231, 231n3, 232, 234, 243
African literature
  and critiques/promotion of by white academics 320–321
  in East Africa 314–315, 318–325
  and Western theft of idea of literature from 315
  see also Heinemann African Writers Series; literature curricula
African National Congress 67, 108, 109, 112, 112–113
African philosophy
  and appropriation of Western forms of knowledge 199
  and negation of African indigenous knowledges 192
  and a postmodern dis-position 198–205
African Renaissance 14, 14–15, 257–258, 263, 301
African research 4, 27, 92–93
African sociology
  conceptual clarification of terms 175–176
  and epistemic reclamation 176–179
  ignorance of 174, 185–186
  works of critical reflection 179–185
  see also sociology; Western sociology
African Studies Centre (UCT) 145, 145n3, 146, 148, 174n2, 329
African universities (excl. SA)
  based on colonialism/European modernity 162, 164
  common denominators of Africanisation 301
  effect of SAPs on 4, 27
  and funding of higher education 74
  need for multilingual studies 142–143
  North African universities 221–222
  and perpetuation of Western thought 4–5, 163
  and relationship with society 283
  in sub-Saharan Africa 75
  tension between global and national priorities 397

  see also entries under higher education; entries under universities; Makerere University (Uganda)
Africanisation
  calls for in SA 1, 103, 104
  common denominators of 301
  of curricula 24, 260, 284, 284–285, 312
  and decolonisation, conflation with 36
  and decolonisation, debates around 33–43
  and decolonisation, only part of the process 284n1
  efforts at Makerere University 302–312
  Hopper's remarks on first-level indigenisation 44
  of knowledge production in post-colonial Ghana 288–293, 294, 295, 296
  overview of efforts in Africa 22–25
  and relationship between universities and society 283
  should encompass all levels of learning 294
  see also entries under curriculum decolonisation/transformation; entries under decolonisation; transformation
Afrikaans, as language of instruction 143, 144
Afrikology, and Diop 256–259, 261
Agger, Ben 178
Ajayi, JF Ade 4, 23, 211, 217, 219, 220
Ake, Claude 4, 5
Akintoye, Banji 217
Akìwowo, Akínsolá 183–184, 185
Alasow, JG 121, 127–128
alienation
  addressed via a fusion of epistemologies 197
  of black staff/students in SA 20, 103, 104, 110–112, 122–123, 147, 149
  of black students in US 5, 25
  in eras of colonialism/slavery 194, 321–322
  in relation to literature 316, 319, 321–322
  and rising global inequality 67
  of universities from their publics 49, 57
Allen, BCM 383, 383n2, 384
Allen, WR 381–382, 385, 389
Altbach, PG 143–144
Amadiume, I 179, 180–181, 182–183, 183
Amin, Idi 309, 311
Amin, Samir 182, 250, 255, 255–256, 256, 405
Ampofo, A 374
Amsden, Alice 249
Anyumba, Henry 24, 322
apartheid era
  and censorship 231–232
  creation of apartheid-enforced identities 21
  creation of historically black universities 2, 53, 81, 90
  and decolonisation as material and not

metaphor 170
and distinction between democratisation and decolonisation 167
knowledge production during 283
legacies for post-apartheid higher education 1–2, 16–17
persistence of apartheid symbols 14
SA as member of 'white dominions' 13–14
see also race; racism
'applied philanthropy' *see* 'Negro Problem': as 'applied philanthropy'
Aptheker, H 346
Archer, M 177, 178
arrests of students 114–115, 131, 132
art and drama studies (UCT) 150–151
Arusha Declaration 234, 238, 243, 251
Asante, Molefi Kete 5, 24
Ashforth, Adam 61
Asiwaju, Anthony I 218, 219
Asmal, Kader 81, 86, 91
Atanda, JA 218, 220
Atlanta School of Sociology 26, 345–346, 349–353, 354–355
autonomy 21, 27
Awe, Bolanle 9, 27, 218, 220
Ayandele, Emmanuel 218, 220
Ayer, AJ 38–39

Babu, Abdul-Rahman Mohammed 247–248
Badat, Saleem 19, 123, 129
Bakare-Yusuf, B 179, 183
Bantu Education Act (SA) 2, 14
Barnett, Clive 273
Basu, Kaushik 66, 67
Beachey, RW 305, 307
Bell, Derrick 387–388
Biko, Steve 44–45, 52, 112
Biobaku, SO 217, 220
Bishop, JM 389
black academic staff
  and Africanisation process 103, 104, 294, 301, 302–304, 310–311, 312
  at Atlanta School of Sociology 349, 350, 351
  and 'Black Studies' curricula in US 25–26
  and embodiment of knowledge 123–124
  and erosion of politics of collectivity 372–373
  at Howard University 357–359, 359–361
  in South Africa 18, 20, 91, 92, 134, 146–147, 148, 149–150
  see also academic staff (SA); white academic staff
black consciousness
  Biko's views on 44–45
  links to current student protests 104, 112

New Black Consciousness 35
  and vision of decolonisation 168n2
black doctorates 359–360, 359n3, 381, 383
black feminist scholarship 26
Black Lives Matter movement (US) 35
'black pain' 37, 43, 45
  see also race; racism
Black Radical Tradition 163
black-serving institutions (US) 381–382, 382
Black Student Movement (Rhodes) 120–121, 125, 127, 127–128, 129–130, 131
black students (SA)
  enrolment figures 17, 71, 87
  graduation rates 18, 71
  and Nyamnjoh's concept of 'whitening up' 137
  and sense of alienation at HWUs 20, 103, 104, 110–112, 122–123, 147
  see also students (SA); white students: in SA
black students (US)
  barriers to higher education 388–389
  calls for curriculum transformation 6, 25
  enrolments in higher education 380, 381, 386–387
  experiences of racism 6, 26, 347, 389, 390
  at historically white institutions 25, 383
  provision of inferior education for 344–345, 346–347
  types of degrees 381, 383
  see also historically black colleges and universities (US); United States of America
'Black Studies' courses (US) 25–26
black women authors 139–140, 276
block grants 68
Blyden, Edward Wilmot 332
Boahen, A Adu 4, 292, 293
Boas, Franz 332, 361n7
Boyo, al-Hajj Ishaq 292
Bozalek, V 89
Brazil 102
Brown v. Board of Education of Topeka (US) 373, 385, 387
Brown, Wendy 160, 161, 164
Bunche, Ralph
  member of Howard University faculty 22, 357, 358
  overseas research 360, 361
  writings on race/racism 22, 362–363, 369n12, 370–371
Bunsen, Bernard 302–303
Burawoy, Michael 178–179
Burbules, NC 202–205
bursaries 18, 69
  see also funding of education
Butler, Anthony 149

411

Cabral, Amilcar 181, 231, 232
capacity building of staff 18, 304, 312
Cape Peninsula University of Technology 87
capitalism
   and globalisation 229–230, 245–246, 246n17
   and hegemonic knowledge systems 230
   and neoliberalism 229–230, 234, 248–250
   research by Atlanta School of Sociology on 352
   and Williams' scholarship on slavery 22, 367–370
Cardoso, Ferdinando 249
Carnegie, Andrew 331–332
case citations 143, 346, 384–386, 387–388
Centre for African Studies (UCT) 145, 145n3, 146, 148, 174n2, 329
Centre for Higher Education Transformation 2
Centwa, Siyanda 122
Césaire, Aimé 176–177
Chakrabarty, Dipesh 279–280
Chengeta, G 120, 132
Chikane, R 110
churches
   mission schools 286–287, 288, 289
   role in US civil rights movement 353
   and roles played by missionaries 286–287, 288, 289, 321, 335, 365, 366, 378–379
citation counts 58, 161
civil rights movement (US) 6, 25, 353, 355, 381n1
Civil War (US) 344–345, 346, 359, 378
Clarke, Rebecca 275–276
Cloete, N 101–102
Cock, Jacklyn 182
Cohen, Andrew (Governor of Uganda) 306
Cohen, T 391–392
collectivism 124–127, 133, 372–373
colonialism
   and 'appropriate' education for Africans 283, 284n1, 288–289, 290
   cause of alienation of Africans 321
   colonial/European Renaissance 14, 39–40
   concept of a 'colonial library' 214
   and decolonisation as material and not metaphor 170
   and distinction between democratisation and decolonisation 167–168
   European experience presented as universal 162–163
   imagining a decolonised South Africa 169
   inseparable from whiteness 157–158
   Marx's observations on India 248, 248n18
   negation of African indigenous knowledges 192–193, 194, 231
   promotion of Western culture as superior 229

   publication of 'popular literature' 322–323
   in South Africa 84, 159, 168
   subversion of position of women 183
   writings about Africa 165, 211–212, 235, 235n6, 236, 334, 335, 338
   see also Western/Eurocentric scholarship
coloured students (SA) 87, 91
commissions on higher education funding (SA) 67–68, 69, 76
community outreach activities 306–307, 310
Connell, Raewyn 179
Cook, David 319, 321
Cook, W Mercer 357n1
Cooper, Dave 145, 145n2
Cornell, J 147
cost-sharing funding model 69–70, 74
Council on Higher Education (CHE) 75–76
court cases 143, 346, 384–386, 387–388
crime 353
critical race theory (CRT) 387, 390
Cuba 102
culture
   and bias in Western scientific research 24
   literature as an expression of 316
   multiculturalism 168, 373
   Western vs 'primitive' cultures 229
   see also African culture
Currey, James 272, 275
Curriculum Change Working Group (UCT) 147–148
curriculum decolonisation/transformation
   and ability of white academics 285
   African-American students' call for 6
   and alternative modalities of intellectual engagement 164–165
   and capacity building of staff 312
   efforts by Ibadan School of History 215–218
   efforts in East Africa 24, 93, 315–318
   global spread of Fallist campaigns 19
   and ignorance/neglect of African scholarship 174–175, 185
   and power to determine what constitutes knowledge 174–175
   in Tanzania 236
   value of courses designed around debates 185–186
   walling off/dilution of 176, 186
   see also Africanisation: of curricula; literature curricula
curriculum decolonisation/transformation (SA)
   background/context 1–3
   critiques of the call for 284
   debates around 17
   and fusion of epistemologies 196–198
   at historically black universities 91–92, 93

and invisible systemic failures 27
need for training of black academics 18
and a postmodern dis-position 198–205
reclamation of indigenous African knowledges 193
Rhodes University, students' call for 120
UCT, #RMF demands for 19–20, 137, 138–147
UCT's responses to #RMF demands 147–151
Wits University, students' call for 103, 104, 109, 110
see also decolonisation (SA)

Dadhich, Naresh 61
Dakar School of Culture (Senegal) 23–24, 255, 256, 259–260, 263
Dar es Salaam School of Political Economy *see* University of Dar es Salaam: School of Political Economy
Davidson, Basil 292
Davis, Angela 26
De Saussure, Ferdinand 261
debt, student 388–389
decolonisation
and Africanisation, conflation with 36
Africanisation only part of the process 284n1
and collectivist approach to knowledge 124–125
of gender relations 183
history of 284n1
and integrating African/Western forms of knowledge 195–196
as matter of education and re-education 278
move towards decoloniality 221, 222
Nyerere's exposé of 'false decolonisation' 233
overview of African countries 22–25
as a radical and multivalent signifier 159
requires transformations at various levels 373
and rewriting Africa's history 228
and work of Howard scholars 358–359, 370–373
see also Africanisation; transformation
decolonisation (SA)
#RMF's distinction from 'transformation' 138–139
black consciousness vision of 168n2
as 'buzzword' 1, 157, 161
and concepts of race/'black pain' 43–45
critical overview of 157–159
debates between Africanists 33–43
earlier decolonial and transformation efforts 3
and institutionalisation of 162–166
lessons from Heinemann AWS 270, 278–281
as material and not metaphor 166–171

neoliberal undoing of 160–162
potential drivers of reconstructing/'decolonising' knowledge 60–63
as struggle against epistemicides 3
and talks between universities 103
and use of indigenous languages 3
see also curriculum decolonisation/transformation (SA)
degrees/doctorates 359–360, 359n3, 381, 383
democratisation, vs decolonisation 167–168, 168–169
Denoon, Donald 237, 309, 310
Department of Linguistics (UCT) 145, 145n3, 146
dependency theory 249
desegregation (US) 372, 385–386, 390
development, discourses on 57–59
development studies (University of Dar es Salaam) 239
developmental universities 75
Dickinson, David 105
Dike, Kenneth Onwuka
overview of 223–225
founder member of Ibadan School of History 23, 211, 212, 215
founder of historical bodies/schemes 215, 216–217
historiographical work 212–213, 217
as vice-chancellor 215, 220
see also Ibadan School of History (Nigeria)
Diop, Cheikh Anta
and African sociological discourses 180–181
and Afrikology 256–259, 261
and genetic relatedness of languages 257, 259, 261–262
leader of Dakar School of Culture 23–24, 255
as organic intellectual 255–256
see also Senegal
Diop, Cheikh Mbacké 258
Diop, Samory Candace 258
discrimination 89, 111, 140, 386, 387
see also racism
diversity 168, 373, 391
Dlamini, Mcebo 108, 113, 114
doctorates, black 359–360, 359n3, 381, 383
'double consciousness' (Du Bois) 352
Douglass, Frederick 354
Dred Scott v. Sandford (US) 384–385, 385
Drew, Charles R 357n1
drop-out rates 71
Du Bois, W.E.B.
and Atlanta School of Sociology 26, 345, 351, 352–353

awards given to 257
and concept of 'scientific' sociology 333, 336, 337–338, 338–339, 340
critical of 'applied philanthropy' on the 'Negro Problem' 335, 335–336, 337, 340
critical of industrial education 334, 379
and divisions between black/white workers 347
Dumas' observations on 388
as first generation of black PhDs 359
a founder of American sociology 329
and 'the future of world democracy' 339–340
rejection of racist depictions of Africa 334
and Talented Tenth 370
and theories of race 361n7
and ties connecting Africans and African Americans 332, 333
writings of 26, 180, 333, 334, 339–340, 349, 355, 372
Du Preez, P 83, 86, 89
Dumas, MJ 388
Duncan, J 106, 132
Durban University of Technology 50, 60, 87
Dussel, E 195
Dzobo Commission (Ghana) 294–295, 296

East Africa
    curriculum transformation efforts 24, 93
    literary traditions/transformation 314–315, 318–322
    publication of 'popular literature' 322–324, 325
    University of East Africa 230, 302, 311, 319
    see also Africa; Kenya; Tanzania; Uganda
East African Literature Bureau 323
East African Publishing House 275, 276, 324
East Africanisation *see* Africanisation: efforts at Makerere University
Economic Freedom Fighters Student Command (Wits) 108, 109, 109–110, 109n6, 112
Education Act (Ghana) 296
Education White Paper 3: *A Programme for Higher Education Transformation* (1997) 2, 17, 18, 49, 56, 68, 85
Egypt and Egyptology 257, 258, 261, 262
Eiselen Commission on Native Education 1–2
Ekeh, Peter 23
embodiment, concept of 121–124
endogeneity 174, 175, 183
    see also African sociology
English language
    and creation of an African elite 320
    as medium of academic discourse 142, 143, 143–144, 164, 314

teaching of 316
see also language
English literature 316, 319, 320
enrolments in higher education
    in SA 17, 71, 87
    in SSA 70
    in US 380, 381, 386–387, 389, 391
equity in higher education
    overview of issues 70–72
    encompasses social justice 66
    promoted by National Plan for Higher Education 18
    questions around current approach to 66
Erskog, M 128
Esters, LT 383, 383n2, 384
Eurocentric scholarship *see* Western/Eurocentric scholarship
excellence, concept of
    and equation with race 21
    and Ramphele's focus on 20
    reduced to statistical accountancy 141
    vs relevance 5
Exclusive Books 24–25
expenditure on education 18, 69, 70–71, 72–73, 74
    see also funding of education
Extension of University Education Act (SA) 2, 81

fallibilism, sense of 202–203
Fallist student movements *see* #FeesMustFall movements; #FeesMustFall (Wits); #RhodesMustFall (UCT); Rhodes University student movement
Fanon, Frantz 181, 231, 237, 245, 284n1
Fáshìnà, Dipo 185
fees
    impact of neoliberal agenda on 160
    in South Africa 71, 71–72, 101, 102, 129
    see also funding of education
#FeesMustFall movements
    background to 1, 15–16, 270
    and exposure of mediocrity of academics 21
    formation of commissions into funding 67–68
    intention of benefiting poor youth 72
    no public defence of universities 49
    as reminder of incomplete knowledge project 56–57
    as space to articulate grievances 75, 111–112
    see also #RhodesMustFall (UCT); Rhodes University student movement
#FeesMustFall (Wits) 103, 104–115
    see also University of the Witwatersrand
feminism

issues in Rhodes student movement 131
issues in Wits student movement 113
feminist scholarship
  as element of a decolonised curriculum 141, 148
  elevation of literature authored by black women 139–140
  ignorance of 179
  and institutionalisation of decolonisation 165
  in US 26
Finland 102
flagship tertiary institutions (US) 381–382
food fermentation 60
forestry research institutes 51, 52
Forster, DA 63–64
Francis, D 89
Franklin, RM 344
Frazier, E Franklin 357, 358, 360, 362, 372
Frazier, Garrison 331
Freeman, KR 391–392
Freire, Paulo 141–142, 197, 251, 251n19, 278, 343
funding of education
  effects of SAPs on 4, 27
  in Ghana 102, 286, 287, 289, 290, 294, 296
  at Makerere University (Uganda) 311–312
  move towards cost sharing 74
  as percentage of GDP 102
  in US 6, 27, 348–349, 379, 383–385, 386, 390
  see also fees
funding of education (SA)
  during apartheid period 51, 53
  fee-free higher education 19, 70, 72–74, 110
  historical imbalances in 18
  insufficient state contributions to 101–102
  modelling funding equity 76–77
  post-1994 overview of 67–70, 71–72
  funding of research 4, 27, 58, 71, 145, 311–312, 349–350
Further Education and Training Colleges Act (SA) 88

Gachukia, Eddah 315–316
Gamedze, Thuli 142, 150
Garuba, Harry 2, 147, 279, 284 285, 293
gender studies
  and African sociology 182–183
  at UCT 145, 145n3, 146
  Western gender discourse 182
Gerwel, Jakes 91
Ghana
  and 'appropriate' education for Africans 288–289
  citizens' views on education 293–294
  funding of education 102, 286, 287, 289, 290, 294, 296
  overview of schooling 286–288, 289, 294, 294–296
  tertiary sector 285–286, 289–293, 294, 301–302
Godsell, G 110
Goldie, Taubman 216
Gqola, P 132
graduation rates (SA) 18, 62, 71, 75
grants, funding 68
'Great Debate' (University of Dar es Salaam) 244–248
Green Papers
  on Higher Education Transformation 17
  on Science and Technology 54
Greenberg, J 261, 262
Griffiths, Gareth 274–275
gross domestic product (GDP) 102
Grutter v. Bollinger (US) 387, 388
Guggisberg, Gordon 287, 288

Habib, Adam 102, 103, 107–108, 116
Hadebe, S 92
Haralambos, M 38
Harney, Stefano 163
Harris, Abram 357, 358, 360, 360–361, 362
Harris, Cheryl 387
Harris, Jerry 246n17
Hassim, S 120, 131
Hastie, William H 357n1
Haupt, Adam 141, 142–143, 144
Hawaii 365–366
Hegel, GW 235n6
Heher Commission of Inquiry 67, 69, 73, 76
Heinemann African Writers Series
  background/overview 24–25, 271–274
  critiques and contestations 269–270, 274–278
  highlighting of East African writers 324
  and lessons for decolonisation in SA 270, 278–281
Hemson, C 89
Henry, Charles 358
Hiddingh Campus (UCT) 150–151
Higgs, Philip 16–17
higher education
  as least progressive of social expenditures 72–73
  as private and public good 74–76, 124, 124–125, 129
  see also entries under universities
Higher Education Act (SA) 3, 49, 56, 86
Higher Education Act (US) 383
higher education (SA)

and Dakar School's relevance to 259–260, 263
and inflation 102
legacies of apartheid era 1–2, 16–17
and post-apartheid transformation processes 2, 17–19, 54, 56–57, 84–89
returns on tertiary education 74
see also funding of education (SA); historically black universities (SA); historically white universities (SA); universities (SA)
Higher Education South Africa (HESA) 2
Hill, Alan 271, 275
Historical Research Schemes (Nigeria) 216–217
Historical Society of Nigeria 216
historically black colleges and universities (US)
overview/history of 5–6, 346–347, 377–380
and barriers to higher education 388, 389
and continuing racial segregation 386
federal/state disinvestment in 383–385, 390
play critical role in black education 382, 382–383
recommendations/future direction of 390–392
and replication of societal racial attitudes 359
research conducted by 372
see also black students (US); United States of America
historically black land-grant universities (US) 383, 383n2, 384
historically black universities (SA)
during apartheid period 2, 53, 81, 90
challenges to transformation of 82, 83, 89–93
focus of student organisations in 101n2
ongoing problems experienced by 17–18
strategies towards transformation 93–94
see also universities (SA)
historically white institutions (US) 6, 383, 383n3, 384, 389
historically white universities (SA)
and alienation of black students/staff 20, 103, 104, 110–112, 122–123, 147, 149
during apartheid period 16
continuing lack of transformation of 18, 19, 127
funding of 51
and transformation of HBUs 90
see also universities (SA)
historiography *see* African historiography; Ibadan School of History (Nigeria); University of Dar es Salaam: School of Historiography
history curricula
Ibadan School of History 215–218
and issues around regionalism 221–222

History Department
Makerere University 305–311, 311, 312
University of Dar es Salaam 235–238, 235n8, 240, 243
Hodgkin, Thomas 291
Holomisa, Bantu 87
hooks, bell 26, 121–122, 122, 123, 125, 128
Hoppers, Catherine Odora
and cognitive crisis in higher education 398
and enlargement of knowledge 40–42, 196
and idea of 'race' 43–44
knowledge as wisdom 198
and negation of African knowledges 194
rediscovery of an African *gnosis* 197
Hountondji, Paulin 175, 177, 277
Houston, Charles H 357n1
Howard School of International Affairs (US)
as constellation of black intellectual leaders 357–359, 359–361
and decolonising transformation of knowledge production 370–373
and demythologising history and whiteness 366–370
paradigms, theories and schools of thought 358–359, 360, 361–366
Howard University 357, 359–360, 360, 361, 371, 372
Hub for Decolonial Feminist Psychologies in Africa 148
Huggan, Graham 276, 277
humanities studies
and appropriate content of 293
impact of neoliberal agenda on 124–125
and relevant research on Africa 291
and transformation of 27
at UCT 145–146, 145n3, 148, 174n2, 329
and unacknowledged inequalities 122–123
Huxley, Elspeth 322–323
Hyden, Goran 233–234, 241

Ibadan School of History (Nigeria)
background to 23, 211, 212, 213, 214, 308
critiques of 218–221
curriculum transformation efforts of 215–218
see also Dike, Kenneth Onwuka
Ibironke, Olabode 275, 277–278, 280
Ibn Khaldūn 180
identity, African 15, 127, 193, 194–195, 214
ideology of black inferiority 334, 342, 343, 345, 347, 348, 350–351, 384–385
see also race; racism
Ifá texts 183–184, 184, 184n7, 185
Ikime, Obaro 9, 23, 211, 216, 218, 219–220
imperialism 214, 245, 246–247, 248n18, 249
income contingent loans 74

India 57, 61, 248, 248n18
Indian students (SA) 87
indigenisation 1, 44
  see also Africanisation
indigenous knowledge systems *see* African indigenous knowledge systems
industrial education (US) 330–331, 331–332, 334, 348, 379
inequality
  and conceptualisations of race 363
  effect of government spending/taxation on 72–73
  global rise in 66–67
  poverty as unacceptable face of 67
  and provision of education in addressing 70
  and student activist voices against 49, 56
  unacknowledgement of embodied inequalities 123
  see also poverty
inflation rates 102
infrastructure of universities 90, 91, 93
Ingham, Kenneth 305–307, 311, 312
innovation systems (SA) 54–55, 55–56
Institute of African Studies (Ghana) 290–293
international relations 358–359, 358n2, 369
  see also Howard School of International Affairs (US)
Islamic education (Ghana) 295–296

Jagarnath, V 123
Jaja of Opobo 216
James, CLR 357, 361, 367, 368
Jansen, J 101n2, 103, 284
Jay, W 343–344
Johnson, Krista 22
Johnson, Mordecai W 357n1, 360
journals
  Journal of Negro Education 357, 364, 364n8, 371–372
  in Nigeria 216
  and publication in 2–3, 4, 5, 92, 141, 161
  used in East African literary education 314
  Journal of Egyptology/African Civilizations 258
judiciousness, sense of 204–205
Julian, Percy 357n1
Julien, Eileen 276–277
Just, Ernest Everett 357n1

kaCanham, H 133
Kajubi, S 303
Kalla, Shaeera 102, 105, 108–109
Kalula, Evance 146
Kark, Sidney 52
Kelley, Robin 164
Kenya

curriculum Africanisation/transformation efforts 24, 315–318
Kenya Literature Bureau 323
Kenya Oral Literature Association 322
Kenzo, MJR 199
Kerner Report 381, 381n1
Kessi, S 147
Khondker, H 83
Kimambo, Isaria 23, 235n8, 236, 243
King, Martin Luther 355
King, Martin Luther Jr 345
knowledge systems
  and Africa, denial of capacity to produce knowledge 175
  and Africa, production of knowledge as ancestors of humankind 262–263
  and alternative modalities of intellectual engagement 164–165
  under apartheid 283
  under capitalism 230
  changing hegemonic visions of 229
  colonial writings about Africa 165, 211–212, 235, 235n6, 236, 334, 335
  and conceptual divide between theoretical/applied knowledges 329, 330, 335–336, 340
  as contribution to the collective 124–125
  and decolonisation, work of Howard scholars 358–359, 370–373
  Marxism as subaltern system 230
  Mode 2 knowledge production 55
  need for hospitality to all knowledge forms 41
  plurality of 'knowledges' 36–37, 40, 61–63, 162–163
  potential drivers of reconstructing/'decolonising' 60–63
  and power to determine what constitutes knowledge 174–175
  and Serageldin's six crucial values 40, 42
  transdisciplinary knowledge 3, 41–42, 55, 258
  universities' monopoly on knowledge production 164
  universities' participation in global systems 59–60
  see also African indigenous knowledge systems; Western/Eurocentric scholarship
Kuper, Adam 237

land-grant universities (US) 383, 383n2, 383n3, 384
language
  Afrikaans 143, 144
  Constitutional Court cases 143
  multilingualism 142–143, 144, 259

see also African languages; English language
Lash, S 38
law
  cases cited 143, 346, 384–386, 387, 387–388
  critiques of legal education 385
  Law Faculty (UCT) 146, 149
  Law Faculty (University of Dar es Salaam) 240, 240n13, 252
Le Grange, Lesley 3, 194
lecturers *see* academic staff (SA); black academic staff; white academic staff
legislation
  Bantu Education Act (SA) 2, 14
  Education Act (Ghana) 296
  Extension of University Education Act (SA) 2, 81
  Further Education and Training Colleges Act (SA) 88
  Higher Education Act (SA) 3, 49, 56, 86
  Higher Education Act (US) 383
  Morrill Acts 379, 380, 383n2, 383n3, 384
  National Defense Education Act VI (US) 6
Leibowitz, Brenda 34, 62, 89
liberation capital 350–351, 372
liberation education 343, 345
liberation movements (Africa) 231, 231n3, 232, 234, 243
Linguistics Department (UCT) 145, 145n3, 146
literature
  differing views on 316
  African Writers Series 316, 319, 320
  see also African literature; Heinemann Western literature
literature curricula
  and birth of Heinemann AWS 24–25
  elevation of black women authors 139–140
  transformation efforts in Kenyan universities 315–318
  see also entries under curriculum decolonisation/transformation
Lo Liyong, Taban 24, 314, 318, 321, 322
loans, student 18, 69, 74, 388–389
Locke, Alain L 357, 360, 361, 361n6, 361n7
Logan, Rayford 357, 360, 361, 372
Low, DA 305, 306
Lule, Yusuf 304
Lushaba, Lwazi 149–150
Lutwama, Joseph 303

Mafeje, Archie 3, 4, 182, 241
Magubane, Bernard 175
Maher, A 194
Mahlangu, Solomon 106, 106n5, 111–112
Makerere University (Uganda)
  Africanisation of History Department 305–311, 311, 312
  Africanisation, overview of efforts 302–305
  funding of 311–312
  government interference in 311
Malan, DF 13–14
Maldonado-Torres, Nelson 147
Mamdani, Mahmood
  and African Studies Centre (UCT) 145n3, 174, 174n2, 329
  and colonial modern roots of African universities 162, 164
  concepts of relevance vs excellence 5
  courses designed around specific debates 185–186
  creation of apartheid-enforced identities 21
  and discipline–area studies conceptual divide 329, 330, 335
  idea of 'decentralised despotism' 182
  impact of apartheid on SA academy 175
  member of Sunday Morning Ideological Classes 241
  participant in 'Great Debate' 244, 245
Mangosuthu University of Technology 87
Manning, Charles 358n2
Marx, Karl 230, 241, 248, 248n18, 343, 352
Marxism
  critiques of Ibadan School of History 220
  and Du Bois' writings 339–340
  scholars' contributions to Dar es Salaam School of Political Economy 23, 240
  scholars' contributions to Dakar School 256
  as subaltern knowledge system 230
  see also political economy scholarship
Maryland (US) 386
Masinjila, Masheti 322
massification 17
Mazrui, Ali
  comments on Africanisation 294
  critiques of Dar es Salaam schools 23, 237
  Nyerere as original thinker 234
  Obote's attack on 311
  position at Makerere University 303
  rejection of Western epistemological dominance 4, 5
  and relations between educational institutions and societies 283, 285
  writings based on the oral tradition 314–315
Mbati, Peter 93
Mbeki, Govan 181
Mbeki, Thabo 14, 14–15
Mbelek, Jean-Paul 258–259
Mbembe, Achille 17, 34–35, 35–36, 36, 43, 45, 111, 141
McCauley, C 45
media studies curriculum 144

medical schools (SA) 52
Medical University of South Africa (Medunsa) 68
Meer, Fatima 182
mergers of SA universities 16, 68, 86–88
Mhone, GCZ 182
Mills, Charles 158
Ministerial Committee on Transformation and Social Cohesion and the Elimination of Discrimination in Public HEIs 88, 88–89
mission (church) schools 286–287, 288, 289
missionaries 286–287, 288, 289, 321, 335, 365, 366, 378–379
Mkabela, Q 127
Mkandawire, Thandika 27, 182
Mkhatshwa, Nompendulo (Wits SRC) 105, 106n4, 108, 112–113, 113n8
Mkhize, N 124
Mngomezulu, Bheki 92, 301
Mode 2 knowledge production 55
  see also knowledge systems
modernity 195, 199–200, 235, 352
  postmodernism in African philosophy 193, 198–205
  transmodernity 195–196, 402
Modiri, Joel 21–22
Mogoeng Mogoeng, Chief Justice 143
Moi University (Kenya) 315, 317
Mokoena, Mduduzi Paulus 60
Moore, Candice 22
Morrill Acts 379, 380, 383n2, 383n3, 384
Morris, Aldon 350–351, 361n7, 372
Morrison, T 151
Motala, S 284
Moten, Fred 163
mother-tongue education 259, 259–260, 260
  see also African languages; language
Mpe, Phaswane 275
multiculturalism 168, 373
multilingualism 142–143, 144, 259
multiple knowledge systems 61–63
  see also knowledge systems
Mungazi, Dickson A 283
Mungwini, P 199, 199–200
Mustaffa, JB 377, 384
Muzenda, M 120

Nabudere, D 241, 242, 244, 246, 258
Naicker, C 123
Natal Technical College 50–51
Natal University *see* University of KwaZulu-Natal (formerly Natal University)
National Commission on Higher Education (NCHE) 2, 17, 49, 54, 56, 85
National Defense Education Act VI (US) 6

National Plan for Higher Education (SA) 18
National Research Foundation (SA) 18
National Student Financial Aid Scheme (NSFAS) 18, 69, 70, 71, 71–72, 76
  see also funding of education (SA)
nationalism, African *see* African historiography
Ndelu, Sandile 71–72, 74
Ndlovu-Gatsheni, S 111, 134
Negro Industrial and Agricultural College 331, 332
'Negro Problem' (US)
  as 'applied philanthropy' 330–334
  from 'applied philanthropy' to empiricist epistemology 334–336
  and discipline–area studies conceptual divide 329–330
  and Du Bois' future of world democracy 339–340
  from empiricism to science 336–339
  see also United States of America
neoliberalism
  adopted by the University of Dar es Salaam academy 228–229
  and capitalism/imperialism 229–230, 234, 248–250
  and co-option of transformation discourse 119
  relationship between campus violence and neoliberal agenda 115
  and undoing of decolonisation 160–162
  and universities' role as a public good 124–125
New Black Consciousness (NBC) 35
  see also black consciousness
New Humanism (NH) 35, 35–36
Ngcobozi, L 128
Ngubane, Ben 54
Ngũgĩ wa Thiong'o
  battle against Western epistemological dominance 4
  efforts to Africanise Kenyan curriculum 24
  and Heinemann AWS 269, 274, 275, 278, 324
  importance of multilingual instruction 142
  need for centring of Africa 127, 139
  provision of assistance to CCWG 147
  and study of literature 316–317, 318, 319, 322
  writings of 314–315, 318, 321, 324
Nigeria
  Historical Research Schemes 216–217
  Historical Society 216
  National Archives of 215
  University of Ibadan 4, 211, 215, 216, 310
  see also Ibadan School of History (Nigeria)

Nketia, Nana Kwabena 292–293
Nkrumah, Kwame
  and assertion of African identity 194–195
  as first chancellor of Ghana University 301–302
  and funding of education 289, 290
  and ideological hegemony of 237
  and Institute of African Studies 290–291, 292, 293
  and vision for schooling 287–288
  writings on imperialism 181
Norment, Nathaniel 25
North African universities 221–222
  see also African universities
Northedge, A 124
Norway 102
NSFAS (National Student Financial Aid Scheme) 18, 69, 70, 71, 71–72, 76
  see also funding of education (SA)
Ntsebeza, Lungisile 148
nuclear physics 257, 258–259
Nyamnjoh, Francis 137, 146
Nyerere, Julius 181, 232–234
Nzegwu, N 179, 182, 183
Nzimande, Blade 90

Obenga, Théophile 24, 257, 259, 260, 261, 262
objectification 34, 40, 122, 123
Obote, Milton 309, 309–310, 311
Ogot, Bethwell A 305–306
Ogude, James 317
Omarjee, Nadira 139
Ominde, Simeon 4
oppression, maintenance of 140, 316, 342, 343–344, 345
oral history sources 23, 217, 235n8, 236, 292
oral literary forms 314–315, 317, 320, 322
organic intellectuals 234, 242, 251, 256, 355, 397–398, 402
Òrúnmìlà logic 184, 184–185, 184n7
Ouma, Joseph 310
Outlaw, L 199
Owuor-Anyumba, Henry 24, 322
Owusu, Maxwell 4
Oyewùmí, Oyèronké 164, 179, 182, 183

Padmore, George 357, 361, 367
Palmer, Colin 369
Pambazuka Press 233
Pambo, Vuyani 104, 108, 112, 113
Pan-Africanism
  and African literature 280, 280–281
  embraced by African-American students 6
  Nyerere's belief in 233
  as prism for Du Bois' writings 339
  SA as most and least Pan-African country 14

as vision for higher education 290
Paremoer, Lauren 140–141, 145
Park, Robert Ezra
  and 'applied philanthropy' on the 'Negro Problem' 330, 332, 333, 335, 335–336, 337
  and concept of 'scientific' sociology 333, 336, 336–337, 338
  a founder of American sociology 329, 333
  and genesis of black self-consciousness 334–335
  Story of the Negro 332, 334, 335, 339
  and ties connecting Africans and African Americans 332–333
patriarchy, politics of 113, 130, 131
p'Bitek, Okot 4, 276, 314, 318, 322
pedagogy
  #RMF calls for decolonisation of 141–144
  and decolonisation as metaphor 169
  and decolonising educational practices 373–374
  and embodiment of knowledge 121–122
  liberation education versus mis-education 343–345
  need for validation of students' collective memories 174
Penguin South Africa 24, 273
Peninsula Technikon 87
Perham, Margery 307
Philadelphia Negro (Du Bois) 26
philosophy
  and postmodernism 199
  see also African philosophy
Piketty, Thomas 66–67
Plessy v. Ferguson (US) 346, 384, 385
plurality of 'knowledges' 36–37, 40, 61–63, 162–163
  see also knowledge systems
plurality, sense of 202
police
  and student protests at Rhodes 127, 130–131, 132, 133
  and student protests at Wits 107, 114, 115
  see also security officials
political economy analysis 228, 230, 241, 244, 250–251
  see also University of Dar es Salaam: School of Political Economy
political science curricula 140, 240, 252, 311
Popper, K 202
positivism 37, 38, 39
postgraduate dissertations 92–93
postmodernism in African philosophy 193, 198–205
poverty
  linked to dropping out of school 344

420

and Ngũgĩ's hypotheses about literature 317
spiritual poverty 44–45
student activist voices against 49, 56, 104, 126
student debt as edifice of 389
as unacceptable face of inequality 67
and universities' role as a public good 129
and viability of free higher education 76
see also inequality
pragmatism, sense of 203–204
Prah, K 35
predatory journals 2–3
Price, Max 20–21, 21n11, 147
professors, black 20, 123
see also black academic staff
Programme for Higher Education Transformation see Education White Paper 3
Progressive Youth Alliance (Wits) 108, 109, 109n7, 112, 114
public sociology 178–179
see also sociology
publication in journals 2–3, 4, 5, 92, 141, 161
publishers
East African Publishing House 275, 276, 324
see also Heinemann African Writers Series

race
and affirmative action in US 386–388
critical race theory 387, 390
and desegregation in US 372, 385–386, 390
domestication of 373
Du Bois' views on 338, 339
Hopper's idea of 43–44
and New Humanism ideas 35
often equated with excellence 21
racial profiles of students 87, 90
as social construct 352–353
and ties connecting Africans and African Americans 332–333
and work of Howard scholars 357, 358, 360, 361–364, 369, 370, 370–371, 371–372
see also entries under 'black'; 'Negro Problem'; segregation
racism
depictions of Africans as 'savages' in schoolbooks 334
as discrimination 89, 111, 140, 386, 387
and 'disgust with blackness' 388
emergence of a new racism 374
in Eurocentric scholarship 24, 34, 211, 370
and goals of Black Studies curricula 26
ideology of black inferiority 334, 342, 343, 345, 347, 348, 350–351, 384–385
inseparable from whiteness 157–158
as an international institution 363
and issue of 'black pain' 37, 43, 45

links to imperialism 214
as part of universities' institutional culture 123, 124
and transformation of higher education 88–89
in US education institutions 6, 26, 347, 389, 390
see also apartheid era
Ram, Atma 48
Ramaphosa, Cyril 18, 76
Ramose, Mogobe B 167, 192, 198, 206
Ramphele, Mamphela 20
Ramugondo, Elewani 147, 148
rankings (university) 136–137
rape *see* sexual violence
rationality
Cartesian conceptions of 204
neoliberal rationality 160–161
and re-vision of Western/European rationality 200, 201
Readings, Bill 48
Reddy, Jairam 54
Regents of the University of California v. Bakke (US) 387
relevance
prioritised over excellence 5
sacrificed for international recognition 137
religion 184, 229
see also mission (church) schools; missionaries
Renaissance
African 14, 14–15, 257–258, 263, 301
colonial/European 14, 39–40
research
activities of University of Dar es Salaam History Department 235n8
and adoption of Western 'standards' 92–93
as 'applied philanthropy' on the 'Negro Problem' 333–334, 335, 336–337, 340
by Atlanta School of Sociology 350–351, 351–352
attitude of Ugandan politicians to 309, 311
and concept of 'scientific' sociology 337–338, 340
conceptual divide between theoretical/applied knowledges 329, 330, 335–336, 340
conducted by HBCUs 372
funding of 4, 27, 58, 71, 145, 311–312, 349–350
Historical Research Schemes in Nigeria 216–217
impact of neoliberal agenda on 161
Nkrumah's views on relevance of 291
and #RMF's call for decolonised curricula 144–146
SA universities' output 58

work of Howard scholars 359, 370–373
see also science and research
research institutes
  in Ghana 296
  in South Africa 51, 52, 53, 148
residence accommodation 121, 125, 126
reverse discrimination 386, 387
Rhodes, Cecil John 13, 19, 20, 20–21, 137–138, 366–367
#RhodesMustFall (UCT)
  demand for a decolonised curriculum 138–147
  global spread of 19
  management's responses to students' demands 147–151
  and removal of Rhodes' statue 19–20, 137–138
  teaching of coursework by #RMF activists 149–150
  see also #FeesMustFall movements; #FeesMustFall (Wits); Rhodes University student movement; University of Cape Town
Rhodes University
  continuing lack of transformation of 19
  heavily influenced by Rhodes' legacy 13
  naming of 19, 118n1, 120
  silencing of black academics 134
  use of indigenous languages 3
Rhodes University student movement
  background to 118–121
  and collectivism 124–127, 133
  and concept of embodiment 121–124
  and concept of re-centring 127–132
  university/state responses to 119, 132–134
  see also #FeesMustFall movements; #FeesMustFall (Wits); #RhodesMustFall (UCT)
Richards, CG 323
Rimmington, TG 301, 311
Robinson, William 246n17
Rodney, Walter 23, 241, 242, 243, 245n16, 246
Royzman, B 45
Rozin, P 45
rural communities
  activities of USARF 243
  and knowledge systems 41, 42, 60

Santos, Bonaventura de Sousa 398
Sawyerr, Akilagpa 296
School of Historiography (University of Dar es Salaam) 235–238
School of History (Ibadan) *see* Ibadan School of History (Nigeria)
School of Political Economy (University of Dar es Salaam) 23, 238–248, 250–252

schooling
  for African Americans 344–345, 346, 385
  in Ghana 286–288, 289, 294, 294–296
Schuerkens, U 83
science and research
  and development 57–58, 58–59
  and Hoppers' call for transdisciplinarity 41, 42
  and positivism's claims 38
  Western scientific research 24, 194
  see also research
science, technology and innovation (SA) 54–55, 55–56
scientific socialism 241
'scientific' sociology 330, 333–334, 336–339
Scott, David 163
security officials
  on Rhodes campus 121, 127
  on Wits campus 107, 115
  see also police
Sefa Dei, GJ 193
Sefako Makgatho Health Sciences University 68
segregation
  Howard scholars' critiques of 372
  introduced in SA by Rhodes 13
  in US education institutions 5–6, 344–345, 346, 385–386
  see also race; racism
self-legislation process 38–39
self, theories of 352
Sembène, Ousmane 4, 24, 273, 324
Senanu, KE 315, 316, 318
Senegal
  Dakar School of Culture 23–24, 255, 256, 259–260, 263
  funding of higher education 102
  see also Diop, Cheikh Anta
Serageldin, Ismail 39–40, 40, 42
sexual violence (Rhodes campus) 118, 119, 131–132, 133
  see also violence
Shivji, Issa 233, 241, 242, 243, 244, 244–245
Sicherman, C 301, 308, 309, 309–310, 310
Sim, S 198–199, 199
Simmonds, S 83, 86, 89
slavery
  links to racism/white superiority 214
  in US 331, 334, 343–344, 346, 378, 385
  Williams' scholarship on 22, 367–370
  writings by European historians 211–212
Smuts, Jan 14, 358n2
Snyman, G 195
social justice
  as agenda for higher education 49, 56
  as basis for funding models 76

and concept of equity 66
students/scholars' calls for 6, 25, 129, 144
social transformation 83, 167
see also transformation
socialism
  concept of scientific socialism 241
  in Tanzania 231, 233, 234, 238, 239
sociology
  Atlanta School of Sociology 26, 345–346, 349–353, 354–355
  concept of 'scientific' sociology 330, 333–334, 336–339
  and origins of discipline-area studies conceptual divide 329–330
  see also African sociology; Western sociology
Sol Plaatje University 68, 88
Soudien, Crain 17
South Africa
  and colonialism 84, 159, 168
  enrolments 17, 71, 87
  fees 71, 71–72, 101, 102, 129
  graduation rates 18, 62, 71, 75
  as Pan-Africanist country 14
  unemployment rates 67, 72
  see also academic staff (SA); apartheid era; black students (SA); curriculum decolonisation/transformation (SA); decolonisation (SA); funding of education (SA); higher education (SA); students (SA); universities (SA)
South African College 137
South African Post-School Education (SAPSE) 68
South African Research Chair in Social Policy 181, 181n6
Southall, Roger 19
Southern Africa 18, 335, 367
Southern Sociological Congress (US) 333
Southern Sociological Society (US) 330
Spivak, Gayatri 147
staff *see* academic staff (SA); black academic staff; white academic staff
statues, as apartheid symbol 14, 19, 19–20, 104, 366–367
Stellenbosch University 16, 19, 87
Stewart, Tonea 344
Story of the Negro (Washington & Park) 332, 334, 335, 339
structural adjustment programmes 4, 27, 272
Student Representative Council (Rhodes) 131
Student Representative Council (UCT) 20
Student Representative Council (Wits) 102, 106, 108, 112
students (SA)
  arrests of students 114–115, 131, 132

coloured students 87, 91
graduation rates 18, 62, 71, 75
Indian students 87
issues around accommodation 121, 125, 126
student–staff ratios 71
white students 71, 87, 90, 91, 147
see also black students (SA)
study groups 164
sub-Saharan Africa
  establishment of developmental universities 75
  expenditure on higher education 70–71
  growing student enrolments 70
  returns on tertiary education 74
sugar research institutes 51, 52
Sunday Morning Ideological Classes (Tanzania) 236, 241–242, 251
Suransky, C 88
Susser, Mervyn 52
Sztompka, P 177–178

Talented Tenth 370, 371, 371n14
Tamuno, Tekena 9, 218, 220
Tandon, Yash 242, 244, 246, 247, 251
Tanzania
  and liberation movements 231n3, 234, 243
  socialist policies 231, 233, 234, 238, 239
  see also University of Dar es Salaam
Tate, Merze 22, 357, 360, 361, 363–366, 369n12
Tawney, R 67
teacher training colleges 286, 289–290, 294, 295
technical and vocational education 68, 69, 76, 88, 294–295, 379
Teelock-Lallah, Yanisha 139–140, 141
Teferra, D 143–144
Temu, AJ 23
tertiary *see* higher education
Tertiary Education Fund for SA 69
  see also funding of education (SA)
Things Fall Apart (Achebe) 24, 271
Thompson, Charles 357, 364n8, 371
Torres, Carlos 401
traditional knowledge systems *see* African indigenous knowledge systems
transdisciplinary knowledge 3, 41–42, 55, 258
  see also knowledge systems
#TransformWits 103–104
  see also #FeesMustFall (Wits); University of the Witwatersrand
transformation
  as daunting task for HBUs 83
  vs decolonisation 138–139
  factors involved in 2
  hooks' definition of 128
  imperatives in SA higher education 401–402

required at a number of levels 373
social transformation 83
see also entries under curriculum decolonisation/transformation; entries under decolonisation
transmodernity 195–196, 402
Tshwane University of Technology 87
Tubman, Harriet 343
Tuck, Eve 169–171
Turner, Lorenzo 357n1
Tuskegee Institute 331, 335, 337

Uganda
and Amin's ban on research 309
and Milton Obote 309, 309–310, 311
see also Makerere University (Uganda)
Umhlangano intervention (UCT) 150–151
underdevelopment 23, 228, 237, 249
unemployment
in Ghana 294
in South Africa 67, 72
United Kingdom
and 'appropriate education' for Africans 289
spread of #MustFall campaigns to 19
and theft of African idea of literature 315
United States of America
and 'appropriate education' for Africans 288–289
Atlanta School of Sociology 26, 345–346, 349–353, 354–355
Black Lives Matter movement 35
'Black Studies' curricula 25–26
civil rights movement 6, 25, 353, 355, 381n1
Civil War era 344–345, 346, 359, 378
flagships and BSIs 381–382
funding of education 6, 27, 348–349, 379, 383–385, 386, 390
higher education landscape 381–382, 385–390
land-grant universities 383, 383n2, 383n3, 384
and slavery 331, 334, 343–344, 346, 378, 385
spread of #MustFall campaigns 19
and theft of African idea of literature 315
see also black students (US); historically black colleges and universities (US); Howard School of International Affairs (US); 'Negro Problem'
universality
and achieving the status of 340
Césaire's conception of 176, 177
'of human reasoning' 178
of white experience 329, 330
universities
community outreach activities 306–307, 310

global trend towards 'market university' 145
and multiple knowledge systems 62–63
role as guardian of wider civic freedoms 151
see also African universities (excl. SA); entries under higher education; histirically black colleges and universities (US)
universities of technology 87
universities (SA)
alienation from their publics 49, 57
and decolonisation as metaphor 166–171
and decolonisation, institutionalisation of 162–166
and decolonisation, neoliberal undoing of 160–162
and dominance of Western/Eurocentric scholarship 1, 2–3, 16–17, 21–22, 92, 158, 163
failure to centre Africa 127
focus on quantitative indicators 141
graduation rates 18, 62, 71, 75
mergers of 16, 68, 86–88
participation in global knowledge systems 59–60
production of research output 58
role in post-apartheid reconstruction 48–49, 50
see also funding of education (SA); higher education (SA); historically black universities (SA); historically white universities (SA)
Universities South Africa (USAf) 2, 76
university–industry partnerships 55
University of Cape Coast (Ghana) 286, 290
University of Cape Town
academic staff 20, 146–147, 148–150
and creation of elites 145
focus on quantitative indicators 141
globally competitive rankings 136–137
heavily influenced by Rhodes' legacy 13
humanities studies 145–146, 145n3, 148, 174n2, 329
Law Faculty 146, 149
and mergers of universities 87
recurrent expenditure of 18
responses to #RMF demands 147–151
views of vice-chancellors 20–21
see also #RhodesMustFall (UCT)
University of Chicago 349–350
University of Dakar 4, 23, 255, 257
University of Dar es Salaam
adoption of neoliberalism 229–230
history/overview of 230–232, 233
School of Historiography 235–238
School of Political Economy 23, 238–248, 250–252

University of East Africa 230, 302, 311, 319
University of Fort Hare 17, 53
University of Ghana
  establishment of 285–286, 301
  Institute of African Studies 290–293
University of Ibadan 4, 211, 215, 216, 310
University of Johannesburg 87, 108, 296
University of KwaZulu-Natal (formerly Natal University)
  and mergers of universities 87
  overview of colonial/apartheid period 50–53
  transition from 'white' to 'black' university 57
  use of indigenous languages 3
University of Limpopo 2, 8, 17, 18, 87
University of London 212, 230, 301, 302, 312
University of Michigan 225, 382, 387, 388
University of Mpumalanga 68, 88
University of Nairobi 24, 283, 315, 315–317, 318
University of Pretoria 19
University of South Africa (Unisa) 51, 71, 259
University of the Free State
  Afriforum and Another v University of the Free State 143
  racist incident at 88
University of the Western Cape 87, 90, 91
University of the Witwatersrand
  background to student struggles 101–105
  continuing lack of transformation of 19
  see also #FeesMustFall (Wits)
University of Transkei 87
University of Venda 17, 90, 93
University of Zululand 2, 8, 17, 90
University Students' African Revolutionary Front (Tanzania) 242–243
Usman, Bala 181

Vaal University of Technology 87
Van der Merwe, JC 88
Venter, R 83, 84
Veracini, L 167
Verhoef, AH 83, 86, 89
Verwoerd, Hendrik 14, 81
vindicationism 165, 165n1
violence
  on Rhodes campus 131, 132, 133
  on Wits campus 103, 105, 106–107, 114, 115
  see also sexual violence
Visvanathan, Shiv 57–58, 62, 398
Vitalis, Robert 358, 358n2, 363
vocational and technical education 68, 69, 76, 88, 294–295, 379
voice
  in academic discourse 124
  African voices 34, 215, 217, 218, 222

Walker, Alice 26
Walter Sisulu University 8, 17, 87, 90
Wandira, A 304
Warren, Bill 248
Washington, Booker T
  and 'applied philanthropy' on the 'Negro Problem' 332, 333
  and genesis of black self-consciousness 334–335
  as important black politician 329
  institutions founded by 331, 335
  rejection of racist depictions of Africa 334
  Story of the Negro 332, 334, 335, 339
  support for industrial education 330–331, 331, 332, 334, 348, 379
  supported by white elites 348–349
  tacit embrace of black inferiority 349
  and ties connecting Africans and African Americans 332
Webster, JB 308, 309, 309–310, 310, 311, 312
Weep Not, Child (Ngũgĩ wa Thiong'o) 318, 324
West, C 198
West Indian colonies 367–369
Western/Eurocentric scholarship
  and ability to capture African experiences 3, 37, 41
  and appropriation by African philosophy 199
  belief in universality/superiority of 39–40, 40–41, 158, 162–163, 171, 176–177
  dismissive of African oral history 217
  gender studies in 182
  and internalisation of Eurocentric curriculum 22
  and negation of other forms of knowing 34, 163, 193–196, 231
  perpetuated in African universities 1, 2–3, 4–5, 16–17, 21–22, 92, 158, 163
  and positivist approach 38, 39
  racist views of 24, 34, 211, 370
  rejected by African-American students 25
  support for oppression 316
  and value of a fusion of epistemologies 196–198
  and voice in academic discourse 124
  see also African indigenous knowledge systems; knowledge systems
Western literature 316, 319, 320
  see also literature curricula
Western scientific research 24, 194
Western sociology
  concept of public sociology 178–179
  distinction between 'Eurocentric' and 'Eurologos' discourses 175–176
  'internationalisation' of 176, 177

see also African sociology; sociology
white academic staff
  and ability to institute curriculum changes 285
  and critiques/promotion of African literature 320–321
  in South Africa 91, 146, 147–148, 157–158, 171
  in US 347, 349–350, 380
  and 'white ignorance' 158
  see also academic staff (SA); black academic staff
White House Initiative on HBCUs 390
White Papers
  Education White Paper 3 (1997) 2, 17, 18, 49, 56, 68, 85
  White Paper on Science and Technology 56
white students
  in South Africa 71, 87, 90, 91, 147
  in US 26, 380
  see also black students (SA); black students (US); students (SA)
whiteness
  cosmological hubris of 34, 44
  dealing with the complexity of 35–36
  endurance of white supremacy 166, 168
  equating competence with 20
  limits the embodiment of knowledge 123
  linked to property 387
  maintaining whiteness of the academy 157–158, 169
  Mills' concept of 'white ignorance' 158
  Nyamnjoh's concept of 'whitening up' 137
  privileging the white body 35
  white experience as 'universal' 329, 330

Wilks, Ivor 291, 292
Williams, Donald 233–234, 241
Williams, Eric 22, 357, 360, 361, 367–370
Williams, George Washington 332
Winston, Michael 371, 372
women
  black authors 139–140, 276
  and differing gender discourses 182–183
  and politics of patriarchy 113, 130, 131
  and sexual violence on Rhodes campus 118, 119, 131–132, 133
  students at HBCUs 380
Woodson, Carter G 343, 359
workers, students' support for
  at Rhodes University 120
  at Wits University 104, 105, 109, 112
Wright Sr, Richard 26

xenophobia 14, 67

Yang, K Wayne 169–171
Yorùbá
  deity of wisdom 184n7
  Research Historical Scheme 216
  sacred texts 183–184
  sayings 174, 184

Zeleza, Paul 230–231, 301–302
Zimbabwe 283
Zuma, Jacob 19, 69, 70, 129